MIDLOTHIAN PUBLIC LIBRARY
3 1614 00036 5735

W9-AGL-654

Midlothian
Public Library
14701 S. Kenton Ave.
Midlothian, IL 60445

THE HARMONY ILLUSTRATED ENCYCLOPEDIA OF JAZZ

THE HARMONY ILLUSTRATED ENCYCLOPEDIA OF

Third Edition

Brian Case and Stan Britt
Revised and Updated by Chrissie Murray

HARMONY BOOKS
NEW YORK

A Salamander Book

Published in the United States in 1987 by Harmony Books, a division of Crown Publishers, Inc., 225 Park Avenue South, New York, New York 10003 and represented in Canada by the Canadian MANDA Group.

Originally published in Great Britain as THE ILLUSTRATED ENCYCLOPEDIA OF JAZZ by Salamander Books Limited, 52 Bedford Row, London WC1R 4LR.

HARMONY and colophon are trademarks of Crown Publishers, Inc.

Manufactured in Belgium.

Library of Congress Cataloging-in-Publication Data

Case, Brian.
  The Harmony illustrated encyclopedia of jazz.

  Rev. and updated ed. of: The illustrated encyclopedia of jazz. 1978.
  Includes discographies and index.
  1. Jazz music-Bio-bibliography. 2. Jazz music—Discography. I. Britt, Stan. II. Murray, Chrissie. III. Case, Brian. Illustrated encyclopedia of jazz. IV. Title.
ML102.J3C34 1987 785.42'092'2 (B) 86-15040
ISBN 0-517-56442-4
ISBN 0-517-56443-2 (pbk.)

10 9 8 7 6 5 4 3 2 1

Third Edition

Cover picture: Miles Davis (photo: David Redfern)

Credits

Editor: John Woodward
Designer: Barry Savage
Picture Research: Kay Rowley
Filmset by H&P Graphics Ltd
Colour Reproduction by Rodney Howe Ltd
Printed in Belgium by Proost International Book Production, Turnhout.

Publisher's Note

Each entry in this book has a selective discography, giving the record title followed by the US and UK labels in brackets; if the second label is European rather than British, this is stated. If a record has a different title in America and the UK, the US title and label are followed by the UK title and label.

Acknowledgments

The Publishers wish to express their sincere thanks to Val Wilmer, who took and/or supplied many of the photographs used in this book. Val Wilmer is a British journalist and photographer who has worked extensively in the music field; her pictures have appeared in publications throughout the world, notably in her own books, *Jazz People, The Face of Black Music* and *As Serious As Your Life*. Her work has also been seen in her own and group exhibitions and in two films. As a journalist, Val Wilmer was associated with the British publication *Melody Maker* for many years, and was also the London correspondent for the American publication *Down Beat*. She is a founder member of Format, Britain's first all-woman photo agency.
The authors acknowledge the debt they owe to the following publications: *The Jazz Book* by Joachim Berendt, *Miles Davis: A Critical Biography* by Ian Carr, *Who's Who of Jazz* by John Chilton, *The Illustrated Encyclopedia of Black Music* by Mike Clifford, *Jazz-Rock Fusion* by Julie Coryell & Laura Friedman, *Stormy Weather: The Music and Lives of a Century of Jazzwomen* by Linda Dahl, *New Edition: The Encyclopedia of Jazz* by Leonard Feather, *Mother! Is the Story of Frank Zappa* by Michael Gray, *Jazz Records A-Z* by Jorgen Grunnet Jepsen, *Blues Records 1943-1966* by Mike Ledbitter & Neil Slaven, *The Freedom Principle* by John Litweiler, *Big Band Jazz* by Albert McCarthy, *Jazz on Record* by Albert McCarthy, Alun Morgan, Paul Oliver and Max Harrison, *Jazz in the Movies* by David Meeker, *Jazzwomen: 1900 to the Present* by Sally Placksin, and *The Jazz Guitar* by Maurice Summerfield. Also the periodicals *Jazz Express* and *The Wire*.

We would like to thank the following record companies who supplied record sleeves for use in this book: A&M, ABC-Blue Thumb, Ace of Hearts, Affinity, Alfa, America, Antilles, Arc, Arista-GRP, Artists House, Atlantic, Beggars Banquet, Bet-Car, Black Lion, Black Saint, Blue Note, Bluesway, Boplicity, Candid, Capitol-EMI, CBS, Classic Jazz, Coda, Collector's Classics, Concord, Contemporary, CTI-Jazz Magazine, Delmark, DJM, Dooto, Double-Up/EMI, ECM, Elektra Musician, Enja, Epic, Epitaph, Esoteric, ESP, Family, Finesse, Fontana, Fountain, Galaxy, George Wein Collection-Concord, GFM, Gramavision, Guest Stars, Hep, Herwin, HMV, Impulse, Incus, In & Out, Ironic, Island, Japo, Jazz Archive, Jazz Kings, Jazz Panorama, Jazz Society. JCOA Virgin, Jika, JMS, Kingdom Jazz, Leo, Liberty, London, Loose Tubes, Major Minor, MCA, Mercury, Metronome, MGM, Milestone, Mode, Mole, Mood, Mosaic, Muse, Next, NYJO, Ogun, Old Masters, Oldie Blues, Original, Pablo, Paladin, Parlophone, Polydor, Prestige, Putti-Putti, Pye, Queen-Disc, RCA, Reprise, Riverside, Rough Trade, Savon, 77 Records, Shoestring, Solid State, Sonet, Soul Note, Spotlite, Steam, Survival, Steinar, Tax, Telefunken, Temple, Transatlantic, Vanguard, Vara Jazz, Vertigo, Verve, Vocalion, Vogue, Warner Brothers, Watt, Wave, Westbrook, Wing, World Record Club, Xtra.

Special thanks is also given to the following for their valuable help: Rob Adams: Jazz Services; Laurence Aston; Hugh Attwooll, CBS (UK); Nick Austin, Coda (UK); Sue Baker; Peter Barnett; Moira Bellas, WEA (UK); Andrew Carnegie; Ian Carr; Buzz Carter; Roy Carter; Sharon Chevin, CBS (UK); Gabrielle Clawson, Count Basie Society (London); Peter Clayton; Willis Connover, Voice of America; Michael Cuscuna, Blue Note/ Manhattan (US); Charles de Ledesma; Fred Dellar; Debbie Dickinson; Lindsay Edwards; Chris Ellis; Leonard Feather; John Fordham, *City Limits*; Niki Fregard, Shankman-De Blasio Inc (US); Simon Frodsham; Kathy Gardner, Blue Note-EMI (UK); Allan Garrick; Mary Greig; Mike Hames; Nick Highton; Adrian Hill; David Hughes; George Hulme; The late Alexis Korner; Steve Lake; Colin Lazzerini; Graham Lock; Don Lucoff, MCA (US); Charlie McCutcheon; Dave Machray; Jack Massarik; Chris May, Street Sounds; Barry A. Menes, Goller, Gillin & Menes (US); Mood Records (Germany); North Sea Jazz Festival 1986; Chris Parsons, *The Wire*; Rob Partridge, Island (UK); Henry Pleasants; Brian Priestley; Ray Purslow; Judy Reynolds, Import Music Service (UK); Jimmy Roche, Major Surgery, Rocket 88; Rita Sanderson; Keith Shadwick, RCA (UK); Julian Shapiro, CBS (US); Colin Smith; Sandy Sneddon, Sonet (UK); Carol Stein; Ron Steggles; Don Stone; Dell Taylor; Brian Theobald; Val, Arista (UK); Vermilion, Ace/Boplicity (UK); Mark Webster, *Blues & Soul*; Matthias Winkelmann, Enja (Germany); David Yeats; and Mike Zwerin.

Authors

BRIAN CASE, for whom jazz has been a consuming interest for the past 35 years, has been a writer on the subject since the early '70s. He has interviewed well over 150 musicians, most of whom appear in this book, and his articles have appeared in the British publications *Let It Rock, Black Music, Time Out, Inside London, Into Jazz, New Musical Express, Melody Maker, Jazz Journal, The Wire, The Observer, The Sunday Times,* and *The Times Literary Supplement*. He has contributed to the book *Jazz Now,* and has written sleeve notes for albums by numerous artists including James Moody, Eric Dolphy and Harry Edison. Prior to his jazz-writing days he wrote a play, *Our Kid,* for British radio, and a novel *The Users* was published in 1968 by Peter Davies in the UK and Citadel/Simon & Schuster in the USA.

STAN BRITT, born in Beckenham, Kent, has been a freelance writer and occasional broadcaster for the past 18 years, commenting almost exclusively on the music scene in general and jazz and blues in particular. Before that, he spent 15 years in various editorial capacities with two leading Fleet Street newspapers, has served periods within the press offices of a couple of leading UK record companies, and has worked in PR, specializing in music. The author of *The Jazz Guitarists* (Blandford Press, 1984), and contributor to both *The Frank Sinatra Scrapbook* (Pop Universal/Souvenir Press, 1982) and *Sinatra & The Great Song Stylists* (Ian Allan, 1972), he has also contributed to a myriad of musical publications, including long-time associations with leading music trade weeklies, *Billboard* and *Music Week*, and has annotated almost 300 liner-notes for a wide variety of record albums. Stan Britt lives in South London, surrounded by a huge collection of records, reference books and memorabilia, all pertaining to a subject which, one way or another, consumes most of his time: music.

CHRISSIE MURRAY was former editor/co-founder of *The Wire* magazine and previously jazz consultant to London's Capital Radio. She has written extensively about jazz and related music for various publications and was music editor of *Ms London* magazine for four years. She has also worked in jazz PR, as a press officer for Charly/Affinity Records, and has presented a 17-week *Jazz Workshop* series for the BBC. She currently contributes to *City Limits* 'Jazz & Improvised Music' section.

Chrissie discovered Miles Davis, Stan Kenton *et al* via Willis Connover's *Voice of America Jazz Hour* broadcasts in 1961 at age 13. She is well known for her anti-élitist views and abhors the 'purist, matrix-number' approach to jazz writing. Rather than 'preaching to the converted', she has deliberately written about jazz as it relates to rock and pop fans. She has also tried to increase the profile of women jazz musicians in what has been a traditionally male-dominated music.

The 1986 revise of this encyclopedia is dedicated to the late Bill Walker, the South London keyboard-player whose musical promise was ended by a tragically early death.

Foreword

Any book that purports to be about jazz must submit to the aesthetic might and magnificence of Louis Armstrong. Louis Armstrong: my home boy. Yes. Pops, the father. Louis Armstrong gave Americans and the whole human race some insights into rhythm and into personality that were different from anything that ever existed before. He defined swing and refined improvization to such a high human degree that he provided the inspiration for people all over America and all over the world to want to swing and want to improvize. Because he was a great artist, Louis Armstrong gave humanity profoundly accurate information within the context of a brand new art form: JAZZ.

In an era like ours, when ignorance and falsehood wear so many crowns, what we need now perhaps more than ever is accurate information. In the interest of truth, we now find ourselves in an era of growing rebellion against the aesthetic denigration of jazz that began when major figures started making fools of themselves and dupes of their listeners. Instead of them refining and elaborating the integral elements of their idiom, those culprit major figures diluted the substance of their art in the name of expansion. This dilution resulted from a combination of arrogance, ignorance, and opportunism of such abominable determination that it threatened the essence of a musical art so profound that its very emergence redefined the history of music as distinctly as the emergence of cubism redefined all we know of visual art. Much of that willingness to dilute a vital art form came from the belief that was mutually held by the Third Reich and Henry Ford: that history is bunk and can be ignored in the pursuit of purely selfish goals that offer no illumination into experience other than further proof of the human capacity for corruption.

But the point of art is not to cultivate but to combat corruption. As Ralph Ellison has pointed out, craft is a substantial aspect of morality. Consequently, the musician who offers the innocent and willing listener an artefact in sound that shows no respect for craft or tradition is being more than inept, is being more than a sell out; this musician is actively corrupting the sensibility of the listening public. And, as the Third Reich proved, determined corruption can lead to catastrophic events.

The corruption we began to face after the misinterpretation of Ornette Coleman's innovation, and after the anger jazz musicians felt toward the success of English rock groups, resulted in a fraudulent cult of the primitive on one side and an equally counterfeit musical dialogue with adolescent passions known as jazz-rock, now "progressive" jazz. The cult of the primitive disdains instrumental technique, harmonic knowledge, specific study of Western forms and of other idioms that they pretend under the battered flag of "world music" to have incorporated into their own so-called art. What distinguishes this cult isn't innovation but the unarguable inability to perform on a professional level in any jazz situation other than the eccentric corner they have so successfully painted themselves into for the last twenty years. The purveyors of "progressive" jazz, of jazz-rock, form a peculiar aesthetic androgyny that has one thing in common with hermaphrodites—sterility.

I say these things not out of opinion but from experience. I have stood on bandstands with cult of the primitive frauds and know, in great detail, how little they have mastered of the specifics required to consider yourself a musician. Owning a scalpel does not make one a surgeon. I also grew up playing in jazz-rock groups. We didn't pretend to be making art; we knew we were only making money. That fact in and of itself separated us from those sellouts who claim to be extending their art instead of their assets.

Fortunately, things are changing and the fugitives from the boot camp of unswerving discipline and dedication can feel the breath of the bloodhounds. Soon they will feel the teeth of the jazz hounds and find themselves incapable of posturing in the seat of sin ever again. Yes, in the corners of America, north, south, east, and west, there are growing numbers of young musicians who are aesthetically arming themselves with the weaponry necessary to overthrow this runaway regime of degeneration. It doesn't matter whether the musicians are men or women, Smitty Smiths or Teri Lynne Carringtons; they are gathering. I recently heard Philip Harper, a young trumpet player, and Don Braden, a young tenor player. Each of them was dead serious about this music. I knew then that what Louis Armstrong gave us all was inspiring another crop of artists who would inspire even more musicians to provide the accurate human information that is the purpose and function of all art. I was also confident that they would some time soon be included in a book like this.

It Don't Mean A Thing, If...

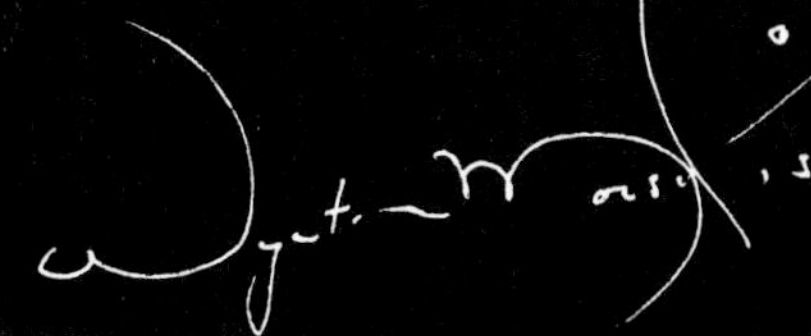

Introduction

The first edition of *The Illustrated Encyclopedia of Jazz*—long regarded as an essential reference work for jazz fans (and, indeed, music writers)—was compiled at the end of the 1970s.

When distinguished authors Brian Case and Stan Britt wrote that first edition, even they couldn't have dreamed that the music they were documenting so lovingly would come to enjoy such a high level of interest in the mid-1980s.

Perhaps none of us ever imagined then that, in the 1980s, veteran drummer Art Blakey would come to be hailed as the 'new messiah of the discos'. Who could have predicted, for instance, that Blakey's Blues March or Lee Morgan's The Sidewinder would be elevated to the top of the jazz play-lists by 16-year-olds who weren't even born when those records first saw the light of day? And, in the late 1970s, it was even harder to envisage that the 10-year-olds of the day would go into huddles six years later to debate, with all seriousness, the 'comparative merits' of Clifford Brown and Kenny Dorham.

As jazz progresses towards the 1990s, we have even more reason for optimism than in the later 1970s. In spite of a world-wide recession, the last half-decade has been marked by some extraordinary events in jazz. Just look at *some* of them...

We celebrated the return of the great master, Miles Davis—undiminished, in good health, still creative and still an inspiration. The innovative Charles Lloyd—a jazz hero in the days of flower-power before going to ground—went back on the road again. There was the reunion of the Modern Jazz Quartet—memorable performances, as though they'd never been away. Herbie Hancock took time out to don tuxedo and tie and recreate a former acoustic age with VSOP. An indication of the pulling-power of jazz was shown in increased commercial sponsorship—the Kool Jazz Festival and the JVC-sponsored festivals. And, in the UK, for a company like Schlitz to put the weighty sum of £200,000 behind their 'Jazz Sounds '86' competition is something that could have happened only in the 1980s. The re-birth of one of jazz's most respected and influential record labels was unprecedented—Blue Note came *back*.

Elsewhere, a massive raid on back catalog has produced the most extensive and breath-taking program of re-issues in jazz history. While at the time of this book's first edition you spent weeks combing the secondhand racks for a coveted classic, you're now so spoiled for choice with gleaming, newly pressed re-releases that you hardly know which to buy first.

Unhappily, since the first edition we've suffered the sad loss of many musical legends and pioneers vital to jazz—Count Basie, Thelonious Monk, Benny Goodman, Stan Kenton, Earl Hines, Art Pepper, Joe Farrell, Vic Dickenson, Zoot Sims, Sonny Stitt, Philly Joe and Jo Jones, Cootie Williams, Shelly Manne, Muddy Waters, Hank Mobley, Benny Morton, Eubie Blake, Big Joe Turner, Harry Miller, Collin Walcott, Pat Smythe and, even as this edition went to press, Teddy Wilson...

Gladly, we've also seen the emergence of many new 'young lions': in the US—trumpeters like Wynton Marsalis and Terence Blanchard, saxophonists Branford Marsalis, Bill Evans, Bobby Watson, Donald Harrison and Chico Freeman, guitarists Stanley Jordan and Emily Remler...; in the UK—pianists like Django Bates (with Loose Tubes and First House), Steve Melling and Mark Fitzgibbon, saxophonists Courtney Pine, Alan Barnes, Iain Ballamy and Jamie Talbot, trumpeter Guy Barker, trombonist Annie Whitehead, the six-piece women's group the Guest Stars...; and in Europe, pianist Michel Petrucciani and guitarist Bireli Lagrene...

A new generation of musicians and fans which has never heard of 'purism' and 'élitism' has probably been the music's salvation in breaking down barrier-making categories. Pop and rock artists like Working Week, Sade, Alison Moyet, Sting—by their association with jazz artists and acknowledgement of jazz styles—have opened up new possibilities for an open-minded generation. For example, through Ms Moyet, many have discovered for themselves the artistry of Billie Holiday. Sting's work with Branford Marsalis and Kenny Kirkland has stimulated interest in both these artists' jazz output. And how many people *outside* jazz had heard of the great Gil Evans before his involvement with the music score for the movie *Absolute Beginners*?

The jealous old guard of 'jazz purists', who once slated rock musician Keith Emerson for 'daring' to cover Meade Lux Lewis' Honky Tonk Train Blues, look on with horror. Their campaign to place jazz in a museum and lock the door has taken a severe battering. The 'exclusivity' tag which hung so heavily round jazz's neck for too many years has been a conspiracy to which much of the media has sadly contributed. In the UK, for instance, jazz has long been conveniently down-classified as 'light entertainment' (therefore, low-priority) by the national broadcasting organizations. This is why a new breed of record-spinners in the clubs and particularly on pirate-radio stations have found such a captive audience. They have become as influential in their way, in the 1980s, as Willis Connover was in the 1960s; they not only helped to *create* the demand for jazz, they actually cater for it by *playing* jazz—and the large national and commercial broadcasting companies have had to pay the price.

As usual, record companies, too, have been slow to react. While the flood of classic re-issues is welcome (and much needed), it would be even better if some of the companies other than Blue Note would put as much energy and enthusiasm into the recording of new and existing jazz talent. And why do they still refuse to accept the marketing reality that a trumpeter like Wynton Marsalis or a guitarist like Stanley Jordan is every bit as 'promotable' as a Michael Jackson or a Madonna? If an artist of the stature of Miles Davis has recorded Cyndi Lauper's pop hit Time After Time, why not promote it and market it like the latest Prince single?

Many of the record companies are confused, worried that 'jazz' is just another of those 'fashion things'—here today and gone tomorrow. But we can prove—just by flicking through this book—that jazz has been here, *today*, since the turn of the century and it's *still* here. How many artists in the current record charts who command such large chunks of company budgets can guarantee equally long-term productivity and interest?

The Illustrated Encyclopedia of Jazz has been extensively revised to take account of this new enthusiasm for the music and to provide an interesting, informed source of reference for the 1980s. Many entries—particularly in the jazz-rock and fusion field (such as George Benson, John McLaughlin, Stanley Clarke, Chick Corea, Herbie Hancock, Weather Report) have been greatly extended while many new (and sometimes unexpected) names have been added (Average White Band, the Brecker Brothers, Chicago, The Crusaders, George Duke, Earth Wind & Fire, Rodey Franklin, Al Jarreau, Mike Mainieri, Manhattan Transfer, Alphonse Mouzon, Jaco Pastorius, Flora Purim, Lee Ritenour, Patrice Rushen, David Sanborn, Stuff, Grover Washington...).

Many of the opinions expressed in the first edition of this book have been revised. An historic artist like Miles Davis, for example, cannot be dismissed as having 'sold out' in the 1970s when you consider the universal influence he *and* his music have had since that decade.

While jazz writers might still agrue about their personal lists of all-time 'greats', there's surely no debate about the contributions made by artists like Toshiko Akiyoshi, Arthur Blythe, George Coleman, Quincy Jones, Airto Moreira, Anita O'Day etc...these artists (conspicuous by their absence in the first edition) have been added with many others.

We've also borne in mind our European readers' wide commitment to jazz, particularly in countries like France, Italy, Germany and Holland, and many of the Eastern bloc countries where the demand for the music is insatiable. As a result, there are many added names of international standing but European interest. These include the Soviet Union's Ganelin Trio, Norway's Jan Garbarek, Czechoslovakia's Jan Hammer and Miroslav Vitous, France's Michel Petrucciani and Jean-Luc Ponty, Alsace-Lorraine's Bireli Lagrene, Poland's Zbigniew Namyslowski, Denmark's Niels-Henning Orsted Pedersen, Turkey's Okay Temiz, Germany's Eberhard Weber as well as the United Jazz+Rock Ensemble.

A concerted effort has also been made to redress the balance regarding women musicians, the dearth of which in the first edition perpetuated the long-held myth that 'women musicians can't, or don't, play jazz'. Some of the many women artists who have made such a vital contribution to the music have been integrated here — among them Jane Ira Bloom, Joanne Brackeen, Betty Carter, June Christy, Amina Claudine Myers, Laura Nyro, Annette Peacock, Nina Simone, Tania Maria, Barbara Thompson, and Kate Westbrook.

New to this edition is an entry specifically on 'British Jazz' — a potted survey of the music in the UK, particularly for the interest of our readers in the US. It has also been a pleasure to have an opportunity to include just some of Britain's world-class musicians who didn't make it into the first edition. These include pianists like Gordon Beck, Michael Garrick and (through the Rocket 88 band) Ian Stewart, trumpeters like Ian Carr and Kenny Wheeler, drummers Tommy Chase and Jon Hiseman, composer Graham Collier, bassist Dave Holland, guitarist Jim Mullen, guitarist and blues pioneer Alexis Korner, bands like the Latin-inspired Paz and hard-bop's Spirit Level, and saxophonists like Don Weller (through the ground-breaking Major Surgery), Dick Morrissey and Trevor Watts.

Also new is the inclusion of two specially significant record labels: Blue Note in the US and Germany's ECM. These two labels are included because they have done so much individually to raise the profile of jazz using professional and strategic marketing, without compromising or 'watering down' the music.

An effort has also been made to list (where humanly possible) some of the classic albums which have been recently re-issued on different labels—a momentous and difficult task in view of the deluge of such re-released material.

With the pressure of so much new information on too little space, there have obviously been casualties. The decision about which artist to leave out, which artist to retain, extend or add, has been agonizing. Sadly, many significant musicians—some long dead—have had to make way for the new and the living. Their immeasurable contribution is acknowledged by their incorporation at the end in the Appendix, although we all agree they deserve a separate book all their own (like a *Who Was Who In Jazz)*.

The best intentions of this 1980s revise of *The Illustrated Encyclopedia of Jazz* is, perhaps, summed up by our last entry—'Z' for Frank Zappa. Here's just one musician who came into the music not so much through jazz, or blues, or even rock but through a much less easily defined 'new music' of the age—yet his influence on the fringes of jazz since the 1970s has been considerable. Zappa is just one example of how this widely accessible music that we term 'jazz' (for want of a better classification) doesn't stand still or wait to be displayed in a glass case with the words 'Do Not Touch' underneath.

In this book, we've tried to show that there are no frontiers to the directions jazz has taken or, indeed, can take. The musicians themselves will continue—as always—to build bridges where others have built barriers. And all they ask is that their music is received in the same spirit in which it is offered.

By listening to their music—going to their live concerts, buying their records, demanding more jazz coverage on radio, TV and in magazines, newspapers and books like this—you, too, are building bridges.

Chrissie Murray, 1986

Directory

Muhal Richard Abrams

After several years of playing hard bop with the Modern Jazz Two + 3, Chicago pianist Muhal Richard Abrams founded the Experimental Band to widen the scope of jazz. This led to his establishment of the Association for the Advancement of Creative Musicians (AACM) in 1965, which attracted many of Chicago's finest young players, Roscoe Mitchell, Joseph Jarman, Lester Bowie, Malachi Favors, Charles Clark, Steve McCall, Henry Threadgill, Bill Brimfield, Fred Anderson, Kalaparusha Maurice McIntyre, Lester Lashley, Leo Smith, Anthony Braxton, Leroy Jenkins, Jack de Johnette. Muhal's first album **Levels & Degrees Of Light,** gives a fair idea of his exploratory scores. Moods fluctuate between eeriness—**Levels & Degrees,** which features the straight, wordless soprano voice—and violent outbursts of unison chaos. **The Bird Song** pitches a read poem against a texture of shrill, sweet instruments such as bird whistles. His next album **Young At Heart, Wise In Time** has plenty of his piano which had evolved by now into a complex mixture of bop, stride, and avant-garde tone clusters.

Muhal's influence upon Chicago's jazzmen has been immense. The Art Ensemble and Anthony Braxton owe much to him and to the free, experimental atmosphere which he established. He can be heard playing piano with the Art Ensemble **(Fanfare For The Warriors)** and piano and oboe on an early album of Joseph Jarman's **(As If It Were The Seasons)** as well as piano, cello and alto clarinet on Braxton's début album, **Three Compositions of New Jazz**.

Anthony Braxton has said of Abrams: 'I have experienced a spectrum of universes from his creativity—from string quartet music to a production of one his plays. In the course of my sixteen years' involvement with Muhal, I have experienced the dynamics of big band music as well as the wonder of stride piano, and along the way, Muhal's spiritual insight has on more than one occasion been a major factor in my own unfolding universe.'

Most recently, much of Abrams' recording output has been on Giovanni Bonandrini's visionary, Italy-based Black Saint label, notably **Rejoicing With The Light** (a work for an extended orchestra) which includes his **Bloodline** composition dedicated to Fletcher Henderson-Don Redman-Benny Carter.

Albums:

Muhal Richard Abrams, Levels & Degrees Of Light (Delmark/Delmark)
Muhal Richard Abrams, Young At Heart, Wise In Time (Delmark/Delmark)
Art Ensemble Of Chicago, Fanfare For The Warriors (Atlantic/Atlantic)
Joseph Jarman, As If It Were The Seasons (Delmark/Delmark)
Anthony Braxton, Three Compositions Of New Jazz (Delmark/Delmark)
Duet (Arista/Arista)
Blues Forever (Black Saint/Black Saint)
Rejoicing With The Light (Black Saint/Black Saint)

Muhal Richard Abrams, Rejoicing With The Light (courtesy Black Saint). The eye-catching painting on the cover is by Abrams' own hand.

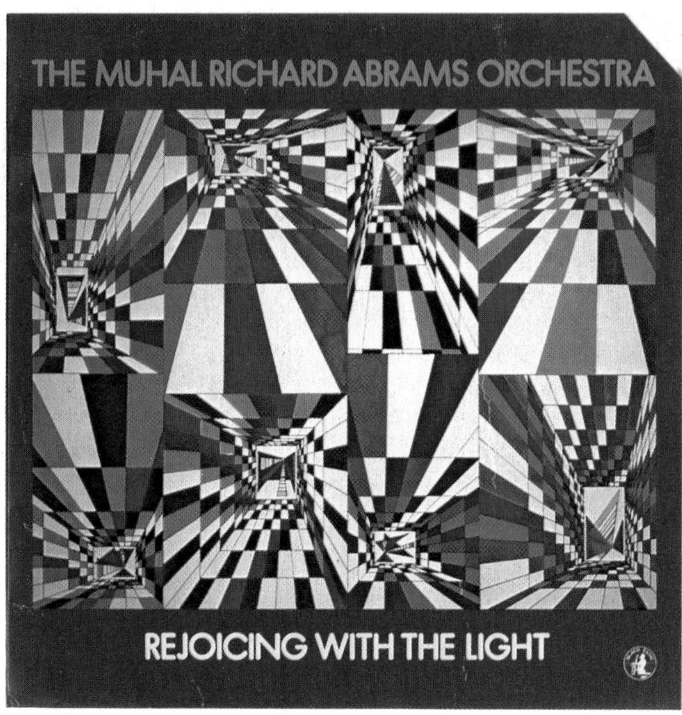

Cannonball Adderley

Julian 'Cannonball' Adderley was born in 1928 in Florida, moving to New York and emphatically into the big league in 1955. Basically a Charlie Parker disciple, the altoist had plenty of bite and a rhythmic directness that became more pronounced in his later work. The meeting with Miles Davis—**Somethin' Else**—proved something of a comeuppance, for the trumpeter was playing with such concision that Cannonball sounded positively garrulous. His work in the Miles Davis group from 1957—**Milestones, Kind Of Blue**—was interesting for the strides he made, learning how to use space, understatement and substitute chords. Chords and modes were very much a preoccupation in that band, with Miles and Coltrane both stretching to escape conventional harmony. Cannonball's association with arranger Gil Evans resulted in a masterly album, **Pacific Standard Time**, which deployed the altoist's legato style in orchestrations which reinterpreted jazz classics—**Manteca, Round Midnight, King Porter Stomp**.

Julian 'Cannonball' Adderley, Somethin' Else (courtesy Blue Note).

Adderley's contract with Riverside paired him with guitarist Wes Montgomery, pianist Bill Evans and a host of other musicians, but the big breakthrough came with his formation of a quintet. The first album, **Them Dirty Blues**, in which he shared the front-line with his cornetist/trumpeter brother, Nat, sold more than the rest of his output combined. Bobby Timmons' soul hit number **This Here** may have had a lot to do with this success, and the unit increasingly featured these bluesy backbeat numbers—**Work Song (The Japanese Concerts)** and **Mercy, Mercy, Mercy (Mercy, Mercy, Mercy)**. With Timmons at the piano, lured away from Art Blakey's Messengers, and the strong rhythm team of Sam Jones on bass and Louis Hayes on drums, the quintet became the spearhead of the commercially successful soul wave. Joe Zawinul joined the band, replacing Timmons, and wrote **Mercy**, and multi-instrumentalist Yusef Lateef was added.

While neither of the Adderley brothers was particularly original, their music, by its heavy emphasis on the roots, helped to popularize jazz at a time when radical upheavals—atonality, polyrhythmic complexity, tonal expressionism—were clearing the halls. Happy music, and none the worse for that. Cannonball's death (of a stroke, on August 8, 1975) hit jazz hard, for he was a kindly man, always ready to promote young talent—for example, Wes Montgomery.

Albums:

Somethin' Else (Blue Note/Blue Note)
Miles Davis, Milestones (CBS/CBS)
Miles Davis, Kind Of Blue (CBS/CBS)
Gil Evans, Pacific Standard Time (Blue Note/Blue Note)
Them Dirty Blues, Now Cannonball & Eight Giants (Milestone/Milestone)
The Japanese Concerts (Milestone/Milestone)
Mercy, Mercy, Mercy (Capitol/Capitol)
Phenix (Fantasy/—)
Coast To Coast (Milestone/Milestone)

Afro-jazz

To escape the strictures and penalties of the South African apartheid system, the cream of the country's jazz musicians trickled away from their homeland in the 1960s. Musicians like Abdullah Ibrahim (Dollar Brand), Hugh Masekela, Jonas Gwanga, Makhaya Ntshoko and Miriam Makeba exiled themselves in the United States. Many others—notably key figures like Harry Miller, Chris McGregor and the Blue Notes, Mike Gibbs, Gwigwi Mrwebi and Ronnie Beer—gravitated first to points in Europe and then to London, England.

Today, London continues to provide a focus for the displaced South African music scene, perpetuating a unique and vibrant brand of inter-racial, traditional, township-based music combined with Afro-American, European and local jazz elements.

Afro-jazz's Brotherhood of Breath, Yes Please (courtesy In & Out).

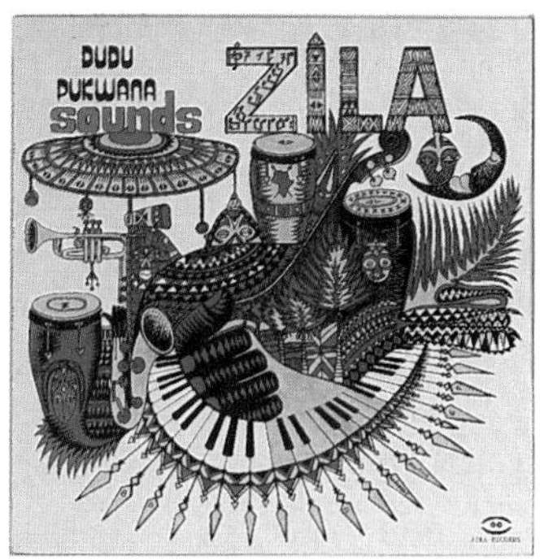

Dudu Pukwana's Zila Sounds (courtesy Jika): township jazz in exile.

Central to the development of the London Afro-jazz movement in the '70s have been musicians like altoist Dudu Pukwana, percussionists Louis Moholo and Julian Bahula, and bassist Johnny Dyani. Tragically, two irreplaceable cornerstones of this vital movement were lost through untimely deaths—the expressive and plaintive trumpeter Mongezi Feza died from double pneumonia in 1975, just 30 years old, while the catalystic bassist-composer Harry Miller was killed in a car crash in 1983.

The '70s and '80s have seen the expansion of local interest in ex-patriate African musicians and their music, not just from South Africa but from all over the African continent including Ghana and Nigeria. More recently, other musicians like South African percussionist Brian Abrahams (District Six) and pianist Mervyn Afrika, Ghanaian saxophonist George Lee (Anansi) and Nigerian percussionist Gaspar Lawal have offered their own significant contribution to the continuing Afro-jazz movement in Britain.

Albums:

Brian Abrahams (District Six), Akuzwale (—/District Six)
Brian Abrahams (District Six), Leave My Name At The Door (—/District Six)
Julian Bahula (Jabula), Let Us Be Free (—/Pläne)
Julian Bahula (Jabula), African Soul (—/Pläne)
Johnny Dyani, Africa (Steeplechase/Steeplechase)
Johnny Dyani-Mongezi Feza, Music For Xaba (Sonet/Sonet)
Gaspar Lawal, Ajomase (—/Cap)
Gaspar Lawal, Abio 'sunni (—/Hot Cap)
George Lee (Anansi), Anansi (—/Ebusia)
Chris McGregor (Blue Notes), Blue Notes In Concert (—/Ogun)
Chris McGregor (Brotherhood of Breath), Yes Please (—/In And Out)
Harry Miller (Quintet), In Conference (—/Ogun)

Harry Miller (Quintet), Down South (—/Vara Jazz)
Louis Moholo, Spirits Rejoice (—/Ogun)
Dudu Pukwana (Zila), Zila Sounds (—/Jika)

Airto

see Airto Moreira

Toshiko Akiyoshi

Pianist-composer-arranger and band-leader Toshiko Akiyoshi was born in Dairen, Manchuria, on December 12, 1929, into a cultured and comfortably off Japanese family. In 1947, as the Chinese Communists consolidated control of the region, the family had to return to Japan with only the possessions they could carry. Akiyoshi's father (himself a Noh exponent) encouraged his daughters to take up ballet, traditional dance and piano, with Toshiko excelling in classical piano studies.

Her first exposure to jazz was hearing the music—particularly Teddy Wilson records—in the wake of the American occupation following World War 2. During the '50s, Akiyoshi was an established musician in Japan with her own band and gigs, and by 1956 was the highest-paid freelance arranger and studio musician there. In 1953, she had recorded with Oscar Peterson for Norman Granz; this, and recommendations from Peterson, won her a scholarship to Berklee College in 1956. On hearing Bud Powell's music in America, she became a great admirer of his style—still evident today in her playing. After working four nights a week at George Wein's Storyville Club in Boston, she made her début at the Newport Jazz Festival.

In 1959 she married saxophonist Charlie Mariano with whom she worked during the '60s. She also worked in small groups, often with bassist Charles Mingus. In 1967, she made her début as composer-conductor at the Town Hall, New York, and two years later married her second husband, saxophonist and flute-player Lew Tabackin. With Tabackin in the '70s she was to create one of jazz's most exceptional big bands—winners of numerous polls both in the States and Japan, and frequent Grammy winners. Their move from California to the East Coast was marked by their concert at the Kool Jazz Festival in 1983.

While Akiyoshi's music is essentially classic Western big band (with its unusual accentuation of the woodwinds in support of lead soloist Tabackin), she incorporates her own cultural background and personal philosophy into her writing. Thus you find a legacy of Japanese traditions and folk forms in her music. For instance, her piece **Sumie** is the Japanese word for a style of traditional brush painting and **Hen-Pecked Old Man** is a character from a favorite Japanese folk-tale.

Akiyoshi dedicated the big band's 1975 **Kogun** to the hapless Japanese soldier who was discovered staked out in the Philippines in 1974, almost 30 years after the war had ended. One of her best-loved works is **Tales Of A Courtesan** (1975) which presents her version of the falsely romanticized Western image of these women during the Edo era; as Akiyoshi explains: '...the contrast between the superficially luxurious life of some of these women and the tragic denial of human rights they suffered.' A further insight into her social conscience is revealed in **Minimata** from her **Insights** album. This was her heartfelt response to the Japanese fishing village tragedy as a result of contamination from industrial mercury pollution.

Toshiko Akiyoshi is, without doubt, an important figure in contemporary music and has won deserved international acclaim with, not surprisingly, a notable following in Japan. The extent of her international appeal is interestingly documented in the 1980 film *Southern Crossing* (Robert Guillemot) with its footage of the Akiyoshi-Tabackin Australian All Stars in Sydney. The 1984 film portrait *Toshiko Akiyoshi: Jazz Is My Native Language* (Renée Cho) charts her life and music from its beginnings to her more recent move to New York and includes performances of **Son Of Road Time, Feast In Milano, Village, Tales Of A Courtesan, Minimata, Remembering Bud** and **Count Your Blessings**. Akiyoshi's contribution to jazz on an international scale cannot be understated.

Albums:
Toshiko Akiyoshi-Lew Tabackin, Insights (RCA/RCA)
Toshiko Akiyoshi-Lew Tabackin, Kogun (RCA/RCA)
Toshiko Akiyoshi-Lew Tabackin, Long Yellow Road (RCA/RCA)
Toshiko Akiyoshi-Lew Tabackin, Road Time (RCA/RCA)
Toshiko Akiyoshi-Lew Tabackin, Tales Of A Courtesan (RCA/RCA)
Dedications (Inner City/—)
Finesse (Concord/Concord)
Toshiko Akiyoshi-Lew Tabackin, March Of The Tadpoles (RCA/RCA)

Akiyoshi-Tabackin, Tales Of A Courtesan (courtesy RCA).

Joe Albany

Born 1924, the legendary pianist had to wait until the '70s to receive his critical due. One of the finest white bebop pianists of the '40s—along with George Wallington, Al Haig and Dodo Marmarosa—Albany played with Charlie Parker, though recordings of their collaboration were not issued until 1976 (**Yardbird In Lotus Land**). For many years, his reputation was based on two records, **The Aladdin Sessions** and **The Right Combination**, separated by an eleven year gap. The former features the pianist on four tracks with Lester Young, and the later date, now deleted, was an informal session recorded in engineer Ralph Garretson's living room, and catches the vastly talented Albany with that other great recluse, tenorist Warne Marsh. Fourteen years elapsed before he surfaced on record again, this time unaccompanied and as good as ever (**Joe Albany At Home**). Since then, there has been a steady flow of albums.

Technically, Joe Albany has everything: touch, timing and a limitless fund of devices to express the range of his imagination. There is a lyrical intensity about his best work that recalls the flights of Parker, his last influence.

Albums:
Lester Young, The Aladdin Sessions (Blue Note/Blue Note)
Charlie Parker, Yardbird In Lotus Land (—/Spotlite)
The Right Combination (—/Riverside)
Joe Albany At Home (—/Spotlite)
Proto-Bopper (—/Spotlite)
Birdtown Birds (—/Steeplechase)
Joe Albany & Niels Pedersen (—/Steeplechase)
Portrait Of An Artist (Elektra Musician/Elektra Musician)

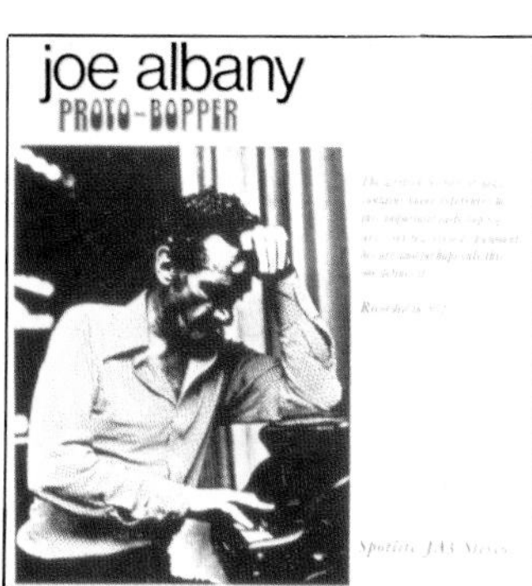

The legendary Joe Albany, Proto-Bopper (courtesy Spotlite).

Henry 'Red' Allen

Henry James 'Red' Allen (born New Orleans, Louisiana, 1908; died New York City, 1967) was, together with Louis Armstrong and Roy Eldridge, the outstanding trumpet stylist of the 1930s. Son of a New Orleans brass-band leader, Henry Allen (1877-1952), Red Allen started on violin and alto-horn, before switching to trumpet. After local work with leading New Orleans musicians like George Lewis and John Handy, as well as with Sidney Desvignes aboard the *SS Island Queen*, Allen became a member of the King Oliver Jazz Band, 1927. Record début—with Clarence Williams same year. Then returned to New Orleans, to work with Walter Pichon and on riverboats with Fate Marable (1928-29). Back in New York (1929), Allen recorded under his own name for the first time (**Henry Red Allen & His New York Orchestra, Vols 1, 2: 1929**) in company with blues singer Victoria Spivey, and instrumentalists Albert Nicholas, J. C. Higginbotham, Charlie Holmes and Luis Russell, all colleagues in a band led by Russell, and of which Allen became a prominent member same year. Music produced at these sessions was of uniformly high standard, with Allen's trumpet playing the individual highlight. Already, as these records show, Allen's basic style had been formed; a style which although obviously influenced by Armstrong, had its own individualism. His playing was distinguished by positive allegiance to the beat, but with rhythmic flexibility few other trumpeters of the period possessed, and an overtly emotional projection; technically, few faults. And Allen's idiosyncratic tonal effects—glissandos, smears, achieved by adroit tonguing—made him, along with Armstrong, a member of the advance guard of the late-1920s/early-1930s.

As with Oliver, already Allen was beginning to think in terms of other than two- and four-bar symmetry. His strong, brassy tone, his fierce attack, together with forward-looking harmonic conception, are demonstrated most handsomely in finest solos with Russell, including **Saratoga Shout, Doctor Blues, Jersey Lightning, Panama, Song Of The Swanee (The Luis Russell Story)** and **It Should Be You, Feeling Drowsy (Henry Red Allen, Vol 1)**.

Allen left Russell (1932), worked with Charlie Johnson (1933), then joined Fletcher Henderson, with whom he had worked, briefly in '32. With Henderson, took several startlingly brilliant solos, on a variety of material, including **Wrappin' It Up, Rug Cutter's Swing (Henderson—1934), 'Yeah Man!, Queer Notions, King Porter Stomp (The Fletcher Henderson Story/ The Fletcher Henderson Story, Vol 4)**, and Night Life, Nagasaki, while there is a different version of **Queer Notions (Jazz Pioneers/Ridin' In Rhythm)**.

With Coleman Hawkins, a colleague of his with Henderson, Allen often produced his best work while, in turn, stimulating the tenorist (eg the two versions of **Queer Notions** cited above). From a Hawkins

Below: The outstanding Henry 'Red' Allen—one of the advance guard of trumpet stylists to emerge from the late 1920s, early '30s.

record date of 1933, Allen's trumpet burned incandescently, on **Jamaica Shout** and **Heartbreak Blues (Jazz Pioneers/Ridin' In Rhythm). Ride, Red, Ride, St Louis Wiggle, Harlem Heat,** and **Red Rhythm** are four other sides which find Allen's playing at its most expressive—this time as a member of The Mills Blue Rhythm Band.

Also recorded with Billie Holiday (1937), **The Golden Years, Vol 2**, as well as with Sidney Bechet (1941), **Sleepy Time Down South** and James P. Johnson, **Father Of The Stride Piano**. Allen recorded fine solos with King Oliver **(King Oliver, Vol 2: 1929-1930)**, Jelly Roll Morton **(Jelly Roll Morton & His Red Hot Peppers (1927-1930), Vol 1)**, and Lionel Hampton **(Lionel Hampton's Best Records, Vol 3: 1939-1940)**. More of the Allen-Russell combination can be found within **Luis Russell & His Louisiana Swing Orchestra**.

Apart from his various recording activities of the 1930s-into-the-1940s, Allen's post-Henderson career encompassed a 25-month stint with the Mills Blue Rhythm Band, and a three-and-a-half-year spell with big band accompanying Louis Armstrong **(V.S.O.P. (Very Special Old Phonography, 1928-1930), Vols 5 & 6)**.

Formed own sextet (end of 1940), of which long-time Allen associate, J. C. Higginbotham, was important member from beginning until 1947 **(The Very Great Henry Red Allen, Vol 1)**. This series of Allen-led bands, with the leader's flaring trumpet and friendly vocals its focal points, lasted into the 1950s, having completed lengthy residencies in major clubs throughout US. Between 1954-65, Allen featured as regular attraction at the Metropole, New York.

First trip to Europe was with band of Kid Ory (1959), returning to Britain as solo act on several occasions during 1960s. Shortly after completing the last of these, in 1967, Allen died in New York of cancer.

One of Allen's finest record dates during the latter part of his career took place in March, 1957, in the company of old friends like Hawkins, Higginbotham, Buster Bailey and Cozy Cole. Session produced much superior jazz from all concerned, including a series of magnificent trumpet solos on each of the ten recorded items, with those on **I Cover The Waterfront, Sweet Lorraine, 'S Wonderful** and a re-make of **Ride, Red, Ride** being especially praiseworthy **(The Very Great Henry Red Allen, Vol 2)**. Allen's playing was, in fact, comparable to the best of his more youthful days; like that to be found on a famous session put together by Spike Hughes **(Spike Hughes & His All American Orchestra)**.

During the latter part of his career, Red Allen was guest in three important TV specials, *Chicago & All That Jazz, The Sound Of Jazz* and *Profile Of The Arts*. Allen's timeless playing, exemplified by two albums made at the tail-end of his career, **The Henry Allen Memorial Album/Mr Allen—Henry Red Allen** and **Feeling Good** was summed up by Don Ellis, a trumpet player from a different era, in the following widely syndicated quote from 1965: 'Red Allen is the most creative and avant-garde trumpet player in New York'.

Albums:

King Oliver, Vols 1, 2 (RCA Victor—France)
Henry 'Red' Allen, Vols 1-4 (RCA Victor—France)
Luis Russell & His Louisiana Swing Orchestra (Columbia/—)
The Luis Russell Story (—/Parlophone)
The Fletcher Henderson Story (Columbia)/ The Fletcher Henderson Story, Vol 4 (CBS)
The Complete Fletcher Henderson (RCA Victor)/ Fletcher Henderson, Vols 1-3 (RCA Victor—France)
Various, Jazz Pioneers (Prestige)/ Ridin' In Rhythm (World Records)
Fletcher Henderson, Henderson—1934 (—/Ace of Hearts)
Coleman Hawkins, Recordings Made Between 1930 and 1941 (CBS—France)
Spike Hughes & His All American Orchestra (London/Ace of Clubs)
The Mills Blue Rhythm Band (Jazz Panorama—Sweden)
Jelly Roll Morton & His Red Hot Peppers (1927-1930), Vol 1 (RCA Victor—France)
Billie Holiday, The Golden Years, Vol 2 (Columbia/CBS)
Sidney Bechet, Vol 1: 'Sleepy Time Down South' (RCA Victor—France)
James P. Johnson, Father Of The Stride Piano (Columbia/—)
Henry Allen & His Orchestra Vols 1-4 (Collector's Classics/—)
The Very Great Henry Red Allen, Vols 1, 2 (Rarities/—)
Various, Harlem On Saturday Night (—/Ace of Hearts)
Lionel Hampton's Best Records, Vol 3 (1939-1940) (RCA Victor—France)
Louis Armstrong, V.S.O.P. (Very Special Old Phonography), 1928-1930, Vols 5 & 6 (CBS—France)
Louis Armstrong, Swing That Music (MCA/Coral)
The Henry Allen Memorial Album (Prestige)/ Mr Allen—Heny Red Allen (Xtra)
Henry Allen, Feeling Good (Columbia/CBS)

Feeling Good (courtesy CBS). Henry 'Red' Allen was described by Don Ellis as ...the most creative and avant-garde player in New York...'

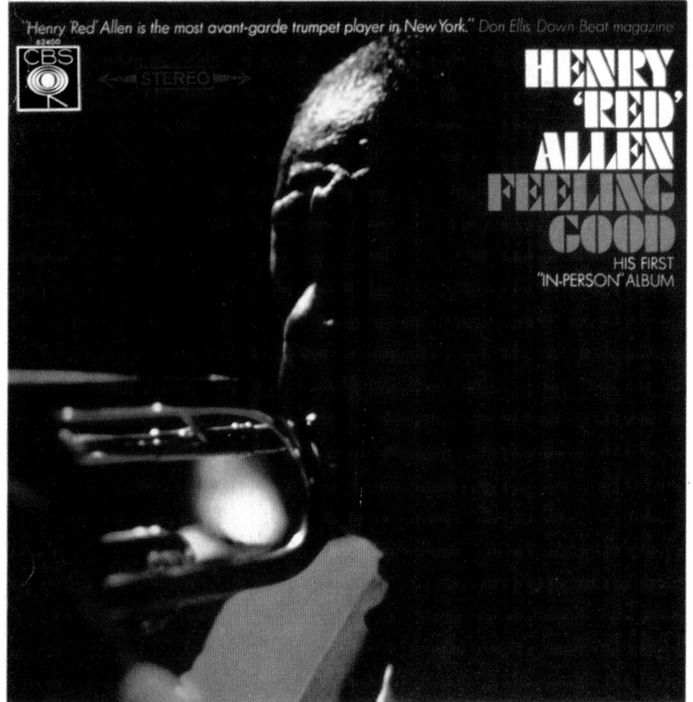

Mose Allison

The pianist-composer was born in Tippo, Mississippi, in 1927, and early blues influences such as Tampa Red, Memphis Slim and Sonny Boy Williamson permeate his work, despite later bebop overlays. His first composition, a series of impressionistic vignettes, **The Back Country Suite (Mose Allison)** remains his best work, and makes a lighter, less self-conscious use of the roots than was usually the case in the late '50s. His singing on numbers like **Blues** or **One Room Country Shack** has an odd appeal, and influenced Georgie Fame. His occasional trumpet playing on later albums is shaky. Allison is an excellent sideman, with Al Cohn, for example, but the charm of his early suites was never recaptured.

In the '50s, Allison was often found in the company of Al Cohn-Zoot Sims, Stan Getz, Gerry Mulligan and Chet Baker but these days he tours as a single. Now a Long Island resident, he works in New York with drummer Tom Whaley and Dennis Irwin or Ratso Harris on bass. His music turns up in some unlikely places, like his song **Meet Me In No Special Place** on Ry Cooder's soundtrack to *Brewster's Millions*. His most recent album was for the now defunct and sadly lamented label Elektra Musician, but there are plans to sign him to Blue Note.

Albums:

Mose Allison (Prestige/Prestige)
Middle Class White Boy (Elektra Musician/ Elektra Musician)
Lessons In Living (Elektra Musician/Elektra Musician)

Albert Ammons

Albert C. Ammons (born Chicago, Illinois, 1907) was perhaps the best-known and foremost exponent of boogie-woogie piano, a style of playing easily recognized by the repetitive ostinato figure played by the left hand, eight beats to the bar, complemented by powerful rhythmic right-hand work.

Ammons, father of the late tenor saxophonist Eugene 'Gene' Ammons, came to the fore during the 1920s as a pianist who appeared at numerous clubs in his native city. First began playing piano at ten, and was featured with Francois Moseley's Louisiana Stompers in 1929; then, as second pianist with William Barbee & His Headquarters (1930-31). By 1934 Ammons had put together own small combo, Chicago-based, which lasted until 1938. 1936: recording début with band that included trumpeter Guy Kelly, bassist Israel Crosby, and drummer Jimmy Hoskins; **Boogie Woogie Stomp**.

Left Chicago in '38 in company with fellow pianist Meade Lux Lewis, at behest of John Hammond. In New York, the pair teamed up with another piano player, Pete Johnson, all three working together, or solo, often with blues shouter Joe Turner. The coming together of the three coincided with sudden craze for eight-to-a-bar music. Trio played at one of Hammond's Spirituals To Swing concerts (December '38) **(John Hammond's Spirituals To Swing)** with Ammons taking part in three-piano showcase **(Cavalcade Of Boogie)** as well as accompanying country-blues singer-guitarist Big Bill Broonzy. Ammons also recorded in 1938 for Library of Congress **(The Complete Library Of Congress Boogie Woogie Recordings)**, and the Ammons-Lewis-Johnson triumvirate cut a torrid two-part **Boogie Woogie Prayer (Café Society Swing & The Boogie Woogie)** in December, a perfect definition of superior boogie woogie playing. **Café Society Rag**, from same session, and with a Turner vocal, identified an important New York venue for the boogie trio. February, '39: Ammons and Johnson (apart) recorded two boogie woogie pieces each with trumpeter Harry James, **(Café Society Swing & The Boogie Woogie)**, an unlikely combination which worked well for all three.

In 1939, too, Ammons recorded several times for Blue Note **(Blue Note's Three Decades Of Jazz—1939 to 1949—Vol 1)**, as soloist **(Boogie Woogie Stomp)**, and as member of Frankie Newton's Port of Harlem Jazzmen **(Port Of Harlem Blues)**. More Ammons solo discs came same year for another famous jazz label, Riverside **(Giants Of Boogie Woogie)**. At end of 1939, Ammons guested again, at a further Spirituals To Swing concert **(John Hammond's Spirituals To Swing)**, contributing two solid choruses to jam-session work-out on **Lady Be Good**, in company with Basie Orchestra and the Goodman Sextet. Ammons-Johnson duo (with rather unnecessary addition of Jimmy Hoskins' drums) laid down some fine boogie sounds for Victor in May, 1941 **(29 Boogie Woogie Originaux)**, but it was to be Ammons' last recording until 1944, due to a musicians' union ban on recordings and to an unfortunate accident which resulted in the pianist cutting off the tip of one finger in attempting to slice a sandwich. He was back in action, for in-person performances, not long after the incident. At this time, Ammons and Johnson worked regularly together, appearing in major US cities—they were great favorites amongst the Hollywood fraternity—but by 1944, Ammons was in recording studios again, this time for Commodore, alone, and in company with his Rhythm Kings **(Commodore Jazz, Vol 1)**, who included Hot Lips Page, Don Byas, Big Sid Catlett, Vic Dickenson, and his old Chicago associate, Israel Crosby. As well as the other's playing on this date, Ammons' powerful keyboard work, especially on **Bottom Blues**, invariably takes solo honors, inspired no doubt by Catlett's catalytic drumming.

Between 1946 and 1949 Ammons recorded for Mercury.

Typical of the music Ammons produced for Mercury is that to be found on **Boogie Woogie Piano Stylings** and **'Jug' Sessions**, the former marred only by some ordinary or indifferent material, the latter featuring on tracks like **St Louis Blues**, Ammons' son, Gene. 1946: Joe Turner and Ammons re-united for National recording date **(Joe Turner Sings The Blues, Vol 2)**, with both big men sounding as electrifying as before. There was, however, a mid-1940s interruption to Ammons' career, due to temporary paralysis of both hands.

He returned to Chicago for the last ten years of his life, where he lived and continued to work. The only deviation from this was in 1949 when he joined Lionel Hampton, recording as well as touring with the vibesman's band. But Albert Ammons, whose Jimmy Yancey-influenced playing had given much pleasure to so many over the years, died in December 1949.

Albums:
Albert Ammons, Boogie Woogie Stomp (Swaggie—Australia)
Various, John Hammond's Spirituals To Swing (Vanguard/Vanguard)
Various, The Complete Library Of Congress Boogie Woogie Recordings (Jazz Piano/—)
Various, Café Society Swing & The Boogie Woogie (Swingfan—Germany)
Various, Blue Note's Three Decades Of Jazz—1939 to 1949—Vol 1 (Blue Note/—)
Various, Kings Of Boogie Woogie (Blue Note/—)
Various, Giants Of Boogie Woogie (Riverside/—)
Various, 29 Boogie Woogie Originaux (RCA Victor—France)
Various, Commodore Jazz, Vol 1 (—/London)
Various, Boogie Woogie Man (RCA Victor—France)
Gene Ammons, 'Jug' Sessions (EmArcy/—)
Various, Boogie Woogie Trio (—/Storyville)
Albert Ammons, Boogie Woogie Piano Stylings (Mercury—Holland)

Gene Ammons

Born 1925, the son of boogie-woogie pianist Albert Ammons, tenor man Gene 'Jug' Ammons was one of Chicago's favorite sons. At the age of 18, he was playing with the King Kolax band, then in the sax section of Billy Eckstine's band. In 1949, he succeeded Stan Getz in the Woody Herman Herd. Starting under the influence of Lester Young, Ammons is best known for the complete antithesis of that style. Big-toned, forthright, often closer to R&B, Ammons projects a party spirit on most occasions. In 1950, he formed an ideal two-tenor combo with Sonny Stitt—simple, functional heads, driving solos, blistering chase choruses. There is little to choose between their albums, **Soul Summit, Blues Up & Down** or **You Talk That Talk**, for the spirit of rugged spontaneity surges through every number. Their final album together, made shortly before Ammons' death in 1974 **(Together Again For The Last Time)**, displays a shrinking of technique, some sloppy note production, but a compensating excitement. His opening solo on **Saxification** says it all—the overwhelming attack, big, blunt, honking, macho sound, the ends of his notes abrupt as a punch in the mouth. Ballads usually ended up as blues, **The More I See You** and **I'll Close My Eyes** feature reiterated phrases and grandstanding finales. Soul sax players like King Curtis owe a great deal to Jug.

Ammons-Stitt, Together Again For The Last Time (courtesy Prestige).

Albums:
Gene Ammons & Dodo Marmarosa, Jug & Dodo (Prestige/Prestige)
Ammons & Stitt, Soul Summit (Prestige/—)
Blues Up & Down (Prestige/—)
You Talk That Talk (Prestige/—)
Together Again For The Last Time (Prestige/—)
Red Top (Savoy/Savoy)

Ivie Anderson

Ivie Anderson (born Gilroy, California, 1904)—a sensitive, musicianly, always tuneful singer—worked with Duke Ellington from February 1931 to August 1942. Even when faced with such daunting material as **Oh Babe!, Maybe Someday** or **Five O'Clock Whistle (The Duke 1940)**, she succeeded, most times, in producing an eminently satisfactory performance.

Ivie Anderson, who died in Los Angeles in 1949, made very few recordings under her own name. But a January 1946 date **(Ivie Anderson & Her All Stars)**, in company with first-class musicians like Charlie Mingus, Lucky Thompson, and Willie Smith, and with band arranged/conducted by Phil Moore, produced some generally first-class singing, best of all on **Empty Bed Blues** and a reprise of **I Got It Bad**, the latter one of her most celebrated feature items with Ellington, viz **The Works Of Duke Ellington, Vol 16** and **In A Mellotone**.

Other Anderson-associated items from the Ellington songbook include **It Don't Mean A Thing (The Complete Duke, Vol 3: 1930-1932), Rocks In My Bed (In A Mellotone), I'm Checking Out Goodbye (The Ellington Era, Vol 2)** and **I Don't Mind (The Works Of Duke Ellington, Vol 18)**. As well as her many in-person appearances and recordings with the Duke Ellington Orchestra, Ivie Anderson also participated in the Marx Brothers' 1937 movie *A Day At The Races*.

The singer received vocal training initially between 9-13 at a convent, then studied for two years in Washington, DC. Her first professional engagement was in Los Angeles. She toured as dancer-singer; worked with several bands as singer only, including Paul Howard's and Anson Weeks' between 1925-30, and made Australian tour with Sonny Clay. Before joining Ellington she worked with Earl Hines in *Grand Terrace Revue* (1930). Opened her own restaurant in Los Angeles after leaving Ellington (1942), still singing regularly on West Coast. An asthmatic complaint restricted her appearances thereafter.

Perhaps the finest collection of Ivie Anderson recordings yet released is **Ivie Anderson** with Ellington.

Albums:
Ivie Anderson (Columbia/—)
Ivie Anderson & Her All Stars (Tops/Gala)
The Works Of Duke Ellington, Vols 10, 16, 17, 18 (RCA Victor—France)
The Complete Duke Ellington, Vol 3 (1930-1932), Vol 5 (1932-1933), Vol 6 (1933-1936), Vol 7 (1936-1937) (CBS—France)
Duke Ellington, The Ellington Era, Vol 2 (Columbia/CBS)
Duke Ellington, In A Mellotone (RCA Victor/RCA Victor)
Duke Ellington, Vintage Duke (Trip)
Duke Ellington (Trip)/ All That Jazz: Duke Ellington (DJM)
Duke Ellington, The Duke 1940 (Jazz Society/—)

Ray Anderson

Born in Chicago, 1952, Ray Anderson is one of the 'baby boom' generation of American improvising musicians. Apart from his fluid, versatile musical techniques, Anderson's music can be relied upon for what can only be described as a likeable and appealing audacity. He has enjoyed an interesting double life as a hard-hitting trombonist in conventional jazz settings (traveling through the avant-garde) into a funk-vocalist/trombonist role with his wild group Slickaphonics.

His first exposure to jazz was his father's Dixieland record collection—the young Anderson being notably impressed with veterans Vic Dickenson and Trummy Young. He took up trombone in the fourth grade, on the same day as his class-mate George Lewis. As a high school senior, Anderson briefly joined harmonica-player Jeff Carp's blues band, as well as contributed to classical recitals. Then, Anderson followed jazz's evolution systematically, from J. J. Johnson to Frank Rosolino to Roswell Rudd (via Archie Shepp) taking in Jimmy Cleveland and Slide Hampton along the way. He worked in Chicago with blues and R&B bands but became increasingly drawn to the improvisational experiments of the local Association for the Advancement of Creative Musicians (AACM).

In the early '70s, he went to California and gained invaluable experience with drummers Charles Moffett and Stanley Crouch. He arrived in New York late '72 to sit in with Charles Mingus, Don Pullen and George Adams and by the mid-'70s, he was working with Keshavan Maslak as part of the Surreal Ensemble. His work in 1977 with Barry Altschul and, later, Anthony Braxton earned him wider recognition. In 1979, he performed in Europe at the Moers Festival with the Leo Smith-Roscoe Mitchell band.

In 1981, Anderson helped form his popular Slickaphonics, described as 'a surreal, witty, funk-new-wave-avant-garde jazz band', including tenorist Steve Elson (formerly with David Bowie), bassist Mark Helias, guitarist Allan Jaffe and drummer Jim Payne. The début of Slickaphonics was quite a tonic on the jazz scene with their somewhat anarchistic, occasionally mischievous, approach to performance, which was informal to say the least.

As well as his rip-roaring input to the high-energy dance rhythms of Slickaphonics (a great hit with young jazz fans), Anderson has recorded a superb album of standards. **Old Bottles—New Wine** (1985) maintains Anderson's distinctive approach and sound alongside pianist Kenny Barron, bassist Cecil McBee and drummer Dannie Richmond. The album was awarded the German jazz critics, prize in 1986.

Always delightfully unpredictable, Anderson's latest project is a recording of 'contemporary New Orleans music' with a sextet including trombone, tuba and cornet. From this musician, you can always expect the unexpected.

Albums:
Bennie Wallace, Twilight Time (Blue Note/Blue Note)
Bennie Wallace, Sweeping Through The City (—/Enja)
Harrisburg Half Life (—/Moers Music)
You Be (—/Minor Music)
Right Down Your Alley (Soul Note/Soul Note)
John Scofield, Electric Outlet (Gramavision/Gramavision)
John Lindberg, Trilogy Of Works For Eleven Instruments (Black Saint/Black Saint)
Slickaphonics, Wow Bag (—/Enja)
Slickaphonics, Modern Life (—/Enja)

Below: Ray Anderson travelling from the AACM to the 'surreal, witty, funk-new-wave-avant-garde' (and decidedly danceable) Slickaphonics.

Above: Louis 'Satchmo' Armstrong. With Duke Ellington, probably the most celebrated figure in jazz—equalled only by the immortal Charlie Parker.

Louis Armstrong

Louis Armstrong (born New Orleans, 1900), formerly of the Crescent City's Colored Waifs Home and the best-known jazz musician of his or any other generation, has few rivals for the title of the greatest of all instrumental soloists. And apart from Billie Holiday (one of the innumerable artists deeply influenced by Armstrong), he remains the greatest jazz vocalist of all time.

Armstrong's development, from an apparently hesitant cornetist (practically untutored) to a position of positive omnipotence, was astonishing. After various mundane non-musical jobs, the young Armstrong formed a band (together with drummer, Joe Lindsay); then, at 18, joined Kid Ory. He worked with Fate Marable, both on Mississippi riverboats and in more conventional settings, between 1918—21. In the latter year, he returned to the city of his birth and played in marching bands as well as with jazz bands of Zutty Singleton, Papa Celestin, and others. His most significant job yet was to follow in 1922, when he joined Creole Jazz Band of King Oliver, like Armstrong a trumpeter of immense importance and ability. Between 1922 and 1924 the two-part team of Armstrong and his mentor was to produce some of the most remarkable music in jazz history.

Cornetists, with Armstrong ostensibly operating as second string to Oliver, are at their most sublime on **Mabel's Dream** (both takes), **Canal Street Blues, Riverside Blues, Snake Rag (Louis Armstrong/King Oliver)** and **Tears, Buddy's Habit** and **Chattanooga Stomp (West End Blues)**. **Tears** was important for the burgeoning talent; not only did he co-compose the piece with Lillian Hardin (the band's pianist and soon to become his second wife), but Louis' nine breaks, each executed impeccably and with rare feeling, point to the kind of virtuoso solo performances he was to produce with frightening regularity in the very near future (**Chimes Blues (Louis Armstrong/King Oliver)**, Armstrong's first solo on records, is less than average). **Weather Bird Rag (Louis Armstrong/King Oliver)** is a glorious example of both Armstrong and Oliver operating in a non-solo capacity but providing superlative breaks in tandem.

When, in June 1924, Armstrong left an already fading Oliver, he had, even at this stage, left an indelible mark on jazz With his induction into the Fletcher Henderson Orchestra as featured trumpet soloist, in September, '24, Armstrong's career took another major step forward. With Henderson, the virtuoso trumpet player really came into focus. His solos on Henderson recordings like **How Come You Do Me Like You Do?, Everybody Loves My Baby, Shanghai Shuffle, Alabamy Bound** and **Copenhagen (Louis Armstrong With Fletcher Henderson, 1924-1925)** are extraordinary in showing off Armstrong's unsurpassed tone, his inexhaustible stamina and fierce attack. His rhythmic powers too are remarkable, with Armstrong breaking up time in a way that made him stand out, with ease, amongst an already star-studded Henderson band (eg Hawkins, Buster Bailey, Redman, Joe Smith, et al).

The next landmark came to pass with the advent of his Hot Five and Hot Seven recordings which have long since passed into the realms of jazz immortality. Chronologically, the Hot Five was first, with Armstrong leading the brothers Johnny Dodds and Warren 'Baby' Dodds, Kid Ory, Lillian Hardin Armstrong (they were married by this time) and Johnny St Cyr through a series of classic performances. The Hot Five was an ideal setting for Armstrong's dexterity, yet only Johnny Dodds could compete with his all-round brilliance, if not technically, then in terms of pure jazz and emotional depth. A few odd failures or disappointments came for Armstrong (eg, **King Of The Zulus**), but generally he sustained incredible heights through the Hot Five recordings (made between 1925-1927). **Cornet Chop Suey (The Louis Armstrong Legend)** is probably Armstrong's first real *tour de force*, but his playing on such as **Heebie Jeebies, Jazz Lips, Skid-Da-De-Dat** and **Gut Bucket Blues (The Louis Armstrong Legend)** are not far behind.

The Hot Seven (1927) produced even more Armstrong fireworks: **Twelfth Street Rag, Melancholy Blues, Wild Man Blues**, and the electrifying **Potato Head Blues (The Louis Armstrong Legend)** set new standards of jazz performance and solo virtuosity. So too did Armstrong's playing on other items: **Gully Low Blues, S.O.L. Blues, Struttin' With Some Barbecue, Once In A while, Savoy Blues**—the last three titles reverting to Hot Five format, with blues guitarist Lonnie Johnson added to **Barbecue** and **Savoy Blues (The Louis Armstrong Legend)**.

By mid-1928, Armstrong had produced still further gems, this time with his Savoy Ballroom Five: **Fireworks, Skip The Gutter** and the magisterial **West End Blues**, with its awesome opening cadenza and final chorus that reaches the ultimate in building to a technical-emotional climax (all **The Louis Armstrong Legend**).

In July 1928, Armstrong recorded with big band accompaniment, this one Carroll Dickerson's **(The Louis Armstrong Legend)**. It was a context in which the Armstrong horn was to be heard, regularly, during most of the next decade. Before finally embarking on this format full-time, there were more Savoy Ballroom Five recordings (seven, actually, with Don Redman added), including beautifully structured solos on **Basin Street Blues** (over dismal vocal-cum-instrumental background) **(The Louis Armstrong Legend)**. And there were inspired duets between Armstrong and an Armstrong-influenced pianist named Earl Hines. At this time, Hines probably was the only instrumentalist in jazz who could offer real challenge to Louis Armstrong, in terms of all-round musical excellence and dazzling solo work. Both men struck sparks off each other—demonstrably so on **Savoyager's Stomp, Muggles** and the mind-boggling **Weather Bird**, which like **West End Blues**, another composition by Armstrong's old boss King Oliver, remains forever one of the all-time great jazz duets (all **The Louis Armstrong Legend**).

Armstrong knocked off yet further opulent trumpet solos on **I Can't Give You Anything But Love** and **Mahogany Hall Stomp (V.S.O.P. (Very Special Old Phonography), Vols 5 & 6)** with an all-star aggregation, including Jack Teagarden, Joe Sullivan, Lonnie Johnson and Luis Russell, the last-named pianist-leader at the disc date. Russell's star-studded orchestra, along with other big bands (Les Hite, Zilner Randolph, etc) provided the backdrop to Armstrong's trumpet for several years. Although these bands produced accompaniments that never remotely approached Armstrong's genius, the succession of one majestic solo after another continued unabated: **When You're Smiling, I'm A Ding Dong Daddy, Confessin' (V.S.O.P., Vols 5 & 6), Body And Soul, Sweethearts On Parade, Shine, Star Dust, Wrap Your Troubles In Dreams (V.S.O.P., Vols 7 & 8)** and **I Gotta Right To Sing The Blues, Dusky Stevedore (Louis Armstrong: July 4, 1900/July 6, 1971)**. By the time the last two items were recorded (1933), the accompanying orchestras were, in every way, nothing more than a cushion to accentuate the bravura work of the Armstrong horn and its owner's inimitable gravel voice.

At this point, it is important to lay stress on the fact that, aside of his cornet/trumpet playing, Armstrong's *vocal* contributions to jazz had been considerable, even thus far. From basic scat of **Heebie Jeebies, Gully Low Blues** and the like, to the more 'conventional' jazz singing of **I Can't Give You Anything But Love, I Ain't Got Nobody** and **I'm A Ding Dong Daddy**, Armstrong had become one of the great jazz vocalists. His voice had warmth, exuded personality, was rhythmically exciting; all in all, a perfect adjunct to the trumpet playing. Whilst on singing, it is also worth noting that Armstrong took part in an impressive number of recordings during the 1920s, as accompanist to numerous blues (or blues-influenced) singers. Most notable of these involved Bessie Smith and Ma Rainey. The Rainey tracks, **See See Rider Blues, Jelly Bean Blues** and **Countin' The Blues (Ma Rainey)**, date from 1924, and demonstrate not only that Armstrong had a natural feel for the genre, but also that, at 24 years old, his blues-playing was astonishingly mature.

With Smith, the following year, this side of his art had improved more than marginally. **St Louis Blues (The Empress)**, probably is the optimum Armstrong-Smith recording, the former's muted horn sounding at times like a logical extension of Bessie's magnificent vocalism. **Cold In Hand Blues, Reckless Blues, Sobbin' Hearted Blues (The Empress), I Ain't Gonna Play No Second Fiddle** and **Careless Love (Nobody's Blues But Mine)** are other supreme examples of one more magical combination.

During the 1920s, the Armstrong trumpet was heard with singers as diverse as Virginia Liston, Margaret Johnson, Sippie Wallace, Eva Taylor (wife of Clarence Williams), Hociel Thomas, Clarence Todd (all **Adam & Eve Had The Blues**), Bertha 'Chippie' Hill, Butterbeans and Susie, Cleo Gibson, Sara Martin, Victoria Spivey, Mamie Smith (all **Jazz Sounds Of The Twenties, Vol 4**) and Maggie Jones, Nolan Welsh, Clara Smith **(Rare Recordings Of The Twenties, Vol 1)**. Overall, the standard of the Armstrong contributions to these and other recordings is astonishingly high.

Later in his career, he was to combine his vocal-instrumental talents with other more pop-orientated singers, the most successful collaboration being with Ella Fitzgerald. This team worked together on record (and in person) on many occasions, nowhere better than during **Porgy & Bess** and **Ella & Louis, Vols 1 & 2/The Special Magic Of Ella & Louis, Vols 1 & 2)**.

Louis Armstrong, the Virtuoso, tended to diminish during the latter portion of the 1930s (and thereafter), but there remained occasions when his trumpet could soar to incomparable heights. Three such performances are: **Struttin' With Some Barbecue** (a remake, and one of the few that can be said to be superior to the original), **Jubilee** and **Swing That Music (Complete Recorded Works 1935-1945)**, the latter title containing four trumpet choruses astonishing even by Louis' own incredible standards, with a stretched-out high-note climax that is unmatched.

Armstrong-with-big-band-backing concept continued into the 1940s, but the decade started promisingly with a stimulating record date that reunited Louis with Sidney Bechet **(Complete Recorded Works 1935-1945)**, with both men trying to outplay the other throughout four titles, best of which is **Coal Cart Blues**. Armstrong had worked alongside Bechet during 1929, with Clarence Williams' Blue Five **(Adam & Eve Had The Blues)** and **Louis Armstrong/Sidney Bechet With The Clarence Williams Blue Five**, and with Josephine Beatty/Red Onion Jazz

Babies **(Louis Armstrong In New York, 1924-1926)**.

In 1947 came the first edition of Louis Armstrong & His All Stars, with the cornet of Bobby Hackett a welcome additional voice, playing some delightful obbligato to Louis' vocals which, since the 1930s, had tended to be more and more a regular feature of recordings, concerts, etc. Also most welcome were the voice and trombone of Jack Teagarden, and the controlled explosiveness of Sidney Catlett's drumming. There are fine studio recordings by this band **(Louis Armstrong: July 4, 1900/July 6, 1971)**, and it was indeed fortuitous that one of its first concerts, at Town Hall in May '47, was recorded for posterity **(Satchmo's Greatest Hits, Vols 4, 5 & 6)**.

There were many moments of magic thereafter, including generally top-class albums like **Louis Armstrong Joue W. C. Handy/Ambassador Satch/Satch Plays Fats**, but often the all-star set-up failed to inspire its leader into producing, during the 1950s/1960s, playing which compared with his innovatory days of the 1920s/1930s. Significant or otherwise, it was during this latter part of his career—following wholly successful international tours which took him to far-off places like Africa, Australia, Europe, the Far East and behind a portion of the Iron Curtain—that Louis Armstrong became an even bigger international music celebrity, his ever-growing number of fans coming more from a strictly non-jazz audience, the people, in fact, who enjoyed his big box office movies like *Hello Dolly!, High Society, A Man Called Adam* or *Where The Boys Meet The Girls*. Or the audience which made his recordings like **Hello Dolly** and **What A Wonderful World** into enormous international successes (**World** went to No. 1 on the US Hit Parade in 1967).

It must be said, though, that by this time the Armstrong All Stars concept (often called a musical circus) had become far removed from that of 20 years before. And as the latter years were to prove, even someone as indomitable as Louis Armstrong could be stricken with poor health, to the extent that, during the final period of his life, there was very little of the glorious trumpet playing of the past; indeed, the accent was mostly on focusing attention to his singing, something that even time and illness could not dim.

Concerts, club appearances, records, TV, movies, documentaries—during his most distinguished career Louis Armstrong conquered them all. Armstrong appeared in over 35 motion pictures or film shorts; he was the subject of the definitive TV special (CBS, 1956—*Satchmo The Great*); was the recipient of innumerable trophies and honors (musical and otherwise); was the winner of countless popularity and critics' polls; and was a long-standing advertisement for Swiss Kriss laxatives which he consumed in large, regular supplies. He played Bottom, onstage, in a 1939 musical production of the Shakespeare travesty, *Swingin' The Dream*, and starred in film specials in Germany and Denmark.

Books by or about the man include: *Satchmo, My Life In New Orleans,* Louis Armstrong; *Swing That Music,* Louis Armstrong; *Louis Armstrong*, Albert McCarthy; *Louis Armstrong*, Hughes Panassie; *Horn of Plenty*, Robert Goffin; *Trumpeter's Tale—The Story of Young Louis Armstrong*, Jeanette Eaton; *Louis Armstrong: A Self-Portrait/The Interview,* Richard Merryman; *From Satchmo To Miles*, Leonard Feather; *Celebrating The Duke, And Louis, Bessie, Billie, Bird, Carmen, Miles, Dizzy And Other Heroes*, Ralph J. Gleason; *Louis: The Louis Armstrong Story 1900-1971*, Max Jones, John Chilton; *Jazz Masters Of The 20s*, Richard Hadlock.

In 1956, Armstrong, assisted by as many relevant musicians as could be assembled at that time, helped put together **Satchmo: A Musical Autobiography**, a four-LP set retracing his career in jazz thus far, with the principal participant adding his own narrative. Louis Armstrong died on July 6, 1971.

Louis Armstrong, more than any other jazz musician, was responsible for bringing the music (of which he was Ambassador No 1) into areas where jazz was anathema. His larger-than-life personality an immense warmth endeared him to millions. Seeing and/or hearing Louis Armstrong was always magical.

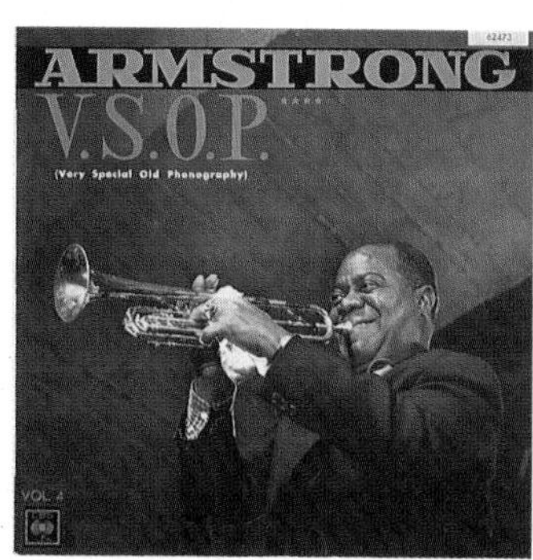

Louis Armstrong, V.S.O.P. Volume 4 (courtesy CBS-France).

Albums:
Louis Armstrong & King Oliver (Milestone)
King Oliver's Jazz Band, 1925 (Smithsonian Collection/—)
King Oliver's Jazz Band (—/Parlophone)
Ma Rainey (Milestone)
Bessie Smith, The Empress (Columbia/CBS)
Bessie Smith, Nobody's Blues But Mine (Columbia/CBS)
Various, Adam & Eve Had The Blues (CBS—France)
Various, Jazz Sounds Of The Twenties, Vol 4 (Columbia—Italy)
Various, Rare Recordings Of The Twenties, Vol 1 (CBS—France)
Louis Armstrong In New York, 1924-1926 (Riverside/Riverside)
Young Louis Armstrong, 1932-1933 (Bluebird/—)
Louis Armstrong: July 4, 1900/July 6, 1971 (RCA Victor/RCA Victor)
Complete Recorded Works 1935-1945 (MCA—France)
Louis Armstrong, Vols 1-3 (—/Saga)
The First Esquire Concert, Vols 1, 2 (—/Saga)
The Second Esquire Concert, Vols 1, 2 (—/Saga)
The Metronome All Stars/The Esquire All Stars (RCA Victor—France)
Louis Armstrong, Louis At The Movies (Privateer)
Satchmo's Greatest, Vols 1-5 (RCA Victor—France)
Satchmo At Symphony Hall, Vols 1, 2 (Decca/Coral)
Louis Armstrong, Swing That Music (Coral)
Louis Armstrong Joue W. C. Handy/ Ambassador Satch/Satch Plays Fats (CBS—France)
Louis Armstrong With Fletcher Henderson 1924-1925 (—/VJM)
Louis Armstrong/Ella Fitzgerald, 'Porgy & Bess' (Verve/Verve)
Louis Armstrong/Ella Fitzgerald, Ella & Louis (Verve)/ The Special Magic Of Ella & Louis, Vols 1, 2 (Verve)
Louis Armstrong, 'Satchmo The Great' (Columbia Special Products/—)
Louis Armstrong/Duke Ellington, The Beautiful Americans (Roulette)
Louis Armstrong, Vols 1, 2 (Trip)/ All That Jazz: Louis Armstrong (DJM)

Art Ensemble of Chicago

In 1965, pianist Muhal Richard Abrams established the Association for the Advancement of Creative Musicians (AACM) out of a sense of dissatisfaction with the constraints of group music. In this workshop atmosphere, the third wave of the avant-garde was born, in many ways the most extreme development to date. The first releases on Delmark **(Abrams: Levels & Degrees Of Light, Joseph Jarman: Song For** and **Roscoe Mitchell: Sound)** showed a very high level of musicianship by hitherto unknowns, and many of the devices later to become the hallmark of AACM music. **The Little Suite (Sound)** pointed the way ahead, and it still is a shocker. Firstly, the players' originality is collective. In the course of this performance they handle upwards of twenty instruments, playing off textures against each other with great humor and a surreal sense of theatre. The history of the music becomes a ragbag of quotes and references within the fabric of a piece—fragments from tent shows, field hollers, bugle calls, blues harmonica, bebop and new wave.

From all this activity, the definitive group emerged: Roscoe Mitchell, Joseph Jarman, playing between them almost the entire saxophone family, flutes, clarinets, drums, sirens, whistles, gongs, bells, vibes etc; Lester Bowie on trumpet, flugelhorn, drums, steer horn etc; Malachi Favors on bass etc. The first album from what was to become the Art Ensemble of Chicago was on the obscure Nessa label **(Numbers 1 & 2)**, although variants of the group **(Congliptious** and **Old Quartet)** follow the same policy. There's a sense of games being played in extremis about much of this music; melody, harmony and rhythm being subjected to the same discontinuity as the plot in the modern novel. Indeterminacy rules, and much of the skill rests upon the reactions of the musicians towards each other, their reflexes. Lester Bowie is probably the key personality, with a solo style, **Jazz Death? (Congliptious)**, that most closely corresponds to the kaleidoscopic methods of the group. Mitchell and Jarman follow broadly the Dolphy-Coltrane trajectory on any one saxophone, but chop about so rapidly that this orthodoxy is obscured.

In 1969 the Art Ensemble embarked for France, establishing a greater reputation there than they had in America. An incredible spate of recording followed, all of it excellent. Arguably the best works are the longest, **Reese And The Smooth Ones**, and the slowly rising dynamic level of **People In Sorrow**; but amazing passages abound throughout their albums. The moving instrumental lament that follows the recitation of the poem **Ericka (A Jackson In Your House)**, or the accurate bebop of **Dexterity (Message To Our Folks)**, shows that they can operate more conventionally.

Joined by drummer Don Moye, their first regular drummer since Philip Wilson left, they cut an album with Bowie's wife, the singer Fontella Bass **(Les Stances A Sophie)**. Over a Motown beat, she renders the erotic words of **Thème De Yoyo**, while the tumbling, free-form saxes, gourds and gym whistles heckle and strafe.

Returning to the United States, the Art Ensemble made their first festival appearance at the Ann Arbor Blues & Jazz Festival in 1972, which was recorded for Atlantic **(Bap-tizum)**. At last, American audiences proved receptive, though the Atlantic contract produced only one further album **(Fanfare For The Warriors)** on which they were rejoined by Muhal Richard Abrams, before being discontinued.

In many ways their music resembles that of Charles Ives, but with the speedo haywire. A little tune will peep out, tiptoe through the funhouse flak, gather confidence as the musicians soar into unanimity, falter into a broken puppet Petrushka waltz-time, and abruptly flop! Some indwelling suspicion of conventional beauty causes them to pull the rug out from under the listener's expectations, open trap doors. Their impatient, scratchy kind of energy ensures that the Art Ensemble will never settle for formula.

Albums:
Roscoe Mitchell, Sound (Delmark/Delmark)
Roscoe Mitchell, Congliptious (Nessa/Nessa)
Roscoe Mitchell, Old Quartet (Nessa/Nessa)
Roscoe Mitchell, Solo Saxophone Concerts (Sackville/Sackville)
Roscoe Mitchell, And The Sound And

Art Ensemble of Chicago, The Third Decade (courtesy ECM).

Below: The extraordinary Art Ensemble of Chicago—l. to r. Lester Bowie, Don Moye, Malachi Favors, Roscoe Mitchell and Joseph Jarman.

Space Ensembles (Black Saint/Black Saint)
Joseph Jarman, Song For (Delmark/Delmark)
Joseph Jarman, As If It Were The Seasons (Delmark/Delmark)
Joseph Jarman/Don Moye, Earth Passage/ Density (Black Saint/Black Saint)
Lester Bowie Numbers 1 & 2 (Nessa/Nessa)
Lester Bowie, Gittin' To Know You All (—/MPS—Germany)
Lester Bowie, Fast Last! (Muse/—)
Lester Bowie, The Great Pretender (ECM/ECM)
Lester Bowie, All The Magic (ECM/ECM)
Lester Bowie, I Only Have Eyes For You (ECM/ECM)
Art Ensemble Of Chicago, Reese And The Smooth Ones (—/BYG—France)
Art Ensemble Of Chicago, Message To Our Folks (—/BYG—France)
Art Ensemble Of Chicago, A Jackson In Your House (—/BYG—France)
Art Ensemble Of Chicago, People In Sorrow (Nessa/Nessa)
Art Ensemble Of Chicago, Les Stances A Sophie (Nessa/Nessa)
Art Ensemble Of Chicago, Tutankhamun (Arista Freedom/Arista Freedom)
Art Ensemble Of Chicago, Chi Congo (Paula/Decca)
Art Ensemble Of Chicago, Phase One (Prestige/America)
Art Ensemble Of Chicago, Bap-tizum (Atlantic/Atlantic)
Art Ensemble Of Chicago, Fanfare For The Warriors (Atlantic/Atlantic)
Old/Quartet (Nessa/Nessa)
Art Ensemble Of Chicago, Message To Our Folks (—/BYG/Affinity)
Art Ensemble Of Chicago, The Third Decade (ECM/ECM)

Lester Bowie, The Great Pretender —solo project (courtesy ECM).

Average White Band

Formed in Scotland early 1972 as a jazz and soul group, the Average White Band's first major exposure was in 1973 as support band to Eric Clapton's comeback gig at London's Rainbow.

The original members were Alan Gorrie (lead vocals, bass), Onnie McIntyre (rhythm guitar, vocals), Malcolm 'Molly' Duncan (tenor sax), Roger Ball (alto, baritone sax, keyboards), Mike Rosen (trumpet) and Robbie McIntosh (drums). Co-lead vocalist-guitarist Hamish Stuart joined six months later, replacing trumpeter Rosen.

Their first album, **Show Your Hand** for MCA, went relatively unnoticed (this first virtually overlooked album was repackaged in 1975, slightly altered, and re-titled **Put It Where You Want It**). Their fortunes changed with a move to Atlantic for the 1974 **Average White Band** (dubbed the 'White album'), beginning their long and creative Atlantic association with producer Arif Mardin. This album produced a big-selling hit single, the funky **Pick Up The Pieces**. As they hovered on success, they suffered a setback with the tragic loss of drummer McIntosh from a heroin overdose in Los Angeles in the September of 1974. A replacement was found in Steve Ferrone (born Brighton, England), formerly with Brian Auger's Oblivion Express.

Throughout the '70s and '80s, AWB have continued to have a string of successes—albums like **Cut The Cake, Soul Searching, Warmer Communications, Feel No Fret, Shine, Live** and **Benny And Us** (recorded with ex-Drifters singer Ben E. King).

Although AWB were credited as the first *British* band to combine the essence of American funk and soul with jazz components, their greatest success has been in the States. Being labeled a 'blue-eyed soul' group hasn't prevented AWB from playing at jazz festivals and their perennial **Pick Up The Pieces** has become a popular inclusion in the practice repertoire of many a budding jazz-funk band.

Apart from their excellent musical accomplishments, AWB is assured a special place in British jazz history as the band which introduced English tenorist Dick Morrissey to occasional AWB guitarist Jim Mullen in New York (two AWB members had played in the Jim Mullen & Co band in Scotland in the '60s). This chance meeting led, two years later, to the acclaimed Morrissey-Mullen partnership (echoing their mutual admiration for the US band Stuff) and Morrisey-Mullen's first album, **Up** for Atlantic, was naturally recorded with the Average White Band.

Album:
Show Your Hand (MCA/MCA)
Average White Band (Atlantic/Atlantic)
Cut The Cake (Atlantic/Atlantic)
Soul Searching (Atlantic/Atlantic)
Average White Band—Ben E. King, Benny And Us (Atlantic/Atlantic)
Warmer Communications (Atlantic/Atlantic)
Feel No Fret (RCA/RCA)
Shine (RCA/RCA)
Cupid's In Fashion (RCA/RCA)

Albert Ayler

Born 1936, died 1970, the great tenorman's brief career provoked fanatical reactions from both ends of the spectrum. Following the innovations of Ornette Coleman and Cecil Taylor, the second wave of New Thing players—Ayler, Shepp, Pharoah Sanders—showed a ferocity in their playing that has never been equalled. The emotional ante had risen in assertion of the black identity, in rejection of European standards of taste and acceptability, and the rise parallels Afro-American political developments in the mid-'60s.

Ayler's apprenticeship lay in R&B bands, where the tenor is used at the extremes of its register, and this characterizes all of his later work. His two earliest recordings, now difficult to obtain, sound more shocking than they were because of the orthodox hard bop context of his Scandinavian sidemen. The first album in compatible surroundings **(Spiritual Unity)**, featured the tenorist with bassist Gary Peacock and the drummer Sunny Murray, whose dramatic, almost frightening crescendos and silences add greatly to the atmosphere of Gothic intensity. **Ghosts, Second Variation** is a musical exorcism of overwhelming force, and Ayler never bettered this performance. The same trio features on the posthumously released live session **Prophesy** and the mood is again Corman-esque. The same year, 1964, saw three more sessions with larger groups, each including Murray. Ayler recorded soundtrack music for an underground film *(New York Eye & Ear Control)* in company with Ornette Coleman's trumpeter, Don Cherry, altoist John Tchicai and trombonist Roswell Rudd, and the results are chaotic. Ayler's move into collective improvisation made more sense when he re-activated the readymade tradition of New Orleans and this was foreshadowed **(Spirits)** in the funeral procession atmosphere of **Witches And Devils** with trumpeter Norman Howard. The collaboration with Don Cherry reaches its peak on **Vibrations** and brings into focus the tenor player's outlandish romanticism on **Mothers**.

The search for ethnic roots showed Ayler's groups back with New Orleans ensemble playing throughout 1965, with spectacular high register work in his solos, **Spirits Rejoice** and **Bells**.

Ayler's contract with Impulse led to a broadening of his range, and a consequent dilution of content in the cause of communication. Thus, the début album **In Greenwich Village** has a skirling Balkan flavor and the joys **(Truth Is Marching In)** and sorrows **(For John Coltrane)** move the listener in a direct and simple way. **Love Cry** saw a pretty re-working of his standard themes, **Ghosts** and **Bells** played fairly straight by Ayler and his brother, trumpeter Don, the horns augmented by the harpsichord of Call Cobbs. The complexity on this album comes from the amazingly fleet drumming of Milford Graves, who embroiders beneath the simple statements. Ayler's rock 'n' roll album **New Grass** upset his followers no end. The meeting between Ayler's avant-garde tenor and the tight beat of Pretty Purdie with yeah-yeah lyrics broke down the categories in some ways, but demonstrated too, that free players needed more rhythmic space.

A concert performance, **Nuits De La Fondation Maeght**, showed a return to form, but Ayler's development was cut short by his suicide in the Hudson River.

Albert Ayler's overwhelming impact tends to conceal the fact that he was something of a throwback, a pre-bebop player with declared roots in Lester Young and Sidney Bechet, and a sound that goes all the way back to the field holler and the brass band. Belches, shrieks, wide register leaps, a vibrato as broad as a busker's and as sentimental as a locket, plus an agility in moving his line in and out of focus, all served to confuse the issue. He had an amazing imagination. His themes and his group concept all point to a search for some ethnic root that springs straight from raw emotion. His critics mistook his work, seeing a gross, bumpkin naïvety, and missing the communicative power and freshness.

Albums:
Spiritual Unity (ESP/ESP)
Prophesy (ESP/ESP)
New York Eye & Ear Control (ESP/ESP)
Vibrations (Arista Freedom/—)
Spirits Rejoice (ESP/ESP)
Bells (ESP/ESP)
Albert Ayler In Greenwich Village (Impulse/Impulse)
Love Cry (Impulse/Impulse)
New Grass (Impulse/Impulse)
Nuits De La Fondation Maeght (Shandar—France)

Roy Ayres

Born in Los Angeles, California, September 10, 1940, the largely self-taught vibes-player Roy Ayres has cut a sizeable swathe through the jazz-funk and disco field. He studied piano and, for a period, steel guitar until his parents bought him a set of vibes in his senior high school year. His earliest influences on vibes were the Latin luminary Cal Tjader (Ayres' high school band was called Latin Lyrics), Milt Jackson and Bobby Hutcherson. In 1959, he spent a year at Los Angeles City College before leaving to become a professional musician.

In the early 1960s, Ayres kept conventional jazz company, notably working with Chico Hamilton, Jack Wilson, Gerald Wilson's big band, Phineas Newborn Jr, Teddy Edwards, Curtis Amy, Leroy Vinnegar and Hampton Hawes with whom he co-led a band. In 1965, Ayres worked with his own quartet for a year, then joined flautist Herbie Manne. The experience with Manne was to bring him into contact with musicians like Reggie Workman, Jimmy Owens, Chick Corea and Larry Coryell. Through Manne, Ayres discovered more about R&B and soul and, taking elements of those styles, he formed Roy Ayres Ubiquity.

Of his influence in the jazz-funk market, Ayres says that he has tried to innovate while simultaneously trying to change his style to a total musical spectrum rather than being limited to just one area of music. Interestingly, his 1981 album **Africa Centre Of The World**, incorporating Nigerian influences, showed something of a return to his early jazz roots.

Albums:
Jack Wilson, Brazilian Mancini (Atlantic/Atlantic)
Herbie Manne, Muscle Shoals Nitty Gritty (Atlantic/Atlantic)
Daddy Bug And Friends (Atlantic/Atlantic)
Mystic Voyage (Polydor/Polydor)
West Coast Vibes (United Artists/United Artists)
Bird Call (United Artists/United Artists)
Change Up The Groove (Polydor/Polydor)
Africa Centre Of The World (Polydor/Polydor)

Azimuth

Influential UK trio created 1977 by pianist/synthesizer-player John Taylor and vocalist Norma Winstone with trumpeter/flugelhorn-player Kenny Wheeler (saxophonist John Surman has substituted for Wheeler on occasions). Azimuth was formed, essentially, as a foil for Taylor's compositions.

Manchester-born Taylor, primarily a self-taught pianist, first attracted wider attention in 1969 with saxophonists John Surman and Alan Skidmore. He worked again with Surman in the '70s with the Morning Glory group which included Norwegian guitarist Terje Rypdal. Taylor also leads an octet (which includes Winstone and Wheeler) and presented his large-scale work **The May Day Suite** at the 1978 Bracknell Jazz Festival. He also appears with the Jan Garbarek group **(Places)**.

London-born Winstone has led her own group, **Edge Of Time** (1972). Her recording début was in 1969 on the Joe Harriott-Amancio D'Silva **Hum Dono** album. She worked with the Mike Westbrook band for a year and her unique vocal range has contributed variously to music by Mike Gibbs, Neil Ardley, John Dankworth, Ian Carr, John Stevens, Keith Tippett and Don Cherry. She is credited as having developed new frontiers for the voice, notably while working extensively with pianist-composer Michael Garrick **(The Heart Is A Lotus)**.

Canadian-born Wheeler leads his own group and has worked with the Globe Unity Orchestra, Anthony Braxton, John Stevens,

Derek Bailey, Keith Jarrett, Dave Holland, Jack De Johnette, Jan Garbarek, John Abercrombie and Ralph Towner.

Azimuth's music has been described as a kind of middle ground between the improvisatory freedoms of new jazz and the strict rhythmic and harmonic disciplines of minimalist music. Their music brings together diverse musical elements from Dave Brubeck and Bill Evans and, perhaps, even a suggestion of early English liturgical music. A recent album, **Départ**, features guitarist Ralph Towner and future projects include a long overdue Taylor-Winstone keyboards-voice duo album.

Albums:
Azimuth (ECM/ECM)
The Touchstone (ECM/ECM)
Départ (ECM/ECM)
Azimuth '85 (ECM/ECM)

Above: Brazil's popular Azymuth—l. to r. Conti, Bertrami and Malheiros.

Azymuth

The vibrant Brazilian instrumental trio Azymuth was formed 1971 by José Roberto Bertrami (keyboards/producer), Alex Malheiros (bass) and Ivan Conti (drums). Based in Rio de Janeiro, Azymuth's music relies heavily on fast-and-furious, updated Latin music encompassing elements of bossa nova, jazz and samba-school rhythms.

Born in São Paulo, Bertrami's early influences were pianists Bill Evans and Luiz Eça. He worked in São Paulo in the mid-'60s, notably with Airto and Flora Purim at the popular Joáo Sebastiáo Bar. In 1967, when Airto and Purim moved to New York, Bertrami went to Rio where he met drummer Conti who had worked with vocalist Roberto Carlos and played with the cream of Brazil's musicians. Malheiros comes from a long line of virtuoso Brazilian bass-players (his father made the first electric bass in Brazil in 1956 from a magazine-ad picture—the family still designs and builds custom basses). Malheiros, whose first influence was acoustic-bassist Scott La Faro, worked as a teenager in a duo with guitarist Egberto Gismonti, as well as with Luiz Eça, Tim Maia and Ed Lincoln.

Together and separately, the trio established themselves as sought-after session musicians, recording with artists like Elis Regina, Deodato and Milton Nascimento as well as for film and TV soundtracks. (Their first album, **O Fabuloso Fittipaldi** of 1973, was actually a film soundtrack.) Azymuth can proudly admit to having contributed to more than a third of the albums made during the '70s samba boom.

The band made its European début at the Montreux Jazz Festival in 1977 and the following year Bertrami gained wide recognition for his contribution as rhythm arranger-keyboardist on Sarah Vaughan's album **I Love Brazil**. Azymuth's international appeal was confirmed in 1979 by their dance floor-oriented **Jazz Carnival** (from their **Light As A Feather** album—the title track being a Stanley Clarke tune), which brought them a huge international audience.

Albums:
Light As A Feather (Milestone/Milestone)
Outubro (Milestone/Milestone)
Telecommunication (Milestone/Milestone)
Cascades (Milestone/Milestone)
Rapid Transit (Milestone/Milestone)
Flame (Milestone/Milestone)
Spectrum (Milestone/Milestone)

Azymuth, Light As A Feather (courtesy Milestone).

Back Door

One of the most exciting British bands to emerge in 1970s and subsequently internationally acclaimed, particularly in the United States. Back Door—bassist-vocalist Colin Hodgkinson, saxophonist Ron Aspery and drummer Tony Hicks—reunited in 1985 making a nostalgic comeback at Ronnie Scott's Club, London.

All three members had worked with Eric Delaney's band in the late '60s. The mainstream grounding with that outfit seemed an unlikely launch-pad for a 3-piece which was to storm across musical barriers with a wholly original and innovative fusion of jazz, rock and blues. Their poll-winning début album, **Back Door**, was a pioneering project in self-production on a small budget.

Since Back Door went separate ways in 1977, each member's reputation has grown individually—notably, Aspery with Sky and Mezzoforte; Hicks with singer-songwriter Chris Rea and as a session-player; and Hodgkinson with Alexis Korner, Jan Hammer, Ian Stewart-Charlie Watts, and Brian Auger.

Back Door's unexpected but electrifying return in the mid-'80s delighted their enthusiastic and loyal following, their music showing no sign of having tarnished in content or performance.

Albums:
Back Door (Warner Brothers/WEA)
8th Street Nights (Warner Brothers/WEA)
Activate (Warner Brothers/WEA)
Starlight (Warner Brothers/WEA)

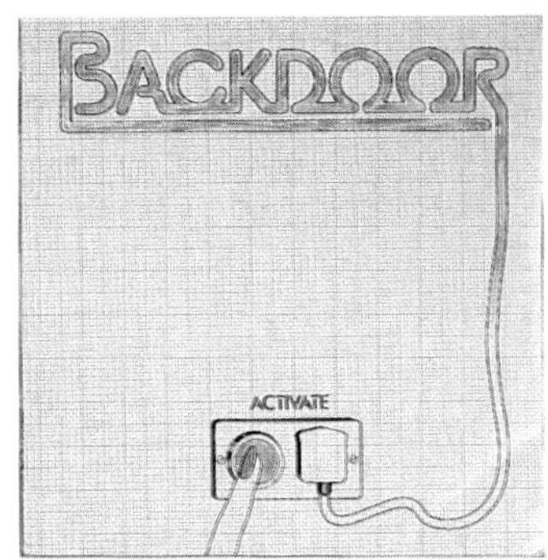

Back Door, Activate (courtesy Warner Brothers).

Derek Bailey

Guitarist Derek Bailey is a leading figure in the European free music scene, pioneering an investigation of sound and texture through electronic variation. Associated with John Stevens' Spontaneous Music Ensemble in the 1960s **(So What Do You Think?)** and the London Jazz Composers Orchestra, Bailey formed a trio with trombonist Paul Rutherford and bassist Barry Guy **(Iskra 1903)**. His work in the duo and solo situation is unfailingly inventive and cliché-free, his tonal manipulations always at the service of the music. A stimulating concert with multi-instrumentalist Anthony Braxton, in 1974, was recorded **(Duo)** and finds both musicians exploring tonal areas and producing startlingly original music through creative friction rather than solo and support. The same general comment applies to the great guitarist's work with saxophonist Evan Parker dating back to an album from 1970 **(The Topography Of The Lungs)** which also includes the Dutch drummer, Han Bennink, and continues through to a magnificently spiky concert performance in 1975 **(The London Concert)**.

Guitarist Derek Bailey and reeds-player Tony Coe, Time (courtesy Incus).

Bailey's fascination with totally free improvisation led to the establishment of Company, an international pool of free musicians, Parker, Steve Beresford, Braxton, Steve Lacy, Rutherford and Lol Coxhill, who play together without forming a permanent group, and the first album **(Company 1)** using Bailey, Parker, cellist Tristan Honsinger and bassist Maarten van Regteren Altena, thoroughly justifies the experiment. From 1971 the guitarist has also been giving solo recitals, and albums like **Derek Bailey Solo** and **Lot 74—Solo Improvisations** confirm his reputation as the most original guitarist on the scene.

Albums:
SME, So What Do You Think? (—/Tangent)
Iskra 1903 (—/Incus)
Duo (Emanem/Emanem)
The Topography Of The Lungs (—/Incus)
The London Concert (—/Incus)
Company 1 (—/Incus)
Derek Bailey Solo (—/Incus)
Lot 74—Solo Improvisations (—/Incus)
Derek Bailey & Tristan Honsinger (—/Incus)
Music Improvisation Company (—/Incus)
Derek Bailey, Tony Coe, Time (—/Incus)
Derek Bailey, Jamie Muir, Dart Drug

(—/Incus)
Derek Bailey, George Lewis, John Zorn, Yankees (Celluloid/Celluloid)
Anthony Braxton, Derek Bailey, Royal Vol 1 (—/Incus)
Company, Epiphany (—/Incus)

Mildred Bailey

Mildred Bailey was, like Ethel Waters before her, and Dinah Washington after, one of those jazz singers who, not content with excelling in one musical genre, had sufficient talent to conquer others. In Mildred Bailey's case she could sing an eloquent blues, had the kind of vocal delivery that appealed to those uninterested in either blues or jazz, and could even make a fair stab at gospel singing. Born Mildred Rinker (in Tekoa, Washington, 1907), sister of Al Rinker (of Rhythm Boys—Bing Crosby-Paul Whiteman fame), was schooled in Spokane, began in music as song demonstrator, then worked in a West Coast revue.

Her initial reputation was achieved through regular work on radio station KMTR as well as at other venues in California. Paul Whiteman signed her to sing with his large orchestra. Worked with Whiteman between 1929-33 (Whiteman probably was first bandleader to feature a solo woman vocalist) during which time she recorded such superb sides as **Stop The Sun Stop The Moon** and **Rockin' Chair (Paul Whiteman & His Orchestra)**; the last-named as closely associated with the name Mildred Bailey as it was to become in later years with the vocal-instrumental duo of Louis Armstrong and Jack Teagarden.

During last year with Whiteman she married the bandleader's ex-xylophone player Red Norvo. They were divorced in 1945. Norvo was to work with her regularly, from 1935 until the end of the 1930s. Her first record had orchestra conducted by Eddie Lang (1929): Hoagy Carmichael's **What Kind O' Man Is You (Her Greatest Peformances 1929-1946, Vol 1)**.

Her curious (yet never unpleasant) high-register voice was rarely, if ever, off-pitch or off-key. Hers was a truly effortless kind of singing, the type which enabled her to encompass a wide variety of material (eg **Old Folks, Peace, Brother!, Gulf Coast Blues** and **There'll Be Some Changes Made** (all **Vol 3**)). Her sense of humor was subtly projected on apposite material, like **Arthur Murray Taught Me Dancing In A Hurry (Vol 3)** and **Week End Of A Private Secretary (Vol 2)**, recorded in 1942 and 1938 respectively. And on recordings like **'Tain't What You Do** and **St Louis Blues (Vol 2)** she worked with the John Kirby Orchestra (augmented by the presence of Red Norvo).

Her finest accompaniments of the period came from her then husband's band, and studio outfits assembled by arranger-composer Eddie Sauter, with outstanding charts written by Sauter for both. She worked also with Benny Goodman (**Vol 1** and **Recordings Made Between 1930 & 1941**), her singing of Frank Loesser's **Junk Man** on the latter disc achieving some minor recognition, sales-wise; she recorded too with Alec Wilder's classically orientated octet (**Vol 3**) and numerous othes with Norvo and studio bands under her own name (viz Mildred Bailey & Her Oxford Greys). Broadcast with Benny Goodman in 1939 (**Benny Goodman, His Stars & His Guests**) but next year worked solo.

Although beset by recurring illnesses during the 1940s, caused as much as anything by constant problems of overweight, she was given her own radio series via the CBS network (*The Mildred Bailey Radio Show—1944-45*). Bailey's consistency of performance on these shows made her a firm favourite, with fans as well as with musicians. Her love for jazz ensured that invariably musicians of the calibre of Norvo, Teddy Wilson and Charlie Shavers were also on hand. 1940s recordings show little or no diminution of her powers (**All Of Me** and **First Esquire Jazz Concert, Vol 1**), but by 1949 her health had deteriorated alarmingly; during that year she was treated for heart and diabetes complaints. Sang again in 1950-51, but was forced thereafter to spend what remained of her life in a New York hospital where she died in December, 1951.

Mildred Bailey's singing was to influence deeply many other vocalists, including Ella Fitzgerald, Peggy Lee, Lee Wiley, Mabel Mercer and Maxine Sullivan.

Mildred Bailey, Her Greatest Performances 1929-46 (courtesy CBS).

Albums:
Paul Whiteman & His Orchestra (RCA Victor/RCA Victor)
Mildred Bailey, Her Greatest Performances 1929-1946 (Columbia)/ Her Greatest Performances 1929-1946, Vols 1-3 (CBS)
Mildred Bailey, All Of Me (Monmouth—Evergreen/Ember)
The Mildred Bailey Radio Show 1944-1945 (Sunbeam)
Mildred Bailey, Me & The Blues (Regal)/ Rockin' Chair Lady (CBS—Realm)
Various, Recordings Made Between 1930 & 1941 (CBS—France)
Tommy Dorsey/Jimmy Dorsey/Eddie Lang, Tommy, Jimmy & Eddie, 1928-29 (—/Parlophone)

Chet Baker

Born 1929, the trumpeter's early career was attended with phenomenal luck, which turned spectacularly sour. 1952 saw him working with Charlie Parker on the West Coast (**Bird On The Coast**) and in the same year joining baritone saxist Gerry Mulligan's famous pianoless quartet. Still very much an apprentice, Baker's work with the group is distinguished less by technique than by his tone, which has an unforgettably plaintive quality, **My Funny Valentine** for example (**Gerry Mulligan, Quartet**). Numbers like **Walkin' Shoes, Bernie's Tune**, show the bright, skating lines of the trumpet as an excellent foil to the burly baritone. But Baker's cool approach sounds diffuse against the ascetic logic of altoist Lee Konitz, who joined the quartet for recording sessions in 1953 (**Revelation**). Also in that year, Baker topped Metronome's trumpet poll, and established his own quartet with pianist Russ Freeman. His work became more outgoing and assured, but none of the recordings remains in the catalog (**Jazz At Ann Arbor), (Chet Baker—Russ Freeman Quartet**).

Association with composers like Freeman, Twardzik and Zieff seemed to develop his limited range, and the group that be brought to Europe in 1955 (**Chet Baker In Paris**) represents the high water mark of promise. Unfortunately, pianist Dick Twardzik died of an overdose at the age of 24, leaving behind a handful of tantalizing examples of his originality, eg **The Girl From Greenland**. Baker's own career began to suffer from narcotics, arrests, headlines, and a critical backlash against his playing that had been so over-praised at the outset. In fact, many of his subsequent albums are excellent—**Playboys, Chet Baker & Crew, Chet In New York**.

In the 1980s, there has been considerable renewed interest in the trumpeter's work, notably in the UK with the successful Boplicity label re-issue of the previously rare Chet Baker-Art Pepper 1956 collaboration **Playboys** and the Baker quintet's **Cools Out**. Such is the legend that Baker's distinctive trumpet can even be heard on a recent Elvis Costello recording.

It is difficult to separate the music from the myth. Chet Baker's good looks, youth and fragile, introverted tone attracted a cult following in the '50s, which his subsequent and tragic track record did nothing to dispel. A likeness to James Dean and a sound reminiscent of Bix Beiderbecke gave a generation of jazz fans their 'Doomed Youth'. Miles Davis was his main inspiration, but there is a sincerity and emotional honesty about his playing that is still very moving.

Chet Baker, Once Upon A Summertime (courtesy Galaxy).

Albums:
Bird On The Coast (Jazz Showcase/—)
Gerry Mulligan Quartet (Prestige/Prestige)
Gerry Mulligan-Lee Konitz, Revelation (Blue Note/Blue Note)
Chet Baker In Paris (—/Blue Star, Barclay—France)
Chet Baker, Baby Breeze (Limelight/Mercury)
Peace (Enja—Germany)
The Touch Of Your Lips (Steeplechase/Steeplechase)
Daybreak (Steeplechase/Steeplechase)
This Is Always (Steeplechase/Steeplechase)
Chet Baker-Paul Bley, Diane (Steeplechase/Steeplechase)
Chet Baker-Art Pepper, Playboys (Vogue/Boplicity)

Leandro 'Gato' Barbieri

Born in Argentina (the nickname 'Gato' is Spanish for 'cat'), the tenorman worked with bandleader Lalo Schifrin before moving to Italy in search of a jazz environment. Quite a few American new wave players fetched up in Rome in the mid-1960s, and Barbieri was fortunate in joining up with Ornette Coleman's trumpeter, Don Cherry. The two albums that Blue Note recorded are classics of free group improvisation (**Complete Communion** and **Symphony For Improvisers**) and show Cherry's brilliant use of the young sideman. A player of enormous power and force, Barbieri tends to operate a very short trajectory, screaming up into the extreme upper register within a few bars, and then back to ground level before starting again. Cherry, deploying tempo changes, demanding interaction, prevents those rhetorical spirals and leads his lowering hurricane in a quadrille. Barbieri also recorded with expatriates like Steve Lacy (**Nuovi Sentimenti**) and South African pianist Dollar Brand (**Confluence**), a duo album of stark drama which unites the florid gestures of Barbieri's tenor with the mission hall blues of the piano.

Barbieri's re-discovery of his Latin American roots led to a series of albums for Impulse which introduced a wider audience to his work, but seems to have led artistically to predictability. There have been several attempts to merge the two cultures—Gillespie and the Cuban drummer Chano Pozo in the '40s, altoman Bud Shank and Brazilian guitarist Laurindo Almeida, Stan Getz and Gilberto, Jobim and Bonfa in the '50s. Barbieri's hybrid centres on the tango, but in spite of the dense rhythmic activity—congas, shakers and rattlers—there is a static feel to the music. The best albums from this period remain the first (**The Third World**), which has the advantage of major contributions by Charlie Haden and Roswell Rudd, and the second (**Fenix**), which has a tenor solo of great balance, as well as the customary vehemence, in **Carnavalito**.

A vast battery of ethnic instruments surrounds the tenorist on an attractive album recorded in Buenos Aires (**Chapter One**). Most of his later work hinges upon lush and beefy romanticism, with high-register kamikaze missions, over latin rhythms (**El Pampero** and **Live In New York**). His appearance on composer Carla Bley's **Tropic Appetites** and the sound track for *Last Tango in Paris* rather confirm that his best work results from collaboration.

His style owes a good deal to Rollins and Coltrane, though the manner is more florid and melodramatic. His initial impact on the listener is overwhelming—the spine-chilling screams, the huge drive—but, like Pharoah Sanders, his undoubted power tends to be dissipated through lack of structure.

Leandro 'Gato' Barbieri, Apasionado (courtesy Polydor).

Albums:
Don Cherry, Complete Communion (Blue Note/Blue Note)
Don Cherry, Symphony For Improvisers (Blue Note/Blue Note)
Giorgio Gaslini, Nuovi Sentimenti (—/HMV—Italy)
Gato Barbieri-Dollar Brand, Confluence

(Arista Freedom/Arista Freedom)
The Third World (Flying Dutchman/—)
Fenix (Flying Dutchman)
El Pampero (Flying Dutchman/RCA Victor)
Chapter One (Impulse/Impulse)
Live In New York (Impulse/Impulse)
Carla Bley, Tropic Appetites (Watt/Watt)
Chapter Three: Viva Emiliano Zapata (Impulse/Impulse)

Charlie Barnet

Charles Daly Barnet (born New York City, 1913) was born to wealthy parents, and raised by mother and a grandfather, who both wanted the youngster to become a corporation lawyer. Barnet Jr. opted to become full-time jazz musician. Piano lessons at a very early age, then on to saxophone at 12. Led first band four years later (aboard steamship); later, played for numerous ships' bands—for Cunard, Red Star, Panama-Pacific, South and Central America. By the time Barnet left Rumsey Academy and put together first (land-based) big band (1933) he was already playing alto, tenor and soprano saxophones and clarinet. First recorded examples of his sax playing, with Red Norvo 1934, give fair indication that basically 'jump' style was already more or less formulated **(Swing Street, Vol 3)**. Influences also apparent: admiration for Coleman Hawkins reflected on tenor; for Johnny Hodges on soprano and some alto; strong elements of Pete Brown, especially from rhythmic standpoint, apparent on all three instruments. Never an extraordinarily gifted improvizer, Barnet always was one of jazz's hardest-driving players. Band-leading/playing career interrupted in 1935 when he disbanded, temporarily moving to Hollywood to become a film actor (with parts in two 1936 movies).

Final breakthrough, as band-leader, in 1939, aided by new RCA-Bluebird contract. (Barnet had recorded for the label a couple of years before **(The Complete Charlie Barnet, Vol 1)** without commercial success.) Subsequent discs on Bluebird became major sellers. These included **Cherokee, Pompton Turnpike, Charleston Alley** and **Redskin Rhumba (Charlie Barnet, Vol 1)**. Barnet, a keen Ellington lover who had played chimes on the latter's Victor recording of **Ring Dem Bells** in 1930, made sure his own band was Ellington-influenced. Often featured Ducal material, such as **Gal From Joe's, Echoes Of Harlem, Harlem Speaks** and **Lament For Lost Love (Charlie Barnet, Vol 2)**. Employed first-class arrangers, principally Horace Henderson, Skip Martin, and, most notably, the gifted Billy May, whose work often has exhibited genuine humor. Barnet himself also contributed scores. Records apart, other major breakthrough came with the band's residence at Famous Door, 52nd Street.

From 1939 until the early-1950s, Barnet continued to lead a succession of excellent big bands, boasting a variety of impressive soloists. Very anti-racial, as shown by choice of sidemen through the years, Barnet at various times employed a series of top-class black musicians, including: Roy Eldridge, Peanuts Holland, Howard McGhee, Clark Terry, Charlie Shavers, Dizzy Gillespie and Oscar Pettiford.

Although 1939-43 bands failed to attain the immense popularity of some other basically white 'swing bands' (ie mostly jazz-influenced dance bands), undoubtedly Barnet's were amongst the most jazz-conscious and hardest-swinging. Mid-1940s Barnet bands followed suit, including amongst personnel listings such names as Buddy De Franco, Dodo Marmarosa, Al Killian, Eddie Safranski, Lawrence Brown, Barney Kessel. Switched record labels, from Victor to Decca, and the recording of **Skyliner (Silver Star Swing Series Presents)** became one of the band's biggest hits. In 1949, formed a fine bebop-based outfit, with arrangers Walter 'Gil' Fuller and Manny Albam, and instrumentalists such as Rolf Ericsson, Claude Williamson, Maynard Ferguson, Tiny Kahn, Dick Hafer **(Bebop Spoken Here)**. Sounded much more 'authentic' than, say, Goodman band of the period, though Barnet himself made no stylistic changes to his own playing. Disbanded October, 1949.

During the following two decades he led jazz units, both large and small, at intermittent periods, including record dates. Very little connection with bebop (or post-bop) about these activities. Best of the latterday recordings was **Big Band 1967** which recaptured the essence of peak days.

During his career Charlie Barnet (he also married 11 times) was a poll-winning instrumentalist **(Benny Carter 1945 + The Metronome All-Stars)**. During its halcyon days the Charlie Barnet Orchestra appeared in several films, or film shorts **(Film Tracks Of Charlie Barnet)**.

Barnet's extraordinary life and career are colorfully documented in *Those Swinging Years: The Autobiography of Charlie Barnet*, published in 1985 (Barnet/Stanley Dance—Louisiana State University Press, Baton Rouge and London). The book takes you through his life—in and out of music and about six marriages.

Silver Star Swing Series Present Charlie Barnet And His Orchestra (courtesy MCA Coral—Germany).

Albums:
Various, Swing Street, Vol 3 (Epic/Columbia)
The Complete Charlie Barnet, Vol 1: 1935-1937 (Bluebird/—)
Charlie Barnet, Vols 1, 2 (RCA Victor/RCA Victor)
Charlie Barnet, King Of The Saxophone (Trip)/ Charlie Barnet & His Orchestra (DJM)
Charlie Barnet, Rhapsody In Barnet (Swing Era)
Charlie Barnet & His Orchestra, Vol 1 (Sounds of Swing)
Film Tracks Of Charlie Barnet (Joyce)
Charlie Barnet & His Orchestra 1944-1949 (Golden Era)
Benny Carter 1945 + The Metronome All-Stars (Queen Disc—Italy)
Charlie Barnet, Some Like It Hot (Swing Era)
Charlie Barnet, Big Band 1967 (—/Vocalion)

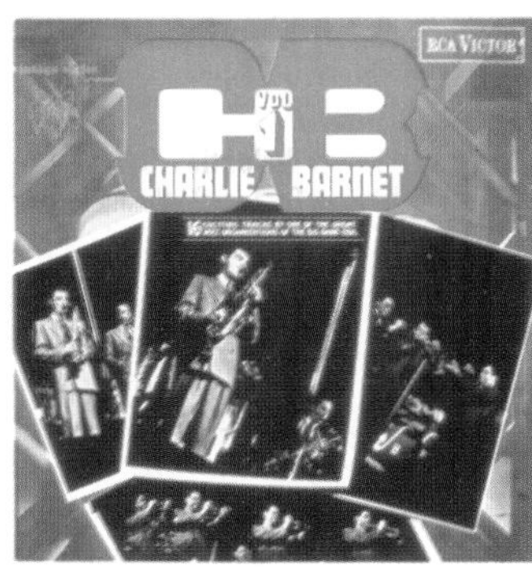

Charlie Barnet Orchestra, Vol. 1 (courtesy RCA Victor).

Gary Bartz

Saxophonist Gary Bartz established himself as a popular crossover artist with successful albums like **Singerella: A Ghetto Fairy Tale, In My Sanctuary, Love Affair, Bartz** etc.

Born in Baltimore, Bartz received his first alto sax aged 11; by his teens, he was playing regularly at his father's nightclub, the North End Lounge. Here, he led his own group and sat in with top musicians like Art Blakey, Max Roach and George Benson. After studying at Juilliard and Baltimore's Peabody Conservatory, he made his professional début in 1964 with the Max Roach-Abbey Lincoln group. Three years later he embarked on a successful solo career, although still finding time to tour and record with McCoy Tyner, Miles Davis and his own group Ntu Troop.

Bartz refused to limit his horizons and his various projects have included, for instance, his interesting involvement with the show *Bebop: The Hip Musical* in the late '70s in which he was musical co-ordinator, arranger and even actor. His musical scope ranges from straight-ahead jazz to R&B, funk and even classical elements (ie his operatically conceived 1975 **Singerella** album).

Albums:
Singerella: A Ghetto Fairy Tale (Prestige/Prestige)
In My Santuary (Capitol/Capitol)
Love Affair (Capitol/Capitol)
Bartz (Arista)

Above: The irreplaceable William 'Count' Basie—the Kid from Red Bank, New Jersey. Legendary leader of an all-time legendary band.

Count Basie

William 'Count' Basie (born Red Bank, New Jersey, 1904) remained one of the supreme jazz catalysts after more than 50 years as a practicing professional musician and a more or less uninterrupted period of 45 years as bandleader. In the latter role, the name 'Basie' connotes all that is best in big-band jazz; at least since 1935, when Basie took over remnants of Bennie Moten Kansas City Orchestra. Basie, leading an outfit called Barons of Rhythm, including Buster Smith, alto sax, was discovered by impresario John Hammond, broadcasting from Reno Club, KC. Hammond helped put together first Basie big band, playing a major role in getting its first national tour. Bill Basie was dubbed 'The Count' before leaving Kansas City. Following 'out of town' appearances, first important New York gig was residency at Roseland Ballroom.

First recordings, 1937 **(The Best Of Basie)**, showed a dynamic outfit, with major soloists in Lester Young, Herschel Evans, Buck Clayton, and Basie himself. Ensemble-wise, a certain raggedness, soon to be obviated with suitable replacements. Band evinced genuine shouting excitement,and underpinning everything was extraordinary rhythm section, comprising, Basie apart, drummer Jo Jones, bassist Walter Page and guitarist Claude Williams (soon to be replaced by the far superior Freddie Green, since his inception a most vital cog in the wheel of all subsequent Basie-led aggregations). Vocals handled by Jimmy Rushing, at first alone, then assisted by Helen Humes and, on occasion, by sax-section leader Earle Warren.

Roseland Shuffle (The Best Of Basie (1937-38)), as well as documenting the band's New York opening, remains an archetypal example of this embryonic stage: introduced by Basie's piano and rhythm section, solos supported by constant riffing by various sections of the band in what has long since become known as Kansas City style. (For chronology's sake, small contingent from main band, including Young, had already made first recordings, with a quartet of sides recorded in Chicago, 1936 under pickup title of Smith-Jones, Inc.) As exciting as the band sounded on record, in live performance it was even more uplifting. Airshot performances from 1937 **(The Count At The Chatterbox, Count Basie & His Orchestra/William & The Famous Door** and **Basie Live!/Count Basie Live)**, although often short on hi-fi, give a more than adequate representation of just how and why it soon became respected as one of the top three big bands. Basie composition called **One O'Clock Jump**, soon to become forever thereafter its theme, also recorded in '37. With Green replacing Williams and Warren taking over from Caughey Roberts on alto sax and clarinet, band received further boost when Billie Holiday joined in same year. However, she was to stay for less than one year during which time she was unable to record with Basie, being personally contracted to another label. Despite initial breakthrough, top commercial success still eluded Basie band. This came only after month-long residency at Savoy Ballroom (January, '38), followed by six months at Famous Door (engineered by agent Willard Alexander), with SRO audiences nightly at latter. This tremendous success was built through early 1940s, even though major blows, like the death of Herschel Evans (1939), and drafting of key figures (Buck Clayton, Jones, Jack Washington), did not help; nor did the exiting of cornerstone sidemen like Young, Page, Benny Morton, or Don Byas. But from late 1930s through the next decade, the records continue to flow unabated; **Super Chief, Blues By Basie, Basie's Back In Town, One O'Clock Jump** and **Basie's Best**. And when sizzling big-band jazz for American servicemen (by way of V-Discs) was called for, Count Basie Orchestra catered splendidly **(Count Basie: V-Discs, 1944-45** and **Count Basie: The V-Discs, Vol 2)**.

The final years of World War II had seen appearance into band's ranks of new faces such as Joe Newman, Emmett Berry, Al Killian, Eugene 'Snooky' Young, J. J. Johnson, Eli Robinson, Illinois Jacquet, Rudy Rutherford, Rodney Richardson and Shadow Wilson. (Buddy Rich sometimes acted as explosive deputy to Wilson.) By mid-1940s, even the seemingly indestructible Basie band was feeling big-band draught. By 1947, even with continued support from Rushing, long-serving Harry Edison, and despite return of Page and Jones and replacement of Jacquet by Paul Gonsalves, both band and repertoire had become stylised. Material-wise, the band was at its lowest ebb. Ironically, Basie (surely not everyone's idea of a pop-style hitmaker) notched up what must be his only Hit Parade smash hit during this period. With Edison's wretched vocal, and very little of what could be called pure Basie, the band's recording of novelty, **Open The Door, Richard!**, topped the US charts at beginning of '47. By 1950, Basie had been forced to cut down to eight pieces, the first and only time since the mid-1930s he had been without a big band under his leadership. First line-up had Basie leading Edison, Dickie Wells, Georgie Auld, Gene Ammons, Al McKibbon, Gus Johnson and omnipresent Green; finally, octet comprising Charlie Rouse (replaced by Wardell Gray), Serge Chaloff, Clark Terry, Buddy De Franco (replaced by Marshall Royal), Jimmy Lewis, Johnson (or Buddy Rich). The latter octet(s) played music often influenced by contemporary jazz sounds. One version of octet appeared on its own and in support of Billie Holiday, in a splendid film short made in 1950.

Basie reverted to big-band formula in 1951, initially for recording purposes **(One O'Clock Jump)**, with a superior array of soloists; Gray, Lucky Thompson, Paul Quinichette, Eddie 'Lockjaw' Davis, Newman, Charlie Shavers, Terry, plus Lewis-Green-Johnson-Basie rhythm to play important roles in Basie big-band renascence. Apart from customary superb solos, Gray's feature **Little Pony** attained somthing of an 'in' reputation with fellow musicians and discerning fans; solo, notated and with words fitted to notes, phrases etc by Jon Hendricks, it was later reactivated in an extraordinary fashion by remarkable Lambert, Hendricks and Ross vocal group (with Annie Ross singing Gray's solo). Arrangers-composers Buster Harding **(Bleep Bop Blues, Nails, Howzit)**, Neal Hefti **(Fancy Meeting You, Little Pony)**, and Ernie Wilkins **(Bread, Bootsie, Hob Nail Boogie)** provided just the right degree of explosive material, blues-based with the accent firmly on swing.

Wilkins, Hefti, Johnny Mandel and saxist-flautist Frank Wess were to exert considerable influence on direction with 'new' (1952) Basie band, first efforts of which were superbly encapsulated on two very successful Norman Granz-supervised LP **(Count Basie Dance Sessions, Nos 1 & 2/Sixteen Men Swinging)**, with Wilkins present also as member of sax section. Johnson, Green, Newman, Wilkins, together with Frank Foster, Eddie Jones and Charlie Fowlkes were each to make substantial contributions in the rejuvenated band of this period, and thereafter. Even more than in earlier years, this 'new' Basie unit offered a togetherness that was almost hypnotic, with a delicious and unparalleled penchant for the ultimate in relaxed rhythmic performance, and a unique sense of dynamic range—from a blistering scream to a muted whisper—which immediately elevated it to the big-band pantheon. Its pinnacle was reached in 1959 with the album which on its original release was entitled **The Atomic Mr Basie (The Atomic Mr Basie, Chairman Of The Board/The Atomic Mr Chairman)**. Solo-wise, the disc presents probably the finest collection of individual statements by Basieites since the war-time period, with especially rewarding contributions from Eddie Davis (**Whirly Bird**, and others), Frank Wess **(Splanky)**, Joe Newman, Thad Jones, and William Basie **(The Kid From Red Bank)**.

But it is the sheer powerhouse dynamism of the band as a collective unit which must take pride of place (alongside Neal Hefti's finest-ever writing for Basie's, or for that matter any other band with whom he has been associated). Prior to **The Atomic Mr Basie**, this powerhouse aggregation had made a succession of top-notch LPs, including **The Band Of Distinction, Li'l Ol' Groovemaker, Basie At Newport, Easin' It** and **Kansas City Suite**. Last-named comprised a series of typically fine arrangements-compositions from Benny Carter which suited the band to perfection. A single popular recording of the 1950s/1960s (and indeed thereafter) was organist Wild Bill Davis' arrangement of **April In Paris (April In Paris)** with its one-more-thrice endings.

Although the Count Basie Orchestra of post-1952 did produce talented soloists like Newman, Thad Jones, Frank Foster, Frank Wess, Benny Powell and Eddie Davis, it is true that, in comparison with the pre-war outfit, its basic strength lay in that unflagging ensemble togetherness. One important figure appeared during the 1950s; his name—Joe Williams. A singer whose basically superior voice allowed him to encompass urban blues, R&B and standard pop (including ballads), with utmost efficiency—if not more. Onstage, Williams' charismatic personality and big handsome voice helped immensely in the Basie 'comeback'; certainly, it is true to say also that behind Williams the band tended often to swing more potently than without his presence. Williams, who sang with Basie between 1955-58, first recorded with the band in 1955, at what, in the event, turned out to be by far the finest collaboration, on record, by the pair **(Count Basie Swings, Joe Williams Sings)**, including musically exciting versions of **Please Send Me Someone To Love, Roll 'Em, Pete, Alright, Okay, You Win** and **Every Day I Have The Blues**, the latter a Memphis Slim tune that became Williams' first hit.

Frankly, following the opulence and electricity of **The Atomic Mr Basie**, the Count Basie Orchestra rarely has produced work of comparable stature. Of course, sometimes repertoire has been less than adequate (viz James Bond movie themes, Beatles tunes and excerpts from *Mary Poppins*). But many times since then the band itself seemed to be going through the motions, often playing over-familiar material in lacklustre, even

Count Basie Orchestra, William & The Famous Door (courtesy DJM). First classic band of the one-and-only Count Basie—live on 52nd Street.

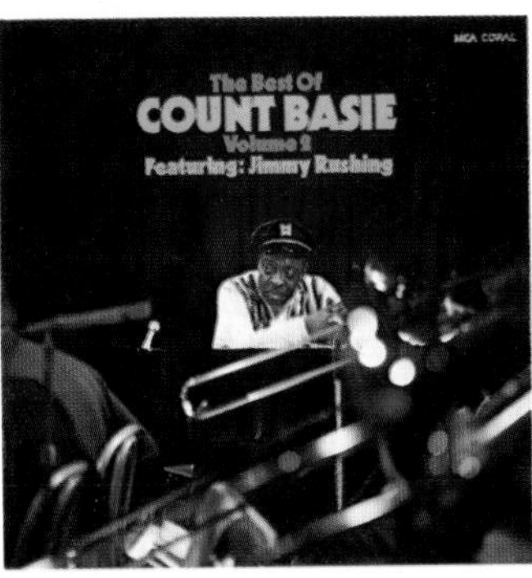

The Best Of Count Basie Volume 2 (courtesy MCA Coral—Germany).

Basie Big Band (courtesy Pablo). The Count and his Orchestra, 1975.

boring fashion. Ironically, its popularity tended to soar during the latterday period, thus its appeal today stretches well outside the thinly disguised jazz boundaries. It was not at all uncommon for Count Basie Orchestra to play regular lucrative engagements at nightspots in Las Vegas. It has appeared on the bill of Royal Variety Show, in London, before Queen Elizabeth II. It has also recorded (as well as appeared in concert) with more pop-based vocal artists such as Billy Eckstine, Tony Bennett, Mills Bros, Sammy Davis Jr, Kay Starr, Bing Crosby, and Frank Sinatra (who has worked extensively with Basie & Co, on record and in person, including joint appearance at 1965 Newport Jazz Festival). In more definite jazz vein, Ella Fitzgerald has performed extremely capably in company with the Basie Orchestra (**On The Sunny Side Of The Street** and **Ella & Basie**). Perhaps best of all vocalist-band collaborations (of those who have not worked regularly with Basie) is to be found on **No Count Sarah** which produced vocal-instrumental fireworks from Sarah Vaughan and the band seldom heard before or since. Whilst the reputation of the band itself lessened during past two decades, the reputation and ability of its leader remained undiminished. For example, Basie was recorded outside as well as inside big-band format, which meant constant re-evaluation of his pre-eminence as a piano player of the first order. Right from his earliest days, Basie was a very good pianist. His early days with Bennie Moten (**Moten's Blues**), indicate a useful performer whose antecedents come from Harlem-stride school, exemplified by Willie 'The Lion' Smith, James P. Johnson and Fats Waller. (Indeed it was Waller, his initial inspiration, who had given fledgling Basie some basic tuition.) Later, outside own big band, Basie's superbly economic piano style (he developed an individual approach which was, in fact, an abbreviated version of Waller-type stride, using time and space to devastating effect) was heard most helpfully as part of Benny Goodman Sextet (**Solo Flight** and **Charlie Christian—Lester Young Together 1940**) or with the Metronome All Stars (**Benny Carter 1945 + The Metronome All Stars**).

Basie also gave life to a star-studded Goodman jam session of '38 (**Famous Carnegie Hall Concert**), as well as to important recording sessions by Lester Young (**Lester Young Leaps Again!** and **Pres/The Complete Savoy Recordings**) and Jo Jones (**The Jo Jones Special**).

In more recent times, record producer Norman Granz placed Basie's timeless keyboard artistry within an intriguing variety of small-group jazz company, ranging from basic piano-trio setting, with Ray Brown and Louis Bellson (**For The First Time**), to situations involving more varied instrumentation. In such circumstances (**Basie & Zoot, Basie Jam, Nos 1 & 2** and **Count Basie Jam Session At The Montreux Jazz Festival 1975**) the Kid From Red Bank acted as catalyst supreme, eliciting from the likes of Roy Eldridge, Lockjaw Davis, Joe Pass, Johnny Griffin, Harry Edison, Clark Terry, Benny Carter and J. J. Johnson, superior solo performances. Nothing new for Basie and Granz—Basie had done the same thing for the producer in the early 1950s when, Basie's piano (and organ too) had paced a line-up that included Stan Getz, Carter, Buddy Rich, and ex-Basieites Edison, Wardell Gray and DeFranco, through some fine musical moments at a fine studio jam session (**Jam Sessions, Nos 2 & 3**).

Basie's occasional outings at the organ demonstrated a pleasing transference of piano technique to the electrical instrument, preferable at up-tempo. Especially memorable here is Basie's organ work with Illinois Jacquet (**Illinois Jacquet & His Orchestra**) as well as with Oscar Peterson (**Satch & Josh**) and own small-band recordings (**Count Basie Sextet, For The First Time, Basie Jam,** etc), and on rarer occasions on big-band albums (**Dance Session No 1**). In late 1976 Basie was hospitalized with a heart attack. But by early next year was back on the road again, in time for yet another European tour; at 74, as indomitable as ever.

How much longer the Basie band could continue to turn out the same kind of music and still retain its popularity was anybody's guess. Certainly, change of musical direction (and policy?) was overdue. Although a strictly one-off affair, the band's 1970 LP **Afrique**, for instance—arranged and conducted by Oliver Nelson and with music by Nelson, Gabor Szabo, Albert Ayler and Pharoah Sanders—demonstrated that dramatic change was possible.

By 1980, however, Basie's deteriorating health was causing serious concern. From that year Basie was having to make his stage entrances in the famous 'Basie buggy' as he could no longer walk unaided—it was a moving sight for fans and band members alike.

On September 23, 1982, Basie was presented with a sincere tribute by the British Count Basie Society at a Royal Festival Hall reception—a silver salver inscribed 'To Bill Basie with our love and respect—Count Basie Society, London'. This affectionate gesture deeply touched Basie and, sadly, it was made on what proved to be his last visit to the UK.

In spite of his poor health, Basie continued to work up till a month before he died. Finally, on April 26, 1984—sadly short of his 80th birthday—the great Count Basie died in hospital at Hollywood, Florida, from cancer of the pancreas complicated by his long-standing diabetes condition.

While the world mourned the passing of one of its most honored and historic musical luminaries, there was speculation about the future of his orchestra. Basie's wish had been for the band to stay together after his death and senior members of the band met to decide that the orchestra should continue to perpetuate the Basie legend under the distinguished leadership of Thad Jones. The Basie band, like the leader himself up to his death, remains an implacable, immovable force that can still, when the adrenalin is flowing, rise to the heights like no other outfit anywhere.

There is much about the early Basie in *Jazz Style In Kansas City & The Southwest* by Ross Russell. Also of interest is *Count Basie & His Orchestra* by Ray Horricks.

Albums:
Count Basie, Good Morning Blues (MCA/—)
The Count Swings Out (1937-38) (—/MCA—Germany)
Count Basie, The Best Of Basie (1937-38) (—/MCA—Germany)
Count Basie, The Blues I Like To Hear (1938-39) (—/MCA—Germany)
Count Basie, Super Chief (Columbia/CBS)
Lester Young With The Count Basie Orchestra (Epic/Epic—France)
Lester Young, The Lester Young Story, Vol 3/ Enter The Count (Columbia/CBS)
The Count At The Chatterbox 1937 (Jazz Archives/—)
(Count Basie & His Orchestra (Trip)/William & The Famous Door (DJM)
Blues By Basie (Columbia/Philips)
Basie's Back In Town (Epic/Philips)
One O'Clock Jump (Columbia/Fontana)
Various, John Hammond's Spirituals To Swing (Vanguard/Vanguard)
Various, Famous Carnegie Hall Concert (Columbia/CBS)
Count Basie, Basie's Best (Columbia/CBS)
Count Basie: The V-Discs—1944-45 (Jazz Society/—)
Count Basie: The V-Discs, Vol 2 (Jazz Society/—)
Count Basie (RCA Victor—France)
Basie Live! (Trip)/Count Basie Live (DJM)
Blues By Basie (Tax—Sweden)
Count Basie, April In Paris (Clef/Columbia—Clef)
Count Basie Dance Sessions, Nos 1 & 2 (Clef)/ Sixteen Men Swinging (Verve)
Count Basie, The Band Of Distinction (Verve/HMV)
The Atomic Mr Basie (Roulette), Chairman Of The Board (Roulette)/ The Atomic Mr Chairman (Vogue)
Count Basie: The Soloist 1941/1959 (Jazz Anthology/—)
Count Basie (—/Vogue)
Count Basie, Kansas City Suite (Roulette/Columbia)
Count Basie, The Newport Years, Vol VI (Verve)/The Live Big Band Sound Of Count Basie (Verve)
Count Basie, Afrique (Flying Dutchman/Philips)
Various, Jazz At The Santa Monica (Pablo/Pablo)
Charlie Christian/Lester Young, Together 1940 (Jazz Archives/—)
Lester Young Leaps Again! (EmArcy/Fontana)
Lester Young, Pres/The Complete Savoy Recordings (Savoy/Savoy)
Benny Carter 1945 + The Metronome All-Stars (Queen Disc—Italy)
Various, Jam Sessions Nos 2 & 3 (Verve/Columbia—Clef)
Illinois Jacquet & His Orchestra (Verve/Columbia—Clef (EP))
Count Basie, For The First Time (Pablo/Pablo)
Count Basie/Joe Turner, The Bosses (Pablo/Pablo)
Count Basie Jam Session At The Montreux Jazz Festival 1975 (Pablo/Pablo)
Count Basie, Basie Jam No 2 (Pablo/Pablo)
Count Basie/Zoot Sims, Basie & Zoot (Pablo/Pablo)
Count Basie Swings, Joe Williams Sings (Verve)/ Swingin' With The Count (Verve)
Joe Williams—Count Basie (Vogue/Vogue)
Count Basie/Sarah Vaughan, No Count Sarah (Mercury)/Sassy (Fontana)
Lambert, Hendricks & Ross, Sing Along With Basie (Roulette/Columbia)
Count Basie/Ella Fitzgerald, On The Sunny Side Of The Street (Verve/Verve)
Montreux '77: Count Basie Big Band (Pablo Live/Pablo Live)
Montreux '77: Count Basie Jam (Pablo Live/Pablo Live)
Count Basie, The Atomic Period (Rarities/—)

Sidney Bechet

Sidney Bechet (born New Orleans, 1897) was amongst the first truly masterful jazz soloists, youngest of seven children in a musical family. First instrument was clarinet; as a child, he sat in with legendary Freddie Keppard, and marched with another New Orleans trumpeter Manual Perez, and throughout his career remained one of the finest of all clarinettists, even though, eventually, clarinet took second place to soprano sax, the latter being the instrument which Bechet, single-handed, turned into a powerful form of expression within jazz vernacular. Other early jazz figures with whom Bechet was associated: Lorenzo Tio (a tutor for Bechet), Buddie Petit, John Robichaux, Bunk Johnson. Bechet even played cornet during New Orleans street parades. Left Crescent City for good in 1917 (had worked for first time with King Oliver the year before), moving on to Chicago, then New York. Became a member of Southern Syncopated Orchestra led by Will Marion Cook, 1919 (second time) and went to Europe. Left Cook in London, by which time he added soprano to his clarinet, playing regularly in the British capital (and Paris), before deportation to the US ('21). Same year recorded for first time. Briefly with Duke Ellington and James P. Johnson, and in same year (1925) toured with *Revue Nègre*, as a member of Claude Hopkins Orchestra which accompanied Josephine Baker.

1926: toured Russia, visited Berlin, organized band for another *Revue Nègre*, re-visiting Europe following year. With Noble Sissle for season in Paris (1928), subsequently serving jail sentence in French capital for involvement in shooting incident. Returned to US, rejoining Sissle, toured with Ellington (1932), then organized the first of his celebrated New Orleans Feetwarmers (with cornettist Tommy Ladnier). Retired from music, becoming proprietor, with Ladnier, of a New York tailoring establishment. But by 1934 had rejoined Sissle, a situation which remained unchanged until 1938. Worked with own and other bands at Nick's, New York jazz club (1938), followed by a lengthy season at Momart Astoria with Willie 'The Lion' Smith, with whom he had worked previously. Regular and much-respected figure on New York jazz scene from then until 1951 with many appearances at the famous Eddie Condon wartime Town Hall concerts, as well as innumerable concert and club dates in the Big Apple, and cities like Boston and Chicago. Appeared at Nice Jazz Festival (1949), where he jammed with Charlie Parker and others. Returned the following year.

From 1951 until his death (in 1959), Paris was to become more or less permanent home for Bechet although he made infrequent trips back to the States for special guest appearances, recordings etc. Visited Britain (1956), South America (1957). In Paris, though, Bechet became something of an institution, a particular favorite amongst Left Bank fraternity. Took part in 1955 movie *Blues*.

Until John Coltrane made it his secondary instrument, Sidney Bechet's position as jazz's premier exponent of soprano saxophone was unchallenged. Using combination of impassioned emotionalism (heightened by use of heavy and wide vibrato) and an unremitting attack, Bechet's fierce playing of the instrument was powerful enough to combat the challenge of all others, including trumpets, in any ensemble. Only Louis Armstrong **(Louis With Guest Stars)** seemed able to resist Bechet, whose approach to ensemble playing was that invariably taken by the trumpet. In his earlier days, often in Armstrong's company, Bechet provided stimulating accompaniments and solos to a variety of blues singers, including Bessie Smith, Mamie Smith, and Margaret Johnson. And with Clarence Williams (Bechet's first recordings of note were with Williams' Blue Five in 1923) he further enhanced vocal records of the 1920s with such as Virginia Liston, Sippie Wallace, Eva Taylor **(Adam & Eve Had The Blues)**. With Williams, Bechet first locked horns with Armstrong **(Louis Armstrong/Sidney Bechet With The Clarence Williams Blue Five)**, the pair sounding beautifully expressive on **Texas Moaner Blues, Papa De Dad', Just Wait Till You See** and the first get-together on **Coal Cart Blues**.

Above: Sidney Bechet, a jazz immortal. A magisterial and influential soloist, both on soprano saxophone and clarinet.

Bechet added his soaring sound to Jelly Roll Morton's New Orleans Jazzmen recording date of 1939, a few months after his own matchless recording of **Summertime (Jazz Classics, Vol 1)** for Blue Note; probably first-ever success on record for jazz ballad performance. Following year, in company with Muggsy Spanier, he committed to record a series of superbly structured solos (in the context, and for Bechet, his flowing solos were admirably restrained) which rank with his finest work elsewhere **(Ragtime Jazz/ Tribute To Bechet)**.

For Blue Note, Bechet recorded some of his most memorable solos **(Jazz Classics, Vols 1, 2)** including poignant clarinet duets with Albert Nicholas in 1946; a splendid Bechet Blue Note Quartet date with Teddy Bunn from 1940; the Bechet Blue Note Jazzmen sides (with Sidney DeParis, Vic Dickenson, et al) from 1944; more fine jazz in company of Max Kaminsky, Art Hodes and the like, from '45; and some joyful, freewheeling music (with Wild Bill Davison and Hodes, again) from 1949.

Then, of course, there were the marvelously integrated, beautifully felt performances by the Feetwarmers **(Sidney Bechet, Vols 1-3)**. And the equally famous recordings which juxtaposed Bechet's ecstatic soprano and clarinet opposite the simple, but heartfelt clarinet of Mezz Mezzrow, made in 1945 for the King Jazz label—**(Bechet-Mezzrow Quintet)**—to be repeated (although not as closely argued as '45) two years later **(The Prodigious Bechet-Mezzrow Quintet & Septet)**. Even though a more gifted front-line partner (eg Armstrong) might have resulted in music of even greater significance, the Bechet-Mezzrow sessions find the New Orleans man achieving moments of total inspiration, rare even in the most exalted jazz circles. During his latter period as one of France's adopted sons, Bechet continued to work extensively, both in live performance as well as on record, using mostly local musicians, although readily taking the opportunity to assert his undiminished authority in the company of visiting US jazzmen, as with **Refreshing Tracks, Vol 1**. And his rare trips back home often produced satisfying results **(Sidney Bechet At Storyville)**. Fronted all-star band of Americans at Brussels International Fair (1958). Autobiography, *Treat It Gentle*, published in 1960.

Of all the non-trumpet front-line instrumentalists, Sidney Bechet was, without doubt, the most powerful voice. A virtuoso peformer, and a complete individualist, Bechet remains one of jazz's most important soloists.

Albums:

Louis Armstrong/Sidney Bechet, With The Clarence Williams Blue Five (CBS—France)
Clarence Williams, Adam & Eve Had The Blues (CBS—France)
Sidney Bechet, The Rarest . . . Vol 1 (After Hours)
Sidney Bechet, Blackstick (1931-1938) (MCA-Coral—Germany)
Various, John Hammond's Spirituals To Swing (Vanguard)/The Legendary John Hammond's Carnegie Hall Concerts 1938/39 From Spirituals To Swing (Vogue)
Sidney Bechet, Unique Sidney (CBS—France)
Various, The Panassie Sessions (RCA Victor/RCA Victor—France)
Jelly Roll Morton & His Red Hot Peppers/New Orleans Jazzmen, Vol 2 (1926-1939) (RCA Victor—France)

Jazz Classics, Volume 1 (courtesy Blue Note)—more gems from Bechet.

Sidney Bechet, Vols 1-3 (RCA Victor—France)
Louis Armstrong, Louis With Guest Stars (MCA Coral—Germany)
Sidney Bechet, Jazz Classics, Vols 1, 2 (Blue Note)
Sidney Bechet/Muggsy Spanier, Ragtime Jazz (Olympic)/Tribute to Bechet (Ember)
Sidney Bechet 1949 (Barclay)
Bechet-Mezzrow Quintet (Concert Hall)
The Prodigious Bechet-Mezzrow Quintet & Septet (Festival—France)
Eddie Condon, The Eddie Condon Concerts, Vol 2 (Chiaroscuro/—)
Various, 'This Is Jazz', Vols 1, 2 (Rarities)
Sidney Bechet Album (—/Saga)
The Genius Of Sidney Bechet (Jazzology/—)
Sidney Bechet & Friends (For Discriminating Collectors)
Sidney Bechet At Storyville (Storyville/Vogue)
Sidney Bechet, Refreshing Tracks Vols 1 & 2 (—/Vogue)
Sidney Bechet, His Way (Pumpkin/—)
Sidney Bechet (Musidisc—France)

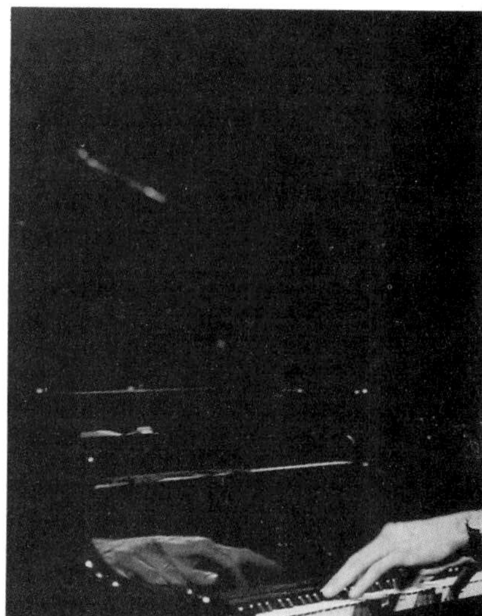

Gordon Beck

The internationally acclaimed Gordon Beck—without doubt, one of Britain's most creative and accomplished pianist-composers—was born in London, September 16, 1935. He studied classical music in his teens, his jazz inspiration coming from George Shearing and Dave Brubeck and, later, Keith Jarrett and Chick Corea. (His 1982 **Reasons** is his beautiful tribute to just some who have influenced his playing.)

His professional music career started at age 26, after ten years in aircraft engineering, but this late start didn't hinder a growing reputation. Throughout the '60s, he worked with established musicians like Tony Kinsey, Bobby Wellins, Alan Skidmore and Tubby Hayes as well as accompanying visiting Americans at Ronnie Scott's Club.

In the late '60s, he formed a trio with

bassist Jeff Clyne, drummer Johnny Butts or Alan Ganley (later, Tony Oxley). Guitarist John McLaughlin joined the band for a year and their **Experiments With Pop** is regarded by many as a long-lost British jazz classic (with its unusual interpretations of pop tunes like **These Boots Were Made For Walking**).

In 1969, Beck succeeded George Gruntz in Phil Woods' European Rhythm Machine, bringing Beck recognition in Europe and the United States. In 1974, he formed his own highly acclaimed but regrettably short-lived Gyroscope—Beck on electric piano, including saxophonist Stan Sulzmann and percussionist Frank Ricotti.

By the late '70s, he formed his European Quartet with guitarist Alan Holdsworth, bassist J. F. Jenny Clarke and drummer Aldo Romano, recording his exceptional **Sunbird**—a complex work dynamically and atmospherically portraying the various stages of bird migration.

During the '80s, Beck has performed less and less in his native England, finding constant work on the Continent, but his contribution and achievement continue to be widely acknowledged. His deserved international reputation, and the high regard accorded him, puts Britain's Gordon Beck indisputably in a class alongside Chick Corea and Keith Jarrett.

Albums:
Experiments With Pop (—/Major Minor)
Gordon Beck-Alan Holdsworth, Conversation Piece—Part 1 & 2 (—/Vinyl)
Sunbird (—/JMS—France)
The French Connection 2 (—/JMS—France)
Reasons (—/JMS—France)

Above: The internationally acclaimed British pianist-composer Gordon Beck—in the same class as Keith Jarrett and Chick Corea.

Gordon Beck, The French Connection 2 (courtesy JMS—France).

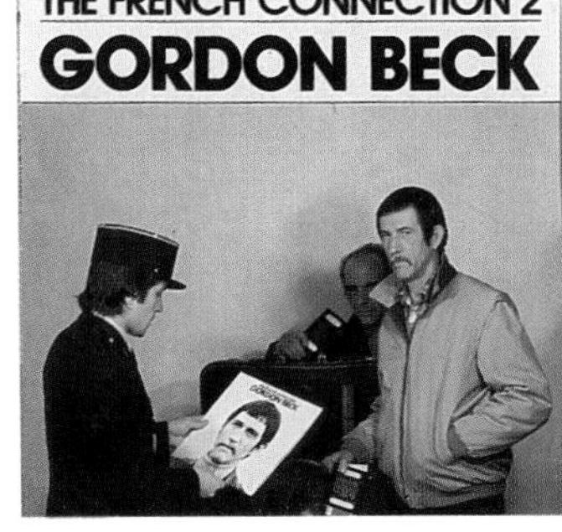

Bix Beiderbecke

More has been written over the years since his death about Leon Bix Beiderbecke (born Davenport, Iowa, 1903) than about the remarkable music he produced during a tragically short career. Indeed, it was not until 1974, with the publication of *Bix: Man & Legend*, written by Richard M. Sudhalter and Philip R. Evans, with William Dean-Myatt, that a totally comprehensive, scholarly and apparently near-flawless account of the life and music of Beiderbecke, complete with discography, made available a more or less satisfactory (and satisfying) account of the man's *music*, as well as his private life. Beiderbecke, who started at piano aged three, moved to cornet at 14, and graduated, musically, through school and local children's band, first expressing a genuine interest in becoming full-time jazzman during his high school period (1919-21).

In 1921 Beiderbecke played on riverboats, enrolled at Lake Forest Military Academy near Chicago (he was expelled a year later), before taking jobs with several Chicago-based bands. Also in '21 sat in with Elmer Schoebel band. Joined the Wolverines (1923), making record début with latter in 1924. Those early recordings **(Bix Beiderbecke & The Chicago Cornets)** show a rather tentative young musician, but thereafter he was to produce a series of recorded performances, on B-flat cornet, that were not only masterfully lyrical and supremely logical in development but also totally unlike anything produced at that time, either by the great black trumpet vinced players or their white counterparts. Further Wolverines recordings demonstrate a growth in stature and confidence, and the formation of a style that was an intriguing counterpoint to those already in use—as personified in the work of say, King Oliver, Louis Armstrong, Tommy Ladnier and Freddie Keppard.

Beiderbecke's was a style which was to exercise its own influence, swiftly and lastingly. Amongst those to be deeply influenced by Beiderbecke were Red Nichols, Jimmy McPartland, Bobby Hackett and Rex Stewart, who showed his admiration for Beiderbecke by producing a solo of Bixian style during a recording by the Fletcher Henderson Orchestra of Beiderbecke's own classic showcase, **Singin' The Blues**.

Beiderbecke left the Wolverines in November, 1924, to join the orchestra of Charlie Straight, but more important was his association during 1925-26 with the band led by saxist Frankie Trumbauer, a name soon to be closely associated with Beiderbecke's. Then both became members of Jean Goldkette Orchestra until temporary disbandment in the fall of 1927. By which time, Beiderbecke had recorded with, amongst other units, the Sioux City Six and his own Rhythm Jugglers **(Bix Beiderbecke & The Chicago Cornets)**, Trumbauer **(The Golden Days Of Jazz: Bix Beiderbecke)** and the Goldkette band **(The Bix Beiderbecke Legend)**.

With Trumbauer, Beiderbecke recorded two remarkable trio sides (also featuring guitarist Eddie Lang) **Wringin' & Twistin'** and **For No Reason At All In C**, not to mention the previously noted **Singing The Blues**, the latter containing probably the single most brilliant solo Beiderbecke produced on record, and certainly one of the most influential, much-copied and widely-discussed solos in jazz history. Of less import, but even more intriguing perhaps was an unaccompanied piano solo recorded the same year, **In A Mist**. Both composition (it was written by Beiderbecke) and performance are cast in distinctly Debussy-like mold. **I'm Coming Virginia** (also with Trumbauer) is another significant track that dates from 1927: beautifully sculpted, effortlessly delivered **(The Golden Days Of Jazz: Bix Beiderbecke)**. Other important recordings during that year, made under the banner of Bix Beiderbecke & His Gang, included such influential sides as **Jazz Me Blues** and **Since My Best Gal Turned Me Down (Bix Beiderbecke & His Gang)**.

Of equal importance was the occasion when Beiderbecke, together with Trumbauer, became a member of the Paul Whiteman Orchestra, the most popular and successful musical aggregation on the US music scene. With Whiteman, Beiderbecke was to receive the kind of international exposure he could not have accomplished alone. Conversely, jazz content of Whiteman's band was given a decided boost with Beiderbecke's induction into its ranks **(The Bix Beiderbecke Legend)**, especially on individual numbers like **You Took Advantage Of Me, Changes, There Ain't No Sweet Man Worth The Salt Of My Tears, Love Nest** and **Dardanella**. Often he was given a mere eight bars. But the eloquence of his playing, even when featured briefly, was in stark contrast to the often ponderous and heavy-handed swing of the huge orchestra.

During this period as principal jazz soloist with Whiteman, Beiderbecke began to lose his growing battle with alcoholism. Absent from the band on several occasions (once, when Whiteman was in Hollywood to make the famous early talkie, *The King Of Jazz*) Beiderbecke's health deteriorated so alarmingly that, after leaving for the second time, in 1929, he never worked with Whiteman again.

Apart from freelance recordings, a rather pathetic final record date of his own, and some erratic live engagements, it was the end of the Bix Beiderbecke Story. He died in his Queen's, New York, apartment, August 6, 1931—aged 28—from lobar pneumonia with oedema of the brain. His body was taken to his native Davenport, where he was buried five days later. The Beiderbecke legend was given fictional renaissance many years after his death by Dorothy Baker's best-selling novel *Young Man With A Horn*, whose principal character obviously was based on the hard-drinking Bix Beiderbecke. Of other publications on Beiderbecke, the following deserve individual recommendation: *Bugles For Beiderbecke*, by Charles H. Wareing & George Garlick, the best, next to the Sudhalter-Evans-Dean-Myatt tome; Richard Hadlock's chapter on Beiderbecke in his *Jazz of the Twenties*; Gunther Schuller's treatise on Bix in *Early Jazz*; and Burnett James' *Bix Beiderbecke*.

With his records being issued and re-issued at impressively regular intervals, the Legend of Bix Beiderbecke, the musical legend, retains its popularity and importance almost 50 years after his death.

The Beiderbecke legend received an unlikely and indirect boost in the UK in 1985 with Alan Plater's brilliant, if low-key, enjoyable television dramatization *The Beiderbecke Affair*—a mystery serial which chronicled a schoolteacher's subsequent offbeat adventures in tracking down a coveted set of exclusive Beiderbecke records. For copyright reasons the musical score was written by Frank Ricotti, featuring trumpeter Kenny Baker, and successfully evoked the Beiderbecke-Trumbauer idiom.

Albums:
Bix Beiderbecke & The Chicago Cornets (Milestone)
Bix Beiderbecke Story, Vols 1-3 (Columbia/CBS—France)
Bix Beiderbecke Legend (RCA Victor—France)
Bix Beiderbecke, Bix & His Gang (—/Parlophone)
Jack Teagarden Classics (Family—Italy)
The Indispensable Bix Beiderbecke (—/RCA Jazz Tribune—France)

Young Bix Beiderbecke & The Chicago Cornets (courtesy Milestone).

Louis Bellson

Louis Bellson (born Louis Balassoni, in Rock Falls, Illinois, 1924) has worked in all manner of jazz contexts from a very youthful age. Respected big-band percussionist, he has worked with Duke Ellington, Harry James, Tommy Dorsey and Count Basie, spending more than one period during his career with each, and Ted Fio Rito, as well as leading a succession of healthy sounding big bands of his own.

A formidable technician, but one who uses his considerable skills constructively and with infinite taste, Bellson is also equally at home within the framework of small-combo jazz. He has worked with countless small bands over many years, including better-known outfits such as the Benny Goodman Quintet and the more disparate Jazz at the Philharmonic all-stars.

Bellson, who during the mid-1940s innovated the concept of twin bass drums as part of the drummer's basic kit, brought a completely new and fresh approach to the Ellington orchestra during his two-year spell. From an all-round standpoint, he must be considered the most accomplished drummer employed, for any length of time, by Ellington. During this period (1950-52), Bellson's reputation was further enhanced, this time as composer and arranger. Amongst his written contributions for Ellington, the best known include **The Hawk Talks** (affectionate dedication to Harry James), **Ting-a-Ling** and **Skin Deep**. Bellson's immaculate drumming featured extensively during the latter, released originally as a two-part single recording which achieved pop-type sales when released (1953).

Apart from work with big bands and small combos, Bellson often has accompanied top-line singers (viz Tony Bennett, Louis Armstrong, Ella Fitzgerald and Pearl Bailey). In fact, Bellson married singer-comedienne-actress Pearl Bailey in 1953. In a small-group setting, Bellson has proved a demonstrably tasteful, always attentive accompanist, especially when accompanying pianists of the calibre of Count Basie **(Basie Jam** and **For The First Time)**, Art Tatum **(Tatum Group Masterpieces)**, Oscar Peterson (with Basie) **(Satch & Josh)** and Duke Ellington **(Duke's Big Four)**.

Under his own name, Bellson has recorded many albums, none of which has proved to be of inestimable importance, but each containing much good music and all-round superior musicianship. Amongst the best of these have been several in-person recordings, including **Louis Bellson At The Flamingo, Big Band At The Summit** and **Louis Bellson's Septet Recorded Live At The 1976 Concord Jazz Festival**. Similarly, Bellson can be heard at his best during a live recording with Count Basie, **Basie In Sweden**.

As a person, Bellson is universally recognized as an endearing, genuinely modest jazz musician. Thankfully, too, his modesty reaches into his musical make-up. Even when leading his own bands Bellson rarely hogs the solo limelight (unlike the vast majority of drummers). Possibly his lengthiest solo on record is to be found during yet another live performance, this time as a member of the Jazz at the Philharmonic troupe **(The Exciting Battle/JATP Stockholm '55)**.

The former boy-wonder drummer, whose teens were spent winning all kinds of drumming contests, remains one of the handful of real virtuoso performers; constantly in demand, readily and easily adaptable.

Albums:

The World Of Duke Ellington, Vol 2 (Columbia)/ The World Of Duke Ellington, Vol 1 (CBS)
The World Of Duke Ellington, Vol 3 (Columbia)/The World Of Duke Ellington, Vol 2 (CBS)
Duke Ellington, A Tone Parallel To Harlem (CBS—France)
Duke Ellington Concert At Carnegie Hall (Trip/DJM)
Duke Ellington & The Ellingtonians (—/Vogue—France)
Duke Ellington, Duke's Big 4 (Pablo/Pablo)
Art Tatum, The Tatum Group Masterpieces (Pablo/Pablo)
Count Basie, Basie Jam (Pablo/Pablo)
Count Basie, Basie Jam No 2 (Pablo/Pablo)
Count Basie, For The First Time (Pablo/Pablo)
Count Basie Jam Session At The Montreux Jazz Festival 1975 (Pablo/Pablo)
Count Basie, Basie In Sweden (Roulette/Columbia)
Duke Ellington, Ellington Uptown (Columbia/CBS—France)
Various, The Exciting Battle/J.A.T.P. Stockholm '55 (Pablo/Pablo)
Ella Fitzgerald/Louis Armstrong, The Special Magic Of Ella & Louis, Vol 2 (—/Verve)
Various (Including Louis Bellson), Kings Of Swing, Vol 2 (—/Verve)
Louis Bellson/(Mills Blue Rhythm Band), Big Bands! (Onyx/Polydor)
Louis Bellson, At The Flamingo (Verve/Columbia)
Louie In London (—/Pye)
The Louis Bellson Explosion (Pablo/Pablo)
At The Thunderbird (Impulse/—)
Big Band At The Summit (Roulette/Columbia)
Louis Bellson's Septet Recorded Live At The Concord Jazz Festival (Concord Jazz/—)
Louis Bellson, Prime Time (Concord Jazz/—)

Drummer Louis Bellson At The Thunderbird (courtesy Impulse).

George Benson

Guitarist George Benson's early contribution to jazz is often overshadowed by his more recent commercial success. Once hailed as the 'natural successor to Wes Montgomery', Benson has offended some of his early jazz followers in later years by succumbing to the demands made on him by pop mega-stardom.

Born in Pittsburgh in 1943, Benson's introduction to the guitar sound was through Charlie Christian recordings with Benny Goodman. Not until the age of 7 was Benson introduced to the guitar itself by his stepfather, who redeemed the instrument from a pawnbroker.

Benson's singing career began earlier than more recent fans imagine, at five, when—known as Little George Benson, the kid from Gilmore Alley—he won a singing contest at a street dance.

In late teens, Benson heard Charlie Parker's **Just Friends** which inspired him to try to develop a guitar 'voice' in the same way that Parker 'vocalized' the saxophone. After a period as back-up guitarist with vocal R&B groups, Benson left Pittsburgh to pursue a jazz career and joined organist Jack McDuff in the early 1960s **(George Benson and Jack McDuff)**. The three years with McDuff were a challenge for young Benson's then limited technique—McDuff was tough on Benson and would tell him 'either *play* it or put it down'. The experience with McDuff's live charts also taught him how 'to fire up very quickly in a short space of time'. This made Benson valuable property in the record business—a solo artist who could play an interesting guitar break against the studio's three-minute clock was, indeed, a useful sideman.

On leaving McDuff, Benson formed and toured with his own group from 1965 which included Lonnie Smith (organ), Ronnie Cuber (baritone) and Phil Turner (drums).

Benson then established a long and creative association with record producer and executive Creed Taylor (first at A&M, then Taylor's own fusion-flavored CTI label). The CTI contract resulted in some big-selling albums **(Body Talk, White Rabbit** and **Good King Bad)**. After the success of **White Rabbit**, particularly, Benson's reputation was further advanced by 'guest' appearances with big jazz names like Freddie Hubbard, Ron Carter, Hubert Laws, Herbie Hancock, Airto Moreira and, of course, Miles Davis (notably the famous if low-profile contribution to Davis' **Miles In The Sky**).

Benson's move to Warner Brothers brought a major hit in 1976 with his début album—the now classic **Breezin'** (the memorable title track being a reworking of guitarist Gabor Szabo's attractive composition). **Breezin'** holds the distinction of being the first record by a jazz musician to go platinum, occupying No. One in pop, R&B and jazz charts simultaneously. That year, **Breezin'** topped 2,000,000 sales—and Benson was voted the world's No. One jazz guitarist by jazz *and* pop polls. **Breezin'** was essentially an instrumental album but the one vocal track—Leon Russell's **This Masquerade**—achieved top spot in the US pop singles chart. The unprecedented vocal success of **This Masquerade** presented Benson with a new and interesting, not to mention economically sensible, direction and most of his output since has found him incorporating lyrics with his inimitable style of 'scatting'.

In Flight—his second Warner album—not surprisingly also went platinum. At the same time, his vocals and guitar-playing were included in the soundtrack of the Muhammad Ali film *The Greatest*—from that album was to emerge a big hit, **The Greatest Love Of All**.

Blue Benson (courtesy Polydor): classic George Benson from 1968 featuring Herbie Hancock, Ron Carter, Billy Cobham et al.

By 1977, Benson's growing status was indicated by his 'Benson x Four' weekend in New York. This featured him in four different concerts: the Metropolitan Museum of Art with diverse guitarists Bucky Pizzarelli, Les Paul and Gabor Szabo; the Palladium Theater with singer Minnie Riperton; Avery Fisher Hall with the Dance Theater of Harlem and, separately, a line-up of Alphonso Johnson, Joe Sample and Grover Washington Jr.

Benson's third Warner album, **Weekend In L.A.** (January 1978), was his first live project for the label and included percussionist Ralph McDonald, drummer Harvey Mason, guitarist Phil Upchurch, pianist Jorge Dalto, keyboardist Ronnie Foster and bassist Stanley Banks. The same year, Benson's now international acclaim was reflected by an ambitious world tour taking in Japan, Europe and Australia. That summer, he was guest performer at President Carter's White House tribute to the Newport Jazz Festival's 25th anniversary . . . George Benson's star status was now confirmed.

Benson's recording output of the last few years has featured his dexterous and inventive guitar-playing less and less and his melodic, velvety vocals more and more. However, in live performance, Benson can usually be relied upon to enthral and delight with at least one full-length guitar showstopper proving that the 'natural successor to Wes Montgomery' lives.

Albums:

George Benson & Jack McDuff (Prestige/Prestige)
Body Talk (CTI/CTI)
White Rabbit (CTI/CTI)
Good King Bad (CTI/CTI)
Miles Davis, Miles In The Sky (Columbia/CBS)
Breezin' (Warner/Warner)
In Flight (Warner/Warner)
Blue Benson (Verve/Polydor)
George Benson (CTI/CTI)
The Electrifying George Benson (—/Affinity)
Weekend In L.A. (Warner/Warner)
While The City Sleeps (Warner/Warner)

Bunny Berigan

Roland Bernard 'Bunny' Berigan (born Fox Lake, Hilbert, Calumet, Wisconsin, 1907) has the dubious distinction of figuring prominently amongst the all-time list of notable jazz musicians who died at tragically early ages. Was less than 30 when he died in 1942 (in New York, from a combination of pneumonia and haemorrhage, accentuated by alcoholism). Berigan's death was a real tragedy insofar as his was a talent of comprehensive proportions. A first-class technician, Berigan's playing was noted for its fire and sheer emotionalism.

Came from a musical family, first learning violin before turning to trumpet. At 13 was playing in a local band. Played regularly for University of Wisconsin dance units, even though he was not a student, and likewise as teenager sat in with New Orleans Rhythm Kings. After working with several Wisconsin bands, made first trip to New York in 1928. Finally, moved from home to New York to join dance band of Hal Kemp (1930). Toured Europe with Kemp during major portion of that year. Returning to New York, freelanced, then became member of Fred Rich's outfit. 1931: Berigan's horn added to Dorsey Bros Orchestra that took part in Broadway show *Everybody Welcome*; the same year he completed summer season with Smith Ballew.

Major breakthrough came when signed by Paul Whiteman (1932-33), after which played, briefly, with Abe Lyman before becoming regular staffman with CBS. Between 1932 and 1935, when he joined Benny Goodman, recorded prolifically, with the likes of the Boswell Sisters, Dorsey Bros Orchestra, Mound City Blue Blowers **(The Great Soloists: Bunny Berigan 1932-1937)**, Adrian Rollini **(Adrian Rollini & His Orchestra 1933-34)**.

His reputation as a constantly rewarding trumpet soloist, influenced jointly by the power and fire of Armstrong and Oliver and the lyricism of Beiderbecke, was matched by the respect he earned from a personal standpoint. Whilst Berigan's reputation soared with Goodman, truth to say, the latter's band benefited most from the flaring trumpet solos its latest star acquisition produced. Both on record **(Benny Goodman, Vols 5, 7)** and in person **(A Jam Session With Benny Goodman 1935-37** and **Benny Goodman & His Orchestra Featuring Bunny Berigan)** Berigan vied with Goodman's clarinet for top solo honors, and often won. During his stay with Goodman, Berigan's solos on **King Porter Stomp, Sometimes I'm Happy, Blue Skies** and others, overnight became individual statements of near-classic proportions. More studio work (CBS, ARC) followed the departure from Goodman, then brief associations with Red McKenzie, Red Norvo and Ray Noble, plus recording date with Billie Holiday **(The Billie Holiday Story, Vol 1)** and others, under his own name **(The Great Soloists: Bunny Berigan 1932-1937)**. At one of the latter Berigan first recorded **I Can't Get Started (Take It Bunny!)** a song that was to play a significant part in his musical life after he re-recorded it with his own orchestra in 1937. Other important record dates included two in December, 1935, made specifically for the UK market, during which Berigan inspired musicians like Bud Freeman, Cliff Jackson, Cozy Cole and Jess Stacy to produce of their best **(Swing Classics 1935/Jazz In The Thirties)**.

After participating in recordings with Tommy Dorsey, which produced more Berigan excellence on, for example, **Song Of India, Melody in F, Marie** and **Liebestraum (Tommy Dorsey & His Orchestra)** Bunny Berigan, with Dorsey's blessing, put together his own big band (1937).

During the following years (1937-40) Berigan's alcoholism worsened, and although he delivered numerous glorious performances, there were many times when his playing was erratic, even downright poor.

Noted musicians who worked with Berigan's post-1937 big band included drummers Davey Tough, Buddy Rich and George Wettling; tenorist George Auld; trombonists Sonny Lee and Ray Coniff; pianists Joe Bushkin and Joe Lippman (the latter also arranged for the band); and saxists/clarinettists Gus Bivona, Mike Doty and Joe Dixon.

Whilst it never achieved any extraordinary musical heights, Bunny Berigan's Orchestra often was better than some others of the many white big bands spawned by the 'Swing Era'. Hardly surprising, but Berigan's trumpet was focal point, and as its records testify **(Bunny Berigan & His Orchestra)** there were few occasions when he did not execute solos of superlative standards. His statements, for example, on **Can't Help Lovin' Dat Man, Prisoner's Song, Jelly Roll Blues, Mahogany Hall Stomp** (interesting comparison to Armstrong's immortal version) and, above all **I Can't Get Started With You**, indeed rank with the great trumpet solos of the decade. **I Can't Get Started**, with warm, friendly vocal contribution from Berigan to add to his definitive trumpet statement, has long since assumed legendary proportions amongst jazz buffs. And this was the nearest he came to producing a hit record. Certainly, the Berigan orchestra managed to acquire for itself an ample share of radio broadcasts, and numerous superior examples of its worth have been made available over the years, inlcuding **'Down By The Old Mill Stream'—Bunny In The '30s, Bunny Berigan—Leader & Sideman, Shanghai Shuffle** and **Bunny Berigan, Vols 1, 2**. Unfortunately, Bunny Berigan was not the most disciplined of bandleaders and this, together with his drinking problem and a penchant towards over-generosity, resulted in the orchestra's eventual demise.

Faced with bankruptcy, Berigan rejoined Tommy Dorsey (one of his staunchest admirers, always) in March, 1940. Dorsey made sure that his ailing friend received his share of solos, as on **Hallelujah (That Sentimental Gentleman)** from a June 1940 broadcast. By August, though, Berigan was again leading his own (small) band, in New York. Then, he put together what was to be his last big band, toured (including Hollywood, where he recorded his contribution to the soundtrack of *Syncopation*), but contracted pneumonia in April 1942. Although discharged from hospital in May, and did in fact play a few club dates, he was admitted to New York Polyclinic Hospital end of same month, where he passed away on June 2.

Together with Bix Beiderbecke (whose own tragically short life followed a similar pathway), Bunny Berigan was the greatest white trumpet player to be produced from the 1920s/1930s period—indeed, one of the greatest of all-time—and truly a giant performer on his chosen instrument.

Trumpeter Bunny Berigan, Volume 2 (courtesy Shoestring)—'on the air'.

Albums:

Bunny Berigan, The Great Soloists: Bunny Berigan (1932-1937) (Biograph)
Benny Goodman & His Orchestra Featuring Bunny Berigan (Golden Era)
Benny Goodman, Vols 5, 7 (RCA Victor—France)
A Jam Session With Benny Goodman 1935-1937 (Sunbeam)
Billie Holiday, The Billie Holiday Story, Vol 1 (Columbia/CBS)
Adrian Rollini & His Orchestra 1933-1934 (Sunbeam)
Bunny Berigan, His Trumpet & Orchestra: Original 1937-1939 Recordings (RCA Victor Vintage/—)
Bunny Berigan, Take It Bunny! (Epic/—)
Various (Including Bunny Berigan), Swing Classics 1935 (Prestige)/
Bunny Berigan, 'Down By The Old Mill Stream'—Bunny In The '30s (Jazz Archives)
Bunny Berigan, Great Dance Bands Of The Thirties (RCA Victor)/ Bunny Berigan & His Orchestra (RCA Victor)
Bunny Berigan, Through The Years—Bunny Berigan—Leader & Sideman (Jazz Archives)
Bunny Berigan, Vols 1, 2 (Shoestring)
Bunny Berigan 1936 (Coral—Germany)
Tommy Dorsey & His Orchestra, Vols 1, 2 (RCA Victor)
The Metronome All Stars (Esquire All Stars) (RCA Victor—France)
Tommy Dorsey, That Sentimental Gentleman (RCA Victor/—)

Chu Berry

Leon 'Chu' Berry (born Wheeling, West Virginia, 1910) probably was, together with Ben Webster and Bud Freeman, the third most important tenor saxophonist during the period from the mid-1930s until his premature death in 1941 (behind Coleman Hawkins and Lester Young). Certainly, it was no minor tragedy when Berry died in October, 1941, from severe head injuries, following a car crash.

Coming from a musical family, Berry played alto sax at high school. During three years at college, played both alto and tenor saxes (he moved on to the bigger horn, permanently, after hearing Hawkins). After turning down the offer of a career as professional footballer, Berry decided on a career in music, starting with Sammy Stewart band (1929-30), followed by spells with Cecil Scott, Otto Hardwick, Kaiser Marshall, Walter Pichon, Earl Jackson and Benny Carter, (1932, and again in 1933). Like Carter, Berry also worked with Charlie Johnson (1932-33); then with Teddy Hill (1933-35) and Fletcher Henderson (1935-37) **(The Fletcher Henderson Story/The Fletcher Henderson Story, Vol 4)** before joining Cab Calloway in 1937.

With Calloway, Chu Berry recorded some of his finest solos **(16 Cab Calloway Classics)**, individual classics such as **Ghost Of A Chance, Lonesome Nights, Take The 'A' Train** and his own **At The Clambake Carnival**. With Lionel Hampton, too, Berry's rich-toned, rolling style (Hawkins-influenced, no doubt, with less staccato in delivery and less overtly rhapsodic in ballads) found a happy stomping ground **(The Complete Lionel Hampton/Lionel Hampton's Best Records, Vols 2, 3, 5)** nowhere better showcased than on **Sweethearts On Parade (Vol 2)**. Whilst with Calloway, Berry participated in a marvelously rewarding record date, featuring Roy Eldridge, Sidney Catlett and others, which resulted in magnificent playing by front-line pair of Berry and Eldridge on **Sittin' In, Starsdust, Body & Soul** and **Forty Six West Fifty Two (The Big Sounds Of Coleman Hawkins & Chu Berry)**. With Eldridge, Berry had previously recorded under Gene Krupa's leadership, in 1936, at another successful date in which both played a major role in proceedings, notably during **Swing Is Here (Benny Goodman, Vol 4: 1935-1939)**. Berry always sounded comfortable too with Teddy Wilson, and during the late 1930s, the pianist used his tenor sax to considerable advantage at several recording sessions **(Teddy Wilson & His All-Stars)** and **(The Teddy Wilson)**.

Surprising, perhaps, but Berry also sounded inspired and at top of his game when he recorded (in 1938) as a member of Wingy Manone's Orchestra **(Chew, Choo Chu & Co.** and **Wingy Manone, Vol 1)**.

Although it has been stated in some publications that Chu Berry joined Count Basie Orchestra, this is erroneous. He did not take the place of Herschel Evans, but did, however, deputize for him at recording date that produced **Oh! Lady Be Good** and a Jimmy Rushing feature, **Evil Blues**.

'Chu' (courtesy Epic—France). The quintessence of Chu Berry.

Amongst other impressive examples of Berry's big-toned, totally swinging tenor sax style are to be found several 1937 recordings made under his own name **(Chu Berry & His Stompy Stevedores)**, also during his Calloway period. Notable amongst these are **Limehouse Blues, Chuberry Jam, Too Marvelous For Words** and **Indiana** (all **'Chu'**). His work with Spike Hughes **(Spike Hughes & His Orchestra)** from four years before the Stompy Stevedores dates, once again illustrates the magnitude of his loss at such a ridiculously youthful stage in his development, musically and personally.

Albums:

Spike Hughes & His All American Orchestra (London/Ace of Clubs)
Benny Goodman, Vol 4 (1935-1939) (RCA Victor—France)
Chu Berry, 'Chu' (Epic—France)
Chu Berry, Penguin Swing: Chu Berry Featured With Cab Calloway (Jazz Archives)
16 Cab Calloway Classics (CBS—France)
Mildred Bailey, Her Greatest Performances, 1929-1946, Vols 1, 2 (Columbia/CBS)
The Fletcher Henderson Story (Columbia)/The Fletcher Henderson Story, Vol 4 (CBS)
The Complete Lionel Hampton (RCA Victor)/ Lionel Hampton's Best Records, Vols 2, 3, 5 (RCA Victor—France)
The Chocolate Dandies (—/Parlophone)
Benny Carter—1933 (Prestige)/Various (Including Benny Carter), Ridin' In Rhythm (World Records)
Teddy Wilson & His All-Stars (Columbia/CBS—Holland)
The Teddy Wilson (CBS Sony—Japan)
Chu Berry, Chew, Choo, Chu & Co. (RCA Victor—France)
Wingy Manone, Vol 1 (RCA Victor)
The Big Sounds Of Coleman Hawkins & Chu Berry (—/London)
Coleman Hawkins/Chu Berry, Immortal Swing Sessions (Sonet/—)

Barney Bigard

Not only is Leon Albany 'Barney' Bigard one of the very finest of the many gifted clarinet players to come from New Orleans, he is also the single most important performer on his instrument to have worked with the Duke Ellington Orchestra. Bigard, born in 1906, joined Ellington at the end of 1927, after gaining valuable experience with several noted bandleaders, both in New Orleans and Chicago, including Albert Nicholas, Luis Russell and King Oliver. Brother of drummer Alex Bigard, he also brought his tenor sax into the Ellington fold, although this latter instrument afforded him comparatively little solo space of any consequence; his premier importance with the band was as clarinettist, another of a succession of star solo instrumentalists to be uniquely showcased.

Bigard, one of the few to use the Albert (as opposed to the more popular Boehm) system of clarinet-playing, always was an original player, but his originality was never more apparent than during his Ellington tenure. Possessor of a beautifully evocative tone, especially in the chalumeau register, Bigard is a warm, fluent improviser who has never needed to show off his undoubted technical skills in any pyrotechnic fashion. Outside Ellington, Bigard has proved his worth in a variety of bands, most memorably in 1929, as member of the Jelly Roll Morton Trio **(Jelly Roll Morton (1929), Vol 6)**, his graceful, yet deeply-felt playing on **Smilin' The Blues Away** being exquisite.

With Ellington, Bigard really came into his

own. Ellington's tone poem for Bigard's clarinet was the 1936 **Clarinet Lament**; a masterpiece of orchestration which allows Bigard to give full rein to his expressive powers, elegant drive and impressive technique **(The Complete Duke Ellington, Vol 7)**. Another early Bigard-Ellington masterpiece is to be found in the 1940 **Across The Track Blues (The Works Of Duke Ellington, Vol 12)** which, even to a casual listener, is ample evidence of his mastery as a blues performer. That blues superiority has been apparent throughout Bigard's career, and was certainly present during Ellington's October 1928 recording of **The Mooche (Duke Ellington In Harlem)**. And a trio of different recordings of **Saturday Night Function** from the following year **(The Works Of Duke Ellington, Vol 2, The Complete Duke Ellington, Vol 2: 1928-1930** and **Rare Duke Ellington Masterpieces)** are further superb examples of his prowess as a bluesman.

On tenor sax, he was an ordinary soloist; one of his best contributions to Ellington on this instrument remains that on **Hot Feet (The Works Of Duke Ellington, Vol 3)**. He was a competent, never brilliant, tenorist with Ellington, Oliver and Russell (though he rarely played the instrument after leaving the former).

After leaving Ellington, in 1942, Bigard worked with own bands, with Freddie Slack (1942-43); undertook some studio work; became a member of Kid Ory's band (1946), then worked as a member of the Louis Armstrong All Stars (1947-52). Subsequently, rejoined All Stars for two periods—1953-55, 1960-61.

Even with a supreme catalyst like Louis Armstrong, Bigard rarely recaptured the brilliance he had demonstrated with Duke Ellington. There were times, however, when he did produce fluent playing which was more reminiscent of the past and Ellington, including a handful of Armstrong recordings **(Satch Plays Fats** and **Louis Armstrong, Vol 3)**. But even those recordings under his own name rarely showed him at anywhere near his best. Better were those with Shelly Manne **(Shelly Manne & Co.)**, Art Hodes **(Bucket's Got A Hole In It)**, Ben Webster and Benny Carter **(BBB & Co.)**.

Since the 1960s Bigard has accepted selective gigs, and even a short British tour in the early 1970s.

Albums:

The Complete Duke Ellington, Vols 1-7 (CBS—France)
The Works Of Duke Ellington, Vols 1-18 (RCA Victor—France)
Duke Ellington In Harlem (Jazz Panorama)
Duke Ellington, At His Very Best (RCA Victor/RCA Victor)
Duke Ellington, In A Mellotone (RCA Victor/RCA Victor)
Rare Duke Ellington Masterpieces (—/VJM)
Duke Ellington, Hot In Harlem (1928-1929) (Decca/MCA—Germany)
Duke Ellington, Rockin' In Rhythm (1929-1931) (Decca/MCA—Germany)
Duke Ellington, The Duke 1940 (Jazz Society)
King Oliver's Dixie Syncopators (—/MCA—Germany)
Jelly Roll Morton, Vol 6 (1929) (RCA Victor—France)
Luis Russell & His Louisianna Swing Orchestra (Columbia/—)
Louis Armstrong, Satch Plays Fats (Columbia/CBS—France)
Louis Armstrong, Vol 3 (—/Saga)
Various (Including Barney Bigard), Ellington Sidemen (Columbia/Philips)
Art Hodes, Bucket's Got A Hole In It: Barney Bigard With Art Hodes (Delmark)
Barney Bigard/Benny Carter/Ben Webster, BBB & Co. (Prestige-Swingville/Xtra)
Shelly Manne & Co. (Flying Dutchman/—)

Black Artists Group

Originally based in St Louis, this group of avant-garde musicians seemed to be working similar collective areas to Chicago's AACM. There is the same concentration on a wide variety of instruments to provide an ever-changing texture to the music. To date, BAG's leading lights appear to be Oliver Lake, Charles 'Bobo' Shaw (an interesting composer of Asian-influenced works) and Lester Bowie's brother, Joseph. The one album under the collective name **(Black Artists Group In Paris)** is a sensitive and dynamically controlled piece, with fine alto and trombone contributions from Lake and Bowie respectively.

Albums:

Black Artists Group In Paris (BAG/BAG)
Joseph Bowie—Oliver Lake (Sackville/—)
Wildflowers, The New York Loft Sessions (Douglas/—)
Charles Bobo Shaw, Junk Trap (—/Black Saint)
Human Arts Ensemble, Live In Trio Performance (—/Circle Records)

Above: Ed Blackwell and Charlie Haden—drum and bass pioneers with Ornette Coleman's trail-blazing quartet late 1950s, early '60s.

Ed Blackwell

One of the great pioneers of free drumming—in company with Sonny Murray and Milford Graves—Ed Blackwell's main body of work remains within the group context of Ornette Coleman's Quartet and Don Cherry's units. Born in New Orleans, his drum concept fitted perfectly the needs of the new collective music—indeed, traditional New Orleans march rhythms combine with an African and Afro-Cuban influence in his work. A master craftsman, his preoccupation with shifting metres and sonics made him the ideal partner for Ornette, although it was Blackwell's student, Billy Higgins, who cut the first albums with the alto player.

The nature of Ornette's music—the rapid shifts of tempo, the mobile textures, the rocking swing—placed immense responsibilities on the drummer. It was a highly specialized function, and Blackwell, unlike Higgins—a looser, less asymmetrical player—doesn't seem to have worked much outside the free school. The leader's wish that rhythm should flow as naturally as patterns of breathing set enormous problems for this group, particularly on the level of avoiding collision. Blackwell's style is simpler, less cluttered than most drummers'; a tight snare sound dominates, propelling the rolling tattoo figures and often echoing the alto phrases. It is concentrated playing that deftly avoids the equally innovative use of rhythm by bassists like Charlie Haden, Scott La Faro or Jimmy Garrison.

Blackwell's solo feature on **T & T (Ornette!)** shows the close links between rhythm and melody in the new music, as well as the drummer's African leanings. Comparisons between Blackwell and Higgins can be drawn from their paired solos **(Free Jazz** and **Twins)** with the former's heart of darkness drum rolls followed by Higgins' flaring cymbal work.

Again, the drummer's work with Ornette's trumpeter, Don Cherry, is pivotal. The music constantly changes direction and requires a rare blend of self-effacement and initiative **(Complete Communion, Symphony For Improvisers** and **Where Is Brooklyn?)**. Cherry's composition for a large group **(Relativity Suite)** features Blackwell on **March Of The Hobbits**. The interaction between trumpeter and drummer is most clearly shown on the two albums made for the deleted French label BYG **(Mu, Parts One & Two)** a duo that never sounds remotely restricted in textural range.

Ill-health has dogged Blackwell's career (in fact, he's on a kidney machine three times a week) and recent years have seen few albums.

Albums:

Ornette Coleman: This Is Our Music (Atlantic/Atlantic)
Ornette! (Atlantic/Atlantic)
Art Of The Improviser (Atlantic/Atlantic)
Ornette On Tenor (Atlantic/Atlantic)
Free Jazz (Atlantic/Atlantic)
Twins (Atlantic/Atlantic)
Science Fiction (Columbia/Columbia)
Friends And Neighbors (Flying Dutchman/—)
Don Cherry: Complete Communion (Blue Note/Blue Note)
Symphony For Improvisers (Blue Note/Blue Note)
Where Is Brooklyn? (Blue Note/Blue Note)
Relativity Suite (JCOA/Virgin)
Mu, Parts One & Two (BYG—France)
Old & New Dreams (Black Saint/Black Saint)
Dewey Redman-Ed Blackwell, In Willisau (Black Saint/Black Saint)
Don Cherry-Ed Blackwell, El Corazón (ECM/ECM)

Eubie Blake

There is little doubt that of all jazz musicians, James Hubert Blake (born Baltimore, Maryland, 1883) was one of the most remarkable. Not only because, at 100, he must have been the oldest practicing jazz musician, but because he retained such remarkable facility as a pianist.

Extraordinary to realize that Blake was playing ragtime piano when that musical form was first in vogue. Not at all surprising, his latterday playing had raggy overtones and indeed he still played ragtime tunes at concert performances. Not a noted practitioner of stride piano, nevertheless he could occasionally evoke, with his strong, two-handed playing, that school of jazz expression; likewise, basic blues.

Eubie Bake sang in a modest friendly manner, and his prowess as raconteur has been positively documented in various record projects of more recent times. Blake's parents, both former slaves, offered musical encouragement to their son, who showed early interest, playing organ from six. Deeply influenced by the playing of itinerant black pianist Jesse Pickett (to whom he first listened in late 1890s). Composed first ragtime tune **(Charleston Rag)** in 1899. First regular job in a sporting house. Initial professional stage appearance with a Dr Frazier's Medicine Show, Fairfield, Pennsylvania (1901), playing melodion and executing buck dance on back of a truck.

Toured as buck dancer before going to New York (1902), returning to Baltimore following year for work as relief pianist in saloon bar joint; later in 1903 worked at another sporting house. Gigged at various establishments, including Goldfield House where he was resident for some time. Atlantic City was his next home and workplace (between 1905-14). During 1914 was heard by visiting piano giant James P. Johnson who called Blake 'one of the foremost pianists of all time'. Met lyricist Noble Sissle during spring of 1915. Pair decided to go into song-writing partnership. First joint composition **(It's All Your Fault)** popularized by Sophie Tucker in her show. (Blake's first copyrighted/published tune: **Chevy Chase**, 1914.)

Prompted by black orchestra leader James Reese Europe, Blake and Sissle teamed up with successful vaudeville team Flournoy

Below: The remarkable Eubie Blake, the 'Peter Pan' of jazz and ragtime who died in 1983 just days after world-wide celebrations for his 100th birthday.

Miller-Aubrey Lyles to produce **Shuffle Along**, as a genuine black musical comedy show (legendary cabaret artiste Josephine Baker a member of chorus line; Florence Mills one of the singers). Sissle-Blake team contributed strongly to **Elsie** (1923), and to revues by Cochran and André Charlot. In 1930, in collaboration with Andy Razaf, Blake composed **Memories Of You**—probably his best-ever pop tune. **I'm Just Wild About Harry**, his other most familiar composition (used as Harry Truman's presidential campaign song in 1948 US election) originated from score of **Shuffle Along; Memories Of You** was written for **Blackbirds Of 1930**. Although Blake continued to write music for shows, mostly with Sissle, much of his output was not used. Blake-Sissle partnership renewed during World War II: together they toured with their own USO show, Blake playing piano and conducting orchestra.

Blake enrolled at New York University after ceasefire, obtaining degree in music with specific reference to Schillinger system. Inactive professionally for several years, Blake's 'comeback' was gradual, via concerts, club appearances, benefits, etc, often being reunited with Sissle. That his piano-playing powers remained undiminished was illustrated by release of **Wizard Of The Ragtime Piano** in 1959, with sparkling keyboard contributions sympathetically accompanied by Bernard Addison, Milt Hinton (or George Duvivier), and Panama Francis (or Charlie Persip). Noble Sissle vocalized on **I'm Just Wild About Harry**.

One other first-class album of the comeback period is **The Marches I Played On The Old Ragtime Piano**, but it was not until release, in 1973, of **The 86 Years Of Eubie Blake** that total proof of his undiminished talents was produced. Through four sides of a fascinating double-LP set, Blake musically and verbally highlighted important events during his career, at the same time citing examples of significant musical influences. Throughout, Blake's strong, ragtime-into-stride playing is astonishingly well-preserved. Vocally, Blake is as charming as ever, with fellow veteran Sissle helping out on three numbers.

After approximately 1969, when Eubie Blake captivated an enthusiastic audience at that year's Newport Jazz Festival, his career was much less than static. He recorded at fairly regular intervals, giving still further insights into his own music as well as that by other ragtime, blues, jazz and vaudeville/pop composers of a bygone age he remembered so well **(Eubie Blake At The Piano** and **From Rags To Classics)** and continued to make a series of absorbing live appearances, including **91 Years Young**, recorded in concert at the 1974 Montreux Jazz Festival.

With the sudden rush of interest in ragtime during the early-1970s, it must have amused—and delighted—Eubie Blake to find that many of his earliest recordings **(Eubie Blake—Blues & Ragtime, Vols 1 & 2)** made perhaps unexpected appearances in modern record catalogs.

In 1976, a remarkably sprightly 93-year-old Blake was still showing willing taking a supporting acting part in Jeremy Paul Kagan's low-budget film biography *Scott Joplin* with Billy Dee Williams in the title role.

As recently as 1981, Blake took the grand concert stand along with a new generation of piano stars including Herbie Hancock, George Duke, Ramsey Lewis and Rodney Franklin. The occasion was a lavish keyboard concert organized by CBS **(One Night Stand: A Keyboard Event)**. The 98-year-old Blake honored a delighted young audience with an unforgettable version of his own, enduring **Charleston Rag**, composed when he was just 16.

The 100th birthday of this ragtime pioneer, pianist and composer on February 7, 1983, was an unprecedented event in jazz history, demanding worldwide celebration into which Blake entered enthusiastically. Eubie Blake had seemed indestructible. Then, just five days later, on February 12, he died from pneumonia.

The irrepressible James Hubert Blake used to say: 'If I'd known how long I was going to live, I'd have taken more care of myself'...

Albums:
Eubie Blake—Blues & Ragtime 1917—1929, Vol 1 (Biograph)
Eubie Blake—Blues & Ragtime, Vol 2 (Biograph)
Eubie Blake, Wizard Of The Ragtime Piano (20th Century Fox/—)
Eubie Blake, The Marches I Played On The Old Ragtime Piano (20th Century Fox/—)
The Eighty-Six Years Of Eubie Blake (Columbia/CBS—Holland)
Eubie Blake, From Rags To Classics (Eubie Blake Music/London)
Eubie Blake At The Piano (Eubie Blake Music/London)
Eubie Blake/Joan Morris/William Bolcomb, Wild About Eubie (Columbia/—)
Eubie Blake, 91 Years Young (RCA Victor—France)
Various, One Night Stand: A Keyboard Event (Columbia/CBS)

John Blake Jr

Born in Philadelphia, 1948, John Blake Jr. has been described by jazz critic Leonard Feather as 'the most important new violinist to reach the jazz forefront in the past several years'. Blake brings a broad and diverse background to his performance, having studied at Settlement Music School, West Virginia State University and the Insitute for Advanced Musical Studies in Montreux, Switzerland. He was also awarded a NEA grant to study India's Southern Carnatic violin style, and studied in Europe with concert violinist Zino Francescotti. Making his first recordings with saxophonist Archie Shepp, Blake later toured with Grover Washington Jr. He has appeared on at least four major labels and composed and arranged for some of the most outstanding names in jazz In recent years, he has toured and recorded as an integral part of the McCoy Tyner group.

As well as working with his own trio and solo, Blake visits college campuses, jazz clubs, societies and community arts series, both performing and lecturing.

Albums:
Archie Shepp, Attica Blues (Impulse/Impulse)
Archie Shepp, Cry Of My People (Impulse/Impulse)
Grover Washington Jr, Live At The Bijou (Kudu/—)
McCoy Tyner, Horizon (Milestone/Milestone)
McCoy Tyner, La Leyenda De La Hora (Columbia/CBS)
McCoy Tyner, The New York-Montreux Connection (Columbia/CBS)
The String Summit—One World In Eight (MPS/—)
James Newton, James Newton (Gramavision/Gramavision)
Jay Hoggard, Love Survives (Gramavision/Gramavision)
The Young Lions (Elektra Musician/Elektra Musician)
Maiden Dance (Gramavision/Gramavision)

Above: Art Blakey, veteran drummer and leader of the Jazz Messengers.

Art Blakey

Born Pittsburg, 1919, drummer Art Blakey remains one of the greatest players and combo leaders in the history of jazz There is such a furious commitment about his playing that soloists are forced to exert themselves, and any notion of coasting goes by the board. Generations of young players have learned their craft in Blakey's groups, left to lead their own groups, leaving him to break in another batch. Along with drummer Max Roach, it was Blakey's contention that drums were frontline instruments. History has proved them right, but initially their dominant role and parallel interchanges with the horns led to critical accusations of obtrusiveness.

It was this conception of heightened rhythmic activity that led to the formation of The Jazz Messengers in 1954 by Blakey and pianist Horace Silver. Their first album—**Horace Silver & The Jazz Messengers**—has tremendous punch, both drummer and pianist working together to lift the horns, trumpeter Kenny Dorham and tenorist Hank Mobley, on an urgent tide of riffs and accents. A live set **(At The Café Bohemia)** has the magnificent **Soft Winds** solo by Dorham, but the general standard of playing is so high that it seems pointless to single out performances. The interaction between drums, piano and the horns is the very essence of hard bop.

With the departure of Silver, the main onus of stoking the boilers fell on Blakey, and subsequent albums with altoist Jackie McLean and trumpeter Bill Hardman show an increase in domination from the drums **(Night In Tunisia)**. The meeting with Monk **(Art Blakey's Jazz Messengers With Thelonious Monk)** produced fine, considered music, and both albums featured the unsinkable tenor of Johnny Griffin. Large drum ensembles **(Orgy In Rhythm** and **The Drum Suite)** were a preoccupation of Blakey's in the mid-1950s, and showed his links with Africa, home of the drum.

The next Messengers line-up laid emphasis on funk. Pianist Bobby Timmons' tune **Moanin'** heralded a return to the gospel atmosphere of Silver's **The Preacher**, and was soon followed by **Dat Dere (The Big Beat)**. Musical directorship passed from tenor-player Benny Golson to trumpeter Lee Morgan, a player of great style and poise, as displayed on **It's Only A Paper Moon (The Big Beat)** and the front line, if that term has any meaning in Blakey's groups, was brought up to strength by tenor-player Wayne Shorter. Shorter's writing soon came to dominate the band book, and a succession of excellent albums restored the ascendancy of the Messengers **(Freedom Rider** and **Night In Tunisia)**. Trumpeter Freddie Hubbard took over from Morgan with no loss of striking power. There is very little to choose between **Buhaina's Delight, Mosaic** and **Free For All**, and the eventual break-up of this unit (Shorter moving to Miles Davis' Quintet), would have been discouraging to anyone less resilient than Blakey. In fact, the 1968 recording at Slugs **(Art Blakey & The Jazz Messengers Live!)** shows the old powerhouse driving the horns with his old unquenchable enthusiasm.

Art Blakey has recorded with a wide range of musicians outside his own group, bringing urgency and sensitivity to the rhythm sections. His contributions to the Thelonious Monk trios **(Thelonious Monk)**, and early quintets **(Genius Of Modern Music)**, show his compatibility with the percussive keyboard style.

His drum style is unmistakable, the chunk of the hi-hat squashing down in silence before the figures start to roll across the skins like big wooden skittle alley balls, the abrupt pause, a flashing woodpecker rattle of sticks on snare-rim before the final titanic swell. Blakey took the bop style from Kenny Clarke and reduced it to its irreduceable essentials. At the centre of his work is the drum roll, tiny tumblings which build to landslide proportions. Weak players tend to be overpowered by his backing, but as a make-or-break academy, Blakey's groups are second to none.

Indeed, at the 1981 Kool Jazz Festival, for example, Art Blakey hosted a specially memorable night when an extraordinary array of Jazz Messengers, past *and* present, took the stage together—Johnny Griffin, Jackie McLean, Billy Harper, Bobby Watson, Bill Hardman, Donald Byrd, Freddie Hubbard, Curtis Fuller, Walter Davis and Cedar Walton . . .

Throughout the late '70s and the '80s, Art Blakey, in his time-honored tradition, has continued to recruit and introduce promising young talent—acclaimed musicians like bassist Charles Fambrough, trumpeters Wynton Marsalis and Terence Blanchard, saxophonists Billie Pierce, Bobby Watson, Donald Harrison and Branford Marsalis, pianists James Williams and Donald Brown all to do well as solo artists.

The interest in Blakey and the personalities in his current line-ups has become almost 'revivalist' in zeal in the '80s, notably in the UK where foremost jazz DJ Paul Murphy was moved to proclaim in the mid-'80s that Art Blakey was 'the new messiah of the discos'. A new dance generation bops to Blakey's latest and re-issued albums while young aficionados heatedly debate the 'relative merits' of Jazz Messengers Lee Morgan and Kenny Dorham.

In spite of overseeing all this awesome, youthful Jazz Messengers activity, Blakey's own musical energy and enthusiasm show no signs of dissipating. As Blakey says: 'I'll play drums until Mother Nature tells me different. I'll retire when I'm six foot under . . .'.

Albums:

Horace Silver & The Jazz Messengers (Blue Note/Blue Note)
The Jazz Messengers At The Café Bohemia (Blue Note/Blue Note)
A Night In Tunisia (Vik/RCA Victor)
Art Blakey's Jazz Messengers With Thelonious Monk (Atlantic/Atlantic)
Orgy In Rhythm (Blue Note/Blue Note)
The Drum Suite (Columbia/CBS)
Moanin' (Blue Note/Blue Note)
The Big Beat (Blue Note/Blue Note)
Freedom Rider (Blue Note/Blue Note)
Night In Tunisia (Blue Note/Blue Note)
Buhaina's Delight (Blue Note/Blue Note)
Mosaic (Blue Note/Blue Note)
Free For All (Blue Note/Blue Note)
Art Blakey & The Jazz Messengers Live! (—/DJM)
Thelonious Monk (Prestige/Prestige)
Thelonious Monk, Genius Of Modern Music (Blue Note/Blue Note)
Art Blakey & The Jazz Messengers, Gypsy Folk Tales (Roulette/Pye)
Art Blakey-Buddy De Franco, Blues Bag (Vee Jay/Affinity)
Art Blakey Big Band and Quintet featuring John Coltrane, Ain't Life Grand (Bethlehem/Affinity)
A Night At Birdland Vols 1 & 2 (Blue Note/Blue Note)
Indestructible! (Blue Note/Blue Note)
In This Korner (Concord/Concord)
Straight Ahead (Concord/Concord)
Keystone 3 (Concord/Concord)
Blue Night (Timeless/Timeless)

Free For All (courtesy Blue Note): one of the finest Art Blakey line-ups.

Blanchard-Harrison, New York Second Line (courtesy George Wein Collection).

Terence Blanchard

In the 1980s, trumpeter Terence Blanchard is one of a long line of exceptionally gifted young musicians to come to prominence as a Jazz Messenger with Art Blakey.

In many ways, Blanchard's career parallels that of his predecessor with Blakey, fellow New Orleans prodigy Wynton Marsalis. Born in 1962, Blanchard learned piano at age 5. At 8, he took up trumpet although not seriously until 14. Initially involved in classical music through the New Orleans Civic Orchestra, his love for jazz was first fired by the enlightened teaching techniques of Wynton's father, pianist Ellis Marsalis, at the New Orleans Center for the Creative Arts (NOCCA).

In 1980, Blanchard went to Rutgers, New York, to study classical trumpet under Bill Fielder and jazz with ex-Thelonious Monk tenorist Paul Jeffrey. Through Jeffrey, Blanchard worked in Lionel Hampton's band and, when Wynton Marsalis left Blakey, Blanchard auditioned in March 1981 and was hired. He lists Clark Terry, Clifford Brown, Freddie Hubbard, Miles Davis and Woody Shaw among his influences but (and in spite of Marsalis) Blanchard has already established an individual voice and style on trumpet.

With altoist Donald Harrison (an ex-Berklee student, hired by Blakey along with Blanchard), their acclaimed **New York Second Line** début was recorded in 1983.

Albums:

Art Blakey and the Jazz Messengers, The New York Scene (Concord/Concord)
Terence Blanchard—Donald Harrison, New York Second Line (George Wein Collection—Concord/George Wein Collection—Concord)

Jimmy Blanton

Jimmy Blanton's life and musical career were both cut drastically short due to his premature death through turberculosis in 1942. He was 21 years old. Blanton's death was particularly unfortunate for within the space of two years he had achieved, virtually single-handed, a complete breakthrough in the concept of bass playing in jazz Instead of merely providing only a rock-solid accompaniment to front-line soloists, Blanton conceived his role along the lines of a horn, utilizing harmonic, melodic and rhythmic ideas that hitherto were unknown to jazz bassists. In those two years, Blanton emancipated the role of the bass player in jazz, and pioneered most, if not all, the directions it was to take in subsequent years. To an already star-studded Duke Ellington Orchestra, with whom he spent these vital two years, he imparted a rhythmic subtlety that even that great organization had not possessed before Blanton's inception into the ranks of Ellingtonia in the fall of 1939.

Before Blanton probably the only bass-player possessing anywhere near his sophistication and subtlety was John Kirby. But with Blanton, the thoughts and ideas for a whole new generation of bass players were crystallized: his fleet-fingered plucking certainly did have profound effect upon the work of Oscar Pettiford, Charles Mingus, and Ray Brown, to name the three finest post-Blanton bassists who would carry on his pioneering efforts a stage further. (When, over 30 years later, Norman Granz persuaded Ellington to re-record a selection of the extraordinary Ellington-Blanton bass duets, the choice of Brown as bassist for the project was obvious and appropriate **(This One's For Blanton)**.)

The original Ellington-Blanton duets **(The World Of Duke Ellington, Vols 11, 14, 15)** today retain their freshness and vitality, especially studio-made masterpieces like **Pitter Panther Patter** and **Mr J. B. Blues (Vol II)**. Of the many sides which Blanton recorded in his two years with the full Ellington orchestra, probably his most memorable individual performances were encapsulated during **Jack The Bear** and **Ko-Ko (The Works Of Duke Ellington, Vol 9)** wherein his superb articulation and beautifully resonant tone are amply displayed, and his unflagging drive lifts the band to further heights of inspiration and achievement. Similarly during **Bojangles, Conga Brava, Harlem Airshaft (Vol 10), John Hardy's Wife (Vol 14)** and **Take The 'A' Train** and **Jumpin' Punkins (Vol 15)**, Blanton's inspired playing adds that vital extra, exciting dimension to already impressive performances.

During his all-too-short period with Ellington (Blanton left the band in late 1941, after being taken seriously ill, and died in a sanitarium near Los Angeles in July 1942) the bassist took part in numerous bands-within-the-band recording projects, under the leadership of Barney Bigard, Johnny Hodges, Rex Stewart and Cootie Williams. Here, too, his unique gifts never failed to enhance the respective sessions.

Jimmy Blanton (born Chattanooga, Tennessee, 1921) started out as violinist, studying theory with an uncle. Turned his attention to bass whilst at college and played in college and local bands. Made riverboat trips with bands of Fate Marable during summer vacations, and after moving to St Louis, became member of Jeter-Pillars Orchestra (1937), continuing to work with Marable during summer. Ellington heard him play in St Louis, signed him, and for a while Blanton and Billy Taylor were both employed as bassists with Ellington band (Taylor left at beginning of 1940).

Like Charlie Christian and Lester Young in their own individual ways, Jimmy Blanton was an innovator of real importance, whose playing looked forward to the bebop innovations which he never lived to hear or, sadly, be part of.

Albums:

Duke Ellington, The Jimmy Blanton Years (Queen Disc—Italy)
The Works Of Duke Ellington, Vols 9-17 (RCA Victor—France)
Duke Ellington, The Duke 1940 (Jazz Society)
Duke Ellington, At His Very Best (RCA Victor/RCA Victor)
Duke Ellington, Braggin' In Brass 1936-1939 (Tax—Sweden)
Duke Ellington 1937-1939 (Tax—Sweden)
Duke Ellington, The Ellington Era, Vol 2 (Columbia/CBS)
Duke Ellington/Ray Brown, This One's For Blanton (Pablo/Pablo)

Carla Bley

Pianist and composer Carla Bley's importance as a musician has become difficult to separate from her importance as organizer of a musical environment for others.

Born Carla Borg in 1938 into a religious family in Oakland, Ca, Carla Bley's first musical experiences centered around the church where her father—a Swedish immigrant—played organ, led the choir and taught piano. She played piano from age 3, performed at recitals and church services, and was composing her first 'opera' at age 8.

Bley dropped out of school at 15 and left home. After a brief aimless period arranging and playing piano for a folk singer on the West Coast, she worked in New York jazz clubs as a cigarette girl. She also began writing for jazz musicians and returned to California briefly, playing in various clubs and bars in and around Los Angeles, before deciding to move to New York permanently. In 1957 she married her first husband, Canadian-born pianist Paul Bley whose music was to influence her own profoundly. (A woman journalist, also an amateur musician, asked Carla Bley to recommend a teacher—'Why don't you marry Paul Bley?' replied Ms Bley sagely.)

Gaining a reputation as a composer of considerable originality, Bley's pieces began to be recorded by influential names—Paul Bley, of course **(O Plus 1** on **Solemn Meditation)**, Jimmy Giuffre **(Ictus)**, George Russell **(Zig Zag** and **Bent Eagle)** and Art Farmer **(Sing Me Softly Of The Blues)**. Music began to take over as a way to make a living. For a while she played at coffee houses in Greenwich Village and in 1964 she became the pianist in Charles Moffett's group with Pharoah Sanders.

She became active in the notorious Jazz Composers Guild. Along with her second husband, trumpeter-composer Michael Mantler, she was responsible for the creation of an orchestra of Guild members which included such New Music luminaries as Roswell Rudd, Archie Shepp and Milford Graves. The orchestra continued to perform even after the Guild collapsed, appearing at the Newport Festival and Museum of Modern Art. This led to the formation of the Jazz Composers Orchestra Association (JCOA), a non-profit foundation to support the orchestra and commission/record new works. During this period, she toured Europe twice as a member of the Jazz Realities Quintet with saxophonist Steve Lacy. Subsequently, Bley's piano playing has contributed to the success of works by Don Cherry **(Relativity Suite)**, Clifford Thornton **(The Gardens Of Harlem)** and Grachan Moncur III **(Echoes Of Prayers)**.

In 1967, Bley's idiosyncratic **A Genuine Tong Funeral**—sub-titled 'Dark Opera Without Words'—was recorded by a nucleus of the Gary Burton Quartet and orchestra featuring Larry Coryell, Gato Barbieri, Steve Lacy and Jimmy Knepper. It was an ambitious venture, as Burton explains: 'I thought it would be nice to do a major project using theatrical, bizarre, programatic music. RCA thought it was a good idea and spent three times as much on it as a normal album. Carla is a unique musician, essentially self-taught and very creative, musically speaking. She has unusual technicalities of her own which turn up fresh ideas. Her music is solid, well-written—always refreshing and interesting.'

On the recording of JCOA's first double album **The Jazz Composers Orchestra**, Bley proved a solid, sympathetic pianist; further evidence of her 'unusual technicalities'

Pianist-composer-arranger Carla Bley—acclaimed as one of the most prolific, respected, individualistic and inimitable writers in contemporary music.

emerged when she was commissioned by bassist Charlie Haden to compose part of and arrange his **Liberation Music** album featuring Don Cherry, Gato Barbieri, Roswell Rudd and Dewey Redman.

Bley's epic **Escalator Over The Hill**—a jazz opera ('chronotransduction') of staggering dimensions—resulted from collaboration with lyricist Paul Haines and took nearly four years (1968-71) to complete. This gigantic work incorporated the combined talents of dozens of musicians including Cherry, Barbieri, Rudd, Haden and British musicians guitarist John McLaughlin and singer-bass guitarist Jack Bruce. JCOA released **Escalator** as a three-record set and, to help promote this unusual project, Bley made several trips to Europe. **Escalator** received high critical acclaim with Bley winning *Downbeat* magazine's International Critics Poll for the third time and receiving composition grants from the Creative Artists Program Service and the National Endowment for the Arts plus the award of a Guggenheim Fellowship. **Escalator** also won the French Oscar du Disque de Jazz and was voted 'LP of the Year' in the UK in *Melody Maker's* jazz poll.

Bley and Mantler looked for a further outlet for their own music—as a result, Watt Works was formed with its own studio, Grog Kill, in New York. A new work with Paul Haines was recorded as Watt's first album, **Tropic Appetites**. This featured British vocalist Julie Tippetts, Howard Johnson, Gato Barbieri, Dave Holland, Toni Marcus and Paul Motian. Soon after, Bley contributed to the second Watt album, Mantler's **No Answer** (based on Samuel Beckett's words) with Jack Bruce and Don Cherry.

Although Bley's involvement with JCOA also continued, she still found time to help develop the New Music Distribution Service (NMDS) for all independently produced albums of new music. She also edited the JCOA/NMDS newspaper *Corrective News Distribution*.

Bley spent a year working on a special commission which she finally entitled **3/4**. The work was premiered at Alice Tully Hall with Keith Jarrett as the piano soloist, and later performed by the St Paul Chamber Orchestra (again, with Jarrett), Speculum Musicae (with pianist Ursula Oppens) and at the Kitchen (with Frederic Rzewski). With the aid of a Ford Foundation grant, Bley was able to record her own version of **3/4** for Watt and also played piano on Mantler's **13**.

While in London recording Michael Mantler's adaptation of the Harold Pinter play **Silence** (with Robert Wyatt, Kevin Coyne, Chris Spedding and Ron McClure), she also sang some John Cage songs on an album produced by Brian Eno for his Obscure Records.

Back home in Watt's Grog Kill studio, Bley recorded her next album, **Dinner Music**, with an interesting if curious line-up of Roswell Rudd, Carlos Ward, Mantler and Bob Stewart with Richard Tee, Eric Gale, Cornell Dupree, Gordon Edwards and Steve Gadd. She produced and played on Mantler's **Movies** album featuring Larry Coryell, Steve Swallow and Tony Williams. She also worked on the music for a play by surrealist painter Leonora Carrington, commissioned by the Theater of Latin America, and participated as Composer-in-Residence at the Hurley Woods Music Festival.

Her own dynamic ten-piece band, formed in the late 1970s, with its taste for theatricality, has toured Europe and the USA extensively. The band has featured, variously, the extraordinary talents of saxophonists Tony Dagradi, Steve Slagle and Carlos Ward, trombonist Gary Valente, tuba-players Earl McIntyre and Bob Stewart, and bassist Steve Swallow. Notable Carla Bley Band albums in the '80s include **Social Studies** (1980) featuring saxophonist Carlos Ward and the excellent **Carla Bley Live!** (at the Great American Music Hall, San Francisco, 1981) with its show-stopping 'old-time religion'-flavoured **The Lord's Listenin' To Ya, Hallelujah!** (with Gary Valente's rousing *pièce de résistance* on trombone).

After such a spectacular and varied career, Bley commands the greatest respect from her peers and has even been described as 'the most original pianist-composer since Monk'; she certainly ranks amongst the most prolific, individualistic and inimitable writers of contemporary music. Carla Bley is also one of the few jazz artists who has managed to establish almost complete control over her music.

Albums:
Don Cherry, Relativity Suite (JCOA/Virgin)
Clifford Thornton, The Gardens Of Harlem (JCOA/Virgin)
Grachan Moncur III, Echoes Of Prayers (JCOA/Virgin)
Escalator Over The Hill (JCOA/ECM)
Tropic Appetites (Watt/Watt)
Michael Mantler, No Answer (Watt/Watt)
Carla Bley-Gary Burton, A Genuine Tong Funeral (RCA/RCA)
Charlie Haden, Liberation Music (Impulse/Impulse)
Michael Mantler-Carla Bley, 13 3/4 (Watt/Watt)
Michael Mantler, The Hapless Child (Watt/Watt)
Dinner Music (Watt/Watt)
European Tour 1977 (Watt/Watt)
Musique Mécanique (Watt/Watt)
Social Studies (Watt/Watt)
Carla Bley Live! (Watt/Watt)
I Hate To Sing (Watt/Watt)
Heavy Heart (Watt/Watt)
Night-Glo (Watt/Watt)
Charlie Haden, The Ballad Of The Fallen (ECM/ECM)

Paul Bley (courtesy Wing)—'Chord changes have never interfered with my own way of hearing melody'.

Paul Bley

Born 1932 in Canada, pianist Paul Bley took over Oscar Peterson's bassist and drummer when the maestro moved to the United States in 1949. Despite popularity and success for the trio, Bley too upped stakes and went to New York's Juilliard to extend his studies. By 1954 he was playing at top venues like Birdland, and the following year worked briefly with Chet Baker. Bley seems to be naturally of the avant-garde, restless, experimental—as he says, 'chord changes have never interfered with my own way of hearing melody'. Ornette Coleman and Don Cherry gravitated to the Bley group in Los Angeles in 1958, which gave a recorded preview **(The Fabulous Paul Bley Quintet)** of the musical revolution to come with Coleman's series of Atlantic albums. In 1960 Bley was working with another experimenter, George Russell **(Jazz In The Space Age)** playing duets with fellow pianist, Bill Evans, on **Chromatic Universe**. He next spent three years with Jimmy Giuffre, and on albums like **Fusion** and **Thesis** showed great empathy for Giuffre's terse austerity, fractured lines and unstated pulse. After a year with tenorist Sonny Rollins **(Sonny Meets Hawk)** Bley formed his own trio with Steve Swallow on bass and Barry Altschul on drums, and released a stream of impressive albums for ESP and ECM **(Closer, Ballads, Open, To Love, Paul Bley & Gary Peacock** and **Bley NHOP)**. Bley's favorite compositions, **Closer** and **Mr Joy**, figure time and again, each version a further disciplined advance of the heart of the matter. More recently he set up his own label, Improvising Artists, and released albums with clarinettist Giuffre **(Quiet Song)**, with tenorist John Gilmore **(Turning Point)** and solo **(Alone Again)**.

In a quiet way Paul Bley has collected quite a few firsts. His pioneering work on the West Coast with Coleman put him in advance of many of the new wave players in New York. He was the first to perform publicly on the synthesizer in 1969—and soon returned to the acoustic piano. Unlike most of the new wave pianists, Bley's style is spare and subtle, introverted and extremely concentrated. His chords are complex and many-layered. Inner voicings are constantly shifting, altering the structure of his pieces. He makes intelligent and sensitive use of the strings inside the piano, plucking and taking up the chord on the keyboard. Bley's originality repays careful listening.

Albums:
The Fabulous Paul Bley Quintet (—/America—France)
George Russell, Jazz In The Space Age (Decca/—)
Jimmy Giuffre, Fusion (Verve/—)
Jimmy Giuffre, Thesis (Verve/—)
Sonny Rollins, Sonny Meets Hawk (RCA/RCA—France)
Paul Bley, Closer (ESP/ESP)
Ballads (ECM/ECM)
Open, To Love (ECM/ECM)
Paul Bley & Gary Peacock (ECM/ECM)
Paul Bley, Niels Henning Orsted Pedersen (—/Steeplechase)
Alone Again (Improvising Artists/Improvising Artists)
Quiet Song (Improvising Artists/Improvising Artists)
Turning Point (Improvising Artists/Improvising Artists)
Sonor (Soul Note/Soul Note)
Tango Palace (Soul Note/Soul Note)
Tears (Owl/—)

Blood Sweat & Tears

Formed in New York, 1967, by Al Kooper, Steve Katz and Bobby Colomby, Blood Sweat & Tears were among the first to fuse jazz imaginatively with heavy rock and R&B influences, creating an almost 'big band jazz-rock' sound, equalled perhaps only by early Chicago. Their first album, **Child Is Father To The Man,** in 1968, predominantly shows up Kooper's earthy influence (possibly better appreciated as a super-session musician and organist on Bob Dylan's **Like A Rolling Stone** and **Blonde On Blonde**). Their second album, **Blood Sweat And Tears** (after Kooper's departure), sold a million copies, produced hit singles like **You And Me So Very Happy**, the enduring **Spinning Wheel, And When I Die**, but was critically denounced (perhaps, in retrospect, unfairly) as a pale shadow of the first album.

BS&T have suffered numerous personnel changes over the years and their varying output has reflected this, although the part played by the fine jazz bassist Ron McClure and the Brecker Brothers cannot be underestimated. However, BS&T must be remembered as important contributors to the jazz-rock explosion of the late '60s and early '70s.

Albums:
Child Is Father To The Man (Columbia/CBS)
Blood Sweat And Tears (Columbia/CBS)
Three (Columbia/CBS)
BS&T 4 (Columbia/CBS)
New Blood (Columbia/CBS)
No Sweat (Columbia/CBS)
Mirror Image (Columbia/CBS)
New City (Columbia/CBS)
More Than Ever (Columbia/CBS)

Jane Ira Bloom

Born in Newton, Mass., in 1955, Jane Ira Bloom—proficient on soprano, alto and tenor saxes—can be numbered among the most respected musician-composers to emerge in the '70s. As well as leading her own group, she has performed to great acclaim in Europe, appeared in the Kansas City Women's Jazz Festivals and the Kool Jazz Festival, as well as featuring in the Broadway musical *The 1940s Radio Hour*.

She turned down an invitation from Mercer Ellington to tour with the Ellington Orchestra and went to Yale where she received a BA and an MA. After graduation in 1977, she went to New York and studied with tenorist George Coleman. At Yale she had met bass-player Kent McLagan, with whom she was to work for three years. Her first album in 1979, **We Are**, was a horn-bass format (with McLagan), self-produced and released on her own label Outline. Two years later, she recorded her second album, **Second Wind**, featuring vibes and marimba-player David Friedman, an association which was subsequently to bring her wider exposure. She has also contributed to vocalist Jay Clayton's work **(All Out)**, highlighted in performance at the 1982 New Music America Festival.

Her exceptional 1982 album, **Mighty Lights**, finds her in the company of bassist Charlie Haden, drummer Ed Blackwell and pianist Fred Hersch. **Mighty Lights** provides a fine example of the individuality of her playing and includes her particularly lyrical and poignant tribute to the late Bill Evans **(The Man In Glasses)**.

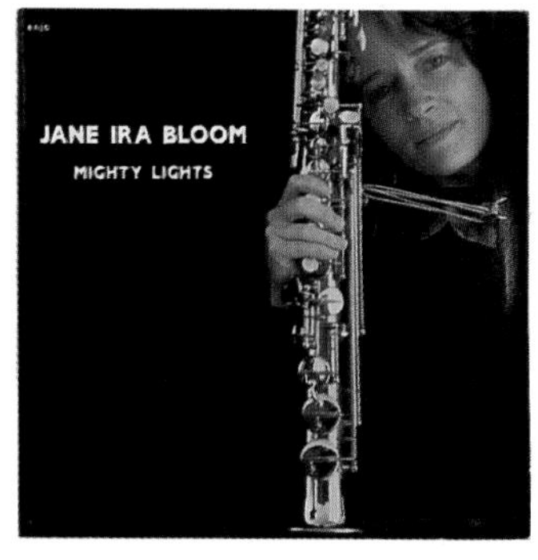

Jane Ira Bloom, Mighty Lights (courtesy Enja).

Albums:
We Are (Outline/—)
Second Wind (Outline/—)
David Friedman, Of The Wind's Eye (—/Enja—Germany)
Mighty Lights (—/Enja—Germany)
Jane Ira Bloom-Fred Hersch, As One (—/JMT—Germany)

Blue Note

Since the Blue Note label's inception in the late 1930s, no other label has equalled the continuous outpouring of jazz legends from its catalogue—in fact, Blue Note *made* jazz legends.

In 1938, Alfred Lion left Nazi-dominated Germany and arrived in New York where, on December 23, he heard boogie-woogie piano masters Albert Ammons and Meade Lux Lewis at Carnegie Hall. Two weeks later, Lion recorded the two pianists in a privately hired studio, pressed up fifty 12-inch 78s of each artist, and the Blue Note label was born. In 1939, Lion was joined by fellow German Francis Wolff and together, over the next quarter of a century, they were to create the most prestigious, distinguished and loved jazz label of all time, with its distinctive sleeve designs by Reid Miles.

The golden age of Blue Note sadly ended in 1966 when it was sold to Liberty Records. Although the label continued to make and release records, things weren't quite the same. In the mid-'80s, Bruce Lundvall announced that this most famous of jazz labels would be reborn, with the assistance of Michael Cuscuna. The news set jazz fans rejoicing around the world.

On February 22, 1985, major Blue Note artists (old and new) gathered at the Town Hall, New York, to celebrate the relaunch of the label (documented on video, *One Night With Blue Note—Preserved Vols 1 & 2*). Assembled Blue Note musical dignitaries included Herbie Hancock, Freddie Hubbard, Art Blakey, Johnny Griffin, Bobby Hutcherson, Kenny Burrell, Grover Washington Jr, McCoy Tyner, Jackie McLean, Woody Shaw, Charles Lloyd, Lou Donaldson, newcomer Stanley Jordan et al.

The revitalised Blue Note arrived with a declaration—to put on display the treasures of its past and present (much of it previously unissued; much of it still to be recorded; all of it avidly awaited).

New signing to Blue Note in the '80s include Stanley Jordan, saxophonist Bill Evans and Tania Maria.

Blue Note has been reborn and, thanks to Michael Cuscuna and Bruce Lundvall, flourishes in the same spirit with which founders Alfred Lion and Frank Wolff created this historic record label.

Above: Arthur Blythe—a great original with an instantly identifiable sound.

Arthur Blythe

Born in Los Angeles on May 7, 1940, the phenomenal alto saxophonist Arthur Blythe seemed to burst on the scene from nowhere, a fully fledged 'star', in his mid-thirties. He wanted to study trombone but his mother, an Earl Bostic and Johnny Hodges fan, had other ideas so he studied alto sax from aged 9. By 13, he was performing in a blues band and, at 16, discovered jazz via Charlie Parker, Thelonious Monk, Miles Davis and, especially, his hero John Coltrane.

In 1963, he joined pianist Horace Tapscott **(The Giant Is Awakening**, 1969) and other experimentalists in the Underground Musicians Association (also known as 'the Union of God's Musicians and Artists Ascension')—an organization for the preservation of black music in the community. During the '60s and '70s, Blythe worked with Tapscott's quartet and his Pan African Peoples Arkestra. He also taught at the Malcolm X Center in Los Angeles and the University of California as a student teacher. Moving to New York in '74, gigs were hard to come by initially and Blythe took day jobs, including his now-famous stint as a security guard in a porn theater. He worked for a few weeks with vocalist Leon Thomas before joining Chico Hamilton's band in '75 **(Chico Hamilton And The Players, Peregrinations, Coonskin** and **Catwalk)**. He has also made a notable contribution to the Gil Evans line-up **(Parabola** and **Live At The Royal Festival Hall)**.

In 1977 he formed his own sextet (including tuba and cello), recording **The Grip** and **Metamorphosis** (India Navigation). Since signing to the major Columbia in the late '70s, Blythe has found a sizeable audience with exceptional albums like **In The Tradition, Blythe Spirit** and **Elaborations** (including his inimitable rendering of **One Mint Julep**). His mid-'80s album **Put Sunshine In It** took a sharp turn towards the funk market and achieved great success in the discos.

His writing for the unusual instrumentation of alto sax, tuba (Bob Stewart), guitar (Calvin Bell) and cello (Abdul Wadud) has produced some of his most enduring work (notably, **Blythe Spirit** and **Elaborations**)—his distinctive alto sound soaring above, below, across, in and out of the whole, his jagged-edged, deliciously blues-tinged lines poised before they fall.

While Blythe's music clearly springs from the adventurous jazz tradition, you often sense a wicked sense of humour lurking (no put-down intended, it's a wry and effective device)—listening to Blythe is always a delightful experience. Of all the new wave alto-players in the late '70s, Blythe has developed a particularly personal and instantly recognizable sound and style. He's undoubtedly one of the great originals.

Albums:
Lennox Avenue Breakdown (Columbia/CBS)
In The Tradition (Columbia/CBS)
Illusions (Columbia/CBS)
Blythe Spirit (Columbia/CBS)
Elaborations (Columbia/CBS)
Light Blue (Columbia/CBS)
Put Sunshine In It (Columbia/CBS)
Da-da (Columbia/CBS)

Earl Bostic

Earl Bostic's hairy tone and basic, hard-driving rhythmic style made him one of the first cross-over jazz artists—in Bostic's case, from jazz to R&B. Born in Tulsa, Oklahoma, 1913, Bostic started on alto sax, clarinet, and after studying music at Xavier University, New Orleans, work followed with numerous outfits (including Charlie Creath-Fate Marable, Don Redman and Edgar Hayes).

In 1939, Bostic fronted own band in New York, sometimes playing also baritone sax, trumpet, guitar. In 1941, worked in Harlem with Hot Lips Page. 1943: joined Lionel Hampton, he had previously played at one of the vibra-harpist's legendary late-1930s all-star record dates **(The Complete Lionel Hampton/Lionel Hampton's Best Records, Vols 3, 5)**. Stayed with Hampton's wildly swinging big band for about a year **(Steppin' Out: Lionel Hampton, Vol 1: 1942-1944)**. Subsequently, worked with small groups, mostly under own leadership.

During 1950s attained a pop-size reputation as best-selling record artist with R&B-styled hits of standards like **Temptation, Flamingo, Sleep, Cherokee, You Go To My Head** and **Moonglow**. Many of the innumerable LPs he made during last 15 years of his life (Bostic died of a second heart attack in 1965, having been stricken by an initial heart seizure in 1956) are of interest more to R&B fans than jazz collectors. But they always swung, with Bostic's sandpaper-edged tone and wailing sax projecting its basic message to great effect. Bostic, who during his career penned arrangements for, among others, Paul Whiteman, Artie Shaw, Hot Lips Page and Louis Prima, was also a composer of some merit: **Let Me Off Uptown** (a hit for Gene Krupa) and **The Major & The Minor** (recorded by Alvino Rey), are amongst his better-known tunes.

Albums:
The Complete Lionel Hampton (RCA/Victor)/ Lionel Hampton's Best Records, Vols 3, 5 (RCA Victor—France)
Steppin' Out: Lionel Hampton, Vol 1 (1942-1944) (MCA—Germany)
Various, Swing Classics, Vol 2 (1944/45) (—/Polydor)
Earl Bostic, Bostic Showcase Of Swinging Dance Hits (—/Parlophone) (EP)
Earl Bostic (King/—)
Various (Including Hot Lips Page), The Sax Scene (—/London)
Various (Including Buck Ram, Hot Lips Page, The Changing Face Of Harlem, Vol 1) (Savoy/Savoy)

Above: Mississippi-born trumpeter Bobby Bradford—a musician with a fine logic and precise articulation.

Lester Bowie

see Art Ensemble of Chigago

Joanne Brackeen

Pianist-composer Joanne Brackeen, born in Ventura, California, 1938, didn't begin performing and recording under her own name until the late '70s. She married saxophonist Charles Brackeen in 1960 and raising four children prevented her from performing regularly. Her career took a long overdue upturn in the late '70s when pianist Bill Evans' formidable producer Helen Keane was taken on as her manager on his recommendation.

She took a few formal piano lessons aged 9 but virtually taught herself, initially copying solos from Frankie Carle records. Her scholarship to the prestigious Los Angeles Conservatory of Music lasted three days, after Brackeen decided that their curriculum was not a natural way to teach music.

By the late '50s, Brackeen was playing piano on the West Coast with top musicians like Dexter Gordon, Harold Land, Bobby Hutcherson and Charles Lloyd but she wasn't particularly anxious to join the big league herself. The family's move to New York changed that. She worked with vibes-player Freddy McCoy first and then, for three years, with Art Blakey's Jazz Messengers prompting one patronizing critic to desribe her as 'the only female Messenger of any tenure in the band's 25-year history'. Stints followed with Joe Henderson and two years with Stan Getz before going it alone in '77.

In 1978, she recorded a well-received duo album **(Prism)** with bassist Eddie Gomez (another long-time Bill Evans associate). **Keyed In** and **Ancient Dynasty**, recorded for Bob James' Tappen Zee label, enhanced a now established reputation. Her superb 1982 album **Special Identity** for Antilles found her with Gomez again and drummer Jack De Johnette, featuring a batch of new Brackeen compositions. Brackeen has become internationally recognized as an original, intuitive and visionary keyboard artist in the '80s—it's a pity it had to take so long.

Below: Joanne Brackeen—a late-starter who has become internationally recognized as a visionary and intuitive pianist.

Albums:
Snooze (Choice/—)
Invitation (Freedom/—)
Joanne Brackeen-Clint Houston, New True Illusions (Timeless/—)
Tring-a-Ling (Choice/—)
Mythical Magic (Pausa/—)
Joanne Brackeen-Eddie Gomez, Prism (Choice/—)
Special Identity (Antilles/Antilles)
Havin' Fun (Concord/Concord)

Bobby Bradford

Born 1934 in Mississippi, the trumpeter paid his dues with Leo Wright, Buster Smith, Wardell Gray, Eric Dolphy and Gerald Wilson. Most importantly, he began playing with revolutionary alto-player Ornette Coleman in the Los Angeles area from 1953. After four years in USAF bands, Bradford studied music at the University of Texas. Between 1961-63, he rejoined Ornette in New York, but unfortunately no records resulted. Back in Los Angeles, he formed the New Art Jazz Ensemble with multi-reed-player, John Carter. In the '70s, Bradford made several trips to Europe, and recorded with the fine British drummer, John Stevens.

A more orthodox, brass-toned player than Ornette's habitual partner, Don Cherry, Bradford's presence on numbers like **Law Years** and **The Jungle Is A Skyscraper (Science Fiction)** brings a deliberate and considered quality to the music. Again, elegance and freedom combined in his own West Coast band with fellow Texan, John Carter, and several excellent musicianly albums followed. The first **(Seeking)** featured the compositions of Carter and covered a wide spectrum of moods in which interaction between the horns and the rhythm section—Tom Williamson, bass, Bruz Freeman, drums—was distinguished by thought and restraint. There is real blues feeling on numbers like **The Sunday Afternoon Jazz Blues Society (Self Determination Music)** which works better than the longer, more rambling pieces. The group deserves to be better known: logic and excitement are infrequent stable-mates.

Bobby Bradford's writing is prominently featured on his album with John Stevens, Trevor Watts and Kent Carter **(Love's Dream)** and the overall feeling is very much in line with Ornette's quartets. Sitting in with Stevens' Spontaneous Music Ensemble **(Bobby Bradford, John Stevens & SME)** Bradford submerges his personality in the dense collective textures.

Albums:
Ornette Coleman, Science Fiction (Columbia/CBS)
Seeking (Revelation/—)
Flight For Four (Flying Dutchman/—)
Self Determination Music (Flying Dutchman/—)
Love's Dream (Emanem/Emanem)
Bobby Bradford, John Stevens & SME (—/Freedom)
Bobby Bradford And The Mo'tel: Lost In LA (Soul Note/Soul Note)

Tiny Bradshaw

Myron 'Tiny' Bradshaw (born Youngstown, Ohio, 1905) was a drummer-pianist-singer during his musical career, but is best remembered for leading a big band that swung the blues and played good, solid, blues-based jazz and R&B from 1934—the year it made its New York début—until early 1950s.

Prior to 1934 Bradshaw, who had majored in psychology at Wilberforce University, Ohio, had sung with Horace Henderson's Collegians, then with Marion Hardy's Alabamians, the Savoy Bearcats, Mills Blue Rhythm Band, and Luis Russell. Like the bands of Lucky Millinder and Todd Rhodes, Bradshaw recorded for important R&B label King (between 1949-58). With King, Bradshaw notched up several hit records, including **Big Town** (with vocal by noted R&B artist Roy Brown) and **Soft**.

During the last 10-15 years of its life, Bradshaw orchestra tended to concentrate more on R&B, although its allegiance to jazz never was forgotten completely. Bradshaw himself, after years of extensive nationwide tours and recording, finally became domiciled in Chicago. But it was in Cincinatti, Ohio—in 1958—that Tiny Bradshaw died. Prior to his death, he had suffered two strokes, the latter having precipitated his enforced retirement from the music business. Amongst the list of musicians who worked with Bradshaw, at one stage or another, can be counted the following: trumpeters Bill Hardman, Henry Glover; saxists Sonny Stitt, Red Prysock, George 'Big Nick' Nicholas, Charlie Fowlkes, Sil Austin; bassist Sam Jones; and singer Arthur Prysock. Blues guitarist-singer Lonnie Johnson recorded with the band in 1951.

Albums:
Various (Including Tiny Bradshaw), Kings Of Rhythm & Blues (Polydor)

Ruby Braff

A marvelously eloquent, always mellifluous player, Reuben 'Ruby' Braff (born Boston, Mass., 1927) is something of a throwback to jazz of pre-World War II except that where Braff is concerned his music sounds fresh and, despite strong influences (ie Armstrong, Berigan, Hackett, James, he does not slavishly copy any of the great

Above: Cornetist Ruby Braff at his most relaxed and often producing his best, touring with George Wein's special all star packages.

trumpeters/cornettists of the past.

A self-taught musician, Braff has tended to concentrate almost exclusively on the warmer sound of the cornet (like, for example, Nat Adderley). His career has seen its share of ups and downs—the latter occurring because of a peculiar situation in the 1950s whereby an up-and-coming player like Braff was unable to find sufficient work because his style was considered out of date. Even in the 'down' days, however, Braff managed to attract the attention of record labels and producers; his not inconsiderable discography thus far gives ample evidence that Braff has been a model of consistency, in various, mostly 'mainstream', settings.

Braff first came to the notice of record-buyers through an appearance as sideman on a 1953 Vic Dickenson record date **(Vic Dickenson Showcase/The Essential Vic Dickenson)**. He tended to steal solo limelight from long-established veterans like Dickenson, Ed Hall and Sir Charles Thompson. His ballad-playing **I Cover The Waterfront** was exquisite, sensitive; his blowing on faster items **(Jeepers Creepers, Keepin' Out Of Mischief Now)** was rhythmically subtle, with Braff exhibiting commendable controlled power, even at moments of climax. Whatever the mood, his playing maintained an impressive sense of logicality and lyricism that showed his obvious debt to Hackett. Further exposure—and in many ways a deeper insight into Braff's technique and mode of self-expression—came the following year when he appeared as one-third of Mel Powell Trio **(Thigamagig)**, then, with a tribute to Billie Holiday **(Holiday In Braff)**, followed by an absolutely delightful cornet-piano date with Ellis Larkins **(Two By Two)**, and a reunion date with Dickenson, this time with Braff as leader **(The Ruby Braff Special)**. In this kind of basically mainstream company, Braff usually is to be heard at his most relaxed, which probably explains why his participation in George Wein's touring Newport All Stars packages **(Tribute To Duke, The Newport All Stars** and **Midnight Concert In Paris)** has usually found him operating at or near to his very best. Much the same can be said with regard to his live appearance at the diner owned by Mr and Mrs Ralph Sutton, with mine host helping out on piano **(Sunnie's Side Of The Street)**.

In the '70s, Braff's unique brand of unruffled elegance was gorgeously show-cased in the chamber setting of the Ruby Braff-George Barnes Quartet—a combo fully operational between 1973-75. With Braff providing the basic spark for the group, ably assisted by guitarist Barnes, plus rhythm guitar and bass, the cornettist had ample opportunity to demonstrate, once again, his dexterity and, in particular, just how effective it can be in utilizing an essentially extrovert instrument sotto voce and still produce music that is of exceptional quality. Indeed, the only complaint was that there were times when the presence of a drummer and/or another horn might have injected more fire into proceedings. Certainly, it is true to say that Ruby Braff operates at a more emotionally satisfying level in more buoyant surroundings. Rather like his 1967 recording date with Buddy Tate, George Wein et al **(Hear Me Talkin'!)** or, in more recent, post Braff-Barnes times, in company with such as Jimmie Rowles, Bucky Pizzarelli and Vic Dickenson **(Them There Eyes)**.

Albums:

Vic Dickenson Showcase (Vanguard)/The Essential Vic Dickenson (Vogue)
Mel Powell, Thigamagig (Vanguard/Vanguard)
Ruby Braff, Holiday In Braff (Bethlehem/London)
Ruby Braff, Ruby Got Rhythm (—/Black Lion)
Ruby Braff/Ellis Larkins, Two By Two (Vanguard/Fontana)
Ruby Braff At Newport (Verve/Columbia—Clef)
Various, The Newport All Stars (Black Lion/Black Lion)
The Newport All Stars, Tribute To Duke (MPS)
The Newport All Stars, Midnight Concert In Paris (—/Philips)
Ruby Braff/Ralph Sutton, On Sunnie's Side Of The Street (Blue Angel Jazz Club/—)
Ruby Braff & His Men (RCA Victor/—)
Ruby Braff, Hear Me Talkin'! (Black Lion)
The Ruby Braff-George Barnes Quartet (Chiaroscuro)/The Best I've Heard . . . (Vogue)
Ruby Braff & His International Jazz Quartet Plus Three (Chiaroscuro)/The Grand Reunion (Chiaroscuro)/Bugle Call Rag (Vogue)
The Ruby Braff Special (Vanguard/Vanguard)
Ruby Braff, Them There Eyes (Sonet)
Ruby Braff-Dick Hyman, America The Beautiful (George Wein Collection-Concord/George Wein Collection-Concord)

Ruby Braff—Ellis Larkins' duet, Two By Two (courtesy Fontana).

Dollar Brand

see Abdullah Ibrahim

Anthony Braxton

Composer and multi-instrumentalist Anthony Braxton has created a valuable bank of work over 20 years which has greatly influenced the shape of today's music. Braxton's music is all-encompassing from masterful solo saxophone improvisations to notated music for multiple orchestras.

Born in Chicago in 1945, his early influences included Ahmad Jamal, Warne Marsh, Paul Desmond, Lee Konitz and Miles Davis. A period in Korea, playing in army bands, enabled him to work on his musical skills. On return to Chicago in 1966, Roscoe Mitchell introduced him to the Association for the Advancement of Creative Musicians.

The most gifted instrumentalist of Chicago's AACM, Anthony Braxton's début album **(Three Compositions Of New Jazz)** in 1968 showed not only the fast, confident alto-player, but also a highly distinctive approach to group improvising. Braxton's compositions, usually named with formulae, are diagrams which allow great scope for interaction and improvisation, so his choice of partners is crucial. His music is well served here by trumpeter Leo Smith and violinist Leroy Jenkins, habitual cohorts. His next album, **For Alto**, offers four sides of unaccompanied saxophone, a daring and at that time unprecedented idea which succeeds through intelligent programming. **To Composer John Cage** is the most savagely violent playing on record, whereas **Dedication To Ann And Peter Allen** meanders gently and lyrically through passages of silence. Further developments in group music followed, including five versions of **Small Composition (This Time)** which effectively shows the process whereby Braxton erodes the melody in favour of textural variation.

The short-lived group, Circle **(Circle Paris—Concert)**, comprising Braxton, pianist Chick Corea, bassist Dave Holland and drummer Barry Altschul, is less angular than previous collaborations, pretty at times, and always empathetic. Duets between Braxton and Corea feature on **The Complete Braxton** as well as encounters with trumpeter Kenny Wheeler. Braxton has an affinity for the European Free Music scene, and has worked fruitfully with others besides Wheeler, notably with that pioneer of avant-garde guitar, Derek Bailey **(Duo)**. Neither player complements the other in the traditional sense, but their separate lines establish an amazing continuity of feeling.

Braxton's writing covers an enormously wide area of sound, reinterpreting traditions such as bebop, **Donna Lee (Donna Lee)**, the Cool School, **You Go To My Head (Donna Lee)**, the chord-change ballad **You Stepped Out Of A Dream (Five Pieces '75)**, as well as near-straight music pieces like the **Side Two, Cut Two** unaccompanied four saxophone composition—**New York, Fall '74**.

Integrated with this activity is Braxton's increasing armory of instruments. His interest in extremes of register has led him to take up the sopranino, the lumbering contrabass clarinet on **Goodbye Porkpie Hat (In The Tradition)** and the clarinet. Anthony Braxton is, in fact, a one-man jazz crusade.

During the '70s, Braxton was able to experiment more with his orchestral writing. He was commissioned by the Ensemble for New and Newer Music to write a work for chamber orchestra which Braxton performed in 1975 at the Alice Tully Hall, New York. He also recorded **Creative Orchestra Music/1976**, recorded a live concert with the Berlin New Music Group, and toured Europe with his own orchestra in 1978. An extended work **For Four Orchestras** was performed and recorded at Oberlin College, and involved 160 musicians.

Braxton has composed music for the French film *Paris Streets* and collaborated on the score of *Un Coup de Dix Francs*. His music has been used by numerous dance companies including those of Merce Cunningham and Sheila Raz Braxton has also been extensively involved in electronic music, first as a member of the Electronic Music at the American Center in Paris in 1970 and later with synthesizer improviser and composer Richard Teitlebaum.

Braxton has continued to explore new musical frontiers throughout the '80s. His duet album with Max Roach, **Birth And**

Above: Influential multi-instrumentalist Anthony Braxton at the chess-board. In lean times, he has earned his living at the game.

Rebirth, won the Italian Jazz Society's Album of the Year award and led to performances in Europe. His work, **Composition 96 For Orchestra And Four Projectors**, was premiered in Seattle in 1981. He has received a Guggenheim Fellowship for **Composition 102 For Orchestra And Puppet Theater**, and was awarded a National Endowment for the Arts grant for creative orchestral work. He has also found time to teach, notably at Oberlin College, and conduct the Copenhagen Radio Orchestra. In 1982, his **Six Compositions: Quartet** was released featuring music composed in the mid-'70s. In 1985, it was announced that Braxton was to become Professor of Composition at Mills College, Oakland.

His current quartet features pianist Marilyn Crispell (associated with Braxton's groups since 1977), percussionist Gerry Hemingway and newcomer Mark Dresser on bass. Braxton's most recent compositional project is a series of 12 operas to be entitled **Trillium** and his ambitions extend to work for 100 orchestras playing simultaneously in four different cities linked by television cameras and satellite.

Albums:
Three Compositions Of New Jazz (Delmark/Delmark)
For Alto (Delmark/Delmark)
This Time (—/BYG—France)
Circle Paris—Concert (ECM/ECM)
The Complete Braxton (Arista/Arista)
Duo (Emanem/Emanem)
Donna Lee (—/America—France)
Five Pieces '75 (Arista/Arista)
New York, Fall '74 (Arista/Arista)
In The Tradition (—/Steeplechase)
Duets (Arista/Arista)
Concerts: Berlin—Montreux (Arista/Arista)
Creative Orchestra Music 1976 (Arista/—)
Six Compositions: Quartet (Antilles/Antilles)
Anthony Braxton-Derek Bailey, Royal Vol 1 (—/Incus)
Four Compositions (Quartet) (Black Saint/Black Saint)
Anthony Braxton-Max Roach, One In Two, Two In One (—/hatArt)
Anthony Braxton-Richard Teitelbaum, Open Aspects '82 (—/hatArt)
For Four Orchestras (Arista/Arista)
For Two Pianos (Arista/Arista)

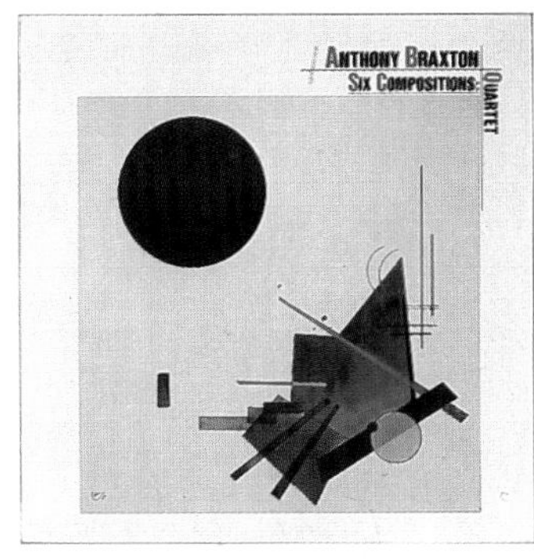

Anthony Braxton, Six Compositions: Quartet (courtesy Antilles).

The Brecker Brothers

Born and raised in Philadelphia, the two Brecker Brothers were to become the most in-demand session musicians in New York.

Mike (tenor sax, flute, drums and piano) was born on 29 March, 1949; Randy (trumpet, flugelhorn, piano and drums), on November 27, 1945. Sons of a piano-playing father, both boys' earliest ensemble-playing experience came from summer big-band stage camps, and both studied at the University of Indiana. Randy was playing in local bar bands in his teens, becoming fascinated with bebop. Mike made his début with an R&B band, Birdsong. Both went to New York to form Dreams (including Billy Cobham and Barry Rogers)—a legendary early jazz-rock fusion band influencing many young New York musicians. They both served apprenticeships with Horace Silver and their performances with Billy Cobham's group in '73 brought them widespread acclaim.

From being the most sought-after session musicians in New York, the Breckers now had the clout to form their own band—the Brecker Brothers. This showcased their abilities as composers, arrangers and producers, as well as musicians, notably on albums like **Heavy Metal Be-Bop** (a good description of their sound).

Together or individually, Randy and Mike Brecker have also performed or recorded with Duke Pearson, Clark Terry, Hal Galper, Charles Mingus, Blood Sweat & Tears, Larry Coryell, Deodato, Art Blakey, Thad Jones-Mel Lewis, Grand Funk, Average White Band, James Brown, Aretha Franklin, Gato Barbieri et al. Mike has also, in recent years, been an integral part of Mike Mainieri's Steps, as well as recording with guitarist John Abercrombie and Kenny Wheeler for ECM.

In spite of their Philadelphia beginnings, the names of Mike and Randy Brecker have become synonymous with 'New York funk'.

Albums:
Dreams, Dreams (Columbia/CBS)
The Brecker Brothers (Arista/Arista)
Back To Back (Arista/Arista)
Don't Stop The Music (Arista/Arista)
Heavy Metal Be-Bop (Arista/Arista)
Detente (Arista/Arista)
Straphangin' (Arista/Arista)

British Jazz

For many years British jazz was thought to be a pale imitation—entirely derivative—of what was happening in the United States. Nothing could be further from the truth. Indeed, saxophonist Ronnie Scott and colleagues were certainly exploring their own brand of hard bop simultaneously with their American counterparts in the early 1950s in spite of their difficult access to the American exponents.

By World War II, Britain was coming out of the golden big-band dance era of the early radio years and rediscovering the sounds of the New Orleans' pioneers. America's involvement in the war brought an unprecedented influx of Afro-American music on records from across the Atlantic. The British jazz scene polarized—the traditionalists looking back to the days of Dixieland, King Oliver, Storyville and South Rampart Street; the modernists taking their lead from the late '40s and the bebop pioneers who had hung out on New York's 52nd Street. By the '50s, the modernists were picking up on hard bop and Cool Jazz drifting over from the US West Coast and making it their own, not to mention the Third Stream (which, anyway, borrowed generously from the European classical tradition).

As the '60s dawned, Britain was still largely unmoved by Ornette Coleman's free-jazz experimentations. If the British traditionalists and modernists were ever to meet, it's interesting that 'the blues' was to offer a significant rendezvous in the early

Above: The Brecker Brothers—Mike and Randy. A dynamic New York-funk partnership, often imitated but rarely duplicated.

'60s. Alexis Korner's great British R&B revival recruited from trad bands (like Chris Barber's) and the modernists blowing at the Ronnie Scott Club. The 'ethnicity' of the '50s trad boom was dealt a severe blow by 'commercialism' in the early '60s—Acker Bilk's **Stranger On The Shore** and Kenny Ball's **Midnight In Moscow** were huge chart hits but had more in common with Denmark Street (London's Tin Pan Alley) than Bourbon Street. British trad jazz was helped on to the skids by the new craze for R&B and the growing popularity of modern jazz.

With '62 came a huge invasion of American stars. Until the mid-'50s, visits from American artists had been severely restricted by an unconditional Musicians Union ban. In '56, the ban had been lifted—foreign musicians could play British concert halls if there was a 'man-for-man' exchange deal. Much of the credit for bringing this vital two-way traffic to *club* level must go to Ronnie Scott and his partner Pete King. The tenacious King pioneered the first exchange just before Christmas '61. After protracted negotiations, British saxophonist Tubby Hayes was booked in to the Half Note Club, New York. In exchange, Zoot Sims arrived at Ronnie Scott's Club. Soon to follow were American jazz legends in their droves . . .

The mid-'60s unfolded in a welter of indigenous free-jazz activity. Musicians exploring the new freedoms included Cornelius Cardew (with AMM), The People Band, John Stevens and his Spontaneous Music Ensemble, Joe Harriott, John Surman, Alan Skidmore, Mike Osborne, Lol Coxhill, Stan Tracey, Derek Bailey, Tony Coe, Elton Dean, Evan Parker, Trevor Watts, Ken Hyder, Maggie Nichols, Tony Oxley among many others. The free jazz in Britain became a much more local *European* movement with British musicians working extensively with improvisers from the Continent.

In the late '60s, British musicians were working in parallel development with Miles Davis' jazz-rock explorations, notably Gordon Beck's 1968 **Experiments With Pops** (with guitarist John McLaughlin) and the John McLaughlin-John Surman **Extrapolation** (1969). Bands like Ian Carr's Nucleus, Back Door, Don Weller's Major Surgery and Barbara Thompson's Paraphernalia extended the electric jazz-rock possibilities even further in the '70s, while bands like Morrissey-Mullen, Tim Whitehead's Borderline and Paz were to help create a wholly indigenous jazz-funk sound and spirit.

In the '80s, a whole new generation of young British musicians has emerged, equally at home with bebop traditions and the improvisational avant-garde (the big band Loose Tubes brings together many of them). Explorative, creative young players like pianists Django Bates and Steve Melling, bassist Mick Hutton, drummer Steve Arguelles, saxophonists Iain Ballamy, Alan Barnes (with hard-bopper Tommy Chase), Courtney Pine and Tommy Smith, trumpeter Guy Barker, trombonist Annie Whitehead and the women musicians of The Guest Stars are at the forefront of a healthy and developing, ever open-minded British jazz scene.

Albums:

AMM, Commonwealth Institute—20th April, 1967 (—/United Dairies)
Back Door, Activate (Warner Brothers/WEA)
Derek Bailey, Notes (—/Incus)
Gordon Beck, Experiments With Pops (—/Major Minor)
Ian Carr's Nucleus, Live At The Theaterhaus (—/Mood)
Tommy Chase-Alan Barnes, Hard! (—/Boplicity)
Tony Coe, Tournée Du Chat (—/Nato)
Tony Coe-Tony Oxley, Coe, Oxley & Co, Nutty (On) Willisau (—/Hat Art)
Lol Coxhill, The Dunois Solos (—/Nato)
First House, Eréndira (ECM/ECM)
Tubby Hayes, Mexican Green (—/Mole Jazz)
Tubby Hayes-Ronnie Scott, The Jazz Couriers (—/Jasmine)
Ken Hyder's Big Team, Under The Influence (—/Konnex)
London Jazz Composers Orchestra, Ode (—/Incus)
Loose Tubes, Loose Tubes (—/Loose Tubes)
John McLaughlin-John Surman, Extrapolation (Polydor/Polydor)
Major Surgery, The First Cut (—/Next)
Morrissey-Mullen, This Must Be The Place (—/Coda)
Maggie Nichols-Pete Nu, Nichols 'N' Nu (—/Leo)
Evan Parker, The Snake Decides (—/Incus)
Paz, Look Inside (—/Coda)
Spontaneous Music Ensemble, 1. 2. Albert Ayler (—/Affinity)
John Surman-Mike Osborne-Alan Skidmore (SOS) (—/Ogun)
Stan Tracey, Captain Adventure (—/Steam)
Barbara Thompson, Mother Earth (—/TM Records)
Tim Whitehead's Borderline, English People: The Subterranean Life At Richmond Lock And Other Locations (—/Spotlight)

Bob Brookmeyer, Through A Looking Glass (courtesy Finesse).

Bob Brookmeyer

Mainly known as a sideman with Stan Getz, Gerry Mulligan and Jimmy Guiffre, Kansas City born valve-trombonist Bob Brookmeyer is a musician of all-round gifts. His trombone playing avoids the rapid-fire evenness of the modern school in favour of a wider bag of e fects. A broad, historically ranging approach has produced several albums under his own name that are robust, witty and inventive **(Traditionalism Revisited** and **Blues Hot & Cool)**. His later work with trumpeter Clark Terry **(Terry-Brookmeyer Quintet)** was a meeting of temperamentally similar players and resulted in warm, optimistic music. Although noted as a trombonist, Brookmeyer is also a competent pianist and composer.

Albums:

Getz At The Shrine (Verve/—)
The Fabulous Gerry Mulligan Quartet (—/Vogue)
The Jimmy Giuffre Trio, Trav'lin' Light (Atlantic/—)
Traditionalism Revisited (Pacific Jazz/Vogue)
Blues Hot & Cool (Verve/—)
The Clark Terry-Bob Brookmeyer Quintet (Mainstream/—)
Back Again (—/Sonet)
Through A Looking Glass (Finesse/—)
Bob Brookmeyer And Friends (Columbia/CBS)

Big Bill Broonzy

Big Bill Broonzy's death (in Chicago in 1958) robbed the blues world of one of its finest practitioners: a highly-rhythmic, flexible guitarist, a singer of great expressivity, and a composer whose songs invariably were remarkably real to life. But Broonzy (born William Lee Conley Broonzy, in Scott, Mississippi 1893) did not die poverty-stricken and unrecognized in his lifetime, as was the fate of so many country bluesmen, great or otherwise. Indeed, during the last ten years of his life, Broonzy's reputation was international, and in some parts of the world he had become something approaching a cult figure.

One of seven children, Broonzy's musical interests were encouraged by an uncle. Raised in Arkansas, where he worked as a share-cropper and part-time preacher (he also worked, at one stage, as coal-miner). His mother, who remembered the days of slavery, died in 1957, aged 102.

Broonzy's first instrument was violin, which he played at country hops. In 1917 he enlisted in US army. After two years was demobilized and made his home in Chicago, by which time he was developing into a first-class guitarist who mixed freely with other itinerant bluesmen, including Papa Charlie Jackson, who taught Broonzy how to play guitar.

Recording début found him playing a country reel **(Blues Origin)**, but thereafter his became one of the most familiar names on blues recording dates—his own and innumerable others, featuring all kinds of musicians. Amongst the latter can be numbered Georgia Tom Dorsey **(Georgia Tom)**, Sonny Boy Williamson **(Blues Classics By Sonny Boy Williamson, Vol 1)**, and Broonzy's brother-in-law, Washboard Sam **(Feeling Lowdown)**. Amongst Broonzy's own earliest recordings **(The Young Big Bill Broonzy 1928-1935)** there are superior examples of his skills, such as **Mississippi River Blues** (1934), **Stove Pipe Stomp** (1932), **Long Tall Mama** (1932) and the bleak **Starvation Blues** (1928). Superb recordings by Broonzy from the years 1936-41 can be found within **Big Bill's Blues** including tremendously evocative performances of Broonzy numbers as vividly real as **Southern Flood Blues, When I Been Drinking, Just A Dream** (one of his finest of all blues compositions), **All By Myself** and **Big Bill Blues.**

Despite his prolificity as recording artist, Broonzy was emloyed often in a non-musical capacity; between 1930-50, for example, he owned a farm in Arkansas, and was working it when John Hammond brought him to New York to appear at his Spirituals to Swing concert **(John Hammond's Spirituals To Swing)** in 1938, and again the following year.

By the late 1940s he was working as janitor at Iowa State College, but Broonzy continued to record and to make appearances in and around Chicago.

Visited Europe, 1951, 1953, where he attained enormous following. During second European tour Broonzy recorded contents from **Big Bill Broonzy: All Them Blues**. 1951: Broonzy recorded an even better collection of fine blues like **Hollerin' & Cryin', Back Water Blues, Low Down Blues**, plus a fresh reworking of **Big Bill Blues**. By this time his repertoire had broadened in size and scope—he must have written, in all, over 300 songs during his career.

However, there were times when his performances, in concert and on record, tended towards the bland. In between the two visits to Europe mentioned above, he toured the continent also in 1952, in tandem with Mahalia Jackson. Alone, he was to return for further sell-out appearances in each year between 1955-7. During 1955 trip he recorded in London, Paris, Baarn and, extensively, in Copenhagen. He continued to be active inside recording studios during '56 and '57—in 1956 was taped in live performance, alone, and on a couple of items together with voice and banjo of Pete Seeger **(Pete Seeger & Big Bill Broonzy In Concert)** and the following year appeared on record with the duo of Brownie McGhee and Sonny Terry **(Blues With Big Bill Broonzy, Sonny Terry, Brownie McGhee)**, the album also containing an interview with Broonzy. He was to repeat the singing-playing-talking format during what turned out to be his final recording dates **(Last Session)** in July 1957. Broonzy's vibrant singing and guitar playing were silenced forever in 1958 when this influential folk-blues artist of exceptional talents died of cancer.

Albums:

Big Bill Broonzy/Sonny Boy Williamson, Big Bill & Sonny Boy (—/RCA Victor)
Jazz Gillum, Vol 1 (—/RCA Victor—France)
Washboard Sam (Blues Classics/—)
Big Bill Broonzy (—/Vogue)
Trouble In Mind (Blues Classics/—)
Pete Seeger & Big Bill Broonzy In Concert (Verve/Verve)
Blues With Big Bill Broonzy, Sonny Terry, Brownie McGhee (Folkways/—)
Big Bill Broonzy, Last Session (Verve/Verve)
Various, Country Blues Encores (Origin/—)
Georgia Tom Dorsey, Georgia Tom (Riverside)
Big Bill Broonzy, Big Bill's Blues (CBS—Realm)
The Young Big Bill Broonzy 1928-1935 (Yazoo)
Big Bill Broonzy Sings Country Blues (—/Xtra)
Big Bill Broonzy: All Them Blues (DJM)
Washboard Sam, Feeling Lowdown (RCA Victor/RCA Victor)
Blues Classics By Sonny Boy Williamson (Blues Classics)
Various, John Hammond's Spirituals To Swing (Vanguard/Vanguard)
Sonny Boy Williamson, Vol 1 (RCA Victor—France)
Big Bill Broonzy (Vogue—France)

'Big Bill' Broonzy (courtesy Blue Bird RCA—France): blues 1934-35.

Clifford Brown

Trumpeter Clifford Brown's death in a car accident at the age of 26 robbed jazz of one of its finest talents. His recording career is spanned **(The Beginning And The End)** by his 1952 début with an R&B unit, Chris Powell and The Blue Flames, and his final, informal jam session recorded in an instrument shop on the eve of his death in 1956. Listening to those last tracks—**Walkin', Donna Lee** and **Night In Tunisia**—it's easy to see why Brownie became a legend. His sound is unmistakable; bright, warm, bubbling with vivacity. There is a joy and a clarity about his work that posterity has proved irreplaceable, and the heritage of hot trumpet—Gillespie, Navarro, Brown—passed into the very different approach of Miles Davis.

Brownie's work for the Blue Note label featured the trumpeter as both leader and sideman, and this has led to a good deal of overlapping on the albums. **Get Happy** turns up on **The Eminent J. J. Johnson** and **Brownie Eyes**; six tracks from **Brownie Eyes** are duplicated on Clifford Brown's **Memorial Album**. Numbers like **Brownie Speaks** or **Cherokee** show off his lyricism at up-tempos, the multi-note, tripping attack riding the furious drumming of Philly Joe Jones and Art Blakey.

He turns up on a Tadd Dameron session **(The Arrangers' Touch)** as part of a ninetet, and his muted trumpet is featured on **Theme Of No Repeat**. The same year, 1953, found Brownie in the Lionel Hampton Band that visited Europe. Despite the leader's ban on individual bandsmen recording, the trumpeter dodged the manager by hopping down the hotel fire escape and cutting an unofficial midnight recording session with trumpeter Art Farmer and the Swedish All-Stars. **Lover Come Back To Me** and **Stockholm Sweetnin'** are classic performances. Further tracks were made in Paris **(The Complete Paris Collection)** with groups of various sizes and combinations of Hampton sidemen. American expatriates and French jazzmen from the 17-piece big band to the quartet. Pianist Henri Renaud plays on most of the tracks, and helped with the organization. There are several takes of numbers like **Brown Skins, Keepin' Up With Jonesy, Salute To The Bandbox** and **The Song Is You**—all featuring the astonishingly mature 22-year-old trumpeter. As *the* hard bop trumpeter, Clifford Brown fitted perfectly into the heated atmosphere of the Art Blakey-Horace Silver combo, later to become The Jazz Messengers. Blue Note recorded the band live **(A Night At Birdland)** and caught the driving excitement, the trumpeter's perfectly executed double-tempo runs and long, supple phrases. His gorgeous tone and melodic fertility made him an excellent foil for singers like Sarah Vaughan and Helen Merrill, and even kept him clear of schamltz on an album with strings.

1954 saw Brownie accorded recognition in the *Down Beat* Critics' Poll, and—more significantly—the start of one of the great partnerships of jazz. Master drummer Max Roach, convinced of the economic viability of a hard bop unit on the West Coast, contacted the trumpeter to return with him to Los Angeles. Before the unit finally settled down with a permanent personnel, various pianists like Kenny Drew and Carl Perkins, saxophonists like Herb Geller and Walter Benton sat in. The definitive personnel comprised Roach and Brownie, either Sonny Rollins or Harold Land on tenor, Richie Powell on piano and George Morrow on bass. This unit was every bit as good as The Jazz Messengers, or Horace Silver's groups, and the output is uniformly excellent.

At Basin Street, Daahoud, Remember Clifford, Study In Brown and **Three Giants** display the great variety of moods and rhythms the group was capable of, from the unusual time-signatures of **Valse Hot** and **Love Is A Many Splendored Thing** to the trumpet-drums duets of **Mildama**. Most of the writing came from within the band, Brownie's **Sandu, Daahoud, Joy Spring;** Rollins' **Pent-Up House;** Land's **Lands End** and Powell's **Gertrude's Bounce**, many of which have passed into jazz standards.

Albums:
Memorial Album (Blue Note/Blue Note)
Brownie Eyes (Blue Note/Blue Note)
The Beginning And The End (Columbia/CBS)
The Eminent Jay Jay Johnson (Blue Note/Blue Note)
Gil Evans-Tadd Dameron, The Arrangers' Touch (Prestige/Prestige)
The Complete Paris Collection (—/Vogue—Pye)
Art Blakey At Birdland (Blue Note/Blue Note)
Max Roach-Clifford Brown In Concert (GNP/—)
Clifford Brown All Stars (Mercury/—)
At Basin Street (Trip/Trip)
Daahoud (Mainstream/Mainstream)
Remember Clifford (Trip/Mercury)
Three Giants (Prestige/Prestige)
Study In Brown (Trip/Trip)
Raw Genius (—/Victor—Japan)
Clifford Brown-Max Roach, Pure Genius, Vol 1 (Elektra Musician/Elektra Musician)
Alternate Takes (Blue Note/Blue Note)

Clifford Brown, The Complete Paris Collection (courtesy Vogue).

Marion Brown

Born in Georgia, 1935, altoist Marion Brown is part of the second generation of New Thing players, though statistically more traditional than most. His début album for ESP **(Marion Brown)** showed a careful player of melodic gifts, not given to the tonal distortions and extremes of the period, and capable of developing a musical argument. After a stint with Sun Ra, and encouragement from Ornette Coleman and Archie Shepp, Brown began to arrive at an original voice. He takes interesting solos on albums by Shepp **(Fire Music)** and Coltrane **(Ascension)**, though his most impassioned playing is to be found in the trio context **(Porto Novo)** with Dutch bassist Van Regteben Altena and the startlingly original Han Bennink on drums. A larger group with Anthony Braxton, Bennie Maupin and Chick Corea **(Afternoon Of A Georgia Faun)** produced pastoral and pastel music of gentle charm, dappled with flutes and voices. **Djinji's Corner** operates on the principles of musical chairs. Brown's Impulse output has been varied, and variable **(Three For Shepp, Sweet Earth Flying** and **Geechee Recollections)**.

Albums:
Marion Brown Quartet (ESP/ESP)
Archie Shepp, Fire Music (Impulse/Impulse)
John Coltrane, Ascension (Impulse/Impulse)
Porto Novo (Arista-Freedom/Polydor)
Afternoon Of A Georgia Faun (ECM/ECM)
Three For Shepp (Impulse/Impulse)
Sweet Earth Flying (Impulse/Impulse)
Geechee Recollections (Impulse/Impulse)
Reeds 'n' Vibes (Improvising Artists Inc/—)

Above: Altoist Marion Brown (left) with trumpter Leo Smith—two musicians who have extended the frontiers of modern music.

Sandy Brown

Clarinettist Alexander 'Sandy' Brown (born Izatnagar, India, 1929, but to all intents and purposes a red-blooded Scotsman) came to the forefront of British jazz during the 1950s with an original approach to his instrument and an enviably broadminded approach to jazz Brown's basic technique was more than adequate, although hardly in the Goodman-De Franco class. But it was his very idiosyncratic phraseology, his hard-brush timbre and often hair-raising rhythmic involvement with his music that made him stand out, not only in British jazz circles, but universally. A most eminently satisfying blues player, he remains, even after his tragically premature death in March 1975, a memorable player and a lovable character. A magnificently earthy soloist, he could raise the level of an already admirable record session **(Doctor McJazz)** to unsuspected heights of passion and brilliance.

Brown, a self-taught musician, was a familiar figure on the British jazz scene in general and the London jazz scene in particular after leaving Scotland in 1946. Worked with such noted traditional figures as Humphrey Lyttelton and Chris Barber, frequently led own bands and appeared as guest soloist on countless other occasions.

But it was as co-leader of the Al Fairweather-Sandy Brown Jazz Band that Brown's individual reputation was really forged, at concert and club appearances as well as through the medium of several excellent mainstream-styled recordings, including **Doctor McJazz**. It was during this period (late 1950s/early 1960s) that Brown's clarinet-playing mirrored his own widening interest in all kinds of jazz, gospel and even African music.

Initially his premier influence was Johnny Dodds, but other influences were added through the years; Ben Webster, Charlie Parker, Louis Armstrong, Duke Ellington and Charles Mingus. A well-nigh perfect introduction of Sandy Brown's artistry is **McJazz Lives On!**, a superior compilation of some of his finest recordings. His pre-eminence as a bluesman can be judged from his impassioned, moving playing on **Careless Love** and, better still, on his own **Two Blue**. His admiration for gospel music manifests itself throughout **Oh Dong, Bang That Gong** (another Brown original) during which he thumps spiritedly through some primitive pianistics.

His clarinet is at its most melodic during a sensitively projected **Willow, Weep For Me**. And his wide tastes in jazz can be judged by the fact that other items to be found on this album included Benny Golson's **Blues March, Mingus**, and **Wednesday Night Prayer Meeting**; Nat Adderley's **Work Song**; and Teddy McRae's **Broadway**, plus several other Brown originals, each different in concept, mood and structure.

Clarinettist Sandy Brown With The Brian Lemon Trio (courtesy 77 Records).

His talent as a composer of intriguing themes is a facet of Brown's talent which tends to be overlooked. A further string of Sandy Brown compositions is to be found within **Sandy Brown & The Brian Lemon Trio** including **Ebun, Legal Pete, Lucky Schiz & The Big Dealer**, and **Louis**, the last-named a moving tribute to Louis Armstrong.

Brown, a respected acoustical architect and, occasionally, a perceptive scribe on the subject of jazz, sometimes took the opportunity of essaying a friendly sounding vocal chorus. As indeed he did in company with US blues pianist Sammy Price during recording of **Barrelhouse & Blues**. But here again, it is the rough eloquence and sheer driving force of his clarinet playing which remains longest in the memory. And even an acknowledged master of the idiom such as Price has to take second place to Brown's blues offering during a supremely rewarding version of **In The Evening**.

Albums:
Sandy Brown, McJazz (—/Nixa)
Sandy Brown/Al Fairweather, The Incredible McJazz (—/Columbia)
Sandy Brown, McJazz Lives On! (—/One-Up)
Sandy Brown With The Brian Lemon Trio (—/77)
Sammy Price, Barrelhouse & Blues (Black Lion)

Tom Browne

Still in his early twenties, New York trumpeter Tom Browne made an enormous impact as a major jazz crossover artist in 1980 with his **Funkin' In Jamaica** single from his **Love Approach** album.

His music training began aged 11 on piano before switching to trumpet. A student at the High School of Music and Art in Manhattan, his first love was classical music, playing in brass and orchestral ensembles. Majoring at Kingsborough College in physics, he discovered jazz through an Ornette Coleman album. His first professional gig was in 1975 with the Weldon Irivine group, going on to work with Sonny Fortune **(Infinity)** and the Fatback Band. His début album, **Browne Sugar** (1979) featured his fluid playing alongside the 14-year-old Marcus Miller on bass.

In spite of his assured fusion success, Browne hasn't forgotten his early influences, paying tribute to John Coltrane and Blue Mitchell on **Yours Truly**.

Albums:
Browne Sugar (Arista/Arista)
Love Approach (Arista/Arista)
Magic (Arista/Arista)
Yours Truly (Arista/Arista)
Rockin' Radio (Arista/Arista)
Tommy Gun (Arista/Arista)

Tom Browne, Love Approach (courtesy Arista)—a fusion success.

Dave Brubeck

Immensely popular with the public and generally denigrated by the critics, pianist Dave Brubeck was the subject of heated arguments throughout the '50s. Classically trained and influenced by modern composers like Darius Milhaud, Brubeck imported many classical devices into jazz, especially atonality, fugue and counterpoint. Bach, Beethoven and Chopin borrowings can be found throughout his work, and his touch is closer to the classical concert hall than the jazz club. Criticism centered on his lack of swing, pomposity of manner and the stultifying effect of his largely block-chorded solos. Most debates on the validity of Third Stream music—the merging of jazz and classical—petered out during the less label-obsessed '60s and '70s, but the fact remains that Brubeck's work has lasted less well than Tristano's.

Starting with an octet, Brubeck pared down to the famous quartet, with altoist Paul Desmond. The early recordings remain the best, particularly those of the college circuit. The Oberlin concert generates considerable emotion, possibly due to the freedom from inhibition (Brubeck and Desmond had quarrelled, the bassist given notice and the drummer had 'flu) and the music, particularly Desmond's solo on **The Way You Look Tonight**, comes over with a rare virility. **Balcony Rock, Don't Worry 'Bout Me** and the Eastern flavored **Le Souk** are again noteworthy for the melodic inventiveness of Desmond, whose tone has some of the purity and thin-spun sharpness of Konitz

Brubeck's later experiments with unusual time signatures, **Blue Rondo A La Turk** in 9/8, and the internationally best-selling **Take Five** in 5/4 **(Time Out)** sound a little self-conscious against the pioneering work of Max Roach, and something of a set-piece in the context of the general freeing-up that was taking place around the late '50s. His extensive world tour in 1958 resulted in an album of pastiche based on ethnic music from Afghanistan, Turkey and Calcutta **(Dave Brubeck Quartet)**.

Hard core jazz fans usually favor drummer Joe Morello, who joined the group in 1956, and bemoan the 19-year restriction on Desmond's talents. In fact, the altoist's work within the quartet was as good as anything that he did outside **(The Paul Desmond Quartet Live)** and after recently rejoining for a reunion tour Desmond died suddenly in 1977.

Brubeck has continued to record and tour in the '80s with a refreshing, updated quartet—tenorist Jerry Bergonzi (notably, **Paper Moon)** taking the saxophone honors and a lively young rhythm section of British-born drummer Randy Jones and son Chris Brubeck on electric bass and occasionally 'gut-bucket' trombone. More recently, clarinettist Bill Smith has renewed an old acquaintance with Brubeck on stage and on record **(For Iola)**, recreating an almost forgotten but interesting and creative partnership.

Dave Brubeck, 'For Iola' (courtesy Concord): dedicated to Mrs Brubeck.

Above: Pianist Dave Brubeck's unprecedented Top-Ten hit with his jazz single Take Five made the pop charts and airwaves reverberate in 1962.

Albums:
Time Out (Columbia/CBS)
Time Further Out (Columbia/CBS)
Dave Brubeck Quartet (Columbia/CBS)
Impressions Of Japan (Columbia/CBS)
Brubeck & Desmond, The Duets (A&M/A&M)
Paul Desmond Quartet Live (A&M/A&M)
Back Home (Concord/Concord)
Tritonis (Concord/Concord)
Paper Moon (Concord/Concord)
Concord On A Summer Night (Concord/Concord)
For Iola (Concord/Concord)

Teddy Bunn

Although his has not been always a fashionable name amongst jazz guitarists, Theodore 'Teddy' Bunn (born Freeport, Long Island, 1909) has long since presented impressive credentials, of the kind which make him indisputably one of the giants on his chosen instrument.

Whether playing single-line solos, combining almost delicacy in approach with inner strength, or essaying chordal work, firmly strummed and with an enviable awareness of dynamics, Bunn has been one of the most consistently rewarding guitar players thus far to be produced by jazz.

Particularly sensitive in the blues idiom, Trixie Smith and Rosetta Crawford **(Out Came The Blues)** are just two blues singers with whom Bunn has recorded. He has also recorded with vaudeville-bluesmen Coot and Grant Wilson **(The Rarest Sidney Bechet, Vol 1)**. And his guitar has been heard in company with clarinettist/soprano saxist Sidney Bechet, himself a comprehensively gifted blues player, on numerous occasions. Most notable Bechet-Bunn recordings include **The Complete Ladnier-Mezzrow-Bechet** set.

Took part in Bechet session ('39), from whence came celebrated version of **Summertime (Sidney Bechet Jazz Classics, Vol 1)**. At same date, with addition of Frankie Newton and J. C. Higginbotham, Bechet-Bunn group cut two superb blues, **Pounding Heart Blues** and **Blues For Tommy Ladnier (Sidney Bechet Jazz Classics, Vol 2)** with guitarist contributing short but telling solo to second title. 1940: Bunn once again inside recording studio with Bechet for further Blue Note date that produced, as part of quartet of fine tracks, a poised version of **Dear Old Southland (Sidney Bechet Jazz Classics, Vol 2)**. Later same year recorded with another noted blues instrumentalist, Oran 'Hot Lips' Page, for Victor.

In quartet setting, Bunn produced series of solos which are as fine as anything he recorded elsewhere. Beautifully delineated statements on **Just Another Woman** and **Do It If You Wanna**, that are miniature masterpieces of blues-tinged jazz guitar. Bunn takes a couple of friendly vocals, but it is his guitar playing which, along with Page's own trumpet/vocal contributions, are focal points of session **(Feelin' High & Happy)**.

Bunn's was very much a musical background; both parents and brother were all instrumentalists. First professional jazz experience in the early 1920s; first recordings with Spencer Williams during same decade. Recorded with Duke Ellington Orchestra (1929) **(Hot In Harlem: 1928-1929** and **Cotton Club Days, Vol 1)**, one of few non-Ellingtonians to do so. (In fact, Bunn did once work with Ellington, briefly, as deputy guitarist.)

In the early 1930s he became more widely known through his excellent playing with both Washboard Rhythm Kings and Washboard Serenaders bands **(Washboard Rhythm Kings/Serenaders 1930-1933)**. Reputation further enhanced as member of his next band, known first as Ben Bernie's Nephews, later changed to Spirits of Rhythm. Left group in 1937 to work for short period with John

Kirby. After leading own combos, rejoined Spirits of Rhythm, 1939. (Numerous references to band's activities in New York to be found in Arnold Shaw's *The Street That Never Slept*.) During '37, recorded with Jimmie Noone **(Jimmie Noone 1937-1941)** and, together with two other members of SOR, broadcast in support of Lionel Hampton **(Great Swing Jam Sessions, Vol 2)**. 1938: in spite of the fact that they had never previously met, musically or socially, Teddy Bunn and Johnny Dodds achieved considerable rapport at recording session that produced richly rewarding music, as illustrated by aural reference to tracks like **Wild Man Blues** and **Blues Galore (Harlem On Saturday Night)**. The Spirits of Rhythm moved to West Coast (1940); the same year he recorded with Lionel Hampton **(The Complete Lionel Hampton/Lionel Hampton's Best Records, Vol 4)** and under his own name, for Blue Note. The SOR disbanded and reformed on several occasions. Bunn settled in California, working with own bands (including his Waves of Rhythm), and others. Worked with Edgar Hayes on more than one occasion; likewise, Jack McVea. Brief spell with Louis Jordan (1959), toured with a rock show, but from 1960s was troubled with failing sight plus recurring illness, including heart attacks and strokes. He died in July 1978.

Albums:

Washboard Kings/Washboard Serenaders 1930-1933 (RCA Victor—France)
Various, Swing Street, Vol 1 (Epic/Columbia)
Jimmie Noone, 1937-1941 (—/Collector's Classics)
Various (Including Johnny Dodds), Harlem On Saturday Night (—/Ace of Hearts)
The Rarest Sidney Bechet, Vol 1 (—/After Hours)
The Complete Ladnier-Mezzrow-Bechet (RCA Victor—France)
Various, Blue Note's Three Decades Of Jazz (1939-1949), Vol 1 (Blue Note/Blue Note)
Sidney Bechet, Jazz Classics, Vols 1, 2 (Blue Note/Blue Note)
Various, Great Swing Jam Sessions, Vol 2 (—/Saga)
Hot Lips Page, Feelin' High & Happy (RCA Victor/—)
Duke Ellington, Hot In Harlem (1928-1929) (MCA—Germany)
Duke Elington, Cotton Club Days, Vol 1 (—/Ace of Hearts)
The Complete Lionel Hampton (Bluebird)/ Lionel Hampton's Best Records, Vol 4 (RCA Victor—France)
Various (Including Rosetta Crawford, Trixie Smith), Out Came The Blues (—/Coral)
Various (Including Big Joe Turner), Roots Of Rock & Roll, Vol 2 (Savoy/—)

Below: Teddy Bunn—one of jazz's finest blues-influenced guitarists. He gained a deserved reputation in 1930's with Washboard Rhythm Kings and Serenaders.

Kenny Burrell

Detroit guitarist Kenny Burrell is one of the most consistent players around. Veteran of countless Blue Note and Prestige sessions, he played with pretty well everybody in the post-bop '50s from Coltrane to Jimmy Smith. Though usually associated with relaxed, after-hours blues, Burrell has fitted well into the more ambitious, arranged setting of big band. With a star-studded studio band playing the arrangements of Gil Evans **(Guitar Forms)** Burrell really stretches out and shows the form that made him Duke Ellington's favorite guitarist. He repays the compliment in one of the few successful tributes to the maestro **(Ellington Is Forever)**, which features his guitar and an amazing collection of sitters-in: Thad Jones, Snooky Young, Jon Faddis, Joe Henderson and Jimmy Smith.

Kenny Burrell seems to be one of the few gutsy ex-organ combo players not to decline into predictable blues licks or inflated soul productions. The catalogs list scores of available albums both as sideman and leader.

Above: The enduring Kenny Burrell—Duke Ellington's favourite guitarist.

Albums:

Jimmy Smith, Back At The Chicken Shack (Blue Note/Blue Note)
Midnight Blue (Blue Note/Blue Note)
All Day Long & All Night Long (Prestige/Prestige)
Kenny Burrell & John Coltrane (Prestige/Prestige)
Guitar Forms (Verve/Verve)
Ellington Is Forever (—/Fantasy)
Kenny Burrell-Grover Washington Jr., Togethering (Blue Note/Blue Note)

Gary Burton

Vibes player Gary Burton was born in 1943 in Indiana, and developed a phenomenal technique using three and four mallets at once. 1964-66 saw the virtuoso working with tenorman Stan Getz **(Getz Au Go Go** and **In Paris)** before launching out with his own group which included guitarist Larry Coryell. During the height of the psychedelic '60s, Burton appeared on the same bill as rock bands, playing that unlikely instrument in beads and buckskins, and incorporating rock influences—particularly Coryell's feedback effects—as well as his own native hillbilly. The growth of non-jazz features shows in the comparison between two albums, **Duster** and **Lofty Fake Anagram**, and when the fashion bubble burst Burton's career found itself in the doldrums. A Montreux recording from 1971 **(Alone At Last)**, which has a side of solo vibes, is accomplished but directionless. His best work results from challenging company, and Carla Bley's composition **(A Genuine Tong Funeral)** using the Gary Burton Quartet and JCOA musicians like Steve Lacy and Gato Barbieri, effectively harnesses his virtuosity.

As with pianists Keith Jarrett and Chick Corea, with both of whom he duetted **(Gary Burton With Keith Jarrett** and **Crystal Silence)**, Burton's career benefited from collaboration with German record producer Manfred Eicher. In 1973 he made what was effectively a comeback album **(The New Quartet)**, using unknown musicians; guitarist Michael Goodrick, bassist Abraham Laboriel and drummer Harry Blazer, and revealing splendid group interplay in a program of Carla Bley, Jarrett, Corea and Mike Gibbs compositions. An album of mainly Mike Gibbs compositions, who also conducted **7 Songs For Quartet & Chamber Orchestra**, is clever, if frigid, Burton. A meeting with bassist Eberhard Weber **(Ring)** produced fine music from the jazz rock feel of **Unfinished Sympathy** to Carla Bley's **Silent Spring**. Two duo albums featured Burton with bassist Steve Swallow **(Hotel Hello)**, multi-tracked and many-layered interpretations of Swallow's complex themes, and Burton with guitarist Ralph Towner **(Matchbook)**, a more overtly romantic session of great charm and empathy.

The compilation album **Works** (1984, a limited edition) brings together a good cross-section of his '70s ECM output featuring Burton in the company of bassist Abe Laboriel, guitarists Pat Metheny, Mick Goodrick and Ralph Towner, bassist Steve Swallow et al.

Towards the end of the '70s, Burton renewed his dynamic partnership with pianist Chick Corea **(In Concert, Zürich, October 28, 1979)**—a memorable live duet performance capturing an impassioned reworking of the enduring **Crystal Silence**. In 1982, **Lyric Suite For Sextet** found Burton and Corea together again—the sextet in question being the duo with the addition of a string quartet doing great justice to Corea's classical-flavored **Lyric Suite**.

During the '80s, Burton—a teacher at Berklee College for many years—has favored touring and recording with groups which include outstanding students from the college, notably altoist Jim Ogden **(Easy As Pie** and **Picture This)**. Most recently, Burton while touring gave considerable international exposure through his group for pianist Makoto Ozone **(Real Life Hits)**.

A Genuine Tong Funeral (courtesy RCA Victor): a Gary Burton classic.

Albums:

Stan Getz, Getz Au Go Go (Verve/Verve)
In Paris (Verve/Verve)
Duster (RCA Victor/RCA Victor)
Lofty Fake Anagram (RCA Victor/RCA Victor)
Alone At Last (Atlantic/Atlantic)
A Genuine Tong Funeral (RCA Victor/RCA Victor)
Gary Burton With Keith Jarrett

(Atlantic/Atlantic)
Crystal Silence (ECM/ECM)
The New Quartet (ECM/ECM)
7 Songs For Quartet & Chamber Orchestra (ECM/ECM)
Ring (ECM/ECM)
Hotel Hello (ECM/ECM)
Matchbook (ECM/ECM)
Dreams So Real (ECM/ECM)
Passengers (ECM/ECM)
Times Square (ECM/ECM)
Duet (ECM/ECM)
Chick Corea-Gary Burton, In Concert, Zürich, October 28, 1979 (ECM/ECM)
Easy As Pie (ECM/ECM)
Picture This (ECM/ECM)
Chick Corea-Gary Burton, Lyric Suite For Sextet (ECM/ECM)
Real Life Hits (ECM/ECM)
Works (ECM/ECM)

Billy Butterfield

Technically skilled, warmly emotional, supremely melodic, and a gifted all-round player—that is Charles William 'Billy' Butterfield (born Middleton, Ohio, 1917). He is as much at home playing in small or large jazz outfits as he is fitting into all kinds of musical contexts to be found inside TV, radio and recording studios as a coveted session player.

As a boy, started on violin, bass and trombone before switching to trumpet (later adding flugelhorn) full-time. Studied medicine at Transylvania College, after graduation from high school. Played in college dance bands, then worked with little-known outfits before obtaining first really important professional job with Bob Crosby, in 1937.

With Crosby, Butterfield became ideal foil to trumpet styles of Yank Lawson and Sterling Bose. Established an enviable reputation as solo player with solos like that on **I'm Free** (later known as **What's New?** and under latter banner achieving even greater popularity) **(South Rampart Street Parade)**. With Bob Crosby's Bob Cats, Butterfield's solo talent likewise utilized to great advantage, most notably on **Mournin' Blues**, where the influence of Bix Beiderbecke, via Bobby Hackett, is clearly discernible **(Big Noise From Winnetka)**. Butterfield stayed with Crosby until 1940, when he joined Bob Strong before accepting offer from Artie Shaw, with whom he was to remain until 1941 (when Shaw disbanded). During this time, Butterfield's mellifluous trumpet was heard at its best on numerous Shavian items, including **Stardust, Concerto For Clarinet, Chantez Les Bas** and **Blues (Concerto For Clarinet)**. As with Crosby, Butterfield played splendidly with Shaw's own small band **(Artie Shaw & His Gramercy Five)** and his driving muted solo did much to help **Summit Ridge Drive** become a million-selling disc several times over. Other Gramercy Five titles with excellent Butterfield contributions are **When The Quail Comes Back to San Quentin, My Blue Heaven** (particularly expressive plunger-mute solo) and **Keepin' Myself For You**.

Worked with Benny Goodman 1941-42 and featured eloquently with big band—**Something New (Benny Goodman Plays Solid Gold Instrumental Hits)** is a fine example of his work with the clarinettist. In 1942, recorded with basically Goodman contingent for Commodore under leadership of Mel Powell **(Swingin' Clarinets)** contributing finely rounded, if brief, solos to session, especially appealing on **When Did You Leave Heaven?**

Left Goodman for Les Brown ('42), then became CBS staffman until entry into US Army (1945). Before service, Butterfield had taken part in a generally excellent record date (in 1944) at which his trumpet was matched opposite the laconic tenor sax of Lester Young **(Pres/The Complete Savoy Recordings)**. Also in '44, was featured at several of the legendary Eddie Condon Town Hall concerts, giving a fine account of himself during a fiercely swinging **Struttin' With Some Barbecue** at one such event **(Eddie Condon & His All Stars)**. Same year, his trumpet and studio orchestra accompanied singer Margaret Whiting on a recording of **Moonlight in Vermont**, which became a million-selling hit. After demobilization, put together own band which toured and recorded during 1946-47. Disbanded, played solo residency at Nick's, New York, before returning to studio work (also New York).

During the late 1940s, into the 1950s, continued making records and in-person appearances with various leaders, including Condon **(We Called It Music, The Golden Days Of Jazz: Eddie Condon** and **Chicago & All That Jazz!)** as well as periodically fronting various own bands.

Produced some of his finest trumpet playing at all-star record date for Capitol in '56 **(Session At Riverside)**. From time to time also worked again with Goodman, and taught trumpet. Then, in 1968, joined newly formed World's Greatest Jazzband of Yank Lawson & Bob Haggart. In company with old friends and musically sympathetic players, Butterfield's playing took on a new lease of life. Certainly, solos like **The Windmills Of Your Mind**, a duet with Lawson, **It Must Be Him (Extra!), This Is All I Ask (The WGJB Of Yank Lawson & Bob Haggart—Project 3/World Record Club)** and **What's New? (The WGJB Of Yank Lawson & Bob Haggart Live At The Roosevelt Grill)** must be ranked with his finest recorded solos taken from any time during his career.

Albums:
Bob Crosby, South Rampart Street Parade (—/MCA)
Bob Crosby, Bob Crosby's Bob Cats 1938-1942 (Swaggie—Australia)
Bob Crosby, Big Noise From Winnetka (—/MCA)
Artie Shaw, Concerto For Clarinet (RCA Victor)
Artie Shaw & His Gramercy Five (—/RCA Victor)
Benny Goodman Plays Solid Gold Instrumental Hits (Columbia/CBS)
Various, Swingin' Clarinets (—/London)
Lester Young, Pres/The Complete Savoy Recordings (Savoy/—)
Eddie Condon & His All Stars (Jazum/—)
Eddie Condon, We Called It Music (—/Ace of Hearts)
Eddie Condon, The Golden Days Of Jazz (Columbia/CBS)
Various, Chicago & All That Jazz! (—/Verve)
The World's Greatest Jazzband Of Yank Lawson & Bob Haggart Live At The Roosevelt Grill (Atlantic)/
Billy Butterfield, Watch What Happens (—/77 Records)
The WGJB Of Yank Lawson & Bob Haggart (Project 3/World Record Club)
Dick Wellstood/Billy Butterfield, Rapport (—/77 Records)
The WGJB Of Yank Lawson & Bob Haggart, In Concert/At Carnegie Hall, Vol 2 (World Jazz/—)
Jack Teagarden, Prince Of The Bone, Vol 2 (1928-1957) (RCA Victor—France)
Various, Session At Riverside (Capitol/Capitol—Holland)
The WGJB Of Yank Lawson & Bob Haggart Plays Duke Ellington (World Jazz/—)

Above: Don Byas, like Coleman Hawkins, was a cross-over tenorist whose playing embraced both the mainstream and bebop.

Don Byas

Carlos Wesley 'Don' Byas (born Muskogee, Oklahoma, 1912) was a 'mid-period' tenor-saxophonist in the truest sense of that expression. He emerged during the early 1930s, to be influenced primarily by Ben Webster and, particularly, Coleman Hawkins. And Byas' peak years coincided with the advent of bebop with which he associated himself with typical gusto and fervor. In the beginning, Byas had started his musical schooling on violin—his mother and father both played instruments—then transferred his allegiance to alto-saxophone. Before his 20th birthday, had gigged with bands like those of Bennie Moten, Walter Page's Blue Devils, and during period at Langston College, Oklahoma, led own Don Byas Collegiate Ramblers. Switched to tenor sax around this time (whilst with Bert Johnson's Sharps & Flats, 1933-35). Left latter band to settle in California, working with Lionel Hampton, Eddie Barefield, Buck Clayton (in 1937). With band accompanying Ethel Waters (1937-39), followed by short stays with Don Redman, Lucky Millinder, before joining Andy Kirk (1939-40). 1940: with Edgar Hayes, Benny Carter. 1941: to Count Basie, in place of exciting Lester Young. Strongly featured during almost three-year stint with Basie band.

Solo highlights on record include **Sugar Blues** and **St Louis Blues (Superchief)**, both of which were, like **Bugle Blues** and **Royal Garden Blues (Blues By Basie)**, recorded by small contingent from full band; **Harvard Blues (Blues By Basie)** probably remains the best.

After leaving Basie, Byas made home in New York, quickly establishing himself as one of the most popular tenorists on 52nd Street. Worked alongside one of his idols, Coleman Hawkins (at Yacht Club), also with Dizzy Gillespie (at Onyx Club), in what must have been the first working bebop band. Byas had recorded with Hawkins in 1944 **(Cattin'** and **Swing!)**. During same year, took part (with Hawkins and Gillespie) in first known bop record date **(The Many Faces Of Jazz Vol 52: Coleman Hawkins)**. Byas had recorded with Gillespie in Trummy Young's band in '44 **(Jazz 44)** and two years later was employed by the trumpeter as sideman for recording date which produced more clearly defined examples of bop **(Greatest Of The Small Bands, Vol 2)** soloing confidently on **52nd Street Theme, A Night In Tunisia** and **Ol' Man Bebop**.

Between 1944-46 Byas recorded numerous titles for Savoy, mostly at sessions under own name, and with sympathetic colleagues like Charlie Shavers, Emmett Berry, Clyde Hart and Max Roach. Typical of the high standard of performances from the tenorist at these dates **(Savoy Jam Party)** are superior examples of his big-toned, rhapsodic ballad playing **(Candy** and **Sweet & Lovely**, both from 1944; **September In The Rain**, 1945; **They Say It's Wonderful** and **September**

Song, 1946), plus a series of comprehensively swinging up-tempo gems like **Savoy Jam Party** and **Bass C-Jam** in '44; **How High The Moon** and **Cherokee** in '45; **St Louis Blues** and **I Found A New Baby** in '46.

Two remarkable virtuoso-class performances (**Indiana** and **I Got Rhythm**) came from a New York Town Hall appearance in 1945 (**Town Hall Concert, Vol 3**). Same year 'The Don' led own bands at various jazz nightspots in the city, including Three Deuces. By September of 1946 Byas was in Europe, as principal soloist with Don Redman. After leaving Redman at tour's conclusion, decided to make his home in France. Later, moved to Amsterdam where, eventually, he settled for good, with Dutch wife and family. 1950: featured with Duke Ellington Orchestra during its European tour that year; recorded with Ellington contingent (plus French pianist Raymond Fol), under Johnny Hodges' leadership (**Mellow Tone**).

Ten years later the emigré tenorist again toured Europe with fellow Americans, this time as member of Jazz At The Philharmonic troupe, during which his bristling, hard-hitting solos compared favorably with work of his colleagues: most interesting to hear Byas' thick tone, unflagging drive in company with two other tenor giants, Hawkins and Stan Getz (**JATP IN Europe, Vol 1**) as well as part of a predominantly mainstream line-up (**JATP In Europe, Vol 3**).

In between, Byas had built up considerable reputation as solo act, visiting most European countries, including Britain, playing at festivals, concerts and in clubs. Twenty-four years after leaving his home country, Byas returned principally for the purpose of making Dutch documentary film about Don Byas. Appeared—to enthusiastic response—at 1970 Newport Jazz Festival and, briefly, elsewhere. 1971: toured Japan with Jazz Messengers of Art Blakey, returning to Holland same year. During 1960s, Byas' playing underwent slight stylistic adjustments as he endeavored to incorporate (sometimes unsuccessfully) some of the devices of John Coltrane and Sonny Rollins (who both acknowledged Byas as personal influence). Basically, though, his style was maintained right up until the time of his death, from lung cancer, in 1972.

Typical of Byas' 1960s performances (and indeed of his playing up to his death) are those to be found on a two-tenor album from 1966 (**Ben Webster Meets Don Byas**). Better still, though, is **Anthropology** from three years before the Byas-Webster date, with Byas steaming through a typical live program, including the title tune and **A Night In Tunisia** from his Gillespie-associated days, helped enormously by the efforts of the phenomenal Danish bassist Niels-Henning Ørsted-Pederson.

Albums:
Count Basie, Blues By Basie (Columbia/Philips)
Count Basie, Superchief (Columbia/CBS)
Count Basie (Queen Disc—Italy)
Count Basie, The V-Discs, Vol 2 (Jazz Society)
Coleman Hawkins, Cattin' (—/Fontana)
Coleman Hawkins, Swing! (—/Fontana)
Various, Jazz 44 (—/Black & Blue—France)
Coleman Hawkins, The Many Faces Of Jazz, Vol 52 (Mode—France)
The Greatest Of Dizzy Gillespie (RCA Victor)/Various, The Greatest Of The Small Bands, Vol 2 (RCA Victor—France)
Shelly Manne & Co. (Flying Dutchman/—)
Various, Town Hall Concert,, Vol 3 (—/London)
Don Byas, Savoy Jam Party (Savoy)
Le Grand Don Byas (Vogue—France)
Various, Mellow Tone (Vogue)
Don Byas, Live At The Montmartre (Debut/Fontana)
Don Byas Meets Ben Webster (Prestige)/Ben Webster Meets Don Byas (BASF)
Don Byas, Ballads For Swingers (—/Polydor)
Don Byas, Anthropology (Black Lion/Black Lion)
Various, Jazz At The Philharmonic In Europe, Vols 1, 3 (Verve/Verve)

Tenorist Don Byas, Anthropology (courtesy Black Lion).

Charlie Byrd

Born 1925 in Virginia, guitarist Charlie Byrd achieved immense popularity on the bossa nova wave in the early '60s. Influenced by none of the usual guitar masters—Christian, Reinhardt—Byrd studied under classical master, Segovia, and much of his improvisation revolves around the classical flamenco. In fact, his status as a jazzman has often been questioned, though there are no doubts about his mastery of the instrument. A quiet, sensitive player, Byrd uses an acoustic classical guitar and concentrates on meandering melodies of great charm and limited drive. In 1959 he joined Woody Herman, and in 1961 took his trio on a State Department tour of Latin America. Collaborating with tenorman Stan Getz on one of the first bossa nova albums (**Jazz Samba**) Byrd began a long preoccupation with that form. The hit number **Desafinado** turns up on his Milestone double album **Latin Byrd** as well as versions of **One Note Samba** and other Jobim compositions. Most of his albums reveal a charming miniaturist, though the jazz content rather depends upon his colleagues.

Albums:
Stan Getz, Jazz Samba (Verve/Verve)
Latin Byrd (Milestone/Milestone)
Triste (Improv/Improv)
Great Guitars (Concord/Concord)
Bluebyrd (Concord/Concord)
Sugar Loaf Suite (Concord/Concord)
Great Guitars At The Winery (Concord/Concord)
Brazilian Soul (Concord/Concord)
Brazilville (Concord/Concord)
Straight Tracks (Concord/Concord)
Great Guitars At Georgetown (Concord/Concord)
Isn't It Romantic? (Concord/Concord)

Donald Byrd

Donald Toussaint L'Ouverture Byrd was born in 1932 in Detroit, a city that had supplied many of the stalwarts of bop and hard bop: Kenny Burrell, Pepper Adams, Sonny Stitt, Milt Jackson, Tommy Flanagan, Barry Harris and the three Jones boys, Thad, Elvin and Hank. After early experience as a sideman with George Wallington, Art Blakey's Messengers and Max Roach, trumpeter Byrd found himself in the lucrative position of recording every day to keep up with the public appetite for long playing albums. Between 1955-58, he made sixty albums for Blue Note, Savoy and Prestige, sharing sessions with Monk, Coltrane, Rollins, Silver, Jackie McLean and Phil Woods. His playing at this time was immature, his tone thin, but—despite over-exposure—his promise was clear. A good example (**House Of Byrd**) collates two mid-'50s sessions, pairing with trumpeter Art Farmer, and sharing a quintet with altoist Phil Woods.

A period with altoist Gigi Gryce produced the Jazz Lab, in which the two music students could experiment with composition and harmony, and this bore fruit in Byrd's excellent Blue Note albums with baritone saxophonist, Pepper Adams. Two of these (**Royal Flush** and **Cat Walk**) show that the trumpeter's writing on **Jorgie's Shangri-La** and **The Cat Walk** avoided the clichés of the period and invented new routes to old destinations, while his playing gained in strength and lyricism.

A combination of factors led to Donald Byrd's subsequent disappearance from jazz circles in favor of fusion music. He attributes his change of direction to the ghetto riots, the influence of singer James Brown, both as a leader of his people and a musician, and the rise of Tamla Motown in his hometown. Byrd is doctor of ethnomusicology, and believes that the black heritage is better represented today through soul music, hence his Blue Note album, **Black Byrd** in the early '70s, that label's first million-seller although a somewhat diluted product in terms of 'pure jazz' content.

Byrd's 1978 album **I Want To Thank You For F.U.M.L. (Funking Up My Life)** was the first time he produced himself and confirmed his position in the funk charts. His first album with his band 125th Street (**And 125th St., N.Y.C.**) included pianist Clare Fisher who had written for the Hi-Los.

While Byrd is credited as one of the first to merge jazz with pop forms, recording has been only one aspect of his musical life. Byrd earned a doctorate from Columbia Teachers College, attended University Law School, and during '60s and '70s taught in New York public schools (including the High School Of Music and Art) and at Rutgers, New York University, Brooklyn College and North Carolina Central State University (where he headed the Department of Jazz Studies). He has directed stage band clinics; lectured on ethnomusicology all over the world; written for numerous radio and television orchestras in Europe; hosted his own TV series in New York; played with the Philadelphia Philharmonic and conducted the Detroit Symphony; and written for films (ie *Cornbread, Earl and Me*).

From 1968-72, Byrd directed the Howard Univeristy Jazz Institute, conducting an experiment with five young musicians. The result was the vocal-instrumental group The Blackbyrds (**City Life, Unfinished Business** and **Action**). He has also been involved with the Howard-based group The Three Pieces and the New Central Connection Unlimited—students from North Carolina State University.

Albums:
House Of Byrd (Prestige/Prestige)
The Cat Walk (Blue Note/Blue Note)
Royal Flush (Blue Note/Blue Note)
Black Byrd (Blue Note/Blue Note)
I Want To Thank You For F.U.M.L. (Funking Up My Life) (Elektra-Asylum/Electra-Asylum)
And 125th St., N.Y.C. (Elektra-Asylum/Electra-Asylum)
Byrd In Hand (Blue Note/Blue Note)
A New Perspective (Blue Note/Blue Note)
Free Form (Blue Note/Blue Note)

Donald Byrd, Royal Flush (courtesy Blue Note): trumpeter before stardom.

Cab Calloway

Cabell 'Cab' Calloway (born Rochester, New York, 1907) is remembered mostly as a jivey vocalist-cum-bandleader of the 1930s-'40s who found fame afresh in another area of music—the stage musical—later in his career.

Calloway was raised in Baltimore where he sometimes sang with local high-school group, and studied at Chicago college when he moved on from Baltimore to the Windy City in his teens. Appeared, together with sister Blanche, at Chicago's Loop Theater; the couple also appeared in a tabloid show. Cab Calloway worked as drummer and master of ceremonies around this time. With the Missourians in New York (1928), then back to Chicago to work with Alabamians (1929), combining job of MC with that of 'personality vocals'. Back again with Missourians, then, after regularly undertaking bandleading chores, changed name of band to Cab Calloway & His Orchestra. 1931: commenced prestigious residency at New York's Cotton Club lasting, on and off, best part of a year. Already, Calloway—later to be dubbed His Highness of Hi-De-Ho—had established more of a reputation than the band itself: recording, in 1931, of **Minnie The Moocher (The King Of Hi-Di-Ho)** tended to confirm this.

Unfortunately, most recordings tended to feature Calloway's averagely funny vocals—scarcely 'jazz singing' in any conceivable way—to the exclusion of all but a comparative handful of solos from his sidemen.

Cab Calloway & His Cotton Club Orchestra recorded some fairly good material for Victor 1933-34, inlcuding **Long About Midnight** and **Moonglow**, plus reprises from recent past of **Minnie The Moocher** and **Kickin' The Gong Around (Cab Calloway & His Orchestra 1933-1934)**. Calloway and orchestra toured Europe (including Britain) in 1934. Calloway himself played alto sax (apparently unconvincingly) on odd occasions during 1930s. Probably best jazz emanated from band of 1937-42 vintage. Principal soloist during most of this time was Chu Berry, whose superior tenor saxophone playing of **I Don't Stand A Ghost Of A Chance** (1940) became a popular recording and today is rightly looked upon as something of a classic (**Chu** and **16 Cab Calloway Classics**). At the time, Berry was most generously featured soloist with Calloway (**Penguin Swing**) but other notable instrumentalists (and their features) were: Hilton Jefferson, **Willow, Weep For Me** (1940); Jonah Jones, **Jonah Joins The Cab** (1941); Cozy Cole, **Crescendo In Drums** and **Paradiddle** (both 1940); Milt Hinton, **Pluckin' The Bass** (1939); and a youthful trumpeter-arranger Dizzy Gillespie, **Pickin' The Cabbage** and **Bye Bye Blues** (1940-41) (all **16 Cab Calloway Classics**).

Calloway band lasted until 1948 (when star sidemen mentioned had all long since departed). After break up, Calloway toured with sextet, putting together big bands from time to time for rare engagements, including trips to Canada, South America. Calloway appeared as solo act in Britain (1948), head-lining London Palladium for season. Toured UK again, in similar fashion, in 1955.

For two years (1952-54 including London run), appeared as Sportin' Life in folk-opera *Porgy & Bess* (Original Broadway Cast LP: **Porgy & Bess**). Was to repeat this role at various times during 1950s. Put together more big bands for seasons at various New York clubs, and elsewhere, during 1950s; midway through decade, undertook tour with Harlem Globetrotters. Was back, few years later, to more stage work, including leading role opposite Pearl Bailey in *Hello Dolly!* During a colorful lifetime in show business has appeared in numerous movies, including *The Big Broadcast of 1933, International House, The Singing Kid, Stormy Weather, Sensations of 1945* and *St. Louis Blues*.

One of Calloway's most welcome screen appearances of later years has been in John Landis' riotous film *The Blues Brothers* (1980) which, in spite of much R&B mayhem from John Belushi and Dan Aykroyd, includes a wonderful cameo recreation of his 1931 **Minnie The Moocher**—perfectly undiminished Calloway even in his seventies.

Albums:

Chu Berry, Chu (Epic)/Chu Berry & His Stompy Stevedores (Epic—France)
16 Cab Calloway Classics (—/CBS—France)
Chu Berry, Penguin Swing: Chu Berry Featured With Cab Calloway (Jazz Archives)
Cab Calloway & His Orchestra 1933-1934 (RCA Victor—Germany)
Cab Calloway & His Cotton Club Orchestra (—/RCA Victor—France)
The King Of Hi-De-Ho (—/Ace of Hearts)
The Blues Brothers—Original Soundtrack Recording (Atlantic/Atlantic)

Harry Carney

There is very little argument that Harry Carney (born Boston, Massachusetts, 1910) was the greatest of all the baritone saxophonists. Certainly, it could be said that Serge Chaloff was a more accomplished improviser and had more speed; and there have been times when Gerry Mulligan, too, has proved to be a more interesting soloist than Carney—especially at length. Having said that, Carney still was in a class of his own, omnipotent on an often cumbersome instrument for around 45 years, unchallenged in terms of sheer tonal quality, ability to swing (Carney was unbeatable in terms of rhythmic drive), and all-round competence.

He was the first to 'tame' the baritone, to make it sound something rather more than a kind of vaudeville throwback. Carney was also an accomplished soloist on alto sax, clarinet and bass clarinet. But it was the hugeness of his baritone sax sound which became so integral a part of the overall sound of the textures and colors devised by Duke Ellington for his various orchestras. And it was to Ellington that Carney, like so many other Ducal soloists over the years, owed a priceless debt of gratitude for providing him with the kind of settings and situations which enabled his innate talent to blossom to the fullest. Carney remained a rock-like figure of absolute permanency within the Ellington fold, while others around him lasted a mere 15, 10, five or less years.

In all, Carney's residence with the Ellington band lasted from 1927 until his employer's death in 1974—just six months before Carney himself passed away. There was a special kind of relationship between Ellington and Carney that did not seem to exist between the bandleader and any of his other star pupils.

Later to become a prolific poll-winner on baritone, Harry Howell Carney joined Ellington in 1927 (his first gig with the band was a one-nighter near the city of his birth) after having worked with local Boston bands, then leaving for New York together with friend altoist Charlie Holmes. His subsequent splendidly consistent work with Ellington and his ability to merge into practically any kind of jazz context found him regular work, especially the kind of pick-up record-session bands put together by Teddy Wilson for singers of the calibre of Billie Holiday (**The Golden Years, Vol 2**) and to showcase the talents of the cream of available jazz instrumentalists (**Teddy Wilson & His All Stars**).

Carney's supremacy as baritone saxist no doubt earned him a two-number spot on the star-studded bill of the legendary Goodman Carnegie Hall concert of January 1938 (**The 1938 Carnegie Hall Jazz Concert**) where his versatility made him an obvious choice for inclusion amongst the list of participants in the jam session on **Honeysuckle Rose**, and his matchless tone and magnificent control earned him an even more appropriate showcase, alongside the soprano sax of Johnny Hodges, during an unforgettable duet performance by both on the little-heard Ellington number **Blue Reverie**. Hodges, incidentally, clearly was the principal influence on Harry Carney's playing, and in the shaping of his style.

Always a major asset with whomever he appeared, Carney's cavernous baritone sound has been majestically and helpfully present throughout a string of first-rate record dates with Hodges as leader (**Ellingtonia '56, Johnny Hodges & The Ellington Men, Hodge Podge** and **Love In Swingtime 1938/9**). Carney performed a similar role in other all-star sessions, including those put together by Lionel Hampton (**The Complete Lionel Hampton/Lionel Hampton's Best Records, Vols 2, 5**). Likewise, with regard to 'official' all-star studio get-togethers like **The Metronome All Stars/The Esquire All Stars** and **Benny Carter 1945 + The Metronome All Stars**) or organized live events cast in a similar vein (**Second Esquire Concert, Vol 2**) the latter as a member of the Ellington Orchestra.

But it is as the anchor member of the most famous of all jazz aggregations that Carney's name is forever linked. And for anyone remotely interested in his work, it is Harry Carney's inimitable renderings of such as **Sophisticated Lady, Prelude To A Kiss** or **La Plus Belle Africaine** which more readily come to mind—the solos, and of course, that unique, all-encompassing sound which for 45 years gave the Ellington ensemble such body and strength.

Albums:

The Works Of Duke Ellington, Vols 1-18 (RCA Victor—France)
The Complete Duke Ellington, Vols 1-7 (CBS—France)
Duke Ellington, Ellington In Concert, Vol 2 (—/World Record Club)
Duke Ellington, The Beginning (1926-1928) (MCA—Germany)
Duke Ellington, Hot In Harlem (1928-1929) (MCA—Germany)
Duke Ellington, Rockin' In Rhythm (1929-1931) (MCA—Germany)
Duke Ellington, The Golden Duke (Prestige/Prestige)
Duke Ellington, Toodle-oo (—/Vocalion)
Duke Ellington, Masterpieces By Ellington (CBS—Holland)
Duke Ellington, Such Sweet Thunder (Columbia/CBS—Realm)
Duke Ellington, His Most Important Second War Concert (—/Saga Pan)
Duke Ellington, Black, Brown & Beige (Ariston—Italy)
Duke Ellington, The Duke 1940 (Jazz Society)
Various (Including Duke Ellington), The Greatest Jazz Concert In The World (Pablo/Pablo)
Duke Ellington, The Great Paris Concert (Atlantic/—)
Duke Ellington, The English Concert (United Artists/United Artists)
Duke Ellington's 70th Birthday Concert (Solid State/United Artists)
Duke Ellington, Latin American Suite (Fantasy/—)
Duke Ellington's Third Sacred Concert, The Majesty Of God, As Performed In Westminster Abbey (RCA Victor/RCA Victor)
Various, Great Ellingtonians Play A Tribute To Duke Ellington (—/Double-Up)
Johnny Hodges, Hodge Podge (Columbia/CBS—Realm)
Everybody Knows Johnny Hodges (Impulse/Impulse)
Johnny Hodges & The Ellington Men (Verve)
Duke Ellington Meets Coleman Hawkins (Impulse/—)
Billie Holiday, The Golden Years, Vol 2 (Columbia/CBS)
Various, The 1938 Carnegie Hall Jazz Concert (Columbia/CBS)
Various, The Second Esquire Concert, Vol 2 (—/Saga)
Benny Carter 1945 + The Metronome All Stars (Queen Disc—Italy)
The Metronome All Stars/The Esquire All Stars (RCA Victor—France)
The Complete Lionel Hampton (RCA Victor)/ Lionel Hampton's Best Records, Vols 2, 5 (RCA Victor—France)
Teddy Wilson & His All Stars (Columbia/CBS)
Rex Stewart Memorial (—/CBS—Realm)
Johnny Hodges, Ellingtonia '56 (Verve/Columbia—Clef)
Johnny Hodges, Love In Swingtime 1938-39 (Tax—Sweden)
Duke Ellington, Souvenirs (Reprise)

Ian Carr

Trumpeter-composer-arranger and distinguished British jazz-rock pioneer, was born in Dumfries, Scotland, 1933.

His reputation was established in the early 1960s with the Newcastle-based EmCee Five (**Let's Take Five** and **EmCee Five Vol 2**, both EPs, now collectors' items). From 1962-69, he co-led the much-vaunted Don Rendell-Ian Carr Quintet (**Shades Of Blue, Phase Three, Change Is**). Over the years, Carr has also worked with such British luminaries as Harold McNair, Joe Harriott, Amancio D'Silva (**Hum Dono**), John McLaughlin, the New Jazz Orchestra (**Le Déjeuner Sur L'Herbe**), Michael Garrick (**Promises, The Heart Is A Lotus**), Mike

Below: Harry Carney, probably the most celebrated baritone saxophonist in jazz history—a rock-like figure within the Duke Ellington fold.

Westbrook, Neil Ardley **(Kaleidoscope Of Rainbows)**, Barbara Thompson, Jon Hiseman, John Stevens-Trevor Watts **(Springboard)** and Keith Tippett **(Septober Energy)**.

1969 was a cornerstone in British contemporary music, the year that Carr founded his ground-breaking band Nucleus exploring jazz-rock fusion and extending the use of electronics producing such memorable albums as the early **Elastic Rock, Solar Plexus, Belladonna** and **Roots** up to the mid-'80s with **Live At The Theaterhaus**. In 1970, Nucleus won first prize at the Montreux International Jazz Festival and were the first British jazz-rock unit to appear in the United States (1970 Newport Festival). In 1978, Nucleus was selected by the British Council for a tour of India, an honor repeated in '84 with a tour of Latin America.

In '86, Carr's extended work *Spirit of Place* was performed at Bracknell featuring Eberhard Weber, Tony Coe and the Kreisler String Orchestra.

As well as being one of Britain's most often commissioned composers, Carr is also one of the music's most articulate and interesting critics and commentators. He is highly regarded as an author. His excellent survey of jazz in Britain, *Music Outside* (Latimer New Dimensions—an updated reprint is long overdue) is regarded as a standard work and his critical biography *Miles Davis* (Quartet/Paladin) was internationally acclaimed. He has also contributed to *The Jazz Companion* (Granada), 1986.

The honors he particularly values are being made a member of the Royal Society of Musicians of Great Britain in 1982; and, in August that year, receiving a special award from the region of Calabria (Southern Italy) for his undeniably 'outstanding contribution in the field of jazz'.

Carr is also actively engaged in jazz education; he's an associate professor at the Guildhall School of Music and Drama, and supervises workshops for gifted young musicians at Interchange in North London.

Carr is also a member of the Europe-based United Jazz+Rock Ensemble.

Trumpeter-composer Ian Carr's Nucleus, Belladonna (courtesy Vertigo).

Albums:
Elastic Rock (—/Vertigo)
We'll Talk About It Later (—/Vertigo)
Solar Plexus (—/Vertigo)
Belladonna (—/Vertigo)
Labyrinth (—/Vertigo)
Roots (—/Vertigo)
Under The Sun (—/Vertigo)
Snakehips Etcetera (Phonogram/Vertigo)
Alleycat (—/Vertigo)
In Flagrante Delicto (Capitol/Capitol)
Out Of The Long Dark (Capitol/Capitol)
Awakening (—/Mood—Germany)
Live At The Theaterhaus (—/Mood—Germany)
United Jazz+Rock Ensemble, 10 Years (—/Mood—Germany)

Benny Carter

Bennett Lester 'Benny' Carter (born New York City, 1907) assuredly is one of the most accomplished, multi-talented musicians to grace the jazz scene, in any era: an excellent trumpet player and clarinettist, proficient on tenor sax, piano; a peerless alto saxophonist; and a writer of immense imagination and all-round skills. Only as an occasional singer can any one aspect of his talents be said to be less than average. Carter's skills as arranger and composer place him high amongst the leaders of his field, his writing for the saxophone section being virtually in a class of it own. Exemplified magnificently on two LPs **(Further Definitions** and **Additions To Further Definitions)** from the late-1960s. Attention must be focused primarily on his contributions to the evolution in jazz of alto saxophone. For Carter usually is ranked (correctly) alongside Johnny Hodges, Charlie Parker and Ornette Coleman in most, if not all, all-time listings of top men on this particular instrument. The jazz-lovers' dream, a record date featuring three of the four, was realized in 1953 **(The Charlie Parker Sides/The Parker Jam Session)** when Carter, Hodges and Parker stood shoulder-to-shoulder inside a recording studio for the first, and only, occasion, along with several other jazz giants or near-giants. Carter's personal influence on the alto sax during the 1930s was at least equal to that of Hodges, and he remains one of a handful of altoists who came to the forefront during that decade successfully to incorporate some of Parker's unique vocabulary into his own musical make-up, without losing his own identity.

Basically, Carter's approach to the alto involves an almost unsurpassed elegance of tone, a most definite sympathy to rhythm (achieved with what has long since been recognized as typical Carter subtlety), and a clean, uncluttered, flowing, essentially melodic mode of improvisation. Technically, his work on alto (as indeed with the several other instruments he has used during his lengthy career) is beyond reproach. Coming from a musical family—both Cuban Bennett (1902-1965), an accomplished trumpeter, and Darnell Howard (1895-1966), a noted clarinettist-violinist, were cousins—Benny Carter started on piano, adding, in turn, trumpet and C-melody sax. Vital change to alto sax took place after first important engagement, with band of June Clark (1924). Same year, first worked with Earl Hines on baritone sax, after which his musical experiences (and education) really began to pick up: Horace Henderson, James P. Johnson, Duke Ellington, Fletcher Henderson **(The Fletcher Henderson Story/The Fletcher Henderson Story, Vols 2, 3)**, Charlie Johnson **(Charlie Johnson & His Orchestra 1927-1929)** and Chick Webb. He worked with several of these bands on more than one occasion.

1931: appointed musical director of McKinney's Cotton Pickers **(McKinney's Cotton Pickers, Vols 2-5)**, a position he held for about a year. Carter also occupied a similar role with pseudonymous Chocolate Dandies band **(The Chocolate Dandies)** between 1930-33, during which time he also worked with Don Redman, and he added trumpet as a regular 'double', still finding time to write scores for several bands for whom he had worked since joining Johnson and others with whom he did not work as an instrumentalist. Between 1932-34 became leader of own bands **(Benny Carter-1933/Ridin' In Rhythm)** and in latter year also arranged for Benny Goodman.

Above: The accomplished and remarkable Benny Carter, multi-instrumentalist, composer, arranger, band-leader—truly a Jazz Giant in every sense.

Then came stints with Willie Bryant **(Willie Bryant/Jimmy Lunceford & Their Orchestras)** before Carter emigrated—temporarily—to Europe (1935).

In Paris, Carter's first job was with Willie Lewis Orchestra **(Willie Lewis Orchestra)** but by 1936 he had crossed the English Channel to take up appointment as staff arranger for Henry Hall Orchestra (although he was not allowed to play). Permission was given for Carter to play on London record date featuring contingent from Hall band **(Swingin' At Maida Vale)**. Tour of Scandinavia (1936) then Holland, France (1937-38), documented in part with recordings made in Holland **(Benny Carter With The Ramblers & His Orchestra)**. In March, 1938, recorded in Paris with cosmopolitan band, including legendary Django Reinhardt **(Django & His American Friends, Vol 2)**, and music which resulted from same was of consistently high quality; similarly pleasing results had been obtained from another Paris session involving Carter and Reinhardt a year before **(Django & His American Friends, Vol 1)**, this time with Coleman Hawkins helping out.

After second Carter-Reinhardt date, returned to US. Between 1939-41, led own big band, at various times featuring noted instrumentalists such as Tyree Glenn, Jonah Jones, Jimmy Archey, Sidney De Paris, Sonny White, Doc Cheatham, Benny Morton, Eddie Heywood, Joe Thomas, J. C. Heard and Coleman Hawkins. Despite fine contributions from sidemen on recordings by these bands **(Melancholy Benny** and **Benny Carter & His Orchestra: 1940-1941)** it is the playing of its leader and his arrangements and compositions which linger longest in the memory. Indeed, his writing for the saxes on **All Of Me**, from 1940 **(Benny Carter & His Orchestra: 1940-1941)** still sounds remarkable today. During 1940, Carter also recorded under Hawkins' leadership **(The Big Sounds Of Coleman Hawkins & Chu Berry)** and with Billie Holiday **(God Bless The Child)**, contributing sensitive clarinet obbligato and solo to **St Louis Blues** at the singer's October 15 record date. In New York, Carter fronted sextet that included Dizzy Gillespie and Jimmy Hamilton. (Carter had written superior arrangements for Cab Calloway Orchestra, of which Gillespie was then member, 1940.)

1943: moved to West Coast. In Hollywood, put together another big band which included some up-and-coming talent, like Max Roach, Henry Coker, Al Grey, J. J. Johnson, Joe Albany, Porter Kilbert, Curley Russell. Once again, recordings (**Big Band Bounce** and **Live Sessions 1943/1945**) do reasonable justice to uniformly fine music produced by Carter and sidemen, further amplified by superior big-band music to be found within **Benny Carter 1945 + The Metronome All-Stars**. 1945: made permanent home in Hollywood. Throughout much of the late-1940s/early-1950s, live appearances drastically reduced. This was because he was to spend much time in Hollywood writing music for various films. Also appeared on screen, as himself, in several films, including *The Snows Of Kilimanjaro*, *Stormy Weather*, *As Thousands Cheer* and *Clash By Night*. During 1950s, occasionally put together own bands, including big-band residency in Los Angeles in 1955; same year he assisted with musical score for *The Benny Goodman Story*. (Did likewise for *The Five Pennies*, as well as for highly successful TV series *M-Squad*.)

Carter's interrupted recording career picked up somewhat when, in 1952, Norman Granz signed him to record a series of albums for his Clef/Norgran labels (**The Formidable Benny Carter, New Jazz Sounds**, etc). For Granz, he also participated in recordings with other top-name artists, including the Parker-Hodges-Carter-&-Co session noted previously, and a rewarding all-star date in 1953 which resulted in **Jam Session, Nos 2, 3**. Latter events were nothing new to Benny Carter. For instance, he had been a meaningful contributor to three of Lionel Hampton's classic all-star dates of 1938-39 (**The Complete Lionel Hampton/Lionel Hampton's Best Records, Vols 2, 3, 5, 6**) and further proved his worth in this kind of organized jam session situation by taking solo honors during a similarly styled Capitol record date in 1955 (**Session At Midnight**). And that Carter's alto had lost none of its opulence or combative spirit during live performance was demonstrated most admirably when he toured for Granz with Jazz At The Philharmonic in 1953 (**JATP In Tokyo**). His **Flamingo** feature, in Ballad Medley portion of the programme, was as graceful, elegant as ever; alongside his peers (eg Webster, Bill Harris, Eldridge, Willie Smith) his impassioned playing on the more rhythmic numbers lost nothing in comparison; and he proved during same tour probably the best sax player to work with Gene Krupa Trio. Carter, at 47, reserved some of his greatest improvisations for another piano-sax-drums session (this one inside the studio) a year later. This time Carter was in company of drummer Louis Bellson and the jazz pianists' pianist, Art Tatum. Never for one moment overawed by the extravagancies of Tatum's keyboard style, Carter produced, even by his own standards, astonishingly good solos throughout, especially on **Blues In B Flat, Undecided, Makin' Whoopee'** and his own **I'm Left With The Blues In My Heart**. That Carter could continue to co-exist in most kinds of jazz company was proved by a thoroughly enjoyable record date for Contemporary in late-1950s (**Benny Carter: Jazz Giant**), with Carter's undiminished artistry en rapport with sympathetic playing of Ben Webster, Barney Kessel, Frank Rosolino, Jimmie Rowles (or André Previn), Leroy Vinnegar and Shelly Manne. Subsequent Contemporary session (**Swingin' The 20s**) with Vinnegar and Manne again present was not as successful because special guest Earl Hines, whilst soloing admirably enough, seemed intent on going his own way elsewhere. Apart from his work on alto and trumpet, Carter also played piano on some tracks. Carter cut three LPs for United Artists between 1959-62, the best of these being **The Benny Carter Jazz Calendar** with his deft, distinctive touch as writer being much in evidence. And as well as Carter and fellow saxists Hawkins, Charlie Rouse and Phil Woods playing, collectively and alone, it was Carter's inventive, fresh-sounding scores for **Further Definitions** that took pride of place at a '61 recording session, including a marvellous re-write for saxes of Hawkins' immortal **Body & Soul** solo from '39. Follow-up LP, **Additions To Further Definitions**, had two different saxes-with-rhythm line-ups, and although not as comprehensively successful as its successor, it did contain much Carter-inspired music-making and more glorious writing for the reeds. Since early-1960s, Benny Carter has been, in turn, active and semi-active as a player. Has toured with JATP on several occasions (**Jazz At The Philharmonic In Europe, Vols 1, 3 (1960)** and **The Greatest Jazz Concert In The World (1967)** and more recently, **JATP At The Montreux Jazz Festival 1975**). Has also made numerous studio recordings with a variety of musicians, but all of a similar free-swinging bent as of previous years. These have included musicians of the calibre of Barney Bigard and Ben Webster (**BBB & Co**), Milt Jackson and Joe Pass (**The King**), Dizzy Gillespie and Tommy Flanagan (**Carter, Gillespie, Inc**) and Count Basie, Eddie 'Lockjaw' Davis and Clark Terry (**Basie Jam No 2**). For a short period, in 1968, Carter lent his alto sax sound to the Duke Ellington Orchestra. Seven years before, he had performed a similar function with Count Basie, and in November, '60 had provided the Basie band with a collection of compositions/arrangements (**Kansas City Suite**) which ranked with anything it has been called upon to play during the past 30 years. Carter's 1970s activities, rather than decreasing, appear to have expanded from the previous decade. In the 1980s, this incredibly well-preserved musician is as unquenchably prolific and musically outstanding as at any comparable period of a truly distinguished career.

Benny Carter, Further Definitions (courtesy Impulse).

Benny Carter, Melancholy Benny, 1939-40 (courtesy Tax-Sweden).

Albums:

Charlie Johnson-Lloyd Scott-Cecil Scott (RCA Victor—France)
McKinney's Cotton Pickers, Vols 2-5 (1928-1931) (RCA Victor—France)
The Chocolate Dandies (—/Parlophone)
The Fletcher Henderson Story (Columbia)/ The Fletcher Henderson Story, Vols 2, 3 (CBS)
Benny Carter-1933 (Prestige)/Various, Ridin' In Rhythm (World Records)
Spike Hughes & His All-American Orchestra (London/Ace of Clubs)
Willie Bryant/(Jimmie Lunceford) & Their Orchestras (Bluebird/—)
Willie Lewis (Pirate—Sweden)
Benny Carter, Swingin' At Maida Vale (—/Ace of Clubs)
Benny Carter With The Ramblers & His Orchestra (—/Decca—France)
Django Reinhardt & The American Jazz Giants (Prestige)/Django & His American Friends, Vols 1, 2 (HMV)
The Complete Lionel Hampton (Bluebird)/ Lionel Hampton's Best Records, Vols 2, 3, 5, 6 (RCA Victor—France)
Coleman Hawkins/Roy Eldridge, Hawk & Roy (Phoenix)
Ethel Waters (1938-1941) (RCA Victor—France)
The Big Sounds Of Coleman Hawkins & (Chu Berry) (—/London)
Benny Carter, Melancholy Benny (Tax—Sweden)
Benny Carter & His Orchestra: 1940-41 (RCA Victor—France)
Billie Holiday, God Bless The Child (Columbia/CBS)
Benny Carter, Big Band Bounce (Capitol/Capitol—Holland)
Benny Carter 1945 + The Metronome All-Stars (Queen Disc—Italy)
The Formidable Benny Carter (Norgran/Columbia—Clef)
Benny Carter, New Jazz Sounds (Verve/Columbia—Clef)
Various, The Charlie Parker Sides (Verve)/ The Parker Jam Sessions (Verve)
Various, Jam Session, Nos 2, 3 (Verve/Columbia—Clef)
Various, J.A.T.P. In Tokyo (Pablo/Pablo)
Various, The Tatum Group Masterpieces (Pablo/Pablo)
Various, Session At Midnight (Capitol/Capitol)
Benny Carter: Jazz Giant (Contemporary/Vogue—Contemporary)
Benny Carter/Earl Hines, Swingin' The 20s (Contemporary/Vogue—Contemporary)
The Benny Carter Jazz Calendar (United Artists/United Artists)
Count Basie, Kansas City Suite (Roulette/Columbia)
Benny Carter, Further Definitions (Impulse/HMV)
Benny Carter, Additions To Further Definitions (Impulse/Impulse)
Benny Carter/Barney Bigard/Ben Webster, BBB & Co. (Prestige—Swingville/Xtra)
Various, The Greatest Jazz Concert In The World (Pablo/Pablo)
Benny Carter, The King (Pablo/Pablo)
Benny Carter/Dizzy Gillespie, Carter, Gillespie, Inc. (Pablo/Pablo)
Montreux '77: Benny Carter 4 (Pablo Live/Pablo Live)
Count Basie, Basie Jam No. 2 (Pablo/Pablo)

Betty Carter

Born Ella Mae Jones in Flint, Michigan, 1930, the indomitable Betty Carter has been called 'the greatest living jazz singer'. Her individual performance, compositions and vocal technique have placed her among the legends, first as a big-band singer in the 1950s and, since the '70s, with her own superlative trio.

Her first 'gig' was in Detroit when Charlie Parker invited her on to the bandstand (skipping school, she altered her birth certificate to avoid the club's 'No Juveniles' rule). In 1948, she joined Lionel Hampton's big band (they weren't always on good terms and he actually fired her seven times—his wife always rehiring her because she loved her voice). It was Hampton who dubbed her, much to her distaste, 'Betty Bebop'. In 1951, she left Hampton's band taking a residency at Harlem's Apollo Bar. Independent ever since, Carter now mainly works the clubs. In the '50s and '60s, she toured with artists like Miles Davis and Ray Charles (recording a now-classic album of duets with Charles in 1961).

In 1969, she founded her own record label, Bet-Car, and her trio has a formidable reputation as a training ground for young musicians—like John Hicks, Curtis Lundy and Kenny Washington. Most recently, her trio has included young pianist Benny Green, bassist Tarik Shah and drummer Winard Harper. A dynamic performer, just listen to her irresistible delivery on her own **New Blues (You Purrrrrr)** and her innovative improvisations on **With No Words** (from the exceptional live **Whatever Happened To Love?**). This live album features Carter with strings conducted by David Amram, plus her own exceptional trio.

Albums:
Betty Carter (1970) (Bet-Car/Bet-Car)
Betty Carter (1976) (Bet-Car/Bet-Car)
The Audience With Betty Carter (Bet-Car/Bet-Car)
Whatever Happened To Love? (Bet-Car/Bet-Car)

Betty Carter, Whatever Happened To Love? (courtesy Bet-Car Records).

Ron Carter

One of the most influential and formidable acoustic bassists to emerge in the 1960s, Ron Carter (born Ferndale, Michigan, on May 4, 1937) learned cello from age 10. At Cass Tech in Detroit, he realized early on that opportunities for black players in classical music were limited. Aware that there were few accomplished bassists among his peers, he switched to bass. He took a six-month crash course in bass studies and won a scholarship to Eastman, New York, graduating with a BA in music education in 1959. In 1962, he was awarded a master's degree at Manhattan School of Music.

Before long he was working with big-name artists like Chico Hamilton, Cannonball Adderley, Eric Dolphy and Jackie Byard. From 1963-68, he worked almost exclusively with Miles Davis in a classic quintet with Herbie Hancock, Wayne Shorter and young Tony Williams. In the early '70s he worked with a diverse selection of artists—Lena Horne, Michel Legrand, the New York Jazz Quartet, Stanley Turrentine, Hubert Laws, Lionel Hampton and Joe Henderson. In 1975, he formed his own quartet and the evidence of his prowess as a composer can be found on solo albums like the 1980 **Patrão** (featuring Chet Baker and Nana Vasconcelos). In the late '70s and early '80s, Carter reunited with his old cohorts from the Miles Davis Quintet, touring and recording with VSOP. Involved in jazz education, Carter has also written a two-volume book *Building A Jazz Line*.

In '86, Carter toured internationally as part of the herbie Hancock Quartet with saxophonist Branford Marsalis.

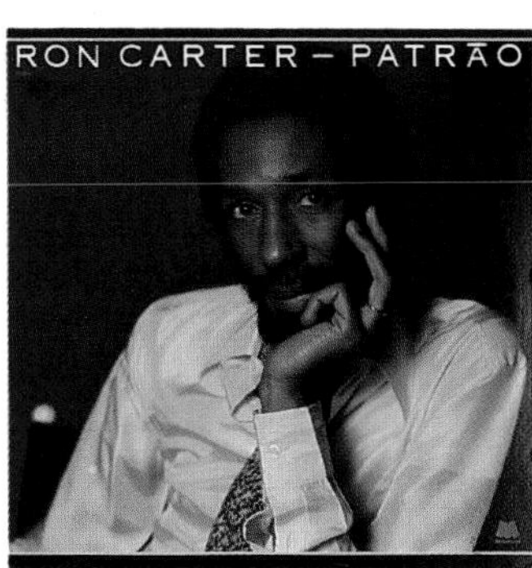

Ron Carter, Patrão (courtesy Milestone)—a celebrated bass-player.

Albums:
All Blues (CTI/CTI)
Ron Carter-Jim Hall, Alone Together (Milestone/Milestone)
Outfront (Prestige/Prestige)
Spanish Blue (CTI/CTI)
Patrão (Milestone/Milestone)
VSOP, The Quintet/VSOP Live (Columbia/CBS)

Casiopea

Likeable, enthusiastic Japanese supergroup whose lively compositions and technical ability have placed them at the top of an international fusion market. Derivative though they might be of a wholly 'New York funk' sound, Casiopea humbly explain that jazz funk is hardly part of Japan's cultural heritage.

The musicians of Casiopea are guitarist Issei Noro (who writes and arranges most of their material), keyboardist Minoru Mukaiya, electric bassist Tetsuo Sakurai and drummer Akira Jimbo. In the United States their music received wide exposure through association with heavyweight fusion artists like Dave and Don Grusin, Harvey Mason, Bob James and Lee Ritenour.

Their studio output is a lesson in Japan's high-tech engineering and production and their 1982 **Mint Jams**, recorded on-stage at Chuo Kaikan Hall, is an introduction to their live instrumental prowess (being only 'slightly' remixed in Tokyo's Alpha studio).

Albums:
The Soundography (Sonet/Sonet)
Down Upbeat (Sonet/Sonet)
Mint Jams (Sonet/Sonet)

Japanese funk supergroup Casiopea, Mint Jams (courtesy Sonet).

Serge Chaloff

Born 1923 in Boston, died 1957, baritone saxophonist Serge Chaloff's father and mother were both classical musicians. The best of the bebop baritones, Chaloff worked with the bands of Georgie Auld and Jimmy Dorsey before joining Woody Herman in 1947. Chaloff is the second soloist on **The Four Brothers (The Best Of Woody Herman)** and featured on **The Goof And I**. Disgracefully, most of his best recordings have been deleted, but four tracks with alternate takes **(Brothers & Other Mothers)** give an idea of his agility on the big horn and his highly original turn of phrase.

Albums:
The Best Of Woody Herman (—/CBS)
Brothers & Other Mothers (Savoy/Savoy)
Blue Serge (Capitol/Capitol)
Stan Kenton Presents...Boston Blow-Up! (Capitol/Affinity)

Above: 'Brother Ray' Charles—'the Genius'. His gospel-inspired performances have had an immeasurable influence on R&B artists of all eras.

Ray Charles

The influence of Ray Charles on a broad spectrum of popular music during the past 25-odd years has been almost immeasurable. Single-handed he was responsible (from middle-to-late-1950s period) for creating huge market for basically black soul music; his concerts and records attracted vast audiences— white and black—and did much in helping bring together various pop music forms.

Charles' own musical mixture comprises various elements of blues, R&B, gospel, jazz and pop. Gospel stems from his own religious (Baptist) upbringing and his participation in church music from a very young age. As a youngster, Charles also listened to jazz, blues, C&W and pop.

Amongst the lengthy list of some who have helped shape his unique style can be numbered the following: Washboard Sam, Sonny Boy Williamson, Mahalia Jackson, Bud Powell, Joe Turner (the singer), Muddy Waters, Charles Brown, Hank Williams, Count Basie, and Nat Cole (both as singer and pianist).

Ray Charles Robinson (born Albany, Georgia, 1932) became totally blind at six, yet taught himself to play piano, organ, alto saxophone, clarinet and trumpet. Also learned to read and write music and make own arrangements (thanks to Braille) during this time at Florida school for deaf and blind. Left school to join dance band in mid-teens. Joined blues band of Lowell Fulsom (for a year), during which time he developed, vocally and pianistically. Played Apollo, alone, put together group to accompany singer Ruth Brown, then returned to Seattle where he had moved after leaving the dance-band. Put together another band for residency (it was sometimes known as Maxim Trio) and band achieved distinction of being first all-black unit to have sponsored TV show in Pacific Northwest.

Previously, in Seattle, Charles had formed a trio modelled closely on celebrated King Cole Trio, with leader's vocals often cast very much in Cole mold (in those days his style varied between Cole and Charles Brown), and between 1949-51 had recorded for Swingtime **(Ray Charles Blues)**. Recorded around 60 sides for the label, mostly unremarkable. With Swingtime's fortunes fading, Atlantic Records paid $2,500 for Charles' contract (1952).

Transformation from average-to-good R&B-based singer-pianist-composer was startling. By end of 1950s, Charles had notched up a string of huge-selling record hits, starting with **It Should've Been Me** (1953), and continuing with **I Got A Woman, Hallelujah, I Love Her So, A Fool For You, Drown In My Own Tears, Yes Indeed, Swanee River Rock, Night Time Is The Right Time, What'd I Say, Just For A Thrill** and **Don't Let The Sun Catch You Cryin' (A 25th Anniversary In Show Business Salute To Ray Charles)**. Each number delivered with maximum of emotional impact, Charles' impassioned singing supported by own gospel-jazz piano and a rough, exciting big band riffing furiously behind him.

Whilst recordings demonstrated just how genuinely exciting Ray Charles could be, it was with his in-person appearances that conclusive judgments could be made. The combination of the Charles voice and piano, a basic-sounding rhythm section, hard-hitting band and, from 1957 onwards, a gospel-based vocal group The Raelettes, tended to make his concerts seem reminiscent of a black church service, with Charles and vocal and band engaged in frantic call-and-response format, with audience adding its own presence in the manner of gospel congregation.

During his stay with Atlantic Charles' jazz proclivities were given full rein in albums specifically designed to show off this side of his talents. Most notable of these is a brace of non-vocal albums **(Soul Brothers** and **Soul Meeting)**, both of which conjoin Charles' instrumental talents (as accomplished pianist, and average, Parker-influenced, weak-toned altoist) with the consummate vibraharp artistry of Milt Jackson. Also on Atlantic is **The Great Ray Charles**, another all-instrumental LP, with Charles' piano accompanied by six-piece band, arranged by Quincy Jones and Ernie Wilkins, apart from two fine trio tracks **(Black Coffee** and **Sweet Sixteen Bars)** which, perhaps more than most of his recordings, admirably define Charles' gospel-based, bop-tinged jazz piano style.

Moving to ABC Paramount (1959), Charles' very first single release (an updating of **Georgia On My Mind**) was a hit, the first of numerous others for the label **(25th Anniversary In Show Business Salute To Ray Charles)** to feature, along with more conventional jazz/blues instrumentation, strings. Arranger for **Georgia** was Ralph Burns.

Over the years Charles has worked with numerous other top-rated jazz writers, including Marty Paich, Gerald Wilson, Gil Fuller, Quincy Jones and Ernie Wilkins. Paich supplied string scores for **Ray Charles & Betty Carter**, a superb, often moving collaboration between two artists both deserving to be called jazz singers, here framed in semi-jazz setting. The Charles-Carter idea was repeated three years after the first, and in many ways best, recording date ('61). After **Georgia** came more ABC hits: **Unchain My Heart, Hit The Road, Jack, One Mint Julep, I Can't Stop Loving You, You Are My Sunshine, Cryin' Time, Busted**, etc.

By this time he was featuring an ever-wider variety of material, including two award-winning albums in which he sang C&W songs **(Modern Sounds In Country & Western, Vols 1, 2** and **Together Again: Country & Western Meets Rhythm & Blues)** his own way. Better by far, though, were LPs like **Genius + Soul = Jazz**, wherein Charles (on organ, and singing only on two tracks) is brought together with the Count Basie orchestra (circa 1960), minus its leader, with superior charts from Jones and Burns.

During latter part of 1960s, and through until the present, Charles has continued to tour with own big band and singers. Left ABC Paramount to start own label (Crossover), which subsequently re-issued much of the Atlantic-ABC Paramount material.

Charles' health was not at its best at the end of the 1970s, helped not at all by addiction to heroin, a situation which led, at one period, to a jail sentence during which time he successfully took a cure. There is no doubt Ray Charles remains a vital and compelling performer, a genuine talent of real importance and continuing influence. In truth, though, there have been many occasions during the past decade when his music appears to have been stylized, and a series of inferior repetitions of the past. As a recording artist, for instance, he has been unable to recapture his almost magical appeal of the 1950s/1960s; and his concert appearances sometimes have given the impression of someone going through the motions, his heart not always completely into his music. There are occasions still, however, when the real Ray Charles is revealed, once again, as the musically charismatic personality who can put other rivals completely in the shade, seemingly without really trying.

Aural references to Charles' live recordings **(Ray Charles Live-The Great Concerts, Ray Charles At Newport** and **Genius Live In Concert)** give more than adequate proof of his in-person greatness in the past. And just how much his very presence can add extra fuel to an already raging inferno can be judged from his impromptu appearance (he was already in the audience, before being called onstage) during a magnificent Aretha Franklin concert—**Live At Fillmore West**.

Ray Charles, What'd I Say (courtesy Atlantic)—at his finest.

Albums:
Ray Charles, Ray Charles Blues (—/Ember)
The Genius Of Ray Charles (Atlantic/Atlantic)
Ray Charles, What'd I Say (Atlantic/Atlantic)
A 25th Anniversary Show Business Salute To Ray Charles (Atlantic/Atlantic)
Ray Charles At Newport (Atlantic/Atlantic)
Ray Charles/Milt Jackson, Soul Brothers (Atlantic/Atlantic)
Ray Charles/Milt Jackson, Soul Meeting (Atlantic/Atlantic)
Ray Charles Live-The Great Concerts (Atlantic/—)
Ray Charles, Genius + Soul = Jazz (Impulse/HMV)
The Great Ray Charles (Atlantic/London)
Ray Charles, The Genius After Hours (Atlantic/London)
Ray Charles, Modern Sounds In Country & Western, Vols 1, 2 (ABC-Paramount/HMV)
Ray Charles & Betty Carter (ABC-Paramount/Pathe Marconi—France)
Ray Charles, Genius Live In Concert (ABC-Paramount/Blues Way)
Ray Charles Sings The Blues (Atlantic)
Ray Charles, Sweet & Sour (ABC-Paramount/—)
Ray Charles, The World Of Ray Charles, Vols 1, 2 (Crossover/London)
Focus On Ray Charles (Crossover/London)
Ray Charles, Message To The People (Renaissance/Probe)
Friendship (CBS/Columbia)

Committed hard-bopper Tommy Chase, Drive (courtesy Paladin).

Tommy Chase

Aggressive British drummer and quartet leader Tommy Chase (born Worsely, Lancashire, 1947) has made a considerable contribution in Britain to the early '80s revival of interest in indigenous hard bop, particularly among the young generation. With an uncompromising line in self-promotion, and boundless energy for the music, Chase arrived in London in the early '70s. He led his own groups, recorded with saxophonist Ray Warleigh and accompanied many visiting Americans including Joe Albany, Jon Eardley, Al Haig and Red Rodney.

Strongly influenced by Art Blakey and Max Roach, Chase shares with Blakey a passion for undiscovered young talent. His regular line-up includes the Jackie McLean-influenced saxophonist Alan Barnes, bassist Alec Dankworth and Australian-born pianist Mark Fitzgibbon—all in their early-mid 20s.

Albums like his 1983 début **Hard!** and its follow-up **Drive!**, as their titles suggest, abrasively encapsulate his steam-rollering hard-bop aspirations delivered, at times, almost with venom. Chase's commitment is total.

Albums:
Hard! (—/Boplicity)
Drive! (—/Paladin)

Doc Cheatham

For more than 50 years, Adolphus Anthony 'Doc' Cheatham (born Nashville, Tennessee, 1905) has been a trumpet player of the first order, an accomplished soloist as well as a top-class lead, without ever achieving the kind of recognition his talents most certainly deserve.

Cheatham, taught trumpet and music theory by Prof. N. C. Davis, in his home town, has been associated mostly with big bands. For example, amongst others, he worked in the 1920s with large-size outfits led by Marion Hardy (his first job as a professional), Albert Wynn, Wilbur De Paris and Chick Webb.

In the following decade, Cheatham's trumpet was heard in such diverse outfits as McKinney's Cotton Pickers **(McKinney's Cotton Pickers, Vol 5: 1930-1931)**, Cab Calloway **(Cab Calloway & His Orchestra 1933-1934** and **16 Cab Calloway Classics)** Teddy Wilson **(Teddy Wilson & His Big Band 1939-1940)**. Spent the years 1933-39 with Calloway, making his second trip to Europe with that band (in '34)—his first had taken place in 1929, as member of Sam Wooding Band.

First gig of 1940s was with Benny Carter, with whom he recorded **My Favourite Blues (Benny Carter & His Orchestra: 1940-41)**, one of his infrequent solos, but one which emphasizes his elegant, poised and warm style.

Worked on record, for Commodore, as part of band backing Billie Holiday at famous 1944 date **(The 'Commodore' Days)**. Leader at that session was Eddie Heywood, for whom Cheatham was then playing trumpet **(Begin The Beguine)**. (Prior to Heywood, Cheatham had worked with Fletcher Henderson and Teddy Hill). Between 1952-55 worked with another fine small combo, led by Vic Dickenson.

Cheatham's reputation was internationalized when he made two further overseas trips, this time as member of the Wilbur De Paris New Orleans Band; first, in 1957, to Africa then, in '60, to Europe. In between these tours, came another European jaunt (in 1958) with pianist Sammy Price. Revisited African continent in 1960, touring with Herbie Mann's band. Member of the Benny Goodman Quintet/Sextet (1966-67). His trumpet regularly featured on showcase items like **When Sunny Gets Blue, I Can't Get Started** and **These Foolish Things**. Yet another trip to Europe—this time to Belgium—in August, '66, also with Goodman, to appear at Comblain-la-Tour Jazz Festival, live and on television. Same year was back in Europe with jazz package titled Top Brass, featuring several of the finest brassmen extant.

From early-1950s through 1960s, worked regularly in Afro-Cuban-styled bands, a genre in which he obviously feels at ease. The bands include: Marcelino Guerra, Perez Prado and Machito (various occasions, including Japanese tour in 1956).

During last decade, has continued to do most of the things he had performed so impeccably in previous decades—recording (including jazz and session work), TV, in big band and small groups alike. A most dependable sideman, whose own individual talents have been showcased thoroughly on one occasion only—a two-LP collection **(Adolphus 'Doc' Cheatham)**—and in sympathetic quartet setting, he produces consistently fine playing throughout. His superior ballad playing (eg **This Is All I Ask** and **That's All)** is complemented admirably by a selection of impressive up-tempo performances, all of

Below: Tennessee-born Adolphus Anthony 'Doc' Cheatham, for more than half a century an accomplished (oft-neglected) horn-player of distinction.

which demonstrates that, as a soloist, Doc Cheatham has been lamentably and unforgivably neglected during an otherwise wholly distinguished career. Perhaps the one other album which does full justice to his talents is **Shorty & Doc**, a delightfully unpretentious, easy-swinging set recorded in 1961, in company of another drastically underrated trumpet man, Harold 'Shorty' Baker. During his career, Cheatham has been heard on record also with Ma Rainey, Max Kaminsky, Pee Wee Russell, and Captain John Handy.

Albums:
McKinney's Cotton Pickers, Vol 5 (1930-1931) (RCA Victor—France)
Cab Calloway & His Orchestra 1933-1934 (RCA Victor—Germany)
Teddy Wilson & His Big Band 1939-1940 (Tax—Sweden)
Eddie Heywood, Begin The Beguine (Mainstream/Fontana)
Wilbur De Paris, That's A Plenty (Atlantic/London)
Wilbur De Paris, The Wild Jazz Age (Atlantic/London)
Juanita Hall Sings The Blues (Counterpoint/Society)
Shorty Baker/Doc Cheatham, Shorty & Doc (Prestige—Swingville/—)
Billie Holiday, Vol 1 (—/SagaPan)
Adolphus 'Doc' Cheatham (Jezebel/—)
Earl Hines, Swingin' Away (—/Black Lion)
Doc & Sammy (Sackville/—)
Hey Doc! (Black & Blue—France)
Buddy Tate, Jive At Five (Mahogany/—)
Sammy Price Five (Black & Blue—France)

Don Cherry

Born in Oklahoma City, 1936, the trumpeter played with orthodox groups before meeting Ornette Coleman in 1956, and falling completely under the influence of the altoist's revolutionary concepts. Cherry is present on all the classic Atlantics, the most compatible foil that the leader ever found. There are parallels for the sorcerer's apprentice role with the young Miles Davis in Charlie Parker's group; both trumpeters are tentative and at their best when restricting their ideas to ranges they can handle; both are most effective as an astringent contrast to their volcanic leaders. Cherry's sound on pocket trumpet is thin, his ideas fragmented and often inconclusive, and the impression is of a neurotic Boy Scout. Nevertheless, within the context of the music, his understanding of his leader's world is complete—contrapuntal numbers like **Mapa (Ornette On Tenor)** show his responsiveness. **Peace (Shape Of Jazz To Come)** displays his growing variety of method, and both **Face Of The Bass (Change Of The Century** and **WRU (Ornette!))** give him a chance to express himself before the leader has mapped out the melodic possibilities. Expressive but rhythmically weak, Cherry's early work is overshadowed by both Ornette and his own subsequent development.

Below: Don Cherry, restless explorer of a wealth of 'world music'.

Cherry left the group and tried out the lessons he had learned with a variety of giants. Sessions with Coltrane **(The Avant-garde)** and Rollins **(Our Man In Jazz)** followed, both proving that Cherry's concept was both lighter and more radical. **Cherryco**, for example, finds Coltrane unable to utilize the theme without resort to the chord changes. The collaboration with tenorist Albert Ayler proved more suitable, although the dense collective **New York Eye And Ear Control** lacks the coherence of **Free Jazz**. The album that they made together in Copenhagen, 1964 **(Vibrations)** catches both players at their best.

Lessons in organizing the New York Contemporary Five, members including Archie Shepp and altoist John Tchicai, between 1963-64, stood Cherry in good stead when he assembled his own group. Now based in Europe, he chose the young Argentinian tenorist, Leandro 'Gato' Barbieri, Henry Grimes on bass and Ed Blackwell drums. The two albums for Blue Note **(Complete Communion** and **Symphony For Improvisers)** are classics of the new music, rich in texture and melodic invention, offering a group empathy that holds the vast range of moods together. By now, Cherry possessed a formidable technique, and his lyrical gifts had been broadened by his travels and exposure to other ethnic musics. As a leader, shaping the direction of the group, his identity is as strongly imprinted as Ornette's was back in the old quartet days. His soloing over the massive Jazz Composers' Orchestra **(The Jazz Composers' Orchestra)** is spikily assured and attacking. However, increasingly there were signs that Cherry's fascination with other folk forms was leading him away from jazz; inevitable, perhaps, for non-harmonic new music has more in common with non-European idioms. The heavy emphasis on flutes and percussion make for an Eastern experience **(Eternal Rhythm)** and much of Cherry's subsequent work cannot be judged by Western 'Art Music' standards, for he seems to be aiming at a religious celebration. The duets with Ed Blackwell **(Mu, 1 & 2)** place him firmly within the jazz mainstream, and his trumpet playing here is angularly brilliant. A final composition **(Relatively Suite)** achieves a balance between his allegiances, from the Tibetan-sounding bells at the opening to the wild, jubilantly sung passage from Cherry.

In 1974, Don Cherry settled in Sweden, and although productive in the fields of schoolchildren's music and Eastern chant, it seemed unlikely that he would return to jazz. Always unpredictable, Cherry re-surfaced with two excellent albums **Don Cherry** and **Old & New Dreams**.

Nowadays, Cherry does not regard the trumpet as his primary instrument, ready to improvise on wood flutes, thumb piano, Balinese gongs, African hunter's harp, percussion, keyboards or voice. As such, Cherry has continued to explore his 'world music' themes into the '80s, notably in association with Codona—featuring Cherry with sitarist Collin Walcott and Brazilian percussionist Nana Vasconcelos. Their 1982 album **Codona 3** continues Cherry's world tour, taking in traditional Japanese music **(Goshakabuchi)**, passing through their idiosyncratic vocal and instrumental improvisations, even echoing the romance of the old American railroad **(Clicky Clacky)**. The death of Walcott in 1985 tragically and abruptly curtailed the creative collective voice Codona had been developing. A duet collaboration with percussionist Ed Blackwell in 1982 **(El Corazón)** is interesting for its reworking of Monk's **Bemsha Swing**.

Albums:
Ornette Coleman's Atlantic Albums (Atlantic/Atlantic)
The Avant-garde (Atlantic/Atlantic)
Our Man In Jazz (RCA Victor/RCA Victor)
New York Eye And Ear Control (ESP/ESP)
Vibrations (Arista-Freedom/Arista-Freedom)
New York Contemporary Five (Sonet/Sonet)
Complete Communion (Blue Note/Blue Note)
Symphony For Improvisers (Blue Note/Blue Note)
Jazz Composers' Orchestra (JCOA/JCOA Virgin)
Eternal Rhythm (BASF/BASF)
Mu, Parts 1 & 2 (—/BYG—France)
Relativity Suite (JCOA/JCOA Virgin)
Don Cherry (A&M/A&M)
Old & New Dreams (Black Saint/Black Saint)
Eternal Now (Sonet/Sonet)
Don Cherry—Live In Ankara (Sonet/Sonet)
Codona 3 (ECM/ECM)
Don Cherry-Ed Blackwell, El Corazón (ECM/ECM)

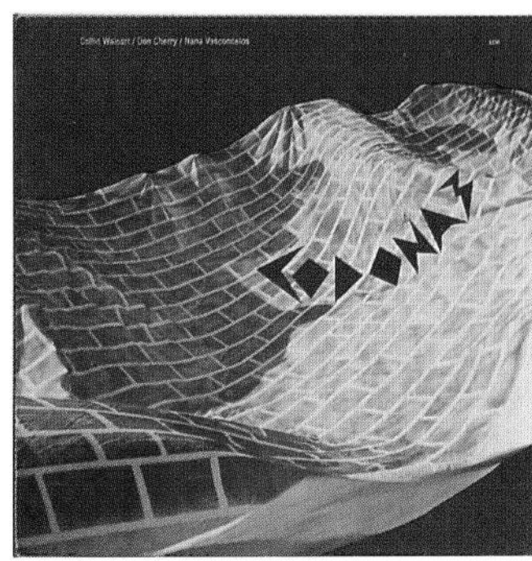

Codona 3 (courtesy ECM)—Cherry with Walcott and Vasconcelos.

Don Cherry-Ed Blackwell, El Corazón (courtesy ECM). Just one facet of an eclectic musician.

Chicago, 1984—the year their Chicago 17 album clocked up five million sales across the world. A remarkable cross-over success story for two decades.

Chicago

Formed in Chicago in 1968 (first as the Big Thing), they abridged their original name of Chicago Transit Authority to plain Chicago when they went to Los Angeles to work with producer James William Guercio. With their first album—called, simply, **Chicago**—they made a big impact on pop-oriented jazz-rock. They created an individual, if commercial, sound—an original jazz-blues approach laid over a funky base with an almost powerhouse big-band brass attack.

Throughout the '70s and '80s, Chicago released a string of singles successes from albums **Chicago**, **Chicago II**, **III**, **IV**, **V** (etc ever onwards), notably their first, the stunning **I'm A Man**, then **25 Or 6 To 4**, **Wishing You Were Here**, **If You Leave Me Now**, **Another Rainy Day In New York City**, **Baby What A Big Surprise**.

In 1985, mainstay bassist-vocalist Peter Cetera left the band just as remaining members (keyboardist Bobby Lamm, drummer Danny Seraphine, reeds-player Walt Parazaider, trumpeter Lee Loughnane, trombonist Jimmy Pankow and keyboardist-guitarist Bill

Champion) prepared to record their 18th album. Interestingly, the 1984 **Chicago 17** notched up five million international sales—their best seller to date—an extraordinary feat for a band whose initial success began in another age two decades earlier.

Albums:
Chicago (Columbia/CBS)
At Carnegie Hall (Columbia/CBS)
Chicago IX—Greatest Hits (Columbia/CBS)
Chicago 17 (Columbia/CBS)

Chicago 17 (courtesy CBS)—the band's best-seller to date.

Chicago IX (courtesy CBS)—compilation of their 'greatest hits'.

George Chisholm

George Chisholm (born Glasgow, Scotland, 1915) has been since the late-1930s probably the finest jazz trombonist produced in Britain. As early as 1936, Chisholm's worth as a technically assured, fiery player had been recognized by musicians outside the British Isles. It was in 1936 that Benny Carter, at that time living and playing in Holland, invited him to participate in a recording session which took place in that country, in company with the Dutch band the Ramblers **(Benny Carter With The Ramblers & His Orchestra)**. Chisholm's perky trombone was second only to Carter's immaculate playing in terms of solo success on that date. Same year, he recorded in company of another famous US jazzman, the great saxophonist Coleman Hawkins. And when Fats Waller visited London in 1939, during which time he undertook several recording engagements, George Chisholm's trombone was a welcome addition to the proceedings at one of these **(The Fats Waller Memorial Album)**.

Soloist and section man with bands of Teddy Joyce (1936), Ambrose (1938), BBC Showband (1952), Kenny Baxter (on numerous occasions), Jack Parnell (1959), and a participant at a special Hungarian relief fund London concert (1958, with Louis Armstrong headlining), Chisholm has attained a wide reputation during the past 15 years as a very funny man (which he is). Unfortunately, his natural flair for comedy often has obscured the fact that he remains a gifted trombonist who can deliver sensitive solos, in a 'serious' vein, with the best, as his playing on tracks like **Here's That Rainy Day, The Boy Next Door** and **Mood Indigo** (all **George Chisholm**) shows quite definitely.

Just how much he can add to the excitement of a live performance—inspiring those around him to give of their very best—can be judged further by his expressive playing as guest at a concert by the Alex Welsh Band **(An Evening With Alex Welsh)**. And his ability to more than hold his own in distinguished company is manifestly displayed within the grooves of **Wild Bill Davison With The Freddy Randall Band**.

Albums:
George Chisholm (—/Rediffusion)
Benny Carter With The Ramblers & His Orchestra (Decca—France)
The Fats Waller Memorial Album (—/Encore)
Various, British Jazz, Vols 1, 2 (—/BBC Records)
Various, Swingin' Britain—The Thirties (—/Decca)
George Chisholm, Jazz Today—Tribute To Benny Carter (—/Jazz Today)
An Evening With Alex Welsh (—/Black Lion)
Wild Bill Davison With Freddy Randall & His Band (—/Black Lion)

Charlie Christian

Guitarist Charlie Christian was, along with Thelonious Monk, Charlie Parker, Dizzy Gillespie and Kenny Clarke, one of the pioneers of bebop. Some of the earliest bop recordings from 1941 find Christian already into his mature style, single note runs and complex chord changes **(The Harlem Jazz Scene)**. Also present are Monk and Clarke and a Dizzy Gillespie still divided between his early influence, Roy Eldridge, and the new developments. **Swing To Bop** shows his intensely rhythmic use of riff, and throughout his blues feeling on the comparatively new instrument, the electric guitar, shows the influence of his Texas and Oklahoma upbringing. In 1939, he joined the Benny Goodman Sextet, and his profound influence on that unit, as well as future generations of guitarists, is shown on **A Smo-o-o-oth One** and **Seven Come Eleven**. **Solo Flight** features the guitarist riding the Goodman Orchestra **(Charlie Christian With The Benny Goodman Sextet & Orchestra)**. Born in 1919, Christian died of tuberculosis in 1942.

Albums:
Harlem Jazz Scene, 1941 (Esoteric/Society)
Charlie Christian With The Benny Goodman Sextet & Orchestra (Columbia/Realm)

Charlie Christian Live! (courtesy Jazz Archive—with Goodman's 1940 sextet.

June Christy

Born Shirley Luster in Springfield, Illinois, on November 20, 1925, 'the misty Miss Christy'—like her Kenton counterparts Anita O'Day and Chris Connor—has enjoyed a revival of interest in the late '70s-early '80s. Their early records have sold particularly well in recent years; notably in the United Kingdom where jazz vocals have enjoyed a latter-day vogue.

As early as 13 she was singing with a local band and worked with society bands around Chicago, including Boyd Raeburn's (in his pre-jazz days), Benny Storey's and Denny Beckner's. Internationally acclaimed as the vocalist with Stan Kenton's orchestra, she replaced Anita O'Day in 1945. When Kenton's band broke up in the late '40s, she worked as a solo throughout the '50s, usually with piano accompanist Jimmy Lyon. She occasionally toured with reunited Kenton line-ups and made some superb albums with bands led by her husband Bob Cooper and Pete Rugolo, sometimes (to no detriment) with strings.

Christy went into semi-retirement in the late '60s, working occasionally in Los Angeles and San Francisco, although 1985 saw her welcome return to the international festival circuit. An impressive compilation of June Christy's solo work with Rugolo and Cooper was issued by Affinity in the UK in 1986 **(The Best Thing For You)**.

Albums:
Artistry In Rhythm (Capitol/Capitol)
The Misty Miss Christy (Capitol/Capitol)
The Song Is June (Capitol/Capitol)
Those Kenton Days (Capitol/Capitol)
Cool School (Capitol/Capitol)
Something Cool (Capitol/Capitol)
June Christy-Bob Cooper, Impromptu (Sea Breeze/—)
The Best Thing For You (—/Affinity)

The 'Misty Miss Christy', The Best Thing For You (courtesy Affinity).

Stanley Clarke

Bassist Stanley Clarke, like drummer Anthony Williams, was something of a teenage prodigy, playing with Horace Silver at 18.

Born Philadelphia on June 30, 1951, Clarke was encouraged to study violin and cello. As he got older, and his hands grew too large for the violin and his legs grew too long to sit at the cello (he stands well over six feet tall), he took up classical bass. Through junior and senior high school, he played with local R&B and rock bands and was part of the All-Philadelphia Musical Academy for three and a half years, majoring in string bass. Clarke's musical tastes span rock, jazz and classical—listing as his early influences Mingus, Paul Chambers, Scott La Faro, Ron Carter, Richard Davis, Jimi Hendrix, James Brown, Motown, Bach, Wagner and Stravinsky.

He arrived in New York late '70 gaining valuable experience with Horace Silver, Stan Getz, Art Blakey, Dexter Gordon, Thad Jones-Mel Lewis, Gil Evans, Joe Henderson and Pharoah Sanders. Late in 1971, Clarke met Chick Corea and early '72 joined Corea's Return To Forever. He made his reputation with Return To Forever, the unusual amount of elbow-room in the group's approach giving him plenty of solo space. Any of their albums **(Hymn To The 7th Galaxy, Light As A Feather, Where Have I Known You Before** and **No Mystery)** illustrate the subtle interaction between the musicians.

In 1976, Clarke launched on a solo career. One of his most interesting projects was the half-studio/half-live album **I Wanna Play For You** in the late '70s. Studio guest stars included saxophonists Tom Scott and Stan Getz, trumpeter Freddie Hubbard, guitarist Lee Ritenour, keyboardists George Duke, Ronnie Foster and Bayete Todd Cochran, drummers Harvey Mason and Steve Gadd, percussionist Airto, singer Dee Dee Bridgewater and vocal trio Hot plus special guest Jeff Beck. The live side was recorded at 1977 dates in Los Angeles and Long Island.

Clarke's albums under his own name **(Stanley Clarke, Journey To Love** and **School Days)** commute between jazz and rock with astonishing passages of near-flamenco classical like **Spanish Phases For Strings & Bass (Stanley Clarke)** and multi-tracked vocal on **Just A Game (School Days)**. More recently, Clarke has been involved with keyboardist George Duke on the Clarke-Duke project. Superstar publicity has both inflated and detracted from his real status as a fine musician.

Albums:
Return To Forever (ECM/ECM)
Hymn To The 7th Galaxy (Polydor/Polydor)
Light As A Feather (Polydor/Polydor)
Where Have I Known You Before (Polydor/Polydor)
No Mystery (Polydor/Polydor)
The Romantic Warrior (Columbia/CBS)
Stanley Clarke (Atlantic/Atlantic)
Journey To Love (Atlantic/Atlantic)
School Days (Atlantic/Atlantic)

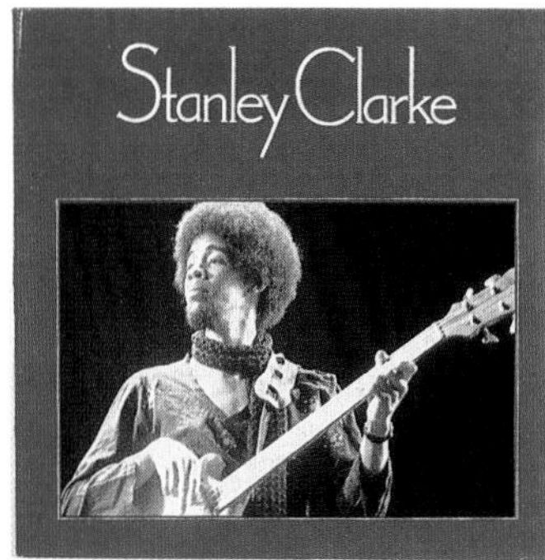

Stanley Clarke (courtesy Atlantic) —commuting between jazz and rock.

Buck Clayton

Wilbur 'Buck' Clayton (born Parsons, Kansas, 1911) has had the kind of distinguished career that should be the envy of most, if not all jazz musicians. Started on piano, aged six, switched to trumpet at 16, taking lessons from his father who played trumpet and tuba. Worked in several non-musical jobs on West Coast before returning to Kansas for completion of high school studies. Went back to Los Angeles to work with several local bands, before leading a 14-piece band, which later was heard by Teddy Weatherford who arranged for its residency in Shanghai. After which, Clayton led another big band in Los Angeles (1936), and his career really began to take shape when he rejoined Count Basie late '36. Since then has continued to demonstrate a consistency in performance that few other jazz trumpeters have matched.

Buck Clayton's first recordings, made in 1937, illustrate the kind of warm, delicate and relaxed swing that marks his playing at all times, as well as showcasing his basic all-round technique. A technique that is much influenced by Louis Armstrong, coupled with much of the sensitivity and lyricism of Joe Smith. Those early recordings—as well as soloist-accompanist on dates featuring Billie Holiday—also demonstrate that by this time Clayton's approach to trumpet was more or less formulated.

Over the years, with slight adjustments here and there, that style has remained virtually unchanged. His elegance of phrase and undeniable rhythmic powers added considerably to Basie-Holiday recordings of '37 (and indeed, for both, thereafter). In addition, his astute use of various mutes, pleasingly evidenced on tracks like **Honeysuckle Rose** (briefly) and **Swinging At The Daisy Chain** further enhanced his growing reputation. Subsequent studio-made Basie-Clayton recordings **(The Best Of Count Basie, Jumpin' At The Woodside, You Can Depend On Basie, The Great Count Basie & His Orchestra, Super Chief, The Lester Young Story, Vol 3** and **Count Basie)** were to produce even more memorable Clayton trumpet work.

Of many consistently fine solos which Clayton delivered during his tenure with Basie, following must rank with the best: **Smarty, Swingin' The Blues, Jumpin' at The Woodside, Time Out, Topsy, Doggin' Around** and **Fiesta In Blue,** plus two Basie sextet items, **Bugle Blues** and **Royal Garden Blues**. One should not forget Clayton's exquisite playing on tracks featuring blues singer Jimmy Rushing **(Blues I Love To Sing)** including **Good Morning Blues, Sent For You Yesterday & Here You Come Today, Blues In The Dark, Boo-Hoo** and **How Long Blues**. And there is potent evidence of Clayton's in-person abilities—with Basie, and sometimes with Rushing—from available airchecks of band and singer in late-1930s **(Count Basie At The Savoy Ballroom 1937, William & The Famous Door** and **The Count At The Chatterbox 1937)**.

Clayton's sensitive contributions added an extra dimension to numerous Billie Holiday record dates, especially from this period. In 1937, for instance, he made particularly significant contributions to such individual titles as **This Year's Kisses, Why Was I Born?, Mean To Me (The Lester Young Story, Vol 1)** and **He's Funny That Way (The Lester Young Story, Vol 2)**.

In '38, as a member of a Lester Young-led pianoless Kansas City Six, Clayton produced some of his most expressive solo work **(Lester Young & The Kansas City Five** *(sic)***)**, nowhere better illustrated than on **Pagin' 'The Devil'** and **I Want A Little Girl**. Young-Clayton partnership also produced memorable results at subsequent reunions **(Spirituals To Swing** and, especially, **Lester Young Leaps Again!)**.

Although hardly a typical Jazz At The Philharmonic representative, even in this pot-boiling atmosphere he never lost his poise and innate good taste **(Jazz At The Philharmonic 1946, Vol 2)** by which time Clayton not only had left Basie, but also had completed period of service in US Army.

Since World War II he has toured with JATP (just under two years), appeared as featured soloist in all manner of pick-up groups, and has led succession of invariably top-class units, basically comprising mid-period jazzmen.

Clayton too has been prime mover in organized jam sessions on record, made possible with advent of LP record. Majority of these, starting in 1953, were recorded for American Columbia label. Probably most celebrated is **Buck Clayton Jam Session** comprising two extended tracks **(The Hucklebuck** and **Robbins Nest)**, and including series of solos—some brilliant, some ordinary—from such as Urbie Green, Henderson Chambers, Joe Newman, Julian Dash, Sir Charles Thompson and, of course, Clayton himself. Jam sessions tended to vary in terms of artistic and creative success, depending upon chosen musicians; **The Golden Days Of Jazz: Swingin' Buck Clayton Jams Count Basie & Benny Goodman** exemplifies the kind of magnificent-plus-mundane results which have emanated from similar Clayton-sponsored recorded jam sessions. One such recording that did produce mostly superior music was **Buck Clayton Band,** which teamed Clayton with fellow trumpeter Ruby Braff. Pair struck sparks off each other, inspiring rest of eight-piece band to give of individual and collective best. Clayton's own favorite jam session recording is **Songs For Swingers** dating from 1958, which also contains splendid tenor saxophone playing by another Basie alumnus, Buddy Tate. Earlier same year, Clayton contributed mightily to a Tate album date **Swinging Like . . . Tate!**, and earlier same month, shone brightly at two other mainstream dates, those fronted, respectively, by Coleman Hawkins **(The High & Mighty Hawk)** and Dicky Wells **(Trombone Four In Hand)**.

In more recent times Buck Clayton was forced to give up playing trumpet completely, due to stomach, lip and hernia ailments. However, he has not ceased to be involved with jam session events. Indeed, he has produced several recordings in past few years, involving even wider range of musicians and styles. His enforced retirement from playing has, of necessity, thrown spotlight on to an area of his talent that too often has gone unnoticed: composing and arranging. As member of Basie band, produced string of commendable charts (including **H&J, Down For Double, It's Sand, Man** and **Taps Miller)**. Has also written for bands of Duke Ellington and Harry James.

Since 1950s his uncomplicated compositions/arrangements have appeared at more regular intervals. After most recent efforts in this direction, including **Buck Clayton Jam Session, Vols 1, 2/Buck Clayton Jam Session**, his writing (as well as his playing) has contributed handsomely to fine music found on more than one album by Humphrey Lyttelton band. Best of these probably is **Le Vrai Buck Clayton, Vol 2**. His talents as soloist, accompanist, composer, arranger and leader are encapsulated equally impressively throughout 1961 live double-LP collection reissued in its entirety during recent past **(Buck Clayton & Jimmy Witherspoon Live In Paris)**. In all these areas of music-making Buck Clayton has been, for around 50 years, a real credit to the world of jazz—and unquestionably he remains one of its most professional as well as important contributors.

Below: Ex-Count Basie trumpeter Buck Clayton—his playing transcends stylistic categories and has brought him a career with many highlights.

Albums:
Count Basie, Swinging At The Daisy Chain (—/Coral)
Count Basie, Jumpin' At The Woodside (Brunswick/Coral)
Count Basie, You Can Depend On Basie (—/Coral)
The Best Of Count Basie (MCA Coral—Germany)
The Great Count Basie & His Orchestra (Joker—Italy)
Count Basie, Super Chief (Columbia/CBS)
Jimmy Rushing, Blues I Love To Sing (Brunswick/Ace of Hearts)
Count Basie At The Savoy Ballroom 1937 (Saga)
Count Basie & His Orchestra (Trip)/William & The Famous Door (DJM)
Count Basie, The Count At The Chatterbox 1937 (Jazz Archives)
Lester Young & The Kansas City 5 (*sic*) (Mainstream/Stateside)
Various, John Hammond's Spirituals To Swing (Vanguard/Vanguard)
Lester Young, Lester Young Leaps Again! (EmArcy/Fontana)
Various, Jazz At The Philharmonic 1946, Vol 2 (Verve)
A Buck Clayton Jam Session (Columbia/CBS—Realm)
Swingin' Buck Clayton Jams Count Basie & Benny Goodman (CBS)
Buck Clayton Band (Vanguard/Vanguard)
Buck Clayton, Songs For Swingers (Columbia/Columbia)
Buddy Tate, Swinging Like . . . Tate! (Felsted/Felsted)
Coleman Hawkins, The High & Mighty Hawk (Felsted/Felsted)
Dicky Wells, Trombone Four In Hand (Felsted/Felsted)
Buck Clayton/Buddy Tate, Kansas City Nights (Prestige/—)
Various, Tootin' Through The Roof, Vol 2 (Onyx/Polydor)
Nat Pierce, Jam Session At The Savoy (RCA Victor—France)
Buck Clayton Jam Session, Vols 1, 2 (Chiaroscuro)/Buck Clayton Jam Sessions (Vogue)
Jimmy Rushing, Who Was It Who Sang That Song (Master Jazz Recordings/—)
Buck Clayton & Jimmy Witherspoon Live In Paris (Vogue)
Buck Clayton, Jazz Party Time (Chiaroscuro)/ Jam Sessions, Vol 2 (Vogue)
One For Buck (World Record Club)
The Lester Young Story, Vols 1-3 (Columbia/CBS)
Buck Clayton/Roy Eldridge, Trumpet Summit (Pumpkin/—)

Buck Clayton Jam Sessions (courtesy Vogue)—includes The Hucklebuck.

Arnett Cobb

Arnett Cleophus Cobb (born Houston, Texas, 1918) is one of a long breed of Texan musicians whose hard-booting, highly-extrovert tenor saxophone playing has for many years become an integral part of jazz. Studied piano with grand-mother as youngster, moved on to violin, trumpet, C-melody sax before turning, finally, to tenor sax.

First professional work (aged 15) with band of drummer Frank Davis. Spent two years (1934-36) with another territorial band, that of Chester Boone. 1936: joined new outfit, put together by Milton Larkin (like Boone a trumpeter). Cobb stayed until 1942, when he moved on to Lionel Hampton. With Hampton, Cobb's became a familiar name, his exciting solos on feature items like **Flying Home No 2 (The Best Of Lionel Hampton)** and **Overtime (Steppin' Out: Lionel Hampton, Vol 2: 1942-1944)** adding considerably to solo strength of band, and making Cobb more than adequate replacement for departed Illinois Jacquet. 1947: left Hampton to put together own band.

Cobb's 1947 recordings with this six-piece band (for Apollo) **(The Fabulous Apollo Sessions)** demonstrate, most convincingly, that he was not just a wild, frenetic big-band blower, with little or nothing to say of any constructive consequence. At the same time, excitement engendered by his playing on titles like **Go, Red, Go, Top Flight** and **Big League Blues**, proved he had lost none of his ability to produce genuinely exciting performances. Also, these tracks were to leave an indelible mark on R&B music scene in general, then and later. 1948: Cobb forced to disband because of recurring back trouble, resulting in operation. Could not resume work until 1950 when he introduced new band. Again, though, career was interrupted by car crash (1956), resulting in serious injuries.

Emergence of soul jazz during late-1950s/early-1960s meant that, for a time, Cobb's masculine tenor sound was back in favor—certainly on record. For Prestige, for instance, he made a stack of always vitally swinging albums, with generally interesting selection of studio colleagues including Eddie 'Lockjaw' Davis, Wild Bill Davison **(Blow, Arnett, Blow!)**, Coleman Hawkins, Buddy Tate **(Very Saxy)**, Red Garland **(Sizzlin')** and Ray Bryant **(Party Time)**. And to show he could still handle ballads in prescribed fashion, he produced masterful readings of **Willow, Weep For Me, Blue & Sentimental** and **P.S. I Love You**, during admirable low-key date **(Ballads By Cobb)**.

Cobb's club work has continued since 1960s, although periods of ill-health have meant further interruptions to career. However, made first trip to Europe in 1973, as part of all-star package show. Following year, played Dunkirk Jazz Festival, returning in '75 with Milt Buckner's band, with whom he essayed a more formal European tour. These days, records by Arnett Cobb are conspicuous by their rarity. Certainly, though, there is much joyous, free-blowing music to be heard on **Jazz At Town Hall, Vol 1** with Cobb and Buckner being supported by drummer Panama Francis, and Illinois Jacquet.

Celebrated tenorist Arnett Cobb, The Fabulous Apollo Sessions (courtesy Vogue).

Albums:

The Best Of Lionel Hampton (—/MCA Coral—Germany)
Steppin' Out: Lionel Hampton, Vol 2 (1942-1944) (—/MCA—Germany)
Arnett Cobb, The Fabulous Apollo Sessions (Vogue—France)
Arnett Cobb, Blow, Arnett, Blow! (Prestige/—)
Arnett Cobb, Very Saxy (Prestige/Prestige)
Arnett Cobb, Sizzlin' (Prestige)
Arnett Cobb, Ballads By Cobb (Prestige—Moodsville)
Arnett Cobb/Illinois Jacquet, Jazz At Town Hall, Vol 1 (JRC/—)
Arnett Cobb & His Mob (Phoenix Jazz/—)

Billy Cobham's Glass Menagerie, Smokin' (courtesy Elektra Musician).

Billy Cobham

Essentially self-taught, Billy Cobham is probably the most influential jazz-rock percussionist of the late '60s-early '70s, developing a unique propulsive style and sound which seemed to test the limits of human endurance. Perched behind a towering multiple drumkit, Cobham didn't 'warm up', he just exploded in an intense electrical storm of rhythms and sound delivered at breakneck speed.

Born in Panama on May 16, 1944, Cobham was influenced from an early age by local carnival music, marches and parades. In 1950, aged 8, his family moved to Brooklyn, New York. In the mid-'60s, he gained early experience with the Jazz Samaritans, Grover Washington Jr, Billy Taylor and the New York Jazz Sextet before receiving wider recognition with Horace Silver in '68. He co-founded the short-lived but influential fusion band Dreams ('69-'70) and contributed to Miles Davis' **Bitches Brew** experiments.

In 1971, he became an inspirational member of John McLaughlin's Mahavishnu Orchestra **(The Inner Mounting Flame, Birds Of Fire, Between Nothingness And Eternity)**. With Mahavishnu, he astounded audiences with his fast and furious barrage of sound delivered in mind-scrambling time signatures, creating apocalyptic crescendos, and his almost empathetic duetting with guitarist McLaughlin. In 1974, he released his first solo album, **Spectrum**, a studio project featuring rock guitarist Tommy Bolin.

He has worked with his own groups since '76, notably Glass Menagerie, and briefly formed an association with keyboardist George Duke. Cobham is also a formidable figure in jazz education—there's 'standing room only' for his entertaining and enlightening drum clinics.

Albums:

Mahavishnu Orchestra, Between Nothingness And Eternity (Columbia/CBS)
Spectrum (Atlantic/Atlantic)
Crosswinds (Atlantic/Atlantic)
Total Eclipse (Atlantic/Atlantic)
Live On Tour In Europe (Atlantic/Atlantic)
Magic (Columbia/CBS)
Billy Cobham Live: Flight Time (—/Sandra)
Glass Menagerie, Observations & (Elektra Musician/Elektra Musician)
Smokin' (Elektra Musician/Elektra Musician)
Power Play (GRP/GRP)

Al Cohn

Born 1925 in Brooklyn, tenor player Al Cohn, in company with Stan Getz, Allen Eager, Brew Moore and Zoot Sims, was initially influenced by Lester Young. Early performances in this idiom **(Brothers & Other Mothers)** featured Cohn with Getz and Sims, and in quartet performances with pianist George Wallington. A busy professional writer and arranger, Cohn's appearances on record have been infrequent, though his compositions—**The Goof And I**, for example, written for Serge Chaloff—often turn up in the jazz repertoire. Big band experience with Woody Herman, Buddy Rich and Artie Shaw gave him a robust, hard swinging sound, and in recent years a Rollins influence has flavored his style. Usually associated with tenor player Zoot Sims, much of his best work has been in that two-tenor relationship, both men hewing to a swinging, melodic and infinitely cheerful approach **(Zootcase, Body & Soul** and **Motoring Along)**. They turn up together in a Miles Davis unit of 1953 **(Dig)**, playing Cohn originals like **Tasty Pudding**. A witty, reliable musician, Cohn's rare albums under his own name **(Play It Now)** are a guaranteed delight.

In recent years, Cohn has often been found in the company of his son Joe, an excellent jazz guitarist—1982's **Overtones** being their first record date together.

Albums:

The Brothers & Other Mothers (Savoy/Savoy)
Zoot Sims, Zootcase (Prestige/Prestige)
Al Cohn-Zoot Sims, Body & Soul (Muse/—)
Motoring Along (Sonet/Sonet)
Al Cohn, Play It Now (Xanadu/—)
Miles Davis, Dig (Prestige/Prestige)
Overtones (Concord/Concord)
Standards Of Excellence (Concord/Concord)

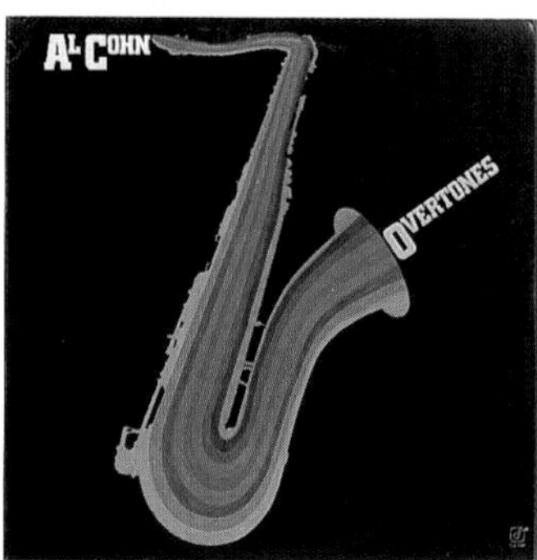

Al Cohn, Overtones (courtesy Concord) — features his guitarist son Joe.

Cozy Cole

William Randolph 'Cozy' Cole (born East Orange, New Jersey, 1909) took up drums and studied music at an early age (two brothers later became professional pianists) before Cole family moved to New York City. First drummed professionally, in late teens, with Wilbur Sweatman, then led own band.

Début on records with Jelly Roll Morton **(Jelly Roll Morton & His Red Hot Peppers: 1927-1930, Vol 1)** in 1930. Worked with orchestra of Blanche Calloway (1931-32), then with string of first-rate bands—Benny Carter, Willie Bryant **(Willie Bryant/Jimmie Lunceford & Their Orchestras)**; Stuff Smith **(Stuff Smith & His Onyx Club Orchestra)** and Cab Calloway.

With Smith, Cole produced some of his finest small-group drumming from this earlier period in his career; with Calloway, with whom he was mainstay of rhythm section between 1938-42, probably his best big-band playing **(Chu Berry Featured With Cab Calloway: 'Penguin Swing', 1937-1941** and **16 Cab Calloway Classics)**, latter containing no less than three excellent drum features for Cole: **Paradiddle, Ratamacue** and **Crescendo In Drums**; each satisfyingly integrated within framework of big-band arrangements.

Apart from brief spell with Raymond Scott ('42), Cole worked for a year as CBS staffman, taking time off to lead own band on 52nd Street. Also featured in Broadway musicals *Carmen Jones* (1954) and *Seven Lively Arts* (1946).

Recorded series of fine sides in 1944, featuring Coleman Hawkins and Cole, with fine Earl Hines piano at one Hawkins-led session **(Swing!** and **Cattin')**. Further Cole-led sessions (with Hawkins, and others), late '44, resulted in equally fine music, with Cole's firm, yet never overpowering beat one of several plus factors **(Jazz 44)**. Early 1945: Cole took part in important embryonic bop record session, together with Charlie Parker and Dizzy Gillespie **(Dizzy Gillespie: The Small Groups: 1945-1946)**. Briefly with Benny Goodman (1946), but mostly engaged in studio work between 1946-48. Fronted own combos, 1948-49, before joining Louis Armstrong All Stars (early '49) **(Louis Armstrong: July 4, 1900—July 6, 1971** and **Louis Armstrong At The Pasadena)**. Appeared in film *Glenn Miller Story*, with Armstrong. Was regular at New York's Metropole during 1950s.

As well as other film appearances, Cole played on the soundtrack of *The Strip* in '51 starring Mickey Rooney.

Started drum tuition school with close friend Gene Krupa, and participated in splendid Henry 'Red' Allen record date ('57) **(Greatest Of The Small Bands, Vol 5)**. Achieved sudden, unexpected commercial success when two-sided single disc, **Topsy**, an old Basie number, became million-selling hit (1958): **Topsy 1** ('A' side) reached US Top 30; then, **Topsy 2** ('B' side) went as high as third place in the charts.

Toured Europe with Jack Teagarden-Earl Hines All Stars (1957). After success with **Topsy** Cole toured with own band for a time; then, it was back to studio and club work. Toured Africa (1962-63) with own band. Since then has kept active in most areas of those spheres in which he has been a regular participant, including productive stint as member of quintet led by Jonah Jones.

Albums:

Jelly Roll Morton & His Red Hot Peppers (1927-1930) (RCA Victor—France)
Stuff Smith & His Onyx Club Orchestra (Collector's)
16 Cab Calloway Classics (CBS—France)
Chu Berry Featured With Cab Calloway: 'Penguin Swing', 1937-1941 (Jazz Archives)
The Complete Lionel Hampton (RCA Victor)/ Lionel Hampton's Best Records, Vols 1, 2, 3, 5, 6 (RCA Victor—France)
Various, The Panassie Sessions 1938 (RCA Victor—France)
Willie Bryant/(Jimmie Lunceford) & Their Orchestras (Bluebird/—)
Chu Berry, Chew, Choo, Chu & Co. (RCA Victor—France)
Coleman Hawkins, Swing! (Fontana)
Coleman Hawkins, Cattin' (Fontana)
Various, The Greatest Of The Small Bands, Vol 5 (RCA Victor—France)
Dizzy Gillespie; The Small Groups (1945-1946) (Phoenix)
(Pete Johnson)/Cozy Cole, All Star Swing Groups (Savoy/Savoy)
Louis Armstrong: July 4, 1900—July 6, 1971 (RCA Victor/RCA Victor)
Louis Armstrong At The Pasadena (Decca/Coral)
Jazz Giants: Cozy Cole/Red Norvo (Trip/—)
Cozy Cole & His Orchestra (Love/London)
Earl Hines-Cozy Cole (Felsted/Felsted)

Nat 'King' Cole, Trio Days (courtesy Affinity)—classic tracks.

Nat King Cole

Nat King Cole, usually associated with the romantic vocal, was one of the finest jazz piano players of the 1940s. Born in Alabama, 1919, he was initially influenced by Earl Hines, but soon developed his own distinctive style. An excellent compilation of his trios from 1944-49 illustrates the logic of his improvisational gifts **(Trio Days)**, while an album with trumpeter Charlie Shavers and tenor player Herbie Haymer from 1945, alternate takes and all, gives a wonderful sense of music in the making **(Anatomy Of A Jam Session)**. Classic trio performances by Lester Young, Cole and Buddy Rich originally billed the pianist as Aye Guy for contractual reasons **(The Genius Of Lester Young)**. His work in the turbulent JATP atmosphere accompanying tenor players Illinois Jacquet and Jack McVea can be found on a compilation of concerts **(Jazz At The Philharmonic 1944-46)**. At the start of the '50s, Cole's success as a singer drew him away from jazz; he died in 1965.

Albums:
King Cole Trio, Trio Days (Capitol/—)
Anatomy Of A Jam Session (Black Lion/Black Lion)
The Genius Of Lester Young (Verve/Verve)
Jazz At The Philharmonic 1944-46 (Verve/Verve)
Trio Days (—/Affinity)

Richie Cole

The personable and irrepressible Richie Cole is a colorful character among the new generation of bebop-inspired alto-players, notably through his lively presentations with Alto Madness.

His earlier career includes stints playing lead alto for the Buddy Rich Band and soloing with Lionel Hampton's orchestra. Cole's Alto Madness is not so much a 'group' but more an ongoing showcase for his breezy style around a constantly shifting personnel. (The columns of Alto Madness assured wide exposure, for instance, for the formidable talents of pianist Bobby Enriques and guitarist Bruce Forman, particularly on tour in Europe.)

Performances with Alto Madness reveal Cole's extraordinary talent for exploring the alto's high register, an entertaining leaning towards showmanship and a jaunty taste in hats. Notable contributors have brought a diversity of styles, including vocalist Eddie Jefferson, Manhattan Transfer and Tom Waits **(Hollywood Madness**, recorded 1979, just two weeks before Jefferson's death). In 1980, Cole teamed up with Phil Woods (an altoist much after his own heart and spirit) for **Side By Side**, Cole responding gleefully to the 'competition'. He's also on record with Ben Sidran-Mark Murphy, Freddie Hubbard **(Back To Birdland)** and Art Pepper **(Richie Cole And . . .)**.

Cole refuses to acknowledge 'musical barriers' and will speak of an ambitious concerto combining Alto Madness with Aaron Copland's American classical music in the same breath as mentioning a project of 'fusionating country music' with Boots Randolph. With Cole's open mind, enthusiasm and eclectic approach, anything's possible.

Albums:
Hollywood Madness (Muse/—)
Freddie Hubbard, Back To Birdland (Real Time/—)
Richie Cole And . . . (Art Pepper) (Palo Alto/—)
Alto Annie's Theme (Palo Alto/—)

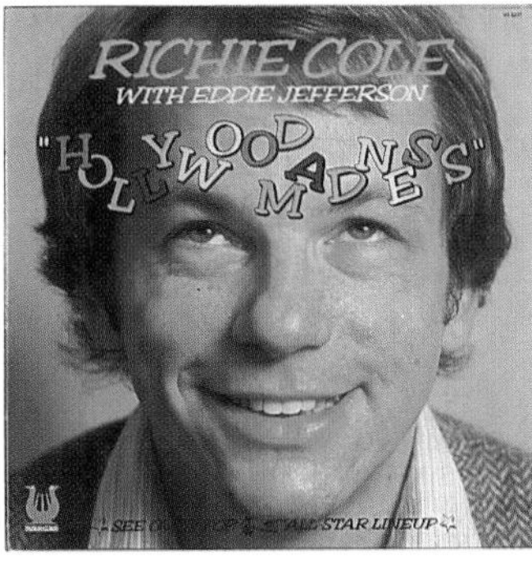

Richie Cole with Eddie Jefferson, Hollywood Madness (courtesy Muse).

George Coleman

For years in criminal danger of being underrated, the inestimable tenorist George Coleman appeared as a compelling sideman in the late '50s and has continued to perpetuate a gritty, undiminished hard-bop style with his own groups well into the '80s.

Born in Memphis on March 8, 1935, his first touring job was at 17 with B. B. King's blues band in the early '50s. He worked in Chicago at age 21 with Ira Sullivan, John Gilmore and Bill Lee. Moving to New York in the late '50s resulted in stints with Max Roach and Slide Hampton. In early '63, he joined the Miles Davis Quintet (the first permanent tenorist since Coltrane's departure) contributing to Miles' **Seven Steps To Heaven** and **My Funny Valentine**. In the mid-'60s, he worked with Lionel Hampton, Lee Morgan and Shirley Scott, toured with Elvin Jones and featured in Cedar Walton's Eastern Rebellion line-up ('75).

He formed his classic octet in '74 which has incorporated such challenging company as fellow saxophonists Frank Strozier, Junior Cook and Sal Nistico. In 1984, he recorded a live quartet album at the Village Vanguard for the Theresa label with pianist Harold Mabern, bassist Jamil Nasser and drummer Idris Muhammed.

A great favorite at festivals and on the club circuit, his ballad-playing on standards like **Body And Soul** are anticipated with delight. Steaming into more uptempo mode, Coleman can still raise the roof with his masterful, blues-edged fat-tenor sound and technique.

Below: 'Big George' Coleman—a powerful saxophonist who never fails to deliver. His influence has extended to a new generation of tenor-players.

Albums:
Miles Davis, Seven Steps To Heaven (Columbia/CBS)
Miles Davis, My Funny Valentine (Columbia/CBS)
Elvin Jones, Poly-Currents (Blue Note/Blue Note)
Big George (Catalyst/Affinity)

Ornette Coleman

Born 1930 in Texas, Ornette Coleman was a largely self-taught musician, and by the age of 14 he was playing with carnival and R&B bands around the Fort Worth area. In the main, the jazz fraternity put him down as harmonically incompetent—not surprisingly, since he was groping towards the most radical innovation that jazz had yet experienced, a revolution that was to de-throne harmony. 'It was when I noticed that I was making mistakes that I realized that I was on the track of something.' By 1954 had most of his style together, and by 1956 a small group of musicians emphatic enough to provide the necessary context. Nevertheless, these were hungry years, with little chance of work, and by 1958 Ornette—in desperation—approached Contemporary records with a bunch of his compositions. Thanks to the open-mindedness of producer Lester Koenig, he was invited to record them himself, plastic alto and all, and the two releases **Something Else** and **Tomorrow Is The Question**, though less than ideal in group terms (a piano was included on the début album, and an orthodox if sympathetic rhythm section on the second) did publicly unveil the revolution.

Where musicians like Coltrane, Rollins, Mingus and Russell sought to find a way out of the harmonic maze of chord progressions, Ornette by-passed the problem. He based his improvisations on melodic and rhythmic planes, developing the solo along a freer-ranging logic than harmony had allowed. The music sounds like a non-European folk survival—direct and moving. Group interaction depended upon intuition to a greater degree than with more traditionally structured music, for there were no pre-set formulae to fall back upon. The demands have whittled the Coleman cohorts to a handful—trumpeter Don Cherry; bassists Charlie Haden, Scott La Faro, Jimmy Garrison and David Izenzon; drummers Ed Blackwell, Billy Higgins, Charles Moffett and Denardo Coleman; tenorist Dewey Redman.

The release of Ornette's albums on Atlantic is the fullest manifesto of the new music, and jazz was never the same again. Two armed camps developed out of the chord players and the free, though in fact the non-musician will find little difficulty in following Ornette's melodic line and logic, and might well wonder what all the fuss was about. Compositions like **Lonely Woman** or **Peace (The Shape Of Jazz To Come)** possess a beauty that would convert the most diehard listener, though the composer's tone might hoist a few eyebrows. Fiercely vocalized and shifting pitch to include squalling dissonances and searing cries, Ornette's alto alternates ambiguously between anguish and exaltation.

The Atlantic series from 1959-61 shows the range of approaches possible within the new music. Performances like **Ramblin' (Change Of The Century)** have the feel of traditional Texas blues, rock as bucolically as a hoe-down. The leader's alto moves in short, jigging phrases, contrasting the attack with great attention to dynamics. The title track, like **Kaleidoscope (This Is Our Music)**, is fast and violent, the key centre discarded as the emotion demands. **Beauty Is A Rare Thing (This Is Our Music)** has a spaciousness about it, and a harrowing beauty that forms and disintegrates and reforms as the four players stretch out the motifs. The medium-fast tempo number, such as **C & D (Ornette!), Congeniality (The Shape Of Jazz To Come), Monk And The Nun (Twins)** and **The Fifth Of Beethoven (The Art Of The Improvisers)**, is the most typical.

Most of these albums comprise the quartet of Ornette, Don Cherry on pocket trumpet, Charlie Haden on bass and either Ed Blackwell or Billy Higgins on drums—a line-up that the leader has never bettered. Scott La Faro's bass **(Ornette!)** though staggeringly innovative, was too prone to ornamentation for the needs of the music, and lacked the selflessness and intuition of Haden's work. Ornette switched to tenor **(Ornette On Tenor)** because, controversially, 'the best statements Negroes have made, of what their soul is, have been on tenor saxophone'. The result was great music, with **Cross Breeding**, a solo of matchless symmetry and logic, contrasting with **Mapa**, which is contrapuntal throughout and group playing of the highest order.

The boldest experiment was yet to come with the double quartet album **(Free Jazz)**, Ornette's regular quartet supplemented by Eric Dolphy, Freddie Hubbard, La Faro and both Higgins and Blackwell. Each man solos, backed by a free collective guided only by an open response to the stream of invention. It is theme-less, unrehearsed, and kept from chaos mainly by the sheer aptness of the altoist's contributions. A classic album, influencing John Coltrane's 'Ascension' experiment, and giving rise to a flood of largely incoherent copyists.

In 1962, Ornette was recorded with his new trio, David Izenzon bass, Charles Moffett drums **(Town Hall)**; one example of an entirely new direction, a composition for string ensemble, **Dedication To Poets And Writers**, was included. The next two years were spent in semi-retirement at his New York studio, where he wrote and worked at two new instruments, the trumpet and the violin. Early in 1965 he returned to public performances with the trio, opening at the Village Vanguard, and then visiting Great Britain to play the legendary Fairfield Hall concert **(An Evening With Ornette Coleman)**.

Starting with a wind quintet composition, Ornette followed by unveiling his concept of trumpet and violin playing **(Falling Stars)** both used unconventionally and largely effective as tone colorings rather than precision instruments. His alto remained unchanged and unrivaled. Izenzon revealed himself as a master of arco bass playing and a considerable innovator, while Moffett—a Fort Worth friend of the leader's—proved himself to be the most conventionally swinging drummer that Ornette had used but none the worse for that.

The same year saw the release of two Blue Note albums by the trio, caught live **(At The Golden Circle)** in Stockholm. The familiar medium-fast tempos of **Antiques, Dee Dee** and **Faces And Places** display the old rocking swing and fertile melodic imagination in full spate. A commission to compose a film score **(Chappaqua Suite)** led to a double album, but the music was judged to be too dominant for the screen images, and not used. The trio was expanded to include tenorist Pharoah Sanders and eleven woodwind, brass and strings players, and Ornette plays for most of the time over an economically written background.

Once again, controversy arose over the use of Ornette's ten-year-old son, Ornette Denardo, as the group's drummer **(The Empty Foxhole** and subsequently **Ornette At 12** and **Crisis)**. Wayward, the youngster's playing certainly adds a random factor to the music. The leader's meeting with Coltrane's drummer, Elvin Jones **(New York Is Now** and **Love Call)**, works well, but at the expense of Elvin's normal style; a meeting of giants, sympathetic but incompatible. By this time, Ornette had found another front line horn in tenorist Dewey Redman, another Fort Worth musician steeped in the blues tradition, and given to half-moaned, half-played tonal manipulations. An album from 1969 **(Crisis)** brings Don Cherry back into the group, and the high spot occurs with the hauntingly beautiful Charlie Haden composition, **Song For Che**.

Following this, Ornette Coleman seems to have retreated into retirement amid a flurry of rumours. His only recorded work in several years was **O.C.**, to be found on album of duets made by Charlie Haden **(Closeness)**, which showed his genius unimpaired by his absence from the scene.

After a period of self-imposed inactivity, the mid/late-'70s saw a flurry of renewed energy from Coleman. Now he was usually found in the company of son Denardo and James Blood Ulmer, who manfully set about the task of translating Coleman's at times impenetrable harmolodic principles to the guitar **(Tales Of Captain Black)**. However, in 1979, Coleman again stopped performing altogether. He re-emerged to appear live again in 1981 and the digitally recorded **Of Human Feelings** with his band Prime Time (Denardo and Calvin Weston, drums; Charlie Ellerbee and Bern Nix, guitars; Jamaaladeen Tacuma, bass) was a minor bombshell in 1982. **Of Human Feelings** was received by Coleman's public with mixed feelings. It presented an updated Coleman sound—lively, raw, electric, iconoclastic new-wave funk which, while it might have lost a few hard-core followers, won him a new generation of young admirers. Also in 1981, Coleman undertook a film score project for Joseph Bogdanovich's *Box Office*, involving 40 musicians.

Apart from his occupation with Prime Time, composing and occasionally touring, Coleman has two special long-term projects in hand—to create an orchestra with members from all 50 American states, and to establish a school in New York for young, under-privileged musicians.

In '86, Ornette Coleman's unexpected but spectacular association with jazz-rock guitarist Pat Metheny was one of *the* most extraordinary events of the '80s, marked by their superb **Song X**.

Below: Ornette Coleman—pioneer of Free Jazz. His mid-1980s collaboration with jazz-rock guitarist Pat Metheny explored exciting and wide-ranging areas.

Albums:
Something Else (Contemporary/Contemporary)
Tomorrow Is The Question (Contemporary/Boplicity)
The Shape Of Jazz To Come (Atlantic/Atlantic)
This Is Our Music (Atlantic/Atlantic)
Change Of The Century (Atlantic/Atlantic)
Ornette! (Atlantic/Atlantic)
Art Of The Improvisers (Atlantic/Atlantic)
Ornette On Tenor (Atlantic/Atlantic)
Free Jazz (Atlantic/Atlantic)
Twins (Atlantic/Atlantic)
Town Hall (ESP/ESP)
An Evening With Ornette Coleman/Ornette Coleman In Europe (Polydor/—)
At The Golden Circle (Blue Note/Blue Note)
Chappaqua Suite (Columbia/CBS)
The Empty Foxhole (Blue Note/Blue Note)
Ornette At 12 (Impulse/Impulse)
Crisis (Impulse/Impulse)
New York Is Now (Blue Note/Blue Note)
Love Call (Blue Note/Blue Note)
Charlie Haden, Closeness (A&M/A&M)
Dancing In Your Head (A&M/A&M)
At The Golden Circle, Stockholm (Blue Note/Blue Note)
Of Human Feelings (Antilles/Antilles)
Song X (Geffen/Geffen)

Ornette Coleman and Prime Time, Of Human Feelings (courtesy Antilles).

Graham Collier

One of Britain's foremost composers, Collier was born in Tynemouth, 1937. After 7 years in a British army military band, he won a *Downbeat* scholarship to America's Berklee School of Music—the first British graduate, 1963. During '63, he toured with the Jimmy Dorsey Band but returned to Britain after a serious car accident.

In 1964, Collier formed his West Coast-influenced Graham Collier Music with which he has toured and recorded extensively—a band including, at some time, virtually every British musician of note. Collier was the first jazz composer in the United Kingdom to be awarded an Arts Council bursary resulting in **Workpoints**—the first of a series of projects demonstrating his belief that jazz composition should, as far as possible, express the essential characteristics of jazz improvisation. This 'freshness in each performance' approach has been further developed in **Mosaics, Songs For My Father** and **New Conditions**.

He has written for many European radio bands including the **Thames Base** suite for Danish bassist Niels Henning. His work on film and TV projects includes scoring John Tydeman's Hi Fi Theatre production of Malcolm Lowry's *Under The Volcano* for the BBC.

Collier is extensively involved in jazz education internationally and is a professor at the Royal Academy of Music in London as co-ordinator of its jazz programme.

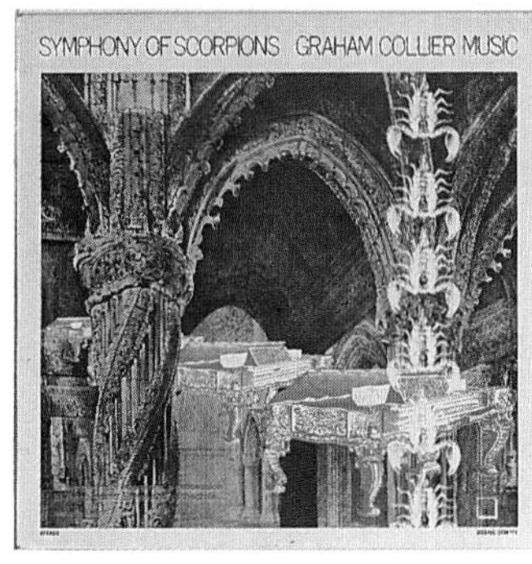

Graham Collier, Symphony Of Scorpions (courtesy Mosaic).

In 1983, Collier was featured in a Channel 4 TV documentary centered around his **Hoarded Dreams**—a 72-minute work for a 20-piece, international orchestra which was performed at the Bracknell Jazz Festival.

In addition to his musical projects, Collier is a broadcaster and author. His *Cleo And John* (Quartet) is a biography of the Dankworths and *Inside Jazz* (Quartet) is a readable and entertaining guide to jazz for the uninitiated.

Albums:
Deep Dark Blue Centre (—/Deram)
Songs For My Father (—/Fontana)
Portraits (—/Saydisc)
Midnight Blue (—/Mosaic)
Symphony Of Scorpions (—/Mosaic)
Down Another Road (—/Fontana)
Mosaics (—/Phillips)
Darius (—/Mosaic)
New Conditions (—/Mosaic)
The Day Of The Dead (—/Mosaic)

Alice Coltrane

Alice Coltrane, the great tenor player's second wife, replaced pianist McCoy Tyner in the John Coltrane group in January 1966, and remained until Coltrane's death in 1967. Coltrane said of her that 'she continually senses the right colors, the right textures, of the sounds of the chords'. Her approach, like the new drummer, Rashied Ali's, was towards a looser, more diffuse design, and the change wrought by the newcomers can be heard on a version of **My Favorite Things (Coltrane Live At The Village Vanguard Again)**. The release of some of her late husband's recordings found Alice dubbing Indian backgrounds **(Infinity)** and her own subsequent output has been characterized by a religious Eastern feel. Proficient on organ, harp and piano, her music concentrates on swirling, transcendental textures.

A recluse in San Fernando for many years, Alice Contrane re-emerged in '86 on a weekly TV programme of meditation, religious devotion and music.

Albums:
John Coltrane, Coltrane Live At The Village Vanguard Again (Impulse/Impulse)
John Coltrane, Concert In Japan (Impulse/Impulse)
A Monastic Trio (Impulse/Impulse)
Journey In Satchidananda (Impulse/Impulse)
Lord Of Lords (Impulse/Impulse)
Ptah The El Daoud (Impulse/Impulse)
World Galaxy (Impulse/Impulse)

John Coltrane

Tenorist John Coltrane was born in North Carolina, 1926, and by his death in 1967 had become one of jazz's great touchstones of spiritual integrity, and a vital linking figure between the '50s and the New Thing. Beginning in R&B outfits, Coltrane joined Dizzy Gillespie in the early '50s, and the classic Miles Davis Quintet in 1955. With Miles, the tenorist showed a debt to Dexter Gordon, with passages of incoherence, and sudden landslides of considerable power and originality. **Round Midnight** gives an early hint of his emotional force **(Miles Davis, Tallest Trees)**. Throughout the year and a half that he stayed with Miles, he worked on his style, trying, as he later told Wayne Shorter, to start in the middle of a sentence and move in both directions at once. In effect, the result was an outrush of arpeggios and semi-quavers spiralling up from the line. Chords obsessed him, and the move to Thelonious Monk's group in 1957 was the necessary next stage. Monk's harmonic sense was totally original, and Coltrane learned how to play buoyantly over the rhythmic stagger of **Monk's Mood** and the jolting, choppy tides of **Nutty (Thelonious Monk & John Coltrane)**.

After the bebop masters—Dizzy, Miles and Monk—he pushed out on his own. His best performances **Good Bait, Lush Life** and **Traneing In**, generated their own rhythmic impetus, the runs cascading into the famous 'sheets of sound', long, spearing legato notes arising from the complexity with chilling force **(More Lasting Than Bronze** and **John Coltrane)**. A meeting with innovator Cecil Taylor **(Coltrane Time)** showed that although Coltrane was moving out of the strictures of hard bop, he was not by-passing the harmonic complex like Taylor or Ornette Coleman. Miles Davis, also casting about for a looser armature, came up with the modal timelessness of Indian music **(Kind Of Blue)** and Coltrane found the melodic freedom of that session highly relevant to his own search.

In 1959 he reached the first real plateau of maturity with two classic albums. His sound was uniformly strong over three octaves, and flexible enough to handle the delicacy of **Naima** or the headlong turbulence of **Mr P.C. (Giant Steps)**. There was a new austerity and discipline in his playing, and the beginnings of a preoccupation with split notes appeared on **Harmonique (Coltrane Jazz)**. His soprano saxophone made its appearance on a number indelibly associated with him, the lyrically lovely **My Favorite Things**, and a great vogue for the instrument began. More imortant was the formation of the great quartet, McCoy Tyner piano, Jimmy Garrison bass, and Elvin Jones drums—a team chosen as a forcing house for his ceaseless explorations: Tyner's strength and dense chordal textures, his ability to sustain vamp figures which would check the leader's slide back into harmony: Garrison's stability and teamwork; Jones' multi-directional rhythms that surrounded Coltrane with choice. Between the 4/4 cymbal beat, the fierce counter-rhythms and the tenor's heavy, incantatory pulse, audiences had to find a new way to move to the music. Recording for Impulse, the quartet produced an unbroken series of exacting, exhilarating and rewarding albums.

Many of the critics who had hailed **Giant Steps** gave an emphatic thumbs down to marathon performances like the seminal **Chasin' The Trane (Live At The Village Vanguard)** but changed their minds with the four-part devotional work, **A Love Supreme**, which in turn became another breakoff point.

Between 1960-65, Coltrane had laid classic performances like **Blues Minor (Africa Brass), Transition (Transition)** and **Out Of This World (Coltrane)**, the strong and tender reading of standard songs **(Ballads)**, and had collaborated successfully with Eric Dolphy on tour and record. With Elvin Jones, he had pioneered a way of making the longer line breathe.

Next, Coltrane sought new stimulation in the young New Thing players. Fascinated by Ornette Coleman's **Free Jazz** experiment, he explored the possibilities of the free ensemble, augmenting the quartet with Archie Shepp, Pharoah Sanders, John Tchicai, Marion Brown, Freddie Hubbard, Dewey Johnson and Art Davis **(Ascension)**. The dense, raging music cried out for a different rhythm, for a looser drummer than Elvin Jones. Coltrane took tenorist Pharoah Sanders into the group, stimulated by his writhing, high-energy playing, and added the mobile, flickering Rashied Ali on drums. The next phase has its riches and its confusions. Arguably, the finest album **(Meditations)** has the two tenorists plaiting, jostling, scouring the music to its emotional quick over the rhythmic groundswell without bogging down into chaos. A performance like **Naima (Live At The Village Vanguard Again)** with the leader's grandeur of expression sandwiching a convoluted solo from Sanders, has great symmetry. With the departure of Tyner and Jones, and their replacement by Alice Coltrane and Rashied Ali, Coltrane once again threw everything back into the melting pot, and this experimental phase was terminated only by his death. Group concept aside, late Coltrane is distinguished by the sheer majesty of his tone, particularly evident on his duo album with Ali **(Interstellar Space)** and on **Offering** from his final album **Expression**. Like Sonny Rollins, his influence on jazz has been enormous and a flood of albums has been released posthumously. Quiet, introspective, humble, John Coltrane's life seems to have been almost totally dedicated to the musico-spiritual search.

Above: The unforgettable John Coltrane: 'I don't know what else can be said in words about what I'm doing. Let the music speak for itself . . .'.

Albums:
Miles Davis, Tallest Trees (Prestige/Prestige)
Thelonious Monk & John Coltrane (Milestone/Milestone)
More Lasting Than Bronze (Prestige/Prestige)
John Coltrane (Prestige/Prestige)
Black Pearls (Prestige/Prestige)
Blue Train (Blue Note/Blue Note)
Paul Chambers & John Coltrane (Blue Note/Blue Note)
Coltrane Time (United Artists)
Miles Davis, Kind Of Blue (Columbia/CBS)
Giant Steps (Atlantic/Atlantic)
Coltrane Jazz (Atlantic/Atlantic)
The Avant Garde (Atlantic/Atlantic)
My Favorite Things (Atlantic/Atlantic)
Live At The Village Vanguard (Impulse/Impulse)
Live At Birdland (Impulse/Impulse)
Crescent (Impulse/Impulse)
Coltrane (Impulse/Impulse)
Africa Brass (Impulse/Impulse)
Transition (Impulse/Impulse)
Sun Ship (Impulse/Impulse)
Ballads/The Gentle Side Of John Coltrane (Impulse/Impulse)
A Love Supreme (Impulse/Impulse)
Ascension (Impulse/Impulse)
Meditations (Impulse/Impulse)
Live In Seattle (Impulse/Impulse)
Concert In Japan (Impulse/Impulse)
Live At The Village Vanguard Again (Impulse/Impulse)
Interstellar Space (Impulse/Impulse)
Expression (Impulse/Impulse)
Om (Impulse/Impulse)
Kulu Se Mama (Impulse/Impulse)
Cosmic Music (Impulse/Impulse)
Miles Davis-John Coltrane: Live In Stockholm (—/Dragon—Sweden)

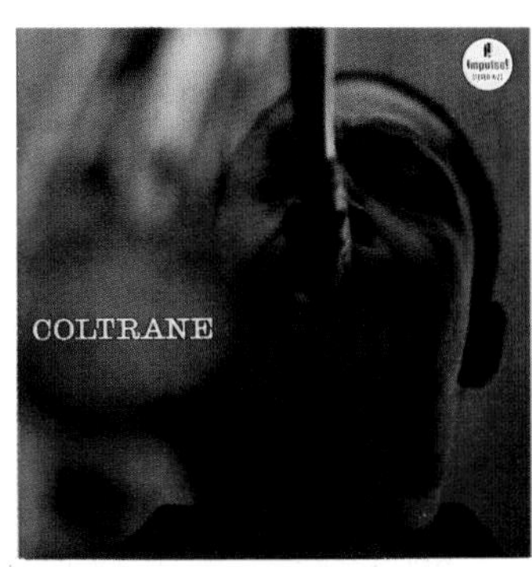

Coltrane (courtesy Impluse)—close up of most-imitated embouchure in jazz.

Eddie Condon

Albert Edwin Condon (born Goodland, 1905) was Hollywood publicity man's dream of the archetypal jazzman: hard drinker, witty, something of a raconteur, characterful . . . in truth, Condon was all these things and more. A living legend for most of his 69 years, whose influence, musically, was felt more than heard. A more than capable rhythm guitarist/banjoist, whose quietly propulsive strumming helped bolster up many a rhythm section. Never in any way a major soloist (nor even a player of minor significance, solo-wise) Condon's premier influence was as a kind of self-appointed entrepreneur, impresario, cheerleader, producer, as well as an indefatigable champion of what was (and is) basically a white-Dixieland jazz school.

A tough little man who taught himself to play, first ukelele, then banjo and guitar, Condon worked as semi-pro musician in his teens, and before he was 20 had played alongside an acknowledged giant like Bix Beiderbecke. Condon associated himself with so-called Austin High School Gang (eg Krupa, Freeman, Teschemacher), and it was with a contingent of these and other Chicago-affiliated musicians that Condon (together with Red McKenzie, vocals, kazoo) produced first of McKenzie & Condon's Chicagoans recordings in December '27, **That Toddlin' Town—Chicago: 1926-1928**, four titles which were to set both standard and style for future 'Chicago jazz'. Other examples of latter: recordings from following year involving Miff Mole & His Little Molers, Eddie Condon's Quartet and Condon's singularly titled Foot-warmers **(That Toddlin' Town—Chicago: 1926-1928)**.

During next few years Condon was to record with an impressive list of important jazzmen, inlcuding Jack Teagarden **(Jack Teagarden: Prince Of The Bone)**, Louis Armstrong **(V.S.O.P.: Very Special Old Phonography, 1928-1930, Vols 5 & 6)**; Red McKenzie's Mound City Blue Blowers **(Recordings Made Between 1930 & 1941)**. Also participated, on banjo, in famous 1932 recording sessions under nominal leadership of meagerly talented Billy Banks **(Billy Banks & His Rhythm-makers)** and it was with orchestra led by Condon that Bud Freeman was to record his most famous solo feature, **The Eel (Home Cooking)**.

Freeman and Condon were to remain close musical associates right up to the latter's death. They worked together in clubs and at concerts on innumerable occasions through the years and recorded in each other's company prolifically, with either Condon playing on Freeman-led bands **(Chicagoans In New York)** or the tenorist guesting with Condon **(Chicago & All That Jazz)**.

After serious stomach illness in 1936, Condon co-led, with clarinettist-saxist Joe Marsala, a fine little band. After working consistently in New York, especially at Dixieland emporium, Nick's, Condon worked with Bobby Hackett, Bud Freeman's Summa Cum Laude Orchestra **(Chicago Styled)**, then both Hackett and Marsala again. Then, in 1942, was responsible for putting together first-ever organized jam session before TV cameras. During this period the ever-gregarious Condon commenced own jam-session type series of concerts at New York's Town Hall, involving lengthy list of prominent jazz musicians, most of whom had been Condon associates for several years.

Condon's Town Hall concerts **(The Eddie Condon Concerts Town Hall 1944-45: Featuring Pee Wee Russell** and **Eddie Condon Town Hall Concerts With Lee Wiley)** did much to help in revival of interest in more traditional jazz forms during 1940s, as well as providing much fine music. These also precipitated kind of studio jam-session recordings which Condon was to oversee in 1950s **(The Golden Days Of Jazz: Eddie Condon)** although there had been similar dates during late-1930s/early-1940s **(Jammin' At Condon's** and **The Roaring Twenties)**, all of which permutated various line-ups of Condon favorites, with quality of music varying from the bland, even messy, to the bright, loosely disciplined and brilliant. Just how poor this kind of music can be is revealed all too illuminatingly on an ill-titled **Jazz As It Should Be Played**.

1945: opened own club, in Greenwich Village, which lasted 12 years. Club changed venue 13 years later. Condon's autobiography, *We Called It Music* (co-written with Thomas Sugrue) first published in 1948, year he started own jazz TV series. Toured Britain in 1967 with own band; visited Japan, Australasia, '64. Underwent two major operations (1964, 1965); reduced own appearances at his club which closed doors in '67. But by 1970 was working in band co-led by Roy Eldridge and Kai Winding. Last recorded evidence of Condon probably dates from 1972 **(Jazz At The New School)**, which demonstrated he was still carrying out the creed which he and others had long since laid down as the Dixielanders' textbook.

Full list of musicians who worked with Condon (who died in 1973) is comprehensive but would certainly include, apart from those already mentioned, Sidney Bechet, Wild Bill Davison, Cutty Cutshall, Lou McGarity, Bob Wilber, Joe Bushkin, Gene Schroeder, Rex Stewart, Vic Dickenson, Edmond Hall, Peanuts Hucko, George Wettling, Billy Butterfield, Jess Stacy, Joe Sullivan, Max Kaminsky and Brad Gowans.

Apart from the aforementioned autobiography, *Eddie Condon's Scrapbook Of Jazz* (by Eddie Condon, with Hank O'Neal) is of absorbing interest to anyone remotely interested in the life and music of Eddie Condon and his numerous musical associates.

Eddie Condon, Condon A La Carte (courtesy Ace of Hearts).

Albums:

Various, That Toddlin' Town—Chicago (1926-1928) (—/Parlophone)
Jack Teagarden, Vols 1, 2 (RCA Victor—France)
The Louis Armstrong Legend (World Records)
Coleman Hawkins, Recordings Made Between 1930 & 1931 (CBS—France)
Billy Banks & His Rhythm-makers (—/CBS—Realm)
Bud Freeman, Home Cooking (Tax—Sweden)
Bud Freeman, Chicago Styled (Swaggie—Australia)
Various, Trombone Scene (—/London)
Various, Great Swing Jam Sessions, Vol 1 (—/Saga)
Various, Chicago Jazz (Decca/Coral)
Eddie Condon, Condon A La Carte (Commodore/Ace of Hearts)
Eddie Condon, Commodore Condon Vol 1 (—/London)
Bud Freeman, Chicagoans In New York (Dawn Club/—)
Various, The Davison-Brunis Sessions, Vols 1-3 (—/London)
The Eddie Condon Concerts, Town Hall 1944-45, Vols 1, 2 (Chiaroscuro/—)
Eddie Condon & His All Stars, Vols 1-18 (Jazum/—)
Jack Teagarden, Big T's Jazz (—/Ace of Hearts)
Eddie Condon, We Called It Music (—/Ace of Hearts)
Eddie Condon, The Golden Days Of Jazz (CBS/CBS)
Various, Chicago & All That Jazz! (—Verve)
Muggsy Spanier & His Ragtimers (—/London)
Eddie Condon's World Of Jazz (CBS—Holland)

Chick Corea

Pianist Armando Anthony 'Chick' Corea was born in Chelsea, Massachusetts, on December 6, 1941. His earliest influence was his father Armando—a jazz trumpeter, bassist, composer and arranger in the 1930s and '40s—who encouraged him to take up piano at 4 years old. Corea played at country clubs with his father in the Boston-Cape Cod area while still very young. In high school Corea was introduced to Latin music and, in 1959, Corea attended Columbia University in Manhattan. He returned to Boston after two months and spent eight months preparing for a Juilliard audition. Once at Juilliard, he became dissatisfied with formal studies and left to become a professional musician. His first major appearance was with Latin luminary Mongo Santamaria in 1962, then with Willie Bobo. While Corea lists his earliest musical interests as Bud Powell and Horace Silver, his classical training had added the strands of Stravinsky, Ravel, Debussy and Bartok which were to become so distinctive in his later playing.

Corea played with Blue Mitchell, Herbie Mann and Stan Getz **(Sweet Rain)**, contributing the complex **Litha** and the lovely waltz **Windows** to the session, and eliciting some of Getz's best work by his sympathetic piano support. A period with Miles Davis during his transition to jazz-rock saw Corea sharing electric keyboard duties with Joe Zawinul **(In A Silent Way, Bitches Brew** and **Big Fun**; though an earlier album **(Filles de Kilimanjaro)** gives a clearer idea of his work.

Typical of his playing in the late '60s—fierce, energetic—is an album with trumpeter Woody Shaw and saxophonist Joe Farrell **(Tones For Joan's Bones)** which is driven along on the surging drumming of Joe Chambers. His formation of Circle in 1970 with multi-instrumentalist Anthony Braxton, bassist Dave Holland and drummer Barry Altschul marked a change in direction. Free interplay is the keynote here, from the driving version of **Nefertiti**—a much wilder, looser performance than Miles'—to the dissonant piano duet with Braxton's extremes of pitch on **Duet (Circle, Paris Concert)**. The group broke up in 1971 when Corea left—'I used to feel very limited and confined and I'd be into a compulsive experimentation on the bandstand' and recorded a pair of solo piano albums for ECM **(Piano Impovisations)**. Fragile, introspective, the music draws extensively from classical, each piece meticulously constructed, from the Monk standard, **Trinkle Tinkle**, to the eight impressionistic vignettes of **Where Are You Now**.

The début album by Corea's new group, **Return To Forever**, featured Joe Farrell, reeds; Stanley Clarke, bass; Airto Moreira, percussion; and Brazilian singer Flora Purim. With Corea on electric piano, and a return to the more overtly stated rhythm, the group played a chamber version of jazz-rock and

Below: Pianist-composer Chick Corea and influential jazz-rock pioneer. His duets with pianist Herbie Hancock and vibist Gary Burton are memorable.

was immensely successful. Subsequent albums (**Light As A Feather, Hymn Of The 7th Galaxy, No Mystery, Where Have I Known You Before** and **Romantic Warrior**) have seen personnel changes, with Corea and Clarke constant, and guitarist Al Di Meola replacing Farrell. One of the crossover supergroups, Return To Forever was careful not to outstrip its following, and Corea in interview places a heavy premium on communication. A scientologist, he believes that his music has a mission, and himself draws inspiration from the scientologist poetry of Neville Potter (**Where Have I Known You Before**).

Away from Return To Forever, Corea has commanded audiences world-wide as a solo performer, as well as touring as an indomitable piano duo with Herbie Hancock. In the late '70s, Corea forged a particularly creative association with vibes-player Gary Burton (notably the enduring **Crystal Silence; Duet;** and **In Concert, Zürich, October 28, 1979**). The Corea-Burton partnership was to be most rewardingly renewed in 1984 with the recording and performance of Corea's 7-part **Lyric Suite For Sextet,** written for the duo and a string quartet. Corea's first venture into writing a complex chamber piece was actually **Septet**, music for string quartet, piano, flute and French horn (not released until 1985)—a five-movement work commissioned by the Chamber Music Society of Lincoln Center for the 1982 New World Festival in Miami.

Early in 1981, Corea recorded **Three Quartets** with saxophonist Michael Brecker, bassist Eddie Gomez and drummer Steve Gadd which included individual 'quartets' dedicated to Duke Ellington and John Coltrane. Later that year, the double album **Trio Music** found Corea in the equally imposing company of bassist Miroslav Vitous and drummer Roy Haynes (recreating their first brief meeting in 1967 on **Now He Sings, Now He Sobs**). While there was space for the trio's individual and collective improvisations, half the album was an affectionate collection of Thelonious Monk tunes which, according to Corea, is 'some of the classic music of the 20th century'.

In 1984, Corea embarked on another duet project, **Voyage**, this time with former Corea group saxophonist Steve Kajula, now playing flute. In 1985, an excellent cross-section of Corea's ECM output ('70s and '80s) was released on the limited edition **Chick Corea/Works** album.

Albums:
Stan Getz, Sweet Rain (Verve/Verve)
Miles Davis: In A Silent Way (Columbia/CBS)
Bitches Brew (Columbia/CBS)
Big Fun (Columbia/CBS)
Filles De Kilimanjaro (Columbia/CBS)
Tones For Joan's Bones (Atlantic/Atlantic)
Circling In (Blue Note/Blue Note)
Circle, Paris Concert (ECM/ECM)
Piano Improvisations, Vols 1 & 2 (ECM/ECM)
Return To Forever (ECM/ECM)
Light As A Feather (Polydor/Polydor)
Hymn Of The 7th Galaxy (Polydor/Polydor)
No Mystery (Polydor/Polydor)
Where Have I Known You Before (Polydor/Polydor)
Romantic Warrior (Columbia/CBS)
Chick Corea-Gary Burton, Crystal Silence (ECM/ECM)
Chick Corea-Gary Burton, Duet (ECM/ECM)
Chick Corea-Gary Burton, In Concert, Zürich, October 28, 1979 (ECM/ECM)
Three Quartets (Warner Bros/WEA)
Trio Music (ECM/ECM)
Again And Again (The Joburg Sessions) (Elektra Musician/Elektra Musician)
Chick Corea-Gary Burton, Lyric Suite For Sextet (ECM/ECM)
Children's Songs (ECM/ECM)
Chick Corea-Steve Kujala, Voyage (ECM/ECM)
Septet (ECM/ECM)
Chick Corea/Works (ECM/ECM)
Chick Corea's Elektric Band (GRP/GRP)
Septet (ECM/ECM)

Chick Corea, Three Quartets (courtesy Warner Brothers).

Above: Larry Coryell and Emily Remler, together—a rewarding, many-faceted and stylistically interesting two-guitar collaboration.

Larry Coryell

Guitarist Larry Coryell was one of the prime movers in electric jazz-rock's development in the late '60s-early '70s.

Born Galveston, Texas, on April 2, 1943, he originally majored in journalism at Washington University because he didn't feel 'talented' enough to pursue a career in music. (His earliest inspiration was Chet Atkins and finger-style country music, before discovering Jimi Hendrix.) However, fortunately, he still studied music privately with Jerry Gray and took classical guitar lessons with Leonid Bolotine in New York, 1965. In 1966, he worked with Chico Hamilton (**The Dealer**) and founded the early fusion band Free Spirits (**Out Of Sight And Sound**). He joined Gary Burton's group in '67 (**A Genuine Tong Funeral, Duster, Lofty Fake Anagram**), a significant association which brought him wider exposure. Coryell can also be found on record to good effect with vocalist Leon Thomas (**Blues And The Soulful Truth**), Herbie Mann (**Memphis Underground**), and Michael Mantler (**The Jazz Composers, Orchestra**).

Coryell has led his own groups since '69, notably the influential Eleventh House (**Level One** and **Aspects**), and has toured often as a solo or in duos with guitarists like Philip Catherine (**Twin House**) and Steve Khan (**Two For The Road**). Most recently, he has been heard in a particularly rewarding and many faceted two-guitar collaboration with Emily Remler.

Solo, Coryell displays an extraordinary technique from jazz and rock, standards and originals, and even into classical works like Stravinsky's *Firebird.*

Albums:
Barefoot Boy (Flying Dutchman/—)
Basics (Vanguard/Vanguard)
Guitar Player (MCA/MCA)
Lion And The Ram (Arista/Arista)
Spaces (Vanguard/Vanguard)
Larry Coryell-Emily Remler, Together (Concord/Concord)
Coming Home (Muse/Muse)

Curtis Counce

Bassist Curtis Counce was born in 1926 in Kansas City, and made his recording début with Lester Young in 1946, followed by stints with Shorty Rogers and Stan Kenton. In 1956 he founded his quintet which lasted until the following year and represents his chief claim to fame. The Curtis Counce Group was arguably the most virile and consistently imaginative outfit on the West Coast in that period, and its four albums, **Landslide, Counceltation, Carl's Blues** and **Exploring The Future**, have not dated like much of that region's more self-consciously experimental music. Tenorist Harold Land, trumpeter Jack Sheldon, pianist Carl Perkins and drummer Frank Butler shared the writing dues with the leader, and between them created a personality that could compete with any combo on the more fashionable East Coast. Underrated at the time, especially Frank Butler whose technique was showcased on numbers like **A Fifth For Frank (Landslide)** and **The Butler Did It (Carl's Blues)**, the only member who continued to add to his reputation was Harold Land.

Albums:
Landslide (Contemporary/Contemporary)
Counceltation (Contemporary/Contemporary)
Carl's Blues (Contemporary/Contemporary)
Exploring The Future (Dooto/Boplicity)

Curtis Counce, Exploring The Future (courtesy Dooto): now on Boplicity.

Ida Cox

Ida Cox (born Knoxville, Tennessee, 1889) was not only one of the most successful blues artists, she was one of the very best. As a child, sang in local African Methodist Choir. Ran away from home to work with F. S. Wolcott's Rabbit Foot Minstrels, making her first appearance at 14. Became solo performer, singing blues, as well as vaudeville and tent-show songs. First recording in June 1923—even before Ma Rainey.

Very first sides (for Paramount) were **Any Woman's Blues, 'Bama Bound Blues** and **Lovin' Is The Thing I'm Wild About (Ida Cox, Vol 1)**. Accompanied only by piano of Lovie Austin, Cox demonstrated at this first session that hers indeed was a voice richly textured, beautifully expressive (especially on **Any Woman's Blues**), deeply immersed in blues idiom, and tinged by her vaudevillian experiences (**Lovin'**). **Bear-Mash Blues**, from a December '23 session (**Ida Cox, Vol 2**), finds her singing with optimum feel, accompanied lovingly by pianist Jesse Crump, also organist, dancer and writer (he composed **Bear-Mash Blues** with Cox), became her husband in 1927. **Graveyard Dream Blues**, from Ida Cox's second record date (**Ida Cox, Vol 2**) must be considered, even by her consistently high standards, one of her very finest offerings. Lovie Austin apart, Jimmy O'Bryant, clarinet, and Tommy Ladnier, cornet, offer accompaniment which is, collectively and individually, beyond reproach. Austin (as leader of her Blues Serenaders, as well as capacity of solo pianist), together with Ladnier and O'Bryant, became basic ingredients of Ida Cox recordings, with minimal additional musicians used at different times. One important addition was Johnny Dodds, who replaced O'Bryant at August '24 session (**Ida Cox, Vol 2**) that produced magnificent blues singing/playing to be found within **Wild Women Don't Have The Blues** and **Worried In Mind Blues**. Declamatory **Blues Ain't Nothin' Else But!**, with unknown accompaniment (**Ida Cox, Vol 2**) is another superlative example of Ida Cox's art.

In late-1920s, she formed own traveling show *Raisin' Caine* which continued through 1930s. After which she toured with Darktown Scandals troupe. Recorded at Carnegie Hall in 1939 **John Hammond's Spirituals To Swing**) executing powerful **Four Day Creep**, accompanied by Dicky Wells, James P. Johnson, Lester Young, Buck Clayton, et al. Same year, recorded with equally potent support from Hot Lips Page, Lionel Hampton, Ed Hall, J. C. Higginbotham and others. **Hard Time Blues** is beautifully representative of overall quality of music resulting from session **(Hard Time Blues)**. Worked through 1950s regularly until career temporarily curtailed by stroke (1945). Retired to live in town of her birth.

Made comeback on record in 1961 when she proved she had retained some of her old potency. Stellar jazz line-up included Coleman Hawkins, Roy Eldridge, Jo Jones and Sammy Price. This Riverside LP, **Blues For Rampart Street**, found her recapturing some of the charisma of past days, particularly on tracks like **Mama Goes Where Papa Goes, Hard Time Blues** and **Wild Women Don't Have The Blues**.

Albums:
Ida Cox, Vols 1, 2 (—/Fountain)
King Oliver Plays The Blues (Riverside/London)
Ida Cox, Blues Ain't Nothin' Else But! (Milestone/—)
Ida Cox, Blues For Rampart Street (Riverside/Riverside)
Various, Ma Rainey & The Classic Blues Singers (CBS)
Various, John Hammond's Spirituals To Swing (Vanguard/Vanguard)
Ida Cox, Hard Time Blues (—/Fontana)

Ida Cox, Volume 1 (courtesy Fountain) —16 tracks of classic blues artistry.

Bing Crosby

Harry Lillis 'Bing' Crosby (born, Tacoma, Washington, 1904) has been best known (and most widely respected) pop singer of past 50 years, with total record sales of almost unassailable proportions. Crosby, star of around 50 movies and Academy Award-winning actor, started his career in music business as solo singer who sometimes played drums. After experience in vaudeville, joined entourage of bandleader Paul Whiteman, as solo vocalist and as member of vocal trio the Rhythm Boys, in 1927. During this time, there is little doubt he could be classified as a jazz singer. With Whiteman, the jazz influence was especially strong on individual items like **Louisiana, From Monday On, You Took Advantage Of Me (The Bix Beiderbecke Legend); 'Tain't So, Honey, 'Taint So, After You've Gone (The Bing Crosby Story)**. Also recorded in company with numerous jazz musicians, including Bix Beiderbecke, Frankie Trumbauer, Don Redman, Dorsey Bros Orchestra and Duke Ellington (all to be found on **The Bing Crosby Story**).

With Ellington orchestra, he recorded a remarkably fine version of **St Louis Blues**. Other jazzmen with whom Crosby recorded include Lionel Hampton, Woody Herman, Jack Teagarden, Joe Sullivan, Count Basie **(Bing 'N' Basie)** and Louis Armstrong. He worked many times with Armstrong over the years—on record, radio, television and films **(Louis Armstrong & Bing Crosby On Stage)**. And although in later years Crosby's singing lost much of its initial basic jazz feel, still there were occasions when the jazz spark returned, as with his singing of **Now You Has Jazz**, during the 1956 film musical *High Society*, in company of Louis Armstrong and the Armstrong All Stars **(High Society, Original Film Soundtrack)**.

When Crosby left Whiteman band he took with him Whiteman's guitarist Eddie Lang. Lang, who can be heard on many Crosby recordings, worked as the singer's personal accompanist between 1930 and his death, two years later. On Lang's death, Crosby replaced him with another guitarist—Perry Botkin—simply because he sounded like and played in the style of Lang.

Crosby collapsed in Spain and died almost immediately from a heart attack after a game of golf on October 14, 1977.

Albums:
The Bix Beiderbecke Legend (RCA Victor—France)
The Bing Crosby Story (Columbia/CBS)
Bing Crosby/Johny Mercer, Mr Crosby & Mr Mercer (—/MCA)
Louis Armstrong & Bing Crosby On Stage (—/Windmill)
'High Society' (Original Film Soundtrack) (Capitol/Capitol)
Bing Crosby/Count Basie, Bing 'N' Basie (Daybreak/Daybreak)
The Early Jazz Years: 1928-1930 (Columbia/CBS)

The Bing Crosby Story, Volume 1: The Early Years, 1928-1932 (courtesy CBS). Bing, Duke, the Dorseys, Whiteman, Redman et al.

Bob Crosby

George Robert 'Bob' Crosby (born Spokane, Washington, 1913) is one of a handful of successful bandleaders who did not play an instrument, could neither read nor write music, and was used only as an up-front personality to effect introductions, wave a casual baton (or arm), and generally look the part of (in his case) the handsome-and-well-groomed type—something which often seemed obligatory during swing era.

Crosby was set on career as lawyer after graduating from college. Instead, in 1932, became professional singer with orchestra of Anson Weeks. 1934: joined Dorsey Bros Orchestra. With Dorseys, Crosby's reputation as modest singer (certainly, not in same class as his elder brother) began to grow amongst record collectors.

Took over group of musicians defecting from Ben Pollack Orchestra, including Gil Rodin, Eddie Miller, Matty Matlock and Ray Bauduc. Thus, the Bob Crosby Orchestra was put together. Début came early-1935, in New York. At first, it had, like Pollack's band, strings, but this was a passing phase, and Crosby Orchestra adopted policy of playing Dixieland favorites, augmenting these with new material in similar vein without strings. Soon it became No. 1 big-band specializing in orchestral Dixieland two-beat jazz. In early days, apart from names mentioned above, other notable sidemen appeared—Yank Lawson and Bob Haggart were two.

Other important musicians to give excellent service to the band: Irving Fazola, Billy Butterfield, Bob Zurke, Joe Sullivan, Jess Stacy, Muggsy Spanier and Eddie Miller.

An important event in the Bob Crosby Orchestra Story was advent of the Bob Cats, a fine band-from-within-the-band unit which produced the best out-and-out jazz performances.

From semi-novelty standpoint, success of **Big Noise From Winnetka (Bob Crosby's Bob Cats/Big Noise From Winnetka)** featuring drummer Bauduc playing on strings of a whistling Haggart's bass, perhaps was the biggest surprise.

Although through the years Crosby was to lose key men—Kincaide, Lawson, Charlie Spivak, all at once, to Tommy Dorsey in '38; Butterfield, Fazola, in '40—somehow adequate replacements (generally) were to be found. (In some cases, too, eg Lawson, departees were to return to the fold.) Eventually, by 1942, what had been basically the original Bob Crosby Orchestra fell apart, tenorist/clarinettist Miller taking a segment of the personnel to form own band.

Crosby, who had appeared in various films, alone and with band—*Let's Make Music, Sis Hopkins, Presenting Lily Mars* and *Holiday Inn* (soundtrack)—went solo to Hollywood. Appeared in further movies, including *As Thousands Cheer, Reveille With Beverly, See Here Private Hargrove*, etc. With US Marines (1944-45). Reformed new band on part-time basis, for special engagements, but during late-1940s and 1950s became better-known as TV, radio personality in solo capacity, often hosting own shows. Since 1960s, has been successful businessman outside music, although from time to time has assembled Crosby-type reunion bands, often containing well-known alumni, for special occasions not entirely divorced from nostalgia (Crosby toured Far East during latter portion of '64).

Albums:
Bob Crosby, The Radio Years (—/London)
The Dorsey Bros., Bring Back The Good Times (MCA—Germany)
Bob Crosby & His Orchestra 1935-1956 (Coral/Vogue—Coral)
Bob Crosby, Five Feet Of Swing (Decca)/ South Rampart Street Parade (MCA)
Bob Crosby's Bob Cats (Decca)/Big Noise From Winnetka (MCA)
The Bob Cats: Bob Crosby's Bob Cats 1938-42, Vol 2 (Swaggie—Australia)

Bob Crosby and the Bob Cats, Big Noise From Winnetka (courtesy MCA).

Israel Crosby

The bassist (born Chicago, Illinois, 1919) first was a trumpet player, adding trombone and tuba. By 13, was playing regularly on all three instruments. At 15, became string bass player, working in Chicago with various leaders, including Albert Ammons. Made début on record with pianist Jess Stacy, November 1935; three days later, recorded again with Stacy, this time as member of Gene Krupa's Chicagoans; one number, **Blues Of Israel**, dedicated to and featuring the talents of the young bass player (both sessions **Benny Goodman & The Giants Of Swing/Ridin' In Rhythm**). Worked with Fletcher Henderson (1936-38), Three Sharps & A Flat (1939), Horace Henderson (1940-41), Teddy Wilson (1941-43). 1944: started session work, an occupation which lasted on regular basis for several years. Worked with Ahmad Jamal Trio (1951-53), then again between 1957-62 **(But Not For Me/The Ahmad Jamal Trio At The Pershing)**, as well as with Benny Goodman (1956-57), with whom he toured Asia. Finally, became member of George Shearing Quintet before dying of a blood clot, in his home town in 1962. Amongst other notable recording dates, Crosby's bass was powerfully present alongside Jimmie Noone **(Jimmie Noone 1937-41)** and during Teddy Wilson's celebrated **Blues In C Sharp Minor** session **(Teddy Wilson & His All Stars)**.

Albums:
Benny Goodman & The Giants Of Swing (Prestige)/Various, Ridin' In Rhythm (World Records)
The Fletcher Henderson Story (Columbia)/The Fletcher Henderson Story, Vol 4 (CBS)
Edmond Hall, Celestial Express (Blue Note)
Teddy Wilson & His All Stars (Columbia/CBS)
Jimmy Yancey, Lowdown Dirty Blues (Atlantic/Atlantic)
Jimmie Noone 1937-41 (Collectors' Classics)
But Not For Me/The Ahmad Trio At The Pershing (Cadet/London)

The Crusaders

With their origins firmly in the mid-1950s, the Crusaders—a nucleus of keyboardist Joe Sample, saxophonist-bassist Wilton Felder and drummer Nesbert 'Stix' Hooper—have built an enviable reputation as one of jazz-funk's most prolific and enduring super-groups. Between them, and individually, they have contributed to more than 200 gold and platinum albums, plus producing a string of successful solo projects.

The Crusaders started life in Houston, Texas, with Sample, Felder and Hooper plus saxophonist Hubert Laws, trombonist Wayne Henderson and bassist Henry Wilson. They worked together through Phyllis Wheatley High and Texas Southern University.

In 1958—as the Modern Jazz Sextet—they took what they called their 'Gulf Coast' sound to Los Angeles and changed their name again to the Night Hawks. Supplementing their club dates with studio work, they became in-demand session players. They released their first album **(Freedom Sound)** as the 'Jazz Crusaders' in 1961, to much critical acclaim. Not wishing to be categorized, they dropped the word 'Jazz' in 1970 to become, simply, The Crusaders. Their reputation grew, assisted by such influential groups as the Average White Band recording their material (like AWB's **Put It Where You Want It**).

With the departure of Wayne Henderson in 1975, the Crusaders remained a trio. Throughout their long career, The Crusaders have been augmented by such inestimable musicians as bassists Abraham Laboriel, Chuck Rainey and Robert 'Pops' Popwell; guitarists Larry Carlton, B. B. King, David T. Walker, Cornell Dupree and Roy Gaines; keyboardist Billy Preston; and vocalists Randy Crawford **(Street Life)**, Bill Withers and Joe Cocker.

In 1975, The Crusaders became the only instrumental group, before or since, to tour with the Rolling Stones. In 1983, Stix Hooper left to pursue a solo career. Felder and Sample recruited drummer Leon Ndugu Chancler and, in 1984, produced their 13th successful Crusaders' album **Ghettoblaster**.

Albums:
Old Shoes And New Socks (Chisa—Rare Earth/—)
Crusaders 1 (Chisa—Blue Thumb/—)
Chain Reaction (ABC/—)
Southern Comfort (ABC/—)
Street Life (MCA/MCA)
Standing Tall (MCA/MCA)
Rhapsody And Blues (MCA/MCA)
Ghettoblaster (MCA/MCA)

Classic Crusaders (1972), Crusaders 1 (courtesy Chisa—Blue Thumb).

Above: Tony Dagradi (ex-Carla Bley band) now a successful solo artist.

Tony Dagradi

Originally from Summit, New Jersey, reeds-player Tony Dagradi (born 1953) has become one of the most exciting and original musicians to emerge from the New Orleans jazz community.

Dagradi has played sax since age 7, studying piano, harmony and theory in New York, and in 1970, he won a *Downbeat* scholarship to Berklee. He spent a few successful years in the Boston-Cape Cod area with his own group Inner Vision before settling in New Orleans. In '77, he toured and recorded with one of New Orleans' most celebrated sons, Professor Longhair **(Crawfish Fiesta)**. After this quick course in New Orleans R&B, Dagradi formed the Afro-Cuban-flavored Astral Project and has worked with the more avant garde-oriented group Lifers, led by bassist Ramsey McLean **(History's Made Every Moment)**.

Towards the end of '80, the eclectic Dagradi joined Carla Bley's much-vaunted line-up, a move which brought him international exposure, particularly in Europe. That same year, his first solo album **Oasis** (including his dynamic hard-bop excursions on **Urban Disturbance**, for example) was highly acclaimed and featured Bley band trombonist and long-time friend Gary Valente. His 1982 **Lunar Eclipse**, with Astral Project, encapsulates his driving approach whether in a hard-bop mode or with a nod to fusion.

Albums:
Carla Bley, Social Studies (Watt/Watt)
Carla Bley, Live! (Watt/Watt)
Carla Bley, I Hate To Sing (Watt/Watt)
Oasis (Gramavision/Gramavision)
Lunar Eclipse (Gramavision/Gramavision)

Tadd Dameron

Born in Cleveland, 1917, died New York, 1965, pianist-arranger Tadley Dameron left a legacy of beauty. He arranged for Vido Musso and Harlan Leonard, making his début as a pianist with Babs Gonzales' Three Bips & A Bop. He was adept at translating bebop, essentially a combo music, to the needs of the big band, and **Good Bait** and **Our Delight**, written for Dizzy Gillespie's band **(In The Beginning)** and **Cool Breeze**, written for Eckstine's, are models of concision and lyricism **(Mr B. & The Band)**. **If You Could See Me Now**, the first bebop ballad, developed out of Gillespie's cadenza to **Groovin' High**, became a vehicle for both Eckstine and Sarah Vaughan. In 1949, he appeared as co-leader with Miles Davis at the Paris Jazz Festival.

Though modest about his piano playing, and usually restricting himself to accom-

Below: Crusaders' mainstays saxophonist Wilton Felder (left) and keyboardist Joe Sample—creators of the successful and influential 'Gulf Coast sound'.

Below: The immortal Tadd Dameron, sadly neglected during his lifetime, one of jazz's finest composers and arrangers for big band.

panying, Dameron's talents went beyond 'arranger's' piano. Between 1947-49 he led his own group, which boasted such talents as trumpeter Fats Navarro, tenors Wardell Gray and Allen Eager, through his own compositions. **The Squirrel, Dameronia, Tadd Walk, Lady Bird, Jahbero, Symphonette** and **The Chase** have become jazz standards **(Prime Source)**, and the combo was tighter than most bebop units. Dameron led his band throughout a lengthy incumbency at the Royal Roost, and developed Navarro's talent to the full. He didn't find a comparable player until trumpeter Clifford Brown in 1953 **(The Arranger's Touch)** and his muted solo on **Theme Of No Repeat** is a classic. Included on the same album is a later session which features **Fontainebleau**, a short composition in three movements of great textural beauty. A session with tenorist John Coltrane, though interesting,falls short of Dameron's high standards **(Mating Call)** though the deleted album **(The Magic Touch)**, using a large ensemble, shows that his genius for voicings and the creation of inspiring springboards remained undimmed.

A great jazz composer, Dameron's work achieves the almost impossible in its balance between form and improvisation. As a judge of talent—Navarro, Eager, Brown, Sarah Vaughan—he ranks with Ellington and Miles Davis.

Albums:
Dizzy Gillespie, In The Beginning (Prestige/Prestige)
Billy Eckstine, Mr B. & The Band (Savoy/Savoy)
Fats Navarro, Prime Source (Blue Note/Blue Note)
The Arranger's Touch (Prestige/Prestige)
Mating Call (Prestige/—)
Fats Navarro (Milestone/Milestone)
The Miles Davis-Tadd Dameron Quintet (Columbia/CBS)

Johnny Dankworth & Cleo Laine

Born 1927, John Dankworth, alto, soprano, clarinet, bandleader, composer, was one of the founder figures of British modern jazz His influential septet, 1950-53, put across the bebop message **(A Lover & His Lass)**. He has led a succession of big bands over the past two decades, taking the Newport Jazz Festival by storm in 1959. Recruiting top British and American talent to perform his larger works, Dankworth has recorded several excellent concept albums **(What The Dickens, Zodiac Variations** and **Million Dollar Collection)**. Often criticized for passionlessness and politeness, his music cannot be faulted on the technical level. A thorough professional, Dankworth has written movie scores and a classical piano concerto.

His wife, singer Cleo Laine, started with the Dankworth Septet in 1951, and their musical partnership has flourished ever since. An international star, she has sung everything from jazz to Schoenberg's Pierrot Lunaire. Most of her albums include jazz or jazz-influenced numbers, and her vocal range and flexibility are phenomenal.

Laine won her first jazz Grammy award in 1986 for **Cleo At Carnegie Hall: The 10th Anniversary Concert**, and she received it while appearing in the Broadway show *The Mystery of Edwin Drood*.

Albums:
A Lover & His Lass (—/Esquire)
What The Dickens (Fontana/Fontana)
Zodiac Variations (Fontana/Fontana)
Million Dollar Collection (Fontana/Fontana)
Cleo Laine Live At Carnegie Hall (RCA Victor/RCA Victor)
Born On A Friday (RCA Victor/RCA Victor)
I Am A Song (RCA Victor/RCA Victor)
Shakespeare & All That Jazz (Fontana/Fontana)
Best Friends (RCA Victor/RCA Victor)

Eddie 'Lockjaw' Davis, 'Straight Ahead' (courtesy Pablo).

Eddie 'Lockjaw' Davis

Born in New York City, 1921, Eddie 'Lockjaw' Davis is largely self-taught. His early tenor influences, Coleman Hawkins, Ben Webster, Don Byas, formed his big-toned, aggressive style, but he has since developed into an immediately identifiable musician. His early experience with the big bands of Cootie Williams, Lucky Millinder, Andy Kirk and Louis Armstrong made him an ideal sideman for Count Basie, whom he joined in 1952. At a time when the Basie band needed an outsize personality in the ranks, Jaws fitted the bill, and the tracks on which he solos, **Flight Of The Foo Birds** and **After Supper (The Atomic Mr Basie)**, leap with vigor and enthusiasm. His work with a studio big band **(Trane Whistle)** inspires everybody and the three-trumpet chase on **Jaws**, followed by the man himself, is a knockout.

In 1955, Jaws teamed with Shirley Scott on organ for a series of straight-ahead bluesy albums **(The Cookbook)** which helped to establish the tenor and organ combo popularity during the late '50s. A number like **The Rev** shows what a master can do with a simple phrase, teasing, squeezing, delaying and hollering in that hoarse, staccato voice until it takes on the contours of emotional conviction. **Have Horn Will Blow** must be one of the hottest solos on record.

He found an ideal partner for a two-tenor band in Johnny Griffin **(The Toughest Tenors)**. Sounding positively mainstream beside the mercurial, bebop Griffin, Jaws' swaggering, melodramatic delivery gives these sessions the stature of a classic boxing bout. Excellent on numerous Norman Granz jam sessions, Lockjaw's feature album **(Straight Ahead)** with the Tommy Flanagan Trio shows all the 'towserish' tenacity that gave him his nickname, and also the Ben Websterish beefy, breathy tenderness on ballads like **I'll Never Be The Same**.

Albums:
The Atomic Mr Basie (Roulette/Vogue)
The Second Big Band Sound Of Count Basie (Verve/Verve)
Trane Whistle (Prestige/—)
The Cookbook (Prestige/Prestige)
The Toughest Tenors (Milestone/Milestone)
Straight Ahead (Pablo/Pablo)
Hey Lock! (Roulette/Pye)

Miles Davis

Trumpeter Miles Dewey Davis was born in Illinois in 1926, the family making a significant removal to East St. Louis when Miles was two. His dentist father bought him a trumpet for his 13th birthday, and his teacher advised him to play without vibrato—'you're gonna get old anyway and start shaking.' St. Louis trumpeters had their own way of playing—sweet, smooth and spacious—quite unlike the pyrotechnic styles of Roy Eldridge and Dizzy Gillespie. Even this early in his career, it was sound that interested Miles.

In 1944, he got his first big break, playing in Billy Eckstine's orchestra which at that time included the cream of young bebop revolutionaries, Charlie Parker, Gillespie and Dexter Gordon. Lost in adulation, Miles enrolled at Juilliard School of Music in New York and spent most of his time tracking Parker through the nightspots. The inevitable happened, Bird encouraging the intimidated student to join him on the bandstand. As a foil to the tempestuous leader, Miles' trumpet was adequate, but his solo spots were marred by poor technique, a meager range and faulty intonation. What he did have was a unique emotional impact. He copied nobody, concentrated on the middle register where he was strongest, and worked tirelessly on the shape of his phrases. Most of Parker's Savoy and Dial output gives a good idea of Miles' development in the middle '40s **(Bird—The Savoy Recordings** and **Charlie Parker On Dial)**.

Leaving Bird in 1948, he studied with arranger Gil Evans, which led to the establishment of the vastly influential nine-piece band. The arrangements of Evans, Carisi and Gerry Mulligan blended the vitality of small combo bebop with a greater range of sound texture and coloration. The band had a light sound and the instrumentation—apart from Miles' trumpet, Lee Konitz's alto and Mulligan's baritone—included a French horn and tuba. It was altogether too far-out for its time, and the band folded after two weeks, leaving recorded evidence **(Birth Of The Cool** and **Pre-Birth Of The Cool)** which set the pattern for jazz on the West Coast for the next decade.

The early '50s were tough on Miles. Bebop had outstripped its audience and the vogue was for singers. Nevertheless, two albums that the trumpeter cut for Blue Note in 1952-53-54 show an intense emotional involvement with his music. The spareness of his style was emerging as an original aestheticism rather than a cover-up for limitations. Irrelevance is rigidly purged. Numbers like **The Leap** or **Take-Off** make use of pedal points, foreshadowing the later modal explorations of **Kind Of Blue**. Some critics contend that these albums are his best **(Miles Davis, 1 & 2)**.

In 1954, Miles recorded **Blue 'n' Boogie** and **Walkin'**, his way of proving that he could play as hot and funky as the old school, a rebuttal of veteran trumpeter Roy Eldrige's verdict 'It's mouse music, man.' The same confident Miles cut the famous Christmas Eve session of that year with pianist Thelonious Monk and vibraphonist Milt Jackson **(Tallest Trees)**, a session tense with quarrels between Miles and Monk. He speared out long legato notes across bar lines, biting them off abruptly in a style that showed trumpeters how to generate excitement without screaming. The lyrical placement and accenting of phrases made **Bags Groove** and **The Man I Love** into classics. In 1955, he found himself the hit of the Newport Jazz Festival: 'What's all the fuss? I always play like that.'

The quintet that set the pattern for most jazz combos in the '50s followed later in the year. Crucial to the blend of simplicity and multi-directional activity that has always characterized Miles' groups was the choice of drummer. Philly Joe Jones had the fire and inventiveness to lift the soloists, one of the great hard bop drummers, and bassist Paul Chambers played long, alert prowling lines. The anchorman was pianist Red Garland, tirelessly solid in his block chord approach. Sharing the front line on tenor was John Coltrane, later to be the greatest trailblazer of the '60s, but at this time still beset by problems. His sound was spinechilling, making his entrances great dramatic events, and then following up with solos composed of fast, multi-note rows of chord changes. Coltrane and Miles were diametrically opposed in aims, the leader editing to the bone, and the contrast worked. Under Miles' direction, the band moved away from harmonic predictability, using fewer chord changes to give more prominence to melody. Any tracks show the unity and sheer streamlined superiority of this quintet **(Miles Davis** and **Workin' & Steamin')**.

With altoist Cannonball Adderley added, and pianist Bill Evans for Garland, Miles made one of the most influential albums of his career **(Kind Of Blue)** in which modes, rather than chords, are used as a basis for

Below: Eddie 'Lockjaw' Davis—his big-toned, aggressive tenor has saved many a session and helped revive the Basie band in the 1950s.

Above: Miles Davis in the 1970s, creating a climate in which popular electronic music flourished.

Miles' celebrated 1981 comeback, The Man With The Horn (courtesy CBS).

improvisation. The resultant music is beautiful, uncluttered and ageless. Miles' playing is epigrammatic, the purity of his tone singing.

Miles continued his collaboration with Gil Evans as featured soloist over a richly textured orchestra **(Sketches Of Spain, Porgy And Bess** and **Miles Ahead)**, all of which sold well and helped to make his trumpet sound the most syndicated in jazz.

Having pioneered at least two new directions for jazz, and helped to promote the careers of future giants like Rollins, Coltrane, Philly Joe and Bill Evans, he decided to change direction again.

He signed up an unknown teenage drummer, Tony Williams, to provide a constantly challenging polyrhythmic surface, with Ron Carter on bass and Herbie Hancock on piano. The rhythm section was capable of playing in different times to each other, and the overall sound was lighter, lither and more sinuous than its predecessor. Following stints with those underrated tenorists, George Coleman **(My Funny Valentine** and **Four)**, and Hank Mobley **(Friday & Saturday Nights—In Person)**, Miles lured tenorist Wayne Shorter from Art Blakey's Jazz Messengers. Shorter was basically in the Coltrane bag, a hard, squalling, legato player, but with a jigging, snake-hipped attack that fitted Miles' new conception.

A series of fine albums followed **(ESP, Miles Smiles, Sorcerer, Nefertiti** and **Miles In The Sky)**, of which **Miles Smiles** is the highpoint. As influential as the 1955 quintet, it brought new patterns of tension and release to big dipper proportions, avoided strong harmonic touchstones and made use of the rhythmic freedoms pioneered elsewhere. Miles was an outspoken critic of the New Thing—Ornette, Taylor, Dolphy etc—and soon began looking elsewhere for his next development. The next album, **Filles De Kilimanjaro**, featured Hancock on electric piano and Carter on electric bass, with the flexible drumming of Williams stiffening up.

Miles' new conception was derived from West Coast acid rock, riff dominated with the trumpeter more economic than ever over a brocade of electric ripples. Using an enlarged personnel—Hancock, Chick Corea and Joe Zawinul on electric pianos, Dave Holland on bass, John McLaughlin on guitar, Shorter on soprano saxophone and Tony Williams on drums (all of whom went on to lead their own units)—Miles cut what, from the jazz purist's viewpoint, was to be his 'last' album **(In A Silent Way)**.

Staring with **In A Silent Way** ('69) and subsequent albums like **Bitches Brew** ('70), **Jack Johnson** ('70, the score written for William Clayton's superb documentary), **Live-Evil** ('72), **On The Corner** ('74) and **Big Fun** ('74), Miles had taken a sharp left turn. His change in direction caused a shock-wave in jazz circles with its heavy rock-influenced rhythms, high-profile electric instrumentation and the 'psychedelic' implications of its spacey electronic FX and phasing. But, like it or not, Miles was to create the climate for much of what was to come after in terms of popular electronic music. Miles didn't so much 'weather' the ensuing storm of protest from the purists, he characteristically ignored it.

Miles enlisted some of the new age's finest experimentalists like pianists Joe Zawinul, Keith Jarrett and Larry Young, electric guitarist John McLaughlin, percussionist Airto Moreira, electric bassist Dave Holland, drummers Billy Cobham and Jack De Johnette. While the diehards debated the new music's validity as 'jazz', the question just didn't arise for a new and open-minded generation: that's what it was—*new* music. No further definition was needed.

For some time, Miles had been in poor health following surgery and a series of medical problems. By '75, his diminishing mobility and deteriorating condition were causing much concern. It was feared that permanent retirement was not far off. Indeed, for the next six years, Miles was rarely seen in any public capacity. Then, in '78, there were rumors that Miles might record again. But it wasn't until '81 that his long-awaited 'comeback' album was finally released to an eager public.

The auspicious appearance of that album, **The Man With The Horn**, called for a special celebration reception on July 1 during the Kool Jazz Festival. Then, on July 5, 1981, the festival closed with an extraordinary musical event—a miraculous return *performance* from Miles Davis. In good spirits, and much better health, he was more relaxed and communicative than he'd ever been before.

It was now definitely business as usual and the double album **We Want Miles** (recorded live in Boston, New York and Tokyo) was issued in '82. At the end of that year, Leonard Feather's famous interview with Miles—the musician who didn't *give* interviews—appeared in *Ebony*. In it, a delightfully contented and forthcoming Miles gave the credit for his incredible recovery after a stroke, and subsequent return, to his wife Cicely Tyson and his Chinese acupuncturist doctor. In '83, he released **Star People**, an album which touchingly included the tribute to his wife **Star On Cicely**. Further proof that Miles Davis was back in blistering form emerged with the release of **Decoy** ('84) and **You're Under Arrest** ('85).

Speaking of the musicians he has used in the past, Miles once said that they have changed the whole style of music today. Few would argue with that. Whether the same will be said of the musicians with whom he is working in the '80s remains a matter for time and the subsequent unfolding of musical history to reveal.

What isn't in doubt is Miles Davis' own immeasurable achievement and contribution to contemporary music. Miles has returned and clearly still believes that what's important is what's happening *now*—the new music and the music of the future.

Albums:

Birth Of The Cool (Capitol/Capitol)
Pre-Birth Of The Cool (—/Durium Italian)
Miles Davis, Vols 1 & 2 (Blue Note/Blue Note)
Walkin' (Prestige/Prestige)
Tallest Trees (Prestige/Prestige)
Miles Davis (Prestige/Prestige)
Workin' & Steamin' (Prestige/Prestige)
Milestones (Columbia/CBS)
Kind Of Blue (Columbia/CBS)
Sketches Of Spain (Columbia/CBS)
Porgy And Bess (Columbia/CBS)
Miles Ahead (Columbia/CBS)
My Funny Valentine (Columbia/CBS)
Four (Columbia/CBS)
Miles In Europe (Columbia/CBS)
Friday And Saturday Nights At The Blackhawk (Columbia/CBS)
ESP (Columbia/CBS)
Miles Smiles (Columbia/CBS)
Sorcerer (Columbia/CBS)
Nefertiti (Columbia/CBS)
Miles In The Sky (Columbia/CBS)
Filles De Kilimanjaro (Columbia/CBS)
Miles In Tokyo (—/CBS Sony—Japan)
In A Silent Way (Columbia/CBS)
Bitches Brew (Columbia/CBS)
At Fillmore (Columbia/CBS)
A Tribute To Jack Johnson (Columbia/CBS)
Live-Evil (Columbia/CBS)
On The Corner (Columbia/CBS)
In Concert (Columbia/CBS)
Big Fun (Columbia/CBS)
Get Up With It (Columbia/CBS)
Agharta (Columbia/CBS)
Water Babies (Columbia/CBS)
Circle In The Round (Columbia/CBS)
Directions (Columbia/CBS)
The Man With The Horn (Columbia/CBS)
We Want Miles (Columbia/CBS)
Live At The Plugged Nickel (Columbia/CBS)
Star People (Columbia/CBS)
Heard 'Round The World (Columbia/CBS)
Decoy (Columbia/CBS)
You're Under Arrest (Columbia/CBS)

Below: Miles, 1980s—his contribution to contemporary music is incalculable.

Blossom Dearie

Born in East Durham, New York, in 1926, Dearie worked with Woody Herman's Blue Flames in the '40s and in Paris with the Blue Stars, '50s. Her fine paino style and witty, fragile-voiced delivery of Dearie 'classics' like **I'm Hip** and **Sweet Georgie Fame** have made her a perennial club favorite.

Albums:
My New Celebrity Is You (Blossom Dearie/Blossom Dearie)
May I Come In? (Capitol/Capitol)
Blossom Dearie Sings (Daffodil/Daffodil)
Needlepoint Magic (Daffodil/Daffodil)

Buddy De Franco

Born Boniface Ferdinand Leonardo De Franco in 1923, the clarinettist who won the *Downbeat* poll ten years running was the victim of fashion: the clarinet supremacy of the swing era had faded, and bebop found no place for the instrument, thus De Franco's virtuosity found little popular outlet. He turns up with the Metronome All Stars of 1947 with Gillespie, Bill Harris, Flip Phillips and Nat King Cole on **Leap Here (All Star Sessions)** and takes his orchestra through the fiendishly complex avant-garde George Russell composition, **A Bird In Igor's Yard (Crosscurrents)**, also leading a sextet with Jimmy Raney and Max Roach on **Extrovert** and **Good For Nothing Joe**. A meeting with piano virtuoso Art Tatum proved that De Franco was technically equipped to keep up with that firework display, and he plays brilliantly **(The Group Masterpieces)**.

From 1966-74, he toured the world as leader of the Glenn Miller Orchestra. Now settled in Florida, he is much in demand for his stage-band arrangements and instruction books like *Buddy De Franco On Jazz Improvisation*.

His welcome return to the international festival circuit in '81, teamed with the enduring bop vibes-player Terry Gibbs, refocused world attention on this rare and gifted performer. A 1983 jazz album with classical clarinettist John Denman is an inspired and rewarding outing for both.

Albums:
All Star Sessions (Capitol/—)
Crosscurrents (Capitol/Capitol)
Art Tatum, The Group Masterpieces (Pablo/Pablo)
The Jazz Ambassadors, Vol 2 (Verve/Verve)
Borinquin (Sonet/Sonet)
Buddy De Franco Presents John Denman; John Denman Presents Buddy De Franco (Lud/—)

De Franco: brilliant on The Tatum Group Masterpieces (courtesy Pablo).

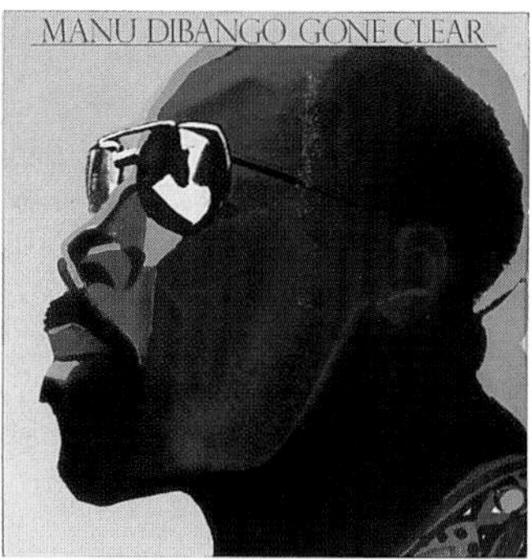

Manu Dibango, Gone Clear (courtesy Island)—'Afro-Quelque Chose'.

Manu Dibango

The unprecedented success of Manu Dibango's **Soul Makossa** in 1974 was significant in opening up the wider interest in African popular music today on such an international scale.

Born in Central Africa (Douala, Cameroon, in 1934), saxophonist Manu Dibango's introduction to music was through traditional African music and the church choir. At 15 he was sent to France to be educated and learned classical piano. He took up saxophone in the early '50s and stayed in Europe until his late 20s, working extensively on the bustling club circuit. In '60, he returned to Africa—to the Congo, where he joined top dance band African Jazz, his popularity spreading across the African Continent, and in the late '60s returned to his native Cameroon.

Listing among his heroes Junior Walker, Duke Ellington and Louis Armstrong, his music is as much rooted in R&B and jazz as it is in his native Makossa and acquired Zairois guitar-band music—a style he has made his own and called 'Afro-Quelque Chose'.

In recent years, he has benefited from a close and creative association with producer Martin Meissonnier—the Meissonnier-produced 12-inch single **Abele Dance** brought Dibango renewed popularity in '84. Of late, he has been exploring the possibilities of merging his special brand of African music with electronics and the new studio technology. In this vein, his **Electric Africa** album appeared in '85, produced by Bill Laswell and featuring Herbie Hancock on keyboards.

Albums:
Manu Dibango (Decca/—)
Afrovision (Decca/Island)
Gone Clear (Island/Island)
Electric Africa (Celluloid/Celluloid)

Al Di Meola

An important early contributor to the jazz-rock revolution, notably with Chick Corea's Return To Forever, Al Di Meola was born in Jersey City, New Jersey, on July 22, 1954.

His earliest influence was classical Italian music from his father. Later he was drawn to the rhythmic possibilities of Spanish and Latin music. Studying jazz guitar from age 8 with Robert Aslanian, Di Meola lists among his early guitar inspirations such legends as Doc Watson, Kenny Burrell, Tal Farlow, Larry Coryell and George Benson.

After a brief period at Berkle in the '70s, Di Meola joined Barry Miles' quintet. In '74, aged 19, he replaced Bill Connors in Return To Forever **(Where Have I Known You Before, No Mystery, Romantic Warrior)**. Since '76, he has pursued a solo course, most recently working with keyboardist Phil Markowitz, drummer Danny Gottlieb, bassist Chip Jackson and percussionist Airto Moreira. Of late, Di Meola has been exploring the combination of electric guitar and a digital-operated, guitar-triggered synclavier **(Soaring Through A Dream)**.

In the '80s, he has toured and recorded as part of a heavyweight trio of acoustic guitarists alongside John McLaughlin and Paco de Lucia **(Friday Night In San Francisco** and **Passion, Grace And Fire)**.

Above: Al Di Meola, jazz-rock guitar pioneer with Return to Forever. In 1985, Di Meola produced Stanley Jordan's début album, Magic Touch, for Blue Note.

Albums:
Land Of The Midnight Sun (Columbia/CBS)
Elegant Gypsy (Columbia/CBS)
Casino (Columbia/CBS)
Splendido Hotel (Columbia/CBS)
Electric Rendezvous (Columbia/CBS)
Tour De Force—Live (Columbia/CBS)
Scenario (Columbia/CBS)
Cielo E Terra (Manhattan/Manhattan)
Soaring Through A Dream (Manhattan/Manhattan)

Baby Dodds

Warren 'Baby' Dodds (born New Orleans, Louisiana, 1898; died Chicago, Illinois, 1959), together with Zutty Singleton and Paul Barbarin, is representative of the very finest drumming to emerge from New Orleans during the early part of jazz history. At 14, worked in a factory, but after drum tuition worked with Bunk Johnson in New Orleans parades. First important job with trumpeter Willie Hightower; then came prestigious gigs with Papa Celestin, Fate Marable (1918-23). Worked with King Oliver for a year (1922-23), joining brother Johnny Dodds who was already playing clarinet with the Creole Jazz Band. Dodds' famed press rolls, rock-steady beat, and an all-round flexibility which many contemporaries did not possess, earned him plaudits of big-name leaders with whom he worked through the years. This meant he obtained regular work after leaving Oliver with Honore Dutrey, Freddie Keppard, Willie Hightower (again), Lil Armstrong, and Johnny Dodds (with whom he worked regularly at Kelly's Stables, 1927-29).

Dodds brothers played numerous varied engagements together in Chicago during 1930s, including regular appearances at the Three Deuces. Baby Dodds also helped brother run fleet of taxis during same decade. With Jimmie Noone (1940-41), Bunk Johnson (1945); at 47, the drummer made first-ever trip to New York with the trumpeter's band. With pianist Art Hodes for two years (1946-47), visited Europe with Mezz Mezzrow ('48) to appear at Nice Jazz Festival. Back in New York with Hodes, them with Miff Mole (1948-49). Suffered stroke in spring of '49; a second in 1950. Was playing again in 1951, and in 1951-52 teamed up with trumpeter Natty Dominique, with whom he had played in Johnny Dodds' Black Bottom Stompers and Washboard Band during late-1920s **(Clarinet King** and **The Complete Johnny Dodds)**.

Taken ill in New York in '52, returned to Chicago for recuperation. Last major appearance in New York in 1952. Partially paralyzed, Dodds nevertheless played from time to time until forced to retire completely in 1957.

Despite difficulties in recording drummers in pre-hi-fi days, Dodds' drumming skills were an integral part of other discs by King Oliver **(Louis Armstrong & King Oliver** and **West End Blues)**, Louis Armstrong **(V.S.O.P.**

(Very Special Old Phonography), Vols 1 & 2, 3 & 4), George Lewis **(George Lewis With Kid Shots)**, Bunk Johnson **(Bunk Johnson's Band 1945)**, Albert Nicholas **(Creole Reeds)**, Sidney Bechet **(Sidney Bechet, Vols 2, 3** and **Jelly Roll Morton Vols 1, 2, 4)**. But best examples of his talents are to be found on a trio of LPs **(Baby Dodds, Nos 1, 2, 3)** recorded in 1946.

Albums:
Louis Armstrong & King Oliver (Milestone)
King Oliver, West End Blues (CBS—France)
King Oliver's Jazz Band (—/Parlophone)
Louis Armstrong, V.S.O.P. (Very Special Old Phonography), Vols 1 & 2, 3 & 4 (CBS—France)
Jelly Roll Morton, Vols 1, 2, 4 (RCA Victor—France)
George Lewis With Kid Shots (American Music/—)
Bunk Johnson's Band 1945 (—/Storyville)
The Complete Johnny Dodds (RCA Victor—France)
Sideny Bechet, Vols 2, 3 (RCA Victor—France)
Albert Nicholas, Creole Reeds (Riverside/—)
Baby Dodds, Jazz A La Creole (GHB)
Various, 'This Is Jazz' Vols 1, 2 (Rarities/—)
Johnny Dodds, Clarinet King (—/Ace of Hearts)
Johnny Dodds, Weary Way Blues (Family—Italy)
Baby Dodds, 'Baby Dodds', Nos 1, 2, 3 (Disc/Melodisc)

Johnny Dodds

To most connoisseurs of early jazz, Johnny Dodds (born New Orleans, Louisiana, 1892) was the greatest of all clarinet players. In many ways, Dodds—brother of drummer Warren 'Baby' Dodds and a clarinettist since 17—*was* the greatest. He may have lacked the technical skills of Sidney Bechet, Jimmie Noone, or Barney Bigard, but he more than made up for any deficiencies with a warmth and passion which only Bechet surpassed.

Tutored by legendary New Orleansian Lorenzo Tio, worked with Kid Ory, and marching bands (both in New Orleans); and on riverboats with Fate Marable; then back with Ory—all before 1920. In latter year, joined King Oliver, working with the trumpeter four years, in Chicago and California. Recorded first solos with Oliver, most eloquent of which are **Canal Street Blues** and **Mandy Lee Blues (Louis Armstrong & King Oliver)**, demonstrating that his was a very basic jazz style; emotional yet with a harsher (but not unmelodic) tone than, say, Noone. Dodds lacked nothing in ability as a blues-player; his contributions to numerous recordings with singers like Ida Cox **(Ida Cox, Vol 2)** were demonstrably right in every way. With leader-pianist-composer Lovie Austin **(Lovie Austin & Her Blues Serenaders)** Dodds' abilities in blues genre were very moving (eg **In The Alley Blues**). As member of Louis Armstrong's Hot Five/Seven combos, Dodds' playing reached new peaks.

Recordings such as **Come Back Sweet Papa, Gut Bucket Blues, Willie The Weeper, Wild Man Blues, Melancholy Blues, Weary Blues (V.S.O.P. (Very Special Old Phonography), Vols 1 & 2)** and **Gully Low Blues, S.O.L. Blues (V.S.O.P., Vols 3 & 4)** benefit enormously from his presence as soloist and ensemble player. Equally superb recordings featuring Dodds' piping clarinet, assisted by Kid Ory and others from Hot Five (sans Armstrong), released under various titles: New Orleans Bootblacks and Wanderers **(Johnny Dodds & Kid Ory)** and Black Bottom Stompers **(Black Bottom Stompers, Vols 1, 2)**. Yet further Dodds excellence to be found within **Weary Way Blues** and **Clarinet King**, the latter containing exquisite clarinet, and with Armstrong comprehensively on form throughout.

Jelly Roll Morton made ample use of Dodds' expressive playing on records by his Red Hot Peppers and, even more impressively, in a trio setting, the group completed by Morton and Baby Dodds **(Jelly Roll Morton, Vols 1, 2, 4)**.

Dodds led own bands during 1930s. Made first (and only) trip to New York in 1938, to record with his Chicago Boys: long-time associate Lil Armstrong, Teddy Bunn; and Charlie Shavers and O'Neil Spencer from the John Kirby band. At 46, his powers seemed undiminished, as shown on five items, including further versions of **Wild Man Blues** and **Melancholy Blues (Harlem On Saturday Night)**. Less than three years later, Dodds died after cerebral hemorrhage (he had moved back to Chicago in '38, suffering a heart attack there a year later).

Probably best all-round examples of Johnny Dodds' playing are to be found on **The Complete Johnny Dodds**. Apart from clarinet, he also played alto, although never outstanding on this instrument.

Albums:
King Oliver, West End Blues (CBS—France)
Louis Armstrong & King Oliver (Milestone)
Ida Cox, Vol 2 (Fountain)
Lovie Austin & Her Blues Serenaders (Fountain)
Johnny Dodds & Kid Ory (Columbia)
Johnny Dodds, Black Bottom Stompers, Vols 1, 2 (Swaggie—Australia)
Jelly Roll Morton, Vols 1, 2, 4 (RCA Victor—France)
Louis Armstrong, V.S.O.P. (Very Special Old Phonography), Vols 1 & 2, 3 & 4 (CBS—France)
Johnny Dodds, Clarinet King (Ace of Hearts)
Johnny Dodds, Weary Way Blues (Family—Italy)
The Complete Johnny Dodds (RCA Victor—France)
Various, Harlem On Saturday Night (—/Ace of Hearts)

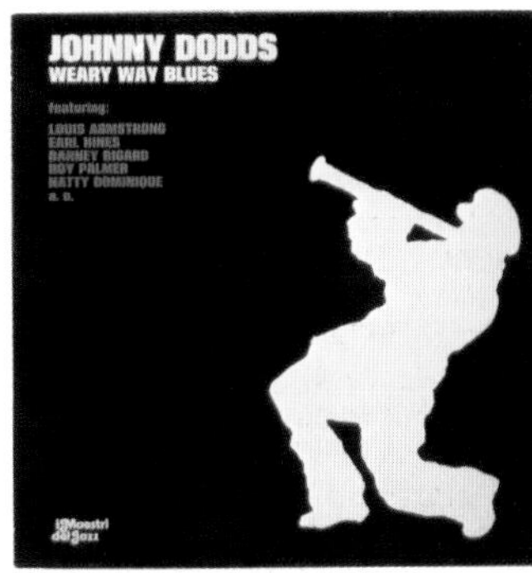

Clarinettist Johnny Dodds, Weary Way Blues (courtesy Family—Italy).

Above: The late, great Eric Dolphy, multi-instrumentalist supreme of the 1960s—alto, flute, bass clarinet. Another irreplaceable musician.

Eric Dolphy

Born 1928 in Los Angeles, the great multi-instrumentalist's earliest influence—in common with most of his generation—was Charlie Parker. Dolphy first came to prominence wih the Chico Hamilton Quintet, playing with a passion that threatened to crack the effete confines of that unit. In 1960, he moved to New York to join Charlie Mingus, where his willingness to challenge conventions found a sympathetic environment. Before his death in 1964, Dolphy was in great demand, playing with Max Roach, George Russell, Ornette Coleman and—most notably—John Coltrane. He wrote the orchestrations for the **Africa Brass** album and joined the Coltrane group as a floating member, accompanying them on their tour of Europe—and staying on. From a career point of view, this was a bad move: the brilliant innovator and the pedestrian local talent. His death cut short his expansion from soloist into the fuller group conception of fellow pioneers like Coltrane and Coleman, and his final album, **Out To Lunch**, is a tragic reminder of his potential.

Dolphy was a transitional figure, neither doctrinaire New Thing, nor wholly content with the harmonic confines of bebop. He seemed to hear differently, to hear high, so that his work on alto, **245 (Eric Dolphy), The Prophet (Five Spot)**, and **Love Me (Memorial)** takes on a shrill, keening quality. Extremes of vocalization mark his playing on both alto and bass clarinet, an instrument that he rescued from limbo and often used in duos with bass players. With Mingus, **What Love (Charles Mingus Presents)** or Richard Davis, **Alone Together (Memorial)**, the dark sonorities are rich and ominous as a dungeon door, whereas on **Music Matador (Memorial)** it snorts like a happy hippo. On both horns, the shape of his phrases is unpredictable, almost wayward, with abrupt, jagged lines flowering suddenly into decoration. His flute, by contrast, is all prettiness and delicacy, never more so than on **Gazzelloni (Out To Lunch)**.

Albums:
Oliver Nelson, The Blues And The Abstract Truth (Impulse/Impulse)
1Eric Dolphy (Prestige/Prestige)
Eric Dolphy At The Five Spot (Prestige/Prestige)
Charles Mingus Presents The Charles Mingus Quartet (CBS Barnaby/—)
Max Roach, Percussion Bitter Sweet (Impulse/Impulse)
George Russell, Outer Thoughts (Milestone/Milestone)
John Coltrane, Africa Brass (Impulse/Impulse)
Eric Dolphy Memorial (Veejay/DJM)
Eric Dolphy, Out To Lunch (Blue Note/Blue Note)

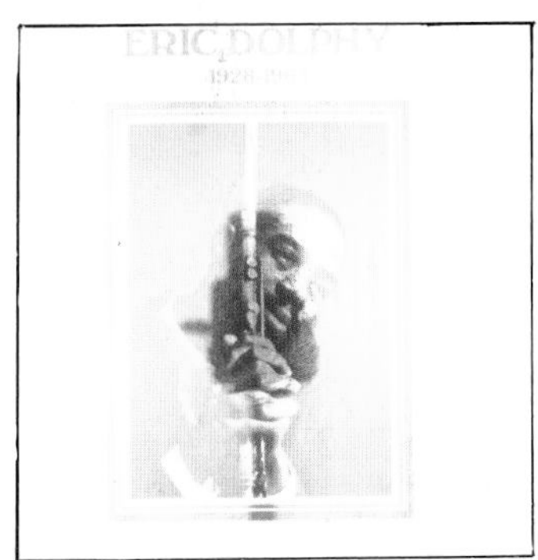

Eric Dolphy (courtesy Epitaph)—half of a mammoth recording session.

Out To Lunch (courtesy Blue Note) —Reid Miles' cover, classic recording.

Kenny Dorham

Born 1924, McKinley Dorham served his apprenticeship during the hectic bebop years, playing trumpet in the Dizzy Gillespie big band, and even acquitting himself honorably in chase choruses with the fabulous Fats Navarro **(Fats Navarro Memorial)**, an early influence. Dorham played with the Charlie Parker Quintet **(Historical Masterpieces)**, his tone already bitingly direct. In the mid-'50s, he was a founder member of The Jazz Messengers, the hard-hitting atmosphere and messianic drumming spurring the

Above: The late trumpet giant Kenny Dorham, overshadowed by Diz, Fats and Miles in his lifetime. His work has found new young fans in the 1980s.

trumpeter to his best work, **Soft Winds (The Jazz Messengers At The Cafe Bohemia)**.

As the decade wore on, Dorham's hard bop style underwent moderate changes, he concentrated on his tone, burnishing it to a muscular lyricism on numbers like **Larue** and **My Old Flame (But Beautiful)**.

Before his death in 1972, he had formed a fruitful association with the young tenorist, Joe Henderson, and their albums for Blue Note feature a wealth of original material utilizing modes and bossa nova rhythms. Kenny Dorham was unfortunate in his contemporaries, Gillespie and Navarro in the '40s, Miles Davis and Clifford Brown in the '50s. He was considerably more than merely reliable, and his work shows a steady and continuous development. A moving and melodic player, he could also drive like a row of sabres. If popularity polls ignored him, his fellow musicians did not, and he features on albums with Monk, Tadd Dameron, Rollins, Hank Mobley, Max Roach and—rather incongruously—with Cecil Taylor.

Interestingly, the '80s 'second wave' of enthusiasm for the legendary Blue Note hard-bop days has elevated Dorham to something like cult status, particularly in the jazz discos where the current generation of 16-year-olds has been heard heatedly comparing the 'relative' merits of Dorham and Lee Morgan.

Albums:

Fats Navarro Memorial (Savoy/Savoy)
Charlie Parker, Historical Masterpieces (Archive of Folk & Jazz/MGM)
The Jazz Messengers At The Cafe Bohemia (Blue Note/Blue Note)
Kenny Dorham, But Beautiful (Milestone/Milestone)
Kenny Dorham, Trompeta Toccata (Blue Note/Blue Note)
Kenny Dorham, Una Mas (Blue Note/Blue Note)
The Bopmasters (Impulse/Impulse)

Jimmy Dorsey

James Dorsey (born Shenandoah, Pennsylvania, 1904) was one of the most accomplished musicians produced by jazz of the Roaring Twenties. Dorsey, elder brother of Tommy Dorsey, started on cornet, moved on to clarinet and alto sax (occasionally baritone sax, too). Played cornet in band of Thomas F. Dorsey, his father, who taught him basic music knowledge. With brother Tommy, started both Dorsey's Novelty Six, then Dorsey's Wild Canaries; latter became one of first jazz outfits to broadcast.

After making recording début with Billy Lustig's Scranton Sirens, joined California Ramblers (1924), then freelanced—on radio, records—with bands of Jean Goldkette, Henry Thies, Ray Miller, Vincent Lopez, Paul Whiteman, Red Nichols. By 1930, had joined Ted Lewis, with whom he toured Europe. Undertook more extensive studio-session work as well as helping Tommy Dorsey to run part-time Dorsey Bros bands which eventually (in 1934) became full-time Dorsey Bros Orchestra (**Dorsey Bros 1928, Dorsey Bros 1928-1929** and **Bring Back The Good Times**). This 1934 band lasted for about a year before violent disagreement between the brothers led to younger Dorsey walking offstage during actual engagement—never to return in that band's lifetime.

Jimmy Dorsey continued to lead what was already a band of growing popularity. Gradually, Jimmy Dorsey Orchestra became leading participant in swing era, playing to enthusiastic ballroom hit records like **Amapola, Tangerine, My Prayer, Yours, Green Eyes, Besame Mucho** and **Star Eyes (The Great Jimmy Dorsey)**, each featuring vocal performances by Bob Eberly, Helen O'Connell and Kitty Kallen—alone or in pairs. Much of jazz content disappeared altogether, although on certain occasions **(Jimmy Dorsey & His Orchestra 1935-1942)** the commercial-pop aspects were (temporarily) forgotten and the band endeavored to swing with eloquent power, as with items such as **Stompin' At The Savoy, Major & Minor Stomp, Mutiny In The Brass Section** and **Waddlin' At The Waldorf**.

Despite demise of big-band era, Dorsey continued to lead own orchestra until 1953 when he was finally reunited with Tommy as a member of his brother's own orchestra. (Musically, pair had appeared in semi-biographical movie, *The Fabulous Dorseys*).

On Tommy's death, in '56, Jimmy Dorsey assumed leadership of the former's band, a position he held until following year when increasing ill-health forced him to retire. Same year, he died of cancer.

Jimmy Dorsey band took part in several World War II movies, including *The Fleet's In, 4 Jacks & A Jeep, That Girl From Paris* and *Shall We Dance?* As jazz instrumentalist, Dorsey's reputation probably is best remembered from earlier days, way back to the 1920s-through-the-1930s, when he worked with innumerable jazzmen, including Jack Teagarden **(J.T.** and **Jack Teagarden Classics)**; Joe Venuti, Eddie Lang and Adrian Rollini **(Benny Goodman & The Giants Of Swing/Jazz In The Thirties)**; Miff Mole **(Miff Mole's Molers 1928-30)** and Red Nichols **(Red Nichols & His Five Pennies, 1926-1928)**.

In the 1920s, his was the most important voice on alto sax; on clarinet, too, his playing was always immaculate, although not quite as distinctive; on coronet (or trumpet), Dorsey could be a more-than-average 'hot' performer, as he proved in company with Venuti-Lang Blue Five **(Benny Goodman & The Giants Of Swing/Jazz In The Thirties)**. On alto and clarinet, his always rhythmic playing was a decided asset, whether heard in context of Whiteman Orchestra **(The Bix Beiderbecke Legend)** or in proximity with such as Bix Beiderbecke and Frankie Trumbauer **(The Golden Days Of Jazz: Bix Beiderbecke)** or in all manner of bands with or without his brother **(Tommy, Jimmy & Eddie, 1928-29)**. And even during the peak days of his orchestra, Jimmy Dorsey's jazz feel, coupled with his technical dexterity, could produce a supremely rewarding performance, as with his astonishingly good version of **I Got Rhythm**, as guest on one of Eddie Condon's legendary war-time concerts **(Eddie Condon & His All Stars, Vol 8)**.

Albums:

Tommy Dorsey/Jimmy Dorsey/Eddie Lang, Tommy, Jimmy & Eddie 1928-29 (—/Parlophone)
The Bix Beiderbecke Legend (RCA Victor—France)
The Charleston Chasers 1925-1928 (VJM)
Jack Teagarden Classics (Family)
Jack Teagarden, 'J.T.' (—/Ace of Hearts)
Various, Benny Goodman & The Giants Of Swing (Prestige)/Jazz In The Thirties (World Records)
Joe Venuti/Eddie Lang, The Sounds Of New York, Vol 2 (1927-1933) (RCA Victor—France)
Miff Mole's Molers—1927, With Sophie Tucker (—/Parlophone)
Miff Mole's Molers 1928-30 (—/Parlophone)
Red Nichols & His Five Pennies, 1926-1928 (MCA Coral—Germany)
Dorsey Bros, 1928-1930 (The Old Masters/—)
Coleman Hawkins, Recordings Made Between 1930 & 1941 (CBS—France)
Dorsey Bros, Bring Back The Good Times (MCA Coral—Germany)
Jimmy Dorsey & His Orchestra 1935-1942 (Swingfan—Germany)
The Great Jimmy Dorsey (Ace of Hearts)

Tommy Dorsey

Tommy Dorsey (born Shenandoah, Pennsylvania, 1905), younger brother by one year of Jimmy Dorsey, started his musical life as a trumpet player and trombonist but during the last 25 years of his life was renowned as leader of a jazz-influenced danceband, who mostly featured himself as a trombone player with a gift for executing superbly controlled pianissimo ballad performances.

His red-blooded temperament led to frequent clashes—even stand-up fights—not only with Jimmy Dorsey, but with a succession of sidemen.

Like Jimmy, Tommy Dorsey was taught to play trumpet by his musician father. Where most of his white contemporaries tended to follow the lyrical pathway of Bix Beiderbecke, Dorsey's impassioned blowing obviously was primarily influenced by the 'hot' solos of the leading black hornmen.

Early examples of Tommy Dorsey's emotionally charged trumpet solos can be found, for example, on tracks like **Daddy, Change Your Mind** and **You Can't Cheat A Cheater**, both included on **Tommy, Jimmy And Eddie, 1928-29**.

During 1927-28, worked as trombonist with the Paul Whiteman Orchestra. Perhaps his most famous solo feature with Whiteman was a first-class contribution to Don Redman's arrangement of **Whiteman Stomp (Paul Whiteman & His Orchestra)**. During the time when he was co-leading one of the early Dorsey Bros bands he recorded **I'm Getting Sentimental Over You**. By the time he had split with his brother and put together own band, Tommy Dorsey had re-recorded the tune **(Tommy Dorsey & His Orchestra)** and thereafter it was to become his very popular signature tune. From 1935, when he formed the Tommy Dorsey Orchestra—using remnants of Joe Haynes Orchestra—until his death in 1956, he was to prove one of the most popular as well as durable bandleaders.

The Tommy Dorsey Orchestra peaked between 1937-44, during which time top jazz sidemen like Bud Freeman, Louis Bellson, Gene Krupa, Buddy Rich, Charlie Shavers, Max Kaminsky, Bunny Berigan, Buddy De Franco, Joe Bushkin and Yank Lawson had passed through its ranks. Likewise, a host of superior pop singers, mostly on the first rungs of the ladder to success, notably Jack Leonard, Jo Stafford, Dick Haymes, Lucy Ann Polk and, Frank Sinatra.

Whilst arrangers Paul Weston and Axel Stordahl handled more commercial aspects of band's charts, Dorsey wisely utilized skills of such jazz-based writers as Dean Kincaide and Sy Oliver, in order to maintain the real spirit of jazz within the band, something all too often absent from many of Dorsey's big-band rivals of the Swing Era. The Clambake Seven—a small group taken from within the ranks of the orchestra—also helped to sustain interest **(Tommy Dorsey, The Clambake Seven)**.

The Dorsey Orchestra featured in several films, including *Ship Ahoy!, Reveille With Beverly, Girl Crazy* and *A Song Is Born*.

Amongst its most popular discs can be numbered **After You've Gone, Lonesome Road** (two-part record arranged by Oliver) (both **Tommy Dorsey, Vol 2**) and **On The Sunny Side Of The Street, Marie** (featuring Berigan and with vocal by Leonard), **Hawaiian War Chant, Opus No. 1** and **Song Of India** (fine Berigan trumpet solo) (all **Tommy Dorsey & His Orchestra**). For Tommy Dorsey, his involvement with jazz went back to his more youthful days, when he blew passionately—both on trombone and trumpet—in company of other eager, fresh-faced youngsters like Benny Goodman **(The Early B.G.)**, Joe Venuti and Eddie Lang **(The Golden Days Of Jazz/Stringing The Blues** and **The Sounds Of New York, Vol 2)**, Bix Beiderbecke **(The Bix Beiderbecke Legend)** and Adrian Rollini **(Jazz In The Thirties)**.

Albums:
Tommy Dorsey/Jimmy Dorsey/Eddie Lang, Tommy, Jimmy & Eddie—1928-29 (—/Parlophone)
Tommy Dorsey & His Orchestra (RCA Victor/RCA Victor)
Tommy Dorsey, Vol 2 (RCA Victor—RCA Victor)
The Best Of Tommy Dorsey, Vols 1-6 (RCA Victor—France)
Dorsey Bros, Bring Back the Good Times (MCA Coral—Germany)
Dorsey Brothers 1928 (The Old Masters)
Dorsey Brothers 1928-1930 (The Old Masters)
The Chocolate Dandies (—/Parlophone)
Benny Goodman, The Early B.G. (Vocalion)
Joe Venuti/Eddie Lang, The Golden Days Of Jazz/Stringing The Blues (CBS/Holland)
Joe Venuti/Eddie Lang, The Sounds Of New York, Vol 2 (RCA Victor—France)
Bix Beiderbecke, The Bix Beiderbecke Legend (RCA Victor—France)
Various (Including Adrian Rollini), Jazz In The Thirties (World Records)
Various, Metronome All Stars/Esquire All Stars (RCA Victor—France)
Paul Whiteman & His Orchestra (RCA Victor/RCA Victor)
Tommy Dorsey, The Clambake Seven (RCA Victor)

Tommy Dorsey, Vol. 2 (courtesy RCA Victor). For years, Tommy Dorsey fronted a successful jazz-based dance band which peaked 1937-44.

George Duke

After a diverse career bordering on the extraordinary (spanning Don Ellis to Frank Zappa to Cannonball Adderley), keyboardist-composer George Duke has emerged as one of the key figures in popular jazz fusion.

Born San Rafael, California, on January 12, 1946, Duke's interest in jazz piano started early, at age 6 when his mother took him to a Duke Ellington concert. After a classical grounding, he put together a Latin band in high school inspired by Les McCann. His time at the San Francisco Conservatory is notable in that Duke majored in trombone and minored in piano. His cousin Charles Burrell, a classical bassist with the San Francisco Symphony, was impressed with Duke's improvisational skills and encouraged him to abandon his classical career to play jazz piano. Duke worked at the Half Note Club with a trio before going on the road with vocal group the Third Wave. **The Primal George Duke**, recorded in '66 when he was just 18, is an interesting if understated example of how he sounded at this time, giving little hint of what genius was to come.

In '68, he worked with Gerald Wilson, Dizzy Gillespie, Bobby Hutcherson and the Don Ellis big band. The following year he recorded and toured with violinist Jean-Luc Ponty. His involvement with Frank Zappa's zany Mothers of Invention in '70 introduced him to the limitless possibilities with synthesizers. Touring with Zappa's line-up gave Duke the opportunity to showcase his own jazz compositions like **The Black Messiah** (a solo spot which, frankly, sat oddly among Zappa's eccentric arrangements even if it did bring the house down).

After a year with Zappa, he spent two years with Cannonball Adderley (replacing Joe Zawinul). A short-lived excursion with drummer Billy Cobham followed and since '76, Duke has concentrated on his solo work and producing, taking time out to work with bassist Stanley Clarke (the **Clarke-Duke Project**).

Duke's exceptional **A Brazilian Love Affair**, recorded in '79 in Brazil with local musicians like Milton Nascimento, Flora Purim, Airto, Simone and Raul de Souza; was a huge commercial success. Still his best project to date, it contains some of his most enduring and explosive work, notably the memorable **Up From The Sea It Arose And Ate Rio In One Bite**, with a stinging guitar solo from Roland Bautista which deserves a special place in fusion history.

Albums:
Frank Zappa, Waka/Jawaka (Bizarre-Reprise/Bizarre-Reprise)
Nat Adderley, Double Exposure (Prestige/Prestige)
Sonny Rollins, Nucleus (Milestone/Milestone)
The Primal George Duke (—/MPS)
The Inner Source (—/MPS)
Feel (—/MPS)
The Aura Will Prevail (—/MPS)
Save The Country (Liberty/Liberty)
Billy Cobham-George Duke, Billy Cobham-George Duke Band Live On Tour (Atlantic/Atlantic)
From Me To You (Epic/Epic)
Reach For It (Epic/Epic)
Don't Let Go (Epic/Epic)
Follow The Rainbow (Epic/Epic)
Master Of The Game (Epic/Epic)
A Brazilian Love Affair (Epic/Epic)
Stanley Clarke-George Duke, Clarke-Duke Project (Epic/Epic)
Thief In The Night (Elektra/Elektra)

Above: George Duke, an eclectic and exceptional keyboard talent. Duke's considerable fusion success includes his all-time classic A Brazilian Love Affair.

Allen Eager

Born 1927 in New York, tenorist Allen Eager is one of the enigmas of jazz A concise, swinging player strongly based on the Lester Young style, Eager was one of the best tenors on 52nd Street in the '40s, but frequently left the scene for high society, skiing, horse-riding and car-racing, settling in Paris in the '50s. Some of his best blowing can be found on a Savoy compilation **(The Brothers & Other Mothers)** which features Lester's white disciples, Stan Getz, Al Cohn, Zoot Sims, Brew Moore and Serge Chaloff. His flowing drive on numbers like **Booby Hatch** is wildly exciting. Two years later, in 1948, he played in Tadd Dameron's sextets and septets, sharing the front line with players like Fats Navarro and Wardell Gray **(Prime Source** and **Good Bait)**. Interesting to contrast his style with Gray's; both men are on the Lester-Bird axis, with Eager lighter, more floating in his attack, **Lady Bird** and **Jahbero**. In the early '50s, Eager played with Gerry Mulligan's large groups with Lee Konitz, Al Cohn and Zoot Sims, switching to alto for some tracks **(Revelation)**.

In the early '80s, Allen Eager made a welcome return to the international touring circuit being received, particularly in Europe, like a long-lost hero.

Albums:
The Brothers & Other Mothers (Savoy/Savoy)
Fats Navarro, Prime Source (Blue Note/Blue Note)
Fats Navarro—Tadd Dameron, Good Bait (Riverside/—)
Gerry Mulligan—Lee Konitz, Revelation (Blue Note/Blue Note)

Earth Wind & Fire

One of the most popular and successful vocal soul-fusion groups, Earth Wind & Fire are included here on the basis of their inspirational musical insights which, for all the commercial gloss, are firmly rooted in jazz and blues courtesy of the visionary Maurice White.

White was born in Memphis but lived in Chicago from age 16—as it turned out, from an impressionable age. Resisting parental pressure to become a doctor, the lure of America's blues capital was too great and he studied music instead at the Chicago Conservatory. While working as session drummer for the influential Chess label, he experienced first-hand the genius and inspiration of such blues and jazz luminaries as Muddy Waters, Howlin' Wolf and John Coltrane.

From '66-'70, White worked with Ramsey Lewis and, while touring the East with Lewis, became captivated by things Egyptological and the mystic sciences—a spiritual enlightenment which was to re-order his life and, subsequently, re-direct his music. Under the influence of his newly raised consciousness, White envisaged a co-operative musical ensemble with multi-cultural potential and appeal—the project was to become Earth Wind & Fire in '71.

In '73, on the **Last Days And Time** album, White introduced an electric version of the ancient African percussion instrument, the kalimba—a symbol which has since become synonymous with the band. Equally as synonymous with EW&F is its brass section (saxophonists Andrew Woolfolk and Don Myrick, trombonist Louis Satterfield and trumpeter Rahmlee Michael Davis), probably the most recognizable and imitated horn section in the world, quite capable of quoting from John Coltrane if necessary. (The British jazz-based group Landscape admitted that riffs on their early '80s album **From The Tea Rooms Of Mars . . . To The Hell Holes Of Uranus** were a deliberate attempt to recreate, through synthesizers, EW&F's distinctive horn sound.)

While EW&F's breath-taking, no-expense-spared stage productions have become famous, complete with levitation acts and spectacular laser light-shows, the group endures as one of the most exceptional and creative vocal-instrumental units to cross the musical sound-barrier. Few others have done it so well.

Albums:
Last Days And Time (Columbia/CBS)
Head To The Sky (Columbia/CBS)
Open Our Eyes (Columbia/CBS)
That's The Way Of The World (Columbia/CBS)
Gratitude (Columbia/CBS)
Spirit (Columbia/CBS)
All 'N' All (Columbia/CBS)
The Best Of Earth Wind & Fire Volume One (Columbia/CBS)
I Am (Columbia/CBS)
Faces (Columbia/CBS)
Raise (Columbia/CBS)
Electric Universe (Columbia/CBS)

Above: In concert, no expense spared—lavish costumes, laser light-shows, even levitation. . . Maurice White and Earth Wind & Fire deliver the goods.

Above: The visionary Maurice White turned his dream of a multi-cultural, co-operative group into a reality when Earth Wind & Fire was born in 1971.

Billy Eckstine

Born 1914 in Pittsburg, singer Billy Eckstine became the first Afro-American pop idol. His rich, bass-baritone voice, perfect pitch and timing, gave him supremacy in the field of the romantic ballad, **I Apologize, Tenderly, Laura, No One But You (Greatest Hits)**. In fact, Eckstine is a hipper musician than his pop following realize. From 1939-43, he was the vocalist with Earl Hines' band, forming his own big band 1944-47 which was years ahead of its time. Excited by the bebop explosion, Eckstine recruited a band of young revolutionaries, including Charlie Parker, Dizzy Gillespie, Fats Navarro, Kenny Dorham, Miles Davis, Sonny Stitt, John Jackson, Dexter Gordon, Wardell Gray, Gene Ammons, Leo Parker, Tommy Potter and Art Blakey. Arrangements by Dizzy Gillespie, Tadd Dameron, Budd Johnson and Jerry Valentine gave the band a distinctive, adventurous sound, and it was probably only the Eckstine vocals that gave it it commercial viability. Sarah Vaughan also sang with the band, showing an Eckstine influence in her wide vibrato. Proficient on trombone and trumpet, the leader took occasional solos, but gave generous space to Dexter Gordon, **Lonesome Lover Blues**; Gene Ammons, **Second Balcony Jump**; Wardell Gray, **Blues For Sale**; Fats Navarro, **Tell Me Pretty Baby**. Two albums catch the band at its peak **(Mr. B. & The Band** and **Together)**, the latter album taken from radio broadcasts.

Eckstine has continued to record with jazz musicians from time to time, including the hilarious **I Left My Hat In Haiti** with Woody Herman, and **St. Louis Blues**, with the Metronome All-Stars, including Lester Young and Warne Marsh **(Greatest Hits)**. With the sort of voice you could stand a spoon up in, the Eckstine baritone influenced many of the bebop singers of the period.

Albums:
Greatest Hits (MGM/MGM)
Mr. B. & The Band (Savoy/Savoy)
Together (Spotlite/Spotlite)

ECM Records

The highly respected and prolific Munich-based record label ECM (originally, Editions of Contemporary Music) has been hailed as the 'European Blue Note'—its individuality, influence and standards of excellence cannot be understated.

Founded in 1970 by German producer Manfred Eicher, ECM's high-quality recordings created a big impact as a viable European alternative to American mainstream jazz ECM has maintained a wholly distinctive artistic policy, reflecting Eicher's personal taste and standards, rather than a frenetic attempt to document every current sound within earshot indiscriminately.

Eicher's own track record is impressive—he studied bass and composition at the Berlin Academy, worked with the Berlin Philharmonic and freelanced as a jazz musician, as well as becoming an independent classical producer with Deutsche Grammophon and Electrola. Under Eicher's guidance, ECM has become influential for its use of combinations without rhythm sections and its chamber-music oriented approach, and legendary for Eicher's unique ability to capture clear transparent sound with all the ringing overtones—'the most beautiful sound next to silence'.

ECM was originally formed to record self-exiled American musicians in Europe. The label's début was Mal Waldron's **Free At Last** (500 copies were originally pressed but eventually over 14,000 were sold). Among ECM's first artists were Paul Bley and several musicians from Miles Davis' late '60s groups—Keith Jarrett, Chick Corea, Dave Holland and Jack De Johnette.

Over the years, ECM has built up an interesting and loyal roster of individualists, noted for its unprecedented diversity. The long list includes the definitive if different styles of Pat Metheny, Gary Burton, Terje Rypdal, Steve Tibbetts, Eberhard Weber, Arild Andersen, Ralph Towner (with and without Oregon), Egberto Gismonti, Jan Garbarek, Charlie Haden, Shankar, Meredith Monk, Steve Reich, the Art Ensemble of Chicago, Codona, Kenny Wheeler, Azimuth, John Surman, John Abercrombie etc.

While Jarrett, Metheny and Corea account for most of ECM's top-ten albums (Jarrett's **The Köln Concert**, for instance, sold more than a million copies), ECM has also generously offered opportunities to many unknowns. A 1985 signing includes the young British band First House (pianist Django Bates, saxophonist Ken Stubbs, bassist Mick Hutton and drummer Martin France)—a group deserving wider recognition but unable to get a satisfactory recording deal in their own country.

In such a short history, no other label can boast such a distinctive personal identity as ECM. The label continues to enjoy an unrivaled influence internationally without once compromising excellence—a considerable achievement for such a young company in the face of commercial pressures.

Gems from Manfred Eicher's unrivalled label: Keith Jarrett's million-seller, The Köln Concert; Garbarek, Haden and Gismonti's Folk Songs (courtesy ECM).

Above: Harry 'Sweets' Edison served an early apprenticeship with Lucky Millinder's band in the late 1930s before becoming a principal Basie soloist.

Harry Edison

Harry Edison (born Columbus, Ohio, 1915) is one of jazz's most gifted and distinctive trumpet players. His sweet-sour tone, deceptively casual approach to what is a straight kind of swing, and splendid all-round qualities have, since the mid-1930s, ensured that his services have been constantly in demand. For conventional jazz record sessions like **Jazz Giants '57/Jazz Giants, Jam Session, Nos 2 3,** and **Jammin' At Sunset**, or bread-and-butter studio sessions with jazz-influenced singers of the calibre of Ella Fitzgerald (**Sings The Cole Porter Song Book)** and Frank Sinatra **(Swing Easy/Songs For Young Lovers)**, or for guest appearances at major international jazz festivals **(Newport In New York '72: The Jam Sessions, Vol 4** and **Jazz At The Santa Monica '72)**.

After commencing on trumpet at 12, Edison's career in music began with work for local Ohio bands. Moved on to Alphonso Trent, then Jeter-Pillars, before gaining valuable, hard-blowing experience with R&B inclined band of Lucky Millinder, starting in February '37. Accepted invitation to replace Karl George in trumpet section of Count Basie Orchestra. Stayed with Basie until leader disbanded in February '50, during which time was employed continuously as a principal soloist. For Basie, Edison produced string of memorable solos, including those on recordings like **Panassie Stomp, Jive At Five (You Can Depend On Basie); Shorty George, Texas Shuffle (Jumpin' At The Woodside); Every Tub, Bolero At The Savoy (Super Chief); Blow Top, Rock-A-Bye Basie, Louisiana, Moten Swing, Easy Does It (Lester Young With Count Basie & His Orchestra); Tuesday At Ten (Basie's Back In Town)**; and **Taps Miller, The Killer** and **Avenue C (Basie's Best)**. Also produced for Basie clutch of Kansas City-inspired compositions, including **H&J, Let Me See, Beaver Junction**, and the eminently durable **Jive At Five**. After leaving Basie, worked with Jimmy Rushing, Jazz At The Philharmonic (1950), then Buddy Rich. Was employed by the drummer for most of two-year period (1951-53).

In 1953 undertook international tour as solo performer with revue of late Josephine Baker. Then moved to West Coast where he set up home, becoming regular studio musician, working often with top artists like Sinatra, Nat King Cole, Nelson Riddle, etc. During period, recorded one of his finest albums, **Inventions/Sweet At The Haig,** live quartet date which showcased all his qualities in most admirable fashion. Undismayed by advent (and eventual passing) of bop, Edison's fetching brand of mid-period jazz often has a quality of timelessness.

In 1958 he moved back to New York, working mostly with own bands, personnel often including such as Ben Webster, Jimmy Forrest and Joe Williams, the singer. With George Auld in '64, touring Europe with another JATP troupe same year. Continued to guest with top bands, like those of Rich, Louis Bellson **(Thunderbird)**, and old boss, Basie; but by end of 1960s was working once again in California.

Apart from those mentioned above, has contributed handsomely to record dates involving Red Norvo **(Greatest Of The Small Bands, Vol 1)**; Jimmy Witherspoon **(There's Good Rockin' Tonight)**; Barney Kessel **(To Swing Or Not To Swing)**; Lionel Hampton **(The Tatum Group Masterpieces)**.

Own dates have been less frequent perhaps than one might have expected, but more often than not resulted in music of highest quality, as with the admirable **Gee Baby, Ain't I Good To You/Blues For Basie** and **Walkin' With Sweets**; both LPs benefiting greatly by presence of Ben Webster. For Edison, a particularly rewarding date was that which placed his trumpet alongside giants like Duke Ellington and Johnny Hodges.

In more recent times, has tended to come into the spotlight again, following period of neglect. After early-1970s re-appearance with JATP **(Jazz At The Santa Monica '72)** Edison signed with Norman Granz' Pablo label. As a result, his playing on records at least **(Oscar Peterson & Harry Edison, Basie Jam, The Trumpet Kings Meet Joe Turner, The Bosses** and, best of all thus far, **Edison's Lights)** give ample proof that, musically, he has taken on a new lease of life. Apart from his many other achievements in an eminently satisfactory career, Edison's squeeze-note style was heard in Gjon Mili's film *Jammin' The Blues* **(Jammin' With Lester)** as front-line colleague to former Basie associates Lester Young, Dicky Wells, and Illinois Jacquet.

Albums:
Count Basie, You Can Depend On Basie (—/Coral)
Count Basie, Jumpin' At The Woodside (—/Coral)
Count Basie, Super Chief (Columbia/CBS)
Lester Young With Count Basie & His Orchestra (Epic—France)
Count Basie, Basie's Back In Town (Epic/Philips)
Count Basie, Basie's Best (CBS—Holland)
Harry Edison, Inventions (Pacific Jazz)/Sweets At The Haig (Vogue)
Frank Sinatra, Swing Easy/Songs For Young Lovers (Capitol/Capitol)
Ella Fitzgerald Sings The Cole Porter Song Book (Verve/Verve)
Various, Jammin' At Sunset (Black Lion/Black Lion)
Buddy Rich, That's Rich (—/Verve)
Buddy Rich, Buddy & Sweets (Verve/Verve)
Various, Jam Sessions, Nos 2, 3 (Verve/Columbia—Clef)
Barney Kessel, To Swing Or Not To Swing (Contemporary/Vogue—Contemporary)
Various, Jazz Giants '57 (Verve)/Jazz Giants (Columbia—Clef)
Harry Edison, Gee Baby Ain't I Good To You (Verve)/Blues For Basie (Verve)
Harry Edison, Walkin' With Sweets (Verve)
Jimmy Witherspoon, There's Good Rockin' Tonight (World Pacific/Fontana)
Art Tatum (Including Lionel Hampton), The Tatum Group Masterpieces (Pablo/Pablo)
Red Norvo, Greatest Of The Small Bands, Vol 1 (RCA Victor—France)
Duke Ellington/Johnny Hodges, Blues Summit (Verve)/Side By Side—Back To Back (Verve)
Various, Jazz At The Santa Monica (Pablo/Pablo)
Various, Newport In New York '72: The Jam Sessions, Vol 4 (Atlantic/Atlantic)
The Trumpet Kings Meet Joe Turner (Pablo/Pablo)
Count Basie/Joe Turner, The Bosses (Pablo/Pablo)
Oscar Peterson & Harry Edison (Pablo/Pablo)
Count Basie, Basie Jam (Pablo/Pablo)
Harry Edison, Edison's Lights (Pablo/Pablo)
Various, Jammin' The Blues (Jazz Archives)
Louis Bellson, Thunderbird (Impulse/—)

Roy Eldridge

David Roy 'Little Jazz' Eldridge (born Pittsburgh, Pennsylvania, 1911) is one of the most important trumpet soloists in jazz history. A superb technician, and a player of extraordinary fire and emotional projection, Eldridge first played drums (at six), and received some tuition on trumpet from elder brother Joe Eldridge (1908-52), himself a first-class alto-saxophonist, violinist. After working with various little-known bands (including his own), first came into prominence with Horace Henderson's Dixie Stompers, then with Zach Whyte (both in 1928), Speed Webb (1929-30), Cecil Scott, Elmer Snowden, Charlie Johnson, Teddy Hill, before co-leading (with brother Joe) local Pittsburgh outfit (1933). With McKinney's Cotton Pickers, then back with Teddy Hill, worked with another of his own bands, before, in 1935, becoming member of one of the principal jazz outfits of the period, that led by Fletcher Henderson. Although Eldridge's trumpet was heard with Henderson only for a comparatively short period (1936-37), he carried on the great tradition of superior trumpet soloists with the band, producing red-hot solos on such as **Christopher Columbus, Stealin' Apples** and **Blue Lou** (all **The Fletcher Henderson Story/The Fletcher Henderson Story, Vol 4**). Around this time, was catalyst supreme on some of the finest small-group recordings of the 1930s: with Gene Krupa's Swing Band, in 1936 **(Benny Goodman, Vol 4: 1935-1939)**; with Teddy Wilson **(The Teddy Wilson** and **Teddy Wilson & His All Stars)**; as well as Wilson-led sessions involving singer Billie Holiday **(The Golden Years, Vols 1, 2** and **God Bless The Child)**. Eldridge was to work with Holiday in later years **(In Concert: Coleman Hawkins with Roy Eldridge & Billie Holiday** and **The Voice Of Jazz, Vol 7)**.

During 1937, he brought an exciting eight-piece band into Chicago's Three Deuces **(Roy Eldridge At The Three Deuces, Chicago—1937)** which featured not only Joe Eldridge on alto, but some of his brother's most exceptional playing up to that time. Roy Eldridge was to become resident at Three Deuces between 1936-38, after which he toured States with same band. That same year left music business for a while to study radio-engineering. Comeback took place in November '38, at 52nd Street's Famous Door. Same month, recorded for Commodore, in company with tenorist Chu Berry **(The Big Sounds Of Coleman Hawkins & Chu Berry)**, and in January following year took one of his best-ever bands into Arcadia Ballroom, New York **(Arcadia Shuffle)** producing one dazzling, solo after another.

His up-tempo statements, with double-time runs executed with facility hitherto unknown, obviously deeply influenced a young, up-coming Dizzy Gillespie. Eldrige's ballad playing was warm and deeply felt. And there was little doubt about his familiarity with the ability to 'feel' the blues.

Following prestigious residencies at the Apollo, Golden Gate Ballroom and Kelly's Stables (1939-40), he returned, in '41, to Chicago for further important season, this one at Capitol Lounge. Next, joined new Gene Krupa big band as featured soloist.

After Krupa's band split in 1943, became, for a time, session player with Paul Baron Orchestra at CBS (1943-44), playing Mildred Bailey radio series. Toured with Artie Shaw, again as featured soloist (1944-45) **(Artie Shaw Featuring Roy Eldridge, Artie Shaw & His Orchestra, Vol 2** and **Artie Shaw & His Gramercy Five)**. Eldridge, an always sensitive, sometimes explosive character, had to undergo various Jim Crow experiences when touring with Shaw—despite conscious efforts by the leader and his other sidemen to prevent such occurrences—which left a scar which lasts until today.

Returned to Krupa in 1949, after leading own bands, then toured Europe with Benny Goodman (1950). Signed with Norman Granz as solo recording artist and to tour with Grantz's Jazz At The Philharmonic packages. In this latter environment, both best and worst of Eldridge could be found. However, there were times when his admittedly extrovert tendencies were channeled into something more memorable and lasting **(J.A.T.P. In Tokyo)**.

Over the succeeding years, has continued to record with many of jazz's finest players, including Dizzy Gillespie **(Trumpet Kings** and **The Gillespie Jam Sessions)**; Ben Webster **(Ben Webster & Associates/Ben Webster & Friends)**; Stan Getz **(Nothing But The Blues)**; Lester Young **(Prez & Teddy)**; Buddy Tate **(Buddy Tate & His Buddies)**; Gene Krupa and Buddy Rich **(Drum Battle)**; Oscar Peterson **(Oscar Peterson & Roy Eldridge)**; Peterson and Sonny Stitt **(Only The Blues/Sittin' In)**; Bud Freeman **(Chicago)**; and Johnny Hodges **(Blues A-Plenty)**. Each of these albums contains much superb Eldridge, especially those with Getz, Peterson, Stitt, Webster and the two Gillespies.

One notable failure was on-record collaboration with Art Tatum **(The Tatum Group Masterpieces)** with Eldridge sounding not at all at ease, or anywhere near his best. (There is rumor that Eldridge and Tatum recorded their contributions at different times. There have been other, more successful, record sessions, including several which took place in Paris, under Eldridge's leadership, during 1950-51 **(Little Jazz Paris Session)** relating to his European trip with Benny Goodman. There were also excellent studio re-creations of Krupa's early days as bandleader in his own right **(The Big Band Sound Of Gene Krupa)**. There have been successful sessions with Joe Turner **(Nobody In Mind)** and Count Basie **(Count Basie Jam Session At The Montreux Jazz Festival 1975)**.

Of records issued under his own name, best by far has been **The Nifty Cat**, which combines all the virtues of his younger days with the maturity of the 60-year-old he was at the time of recording. Roy 'Little Jazz' Eldridge still retains most of those elements which long ago made him an acknowledged giant of jazz, as well as the vital link between those two other great trumpet stylists, Louis Armstrong and Dizzy Gillespie.

Albums:

The Fletcher Henderson Story (Columbia)/ The Fletcher Henderson Story, Vol 4 (CBS)
Benny Goodman, Vol 4 (1935-1939) (RCA Victor—France)
The Teddy Wilson (CBS/Sony-Japan)
Teddy Wilson & His All Stars (Columbia/CBS)
Billie Holiday, The Golden Years, Vols 1, 2 (Columbia/CBS)
Billie Holiday, God Bless The Child (Columbia/CBS)
Billie Holiday, The Voice Of Jazz, Vol 7 (Verve)
Roy Eldridge At The Three Deuces, Chicago—1937 (Jazz Archives)
The Big Sounds Of Coleman Hawkins & Chu Berry (—/London)
Roy Eldridge, Arcadia Shuffle (Jazz Archives)
Montreux '77: Roy Eldridge 4 (Pablo Live/Pablo Live)
Artie Shaw & His Orchestra, Vol 2 (RCA Victor/RCA Victor)
Artie Shaw & His Gramercy Five (—/RCA Victor)
Roy Eldridge, Little Jazz Paris Session (—/Vogue)
Coleman Hawkins, Swing! (Fontana)
Roy Eldridge, Swing Along With Little Jazz (MCA Coral—Germany)
Coleman Hawkins/Chu Berry, Immortal Swing Sessions (—/Sonet)
Roy Eldridge/Tiny Grimes, Never Too Old To Swing (—/Sonet)
In Concert: Coleman Hawkins With Roy Eldridge & Billie Holiday (Phoenix)
Various, J.A.T.P. In Tokyo (Pablo/Pablo)
Various, The Gillespie Jam Sessions (Verve)
Dizzy Gillespie/Roy Eldridge, Trumpet kings (Verve)
Ben Webster & Associates (Verve)
Ben Webster & Friends (Verve)
Herb Ellis/Stan Getz/Roy Eldridge, Nothing But The Blues (Verve/Columbia—Clef)
The Big Band Sound Of Gene Krupa (Verve/Verve)
Lester Young/Teddy Wilson, Prez & Teddy (Verve)
Buddy Tate & His Buddies (Chiaroscuro/—)
Sonny Stitt/Roy Eldridge/Oscar Peterson, Only The Blues (Verve)/Sittin' In (Verve)
Bud Freeman, Chicago (Black Lion/Black Lion)
Johnny Hodges, Blues A-Plenty (Verve/HMV)
Art Tatum, The Tatum Group Masterpieces (Pablo/Pablo)
Joe Turner, Nobody In Mind (Pablo/Pablo)
Count Basie, Montreux '77: Count Basie Jam (Pablo Live/Pablo Live)
Oscar Peterson & Roy Eldridge (Pablo/Pablo)
Various, Jazz At The Santa Monica '72 (Pablo/Pablo)
Roy Eldridge, The Nifty Cat (Master Jazz Recordings/—)

Above: Roy 'Little Jazz' Eldridge, one of the most rewarding and important trumpet soloists—a vital stylistic link between Armstrong and Gillespie.

Duke Ellington

Because of the multiplicity and significance of his achievements within the field of music in general, and his unsurpassed contributions to jazz in particular, Edward Kennedy 'Duke' Ellington (born Washington, DC, 1899) remains one of seminal figures of 20th century music.

In total, the music produced by Ellington in over 55 years was colossal; and the overall standard of that prodigious output—written as well as played—is equal to any other comparable contributor to music of the past near-80 years. It is unlikely that in the foreseeable future there will emerge another ultra-prolific composer and orchestrator who, during over a half-century of continuous writing, will also find time to lead, non-stop, a succession of orchestras or bands—undertaking regular recording dates and an exhausting year-by-year touring schedule, at home and abroad—play fine piano with those various aggregations, and act as official spokesman and master of ceremonies.

If the final story is ever told, it seems unlikely that a complete assessment of Ellington's output as writer can be made. Certainly, though, his compositions run into the thousands, extended works as well as shorter (usually 32-bar) 'tunes'. His capacity for work was almost inhuman, and Ellington's was a mind which continually explored the possibilities opened up by various outlets, other than those presented by his own orchestra. For example, Duke Ellington composed music for such stage shows as *Jump For Joy* and *My People*; he has written musical scores for movies like *Anatomy of a Murder* **(Anatomy Of A Murder)**, *Assault On A Queen* and *Paris Blues*.

During the latter period of his career, Ellington was profoundly involved with a series of sacred concerts (he was a deeply religious man) for which, of course, he composed the music. (This latter-day preoccupation was, for Ellington, his most important contribution to music of any kind. In truth, though, it might be said that in some ways—especially with regard to respective libretti—projects like **Concert Of Sacred Music, Second Sacred Concert**, and **Duke Ellington's Third Sacred Concert, The Majesty Of God** were not as comprehensively successful as a majority of Ellington's other larger compositions.)

Ellington's involvement with extended works of secular nature resulted in music of extraordinary quality. First examples of Ellington extending his compositional genius beyond a basic 32-bar format came in 1931 with two-part **Creole Rhapsody (The Works Of Duke Ellington, Vol 6)** followed by the 1935 four-part **Reminiscin' In Tempo (The Ellington Era, 1927-1940, Vol 2** and **The Complete Duke Ellington, Vol 6: 1933-1936)**. Both allowed Ellington, master music painter, to fill his canvas with additional textures of color, contrast and excitement.

Ellington's first composition in truly extended vein remains one of his most brilliantly evocative: **Black, Brown & Beige**. In many ways **Black, Brown & Beige** was an in-depth summation of Ellington's many achievements up to that time (1943). Because of a recording ban, only excerpts from the entire suite were committed to record **(The Works Of Duke, Vol 19)** although Ellington did record the piece in 1958, with gospel singer Mahalia Jackson reprising the moving **Come Sunday** vocal passage **(Black, Brown & Beige)**. Best of all (and, of course, of historical significance) was complete **Black, Brown & Beige** as premiered at Carnegie Hall in January 1943 **(Duke Ellington: Black, Brown & Beige)**.

Other notable successes in an extended vein have been **Such Sweet Thunder, Liberian Suite/A Tone Parallel To Harlem: The Harlem Suite, A Drum Is A Woman, The Far East Suite, The Latin-American Suite, New World A-Coming: Harlem: The Golden Broom & The Green Apple, The Togo Brava Suite/The English Concert, Suite Thursday (Suite Thursday/Peer Gynt Suites Nos 1 & 2)** and **Deep South Suite** (last movement of which **Happy-Go-Lucky Local** is a magnificent 12-bar train blues).

Superb as these and other extended works are, they are no better than the countless miniature masterpieces written by Ellington during his career. Many of these have not only become an integral part of jazz composing history but are acknowledged as being meaningful contributions to the standard library of popular song. Amongst other famous (and in many cases these rank with Ellington's finest) are the following: **Sophisticated Lady, Do Nothing Till You Hear**

From Me (originally known as **Concerto For Cootie** before lyric was written and its title changed), **I Got It Bad, I'm Beginning To See The Light, Solitude, Satin Doll, I Let A Song Go Out Of My Heart, Mood Indigo** (first recorded as **Dreamy Blues**), **In A Sentimental Mood, Drop Me Off At Harlem, Just Squeeze Me** and **Prelude To A Kiss** (probably his best-ever song).

Although his lyric-writing collaborators included John LaTouche, Johnny Mercer, Ted Koehler, Don George, Peggy Lee, Johnny Burke and Mitchell Parish, often Ellington's songs were poorly served by inferior lyrics. An innovation by Ellington during the 1920s was his use of a singer (Adelaide Hall) using her voice in the manner of a jazz instrumentalist. Adelaide Hall's wordless vocals on **Creole Love Call** and **Blues I Love To Sing (The Works Of Duke, Vol 1)** succeeded in a definite, if startling fashion. Ellington was to use the human voice in similar manner more than once in future, including a stunning **Transblucency** from 1946 **(At His Very Best)**, with Kat Davis as singer.

From an instrumental standpoint the list of masterpieces is, of course, even greater. For Ellington's genius extended to possessing an uncanny knack of selecting the kind of players whose wholly individual sounds and styles would suit his musical creations to perfection. Apart from their 'normal' use within a typical Ellington framework, several of his major soloists were accorded their own individual showcases, including Barney Bigard, with **Clarinet Lament (The Complete Duke Ellington, Vol 7: 1936-1937)** and Cootie Williams, with **Concerto For Cootie (The Works Of Duke, Vol 10)** and **Echoes Of Harlem (The Complete Duke Ellington, Vol 7: 1936-1937)**.

As well as saluting his own musicians, Ellington also offered delicious tributes to other musical personalities, like jazz dancer Bill Robinson **(Bojangles)** and black comedian-vaudeville artist Bert Williams **(Portrait Of Bert Williams)** (both **The Works Of Duke, Vol 10**) and Willie 'The Lion' Smith **(Portrait Of The Lion) (The Ellington Era, 1927-1940, Vol 1/The Ellington Era, 1927-1940, Vol 1-Part 3)**.

Mostly, Ellington used material written by himself, or by his sidemen, including Mercer Ellington, his son; Juan Tizol (**Caravan, Perdido, Bakiff, Conga Brava**, etc); Barney Bigard, and, most prominently, Billy Strayhorn, his closest collaborator. But he was not averse to using compositions from other jazz writers, or pop tunes. In the latter category, not even Duke Ellington could make totally satisfying jazz out of the score from *Mary Poppins* **(Souvenirs)** but was more successful with repertoire from two classical composers: Edvard Grieg **(Peer Gynt Suites Nos 1 & 2/Suite Thursday)** and Piotr Ilyich Tchaikovsky **(The Nutcracker Suite)**.

Like all great jazz organizations, the Ellington orchestra was usually at its most exciting during live performance. Some other jazz big-bands (viz Count Basie, Jimmie Lunceford, Chick Webb) are known to have out-swung it during the kind of cutting contests which once were possible in ballrooms and theatres. Certainly, though, recorded evidence has been made available over the years to prove that when the occasion was right, the band could drive, wail and stomp with the best. Such occasions are apparent during the following: **The Duke 1940, Ellington At Newport**, with its legendary 27 consecutive choruses by tenorist Paul Gonsalves during **Diminuendo & Crescendo In Blue; (The Great Paris Concert, The Greatest Jazz Concert In The World, The Togo Brava Suite/The English Concert** and **Duke Ellington's 70th Birthday Concert)**.

With such an embarrassment of riches throughout 50 years, it is no easy task to select a particular period that could be said to be representative of the absolute peak of Ellington's achievements. But the 1940-42 period found Duke Ellington scaling peaks of artistic invention that rarely have been approached, before or since. In many ways, the list of soloists at his disposal during this time could not be bettered, in terms of individual and collective brilliance: Williams, Rex Stewart, Ray Nance, Joseph 'Tricky Sam' Nanton, Lawrence Brown, Bigard, Ben Webster, Harry Carney, Johnny Hodges and the leader himself. The additional presence of bassist Jimmy Blanton until 1941 was another plus factor.

Cotton Club Days (courtesy Ace of Hearts, Decca). Memories of the early days—reliving a classic Ellington era in New York's Harlem.

Below: Edward Kennedy Ellington—'The Duke'. For over 50 years, a prolific, influential composer and seminal figure of 20th century music.

Between 1940 and 1942 Ellington wrote an astonishing number of classic masterpieces-in-miniature, including: **Ko-Ko, Jack The Bear (The Works Of Duke, Vol 9), Conga Brava, Concerto For Cootie, Cotton Tail, Don't Get Around Much Anymore, Bojangles, Portrait Of Bert Williams, Harlem Airshaft, Rumpus In Richmond (Vol 10), Sepia Panorama, In A Mellotone (Vol 11), Warm Valley, Across The Track Blues (Vol 12), Take The 'A' Train** (written by Strayhorn), **Blue Serge** (written by son Mercer) **(Vol 15), Chelsea Bridge** (also by Strayhorn), **C Jam Blues (Vol 17)**. Over the years, there were comparatively few 'outsiders' invited to participate in Ellingtonian activities (although drummers Elvin Jones, Max Roach and trumpeters Dizzy Gillespie and Gerald Wilson deputized at various times).

Apart from previously mentioned Mahalia Jackson-Ellington session, visiting artists like Ella Fitzgerald **(... Sings The Duke Ellington Songbook, Vols 1, 2, Ella At Duke's Place** and **Ella & Duke At The Côte d'Azur)**; Jimmy Rushing **(Jazz At The Plaza, Vol 2** and **Ellington Jazz Party)**; Billie Holiday **(Jazz At The Plaza, Vol 2)**; and Gillespie **(Ellington Jazz Party)**, have all sat in, with generally worthwhile results. A sit-in of a more unusual nature took place in 1961, when the full might of both the Ellington and Basie bands met inside the recording studio **(First Time/Basie Meets Ellington)** in fierce and friendly musical combat.

One aspect of Duke Ellington's lifetime in music which attracted less attention than was merited (mostly due, like Count Basie, to a genuinely modest assessment of his own abilities in this direction) was his competence as a piano-player. Ellington, apart from his talents as band pianist, was a very good soloist—sometimes a superb one.

His early recordings show him to be an average-only solo player, **The Duke—1926**, showing traces of his prime influences, James P. Johnson, Willie 'The Lion' Smith and Luckey Roberts but without their flair and drive. He was no more than competent during the formative years of his orchestra **(Duke Ellington In Harlem, Duke Ellington, Vol 1, 1926-1928** and **Toodle-Oo)** but by the 1930s, even though he allowed himself little solo space, there was a definite improvement. In 1941, he recorded piano solos **(The Works Of Duke, Vol 15)** which indicated he should feature himself more at the keyboard with his band. Included was a wistful, introspective version of **Solitude**, about which there could be few complaints.

The impact of Jimmy Blanton was felt not only with the Ellington orchestra during his brief tenure, but also on the piano-playing of Ellington. The delightful duets the pair recorded in 1940 **(The Works Of Duke, Vol 11)** demonstrate just how good a solo pianist (and accompanist) Ellington could be. Six years later, Ellington and Billy Strayhorn recorded a series of duets, with bassist Wendell Marshall **(The Golden Duke)** which, on the whole, worked well; three years after which Ellington (in trio setting) produced his finest playing yet **(Piano Reflections)**, essaying a program of new as well as established material.

During the 1960s and thereafter—mostly at prompting by others—Ellington featured himself more at the piano. His work features throughout recordings such as **Solo** (an album which has a remarkable, lengthy version of **Symphonie Pour Un Monde Meilleur** and a typical medley of Ellington tunes); **Duke Ellington—The Pianist** and **This One's For Blanton!** (a tribute to Blanton, in company with bassist Ray Brown) and **Duke's Big 4**.

Perhaps the finest examples of Ellington, solo pianist, emanate from a superb studio date **Blues Summit/Back To Back & Side By Side** which featured also the talents of Harry Edison and Johnny Hodges. Both latter musicians played at their considerable best—but Ellington took solo honors with ease. More fine Ellington piano highlighted recordings at which non-Ellington instrumentalists like Max Roach and Charles Mingus **(Money Jungle)**, John Coltrane **(Duke Ellington Meets John Coltrane)** and Coleman Hawkins **(Duke Ellington Meets Coleman Hawkins)** got joint top billing.

Duke Ellington came from a well-to-do Washington, DC, family, and after winning poster-designing contest at high school became proprietor (for a while) of own sign-writing business. First played piano in public while at high school. After graduation, began to play local gigs. First composition, **Soda Fountain Rag**. Concentrated exclusively on music, playing piano with various bands, including Elmer Snowden. Put together own Duke's Serenaders, then worked with Wilbur Sweatman, in New York. In 1924 he took over leadership of Washingtonians group, touring regularly, playing residencies (including lengthy stay at Kentucky Club), before commencing important residency at Cotton Club (1927-31) in Harlem, which was interrupted only by national tours and recording dates.

Amongst the most important recordings to make an impact on the jazz world during this period were **East St Louis Toodle-oo** (Ellington's first theme), **Black Beauty** and **Birmingham Breakdown** (all **The Beginning: 1926-1928), The Mooche, Awful Sad** and **Jungle Jamboree** (all **Hot In Harlem: 1928-1929); Mood Indigo, Rockin' In Rhythm** and **Creole Rhapsody** (all **Rockin' In Rhythm: 1929-1931**). Band also appeared in film *Check & Double Check* (1930), and made its first trip to Europe (London, Paris) in 1939. Ellington wrote music for, and his band participated in, revue *Jump For Joy*, which opened in Los Angeles in 1941.

First of the legendary Carnegie Hall concerts took place in 1943 (featuring première of **Black, Brown & Beige**), continuing annually, up to and including 1950. In 1951, Ellington band combined with Symphony of the Air for première of *Night Creature*, at same venue. Ellington took trumpeter-violinist-singer Ray Nance and singer Kay Davis on tour to UK (1948); full Ellington band (plus of course, its leader) returned ten years later and on numerous other occasions in subsequent years. During the 1960s, Ellington visited Far East, Middle East, India, Australasia, etc., and constant schedule of touring—at home as well as overseas—continued up until Ellington's death in May 1974.

During his career, Duke Ellington received innumerable honors and awards. These included the President's Medal, the Spring-arn Medal, Presidential Medal of Freedom, 15 honorary degrees; was given Key to 18 cities (as far afield as Niigata, Japan, to Savannah, Georgia, to Amsterdam, Holland); and was presented before Her Majesty Queen Elizabeth II.

The 87th anniversary of Ellington's birth was paid a special tribute in the United States on April 29, 1986, with the official release of a postage stamp bearing Duke's portrait.

Ellington's long-awaited autobiography *Music Is My Mistress* was published in 1974. Other notable literary works on Duke Ellington include the following: *Duke—A Portrait of Duke Ellington* by Derek Jewell; *Duke Ellington* by Barry Ulanov; *Duke Ellington: His Life & Music*, anthology, edited by Pete Gammond; *Duke Ellington* by G. E. Lambert; *The World of Duke Ellington* by Stanley Dance.

Albums:

Duke Ellington, The Duke—1926 (Riverside/London)
Duke Ellington In Harlem (Jazz Panorama—Sweden)
Duke Ellington, Vol 1 (1926-1929) (MCA Coral—Germany)
Duke Ellington, The Beginning (1926-1928) (Decca/MCA—Germany)
Duke Ellington, Hot In Harlem (1928-1929) (Decca/MCA—Germany)
Duke Ellington, Rockin' In Rhythm (1929-1931) (Decca/MCA—Germany)
Duke Ellington, Toodle-Oo (—/Vocalion)
Duke Ellington, The Works Of Duke, Vols 1-18 (RCA Victor—France)
The Complete Duke Ellington, Vols 1-6 (CBS—France)
The Ellington Era, 1927-1940, Vols 1, 2 (Columbia/CBS)
Duke Ellington, Braggin' In Brass 1936-1939 (Tax—Sweden)
Duke Ellington, 1937-1939 (Tax—Sweden)
Duke Ellington, Masterpieces (1938-40) (RCA Victor—France)
Duke Ellington, Ellington Uptown (Columbia/Philips)
Duke Ellington, Masterpieces By Ellington (Columbia/CBS—Holland)
Duke Ellington/Mahalia Jackson, Black, Brown & Beige (Columbia/CBS—Holland)
Duke Ellington: Black, Brown & Beige (Ariston—Italy)
Duke Ellington, Liberian Suite/A Tone Parallel To Harlem (Columbia/CBS—France)
Duke Ellington, Peer Gynt Suites Nos 1 & 2/Suite Thursday (Columbia/CBS)
Duke Ellington, The Nutcracker Suite (Columbia/CBS)
Duke Ellington, A Drum Is A Woman (Columbia/Philips)
Duke Ellington, Such Sweet Thunder (Columbia/CBS—Realm)
Duke Ellington, New World A-Coming: Harlem: The Golden Broom & The Green Apple (Decca/—)
Duke Ellington, The Far East Suite (RCA Victor/RCA Victor)
Duke Ellington, The Latin-American Suite (Fantasy/—)
Duke Ellington, The Togo Brava Suite (United Artists)/The English Concert (Sunset)
Duke Ellington, Afro-Eurasian Eclipse (Fantasy/—)
Duke Ellington, Concert Of Sacred Music (RCA Victor/—)
Duke Ellington, Second Sacred Concert (Fantasy/—)
Duke Ellington's Third Sacred Concert, The Majesty Of God, As Performed In Westminster Abbey (RCA Victor/RCA Victor)
Duke Ellington, The Duke 1940 (Jazz Society/—)
Duke Ellington, Ellington At Newport (Columbia/CBS)
Various (Including Duke Ellington), The Greatest Jazz Concert In The World (Pablo/Pablo)
Duke Ellington's 70th Birthday Concert (Solid State/United Artists)
Ella Fitzgerald Sings The Duke Ellington Songbook, Vols 1, 2 (Verve/Verve)
Ella Fitzgerald/Duke Ellington, Ella At Duke's Place (Verve/Verve)
Ella Fitzgerald/Duke Ellington, Ella & Duke At The Côte d'Azur (Verve/Verve)
Various (Including Ellington/Rushing/Gillespie/Holiday), Ellington Jazz Party (Columbia/Philips)/Jazz At The Plaza, Vol 2 (Columbia/CBS)
Duke Ellington, The Radio Transcriptions, Vols 1-5 (Hindsight/London)
Duke Ellington/Count Basie, First Time (Columbia)/Basie Meets Ellington (Embassy)
Duke Ellington, Piano Reflections (Capitol/One-Up)
Duke Ellington, Solo (President—France)
Duke Ellington—The Pianist (Fantasy/—)
Duke Ellington/Johnny Hodges, Blues Summit (Verve)/ Back To Back & Side By Side (Verve)
Duke Ellington, Money Jungle (United Artists/United Artists)
Duke Ellington/Ray Brown, This One's For Blanton! (Pablo/Pablo)
Duke Ellington Meets John Coltrane (Impulse/Impulse)
Duke Ellington Meets Coleman Hawkins (Impulse/Impulse)
Duke Ellington, The Great Paris Concert (Atlantic/—)
Duke Ellington . . . And His Mother Called Him Bill (RCA Victor/RCA Victor) (A tribute to long-time collaborator Billy Strayhorn)
Duke Ellington, Souvenirs (Reprise/Reprise)
Duke Ellington, The Ellington Suites (Pablo/Pablo)

Duke Ellington Meets Coleman Hawkins (courtesy Impulse).

Duke Ellington At Carnegie Hall (courtesy Queen-Disc—Italy).

Mercer Ellington

To Mercer Kennedy Ellington (born Washington, DC, 1919) fell the utterly unenviable task of trying to achieve the almost impossible when, following the death of Duke Ellington in 1974, he agreed to become front man of his father's orchestra—the most celebrated and important jazz aggregation of all time. But in typically modest and unassuming fashion, Ellington Jr endeavored to pick up the pieces. A formidable task, especially with many of the most illustrious sidemen having died.

Still, Mercer Ellington—arranger, composer, trumpeter, and one-time tour manager for Duke Ellington band—was no newcomer to the rigors of band-leading. As a youth he studied trumpet and also sax, subsequently enrolled as student at Columbia University, Juilliard, and New York University. Put together his very first band as long ago as 1939: Dizzy Gillespie, Clark Terry and Calvin Jackson were amongst sidemen; Billy Strayhorn composed-arranged for the band prior to joining entourage of Ellington Sr).

Following conscription into US Army, Mercer Ellington put together another big band, this one lasting until 1949 (singer Carmen McRae, then known as Carmen Clarke, worked with his outfit). In 1950 Mercer played trumpet and E-flat horn with his father. Started own Mercer Records label (1950-52), leaving music altogether to work as salesman following its demise. He became trumpeter and road manager for Cootie Williams' band (1954), then acted as general assistant to his father (1955-59), after which he took up trumpet again—and bandleading.

Over the years, he has written numerous jazz compositions, many of which have been featured by the Ellington Orchestra. Included are: **Things Ain't What They Used To be** (also known as **Time's A-Wastin'), Piano Reflections (Greatest Jazz Concert In The World** and **The Works Of Duke, Vol 17); Moon Mist (His Most Important Second War Concert** and **Duke Ellington, Vol 2); Blue Serge (Duke Ellington, Vol 2, Duke Ellington, 1943-1946** and **Jumpin' Punkins (The Works Of Duke, Vols 15** and **17).**

Apart from sundry other contributions to the Duke Ellington repertoire, Mercer occasionally also helped his father on more ambitious scores, like **Latin American Suite.** His own album **Continuum** proved encouraging augury for future. Apart from his own **Blue Serge,** this first Ellington album to be made after Duke Ellington's passing included a dedication to another Ellington alumnus, **Carney,** wfitten by saxist Rick Henderson; plus a healthy selection of not over-familiar material by Duke or Strayhorn, including **Drop Me Off In Harlem, Rock Skippin' At The Blue Note, Ko-Ko, All Too Soon** and **Jump For Joy,** most of which had lain dormant for years.

Of recordings made by previous Mercer Ellington bands, the best are **Black & Tan Fantasy, Steppin' Into Swing Society** and **Colors In Rhythm.** He also contributed to numerous record dates featuring the saxophone artistry of Johnny Hodges, including exemplary **Bouquet Of Roses** and **Viscount** for a 1950s recording date **(The Big Band Sound Of Johnny Hodges).**

Albums:

Duke Ellington, Piano Reflections (Capitol/One-Up)
Duke Ellington, The Works Of Duke, Vols 14, 15, 17 (RCA Victor—France)
Duke Ellington, His Most Important Second War Concert (—/Saga)
Duke Ellington, Vol 2 (—/Saga)
Dule Ellington 1943-1946 (Jazz Society)
Various (Including Duke Ellington), The Greatest Jazz Concert In The World (Pablo/Pablo)
Duke Ellington, Latin American Suite (Fantasy/—)
Mercer Ellington, Steppin' Into Swing Society (Coral/—)
Mercer Ellington, Colors In Rhythm (Coral/—)
Mercer Ellington, Black & Tan Fantasy (MCA/—)
Mercer Ellington/Duke Ellington Orchestra Continuum (Fantasy/Fantasy)
The Big Band Sound Of Johnny Hodges (—/Verve)

Don Ellis

Trumpeter Don Ellis was born in Los Angeles in 1934, and gained big band experience with Woody Herman, Claude Thornhill, Lionel Hampton and Charlie Barnet. He spent 1961-62 with the experimental units of George Russell **(Outer Thoughts),** cutting excellent solos on **Pan Daddy** and **The Stratus Seekers.** Much of Ellis' exploratory work was inspired by contemporary straight music rather than jazz, and performances like **Despair To Hope** sprang from John Cage's indeterminancy **(New Ideas).** Surprisingly, Ellis' 21-piece orchestra, using unusual meters, multividers and choirs, achieved great commercial success during the psychedelic '60s. In fact, the band had a walloping impact, never sounding in the least pretentious or Third Stream. The eeriness of **Milo's Theme** with its electronically processed flutes is curiously plaintive, and the distant chorus and Indian dronings of **Star Children** provides a highly original setting for Ellis' precise trumpet **(Shock Treatment)**. An atmospheric live performance **(Don Ellis At Fillmore)** shows the leader's amazing instrumental control in the unaccompanied grotesqueries of **The Blues. Hey Jude** begins on trumpet, but so distorted by a ring modulator that it resembles Morton Subotnick's **The Wild Bull.** He has since turned to movie scores, including the hugely successful **The French Connection.**

Albums:
George Russell, Outer Thoughts (Milestone/Milestone)
New Ideas (Prestige/—)
Electric Bath (Columbia/CBS)
Shock Treatment (Columbia/CBS)
Don Ellis At Fillmore (Columbia/CBS)

Bill Evans (pianist)

Born in New Jersey on August 16, 1929, pianist Bill Evans had one of the most distinctive touches in jazz; four bars, and the identity was clear. He credited George Shearing for opening his ears to the beauties of tone, and Horace Silver and Bud Powell were also among those who contributed to his formative period.

His mother, also a pianist, encouraged him to play and he also learned flute and violin. He won a music scholarship to Southeastern Louisiana College, graduating in '50 with a teaching degree. Guitarist Mundell Lowe diverted him from a teaching career, urging him to try his luck as a pianist in New York. Evans worked with commercial bandleader Herbie Fields and, when he was drafted, he played flute in the Fifth Army Band. Evans eventually joined Lowe in clarinettist Tony Scott's quartet, the group which brought Evans to the keen attention of Riverside Records' Orrin Keepnews.

After sessions as a sideman with George Russell and Charlie Mingus in the mid-'50s, Evans joined Miles Davis on the classic **Kind Of Blue** album, contributing considerably more than backing. In fact, like Miles, the pianist was moving steadily towards greater concision, paring away excess to free melody and making good use of modes to achieve this end.

As a soloist, Bill Evans had tremendous, unshowy technique. Chords were meticulously dissected and rearranged, probed for inner resonances, the whole method used to lyrical ends. This introverted, romantic approach seemed to come out of left field in the violent, hard bop atmosphere of the late '50s, but in many respects Evans was in the forefront of developments. His work has influenced such pianists as Paul Bley, Keith Jarrett, Chick Corea, Herbie Hancock and Joe Zawinul, themselves influential stylists in the late '60s and '70s. An Evans solo like **Peace Piece (Peace Piece & Other Pieces)** shows just how adventurous he was on this spontaneously evolving, harmonically free work.

He was one of the pioneers of free melodic interplay within the group, allowing the original members of his trio scope to create independent lines. The staggeringly original young bassist, Scott La Faro, roves parallel to the piano, building structures of his own, intersecting briefly with a walking line or synopsizing the piano's direction with an appropriate chord. The role of the drummer is less spectacular but Paul Motian tracks the subtle rhythmic shifts and adds to the overall texture. This trio's début album **(Spring Leaves)** shows a rare empathy on numbers like **Autumn Leaves** or **Blues In Green**, and also an attacking spirit not normally associated with Evans. A live session **(The Village Vanguard Sessions)** rises to the heights of simultaneous improvisation, a near-telepathic rapport between the three players that goes beyond the earlier album's achievement. **Solar** seems to move in several dimensions, while the reworking of **Milestones** sees Motian, too, working more loosely than usual in the foreground. **Jade Visions** explores similar emotional territory to **Peace Piece**, each note sustained like a glowing ember before being supplanted by the next. Possibly Evans' most popular composition, **Waltz For Debby**, receives a definitive treatment here, while versions of **Porgy** and **My Romance** are unexpectedly robust by comparison.

The tragic death of La Faro in a car accident in 1961 brought bassist Chuck Israels into the group, followed by Gary Peacock, the difficult role finally settling on the most sympathetic player of the lot, Eddie Gomez Apart from Shelley Manne and Jack De Johnette, Evans had difficulty in finding the perfect drummer. Various editions of the trio recorded Evans' familiar choice of standards, the range of mood comparatively narrow but the interpretation profound **(Trio '64, At Town Hall** and **The Tokyo Concert)**.

Bill Evans continued to record as a solo artist **(Alone** and **Conversations With Myself)** utilizing multi-tracking to excellent effect, so that the three pianos recede in dynamic perspective. A meeting with trumpeter Freddie Hubbard and guitarist Jim Hall **(Interplay)** resulted in some miraculous ensemble improvisation, though a festival meeting with the tigerish drummer, Tony Oxley, did not **(Live At The Festival)**. His recording with the singer Tony Bennett **(The Tony Bennett—Bill Evans Album)** displays a shared love of the song form.

Evan's death—aged just 51—on September 15, 1980, was an immeasurable loss to the music. Excellent Evans material continues to be issued posthumously (much of it live in concert) and his later work, particularly shortly before his untimely death, shows a more freely improvised quality than we were used to hearing. Compare, for instance, the dynamic new ground he was exploring on **Nardis** on 1979's **The Paris Concert, Edition Two** with the 1968 version **At The Montreux Jazz Festival**. The feeling that we still had so much to learn from this influential pianist makes his loss that much harder to bear.

Albums:
Peace Piece & Other Pieces (Milestone/Milestone)
Spring Leaves (Miletone/Milestone)
The Village Vanguard Sessions (Milestone/Milestone)
Trio '64 (Verve/Verve)
At Town Hall (Verve/Verve)
The Tokyo Concert (Fantasy/—)
Alone (Verve/Verve)
Conversations With Myself (Verve/Verve)
Interplay (United Artists/—)
Live At The Festival (Enja/Enja)
The Tony Bennett-Bill Evans Album (Fantasy/—)
Empathy (Verve/Verve)
Bill Evans At The Montreux Jazz Festival (1968) (Verve/Verve)
The Bill Evans Album (Columbia/CBS)
Bill Evans—Re: Person I Knew (Fantasy/Fantasy)
Bill Evans—The Paris Concert, Editions One and Two (Elektra Musician/Elektra Musician)

Pianist Bill Evans, The Paris Concert (courtesy Elektra Musician).

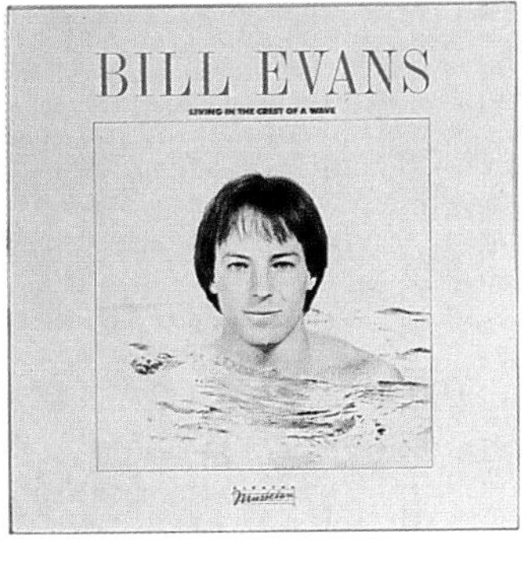

Saxophonist Bill Evans, Living In The Crest Of A Wave (Elektra Musician).

Bill Evans (saxophonist)

Miles Davis has described young saxophonist Bill Evans as 'one of the greatest musicians I've ever come upon'—praise indeed from a master musician and a suitable endorsement for one of the music's most original, inventive and exciting new entrants.

Born in Clarendon Hills, Illinois, in 1959, Evans studied classical piano from age 5. By 13, he was playing clarinet and tenor sax. By 16, he had also reached concert standard as an accomplished classical pianist. A year at North Texas State University was followed by graduation from New Jersey's William Paterson College. He also took private saxophone lessons with Bunky Green in Chicago and Dave Liebman in New York. It was Liebman who recommended Evans as saxophonist for Miles Davis' acclaimed comeback band in '80.

Since his emergence in the early '80s, Evans has also effectively contributed to the band Elements with bassist Mark Egan and drummer Danny Gottlieb, John McLaughlin's revamped Mahavishnu Orchestra, and has recorded and toured with singer-songwriter Michael Franks.

In '84, Evans left the Davis band and recorded his breath-taking solo album **Living In The Crest Of A Wave**—an album so brimming with vitality, exceptional arrangements and atmosphere, it stands as a remarkable first effort.

In '85, Bill Evans' growing stature in jazz was confirmed when he became one of the first new musicians to be recorded by the reawakened Blue Note label. His '85 **The Alternative Man** is an advance on even his excellent first album and features six guitarists—John McLaughlin, Hiram Bullock, Jeff Golub, Sid McGinnis, Dave Hart and Chuck Loeb.

Whether playing flute, keyboards, soprano or tenor saxes, or arranging and producing his own fine compositions, Evans is undoubtedly a musician with an extraordinary depth of vision. Bill Evans has brought with him a much-needed breath of fresh air—he is definitely one of *the* finds of the '80s.

Albums:
Miles Davis, The Man With The Horn (Columbia/CBS)
Miles Davis, We Want Miles (Columbia/CBS)
Miles Davis, Star People (Columbia/CBS)
Miles Davis, Decoy (Columbia/CBS)
David Sanborn, As We Speak (Warner Brothers/Warner Brothers)
Elements, Forward Motion (Antilles/Antilles)
Elements, Elements (Antilles/Antilles)
Ron Carter, Etudes (Elektra Musician/Elektra Musician)
Mahavishnu Orchestra, Mahavishnu (Warner Brothers/Warner Brothers)
Michael Franks, Skin Dive (Warner Brothers/Warner Brothers)
Living In The Crest Of A Wave (Elektra Musician/Elektra Musician)
The Alternative Man (Blue Note/Blue Note)

Below: A multi-talented newcomer, saxophonist Bill Evans' first two solo albums revealed an exceptional potential and an extraordinary depth of vision.

Above: Gil Evans tracking his Blues In Orbit? From the Birth of the Cool to Jimi Hendrix, one of the most open-minded and influential arrangers.

Gil Evans

Born 1912, arranger Gil Evans is, along with Duke Ellington and Tadd Dameron, one of the greatest orchestrators in jazz His deployment of instruments brings out the richness of tone in textures that almost activate the taste buds. Evans devises structures that are continually shifting and refining around the soloist, the writing never conflicting with that sense of spontaneity vital to jazz Starting as an arranger with the Claude Thornhill orchestra in the early '40s, Evans' reputation grew beyond the dance band connection with his work for Miles Davis' 1949 nine-piece band. On **Boplicity** and. **Moondreams (Birth Of The Cool)** Evans' characteristic blendings of French horn and tuba became widely influential. His first album with a unit of his own **(The Arranger's Touch)** has excellent playing from soprano saxophonist Steve Lacy on **Ella Speed** and **Just One Of Those Things**, and sumptuous use of French horn, muted trumpet and bassoon in the ensembles, while **Big Stuff** features lower register textures in a highly original arrangement.

The collaboration with Miles Davis was resumed in 1957, the soloist playing flugelhorn over Evans' voicings for a 19-piece orchestra **(Miles Ahead)**. The album has ten pieces by different writers from Dave Brubeck to Johnny Carisi, and Davis' role is assimilated into the general orchestral fabric. The artistically successful partnership continued with two further albums; on **Porgy & Bess**, the Gershwin score is considerably altered on performances like **Summertime**, which is stately rather than crooning, with Davis riding the ensemble swells with great economy and his unique brand of choked melancholia. The final album **(Sketches Of Spain)** mixes flamenco patterns with jazz, and Davis' playing is often cast in a tragic mold. Throughout the series, Evans' writing is tailored to fit the trumpeter's musical temperament, the prevailing sadness of mood achieved through the quality of sound. Some critics have found Evans' work lacking in drive, swing, and the explosive power of impassioned playing—a shot-silk canvas. In fact, driving performances like Lacy's over a thrusting ensemble on **Straight No Chaser (Pacific Standard Time)** show that Evans' aesthetic is by no means effete. Budd Johnson's work on Don Redman's **Chant Of The Weed**, Jimmy Cleveland's trombone on **Ballad Of The Sad Young Men** and trumpeter Johnny Coles on Beiderbecke's **Davenport Blues** show no lack of virility. A programme of jazz classics featuring altoist Cannonball Adderley **(Pacific Standard Time)** includes **Lester Leaps In** and the brilliantly scored **Manteca**, with Adderley at his best on Monk's **Round Midnight** and Jelly Roll Morton's **King Porter Stomp**. Further albums followed on which the ensemble was showcased as much as the soloist, tonal combinations that seem to hover like painter Morris Louis' veils. The best of these **(Out Of The Cool, The Individualism Of Gil Evans** and **Gil Evans)** show a harmonic subtlety and originality of mind that remain unsurpassed.

In recent years, Gil Evans has continued to work with his orchestra from whose ranks have emerged some of the most exciting soloists of the age like saxophonists Billy Harper, Arthur Blythe and David Sanborn, tuba-players Bob Stewart and Howard Johnson, trumpeter Hannibal Marvin Peterson and percussionist Susan Evans **(Blues In Orbit** and **Priestess)**. While his latter-day ensembles haven't always been as tight as earlier ones, they still manage to turn up evocative Evans-inspired moments like Dave Sanborn's spine-chilling blues-wailing blow on **Short Visit** from **Priestess**. In '83, Evans was recorded live with **The British Orchestra** in Bradford, England, including such UK luminaries as saxophonist John Surman, Stan Sulzmann, Don Weller and trumpeter Henry Lowther.

Always intrigued by the musical developments around him, a promising project with rock guitarist Jimi Hendrix was curtailed by Hendrix's sudden death in September '70. However, in '74, Evans was able to realize at least a measure of the Hendrix spirit on **Gil Evans/Plays Hendrix** (with guitarists John Abercrombie and Ryo Kawasaki).

In the mid-'80s, at age 74, Evans agreed to write most of the '50s arrangements for one of the '80s' most ambitious 'pop' projects—his brilliant score for Julien Temple's film *Absolute Beginners* marked Evans' musical screen début.

Albums:

Miles Davis, Birth Of The Cool (Capitol/Capitol)
Miles Davis, Miles Ahead (Columbia/CBS)
Miles Davis, Porgy & Bess (Columbia/CBS)
Miles Davis, Sketches Of Spain (Columbia/CBS)
The Arranger's Touch (Prestige/Prestige)
Pacific Standard Time (Blue Note/Blue Note)
Out Of The Cool (Impulse/Impulse)
The Individualism Of Gil Evans (Verve/—)
Gil Evans/Plays Hendrix (RCA/RCA)
Blues In Orbit (—/Enja—Germany)
Priestess (Antilles/Antilles)
Gil Evans—The British Orchestra (—/Mole Jazz)
Live At Sweet Basil (—/King—Japan)

Gill Evans, 1983, The British Orchestra (courtesy Mole Jazz).

Jon Faddis

The technical mastery of high-spirited trumpet prodigy Jon Faddis elevated him to the ranks of the new 'young lions' as early as age 15.

Born Oakland, Ca, on July 24, 1953, Faddis took up the instrument aged 7 after seeing Louis Armstrong on *The Ed Sullivan Show*. By age 11, he was studying with ex-Kenton musician Bill Catalano who introduced him to the Dizzy Gillespie style of playing—a technique to which Faddis has been faithful ever since. At 13, he played dances with local soul bands and gained some early experience with big bands and rehearsal bands. As early as 15, Faddis sat in with his hero Dizzy Gillespie, from which encounter was to develop a special relationship between the two trumpeters (apart from anything else, they both share a notorious reputation for wise-cracking).

In '71, just two days before his 18th birthday, Faddis went on the road with Lionel Hampton's line-up and subbed in the Thad Jones-Mel Lewis band. In '72, he left Hampton, attracting much attention touring with Charles Mingus. Faddis joined Jones-Lewis on a regular basis until '76, gaining a daunting reputation around New York. As a result, Faddis has been much in demand as a session musician, which explains his late appearance on the scene as a soloist. He has worked with an extraordinary cross-section of artists, from Frank Sinatra to the Rolling Stones, and has written extensively for TV.

From the mid-'80s, Faddis has toured and recorded with his own group. A solo outing, **Legacy** in '85 (in the top-class company of tenorist Harold Land, bassist Ray Brown, drummer Mel Lewis and pianist Kenny Barron), is a sterling tribute to such masters as Armstrong, Gillespie and Roy Eldridge.

Albums:

Legacy (Concord/Concord)

Above: Trumpeter Jon Faddis—high notes and even higher spirits.

Art Farmer

Flugel-hornist Farmer was born in Iowa, 1928, playing in the bands of Horace Henderson, Benny Carter and Lionel Hampton. In 1953 he went with Hamp's outfit to Europe and recorded several tracks with distinguished fellow bandsman, Clifford Brown, **Stockhold Sweetnin', Scuse These Blues, Falling In Love With Love** and **Lover Come Back To Me**, and the Swedish All Stars **(Clifford Brown Memorial)**. The previous year, Farmer turned up on another historic session with tenorist Wardell Gray, playing his own **Farmer's Market (Central Avenue)**. In fact, Farmer is an extremely adaptable musician, and has played with experimenters like George Russell as well as the boppers.

A collection of his early work **(Farmer's Market)** finds him in a variety of groups including those of Sonny Rollins and Horace Silver. **Alone Together** is his best track, displaying a certain debt to the lean phrasing of Miles Davis, but technically superior. A session from 1955 is by the Art Farmer-Gigi Gryce Quintet, and in its meticulous charts shows an impatience with the prevailing casual blowing sessions of hard bop. A later group, the Art Farmer-Benny Golson Jazztet **(Tonk** and **Farmer-Golson Jazztet)** proved an ideal setting for his lyrical gifts.

Albums:

Clifford Brown Memorial (Prestige/—)
Wardell Gray, Central Avenue (Prestige/Prestige)
Farmer's Market (Prestige/Prestige)
Tonk (Mercury/Mercury)

Farmer-Golson Jazztet (Cadet/—)
Portrait Of Art (Contemporary/—)
A Sleeping Bee (Sonet/Sonet)
To Duke With Love (Inner City/—)
The Summer Knows (Inner City/—)
A Work Of Art (Concord/Concord)
Warm Valley (Concord/Concord)
Manhattan (Soul Note/Soul Note)

Above: Art Farmer, long-time collaborator with Benny Golson. Creator of the warmest flugel-horn sound on earth?

Joe Farrell

There were no bounds to the versatility of Joe Farrell—indeed, with his always questing, urgent saxophone style his horizons seemed limitless. With a remarkable and equal facility on the reed instruments (he played them all except bassoon), Farrell developed into an important influence on young reeds-players in the '70s, notably through his pioneering work with the band Return To Forever.

Born in Chicago Heights, Illinois, on December 16, 1937, Farrell played a clarinet from age 10, encouraged by his musician brother-in-law and inspired by a well-played stack of Benny Goodman 78s. In '53, he took tenor studies at Roy Knapp Music School in Chicago with Joe Sirolla, majoring at the University of Illinois in flute from which he graduated with a BS in music education.

By now he had moved on from Goodman's swing-era clarinet to the raging hard-bop tenor style of saxophonists like Johnny Griffin. Stan Kenton, George Shearing and Charlie Parker were all to inspire him and help shape his musical direction. He worked with local Chicago musicians like Ira Sullivan and Nicky Hill before arriving in New York in '60. During the '60s, still in his early 20s, he worked with a daunting list of established musicians—Maynard Ferguson, Slide Hampton, Tito Rodriguez, George Russell's sextet, Jaki Byard and three years with the Thad Jones-Mel Lewis band. In '67, he formed a trio with drummer Elvin Jones and bassist Jimmy Garrison, following a path formerly trodden by John Coltrane.

In the early '70s, he turned to yet another area—jazz-rock, becoming a founder member of Chick Corea's Return To Forever, and from '74 worked with his own quartet, touring again with RTF in '77.

During the '70s his dynamic saxophone-playing was heard with a diversity of musicians—Woody Herman, Herbie Hancock, John McLaughlin, Santana, Al Kooper, Billy Cobham, James Brown, Aretha Franklin, and his contribution to the Mingus Dynasty was stunning. A period of personal problems took him off the scene in the early '80s but his 'comeback' in '84 (touring internationally with pianist Joanne Brackeen) showed a magnificent return to form and activity. He was working with a new quartet and things were looking up. At the beginning of '86, Farrell's return of spirit and success was to be sadly cut short. On January 10, Joe Farrell died in a Los Angeles hospital from bone cancer. He was 48. Another of jazz's great tragedies.

Albums:
Return To Forever, Musicmagic (Columbia/CBS)
Return To Forever, Return To Forever (ECM/ECM)
Maynard Ferguson, Newport Suite (Roulette/Roulette)
Elvin Jones, Putting It Together (Blue Note/Blue Note)
Charles Mingus, Mingus Revisited (Trip/—)
Thad Jones-Mel Lewis, Live At The Village Vanguard (Solid State/—)
Mingus Dynasty, Mingus Dynasty Live At Montreux (Atlantic/Atlantic)
Joe Farrell—George Benson, Benson & Farrell (CTI/CTI)
La Catedral Y El Toro (Warner Brothers/Warner Brothers)
Upon This Rock (CTI/CTI)
Song Of The Wind (CTI/CTI)
Penny Arcade (CTI/CTI)
Out Back (CTI/CTI)
Moon Germs (CTI/CTI)
Canned Funk (CTI/CTI)
Flute Talk (Zanadu/—)

Maynard Ferguson

Born in Montreal, 1928, trumpeter Maynard Ferguson made his name with the Stan Kenton Orchestra, where his phenomenal upper register technique allowed him to scream an octave above the rest of the trumpet section **(Artistry In Jazz)**. Shorty Rogers used him to good effect in his own driving band **(Blues Express)** and he also worked for the movie studios, notably on Cecil B. De Mille's *The Ten Commandments*. In 1956, he formed his own big band, using largely unknowns who went on to establish a reputation—Slide Hampton, Don Ellis, Joe Farrell and Jaki Byard. The first and best album **(A Message From Newport)** has a colossal impact, largely due to the bite and precision of the brass. Subsequent Ferguson bands show a similar emphasis on hard swing, though his more recent work shows a fusion orientation.

His '82 **Hollywood** album, for instance, was produced, directed and contributed to by bassist Stanley Clarke plus featuring such funk favorites as pianists George Duke and Greg Phillinganes, guitarists Lee Ritenour and Michael Sembello, and altoist Dave Sanborn.

Albums:
Stan Kenton, Artistry In Jazz (Capitol/—)
Shorty Rogers, Blues Express (RCA—France)
A Message From Newport (Roulette/—)
Alive & Well In London (Columbia/CBS)
Chameleon (Columbia/CBS)
Live At Jimmy's (Columbia/CBS)
Primal Scream (Columbia/CBS)
Hollywood (Columbia/CBS)

Ella Fitzgerald

Born 1918 in Virginia, singer Ella Fitzgerald got her first big break when she was spotted by altoist Benny Carter in the amateur hour at Harlem's Apollo. This led to bandleader Chick Webb taking her on as vocalist, and with her first smash hit, **A-Tisket A-Tasket**, her career was assured. She conducted Webb's orchestra after his death. Over the years, her voice has matured from its first piping prettiness into a rich contralto. The old argument still continues over Ella's status as a jazz singer and her lack of emotional depth. She does not move the listener like Billie Holiday, nor amaze with her imagination like Sarah Vaughan, and her swoops through the scales are practiced, glossy and often predictable. Nevertheless, her voice is an unrivaled instrument when handling the classier popular songs. Her signing to Norman Granz saw the release of a series of songbooks covering Jerome Kern & Johnny Mercer, Rodgers & Hart, Harold Arlen, Irving Berlin, Cole Porter and Duke Ellington, the latter—particularly with the small groups—being the most jazz-orientated. She is also a great favorite with Jazz at the Phil audiences, and her scat-singing on numbers like **Lady Be Good** or **How High The Moon** is by now obligatory. The re-emergence of Granz produced a crop of fine Ella albums in the small group context **(Take Love Easy, Ella In London, Ella At Montreux** and **Ella & Oscar)**.

Albums:
Ella Fitzgerald & Louis Armstrong, Ella & Louis (Verve/Verve)
Ella Sings The Duke Ellington Songbook (Verve/Verve)
JATP In Tokyo (Verve/Verve)
Ella Fitzgerald & Joe Pass, Take Love Easy (Pablo/Pablo)
Ella In London (Pablo/Pablo)
Ella At Montreux (Pablo/Pablo)
Ella Fitzgerald & Oscar Peterson, Ella & Oscar (Pablo/Pablo)
These Are The Blues (Verve/Verve)
Ella Abraca Jobim/Ella Fitzgerald Sings The Antonio Carlos Jobim Song Book (Pablo/Pablo)
'Nice Work If You Can Get It'—Ella Fitzgerald And André Previn Do Gershwin (Pablo/Pablo)

Rodney Franklin

One of the most talented and successful young fusion pianists to dazzle all in the late '70s, Rodney Franklin was an exceptionally early-starter.

Born in Berkeley, California, on September 16, 1958, Franklin showed an unusual talent for keyboards as early as age 3. At 6, he was playing alto sax and organ at Washington Elementary School's jazz workshop, part of Dr Herb Wong's experiment in music education for the very young. Inspired by Herbie Hancock, Chick Corea, Oscar Peterson, Art Tatum and Horace Silver, Franklin decided to concentrate on keyboards. At 9, Franklin received an All-Star band award as top soloist at the Reno Jazz Festival; at 16, he became the youngest person to receive *Contemporary Keyboards'* piano award.

In '77, he left school and worked with percussionist Bill Summers. An encounter with Columbia Records' George Butler led to his début album **In The Center** and subsequent hit single **The Groove**, the catchy tune which generated the popular late-'70s disco-dance craze 'the Freeze'. His fourth album, **Endless Flight**, provided another hit for Franklin with his cover of Mike Post's theme for TV's *Hill Street Blues*.

Franklin has also worked with Freddie Hubbard, John Handy and vocalist Marlena Shaw, as well as touring Cuba as part of the CBS Jazz All-Stars in '79.

Albums:
In The Center (Columbia/CBS)
You'll Never Know (Columbia/CBS)
Rodney Franklin (Columbia/CBS)
Endless Flight (Columbia/CBS)
Skydance (Columbia/CBS)

Below: Fusion pianist Rodney Franklin —an exceptionally early starter.

Michael Franks

With a large cult following, popular singer-songwriter and all-rounder Michael Franks has the distinction of being one of the few cross-over vocalists to have his songs recorded by blues luminaries Sonny Terry and Brownie McGhee.

Born in La Jolla, California, on September 18, 1944, Franks played folk and rock in high school. While working part-time as a musician, he majored in contemporary literature at UCLA. In the late '60s, he took a master's degree in contemporary culture at Montreal University.

In the early '70s, Franks taught music courses to undergraduates and worked towards a PhD, undertaking a vast doctoral dissertation on 'Contemporary Songwriting and How it Relates to Society'. When blues masters Terry and McGhee recorded three of his songs in '72, Franks accompanied them on banjo and mandolin.

His own albums have attracted the support of major fusion artists like the Crusaders **(The Art Of Tea)** and he worked with Brazilian musicians on **Sleeping Gypsy**. His songs have also been covered by Manhattan Transfer.

Albums:
Michael Franks (Brut/—)
The Art Of Tea (Reprise/Reprise)
Sleeping Gypsy
(Warner Brothers/Warner Brothers)
Birchfield Nines
(Warner Brothers/Warner Brothers)
Tiger In The Rain
(Warner Brothers/Warner Brothers)
One Bad Habit
(Warner Brothers/Warner Brothers)
Objects Of Desire
(Warner Brothers/Warner Brothers)

Bud Freeman

Lawrence 'Bud' Freeman (born Chicago, Illinois, 1906) tried out his first saxophone—a C-melody sax—in 1923 (the switch to tenor followed two years later).

Tonally, Freeman's work on tenor has been compared with that of Lester Young, though Freeman's tone has more of an edge than Young's; rhythmically, there are similarities with the earlier style of Coleman Hawkins.

Bud Freeman always has been an individualist, instantly recognizable, and something of a style-setting innovator. Certainly, he remains the archetypal tenor player of the so-called Chicago school, of which Freeman was one of the early protagonists.

Freeman's musical training included some tuition from the father of cornettist Jimmy McPartland. At the beginning of his career he was closely associated with Austin High School Gang, in Chicago; he and associates were deeply affected by the music of Louis Armstrong, Jimmy Noone, King Oliver, Bix Beiderbecke, the New Orleans Rhythm Kings et al. Together with his Austin High colleagues, Freeman worked with a variety of bands between 1925-27, not always strictly jazz, mostly in Chicago.

In 1927, Freeman, Frank Teschemacher and McPartland recorded as members of (Red) McKenzie & (Eddie) Condon's Chicagoans. The results have long since passed into annals of recorded jazz as classic definitions of white 'Chicago' jazz **(That Toddlin' Town—Chicago: 1926-28)**. Also in '27, Freeman joined orchestra of Ben Pollack, with whom he was to remain for almost a year before joining a band aboard the *Ile de France*. Also worked for a fortnight in Paris with drummer friend Davey Tough. Returning to US, Freeman joined Red Nichols, before working with succession of jazz and dance bands, including Roger Wolfe Kahn, Zez Confrey.

In 1935 he worked with the prestigious Ray Noble Orchestra, Noble giving Freeman generous allocation of solo space (viz **Dinah (With All My Heart)**) with the tenorist producing bubbling, infectious solo). Spent two years (1936-38) as featured soloist with Tommy Dorsey. Again, was given ample solo space, notably on such Dorsey items as **Smoke Gets In Your Eyes, Who?, Maple Leaf Rag, Marie (Tommy Dorsey & His Orchestra)** and **After You've Gone, That's A-Plenty, Blue Danube** and **Beale Street Blues (Tommy Dorsey, Vol II)**.

Joined Benny Goodman, remaining for nine-month period in1938.

In 1939 he was appointed nominal leader of Summa Cum Laude Orchestra (originally assembled for one-night gig by Eddie Condon previous year). Records testify handsomely **(Chicagoans In New York: Bud Freeman** and **Chicago Styled)** to the freshness and spring-heeled vitality of the band during its almost one-and-a-half-year lifetime. SCLO took part in short-lived revue *Swingin' That Dream*, also featuring Louis Armstrong and Benny Goodman Septet. Apart from comprehensive association with large size bands during 1930s, Freeman worked with numerous small combos during this decade, in person and on record.

Two important recording dates under Condon's leadership really established Bud Freeman as major soloist. Most significant for Freeman was feature item entitled **The Eel (Home Cooking)** which was recorded twice, at both sessions. In itself, **The Eel** encapsulates the quintessence of Bud Freeman's approach to tenor sax.

In 1938, he demonstrated the ability to more than hold his own, even in strongest company, eg Armstrong, Teagarden, Waller, laying down some of his most dynamic playing during a broadcast date from New York **(All That Jazz: Louis Armstrong)**. Freeman's long association with Condon continued productively into the 1940s. These collaborations ranged from a 1939 date which recaptured the spirit if not the essence of McKenzie & Condon Chicagoans **(Chicago Jazz)** through a trio of 1940 studio sessions, two in March **(Commodore Condon, Vol 1)** and one in July (under Freeman's name) **(Home Cooking)**. When SCLO disbanded, he toured with yet another big band—this one his own. The venture, however, lasted only a few months before its leader joined the combo of Joe Marsala.

Following a move back to the city of his birth, plus another unsuccessful attempt at leading big band, Freeman served with the US Army (1943-45). Appointed leader of Service band at Ft George, Maryland; likewise for another band in Aleutian Islands. Out of uniform, he was soon back on the New York music scene, including regular work, once again, with Condon (1946-47). Early in '47, accepted offer to lead trio for hotel residence in Rio de Janeiro. Five years later, was to tour Chile, Peru. Some of Freeman's finest playing of 1950s was captured on record during a 1954 Condon jam session in New York **(The Golden Days Of Jazz: Eddie Condon)**. During this decade he studied with pianist-composer Lennie Tristano, although he maintains this did nothing to change his musical thoughts or basic approach to jazz

Since the 1950s, he has continued to tour extensively, throughout the US and abroad. A regular visitor to the UK and Europe either as leader of own groups, or as solo act. Between 1969-70 was member of World's Greatest Jazzband. Has also appeared with saxist-clarinettist Bob Wilber **(Song Of The Tenor, The Music Of Hoagy Carmichael** and **The Compleat Bud Freeman)**.

Bud Freeman has written two autobiographical books—*You Don't Look Like A Musician* and *If You Know Of A Better Life*.

Below: Bud Freeman—archetypal tenorist of the Chicago school—always an individualist, instantly recognizable, a style-setter and innovator.

Bud Freeman, Home Cooking (courtesy Tax-Sweden)—the tenorist at his best.

Albums:
Various, That Toddlin' Town—Chicago: 1926-28 (Parlophone)
Benny Goodman, The Early B.G. (—/Vocalion)
Various, Jack Teagarden Classics (Family—Italy)
Various, Swing Classics—1935 (Prestige)/ Jazz In The Thirties (World Records)
Bud Freeman, Home Cooking (Tax—Sweden)
Bud Freeman, Chicagoans In New York (Dawn Club)
Bud Freeman, Chicago Styled (Swaggie—Australia)
Mezz Mezzrow/(Frankie Newton), The Big Apple (RCA Victor—France)
Louis Armstrong (Trip)/All That Jazz: Louis Armstrong (DJM)
Benny Goodman, Vols 5, 7 (RCA Victor—France)
Tommy Dorsey, Tommy Dorsey & His Orchestra (RCA Victor/RCA Victor)
Tommy Dorsey, Vol II (RCA Victor/RCA Victor)

Various (Including Eddie Condon), Chicago Jazz (—/Coral)
Eddie Condon, Commodore Condon, Vol 1 (—/London)
Lee Wiley, Sweet & Lowdown (Monmouth-Evergreen/—)
Various (Including Eddie Condon/ Bud Freeman), The Commodore Years (Atlantic/—)
Jack Teagarden, Vol 2: 'Prince Of The Bones' (RCA Victor—France)
The Golden Days Of Jazz: Eddie Condon (CBS—Holland)
The Bud Freeman Trio (—/London)
Eddie Condon, Chicago & All That Jazz! (—/Verve)
Various, The Big Challenge (Jazztone/Concert Hall)
The Compleat Bud Freeman (Monmouth-Evergreen/Parlophone)
Bob Wilber/Maxine Sullivan, The Music Of Hoagy Carmichael (Monmouth-Evergreen/Parlophone)
The World's Greatest Jazzband Of Yank Lawson & Bob Haggart, Extra! (Project 3/Parlophone)
The World's Greatest Jazzband Of Yank Lawson & Bob Haggart, (Project 3/World Record Club)
The World's Greatest Jazzband Of Yank Lawson & Bob Haggart—Live At The Roosevelt Grill (Atlantic/Atlantic)
The World's Greatest Jazzband Of Yank Lawson & Bob Haggart In Concert, Vol 2, At Carnegie Hall (World Jazz/—)
The World's Greatest Jazzband Of Yank Lawson & Bob Haggart, Century Plaza (World Pacific/—)
Bud Freeman, The Joy Of Sax (Chiaroscuro/—)
Bud Freeman, Song Of The Tenor (Philips)
The Real Bud Freeman 1984 (Principally Jazz/—)

Chico Freeman

Chicago's Chico Freeman is undoubtedly one of the most authoritative and intelligent young saxophonists to emerge in the late '70s-early '80s. His has become a dominant and uncompromising voice, both in performance and through his commanding compositions.

Born on Chicago's Calumet Avenue, Chico Freeman arrived into an exceptionally musical family. His father, the indomitable tenorist Earl Lavon 'Von' Freeman, worked with Sun Ra and Dexter Gordon; his Uncle Bruz was a drummer and Uncle George was a guitarist; while his grandfather was a close friend of Louis Armstrong.

Chico Freeman's first instrument was piano, then trumpet, but in spite of the family's strong musical tradition, he was encouraged to take up a mathematics scholarship at Northwestern University. He didn't even pick up a saxophone until he began majoring in music at Northwestern—a response to his trumpet tutor telling him he wasn't destined to be a Miles Davis—and he subsequently developed an equal facility on bass clarinet and flutes.

In Chicago, his association with Muhal Richard Abrams and the AACM musicians opened up his ears to the freer side of improvisational playing—Freeman always anxious to learn, to improve his technique.

Although father Von had remained in Chicago, and become a stalwart of the local scene, Chico decided he had to go to New York. In '76, his 'three-day visit' became permanent, finding immediate employment with Jeanne Lee and Mickey Bass, then Elvin Jones and Sam Rivers around Lower Manhattan's burgeoning loft scene.

Since the late '70s, Chico Freeman has led his own groups which have included the challenging company of bassist Cecil McBee, vibes-players Jay Hoggard and Bobby Hutcherson, drummers Jack De Johnette, Billy Hart and Ronnie Burrage, trumpeter Wynton Marsalis and vocalist Bobby McFerrin.

Freeman, a harsh critic of commercially diluted and 'compromise' music, believes that jazz in the '80s is in transition. His refusal to be categorized and his willingness to change and explore promise to make his musical quest even more interesting as time passes.

Albums:
Cecil McBee, The Source (—/Enja—Germany)
Don Pullen, Warriors (Black Saint/Black Saint)
Kings of Mali (India Navigation/—)
Chico (India Navigation/—)
Morning Prayer (Whynot-Trio—Japan)
Spirit Sensitive (India Navigation/—)
Destiny's Dance (Contemporary/Contemporary)
Tradition In Transition (Elektra Musician/Elektra Musician)
Tangents (Elektra Musician/Elektra Musician)

Saxophonist Chico Freeman, Destiny's Dance (courtesy Contemporary).

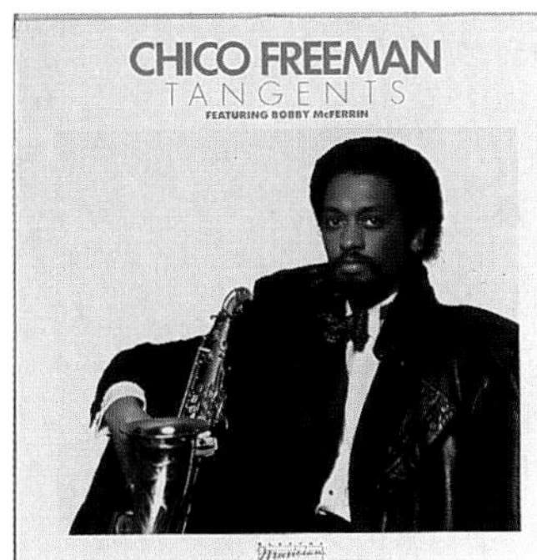

Tangents featuring Bobby McFerrin (courtesy Elektra Musician).

Steve Gadd

Since arriving in New York City in 1971, multi-talented drummer-percussionist Steve Gadd has become one of the most versatile, valuable and employable session musicians in the United States. His innovations with the fusion group Stuff in the late '70s were to influence a generation of young drummers.

Born Rochester, New York, on September 4, 1945, Gadd learned about rhythm early—on his feet, tap-dancing at a local club. From age 3, his uncle taught him to play drums and his early interest in Sousa marches is evident even today in his playing. His growing interest in percussion received a further boost working with a drum corps where he discovered just how many different ways there were to play the instrument.

He studied privately with Bill and Stanley Street, then with John Beck, spending two years at Manhattan's School of Music before going to Eastman in Rochester. His first gigs were with Chuck Mangione and Chick Corea. Working with Corea was a revelation for Gadd. Corea introduced him to limitless creative possibilities and subtleties of jazz-rock. The experience was to influence Gadd's whole approach to drum technique and change his style completely, evolving into his exceptional lightness of touch and formidable rhythmic dexterity.

From '71, Gadd became one of New York's most coveted session-players, performing briefly with Chick Corea, Mike Mainieri and Herbie Mann. In '76, along with Eric Gale, Richard Tee & Co, Gadd worked with revolutionary fusion band Stuff, gaining a world-wide reputation as *the* funk drummer.

Gadd's studio output as a side-player has been prolific and, not surprisingly, his influence as one of the most innovative and technically accomplished percussionists continues to dominate the scene internationally into the '80s.

Albums:
Chick Corea, The Mad Hatter (Polydor/Polydor)
Joe Farrell, La Catedral Y El Toro (Warner Brothers/Warner Brothers)
Maynard Ferguson, Primal Scream (Columbia/CBS)
Chuck Mangione, Main Squeeze (A&M/A&M)
Herbie Mann, Waterbed (Atlantic/Atlantic)
David Sanborn, Taking Off (Warner Brothers/Warner Brothers)
John Tropea, Tropea (Marlin/—)
Michal Urbaniak, Fusion 3 (Columbia/CBS)
Jim Hall, Concierto (CTI/CTI)
Ron Carter, Anything Goes (Kudu/Kudu)
Hank Crawford, Hank Crawford's Back (Kudu/ Kudu)
Gaddabout (—/King-Japan)

Slim Gaillard

The proto-typical '40s hipster, Gaillard sang, danced, played guitar and practically every other instrument but is usually remembered for his jive talk which he called 'vout'. He had a string of hits, **Tutti Frutti, Flat Foot Floogie, Cement Mixer, A-Reet-a-Voutee**, some in partnership with bassist Slam Stewart. Charlie Parker and Dizzy Gillespie turned up on one of his novelty sessions, cutting four tracks including the splendid **Slim's Jam (Charlie Parker, Bird/The Savoy, Recordings)**. A collection with Bam Brown, Harry The Hipster Gibson and Leo Watson, the most gymnastic of scat-singers, catches precisely the period flavor. **Avocado Seed Soup Symphony** is a surreal masterpiece **(McVouty)**.

In '41, he moved to Hollywood, appearing in films like *Star Spangled Banner, Almost Married* and the legendary *Hellzapoppin!*; in more recent years, he made a special guest appearance in the TV epic *Roots—The Next Generation*.

Since the early '80s, Gaillard has taken up residence in London, England, where he still cuts a dash as a colorful figure and is a popular attraction around the clubs.

Slim 'McVouty' Gaillard, Opera In Vout (courtesy Verve).

Albums:
Slim Gaillard & Bam Brown, McVouty (Hep/Hep)
Son Of McVouty (Hep/Hep)
Charlie Parker Memorial Volume 2 (Spotlite/Spotlite)
The Voutist (Hep/Hep)
Slim Gaillard At Birdland (Hep/Hep)
Collectibles (MCA/MCA)
Slim Gaillard/Opera In Vout (Verve/Verve)
Roots Of Vouty (Putti-Putti/Putti-Putti)

Eric Gale

Widely admired guitarist Eric Gale shot to prominence as one of the most revered (and, subsequently, most imitated) stylists of the late '70s fusion with a sound as individual as his fingerprints. He thinks like a horn-player, phrases like a sax-player and coaxes sounds like the human voice from his guitar.

Gale's distinctive, cutting technique evolved after years of listening to John Coltrane, Lester Young, Dexter Gordon, Ray Charles, Jimmy Smith and Charlie Parker (his '80 album **Touch Of Silk**, produced by Allen Toussaint, includes Gale's personal tribute to Parker with his special interpretation of **Au Privave)**.

Born in Brooklyn on September 20, 1938, of Barbadian parents, Gale's first instrument was double-bass at age 12. He soon switched to guitar, finding it easier to carry. After a year of guitar lessons, Gale bought style and technique books and taught himself, later becoming adept on tenor sax, trombone and tuba.

He majored in chemistry at Niagara University but his goal was to become a recording musician. He worked on the R&B circuit in the '50s and '60s with artists like the Drifters, Jackie Wilson, the Flamingos, Jesse Belvin, Baby Washington and Maxine Brown before realizing that studio ambition. After recommendations from King Curtis and Jimmy Smith, Gale found himself very busy in the studio and, in the early '70s, he became house guitarist for Creed Taylor's CTI label.

After a long period of unrelenting studio activity, Gale quit for four years, living on his Ohio farm and getting into reggae in Jamaica.

In '76, Gale made an auspicious return when he formed the band Stuff with fellow innovators Richard Tee, Cornell Dupree, Gordon Edwards, Chris Parker and Steve Gadd. Soon, Stuff was packing out Mikell's in Manhattan—musicians coming from all over the world to hear the band. The success of this band—which never rehearsed but just got up and played some of the liveliest, most spontaneous and ground-breaking funk—was unprecedented. Subsequently, Stuff still stands as one of the most influential groupings in fusion history.

Since '80, having worked with Bob James and Ralph MacDonald, Gale has devoted time to his solo projects. Gale's instantly recognizable style—like that of Larry Carlton and Lee Ritenour—remains enduringly persuasive. There can't be many guitarists since the late '70s who haven't listened to, and tried to ape, Gale's unique sound and technique as displayed on albums like **Stuff, More Stuff** and **Multiplication** or Grover Washington Jr's **Winelight**.

Albums:
Quincy Jones, Gula Matari (A&M/A&M)
Quincy Jones, Body Heat (A&M/A&M)
Tom Scott, New York Connection (Ode/—)
Bob James, Bob James Three (CTI/CTI)
Bob James, Heads (Columbia/CBS)
Ralph MacDonald, The Path (Marlin/—)
George Benson, Space (CTI/CTI)
Richard Tee, Strokin' (Columbia/CBS)
Grover Washington Jr, Winelight
(Elektra—Asylum/Elektra—Asylum)
Sadao Watanabe, Orange Express
(CBS-Sony/CBS-Sony)
Stuff, Stuff
(Warner Brothers/Warner Brothers)
Stuff, More Stuff
(Warner Brothers/Warner Brothers)
Stuff It (Warner Brothers/Warner Brothers)
Stuff, Live In New York
(Warner Brothers/Warner Brothers)
Forecast (CTI-Kudu/CTI-Kudu)
Ginseng Woman (Columbia/CBS)
Multiplication (Columbia/CBS)
Part Of You (Columbia/CBS)
Touch Of Silk (Columbia/CBS)
Blue Horizon
(Elektra Musician/Elektra Musician)
Island Breeze
(Elektra Musician/Elektra Musician)

Ganelin Trio

Russia's improvisational Ganelin Trio—described from 'a Russian equivalent of the Art Ensemble of Chicago' to 'the new voice of free jazz in Russia'—has become an established force on the Soviet Union's 'new music' scene, touring the USSR extensively and having the distinction of being sent to the West to perform under the auspices of the official government booking agency.

Now based in Leningrad, the Ganelin Trio—Vyacheslav Ganelin, Vladimir Tarasov and Vladimir Chekasin—was formed in 1971 in Vilnius, Lithuania. Their personal and energetic brand of improvised music was first heard in the West in '80 when they performed to great acclaim at the Berlin Jazz Days festival. Between them, they play more than a dozen instruments: Ganelin on piano and basset keyboard; Tarasov—drums, percussion and trumpet; and Chekasin—clarinet, basset horn, trombone, ocarina, flute, double flute and two alto saxophones (played simultaneously).

Vyacheslav Ganelin, born 1944, has played piano since age 4; a graduate from Vilnius Conservatory, he is a member of the USSR Composers Union and has also written operas and film scores. Vladimir Tarasov, born 1947, has played drums since '61; self-taught, he also performs with the Lithuanian State Symphony and Lithuanian Radio Symphony Orchestras. Vladimir Chekasin, born 1947, played violin from age 6, clarinet by 11, alto sax at 18; a graduate of Sverdlovsk Conservatory, he was awarded top honors in '70 at the international competition organized by the Czechoslovak Society of Composers.

The Ganelin Trio has emerged as an important example of the 'first wave' of Russian improvisers and their performances have attracted much interest outside the USSR. Their recordings would be hard to come by in the West but for a concerted issue program by Leon Feigin's British-based Leo Records.

Albums:
Catalogue—Live In East Germany (—/Leo)
Con Fuoco (—/Leo)
Ancora Da Capo Parts 1 and 2 (—/Leo)
New Wine (—/Leo)
Non Troppo (—/Enja—Germany)
Vide (—/Leo)
Strictly For Our Friends (—/Leo)

Ganelin Trio, Catalogue—Live In East Germany (courtesy Leo Records).

Jan Garbarek

The distinguished Norwegian tenor saxophonist Jan Garbarek has been described by George Russell as 'just about the most uniquely talented jazz musician Europe has produced since Django Reinhardt'. Garbarek is undoubtedly one of the most original individualists on saxophone to have emerged since the '70s.

Born in Mysen, Norway, 1947, Garbarek taught himself to play saxophone at age 14, inspired by hearing John Coltrane's **Countdown** on the radio. A year later, he was fronting the leading quartet in the non-traditional section of the '62 Norwegian Amateur Jazz Championship. In '65, a significant encounter with George Russell at the Molde Jazz Festival resulted in Garbarek's fascination with Russell's 'Lydian Chromatic Concept of Tonal Organization', with Garbarek becoming an important soloist in the composer's works.

Garbarek has subsequently presented a wide body of his own work from acoustic and electric trios, quartets, through duos with piano, classical guitar, windharp, brass sextet and pipe organ to solos and trios with string orchestras. In the late '70s, he supplied a much-acclaimed series of solo improvisations for Edith Rogers' production of Ibsen's *Brand* at Oslo's National Theater. He has also written music for her production of *Peer Gynt* at Sweden's Malmö State Theater, been commissioned by Amsterdam's Plain Musicke Ensemble, and composed for mixed choir and jazz quartet. The '84 **It's OK To Listen To The Gray Voice** is Garbarek's interpretation of the works of poet Tomas Tranströmer.

Among the first artists to be recorded by Manfred Eicher for ECM, Garbarek's poignant saxophone can be heard on more than 30 albums for the label, either as leader or in an unprecedented variety of settings. His individualistic contributions to Keith Jarrett's projects (notably, **Luminessence, Arbour Zena** and the '74 small group's go-for-bust **Belonging**) helped bring Garbarek's plaintive, stark, almost alto-sounding tenor to a wider audience. An important factor in his individual sound is his love for the Nordic folk tradition which manifests itself with his every breath (just listen to his contributions to the classic, beautiful **Folk Songs** album in the compelling company of bassist Charlie Haden and guitarist-pianist Egberto Gismonti).

Garbarek's highly distinctive tone—a desolate, stinging sound, floating in simplicity and haunting clarity—has proclaimed him as one of the most important saxophone stylists in contemporary jazz

Above: Norway's Jan Garbarek—one of contemporary jazz's most important tenorists with a stark, plaintive sound atmospheric of his native fjords.

Jan Garbarek, It's OK To Listen To The Gray Voice (courtesy ECM).

Albums:
Keith Jarrett, Luminessence (ECM/ECM)
Keith Jarrett, Belonging (ECM/ECM)
Keith Jarrett, Arbour Zena (ECM/ECM)
Ralph Towner, Solstice (ECM/ECM)
Torgrim Sollid, Østerdasmusikk
(—/Mai—Scandinavia)
Jan Garbarek—Charlie Haden—
Egberto Gismonti, Magico (ECM/ECM)
Jan Garbarek—Charlie Haden—
Egberto Gismonti, Folk Songs (ECM/ECM)
George Russell, Electronic Sonata For Souls
Loved By Nature (Soul Note/Soul Note)
Afric Pepperbird (ECM/ECM)
Sart (ECM/ECM)
Triptykon (ECM/ECM)
Witchi-Tai-To (ECM/ECM)
Dansere (ECM/ECM)
Dis (ECM/ECM)
Aftenland (ECM/ECM)
Eventyr (ECM/ECM)
Paths, Prints (ECM/ECM)
Wayfarer (ECM/ECM)
It's OK To Listen To The Gray Voice
(ECM/ECM)
Works (ECM/ECM)

Erroll Garner

Pianist Erroll Garner was one of jazz's great romantics. Basically a swing musician, his piano conception was firmly rooted in an orchestral style with a powerful, two-handed attack which built towards great crescendos. Rich chords and a percussive left hand that drove with a tireless energy, warmth and humor and great melodic gifts made Garner a popular concert performer.

A session from 1947, Charlie Parker's first after his breakdown, found Garner coping well in an unsuitable setting, both men hitting the heights on **Cool Blues**, and accompanying singer Earl Coleman on **This Is Always**, which became a hit **(Charlie Parker On Dial, Vol 2)**. Stunning Garner can be heard on **Blue Lou** from a Gene Norman concert with Wardell Gray **(Jazz Scene USA)**, and a collection of excellent '40s performances by the diminutive titan in the more usual trio setting are on Savoy **(The Elf)**.

A Columbia collection from the '50s gives a fine cross-section of his talent, from the lyrical **Am I Blue** and **Dreamy**—his own composition—to the charging **Avalon (Play It Again, Erroll!)**. His most popular album **(Concert By The Sea)** has the performer pulling out all the stops, the long teasing introductions, the vast range of resource, the overwhelming attack. Playing mainly standards like **Autumn Leaves**, and **April In Paris**, Garner stamps his material with his own unique personality. A self-taught musician, Garner's inability to read music didn't prevent him from writing some beautiful tunes, including **Misty**. Four compositions turn up on a late session from the '70s **(Magician)** which shows all the vitality of three decades ago, and the same determination to wring the listener's heartstrings.

Born in 1923, Garner died in 1977, leaving scores of albums behind on a many labels.

Albums:
Charlie Parker On Dial, Vol 2 (Spotlite/Spotlite)
Jazz Scene USA (—/Vogue—France)
The Elf (Savoy/Savoy)
Play It Again, Erroll (Columbia/CBS)
Concert By The Sea (Columbia/CBS)
Magician (London/Pye)
The Greatest Garner (Atlantic/Atlantic)
Erroll Garner: The Complete Savoy Sessions Volumes 1 and 2 (RCA/RCA)

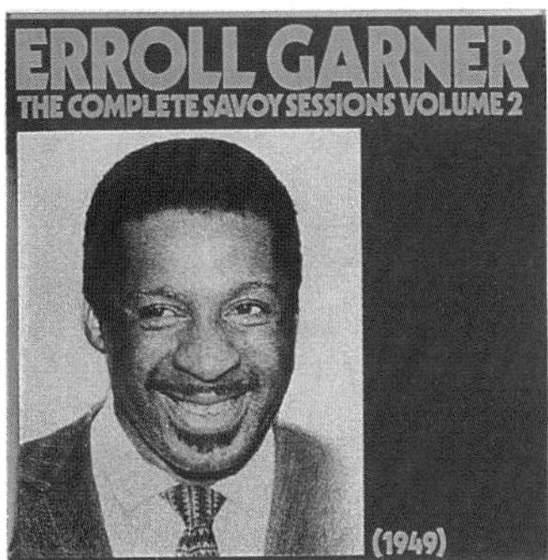

Erroll Garner, The Complete Savoy Sessions Volume 2 (courtesy RCA).

Michael Garrick

Since the early 1960s, Michael Garrick has been one of Britain's most prominent pianists and composers as well as being at the forefront of jazz education from junior schools to the Royal Academy of Music.

Born in Enfield, Middlesex, his first piano tuition was from his mother Olive, a primary-school teacher who bravely supported his ambitions throughout, though despairing that jazz had so much to do with them. After a distinguished academic education (including a BA Honors in English plus a Post Graduate Certificate in Education), Garrick was later awarded an Open Fellowship at Berklee College of Music, United States.

Listing his early influences as Pinetop Smith, Meade Lux Lewis, George Shearing, the MJQ, Charlie Parker, Duke Ellington and Herbie Hancock, Garrick began composing at college in the late '50s for his first quartet (**Kronos**, '59). In '63, he directed his now-historic first Poetry and Jazz In Concert project writing musical settings for poets like Laurie Lee, Dannie Abse, Adrian Mitchell, Spike Milligan, Vernon Scannell, John Smith, Thomas Blackburn, Stevie Smith, Ted Hughes, Christopher Logue, Peter Porter, Charles Causley and Jeremy Robson.

From the early '60s, Garrick became inspired to write pieces which combined 'the fire of jazz with the sublimity of fine church music', his compositions like **Anthem** ('65), **Jazz Praises** ('68) and **Epiphany** ('70) being highly acclaimed and which remain in a class of their own. From '65-'69, in a more secular vein, he was pianist with the Don Rendell-Ian Carr Quintet (**Dusk Fire, Live, Phase III** and **Change Is**).

Since '66, vocalist Norma Winstone has been a mainstay of Garrick's music, adding an extra dimension with her inventive wordless vocals (**The Heart Is A Lotus**). In '77, he formed Threesome—featuring Norma Winstone and guitarist Phil Lee—performing extended works such as **Underground Streams** (based on Rudolph Steiner's lectures of 1913).

Suites for his sextet include **Fire Opal And Blue Poppies, Carioca Celebration, Kicking The Hobbit** (later orchestrated for big band), **The Hidden Colours, Jazz Portraits** and **When The Bluebirds Are Bitter Crazy**. Garrick also performs in duos with saxophonist Lol Coxhill, trumpeter Guy Barker, guitarist Phil Lee and two-piano combinations with Eddie Thompson and John Taylor. In November '85, he led a broadcast début of a 22-piece big band playing his suite **New Flower Of Europe** (dedicated to the memory of poet Wilfred Owen), the jazz portrait **Webster's Mood** and selections from **Kicking The Hobbit**.

Garrick sees the jazz impulse as something which can enrich and transform art and society generally since its fundamentals are primarily personal freedom in co-operation with others. He has published poems under the title *Cautionary Tales Of A Jazz Musician* and has written most of the lyrics for his own songs.

He has been director of Travelling Jazz Faculty since '79, John Dankworth's Wavendon Annual Summer Jazz Course since '76, and a member of the Royal Society of Musicians since '84.

Albums:
Kronos (—/Hep)
Moonscape (—/Airborne)
Poetry And Jazz In Concert (—/Argo)
A Case Of Jazz (—/Airborne)
October Woman (—/Argo)
Promises (—/Argo)
Anthem (—/Argo)
Black Marigolds (—/Argo)
Jazz Praises (—/Airborne)
The Heart Is A Lotus (—/Argo)
Epiphany (—/Argo)
Mr Smith's Apocalypse (—/Argo)
Home Stretch Blues (—/Argo)
Cold Mountain (—/Argo)
Troppo (—/Argo)
You've Changed (—/Hep)

Michael Garrick, You've Changed (courtesy Hep)—with Don Weller.

Stan Getz

Born 1927, Philadelphia, tenorist Stan Getz achieved fame early with his lyrical **Early Autumn** solo with Woody Herman's Second Herd, and as part of the **Four Brothers** saxophone feature (**Early Autumn**).

A Savoy collection from the late '40s assembles the white Lester Young disciples, Getz, Al Cohn, Serge Chaloff, Brew Moore and Allen Eager—**Lester's Gray Boys (Brothers & Other Mothers)**. More early Getz exemplifies the cool approach, subtle, unassertive playing that flows lyrically on ballads like **Indian Summer, Wrap Your Troubles In Dreams** and **Too Marvelous For Words (Stan Getz)**.

Following a tour of Scandinavia which left scores of Getz imitators in its wake, the tenorist began to show more virility in his attack, and a live date from 1951 (**Getz At Storyville**) shows a rare blend of relaxation and drive. With model accompaniment, Al Haig on piano, Jimmy Raney, guitar, Tiny Khan, drums, Getz flows through uptempo numbers like **Parker '51**, and **The Song Is You**, and endless melodic variations on **Thou Swell**.

Above: Tenorist Stan Getz, enduring master of the ballad. His Desafinado 'hit' created an insatiable market for the bossa nova in the early 1960s.

The '50s found him recording for Clef in a series of variable meetings with the giants. Most of these are deleted, but the session with Lionel Hampton produced the driving **Cherokee** and **Jumping At The Woodside**, and the more compatible date with West Coast musicians, trumpeter Conte Candoli and drummer Shelly Manne, found Getz in peak form, especially on the unaccompanied introduction to **Shine**. A session with Dizzy Gillespie (**Diz & Getz**) shows the near-honking side of tenorist, subtlety thrown to the winds, as he responds to Gillespie's ebullience. In the mid-'50s, he formed a quintet with trombonist Bob Brookmeyer. An encounter with another trombonist, J. J. Johnson, at the Chicago Opera House, resulted in some of Getz's finest work, from the sinuous attack of **Crazy Rhythm** to the lyrical loveliness **It Never Entered My Mind (Getz & J.J. 'Live')**. A year later, Getz moved to Scandinavia, disenchanted with current jazz fashions, returning in 1961 and recording one of the few successful albums with strings (**Focus**) which owes much to the brilliant writing of Eddie Sauter.

Following in the footsteps of Gillespie and Bud Shank, Getz made a highly profitable fusion with Latin American music, cutting the first album of the bossa nova fad (**Jazz Samba**) which contained the hit **Desafinado**. He followed this up with two albums on which he collaborated with the Brazilians, Jobim and Bonfa (**Jazz Samba Encore** and **Getz-Gilberto**), the latter containing the Astrud Gilberto version of **Girl From Ipanema**.

By the mid-'60s, he was back in the straight-ahead groove again, leading a quartet of Gary Burton, vibes, Steve Swallow, bass and the great Roy Haynes, drums (**Getz Au Go-Go**). Though not attracted to the expressionism of the New Wave players, the tenor did loosen up considerably under the influence of young sidemen, and albums like the two with pianist Chick Corea (**Captain Marvel** and **Sweet Rain**) show a greater degree of group interplay and shifting tempos than before.

Stan Getz is one of the acknowledged masters of the tenor—not a radical innovator, but an artist who has always gone his own way, and concentrated on working out the details of his style. His tone is one of the loveliest in jazz, and can carry him through a fairly lush programme without losing the attention of the jazz fan (**The Special Magic Of Stan Getz & Burt Bacharach**).

Albums:
Woody Herman, Early Autumn (Capitol/—)
Brothers & Other Mothers (Savoy/Savoy)
Stan Getz (Prestige/Prestige)
Getz At Storyville (Roost/Sonet)
Stan Getz-Dizzy Gillespie, Diz & Getz (Verve/Verve)
Getz & J.J. 'Live' (Verve/Verve)
Focus (Verve/Verve)
Jazz Samba (Verve/Verve)
Jazz Samba Encore (Verve/Verve)

Getz-Gilberto (Verve/Verve)
Getz Au Go-Go (Verve/Verve)
Captain Marvel (Verve/Verve)
Sweet Rain (Verve/Verve)
The Special Magic Of Stan Getz & Burt Bacharach (Verve/Verve)
The Peacocks (Columbia/CBS)
The Steamer (Verve/Verve)
West Coast Jazz (Verve/Verve)
The Girl From Ipanema/The Bossa Nova Years (Verve/Verve)
Pure Getz (Concord/Concord)
Stan Getz-Chet Baker, Line For Lyons (Sonet/Sonet)
Stan Getz-Albert Bailey, Poetry (Elektra Musician/Elektra Musician)

Terry Gibbs

Vibraphonist Terry Gibbs was born in New York, 1924. His style was based on Lionel Hampton's, and he first came to prominence with Woody Herman, 1948-49, moving on to the bands of Tommy Dorsey and Benny Goodman before branching out on his own. The best examples of his work in the catalog are the small group comprising Sam Jones, Louis Hayes and Kenny Burrell **(Take It From Me)** and the big band formed in 1959, including Conte Candoli, Frank Rosolino, Bill Perkins and Mel Lewis, a shouting, extrovert outfit **(The Big Band Sound Of Terry Gibbs)**.

Albums:
Take It From Me (Impulse/—)
The Big Band Sound Of Terry Gibbs (Verve/Verve)

Dizzy Gillespie

Born John Birks Gillespie in South Carolina, 1917, the trumpeter took over his idol, Roy Eldridge's chair in the Teddy Hill band, where his penchant for clowning and horseplay soon earned him his nickname (and gained him the sack from the Cab Calloway band). An early example of his playing can be found on **Kerouac** and **Stardust** from 1941 **(The Harlem Jazz Scene)**, which contain both the Eldridge influence and some of the harmonic ideas that led him into bebop. A period as trumpeter and arranger with the revolutionary Billy Eckstine band of 1944 set the seal on his emergence as the leading trumpeter of the new music, and his small combo recordings between 1944-46 with young modernists like Milt Jackson and Al Haig—**52nd Street Theme, Night In Tunisia, Ol' Man Rebop, Anthropology (The Greatest Of Dizzy Gillespie)** or with tenorist Dexter Gordon or Sonny Stitt—**Blue 'n' Boogie, One Bass Hit, Oop Bop Sh'Bam, A Handful Of Gimme, That's Earl, Brother (In The Beginning)** are classics of the genre.

In 1945, collaboration with bebop's greatest figure, Charlie Parker, produced the magnificent **Groovin' High, Dizzy Atmosphere, All The Things You Are, Salt Peanuts, Shaw 'Nuff, Lover Man** and **Hot House (In The Beginning)**, while a vast and confusing tangle of recordings covers their work together in the studio, concert hall and broadcast **(Lullaby In Rhythm, The Definitive Charlie Parker, Vol 2, Bird & Diz, Diz 'n' Bird In Concert** and **The Quintet Of The Year)**, all of it the finest music that modern jazz has to offer. Unlike Parker, however, Dizzy combined imaginative genius with a talent for public presentation and his beret, horn-rim glasses and goatee soon became the bebop uniform.

In 1946 he organized a big band and worked with arrangers like Gil Fuller, Tadd Dameron, George Russell and John Lewis to transplant what was essentially a combo music into a wider format. The finest pieces, **Emanon, Things To Come** and **Our Delight (In The Beginning)** show the excitement and incredible technique of the band in playing the complex scores, while Dizzy's pioneering work with Latin American rhythms is illustrated by the blasting **Manteca** and **Cubano Be, Cubano Bop (The Greatest Of Dizzy Gillespie)**. By late 1949 the crisis hit the big-band scene, and Dizzy was forced to pander to popular tastes with numbers like **You Stole My Wife You Horsethief (Strictly Bebop)** and in 1950 it was disbanded. A good deal of hilarious scat-singing accompanies some brilliant trumpet playing on numbers like **Swing Low, Sweet Cadillac** and **School Days** from a Salle Pleyel concert of 1953, while earlier combos, one including a young John Coltrane, showcase the leader's lyricism, drive and rhythmic assurance on **Tin Tin Deo** and **Birks Works; The Champ (Dee Gee Days)** was the biggest-selling bebop number of the period.

A studio big band from 1954 showed that Dizzy could generate wild enthusiasm and excitement even in those frigid surroundings, and the arrangements by Buster Harding of numbers like **Hob Nail Special** or **Pile Driver** are eminently suitable **(The Big Band Sound Of Dizzy Gillespie)**. Other tracks on the album feature another studio band from 1955, and a regular big band which Dizzy assembled for a US State Department tour 1956-58. Numerous '50s jam sessions followed, under the aegis of Norman Granz, including several with Dizzy's one-time mentor, Roy Eldridge **(Trumpet Kings** and **The Gillespie Jam Sessions)**, while an encounter with Stan Getz provokes the seamless tenorist to some of his wildest playing on record **(Diz And Getz)**. Using his regular quintet and familiar numbers, the trumpeter recorded wonderfully lyrical versions of **There Is No Greater Love** and **Moonglow (Have Trumpet, Will Excite)**.

The '60s saw no decline in his powers, though on some albums he seems less than fully committed, a charge that can hardly be leveled in the next decade. An album cut in Europe with the dynamic tenorist Johnny Griffin **(The Giant)** has Dizzy playing throughout with daring and ferocity, lyrical on **Serenity**, incisive on **Stella By Starlight**. A new contract with Granz's Pablo produced a great renaissance, from the duet with Oscar Peterson **(Oscar Peterson & Dizzy Gillespie)**, the quartet with Joe Pass, Ray Brown and Mickey Roker **(Dizzy Gillespie's Big 4)** and the Montreux Festival recordings from 1975 **(Dizzy)**. A big band **(Dizzy Gillespie & Machito)** and a septet **(Bahiana)** continue Dizzy's fusion of jazz and Latin American music.

An undisputed trumpet master, Dizzy Gillespie's ability to swing at the softest volume, or to vary his attack from squeezed notes to high register screams remains unrivaled. His abilities as a conga drummer and singer are often overlooked amid his stage antics.

Below: Dizzy Gillespie, pioneer of bebop, Afro-Cuban and the angled trumpet, his standard instrument (so he could hear himself better) since 1954.

Albums:
Charlie Christian, The Harlem Jazz Scene (Esoteric/Saga)
Charlie Parker, Lullaby In Rhythm (Spotlite/Spotlite)
The Definitive Charlie Parker, Vol 2 (Verve/Metro)
Bird & Diz (—/Saga)
Charlie Parker/Miles Davis/Dizzy Gillespie (Vogue/Vogue)
The Quintet Of The Year (Debut/Vogue)
The Greatest Of Dizzy Gillespie (RCA/RCA)
In The Beginning (Prestige/Prestige)
Strictly Bebop (Capitol/Capitol)
Live At The Spotlite, '46 (Hi-Fly/Hi-Fly)
Trumpet Masters, Dizzy Gillespie (GNP Crescendo/Vogue)
Dee Gee Days (Savoy/Savoy)
The Big Band Sound Of Dizzy Gillespie (Verve/Verve)
Trumpet Kings (Verve/Verve)
The Gillespie Jam Sessions (Verve/Verve)
Stan Getz & Dizzy Gillespie (Verve/Verve)
Have Trumpet, Will Excite (Verve/—)
The Giant (Prestige/America)
Oscar Peterson & Dizzy Gillespie (Pablo/Pablo)
Dizzy Gillespie's Big 4 (Pablo/Pablo)
Dizzy (Pablo/Pablo)
Dizzy Gillespie & Machito (Pablo/Pablo)
Bahiana (Pablo/Pablo)
Dizzy's Party (Pablo/Pablo)
Diz & Getz (Verve/Verve)
Dizzy Gillespie At Newport (Verve/Verve)
Dizzy Gillespie & The Double Six Of Paris (Philips/Philips)
The Bop Session (Sonet/Sonet)
Free Ride (Pablo/Pablo)
Dizzy Gillespie/One Night In Washington (Elektra Musician/Elektra Musician)
At The Downbeat Club (Phontastic/Phontastic)
Giants Of Jazz (George Wein Collection/ George Wein Collection)
New Faces (GRP/GRP)
Closer To The Source (Atlantic/Atlantic)

Above: Egberto Gismonti—widely admired guitarist, pianist, composer.

Egberto Gismonti

Refusing to accept any gulf between 'popular' and 'serious' music, the multi-dimensional guitar-playing of classically trained Egberto Gismonti has put him in the front line of Brazil's musical masters, with an enviable reputation and influence outside his homeland.

Born Carmo, Brazil, in 1947, Gismonti studied piano from age 6 for the next 15 years. He went to Paris to study orchestration and analysis with Nadia Boulanger; then composition and practical orchestration with 12-tone composer Jean Barlaque, a disciple of Schoenberg and Webern. He returned to Brazil initially as a classical concert pianist and conductor. In '66, Gismonti was struck by Ravel's adaptations of George Gershwin's ideas of orchestrations and chord voicings. As a result, he became interested in improvisation-based music.

It was Brazil's own *choro* (he describes it as the 'Brazilian form of funk') which made him turn to 6-string guitar, strongly influenced by local luminaries Baden Powell and Deno. By '70, the anti-élitist Gismonti was looking to the likes of Django Reinhardt and Jimi Hendrix for inspiration. In '73, he switched to 8-string guitar, experimenting with different tunings, and explored new possibilities in sound with flutes, kalimbas, sho, voice and bells, before recording the innovative **Dança**

Das Cabeças for ECM with Brazilian percussionist Nana Vasconcelos.

In '77, for **Sol Do Meio Dia** (an album dedicated to the Xingu indians of the Amazon), the Gismonti-Vasconcelos partnership was augmented by ECM stablemates saxophonist Jan Garbarek, sitar-and tabla-player Collin Walcott and 12-string guitarist Ralph Towner. Some of Gismonti's finest playing can be heard on **Magico** and **Folk Songs** ('79)—both collaborations with bassist Charlie Haden and, again, saxophonist Jan Garbarek, taking further a musical format originally explored in the '50s by Jimmy Giuffre's drummerless trio. **Folk Songs** remains an ECM classic—an acoustic *pièce de résistance* in emphatic interplay, full of light and shade, imaginative voicings and harmonics, and dynamic, constantly shifting structures.

Gismonti's skills as an orchestrator—an interesting reminder of his early training—are given full rein on Vasconcelos **Saudades** ('80) with the Stuttgart Radio Symphony Orchestra, and the Gismonti-Vasconcelos duet **Duas Vozes** ('85) recreates so much of the magic of their earlier collaborations.

The exceptional Gismonti is held in great esteem by other composer-guitarists—John McLaughlin, for instance, pays him tribute on his '82 album **Music Spoken Here** by including his own interpretation of the Brazilian's composition **Lôro**.

Albums:

Dança Das Cabeças (ECM/ECM)
Sol Do Meio Dia (ECM/ECM)
Solo (ECM/ECM)
Egberto Gismonti-Charlie Haden-
Jan Garbarek, Magico (ECM/ECM)
Egberto Gismonti-Charlie Haden-
Jan Garbarek, Folk Songs (ECM/ECM)
Nana Vasconcelos-Egberto Gismonti,
Saudades (ECM/ECM)
Egberto Gismonti, Academia de Danças,
Sanfona (ECM/ECM)
Egberto Gismonti-Nana Vasconcelos, Duas
Vozes (ECM/ECM)
Works (ECM/ECM)

Jimmy Giuffre

Multi-reed player Jimmy Giuffre's conception has developed further and foreshadowed more radical change over thirty years than most. Born in 1921, his best known early work was the composition **Four Brothers** for Woody Herman's 2nd Herd. A West Coast musician, Giuffre's output varied between the typical, chirpily swinging sessions with Shorty Rogers **(West Coast Jazz)** and the highly experimental **Shelly Manne, The Three & The Two**, on which Giuffre, Rogers and Manne indulge in simultaneous improvising. Giuffre began to concentrate on the clarinet, restricting himself to the broody, breathy chalumeau register, and his writing grew spare and concerned with emotive sound qualities. An album, **The Jimmy Giuffre Clarinet**, casts a reflective, pastoral mood, and shows his methodical advance into new territory. Two trio albums **(The Jimmy Giuffre Trio** and **Trav'lin' Light)** approach the often rustic themes with all the nimble footwork of may-pole dancers, no individual predominating.

The Train And The River, a 22-carat classic of the late '50s—Giuffre in a ground-breaking drummerless trio with guitarist Jim Hall and bassist Ralph Pena—is a lesson in spontaneous, blues-laced improvisation and staggering musical empathy. A version of the title track is heard to good effect in the '58 documentary *Jazz On A Summer's Day*.

Dispensing with the sounded beat and reviving a pre-harmonic melodic directness, Giuffre was ahead of Ornette Coleman, for example, by several years. His later trios with pianist Paul Bley and bassist Steve Swallow **(Free Fall, Fusion** and **Thesis)** brought this conception to its fullest ensemble realization. More recent work, like **Quiet Song**, confirms his status as one of the few avant-garde clarinettists and an artist of great originality.

Albums:

Shorty Rogers, West Coast Jazz
(Atlantic/Atlantic)
Shelly Manne, The Three & The Two
(Contemporary/—)
The Jimmy Giuffre Clarinet (Atlantic/—)
The Jimmy Giuffre Trio (Atlantic/—)
Trav'lin' Light (Atlantic/—)
Free Fall (Columbia/—)
Fusion (Verve/—)
Thesis (Verve/—)
Paul Bley, Quiet Song
(Improvising Artists Inc/—)
Mosquito Dance (—/DJM)
Four Brothers (—/Affinity)
Tangents In Jazz (—/Affinity)
The Train And The River
(Atlantic/Atlantic)
The Easy Way (Verve/Verve)
In Person (Verve/Verve)
Quasar (Soul Note/Soul Note)

Below: The distinguished and path-finding Jimmy Guiffre (right) with swinging tenor team Zoot Sims and Al Cohn.

Benny Goodman

Benjamin 'Benny' Goodman (born Chicago, Illinois, 1909) probably was the most technically accomplished clarinettist to make a living (primarily) from jazz Goodman was 12 when he made his first public appearance as a player at a talent contest, imitating Ted Lewis; he was as much at home playing clarinet concertos of Mozart, Weber et al as he was playing music by Fletcher Henderson, Eddie Sauter, Mel Powell, or any one of the numerous standard pop composers.

Indeed, since 1938, Goodman worked, in person and on record, with leading personalities and aggregations from the world of classical music. In 1940, for example, Goodman commissioned Béla Bartók to write **Contrasts**, which he recorded with violinist Joseph Szigeti. Aaron Copland's Clarinet Concerto and a similar piece by Paul Hindemith also have been written on commission from Benny Goodman. But, of course, it is as a jazz clarinet player, first and foremost, that Goodman inevitably will be remembered.

Some feel that despite his increasing technical mastery during the post-1930 period, Goodman's jazz playing during the earliest part of his career has rarely been surpassed. Recordings from Goodman's earlier period, leading his Benny Goodman's Boys, or in the role of side-player with Irving Mills & His Hotsy Totsy Gang, Red Nichols' Orchestra (all **The Early BG**) or Ben Pollack's Orchestra **(Ben Pollack & His Orchestra: 1933-1934)**, show a genuine talent in the making. Probably most outstanding recordings of this time were those with Joe Venuti/Eddie Lang All Stars **(Nothing But Notes)**.

By the early 1930s it was obvious, too, that, apart from his instrumental talents, Benny Goodman took to the role of leader with flair and relish. With assistance from John Hammond, Goodman fronted accompanying outfits on Billie Holiday's first recording dates, in 1933, 1935 **(The Golden Years, Vols 1, 2)**. He was to play on numerous subsequent Holiday sessions **(The Lester Young Story, Vol 1, The Billie Holiday Story, Vol 1 and The Golden Years, Vols 1, 2)** producing immaculate clarinet performances which, admittedly, sometimes tended to sound a trifle reserved when measured against contributions by, say, Lester Young, Buck Clayton, Teddy Wilson.

During the early-1930s, as with the previous decade, Goodman's appearances on record were many. Amongst those who benefited from his appearances were Red Nichols (with whom Goodman worked extensively between October 1929-January 1930, and, on record at least, for a period thereafter) **(J.T.)**; Adrian Rollini; Gene Krupa (both **Benny Goodman & The Giants Of Swing/Jazz In The Thirties**). Krupa was to become a seminal figure in the meteoric rise to fame Goodman was to experience following ecstatic reaction to his music at a dance date in August 1935, at Palomar Ballroom, LA. The Palomar date, almost single-handed, signaled start of swing era. By the end of 1930s Goodman had indeed become 'King of Swing'.

Krupa's drumming apart, notable side-players whose instrumental talents helped contribute much to what became the international success of the clarinettist's bands—large and small—included trumpeters Bunny Berigan, Ziggy Elman, and, especially, Harry James, pianist Jess Stacy, guitarist Charlie Christian, and two important black musicians, Teddy Wilson and Lionel Hampton, both of whom were prime movers the in success of various Goodman small combos. But as far as the big band was concerned, the most significant figure was Fletcher Henderson, who from time to time played piano on Goodman small-group recordings and contributed an impressive number of superb arrangements for Goodman—arrangements already featured by Henderson-led big bands of previous years. It could be said the Goodman band lacked the heart of Henderson's, and that in terms of drive and depth it compared poorly with Henderson, Basie, Ellington, Lunceford, and most of the black big bands. Yet certainly there were times when it was lifted to exceptional heights, exemplified superbly throughout **1938 Carnegie Hall Jazz Concert** and **The Big Band Sound Of Benny Goodman**, significantly, perhaps, both live recordings. Later, at the beginning of 1940s, the band achieved further splendor, thanks, in the main, to fresh-sounding arrangements-compositions by Eddie Sauter, Mel Powell, Buster Harding and Jimmy Mundy **(Benny Goodman Plays Solid Gold Instrumental Hits)**. With the big-band era waning, Goodman flirted, half-heartedly, with bop; to most fans, the flirtation was unsuccessful.

Since late-1940s, Goodman continued to lead various groups—of all sizes—but in later years his activities as bandleader were nothing like the halcyon King-of-Swing days. Since first-time visit to London in 1949, he made numerous tours to many parts of the world, including a successful visit to Russia (1962) (first US jazz outfit to be invited by the Russians).

There is little doubt that most of the best jazz produced by Goodman-led groups came from Trio (most famous, original line-up: Teddy Wilson, Krupa, Goodman); Quartet (same as Trio, plus Hampton); plus variety of Quintets, Sextets, Septets, etc. (which have starred, most notably, George Auld, Cootie Williams, Count Basie, Hampton, Johnny Guarnieri, Christian, Gray and Zoot Sims. Christian, something of a Goodman protégé, came to fame with, and died whilst still officially a member of, the Goodman organization. It was he, more than anyone, who helped to make the small-combo sides of 1939-41 so memorable and of lasting value, both with his forward-looking guitar solos and his rhythmically infectious riff-type compositions. Certainly, Christian's presence seemed to inspire Goodman into producing some of his finest playing.

A comprehensive bio-discography, *B.G.—On The Record*, researched and written by D. Russell O'Connor & Warren W. Hicks, was first published in 1969. *The Kingdom Of Swing*, co-written by Goodman and Irving Kolodin, first appeared 30 years before *B.G.—On The Record*. Goodman appeared in the film *A Song Is Born* (1948), having an acting as well a musical role. He and the orchestra featured in several movies, including *Stage Door Canteen, Hollywood Hotel* and *The Big Broadcast of 1937*. Many times a poll-winner—as band-leader, clarinettist—also played soprano, alto and tenor saxes on occasion; and during one eventful recording date in 1928, in addition to clarinet, he played baritone sax **(Room 1411)**, baritone and alto **(Blue)**, and even cornet **(Jungle Blues)**, (all **The Early B.G.**).

Goodman did much to help break down the racial barriers which existed in the music business during 1930s, by hiring Hampton and Wilson on a permanent basis, then Henderson and others. *The Benny Goodman Story*, a typical Hollywood interpretation of the life of a jazzman and with only the barest biographical reference to his real life-story, was completed and first shown in 1955.

The real 'Benny Goodman Story' could have ended with his passing (peacefully in his sleep) on June 13, 1986, aged 77. But the enduring legend and memory of the King of Swing lives on thanks to a multitude of classic recordings Goodman left as his legacy to succeeding generations.

Benny Goodman and his Boys, The Early B.G. (courtesy Vocalion, Decca).

Albums:
Ben Pollack & His Orchestra: 1933-1934 (—/VJM)
Various (Including Benny Goodman), The Early B.G. (—/Vocalion)
Joe Venuti, Nothing But Notes (1931-1939) (MCA—Coral—Germany)
Benny Goodman, A Jazz Holiday (MCA/—)
Various, Benny Goodman & The Giants Of Swing (Prestige)/Jazz In The Thirties (World Records)
Adrian Rollini & His Orchestra 1933-34 (Sunbeam)
Various (Including Benny Goodman), Recordings Made Between 1930 & 1941 (CBS—France)
A Jam Session With Benny Goodman 1935-37 (Sunbeam)
Benny Goodman & His Orchestra Featuring Bunny Berigan (Golden Era)
Benny Goodman, Vols 1-12 (RCA Victor/—)
The Big Band Sound of Benny Goodman (—/Verve)
Benny Goodman Trio & Quartet Live 1937-38, Vols 1, 2 (CBS—France)
Benny Goodman, 1938 Carnegie Hall Jazz Concert (Columbia/CBS)
The Genius Of Charlie Christian (Columbia)/ Solo Flight (CBS)
Charlie Christian With The Benny Goodman Sextet & Orchestra (Columbia/CBS—Realm)
Charlie Christian With Benny Goodman & The Sextet (Jazz Archives)
Benny Goodman, Plays Solid Gold Instrumental Hits (Columbia/CBS)
Various (Including Benny Goodman), John Hammond's Spirituals To Swing (Vanguard/Vogue)
Various, The Metronome All Stars/(Esquire All Stars) (RCA Victor—France)
Benny Goodman/(Charlie Barnet), Bebop Spoken Here (Capitol/Capitol—Holland)
Benny Goodman In Moscow, Vols 1, 2 (RCA Victor/RCA Victor)
Billie Holiday, The Golden Years, Vols 1, 2 (Columbia/CBS)
The Lester Young Story, Vol 1 (Columbia/CBS)
Benny Goodman, All-Time Greatest Hits (Columbia/CBS)
Benny Goodman—A Legendary Performer (RCA/RCA)

Benny Goodman, The Famous 1938 Carnegie Hall Jazz Concert (courtesy Columbia). Acknowledged as one of the greatest live records in jazz history.

Dexter Gordon

Born Los Angeles, 1923, the son of a doctor, Dexter Gordon became *the* bebop tenorist. Dexter served his apprenticeship in the big bands, blowing two-tenor chase choruses with Illinois Jacquet in Lionel Hampton's band from 1940-43. His style was a combination of the laid-back Lester Young and the huge tone of Coleman Hawkins, adapted to the more complex harmonic world of Charlie Parker. After Hamp, he spent a year home playing the clubs. Los Angeles around the mid-'40s was a jumping town, and Bird's visit set the seal on emergent bebop. Central Avenue was the West Coast's 52nd Street.

Dexter joined Louis Armstrong's band for several months and then the more suitable environment of Billy Eckstine's band, which included Dizzy Gillespie, Sonny Stitt, Gene Ammons, Leo Parker and John Jackson, with Fats Navarro taking Dizzy's chair. Two-tenor chases were again carving at each other over Art Blakey's relentless drumming. With most of the musicians under 25, the band played with wild enthusiasm, preaching the message of bebop. Dexter left in 1945 after 18 months and went to New York where he became a favorite along the 52nd Street clubs. He recorded **Blue 'n' Boogie** with Dizzy Gillespie **(In The Beginning)** and, with his own groups, including baritonist Leo Parker, Bud Powell or Tadd Dameron on piano and driving drummers like Blakey or Max Roach, cut a set of high-spirited tracks like **Dexter's Minor Mad, Blow Mr Dexter** and **Dexter Rides Again (Long Tall Dexter, The Savoy Sessions)**.

Back in Los Angeles, Dexter teamed with tenorist Wardell Gray fo a series of exhilarating chases like **The Chase** and **The Steeplechase (The Chase); Rocks 'n' Shoals (Jazz Concert-West Coast)** and, with tenorist Teddy Edwards, for **The Duel (The Foremost!)**. A later reunion with Gray **(Move)** is included on the Prestige memorial album to Gray **(Central Avenue)**.

Following Miles Davis' pace-setting **Birth Of The Cool** album, the West Coast jazz scene underwent a sea-change, and Dexter Gordon's robust, hard-driving style fell from grace. After a spell in Chino prison for narcotics, the tenorist made few recordings in the '50s, though his playing on a session with pianist Carl Perkins **(Dexter Blows Hot And Cool)** showed that he had lost none of his vigor.

Strangely enough, it was acting that boosted his comeback. In 1960, he acted in and performed and wrote music for Jack Gelber's play *The Connection*. The following year, he signed to Blue Note for a series of classic albums **(Doin' Allright, Dexter Calling, Go, A Swingin' Affair, Our Man In Paris** and **One Flight Up)**. All the old virtues of drive, tone and imagination are here in abundance, the sardonic, guffawing quotes, the massive, loping swing. By this time, hard bop was in the ascendant and Dexter was back in fashion—in fact, the most influential tenorist, John Coltrane, had borrowed Dexter's legato, spearing cry. There is an incantatory power about Dexter's playing which makes the simplest, repeated phrases sound less predictable than inevitable. His double-tempo flights shed not an ounce of weight. His beefy treatment of ballads can be overwhelmingly moving; **Guess I'll Hang My Tears Out To Dry (Go)** and **You've Changed (Doin' Allright)**, and his lasting affiliation to bebop is displayed on **Scrapple From The Apple** and **A Night In Tunisia (Our Man In Paris)** where he shares the honors with other 52nd Street veterans like pianist Bud Powell and drummer Kenny Clarke. At 6 foot 5, Dexter Gordon seems to straddle sessions like an enforcer—always reliable, sometimes great.

In his time, he has influenced tenorists Gene Ammons, Allen Eager, Stan Getz, John Coltrane and Sonny Rollins. Dexter Gordon remains one of the most well-loved performers in jazz

Albums:
The Foremost! (Onyx/Polydor)
The Chase (—/Spotlite)
Dizzy Gillespie, In The Beginning (Prestige/Prestige)
Billy Eckstine, Together (—/Spotlite)
Long Tall Dexter, The Savoy Sessions (Savoy/Savoy)
The Hunt (Savoy/Savoy)
Dexter Blows Hot And Cool (Dooto/Boplicity)
Wardell Gray, Central Avenue (Prestige/Prestige)
Doin' Allright (Blue Note/Blue Note)
Dexter Calling (Blue Note/Blue Note)
Go (Blue Note/Blue Note)
A Swingin' Affair (Blue Note/Blue Note)
Our Man In Paris (Blue Note/Blue Note)
One Flight Up (Blue Note/Blue Note)
Montmartre Collection (Black Lion/Black Lion)
Blues Walk (Black Lion/Black Lion)
Homecoming (Columbia/CBS)
Sophisticated Giant (Columbia/CBS)
Manhattan Symphonie (Columbia/CBS)
The Bethlehem Years (Bethlehem/—)
Billie's Bounce (Steeplechase/Steeplechase)
At Montreux With Junior Mance

Below: The incomparable Dexter Gordon, a champion of the two-tenor chase. Much of his earlier Blue Note output has been re-issued in the mid-1980s.

(Prestige/Prestige)
Nights At The Keystone (Blue Note/Blue Note)
Gotham City (Columbia/CBS)
American Classic
(Elektra Musician/Elektra Musician)

Dexter Blows Hot And Cool with pianist Carl Perkins (courtesy Boplicity).

Stephane Grappelli

Stephane Grappelli (originally surname was spelled with a 'y') would have earned himself a place in jazz history books if only for his important role in the Quintette of the Hot Club of France, featuring the dazzling virtuosity of Django Reinhardt. Grappelli's violin was the perfect foil to Reinhardt's guitar in this pianoless group.

Fired by Reinhardt's tremendous rhythmic powers, Grappelli's contributions to recordings by the Quintette like **Limehouse Blues, China Boy** and **It Don't Mean A Thing** (all 1935) and **Them There Eyes, Three Little Words** and **Swing '39** (these latter three tracks from 1938-39) (all **Swing '35-'39)** were admirable in their execution.

Occasionally, Grappelli would play piano, as when harmonica virtuoso Larry Adler recorded with the group in 1939, the year when Reinhardt and Grappelli, violin, recorded (with delightful results) as a duo (all **Django Reinhardt**).

Grappelli, born (1908) and raised in Paris, was involved with music from a very early age. By 12 years, he had acquired his first violin—just one of several instruments he learned to play. He began professionally with theatre bands, eventually being introduced to jazz music. A French jazz musician, Philippe Brun, introduced Grappelli to Reinhardt. Soon after that meeting, they put the idea of the Quintette into practice.

When World War II commenced, Grappelli and the band were touring Britain. While the others returned to Paris, Grappelli opted to stay. During the next six years, he became a popular figure in London with habitués of nightlife in general and in musical entertainment in particular (such as it was), working with local musicians in various clubs. In 1946 he returned to Paris and renewed association with Reinhardt, but the magic of pre-war days did not re-appear too often. Between 1948-55, worked in Club St Germain, Paris, and in the latter year played nine-month residency in St Tropez

During past years Grappelli has played throughout Europe, in clubs, at concerts and festivals, has and broadcast televised extensively, and has been a regular visitor to the recording studio.

In 1966, Grappelli was recorded in concert in Switzerland, together with fellow jazz violinists Jean-Luc Ponty, Stuff Smith and Svend Asmussen **(Violin Summit)**. Since then he has recorded frequently in London (where he has become a perennial favorite with audiences at Ronnie Scott's Club). A live date at the Queen Elizabeth Hall **(Stephane Grappelli 1972)** finds him responding to an enthusiastic audience.

Elsewhere he has recorded with much success, with Americans Gary Burton **(Paris Encounter)**, Bill Coleman **(Stephane Grappelli—Bill Coleman)**, Roland Hanna **(Stephane Grappelli Meets The Rhythm Section)** and Barney Kessel **(I Remember Django)**.

Albums:
Django Reinhardt, Swing '35-'39
(—/Decca/Eclipse)
Django Reinhardt & Stephane Grappelli
With The Quintet Of The Hot Club Of France
(GNP Crescendo/—)
Django Reinhardt, Parisian Swing
(GNP Crescendo/—)
Django Reinhardt (Columbia—Germany)
Various (Including Stephane Grappelli),
Violin Summit (Saba/Polydor)
Stephane Grappelly & Friends (—/Philips)
Stephane Grappelli 1971 (—/Pye)
Stephane Grappelli 1972 (—/Pye)
Stephane Grappelli, Just One Of Those
Things (Black Lion)
Stephane Grappelli, I Got Rhythm (Black Lion)
Stephane Grappelli, Violinspiration
(MPS/BASF)
Stephane Grappelli/Gary Burton, Paris
Encounter (Atlantic/Atlantic)
Stephane Grappelli—Bill Coleman (Inner City)
Jean-Luc Ponty-Stephane Grappelli (Inner City)
Stephane Grappelli Meets The Rhythm
Section (Black Lion)
Stephane Grappelli/Barney Kessel,
I Remember Django (Black Lion)
Stephane Grappelli/Stuff Smith, Stuff & Steff
(Barclay)
Feeling + Finesse = Jazz
(Atlantic/Atlantic)

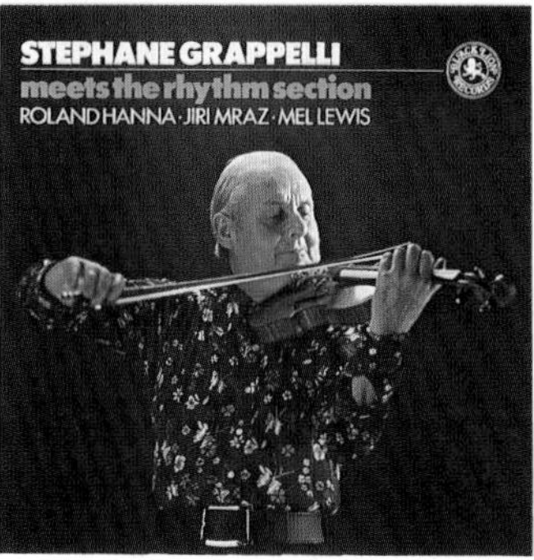

Stephane Grappelli Meets The Rhythm Section (courtesy Black Lion).

Milford Graves

Free drummer Milford Graves first unveiled his concept of non-metrical playing on an all-percussion album **(Milford Graves Percussion Ensemble)** with Sunny Morgan, revealing a wide dynamic range, lightning reflexes, and a total re-thinking of the traditional roles of the components of the kit. How this could be applied within the group context was revealed by Graves' work with the New York Art Quartet **(New York Art Quartet)** where his fast, crisp darting drumming contributes much to the success of contrapuntal sections between Roswell Rudd and John Tchicai.

A partnership, begun in the Giuseppi Logan group between pianist Don Pullen and Graves, developed into amazing free interplay and dissonant structures. Two albums recorded live at Yale University on the artists' own label are unfortunately difficult to come by **(Nommo** and **In Concert)**.

Graves' eruptive work on an Albert Ayler session **(Love Cry)** seems to add density to the simple, melodic approach of the horns. Subsequently, Graves seems to have returned to the all-drum concept, and with Andrew Cyrille, summons up a percussion choir of drums, bells, voice, gongs, whistles etc **(Dialogue Of The Drums)**.

Above: Drum innovator Milford Graves. His explorative, non-metrical playing with his Percussion Ensemble was extended with Albert Ayler and Don Pullen.

Albums:
Milford Graves Percussion Ensemble
(ESP/ESP)
New York Art Quartet (ESP/ESP)
Don Pullen-Milford Graves, Nommo
(SRP/—)
Don Pullen-Milford Graves, In Concert
(SRP/—)
Albert Ayler, Love Cry (Impulse/Impulse)
Dialogue Of The Drums
(Institute of Percussive Studies/—)
Milford Graves & Babi Music
(Institute of Percussive Studies/—)

Johnny Griffin

Born 1928, the Chicago tenorist is undoubtedly one of the fastest players in the history of the saxophone and, in Griffin's case, this is no empty, facile display. His imagination streaks ahead of his flying fingers, throwing out ideas in prodigal handfuls. Obviously not a master of the extended structure (few jazz musicians are), his solos are a string of great breaks, cliff-hanging climaxes and startling tonal devices, the whole held together by his colossal drive. Johnny Griffin is the prototypical hard bopper.

His early experience with the wild Lionel Hampton band set the pattern. His early Blue Note albums **(Chicago Calling, Introducing Johnny Griffin** and **The Congregation)** are memorable for their sheer youthful ebullience. Griffin's meeting with Coltrane and Mobley catches the newcomer to the New York scene at his most competitive, calling the breakneck tempos and generally proving his superiority in this context **(Blowin' Sessions)**.

He proved an ideal member of Art Blakey's hard-hitting Jazz Messengers, his short fuse flaring into hysterical excitement as the drummer bore down. **Art Blakey's Jazz Messengers With Thelonious Monk** is excellent, though atypical. Griffin's association with Monk continues on a pair of deleted quartet albums **(Thelonius In Action** and **Misterioso)** but, though exciting, the tenorist's interpretation of Monk's themes lacks the weight that a thematic player like Rollins could muster. Nevertheless, Griffin is clearly attracted by the challenge, and returns time and again to this material on some of his subsequent albums **(The Toughest Tenors)**.

In the late '50s and early '60s, a fashion for 'soul' redirected the thrust of hard bop away from the sensurround drumming to a baptist backbeat. Predictability soon crept in, and the only player to resist the formula was Johnny Griffin. **Wade In The Water** is a classic in this genre **(Big Soul)**. Forming a two-tenor unit with Eddie 'Lockjaw' Davis, a swinging, partying player, Griffin cut a series of hard-driving albums that recall the great tenor partnerships of Dexter Gordon and Wardell Gray, or Sonny Stitt and Gene Ammons.

In 1962, Griffin moved to Europe, joined the Kenny Clarke-Francy Boland Big Band, and also toured extensively, using pick-up rhythm sections. Two of the best albums **(Blues For Harvey** and **The Man I Love)** are fueled by expatriate American drummers, Ed Thigpen and Albert Heath, who supply the strong direct beat that Griffin needs.

The tone is light and mobile, shooting up to the tip-toe top of the register in moments of overheating, or blasting suddenly from the depths. He's a witty player, projecting the most convoluted phrases from his horn with evident enjoyment.

Johnny 'Little Giant' Griffin, The Congregation (courtesy Blue Note).

Above: Johnny Griffin, often claimed to be the fastest tenorist of all time, ran a popular, hard-driving two-tenor unit with Eddie 'Lockjaw' Davis.

Albums:
Blowin' Sessions (Blue Note/Blue Note)
Art Blakey's Jazz Messengers With Thelonious Monk (Atlantic/Atlantic)
The Toughest Tenors (Milestone/Milestone)
Eddie 'Lockjaw' Davis-Johnny Griffin, Live At Minton's (Prestige/Prestige)
Big Soul (Milestone/Milestone)
Blues for Harvey (—/Steeplechase)
The Man I Love (—/Polydor)
Introducing Johnny Griffin (Blue Note/Blue Note)
The Congregation (Blue Note/Blue Note)
Little Giant (Milestone/Milestone)
To The Ladies (Galaxy/Galaxy)

Dave Grusin

Arranger, composer, performer, record-company executive . . . pianist Dave Grusin has to be one of the busiest, most prolific musicians in the field of fusion.

Raised in Littleton, Colorado, Grusin was urged by his immigrant father—a watchmaker and violinist—to follow a musical career. Although Grusin showed an early talent for piano, he resisted making music his life, initially opting for veterinary college. In deference to his father, Grusin changed his mind at the last moment and entered Colorado University to major in piano studies where he developed his interest in jazz Later at Manhattan School of Music, New York, he planned to teach, until singer Andy Williams offered him a chance to go on the road, the pianist subsequently becoming musical director for Williams' popular TV show. Working for Williams sharpened Grusin's orchestral skills, writing scores for films (*The Graduate, Heaven Can Wait, Three Days of the Condor, The Champ, On Golden Pond, Tootsie* etc) and TV shows (e.g. *It Takes A Thief, Roots—Part II* and *St. Elsewhere*).

Grusin also became highly sought after in the recording studio both as a pianist and a producer: **Subways Are For Sleeping** in '65 was followed by **Piano, Strings And Moonlight,** and **Kaleidoscope** which also featured Thad Jones and Frank Foster.

In '76, Grusin and long-time friend and associate Larry Rosen, the former drummer, founded Grusin/Rosen Productions, the forerunner of today's successful GRP Records company which they describe as 'documenting a new age in jazz'.

Grusin has been involved in the production and/or distribution of some widely selling fusion artists including—from a very lengthy list—Tom Browne, Earl Klugh, Lee Ritenour, Dave Valentin, Bobby Broom, Bernard Wright, Al Jarreau, Sadao Watanabe, Sergio Mendez, and 'old-stagers' Gerry Mulligan **(Little Big Horn)** and Dizzy Gillespie **(New Faces)**.

Albums:
Lee Ritemar, The Captain's Journey (Elektra-Asylum/Elektra-Asylum)
Dave Valentin, Legends (GRP/GRP)
Dave Valentin, The Hawk (GRP/GRP)
Tom Browne, Browne Sugar (GRP/GRP)
One Of A Kind (GRP/GRP)
Mountain Dance (GRP/GRP)
GRP All-Stars Live In Japan (GRP/GRP)
Out Of The Shadows (GRP/GRP)
The NY-LA Dream Band (GRP/GRP)
Night-Lines (GRP/GRP)

The Guest Stars, Out At Night (courtesy Guest Stars).

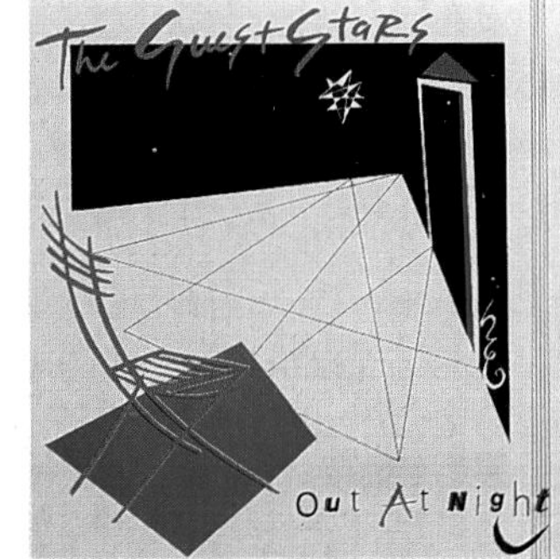

Guest Stars

This group of six women musicians has rapidly grown into one of Britain's most popular and travelled bands. Their lively blend of jazz, pop, soul, Latin and African musics has taken them from the claustrophobic backrooms of London pubs to several international festivals. They have toured America (with no financial assistance, they literally 'sang their way across' on a Virgin Atlantic flight), Germany, Spain and the Middle East (the latter trip sponsored by the British Council). Their self-financed album **The Guest Stars** (July '84), promoted a second—**Out At Night** (December '85).

The Guest Stars, formed in '80, have recruited their members equally from the jazz and rock spheres. Ruthie Smith (saxophones, voice) has worked with Stepney Sisters, Soulyard, Sisterhood of Spit, the Lydia D'Ustebyn Swing Orchestra, Toot Sweet, District Six and the acapella group The Hipscats. Linda Da Mango (congas, percussion, voice) has been heard with The Basement Band, Soulyard, Sisterhood of Spit, Holloway All-Stars and Lydia D'Ustebyn, while Josefina Cupido (drums, percussion, voice) has been a member of Just Good Friends, Red Brass, River, Elephant and Hipscats. Alison Rayner (fretless bass, voice) co-founded Jam Today and has worked with the Interval Band. Deirdre Cartwright (guitar) has played with Jam Today, Painted Lady and Tour de Force, and co-presented BBC TV's *Rockschool* series. Laka Daisical (piano, voice) has performed with Witches Brew, 'The Entire Population of China', Soulyard, The Interval Band, Jazz Rats, Sisterhood of Spit, Lydia D'Ustebyn, Hipscats and trombonist Annie Whitehead's sextet.

Working in the predominantly male context of jazz, their concern is to create a way of working which reflects their experience as women performers—collective rather than competitive. The Guest Stars have never tried to pander to musical fashion—what comes through is a strength and belief in themselves and what their music has to offer.

Plans for the future include tours of Europe, Cyprus, Greece, Turkey, Spain, a return to the United States, and even a trip to Russia.

Albums:
The Guest Stars (—/Guest Stars)
Out At Night (—/Guest Stars)

Charlie Haden

Missouri-born bassist, Charlie Haden (August 6, 1937) first came to prominence in the Ornette Coleman quartet in the late '50s. The first and best of a succession of white bassists to play with the great innovator, Haden had to find a way of responding to the free flow of melodic and rhythmic invention. The established role of the bass—Blanton, Pettiford and Ray Brown—was unsuitable, and Haden evolved a way of playing a roving line that sometimes complemented the soloist, sometimes moved independently. 'Forget about the changes in key and just play within the range of the idea' was the leader's instruction, and Haden was imaginative and intuitive enough to handle this freedom. Most of Ornette Coleman's Atlantic albums show how far the success of the music was due to the great bassist's contribution. **Ramblin' (Change Of The Century)** shows the propulsive power of Haden's near-sitar sound, his uncannily apt use of suspensions and accelerations around the soloist, the use of double stops in his solo.

The contrast between Haden and the late Scott La Faro is well illustrated on Ornette's great collective album **Free Jazz**. La Faro, technically brilliant and, Bill Evans' trio fulfilling a similarly independent role, comes out as over-decorative by contrast with the sheer taste and restraint and ability to listen shown by Haden.

Since leaving Ornette, Haden has played with many fine musicians, most notably in the Keith Jarrett group for a series of fine Impulse recordings. He is a fine composer, **Song For Che (Crisis)**, and in 1969 drew upon the resources of the JCOA for a large musico-political work **(Liberation Music Orchestra)**. Arranged by Carla Bley, the work ranges from the Spanish Civil War to the Chicago Convention, using both Spanish songs and expressionist devices.

Haden's album of duets with old friends Ornette Coleman, Keith Jarrett and Alice Coltrane **(Closeness)**, released late '70s, is magnificent.

Also in the late '70s, Haden instigated the empathetic drummerless trio with Norwegian saxophonist Jan Garbarek and Brazilian guitarist-pianist Egberto Gismonti. Rarely have three such individualistic improvisers performed with such compatibility, as evidenced by their two enduring albums **Magico** ('79) and **Folk Songs** ('81). Haden

Below: (L. to r.) Deirdre Cartwright, Alison Rayner, Josefina Cupido, Ruthie Smith, Linda Da Mango, Laka Daisical—the Guest Stars (photo: Allan Titmuss).

Above: Bassist Charlie Haden, pioneer of Free Jazz with Ornette Coleman. His Liberation Orchestra brings songs of hope for the oppressed.

is also an integral member of the Old and New Dreams quartet with Don Cherry, Dewey Redman and Ed Blackwell, their second album **Playing** being voted Record of the Year in the '82 *Downbeat* critics' poll.

In '82, Haden reassembled his Liberation Music Orchestra and recorded his deeply moving **The Ballad Of The Fallen** (released '83)—again using folk music (from the Spanish Civil War, El Salvador, Chile and Nicaragua) to stress political points in a formal and free contemporary jazz setting. Songs of the liberation movement, of hope and resistance were beautifully adapted and passionately re-arranged by Carla Bley.

An '83 album, **Rejoicing**, finds Haden in unusual collaboration with guitarist Pat Metheny featuring 'standards' from the Ornette Coleman book **(Tears Inside, Humpty Dumpty, Rejoicing**—prefacing Metheny's later work with Coleman) and Horace Silver's **Lonely Woman**, plus the brief but enjoyable Metheny-Haden interchange on **Waiting For An Answer**.

CHARLIE HADEN
THE BALLAD OF THE FALLEN
CARLA BLEY

DON CHERRY
SHARON FREEMAN
MICK GOODRICK
JACK JEFFERS
MICHAEL MANTLER
PAUL MOTIAN
JIM PEPPER
DEWEY REDMAN
STEVE SLAGLE
GARY VALENTE

Charlie Haden, The Ballad Of The Fallen (courtesy ECM).

Albums:
Ornette Coleman's Atlantic Albums (Atlantic/Atlantic)
Keith Jarrett's Impulse Albums (Impulse/Impulse)
Liberation Music Orchestra (Impulse/Impulse)
Closeness (A&M/A&M)
The Golden Number (A&M/A&M)
Charlie Haden-Jan Garbarek-Egberto Gismonti, Magico (ECM/ECM)
Charlie Haden-Jan Garbarek-Egberto Gismonti, Folk Songs (ECM/ECM)
Old And New Dreams, Playing (ECM/ECM)
Liberation Music Orchestra, The Ballad Of The Fallen (ECM/ECM)
Pat Metheny, Rejoicing (ECM/ECM)

Pianist Al Haig Trio And Quintet! (courtesy Prestige).

Al Haig

Pianist Al Haig was born in New Jersey in 1924. One of the earliest and best of bebop pianists, Haig was influenced originally by Nat King Cole and Teddy Wilson, influencing in his turn Hank Jones, Tommy Flanagan, Henri Renaud and Bill Evans. Charlie Parker's and Stan Getz's favorite accompanist, he was the pianist in Bird's classic 1945 quintet, which included Dizzy Gillespie, Tommy Potter on bass and Max Roach drums, playing at the Three Deuces on 52nd Street. His second engagement with Bird lasted from 1948-50 **(Bird On 52nd Street/Bird At St Nicks)**. He also played with Gillespie's small combos in the mid-40s **(The Greatest Of Dizzy Gillespie** and **In The Beginning)** and with tenorist Wardell Gray **(Central Avenue)**.

One of the few albums under his own name resulted from a trip to Paris with Bird **(Al Haig Trio & Quintet)** with James Moody depping for Bird. Great bebop resulted, with all of Haig's characteristic logic and precision on display even at fast tempos like **Maximum**. The B side is trio recordings from 1954, including a version of **Round Midnight** which effectively distinguishes Haig's approach from Bud Powell's or the composer's, Thelonious Monk—cooler, smoother; in fact all of Haig's work is elegant and graceful. In the early '50s he played with Stan Getz, perfectly matching Getz's currently cool approach on numbers like **There's A Small Hotel** and eclipsing the leader on **Indian Summer (Stan Getz)**.

A more virile spirit is to be found on a live recording of 1951 **(Stan Getz At Storyville)**. Al Haig's career throughout the '50s and '60s suffered from public neglect, and not until 1974 did he record an album of his choice **(Invitation)**, his fourth in thirty years.

Albums:
Al Haig Trio & Quintet (Prestige/Prestige)
Invitation (Spotlite/Spotlite)
Al Haig-Jamil Nasser Combo, Expressly Ellington (Spotlite/Spotlite)/Bebop Live! (Spotlite/Spotlite)

Jim Hall

Guitarist Jim Hall was born in Buffalo in 1930, and, like most modern guitarists, was first influenced by Charlie Christian. In 1955 he joined the Chico Hamilton Quintet, moving on to the revolutionary, drummerless, Jimmy Giuffre Trio **(The Train & The River)**. Following a tour of South America with Ella Fitzgerald, Hall became interested in the bossa nova; he joined Sonny Rollins' Quartet in 1961, his often contrapuntal lines alongside the tenorist casting a strong spell on the moving **Where Are You**, and driving on **John S (The Bridge)**.

Hall has recorded with a vast number of musicians, always fitting in, always inventive. One of the best meetings was with pianist Bill Evans **(Interplay)**, both players specializing in subtle shadings and gentle lyricism. A duo with bassist Ron Carter **(Alone Together)** results in the expected sensitivity, and on numbers like Rollins' **St Thomas** and **Whose Blues** shows a virile drive. Hall has played with John Lewis, Sonny Stitt, Zoot Sims, Paul Desmond and Lee Konitz in the '60s, and in recent years recorded with his own trio **(Jim Hall Live)**.

Albums:
Jimmy Giuffre, The Train & The River (Atlantic/Atlantic)
Sonny Rollins, The Bridge (RCA/RCA)
Bill Evans, Interplay (United Artists/United Artists)
Alone Together (Milestone/Milestone)
Jim Hall Live (A&M/A&M)
Concierto (CTI/CTI)
Gary Burton, Something's Coming (RCA/RCA)
Jim Hall-Ron Carter, Live At Village West (Concord/Concord)

Chico Hamilton

Drummer Chico Hamilton is probably best known for his crisp, tasteful time in the famous Gerry Mulligan Quartet **(Mulligan/Baker)** and for his own quintets which included the then oddball choice of cello. The original group, Buddy Collette, reeds, Jim Hall, guitar and Fred Katz, cello, played an often swinging jazz chamber-music that seemed to typify much of West Coast jazz in the '50s. The best album **(The Chico Hamilton Quintet)** included **Walking Carson Blues** and **The Sage**, which the group featured effectively in an excellent film, *Sweet Smell Of Success*. A compilation of later quintets includes early performances by Eric Dolphy and Charles Lloyd **(Chico Hamilton)**. Various albums including Lloyd and Hungarian guitarist Gabor Szabo followed, marking a more aggressive outlook **(Passin' Thru** and **Man From Two Worlds)**. A master of the brushes, Hamilton's drumming is a marvel of flexibility and drive.

Albums:
Gerry Mulligan/Chet Baker (Prestige/Prestige)
Chico Hamilton (Atlantic/Atlantic)
Passin' Thru (Impulse/Impulse)
Man From Two Worlds (Impulse/Impulse)
Chic Chic Chico (Impulse/Impulse)
The Dealer (Impulse/Impulse)

Jan Hammer

Czechoslovakian-born Jan Hammer has emerged as one of the most adaptable keyboardists of '70s jazz-rock, cutting a swathe as a particularly inventive improviser on synthesizers. Coming to international prominence through John McLaughlin's influential Mahavishnu Orchestra, Hammer has been profoundly inspired by Indian music and East European folk forms.

Born in Prague on April 17, 1948, Hammer played piano from age 6 and, at 14, was playing in a band alongside Miroslav Vitous and his brother. After winning the International

Below: Chico Hamilton—straight-ahead or improvising, one of the most creative percussionists in jass and a master of the brushes.

Music Competition in Vienna, Hammer majored in composition and piano at Prague's Academy of Muse Arts from '66-'68. In '68, after briefly taking up a sholarship at Berklee College of Music in Boston, he worked around the Boston area, spending a year at the Playboy Club. In early '70, Hammer worked extensively with vocalist Sarah Vaughan, the following year performing with Jeremy Steig and Elvin Jones **(Merry-Go-Round)**.

Hammer entered previously uncharted waters when he joined John McLaughlin's revolutionary Mahavishnu Orchestra in May '71 (until December '73); the experience with the Mahavishnu enabled Hammer to experiment liberally with synthesizers **(Birds Of Fire)**, a necessary extension of his keyboard skills if only to be heard above Billy Cobham's deafening drums.

Hammer worked with guitarist Jeff Beck **(Wired)** until the late '70s and since has worked mostly with his own groups. An excellent ECM release, **Night** ('84), finds Hammer in the challenging company of guitarist John Abercrombie, tenorist Mike Brecker and drummer Jack De Johnette (Hammer contributing the composition **Ethereggae**).

Albums:

John McLaughlin's Mahavishnu Orchestra, Inner Mounting Flame (Columbia/CBS)
John McLaughlin's Mahavishnu Orchestra, Birds Of Fire (Columbia/CBS)
Al Di Meola, Elegant Gypsy (Columbia/CBS)
Santana, John McLaughlin, Love Devotion Surrender (Columbia/CBS)
Elvin Jones-Chick Corea, Merry-Go-Round (Blue Note/Blue Note)
John Abercrombie, Night (ECM/ECM)
Jeff Beck With The Jan Hammer Group Live (Epic/Epic)
First Seven Days (Nemperor/—)
Timeless (ECM/ECM)
Make Love (MPS/MPS)
Like Children (Nemperor/—)

Lionel Hampton

Lionel Hampton (born Louisville, Kentucky, 1913) is the kind of jazz musician whose very name conjugates the verb 'to swing'. He is also one of jazz's great catalysts, always in the thick of all kinds of musical events—especially the jam-session kind of get-togethers involving musicians who just want to blow.

Apart from Milt Jackson, Lionel Hampton's pre-eminence as the most celebrated exponent of vibes in jazz which he plays, like his other instruments, with unremitting swing and power and an almost fanatical adherence to the beat, has long since become part of jazz lore. No surprise, therefore, to learn that Hampton's first love was drums, which he first played in a 'Chicago Defender' Newsboys' Band, after he and his mother had moved from Louisville to, first Wisconsin, then Chicago. Received tuition on xylophone from one-time Erskine Tate percussionist Jimmy Bertrand. Worked with several Chicago bands, then joined orchestra of Paul Howard, with whom he made his début on records. Next came jobs with Vernon Elkins and Les Hite. With Hite, he recorded in company of Louis Armstrong (both on drums and vibes); first recorded solo, using latter instrument, **Memories Of You (V.S.O.P. (Very Special Old Phonography), Vols 7 & 8)**.

Studied music at University of Southern California early-1930s; appeared in films featuring Hite and Armstrong (played masked drummer in *Pennies From Heaven*) and own band. 1936: fronted big band at Paradise Cafe, Hollywood, occasionally guesting as member of Benny Goodman Quartet. Joined Goodman full-time, November of same year, playing vibes as important ingredient of Goodman Quartet (later with Quintet, Sextet, Septet too), and on occasion deputizing as drummer with big band. (Was one of several replacements for Gene Krupa when latter left Goodman in '38.) With Goodman, Hampton's reputation as major soloist was realized. In turn, he gave various Goodman units in which he appeared extra fire and dynamism. His recordings with the Quartet are legion.

Most memorable moments originate from **1938 Carnegie Hall Jazz Concert** wherein his indefatigable, good-humored playing inspired his colleagues in quartet to real heights of inspiration. He is particularly outstanding on exhilarating performances of quartet favorites like **Stompin' At The Savoy, Dizzy Spells** and **Avalon**. The other side of his playing is represented here by reflective, almost low-key dexterity on **Man I Love**. During his term with Goodman (until 1940), Hampton organized a series of the most remarkable jam-session recordings to emanate from inside a studio. Not only were Hampton's multi-talents amply on display, including composing and arranging, but he proved himself an impeccable assembler of major talents, borrowed mainly from important big bands of the day (viz Ellington, Basie, Goodman, Kirk, Calloway) together with other top-notch instrumentalists like Nat Cole, Benny Carter, Coleman Hawkins and John Kirby. Typical of the miniature Who's Who of Jazz personnel Hampton assembled for such dates was that which participated in session (like all others, for Victor) in September '39 **(The Complete Lionel Hampton/Lionel Hampton's Best Records, Vol 3: 1939-1940)** which boasted sax section of Hawkins, Webster, Chu Berry and Carter, plus Dizzy Gillespie, trumpet, Hampton, Charlie Christian, Milt Hinton, Clyde Hart, Cozy Cole. And the music resulting therefrom was in keeping with the line-up.

Put together his own big band after leaving Goodman, first of a long line of Hampton big bands that sold musical excitement in a most blatantly extrovert way. Music from these bands was basic, dynamic, often uplifting; Hampton's playing was cast in apposite mold. Apart from which a string of talented soloists passed through the ranks of succession of Hampton bands, including following: Quincy Jones, Wes Montgomery, Clifford Brown, Art Farmer, Jimmy Cleveland, Alan Dawson, Milt Buckner, Dexter Gordon, Illinois Jacquet, Arnett Cobb, Chico Hamilton, Shadow Wilson, Cat Anderson, Gigi Gryce, Al Grey, Earl Bostic, Johnny Griffin and Dinah Washington. At the same time, Hampton never completely deserted the small group setting which helped make him famous, although, from time to time, has led galvanic orchestras **(Newport Uproar!** and **The Exciting Hamp In Europe)**, often with devastating effect.

But in a small-group context, there have been more clearly defined examples of his vibraphone playing, even though there have been times (parts of **The Jazz Ambassadors, Vols 1, 2**) when his solos have tended to ramble on for longer than his creative powers have been able to sustain real interest. Nevertheless, Hampton rarely fails to spark a record session. For example, he succeeded in inspiring tenorist Stan Getz into producing harder swinging solos than was usual at the time (1955) during a Hollywood date involving both men **(Hamp & Getz)**. And during live date **(Memorable Concerts, Part 1)** inspired basically extrovert musicians like Charlie Shavers and Willie Smith to play to their passionate best. Conversely, at same concert **(Memorable Concerts, Part 2)** Hampton himself, during a ballad performance of some duration, proved that his finest work is not always at fast, hard-swinging tempos.

His lengthy, dazzling work-out on **Stardust** stands as testimony of his true greatness; certainly, his statement here remains as vital and inspiring as his countless up-tempo

Below: Lionel Hampton—the fountainhead for all vibes-players. Innovator, catalyst, extrovert. A jazz giant in every way.

offerings, but it contains also elements of real creativity not always readily apparent in his more extrovert moments. Whatever the personnel, whatever the situation, Hampton fits—situations like his own all-star date of July '55 which featured Art Tatum, Buddy Rich, Barney Kessel, Harry Edison, and others. On this and another date from the day before which featured Hampton, Tatum and Rich, he refused to be overawed or even intimidated by Tatum's totally individualistic playing throughout (both **The Tatum Group Masterpieces**).

Two years before those two meetings of the giants, Hampton, in Paris as part of a European tour with his then big band, was again a catalytic figurehead, accompanied by small contingent from his band, plus Mezz Mezzrow, and two local musicians. At this date, Hampton produced one more extraordinary ballad performance, **September In The Rain (The Complete 1953 Paris Sessions)**.

In recent years, Hampton has been a victim of ill-health (he has been hospitalized on more than one occasion), and his appearances—both on record and in concert—have been less than prolific.

During early-1960s, Hampton recorded for Glad-Hamp, the label started by late wife Gladyse Hampton (who also acted as manager). During his career, he has composed a number of durable jazz standards, best-known of which are: **Hamp's Boogie Woogie, Midnight Sun, Gin For Christmas, 'Till Tom Special** and the perennial **Flying Home**.

Even in more recent times, Hampton has continued his famous role as an inspirational catalyst. An exuberant Eutin Festival jam in '79 with the young, long-haired, Hamburg-based, boogie-woogie pianist Axel Zwingenberger resulted in their touring in '80 and recording together in '82 **(Lionel Hampton Introduces Axel Zwingenberger In The Boogie Woogie Album)**. It might sound like an unlikely combination but, with Hampton at the helm, what develops is pure magic.

Albums:

Louis Armstrong, V.S.O.P. (Very Special Old Phonography, 1931-1932), Vols 7 & 8 (CBS—France)
The Complete Benny Goodman, Vols 1-3 (RCA Victor/—)
Benny Goodman, Vols 1-3 (RCA Victor—France)
Benny Goodman Trio & Quartet Live (1937-1938), Vols 1, 2 (CBS—France)
Various (Including Benny Goodman), 1938 Carnegie Hall Jazz Concert (Columbia/CBS)
The Genius Of Charlie Christian (Columbia)/Solo Flight (CBS)
The Complete Lionel Hampton (1937-1941) (Bluebird)/Lionel Hampton's Best Records, Vols 1-6 (RCA Victor—France)
Lionel Hampton, Steppin' Out (1942-1944) (MCA—Germany)
The Best Of Lionel Hampton (MCA Coral—Germany)
Lionel Hampton, Slide Hamp Slide (1945-1946) (MCA—Germany)
Lionel Hampton, Sweatin' With Hamp (1945-1950) (MCA—Germany)
Various (Including Lionel Hampton), Gene Norman Presents 'Just Jazz' (Decca/Coral)
Lionel Hampton, The Exciting Hamp In Europe (Ember)
Lionel Hampton, Memorable Concerts (Vogue)
Lionel Hampton, The Complete 1953 Paris Sessions (Vogue)
The Big Band Sound Of Lionel Hampton & His Orchestra (—/Verve)
Various (Including Lionel Hampton), The Jazz Ambassadors, Vols 1, 2 (—/Verve)
Various, Kings Of Swing (—/Verve)
Lionel Hampton/Stan Getz, Hamp & Getz (Verve/Verve)
Lionel Hampton, Hamp! (Verve/Music For Pleasure)
Art Tatum, The Tatum Group Masterpieces (Pablo/Pablo)
Lionel Hampton, Live! (Fontana)
Lionel Hampton, Newport Uproar! (RCA Victor/RCA Victor)
Lionel Hampton/Svend Asmussen, As Time Goes By (—/Sonet)
Chick Corea-Lionel Hampton, Chick & Lionel—Live At Midem (—/Kingdom Jazz)
Leaping With Lionel (—/Affinity)
Lionel Hampton Introduces Axel Zwingenberger In The Boogie Woogie Album (—/Teldec—Germany)

The Best Of Lionel Hampton (courtesy MCA Coral—Germany).

Herbie Hancock

Pianist Herbie Hancock was a child prodigy, performing Mozart piano concertos with the Chicago Symphony Orchestra at the age of 11. Born Chicago, 1940, he went to New York as a protégé of trumpeter Donald Byrd, and soon established himself as a recording artist for Blue Note. His début album **(Takin' Off)** with sidemen Freddie Hubbard and Dexter Gordon demonstrated his compositional gifts, from the gospel-funk of the hit number, **Watermelon Man**, to the rhythmically adventurous **The Maze. Blind Man, Blind Man** proved his talent for catchy tunes **(My Point Of View)** while a further album without horns spotlighted his keyboard technique **(Succotash)** which, while owing something to Bill Evans, Red Garland and Wynton Kelly, showed a graceful balance between single-note runs and texturally thick chord passages.

In the early '60s, Blue Note artists like Sam Rivers, Wayne Shorter, Grachan Moncur III, Andrew Hill, Bobby Hutcherson and Anthony Williams involved themselves in experiments with modes, free rhythms and tone colors, and Hancock proved a useful sideman, shaking rocks in a box for Bobby Hutcherson's **The Omen (Happenings)** and helping in the arrangements on Anthony Williams' first album **(Life Time)**.

His finest work as a composer comes from this fertile period **(Maiden Voyage** and **Empyrean Isles)** both using Freddie Hubbard, Ron Carter and Anthony Williams. There is a litheness and melodic charm about tunes like **Dolphin Dance** that is worlds away from Hancock's current output. Miles Davis picked his new quintet from this stable of talent, Herbie Hancock, Wayne Shorter, Ron Carter and Anthony Williams, aiming at a unit capable of great rhythmic mobility and free of harmonic restrictions.

Miles' subsequent exploration of modes, unison playing, suspended and multiple rhythms was well served by Hancock's and Shorter's writing talents. **Sorcerer, Madness** and **Riot** are typical Hancock scalar pieces built on shifting rhythms, while the pianist's role on his own **Little One** shows how important his atmospheric chording could be for the horns **(ESP)**. Within the rhythm section, his lightly lyrical lines fit into the intricate web of support from bass and drums. Switching to electric piano at Miles' suggestion, Hancock became part of an electric keyboard choir for the trail-blazing jazz-rock album **In A Silent Way**, a role which continued throughout subsequent releases.

In 1968, Hancock left Miles Davis to form his own band, a sextet with tenorist Joe Henderson. **Fat Mama**, a near-R&B original, gives an indication of what was to come **(Fat Albert Rotunda)**, though the next group with saxophonist Bennie Maupin saw Hancock once more experimenting, this time with percussion and electronic voicings **(Crossings)**. **Ostinato** is mainly an exercise in riff, using 15 beats on 4/4 and 7/8 **(Mwandishi)**. **Hidden Shadows (Sextant)** continues this pre-occupation. The commercial turning point came in 1973, thanks to the overwhelming bass riff **(Headhunters)**. Except for the short, sneaky re-vamp of **Watermelon Man**, the entire album was dominated by rhythmic riff, **Chameleon** for example motoring on for fifteen minutes with little solo top-dressing. On a par with Donald Byrd's **Black Byrd** album for jazz-rock sales, Herbie Hancock was established as a superstar.

From this point on, the minimum quantity of pure jazz interest comes mainly from Bennie Maupin, and Hancock's main influences are Sly Stone and James Brown. Apart from the steady stream of best-sellers, he has also composed for the movies, most notably **Blow-up** and **Death Wish**. A convert to Shoshu Buddism, Hancock believes now 'the whole thing is making people happy'.

In late '76, Hancock enlightened his funk fans by touring and recording extensively, in tuxedo and tie, with VSOP—recreating an earlier era and reuniting members of the earlier Miles Davis quintet (bassist Ron Carter, drummer Tony Williams and saxophonist Wayne Shorter with the addition of trumpeter Freddie Hubbard). In '84, Hancock repeated the experiment with VSOP II—this time without Shorter but augmented by bright rising stars trumpeter Wynton Marsalis and his brother, saxophonist Branford Marsalis.

Early in '78, Hancock teamed up with Chick Corea for a series of breath-taking duo acoustic performances in which they topped heights previously unscaled even by them—further bridging the gap between the individual 'mainstream' connections and their contemporary audience. In direct contrast, that year Hancock began using the voice-synthesizing Vocoder, providing his huge vocal pop-chart hit **I Thought It Was You** (from **Sunlight**).

While continuing with his own fusion projects, in the mid-'80s Hancock turned up as a surprise guest pianist on Manu Dibango's **Electric Africa** album, recorded in Paris, '85.

Albums:

Takin' Off (Blue Note/Blue Note)
My Point Of View (Blue Note/Blue Note)
Succotash (Blue Note/Blue Note)
Maiden Voyage (Blue Note/Blue Note)
Empyrean Isles (Blue Note/Blue Note)
Miles Davis:
  ESP (Columbia/CBS)
  Miles Smiles (Columbia/CBS)
  Sorcerer (Columbia/CBS)
  Filles De Kilimanjaro (Columbia/CBS)
  In A Silent Way (Columbia/CBS)
  On The Corner (Columbia/CBS)
Herbie Hancock:
  Fat Albert Rotunda (Atlantic/Atlantic)
  Crossings (Warner/Warner)
  Mwandishi (Warner/Warner)
  Sextant (Columbia/CBS)
  Headhunters (Columbia/CBS)
  Thrust (Columbia/CBS)
  Man-Child (Columbia/CBS)
  Secrets (Columbia/CBS)
  Sunlight (Columbia/CBS)
  Feets Don't Fail Me Now (Columbia/CBS)
  The Best Of Herbie Hancock (Columbia/CBS)
  Herbie Hancock: Quartet (Columbia/CBS)
  Rock-It (Columbia/CBS)
  Manu Dibango, Electric Africa (Celluloid/Celluloid)
  Herbie Hancock-Foday Musa Suso, Village Life (Columbia/CBS)
  Jo Jo Dancer, Your Life Is Calling (Warner Brothers/Warner Brothers)

Pre-funk John Handy Quintet, New View! (courtesy CBS).

John Handy

From early Gregorian chants to the full cry of civil rights, across Eastern folk music and into funky fusion . . . few saxophonists have traveled as great a musical distance as John Handy.

Born in Dallas, Texas, on February 3, 1933, Handy taught himself clarinet at 13, meanwhile showing an early talent for boxing (he became an amateur featherweight champion at 14). Moving to California at 16, he took up alto sax, then tenor, later flute, jamming with local San Francisco musicians. Arriving in New York in '58, Handy came to wide attention with Charles Mingus' groups **(Blues & Roots, Mingus Ah-Um)** and Randy Weston in '59.

In the mid-'60s, he formed a quartet with violinist Michael White **(Jazz At Monterey)**, showing his eagerness to explore horizons beyond the traditional horn-piano-bass-drums group-format. In the late '60s, Handy was to document his involvement in that decade's civil rights issues on **New View!**, containing far-sighted improvisational exchanges with guitarist Pat Martino and vibist Bobby Hutcherson. **Tears Of Ole Miss (Anatomy Of A Riot)**, which covers one side of **New View!**, was inspired by James Meredith's attempt to enter Mississippi University in '62. The piece also recalls Handy's 10-piece Freedom Band organized in San Francisco after he had taken part in the civil rights march on Washington DC, in '63. The Freedom Band proved a useful fund-raising device for the cause because, without being overtly political, it was able to reach wide audiences.

Always a multi-faceted player, Handy's love affair with Indian and other ethnic music resulted in the Eastern-flavored **Karuna Supreme** in collaboration with Ali Akbar Khan, and Handy's group Rainbow included legendary Brazilian folk guitarist Bola Sete alongside Khan and Zakir Hussain.

It's in the funk field, perhaps, that Handy

has found his greatest commercial success, notably since his huge disco-hit **Hard Work** in the late '70s. However, outings with the San Francisco-based Bebop and Beyond sextet in the mid-'80s finds Handy effortlessly returning to his earthier roots. On **Bebop And Beyond** he's in fine form alongside the uplifting company of trumpeter Warren Gale, saxophonist Mel Martin, pianist George Cables, bassist Frank Tusa and drummer Eddie Marshall.

Albums:
Charles Mingus, Blues & Roots (Atlantic/Atlantic)
Charles Mingus, Mingus Ah-Um (Columbia/CBS)
New View! (Columbia/CBS)
Jazz At Monterey (Columbia/CBS)
Karuna Supreme (—/MPS—Germany)
Hard Work (Impulse/Impulse)
Carnival (Warner Brothers/Warner Brothers)
Bebop And Beyond, Bebop And Beyond (Concord/Concord)

W. C. Handy

W. C. Handy, 'The Father Of The Blues', was a composer of stature, a bandleader and music publisher, but by no means the source of the blues. One of the first to recognize the commercial potential of Afro-American folk music, Handy incorporated the form into over-formal orchestrations for his nine-piece orchestra. Chiefly remembered as the composer of **St Louis Blues**, Handy also wrote **Aunt Hagar's Blues, Beale Street Blues, Memphis Blues** and many others.

Billy Harper

One of the younger generation of tenor-players steeped in the spirit of John Coltrane, Billy Harper has emerged as an individual voice.

Born in Houston, Texas (on January 17, 1943) into a musical and church-inspired family, Harper was singing before he could walk. He began playing tenor sax at 12, encouraged by his trumpeter uncle Earl Harper who introduced him early to Sonny Rollins and Kenny Dorham records. Throughout high school and North Texas State University (where he graduated with a Bachelor of Music degree in '65), he gigged as a saxophonist and vocalist, playing with local R&B bands and working with saxophonist/flute-player James Clay.

In '66, Harper moved to New York, his career taking off after meeting Gil Evans in '67 and joining the Evans' orchestra ranks. Harper spent two years with Art Blakey's Jazz Messengers and subsequently worked with Elvin Jones, Max Roach, Donald Byrd and the Thad Jones-Mel Lewis Big Band. He has also recorded with Louis Armstrong, Lee Morgan, Jimmy Owens and Randy Weston.

But it's with his own groups that Harper has produced some of his most enduring work. One of his finest albums is his first as leader—the earth-moving **Capra Black** in '73, on which he produced, arranged and wrote all the tunes backed up by Julian Priester, Jimmy Owens and drummers Billy Cobham and Elvin Jones. Originally issued on Charles Tolliver's US-label Strata East, **Capra Black** was released in the early '80s on the Japanese Denon label (through Nippon Columbia), a company which has also issued Harper's '77 quintet album **Love On The Sudan** (notable for its definitive version of Harper's **Priestess**).

For Harper, his saxophone is an instrument of spiritual communication and as well as extending this communication through his own groups, he is higly regarded as a writer—many of Harper's compositions **(Thoroughbred, Cry Of Hunger, Priestess)** have become staples of the Gil Evans book.

Albums:
Capra Black (Strata East/Denon—Japan)
Black Saint (Black Saint/Black Saint)
Love On The Sudan (—/Denon—Japan)
Soran-Bushi B.H. (—/Denon—Japan)
Trying To Make Heaven My Home (—/MPS—Germany)

Joe Harriott

Born in the West Indies, 1928, alto-player Joe Harriott arrived in Britain in 1951. Initially a hard bebopper, Harriott's naturally adventurous mind led him independently into many of the free areas that Ornette Coleman was exploring. Dispensing with bar lines, set harmony and predetermined structure, Harriott led a fine combo with trumpeter Shake Keane, pianist Pat Smythe, bassist Coleridge Goode and drummer Phil Seaman on a successful album **(Free Form)**.

In the mid-'60s, he collaborated with Indian musician John Mayer on a fusion of Indian music and jazz, using both modes and free-jazz techniques. With a five-piece jazz unit and four Indian musicians—violin, sitar, tabla, tambura—Harriott and Mayer recorded the compositions of Mayer **(Indo-Jazz Suite)**. Joe Harriott died in 1972.

Albums:
Free Form (Jazzland/—)
Indo-Jazz Suite (Columbia/Columbia)
Indo-Jazz Fusions (—/Double-Up—EMI)

Hampton Hawes

The son of a preacher, pianist Hampton Hawes was born in Los Angeles in 1928. At the age of 19 he was playing in trumpeter Howard McGhee's combo with Charlie Parker **(Lullaby In Rhythm)** and the Bird influence never left his playing. Bebop bands were everywhere in LA in the late '40s and early '50s, and Hawes played with many of the giants, Dexter Gordon, Teddy Edwards and Wardell Gray **(Jazz Concert—West Coast** and **Wardell-Gray—Central Avenue)**.

In 1955 he landed a contract with Contemporary, and his début album **(The Trio)** displayed his characteristic surging attack and deep feeling for the blues. All of his subsequent output swings with great inventiveness and vigor, and the three albums cut at one session **(All Night Session)** with guitarist Jim Hall, bassist Red Mitchell and drummer Bruz Freeman, show an inexhaustible drive and jubilation.

The meeting with two members of the Curtis Counce group, tenorist Harold Land and the phenomenal Frank Butler on drums, plus the innovative bassist Scott La Faro, produced an album of surging power. Hawes' later work is rigorously controlled, with a greater emphasis laid on structure, and **The Green Leaves Of Summer** represents the high point.

Addiction and prison sentences left his talent undiminished—in fact his autobiography *Raise Up Off Me* gives a revealing picture of the bebop hothouse.

His later album recorded in concert at the Great American Music Hall, San Francisco (June '75), and the Art Pepper album **Living Legend** (August, same year) showed he was still more than capable of making a blazing attack on the piano with sparks to spare. Sadly, **Living Legend**, ironically, must remain Hampton Hawes' swansong as he died on May 24, 1977.

Albums:
The Trio (Contemporary/Contemporary)
All Night Session (Contemporary/Contemporary)
For Real (Contemporary/Contemporary)
The Green Leaves Of Summer (Contemporary/Contemporary)
Seance (Contemporary/Contemporary)
Live At The Monmartre (Arista Freedom/—)
Hampton Hawes Recorded Live At The Great American Music Hall (Concord/Concord)
Art Pepper, Living Legend (Contemporary/Contemporary)

The Hampton Hawes Trio (courtesy Contemporary)—early piano.

Below: Alto innovator Joe Harriott. His experiments in free playing and fusions with Indian music were prophetic. A sadly missed musician, he died in 1972.

Coleman Hawkins

To say that Coleman Hawkins (born St Joseph, Missouri, 1904) virtually single-handedly brought the saxophone into prominence as a solo instrument of individuality and believability is not so far from being the truth. Before Hawkins wrought his miracle, some time during late-1920s (and indeed, progressively, for several years thereafter), the saxophone had been looked upon as something almost akin to a musical joke. Not only was Hawkins to pioneer (along with Sidney Bechet, on soprano) the jazz saxophone in general but he also became first and undisputed master of the tenor sax. Indeed, apart from Lester Young, Ben Webster, John Coltrane, and Sonny Rollins, his remains the instrument's principal voice. A situation which is hardly likely to change.

Although his blues-playing often left something to be desired (his prowess in this genre really only blossomed during the last 15-20 years of his life), Hawkins never lacked in any other department during a career which commenced as side-player with singer Mamie Smith's Jazz Hounds (with whom he made his record début, in 1923), continued through an important developmental period as premier soloist (apart from Louis Armstrong, for a short spell) with the orchestra of Fletcher Henderson (1923-34), passing on to his first acclaim as one of jazz's greatest solo virtuosi (1934-39).

His career progressed with initial experience as leader of his own big band (1940); thence, through the bebop era (1943-49); his involvement with touring jazz packages such as Jazz At The Philharmonic (1946-68), as well as with an amazing variety of small combos and literally hundreds of record dates which found his indomitable horn showing the

Above: Bebop meets Beefeater. The late piano giant Hampton Hawes visiting the Tower of London. His autobiography offers a revealing insight into the bebop life.

way to such bands and fellow instrumentalists as the Mound City Blue Blowers **(The Complete Coleman Hawkins, Vol 1 (1924-1940/Body & Soul)** in 1929; Lionel Hampton **(The Complete Lionel Hampton/Lionel Hampton's Best Records, Vols 3, 6)** from 1939; Duke Ellington **(Duke Ellington Meets Coleman Hawkins)** 1962; Sonny Rollins **(The Bridge/Sonny Meets Hawk)** 1963; Django Reinhardt **(Django Reinhardt & The American Jazz Giants/Django & His American Friends, Vol 1)** 1937; and his closest rival, Lester Young **(Coleman Hawkins/Lester Young)**. Juxtaposition of tenor saxes of Young and Hawkins on latter album makes for absolutely fascinating listening, if for no other reason than the different approaches of the pair to the same instrument are brought dramatically into focus; Young's lazy-sounding, legato playing, with its great rhythmic subtlety and occasional penchant for riff-type honks in the lower region of the tenor, contrasting with Hawkins' rich, rhapsodic and more roco style—big-toned, reliance on eighth note-dotted sixteenth patterns.

Hawkins' first recordings provide evidence that even he had to learn to get rid of the obligatory slap-tongue style prevalent amongst early-jazz saxophonists **(The Fletcher Henderson Story, Vol 1)**. Yet even in those early days, Hawkins' adventurous spirit asserted itself, as in **Old Black Joe's Blues (The Henderson Pathés)** from '23.

Apart from his recordings with Mamie Smith, Hawkins also took part in sessions involving Bessie Smith **(The Empress** and **Nobody's Blues But Mine)**; and Ma Rainey **(Ma Rainey)**, the last-named finding Hawkins sounding stiff uncomfortable on bass-saxophone, an instrument which, like clarinet, he occasionally played with Henderson, although he forsook both when leaving the band. With Henderson, his reputation as tenorist was built on feature items such as **The Stampede (Fletcher Henderson Story, Vol 1); Whiteman Stomp, Hop Off** and **Feeling Good (Vol 2); Freeze An' Melt, Blazin', Sweet & Hot** and **Hot & Anxious (Vol 3)**. An intriguing look-ahead solo with Henderson, also featuring another 'progressive' of late-1920s, Henry 'Red' Allen, was **Queer Notions** (a Hawkins composition). Hawkins re-recorded the number (with Henderson, with Allen again soloing on trumpet) a month later. Both versions still sound avant-garde for the time (1933).

Hawkins left Henderson in 1934 to accept an invitation to become featured soloist with British dance band-leader Jack Hylton. With Hylton, he toured Britain and France, during which time he recorded at regular intervals.

The mixed company Hawkins kept during his European sojourn can be judged from records he made during the period: with fellow American Benny Carter and Dutch jazz band **(Benny Carter With The Ramblers & His Orchestra)**; Django Reinhardt, Carter, plus sundry French musicians **(Django Reinhardt & The American Jazz Giants/Django & His American Friends, Vol 1)**; British pianist Stanley Black and rhythm section **(Jazz Pioneers—1933-36/Ridin' In Rhythm)**; the aforementioned Dutch band, the Ramblers **(The Hawk In Holland)**; and with the Hylton Orchestra **(Ridin' In Rhythm)**.

With World War II imminent, Hawkins returned to the US. There, in October 1939, he recorded what was to become the single most celebrated track with which to identify the unique artistry of Coleman Hawkins, **Body & Soul (The Complete Coleman Hawkins, Vol 1: 1924-1940: 'Body & Soul')**; a recording which soon after its release was to pass into jazz immortality. **Body & Soul** was, in many ways, a new beginning for, during the next decade, Hawkins was to produce probably his consist ently finest playing (certainly on record) of his career.

Despite inherent problems presented by a world war, and in spite of two major musicians' union bans, involving recording, Hawkins spent more time than most inside recording studios. Typical of his awesome consistency in performance during this period is his irresistibly brilliant playing during first-ever concert sponsored by *Esquire* magazine **(The First Esquire Concert, Vols 1, 2)** and for Hawkins' and Leonard Feather's Esquire All Stars the year before, in 1943 **(The Big Sounds Of Coleman Hawkins & Chu Berry)**, both containing typical rhapsodic Hawkins interpretations of the ballad, **My Ideal**. The tenorist recorded exclusively during 1943-44, particularly for Signature **(Classic Tenors)** and Keynote **(Cattin'** and **Swing!)**.

Most important recordings during the 1940s, however, took place between years 1944-46. First, and most important, were two Apollo sessions from February '44. With trumpeter Dizzy Gillespie and saxist-composer-arranger Budd Johnson figuring prominently in 11-piece band, this is generally recognized as being first bebop record date **(The Many Faces Of Jazz Vol 52: Coleman Hawkins)**.

Although Hawkins' basic style has not undergone any drastic metamorphosis, he fits in with the young boppers with obvious enthusiasm, as on Gillespie's **Woodyn You** or **Bu-De-Dah** (composed by Johnson and pianist Clyde Hart). Hawkins never was a proto-bopper but, as subsequent recordings demonstrated, again he was very much en rapport with the younger musicians' ideas even though some critics have tried to minimize this period in Hawkins' career.

Soon after this historical date, another bop figurehead, Thelonious Monk, was hired by Hawkins to work with him on 52nd Street; the two recorded together for the short-lived Joe Davis label **(The Hawk Flies)**. At end of same year, Hawkins put together a bop-tinged band, featuring the trumpet of Howard McGhee for a California trip. This fine band, with 'extras' like Vic Dickenson, trombone, Allan Reuss, guitar, and John Simmons, bass, added at one or more of three sessions, resulted in one of Hawkins' most eminently satisfying of all albums **(Hollywood Stampede)** with sumptuous ballad playing **(What Is There To Say?, I'm Thru With Love, April In Paris,**etc) being matched by Hawkins' fiercely-blown, exciting and beautifully etched solos on the swingers, of which **Rifftide** is the most interesting. A Hawkins bop original (using chord sequence of **Lady Be Good**, it was recorded nine years later by Monk under the title **Hackensack** and has been credited to at least two other composers, under different titles).

Monk was to be reunited with Hawkins at a Riverside record date in '57 **(Thelonious Monk & John Coltrane)**, once again sounding neither out of place nor an anachronism. Made numerous tours as a member of Jazz At the Philharmonic, and whatever selection of other musicians was available, Hawkins roared like the proverbial lion **(Jazz At The Philharmonic 1946, Vol 2** and **Jazz At The Philharmonic In Europe, Vols 1, 3)**.

During late-1940s, he continued to work with an extraordinary variety of jazzmen, young and old, and including the boppers **(Greatest Of The Small Bands, Vol 2, The Hawk Flies** and **Essen Jazz Festival All Stars With Bud Powell/Hawk In Germany)** as well as the then more contemporary mainstreamers like the trumpeters Henry 'Red' Allen **(Henry 'Red' Allen & His All Stars, Vol 5)**; Roy Eldridge **(The Moods Of Coleman Hawkins)**; Buck Clayton **(The High & Mighty Hawk)**; and Clark Terry **(Giants Of The Tenor Saxophone: The Genius Of Ben Webster & Coleman Hawkins)**. And amongst a clutch of veterans, as with **Jam Session At Swingville, The Big Challenge, Henry 'Red' Allen, Vols 4, 5, The Big Reunion** and **Hawk Eyes**, as well as with sympathetic mainstream-modernists, as with **Sittin' In** and **The Greatest Jazz Concert In The World**, Hawkins inevitably rose to any challenge, with a majestic drive and bristling passion that bordered on the angry. One out-of-the-ordinary challenge involved a 1963 record date, with Hawkins locking horns with Sonny Rollins **(The Bridge/Sonny Meets Hawk)**, the two vitally important musicians generally interacting in most productive fashion.

There is a story that towards the end of his life Hawkins was a bitter, frustrated man. Apocryphal or not, his playing certainly evinced new-found ferocity after he had passed 55, continuing right through to his death from bronchial pneumonia in May '69 in New York City. This was especially true of his live performances during early-1960s, handsomely documented by airshots like those from 1962, 1969 **(Centerpiece)**, as well as with numerous record dates, such as the friendly-yet-combative get-together with fellow tenorist Ben Webster **(Blue Saxophones)**; a far cry, in time at least, from his virtuoso performances on classic Hawkins features like **It's The Talk Of The Town (The Big Bands—1933/Ridin' In Rhythm); The Man I Love, How Deep Is The Ocean? (Classic Tenors); Georgia On My Mind (Recordings Made Between 1930 & 1941); I Can't Believe That You're In Love With Me (Coleman Hawkins Memorial—1940); Chicago (Coleman Hawkins At The Savoy 1940);** or the marvelously inventive, superbly evocative, unaccompanied **Picasso (The Moods Of Coleman Hawkins)**. But then, Coleman Hawkins always was a leader amongst jazz virtuosi, keeping a watchful eye (and ear) on the stylistic changes and developments that occurred in jazz during his lifetime yet going his own majestic way to the very end.

In his personal life, he often kept much to himself, acknowledging few close friends. During his last years, it has been reported that some of those friends helped keep him alive—literally—by insisting he supplement his daily intake of brandy by consuming at least one meal per week (he would accept Chinese food only).

One of Hawkins' last important engagements took place a few weeks before his death when, together with long-time musical associate and friend Roy Eldridge, he appeared on a Chicago-originated TV show.

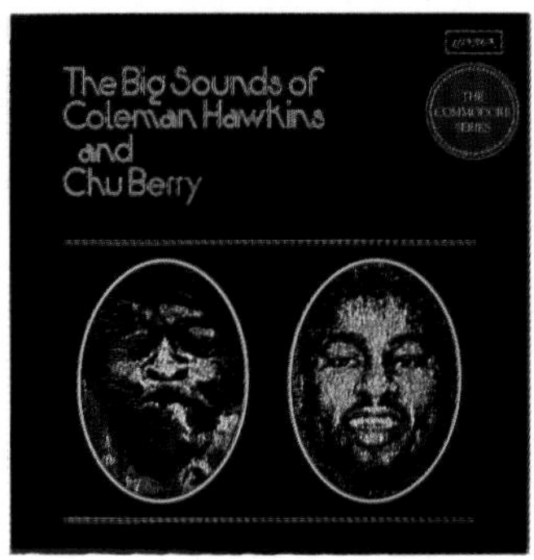

The Big Sounds Of Coleman Hawkins And Chu Berry (courtesy London).

Albums:

The Complete Fletcher Henderson (RCA Victor/—)
Fletcher Henderson, Vols 1-3 (RCA Victor—France)
The Fletcher Henderson Story (Columbia)/ The Fletcher Henderson Story, Vols 1-4 (CBS)
Fletcher Henderson, The Henderson Pathés (—/VJM)
Ma Rainey, Ma Rainey (Milestone)

Bessie Smith, The Empress (Columbia/CBS)
Bessie Smith, Nobody's Blues But Mine (Columbia/CBS)
Coleman Hawkins, Recordings Made Between 1930 & 1941 (CBS—France)
Spike Hughes & His All American Orchestra (London/Ace of Clubs)
The Chocolate Dandies (Parlophone)
Various, The Big Bands—1933 (Prestige)/Ridin' In Rhythm (World Records)
Various, Django Reinhardt & The American Jazz Giants (Prestige)/Django & His American Friends, Vol 1 (HMV)
The Complete Coleman Hawkins, Vol 1 (1924-1940): 'Body & Soul' (RCA Victor—France)
Coleman Hawkins, Swing! (Fontana)
Coleman Hawkins, Cattin' (Fontana)
Coleman Hawkins Memorial—1940 (Jazz Society)
Coleman Hawkins At The Savoy 1940 (Sunbeam)
Coleman Hawkins, The Hawk In Holland (—/Ace of Clubs)
Benny Carter With The Ramblers & His Orchestra (Decca—France)
The Complete Lionel Hampton (Bluebird)/ Lionel Hampton's Best Records, Vols 3, 6 (RCA Victor—France)
Coleman Hawkins, The Many Faces Of Jazz, Vol 52 (Mode—France)
Coleman Hawkins, The Hawk Flies (Milestone/—)
Various, Jazz At The Philharmonic, Vols 1, 2 (Verve)
Coleman Hawkins-Lester Young (Spotlite)
Coleman Hawkins/Lester Young, Classic Tenors (Contact/Philips—International)
Coleman Hawkins, Hawk Eyes (Prestige/Xtra)
Various (Including Coleman Hawkins), The Big Three (Bob Thiele Music/RCA Victor)
Coleman Hawkins, Hollywood Stampede (Capitol/Capitol—Holland)
The Moods Of Coleman Hawkins (—/Verve)
Coleman Hawkins, The Real Thing (Prestige/—)
Various (Including Coleman Hawkins), The Tenor Sax Album (Savoy/Savoy)
The Big Sounds Of Coleman Hawkins & Chu Berry (—/London)
Coleman Hawkins, The High & Mighty Hawk (Felsted/Vocalion)
Coleman Hawkins All Stars (Prestige—Swingville)
Coleman Hawkins, Centerpiece (Phoenix)
Coleman Hawkins/Ben Webster, Blue Saxophones (Verve/Verve)
Coleman Hawkins/Bud Powell, Essen Jazz Festival All-Stars With Bud Powell (Fantasy)/ Hawk In Germany (Black Lion)
Giants Of The Tenor Saxophone: The Genius Of Ben Webster & Coleman Hawkins (Columbia/CBS)
Duke Ellington Meets Coleman Hawkins (Impulse/Impulse)
Various, The Greatest Jazz Concert In The World (Pablo/Pablo)
Sonny Rollins, The Bridge/Sonny Meets Hawk (RCA Victor—France)
Various, Jazz At The Philharmonic In Europe, Vols 1, 3 (Verve/Verve)
Thelonious Monk & John Coltrane (Milestone)
Various, Jam Session At Swingville (Prestige/Prestige)
Various, The Big Challenge (Jazztone/Concert Hall)
Various, The Big Reunion (Jazztone/—)
Coleman Hawkins/Roy Eldridge, Hawk & Roy (Phoenix)
Henry 'Red' Allen, Vols 4, 5 (RCA Victor—France)
Various, The First Esquire Concert, Vols 1, 2 (—/Saga)
Various (Including Coleman Hawkins), The Greatest Of The Small Bands, Vol 2 (RCA Victor—France)

THE MANY FACES OF JAZZ vol. 52

COLEMAN HAWKINS

BUH DE DAH * YESTERDAYS * WOODYN' YOU * RAINBOW MIST * DISORDER AT THE BORDER * FEELING ZERO * BEAN'S TALKING AGAIN * I SURRENDER DEAR * BAH U BAH * IT'S ONLY A PAPER MOON * SOPHISTICATED LADY * SIH SAH

Coleman Hawkins, The Many Faces Of Jazz Vol. 52 (courtesy Mode-France). The irreplaceable Hawk enjoying himself with some proto-boppers in the 1940s.

Heath Brothers

Having assisted in the birth of bebop in the late 1940s, the Heath Brothers' entry into the fusion charts three decades later was a surprise, perhaps even more so considering Percy Heath's 22-year contribution to the MJQ's sedate 'Third Stream' innovations of the '50s—a far cry from the high-profile rhythms of late '70s funk.

Born in North Carolina (April 30, 1923), Percy Heath began as a child violinist, buying his first bass with his army severance pay in '46. Jimmy Heath (born Philadelphia, October 25, 1926) started out as an alto saxophonist (and, nicknamed 'Little Bird', it wasn't hard to see where he was coming from). In '48, the brothers went on the road with trumpeter Howard McGhee, two years later working in Dizzy Gillespie's big band. In the '50s, they performed with just about every major name of the bebop era. In '51, Percy joined his Gillespie rhythm-section cohorts (vibist Milt Jackson, pianist John Lewis and drummer Connie Kay) in founding the revolutionary Modern Jazz Quartet. Jimmy performed with Miles Davis traveled with his own band, and his compositions **Gingerbread Boy** and **Gemini** became jazz standards. In '75 Jimmy completed a project for a 40-piece band, *The Afro-American Suite Of Evolution*.

Tubby Hayes

Born in London, 1935, multi-instrumentalist Tubby Hayes died in 1973. He played tenor with the Kenny Baker Sextet, and spent four years with the big bands of Vic Lewis, Ambrose and Jack Parnell before forming his own short-lived octet in 1955.

In 1957 he joined up with fellow tenorist Ronnie Scott to form the Jazz Couriers, a popular hard bop outfit which lasted for two-and-a-half years. Hayes, apart from his charging, high-speed tenor, played excellent vibes: **Whisper Not (The Message From Britain)** and **Some Of My Best Friends Are Blues (Jazz Couriers In Concert)**; while **If This Isn't Love** and **What Is This Thing Called Love** are typical Courier tear-ups.

In '61, the historic transatlantic 'club exchange' of Hayes for Zoot Sims began an exciting new era for UK jazz.

The Tubby Hayes Big Band featured many of Britain's finest musicians, including saxophonists Pete King and Bobby Wellins and trumpeter Jimmy Deuchar **(Tubbs Tours)**, while the Hayes Quartet of 1967 had Mike Pyne on piano, Ron Mathewson bass and Tony Levin drums. The definitive album **Mexican Green** includes a brilliant, lengthy, open-ended title track, which shows that Hayes was aware of the possibilities of post-Coltrane/Coleman improvising.

The finest talent to emerge in Britain in the '50s, Hayes' premature death dealt a severe blow to modern jazz.

Albums:
The Jazz Couriers, The Message From Britain (Jazzland/—)
The Jazz Couriers, In Concert (—/Music For Pleasure)
The Jazz Couriers (—/Jasmine)
Tubbs Tours (—/Mole Jazz)
Mexican Green (—/Mole Jazz)

Right: The phonomenally gifted Tubby Hayes—co-leader of the two-tenor Jazz Couriers, leader of one of Britain's best big bands, and vibist of distinction.

After the MJQ disbanded in '74, Percy inaugurated the Heath Brothers with Percy (and, initially, with younger brother Albert 'Tootie' Heath on drums) plus pianist Stanley Cowell. Albums like the '78 **Passing Thru, In Motion** ('79), **Live At The Public Theater** ('79), **Expressions Of Life** ('81) and **Brotherly Love** ('81) brought them unprecedented success in the fusion charts.

From their early beginnings 'in the tradition' to their exceptional adaptability of later years, the Heath Brothers' music today 'reflects everything that has gone before in the art form of jazz'—as such they remain important in bringing a wealth of jazz history in a modern language to a whole new generation.

Albums:
Marching On (Strata East/—)
Passing Thru (Columbia/CBS)
In Motion (Columbia/CBS)
Live At The Public Theater (Columbia/CBS)
Expressions Of Life (Columbia/CBS)
Brotherly Love (Antilles/Antilles)

The Heath Brothers, Brotherly Love (courtesy Antilles).

Fletcher Henderson

A four-disc re-issue set of important recordings by the Fletcher Henderson Orchestra (1923-38), and released many years ago, was subtitled **A Study In Frustration**. The reason was that Henderson, one of three great pioneers of big-band jazz, never did gain the full recognition and all-round acclaim that fell to Benny Goodman during swing era when Goodman used many of the original arrangements Henderson had written for his own trail-blazing aggregation in previous years, not forgetting Goodman's use of the kind of big-band structure which the older man had innovated during 1920s/1930s. Although perhaps too much has been made of this over the years, it is true that Fletcher Hamilton Henderson (born Cuthbert, Georgia, 1898) did not receive the kudos his pioneering work so richly deserved.

His early bands, in comparison with later versions, sound primitive, stiff-swinging, and not especially exciting, but by the time the 1930s had arrived, Henderson had established an individual style that was at least as influential as Duke Ellington during same period.

Henderson came from a well-to-do family; father was principal of a Macon, Georgia, training school; and he attended college as well as graduating from Atlanta University. Played piano at school dance dates. In 1920, after receiving AB degree from University, Henderson came to New York, ostensibly to enroll at Columbia University. Instead took job as song demonstrator for Pace & Handy Music Co. Left next year to assemble band to accompany singer Ethel Waters and her troupe with which he toured for a year. Recorded with Waters on regular basis (**Oh Daddy!** and **Jazzin' Babies' Blues**).

Back in New York, he became house pianist for record companies, accompanying many noted blues singers, including Bessie Smith (**Nobody's Blues But Mine** and **The World's Greatest Blues Singer**); Mamie Smith, Alberta Hunter, Trixie Smith and Ma Rainey (**Ma Rainey**).

Frankly, Henderson was a competent rather than inspired accompanist—his work behind Bessie Smith, for instance, compares very unfavorably with that of James P. Johnson. In 1924 he was appointed leader of a recently put-together band to play two lengthy residences in New York's Club Alabam and Roseland Ballroom, plus gigs at further New York venues and in other major cities. Probably first important recordings by this band made for Pathé (**The Henderson Pathés**) during which time several important contributors to Hendersonia emerged, notably arranger - composer - saxist - clarinettist Don Redman, trombonist Charlie Green, clarinettist-saxist Buster Bailey, drummer Kaiser Marshall, and, most significant of all, saxist-clarinettist Coleman Hawkins. These early recordings are more important for the respective solo contributions rather than the sometimes pedestrian arrangements and sloppy ensemble playing.

The first real significant solos, however, were provided by Louis Armstrong, who worked with Henderson for around 14 months (1924-25). Armstrong's electrifying playing on such titles as **Go 'Long Mule, Shanghai Shuffle, Copenhagen, Everybody Loves My Baby, How Come You Do Me Like You Do?, Sugarfoot Stomp** and **T.N.T.** (**The Fletcher Henderson Story/The Fletcher Henderson Story, Vol 1**); and **Tell Me Dreamy, My Rose Marie** and **Twelfth Street Blues** (**The Henderson Pathés**) tend to relegate the rest of his surroundings to another league. Redman was responsible for many of the earliest arrangements—certainly the better ones. (Difference between the well-nigh aridity of earlier efforts like **Dicty Blues** and a later score like that for **Dippermouth Blues** is interesting and marked.)

Fletcher Henderson did not come into his own in this area until 1933-34, and even then he was wise enough to invest in arranging talents of others, most notably Benny Carter, and his own younger brother Horace Henderson. Both latter produced superior charts for the band. Henderson also used stock arrangements, **Singin' The Blues, My Gal Sal** (**The Fletcher Henderson Story/The Fletcher Henderson Story, Vol 3**). Amongst Fletcher Henderson's own most memorable arrangements were **Blue Moments, Sing You Sinners, Moten Stomp, Can You Take It** (**The Fletcher Henderson Story/The Fletcher Henderson Story, Vol 4**); **Shanghai Shuffle** (**First Impressions 1924-1931**); **Down South Camp Meetin', Wrappin' It Up, Hotter Than 'Ell** (**Swing's The Thing 1931-1934**).

In 1935, Henderson had no band at all. Accepted an offer to become chief arranger for up-and-coming Benny Goodman Orchestra. (There is an illuminating chapter on Fletcher Henderson and his early big-band associate Don Redman in Richard Hadlock's book *Jazz of the 20s*. And for comprehensive fact-documentation on Henderson, his bands, side-players, etc, one need go no further than Walter C. Allen's *Hendersonia: The Music Of Fletcher Henderson & His Musicians*, a bio-discography of monumental proportions.)

The Goodman-Henderson association was mutually profitable and for Henderson it meant that, in 1936, he was able to re-start his own orchestra that contained exceptional musicians of the calibre of Chu Berry, Big Sid Catlett, Hilton Jefferson, Eddie Barefield, and two former alumni, Buster Bailey and John Kirby. The rejuvenated band got off to fine start with hit record (**Christopher Columbus**—its first disc) but it could not follow through.

Finally, in mid-1939, Henderson gave up again, to rejoin Goodman. Perhaps surprisingly, Goodman also made Henderson band pianist, in place of far superior Jess Stacy, as well as with various small groups (taking over from departed Teddy Wilson). This situation lasted only until March 1940, when Johnny Guarnieri took his place (Henderson had been given a tough time by many critics for his keyboard inadequacies with Goodman). As arranger, composer, he was to stay until following January when he left again, to form another big band.

For Goodman, he had helped immeasurably in making the clarinettist King of Swing and his band immensely popular, supplying superior charts to such items as **Remember, Three Little Words, When Buddha Smiles, Honeysuckle Rose** (**The Big Band Sound Of Benny Goodman**); **Down South Camp Meetin', Sugarfoot Stomp, Bugle Call Rag, Sometimes I'm Happy, Blue Skies, King Porter Stomp** (**The Complete Benny Goodman, Vols 1-3/Benny Goodman, Vol 5 1935-1938**); **Changes, Wrappin' It Up, Please Be Kind, Get Happy** and **I Can't Give You Anything But Love** (**The Complete Benny Goodman, Vols 1-3/Benny Goodman, Vol 6** (**1935-1938**): **The Fletcher Henderson Arrangements**); arrangements which, for Henderson's own bands, never gained for him any King-of-Swing type of accolade but which, to be fair to Goodman & Co, were played by the latter with more collective skill and, at times, a fair degree of excitement. (More interesting background on Goodman-Henderson relationship to be found in *The Kingdom of Swing*, by Benny Goodman, Irving Kolodin.)

With Goodman's blessing, Henderson tried again (in 1941) to lead his own band. But things never really worked out. Although this and subsequent line-ups included, between 1941-45, many promising instrumentalists—amongst these were Art Blakey, Dexter Gordon, Sahib Shihab, Vic Dickenson and Emmett Berry—Henderson never was able to revive the magic of earlier times.

During 1947, he was back again as staff arranger with Goodman. Between 1948-49, was re-united with Ethel Waters, with whom he toured. Together with pianist-composer J.C. Johnson, wrote revue called *Jazz Train*, assembling special band for the show at Bop City, NYC. Fronted sextet at Café Society Downtown, including Lucky Thompson and Jimmy Crawford; engagement cut short in December, '50 when Henderson suffered a stroke. Special radio show involving the original Goodman Trio and guests like Buck Clayton, Johnny Smith and Lou McGarity. Results released on record (**Benny Goodman Trio For The Fletcher Henderson Fund**), proceeds going to the ailing musician.

A heart attack, followed by another (in '52) was too much, and in December 1952 Fletcher Henderson died in Harlem Hospital. Following reunion by Fletcher Henderson All Stars in 1957 Great South Bay Jazz Festival, Long Island, New York, the participants (including past Henderson sideplayers like Rex Stewart, Benny Morton, J.C. Higginbotham, Buster Bailey, Dicky Wells and Coleman Hawkins) recorded for Jazztone (**The Big Reunion**) using original charts of some of the most famous numbers. And unlike many such reunions, the music produced by this illustrious line-up was exceptional; something which, although it came too late for him to appreciate, undoubtedly would have pleased Fletcher Henderson immensely.

Albums:
Ethel Waters, Oh Daddy! (Biograph/—)
Ethel Waters, Jazzin' Babies' Blues (Biograph/—)
Bessie Smith, Nobody's Blues But Mine (Columbia/CBS)
Bessie Smith, The World's Greatest Blues Singer (Columbia/CBS)
Trixie Smith (Collector's Classics)
Ma Rainey, Ma Rainey (Milestone)
Fletcher Henderson, The Henderson Pathés—Fletcher Henderson & His Orchestra (1923-1925) (—/Fountain)
The Fletcher Henderson Story (Columbia)/ The Fletcher Henderson Story, Vols 1-4 (CBS)
Fletcher Henderson, First Impressions (1924-1931) (—/MCA—Germany)
Fletcher Henderson, Swing's The Thing (Decca/MCA—Germany)
Fletcher Henderson Orchestra 1923-1927 (Riverside)
The Complete Fletcher Henderson (RCA Victor)/Fletcher Henderson, Vols 1-3 (RCA Victor—France)
Fletcher Henderson & His Orchestra, Vols 1, 2 (Collector's Classics)
Various (Including Fletcher Henderson), The Big Bands (Prestige)/Ridin' In Rhythm (World Records)
Benny Goodman, Vols 5, 6 (1935-1938): The Fletcher Henderson Arrangements (RCA Victor—France)
The Big Band Sound Of Benny Goodman (—/Verve)
Various, 1938 Carnegie Hall Jazz Concert (Columbia/CBS)
Benny Goodman Trio For The Fletcher Henderson Fund (Columbia/Fontana)
Fletcher Henderson All Stars, The Big Reunion (Jazztone/—)
Rex Stewart/Henderson All Stars, Henderson Homecoming (United Artists)

Joe Henderson In Japan (courtesy Milestone)—tenorist at his peak.

Joe Henderson

Born in Ohio in 1937, tenorist Joe Henderson got his musical schooling in Detroit. His earliest influences were the Jazz at the Phil albums and R&B but the Coltrane-Rollins dominance of the tenor shaped his approach. He seemed to turn up as a sideman on scores of Blue Note sessions in the '60s, always reliable, trenchant. Like many professionals in his age group, he has incorporated the newer approaches—modes, free playing—into a basically bebop outlook, and he is flexible enough to accommodate the difficult challenge of Andrew Hill's music **Refuge** (**Point Of Departure**) or the basic bluesiness of Lee Morgan's **Sidewinder** (**Sidewinder**). His collaboration with trumpeter Kenny

Dorham, particularly in the field of Latin rhythms—**Blue Bossa, Recorda-Me (Page One); Trompeta Toccata, Mamacita (Trompeta Toccata)**—produced a series of workmanlike albums **(In 'N' Out, Our Thing** and **Una Mas)**.

The contract with Milestone, too, produced solid work. An exciting, beefy player, his mannerisms include a furious, circular stirring that can sound repetitive or mesmerizing depending on taste and context. One of his most successful exercises in controled freedom occurs on **The Bead Game (Tetragon)** where momentum alone seems to advance the piece.

Live performances usually bring out the best in Joe Henderson, and both albums cut at The Lighthouse Café in 1970 are excellent **(If You're Not Part Of The Solution, You're Part Of The Problem** and **In Pursuit Of Blackness)**. Using his regular group, he reworks old material.

An album cut in Tokyo the following year, using a Japanese rhythm section **(Joe Henderson In Japan)**, catches him at his peak. Some of his later output has been in the funky, easy-listening bag **(Canyon Lady)** but on the evidence of his more recent work **(Black Narcissus** and **Relaxin' At Camarillo)** he still functions as a committed player.

Albums:

Page One (Blue Note/Blue Note)
In 'N' Out (Blue Note/Blue Note)
Our Thing (Blue Note/Blue Note)
Mode For Joe (Blue Note/Blue Note)
Inner Urge (Blue Note/Blue Note)
Tetragon (Milestone/Milestone)
If You're Not Part Of The Solution (Milestone/Milestone)
In Pursuit Of Blackness (Milestone/Milestone)
Joe Henderson In Japan (Milestone/Milestone)
Power To The People (Milestone/Milestone)
Black Narcissus (Milestone/Milestone)
Relaxin' At Camarillo (Contemporary/Contemporary)

Below: The exciting Joe Henderson, driving tenorist. His solo on Horace Silver's Song For My Father will remain for ever a memorable Blue Note classic.

Woody Herman

Bandleader Woody Herman was born Woodrow Wilson Herman in 1913, starting in vaudeville with his parents at the age of 9, where he was billed as 'Boy Wonder Of The Clarinet'. By 1936, he had taken over the Isham Jones Orchestra, **The Band That Plays The Blues (The Best Of Woody Herman)** and was featured extensively on clarinet and alto in arrangements that fluctuated between Dixieland and swing.

In 1939, the band recorded the million-selling **Woodchopper's Ball** and popularity was assured. The First Herd was recruited in 1944, a glittering array of outsize personalities like trombonist Bill Harris, tenorman Flip Phillips, drummer Dave Tough, trumpet prodigy Sonny Berman and arranger-pianist Ralph Burns. It was a band of enthusiasts, and it still sounds like it on record. The good-humored vocal on **Caldonia** capped by the wildly exciting trumpet unison, Phillips' booting solo on **The Good Earth**, Harris' idiosyncratic brilliance on **Bijou**, all remain classics of the period **(The Best Of Woody Herman, CBS)** while the sheer exuberance of the band on **Apple Honey, Wild Root** or **Your Father's Moustache** has seldom been equaled. With arrangements by Neal Hefti, Burns and Shorty Rogers, the First Herd scored a radio show sponsored by Wildroot Cream Oil, hosted by Wildroot Cream Oil Charlie, that took the sound into a million homes. Airshots capture the spontaneity of the band better than studio dates, and the trio of releases is worth hunting down **(The Great Herd 1946** and **Woody Herman—His Orchestra & The Woodchoppers, Vols 1 & 2)**.

Personnel changes occurred before the band broke up in 1946, Don Lamond replaced Tough at the drums, Shorty Rogers replaced Hefti and vibraphonist Red Norvo replaced Marjorie Hyams.

Above: Band-leader of renown, Woody Herman, has headed countless Herds since 1944. Even in the '80s, the verve and vitality of Herman's bands seem indestructible.

The Second Herd, despite pessimistic predictions, proved every bit as good. The sax section comprised Stan Getz, Zoot Sims, Herbie Steward and Serge Chaloff, three tenors and a baritone. Jimmy Giuffre scored the famous **Four Brothers** to spotlight the section, and the smooth, low, close-formation ensemble became a trademark: bebop out of Lester Young **(The Best Of Woody Herman, CBS)**. The Ralph Burns feature for Getz, **Early Autumn**, made the tenorist's cool lyricism famous overnight. Bebop began to show in the trumpet section with the arrival of Red Rodney, while Shorty Rogers wrote bebop numbers like **Keeper Of The Flame** and **Lollypop**, the latter a follow-up to George Wallington's famous **Lemon Drop (Early Autumn)**. Again, airshots are worth a listen **(Boiled In Earl)** particularly as the recording ban kept the Second Herd out of the studios for a year.

At the end of 1949, Herman disbanded the Herd, formed another, but due to the decline of the big-band market, he was forced to follow a more conservative line. The Third Herd is a blurred category, covering a multitude of personnel changes, though the arrangements remained the province of Burns and Giuffre. 1959 saw the reassembly of many of the Herman stalwarts, Zoot Sims, Conte Candoli, Bill Perkins, Urbie Green, for the Monterey Jazz Festival. With Mel Lewis on drums, the band tears into **Four Brothers (Live At Monterey)** while **Monterey Apple Tree** is the classic **Apple Honey**. An album from 1963 **(Live At Basin Street West)** reveals a vigorous talent; high-note specialist, trumpeter Bill Chase, lifting the trumpet section for the exciting **Caldonia**, the fast, driving tenorist Sal Nistico on **El Toro Grande**, or trombonist Phil Wilson on **Body & Soul**.With Nat Pierce writing the arrangements, this version of the Herd was a fine mixture of tradition and innovation. An album from the late '60s **(Jazz Hoot)** showcases the flaring trumpet section of Bill Chase, Dusko Goykovitch, Don Rader, Bob Shew and Gerald Lamy, plus solos by Nistico.

Woody Herman's own playing has remained consistently excellent over the decades, still indebted to Frank Trumbauer, The Glissando Kid, for his alto sound, and still apposite on the unfashionable clarinet. In later years, the Herd's sax section hews close to Coltrane, and the electric piano has appeared, but the identity of the band seems indestructible.

Recordings for Concord in the mid-'80s show that the Herman Big Band can still recreate history when reworking classics like **Four Brothers** and **Perdido** in the company of Sal Nistico, Flip Phillips and Al Cohn **(World Class)**.

Albums:

The Best Of Woody Herman (MCA/MCA)
The Best Of Woody Herman (Columbia/CBS Realm)
Early Autumn (Capitol)
The Great Herd, 1946 (Swing Treasury/Swing Treasury)
Woody Herman—His Orchestra & The Woodchoppers, Vols 1 & 2 (First Heard/First Heard)
Boiled In Earl (Swing Treasury/Swing Treasury)
Live At Monterey (Atlantic/Atlantic)
Live At Basin Street West (Phillips/Phillips)
Jazz Hoot (Columbia/CBS)
The Kings Of Swing, Vol 2 (Verve/Verve)
Hey! Heard The Herd? (Verve/Verve)
The Band That Plays The Blues (—/Affinity)
Feelin' So Blue (Fantasy/Fantasy)
The Woody Herman Big Band—World Class (Concord/Concord)
Woody Herman Presents A Great American Evening (Concord/Concord)

Woody Herman, Live At Basin Street West (courtesy Philips).

Andrew Hill

Pianist Andrew Hill was born in Haiti in 1936, and brought up in Chicago. His early influences were Tatum, Monk and Powell, and his interests remain within the harmonic framework despite the avant-garde label.

As a result of his work as a sideman on Joe Henderson's **Our Thing** album, he landed a contract with Blue Note during the heady days of that label's patronage of experiment. Andrew Hill's work as composer and pianist remains the most natural-sounding of the sometimes self-conscious Blue Note school, which included Herbie Hancock, Anthony Williams and Bobby Hutcherson.

His début album **Black Fire** displayed a mobile concept of trio, with Roy Haynes and bassist Richard Davis—an habitual collaborator—tugging the rhythms this way and that. Intense music, oblique, the leader's piano characterized by unusual intervals and a percussive drive that cloaks the lyricism of **Subterfuge** with sinew. Adding vibraphonist Bobby Hutcherson, Hill's next album **(Judgement)** was again an object lesson in combining freedom and discipline. The interaction over the basic vamp figure on **Siete Ocho** is fascinating, and the scurrying yet powerful piano on **Yokada Yokada** gives an idea of Hill's originality.

With the great album **Point Of Departure** he gave notice of his arrival in the front rank, developing the talents of trumpeter Kenny Dorham, multi-instrumentalist Eric Dolphy and tenorist Joe Henderson like a master of color and texture. The compositions, again originals, revolve around the tonal centres, and seem to have been written for these specific sidemen. **Dedication,** a slow and beautiful piece, is a haunting choreography of stately movements. Using an expanded rhythm section, drums, African drums, conga, the pianist-composer recorded a work in four movements **(Compulsion)** to express 'the legacy of the Negro tradition'. From the opening—the dark, threshing drums, the jab of the horns, the rumbling, percussive piano and bass—the sheer power of Hill's musical conception is quite overwhelming.

The consistency of his output **(Andrew!** and **One For One)** makes Blue Note's shelving of this artist a tragedy. After a three-year hiatus in his recording career, he again reappeared with a trio for Steeplechase **(Invitation)** and also cut an album of quintets, quartets and a duo with Lee Konitz **(Spiral)** which proved that he has lost none of his brillance.

Recordings:
Black Fire (Blue Note/Blue Note)
Judgement (Blue Note/Blue Note)
Point Of Departure (Blue Note/Blue Note)
Compulsion (Blue Note/Blue Note)
Andrew! (Blue Note/Blue Note)
One For One (Blue Note/Blue Note)
Invitation (Steeplechase/Steeplechase
Spiral (Freedom/Freedom)

Andrew Hill, Judgement! (courtesy Blue Note)—with Bobby Hutcherson.

Below: Pianist-composer Andrew Hill. His highly original albums for Blue Note like Point of Departure, Compulsion and Andrew! place him near the summit.

Above: Earl 'Fatha' Hines—one of the first great keyboard virtuosi, for over 50 years untouched and undimmed, a seminal figure among piano-players.

Earl Hines

Earl Kenneth 'Fatha' Hines (born Duquesne, District of Pittsburgh, Pennsylvania, 1905) was a seminal figure amongst jazz keyboard players for over 50 years—fashions and new styles come and go, but Hines continued to reproduce technically astonishing performances of great rhythmic, harmonic and improvisational strength which few, if any, can match, even today.

Earl Hines came from a musical family: father played cornet in brass bands, sister was pianist-bandleader during 1930s. Started on cornet, but was quickly switched to piano, commencing with lessons and studies at nine. Majored in music at Schenley High School.

First professional jobs were with singer Lois B. Deppe. After undertaking first job as leader of own band, worked with Carroll Dickerson, Erskine Tate, and others. In 1927 worked as member of Louis Armstrong's band at Chicago's Sunset Cafe: during same year, Armstrong, Hines and Zutty Singleton ran own Chicago club, but venture did not last long. Late in '27, joined forces with Jimmie Noone, their five- or six-piece (trumpetless) band producing some of the finest small-group jazz to be heard in the Windy City (at Apex Club), or indeed anywhere, at that time. Titles like **Apex Blues, Sweet Lorraine, I Know That You Know** and **My Monday Date** (one of Hines' most popular compositions) derive from the Apex Club engagement, especially the recordings of same **(Jimmie Noone & Earl Hines At The Apex Club, Vol 1: 1928).** By which time, it had become blatantly obvious to musicians and fans alike that Earl Hines was in the process of taking the story of jazz piano-playing several steps forward.

Hines' so-called 'trumpet style' had evolved from his deep admiration for the instrumental genius of Louis Armstrong. Hines even managed to recapture the essence of the Armstrong vibrato in his playing: his right-hand use of octaves and tremolo effects, his freeing of the left hand from a more or less obligatory heavy chording and use of unrelieved bass patterns by Waller-Smith-Johnson school, and his startling single-note right-hand attack, together made him jazz's most outstanding technician and most important keyboard innovator of the 1920s. His trumpet style was never more admirably showcased than in tandem with Armstrong for the first time. **Weather Bird (The Louis Armstrong Legend)** moved forward the creative processes of jazz about a decade when issued in 1929.

Hines' first recorded solos **(Earl 'Fatha' Hines)** confirm he was, without a doubt, jazz's first virtuoso of keyboard. His playing on tracks like **Caution Blues, My Monday Date** and appropriately titled **Fifty-Seven Varieties** shows an overall conception that had been barely hinted at by other jazz pianists of the decade.

During succeeding decade, Hines and the band played so many regular engagements at Grand Terrace that his became known as Grand Terrace Band. Recordings by same from the 1930s, apart from further showcasing the sustained brilliance of its leader's playing, were models of consistency, both in solos as well as in ensemble playing.

Rhythm was the strong point of various Grand Terrace bands, and it never sounded more dynamic than when Alvin Burroughs, drums, joined from Horace Henderson's orchestra. Although Hines disbanded, temporarily, at beginning of 1940, he had re-formed by end of same year.

The band led by Hines 1942-43 is of historic importance—although it was never to record, due to prolonged musicians, union ban. At various times the band contained Charlie Parker (playing tenor, not alto sax); Jerry Valentine, arranger, trombone; trumpeters Freddie Webster, Shorts McConnell, and Bennie Harris; trombonist Bennie Green; and singers Sarah Vaughan and Billy Eckstine; soon all to become important contributors to burgeoning bebop revolution.

Only the rear portion of Hines' association with bop and some of its protagonists was documented, via gramophone records, and then its total output was minimal; two extended-play discs **Earl Hines Orchestra (1)** and **Earl Hines Orchestra (2)),** give something less than thorough examples. Hines disbanded, finally, in 1947 and, once again, became Chicago club-owner. But by beginning of following year he was once more on the road (and in the recording studios), this time as member of Louis Armstrong's All Stars **(Louis Armstrong, Vols 2, 3** and **Satchmo At Symphony Hall, Vols 1, 2)**, a situation which lasted until 1951, when Hines put together own sextet.

Long residency at Hangover Club, San Francisco, with quartet, starting fall of '55. In 1957 he went to Europe, as member of Jack Teagarden-Earl Hines All Stars, although during the 1950s, for some inexplicable reason, Hines' playing went out of fashion, and he fell into totally unwarranted neglect.

The situation changed dramatically early-1960s. Suddenly, he was back in favor with a vengeance. Appeared at special concerts, to rapturous applause from critics and public alike. And, whereas his recorded output during the previous decade had been less than prolific, new recording projects came thick and fast. What is more, the standard of performances on the newer recordings was infinitely superior to those from the 1950s. Perhaps a major reason for their superiority has been a tendency often to record Hines as solo artist. And like his once greatest rival (and friend) Art Tatum, Hines invariably is at his magical best when performing alone. Probably the finest of these exceptional albums to appear was that which Hines made for Contact **(Earl Hines At Home)** in 1964, with the pianist's dazzling technique sounding at least as superb as in his younger days.

Further solo albums of similar brilliance have included **Hines '65, Tea For Two, Earl Hines At Home, Hines Does Hoagy, Dinah, Tour De Force** and **Earl Hines Plays Duke Ellington,** each containing substantial quantities of awesome piano-playing.

Just how tremendous Hines remains as a live performer can be gauged by the keyboard pyrotechnics he produced throughout his appearance, unaccompanied, at the 1974 Montreux Jazz Festival **(West Side Story)**, nowhere better illustrated than during a torrid **Why Do I Love You?**

Apart from a tiresome gimmick of sustaining a right-hand tremolo for four or five minutes during concert performances, as with **Don't Get Around Much Anymore (West Side Story),** Fatha Hines remained the greatest living jazz pianist and possibly, overall, the greatest pianist in the entire history of jazz until his death in Oakland, California, on April 22, 1983, aged 77.

Recordings:
Louis Armstrong, The Louis Armstrong Legend (World Records)
Louis Armstrong, V.S.O.P. (Very Special Old Phonography, 1928-1930), Vols 5 & 6 (CBS—France)
Louis Armstrong/Earl Hines, Armstrong & Hines (Smithsonian Collection/—)
Jimmie Noone & Earl Hines At The Apex Club, Vol 1 (1928) (MCA—Germany)
Earl 'Fatha' Hines (Columbia/Philips)
The Young Earl Hines (RCA Victor—France)
The Indispensable Earl Hines, Vols 1-3 (RCA Victor—France)
Hines Rhythm (Epic/—)
South Side Swing (Decca) Swinging In Chicago (Coral)
Earl Hines, Fire Works (RCA Victor—France)
Earl Hines, RCA Masters (RCA Victor—France)
Earl Hines Orchestra (1) (Vogue) (EP)
Earl Hines Orchestra (2) (Vogue) (EP)
Louis Armstrong, Vols 2, 3 (RCA Victor—France)
Louis Armstrong, Satchmo At Symphony Hall (Decca/Coral)
The Father Jumps: Earl Hines & His Orchestra Featuring Billy Eckstine (1940-1942) (Bandstand)
Earl Hines, Fatha Blows Best (Decca/—)
Earl Hines/Johnny Hodges, Stride Right (Verve/Verve)
Earl Hines/Jimmy Rushing (Master Jazz Recordings/World Record Club)
Earl Hines, Spontaneous Explorations (Contact/Stateside)
Earl Hines, Once Upon A Time (Impulse/Impulse)
Earl Hines, A Monday Date: 1928 (Milestone)
Earl Hines/Muggsy Spanier, Tin Roof Blues (Vogue/Pye)
Earl Hines, Quintessential Recording Sessions (Chiaroscuro/—)
Earl Hines, Quintessential Continued (Chiaroscuro/—)
Earl Hines, Hines '65 (Master Jazz Recordings/ World Record Club)
Earl Hines At Home (Delmark)
Earl Hines, Hines Does Hoagy (Audiophile/—)
Earl Hines, Tea For Two (Black Lion/Black Lion)
Earl Hines Plays Duke Ellington (Master Jazz Recordings/Parlophone)
Earl Hines, West Side Story (Black Lion/Black Lion)
Earl Hines, Dinah (RCA Victor—France)
Earl Hines Plays George Gershwin (Festival—France)
Earl Hines/Maxine Sullivan, Live At The Overseas Press Club (Chiaroscuro/—)
Earl Hines, My Tribute To Louis (Audiophile/—)
The Incomparable Earl Hines (Fantasy/—)
Earl Hines/Budd Johnson, The Dirty Old Men (Black & White—France)
Earl Hines, Hits He Missed (Real Time/—)
Fatha (Columbia/CBS)

Once Upon A Time (courtesy Impulse). The inimitable Earl Hines tells a story and makes exceptional music with Hodges, Pee Wee, Gonsalves & Co.

Jon Hiseman

Above: Drummer Jon Hiseman—at the forefront of jazz-rock fusion since the 1970s. Since '79, he has contributed to groups led by his wife, Barbara Thompson.

One of Britain's most inventive and dynamic percussionists, the versatile Jon Hiseman has been at the forefront of jazz-rock fusion in the UK and, indeed, in Europe since the 1970s.

Born in Woolwich on June 21, 1944, Hiseman studied piano and violin as a child but became intensely interested in percussion in his early teens. His first performances were on timpani with a small orchestra but, by 18, he was working semi-professionally on the London scene with R&B and jazz groups. He gained early experience in a jazz-based group which included keyboardist Dave Greenslade and bassist Tony Reeves and worked with the Don Rendell Quintet (alongside Graham Bond). He turned professional in '66, replacing Ginger Baker in Bond's newly formed Graham Bond Organization, followed by stints with Georgie Fame, John Mayall and the New Jazz Orchestra.

From '69-'78 he led three pioneering British blues-based rock groups — Colosseum, Tempest and Colosseum II. Since '79 he has been a member of Paraphernalia and in '75 (with his wife, multi-reeds-player Barbara Thompson) was a founder-member of the United Jazz + Rock Ensemble, the European-based band known as the 'Band of Band Leaders'.

Hiseman's first solo album, **A Night In The Sun** (an LP full of musicality and vitality in the company of top Brazilian musicians) was recorded in Rio de Janeiro in '82. He has also produced and performed on Paraphernalia's **Mother Earth** and **Pure Fantasy,** recorded in the Hiseman-Thompson studio and released on their own record label.

Together with Thompson, vocalist-keyboardist Rod Argent and bassist John Mole, Hiseman played on **Ghosts** ('82). This line-up, plus Clem Clempson (guitarist with the original Colosseum), forms the nucleus of **Shadowshow** ('84).

Hiseman's direct and dynamic drumming technique is frequently in demand by composers such as Andrew Lloyd Webber and John Dankworth. Hiseman's distinctive style can also be heard on recordings with Mike Taylor **(Pendulum, Trio)**, Jack Bruce **(Things We Like)**, Howard Riley **(Angle)** and the New Jazz Orchestra **(Western Reunion, Le Déjeuner Sur L'Herbe)**.

Albums:
Colosseum, Those Who Are About To Die Salute You (Morituri Te Salutant) (Fontana/Fontana)
Colosseum, Valentyne Suite (—/Vertigo-Bronze)
Colosseum, Daughter Of Time (—/Vertigo-Bronze)
Colosseum, Colosseum Live (—/Bronze)
Tempest, Tempest (—/Bronze)
Tempest, Living In Fear (—/Bronze)
Colosseum II, Strange New Flesh (—/Bronze)
Colosseum II, Electric Savage (MCA/MCA)
Colosseum II, Wardance (MCA/MCA)
United Jazz + Rock Ensemble, Live Opus Sechs (—/Mood—Germany)
10 Years—The United Jazz + Rock Ensemble (6 LP box set) (—/Mood—Germany)
Paraphernalia, Mother Earth (—/TM Records)
Paraphernalia, Pure Fantasy (—/TM Records)
A Night In The Sun (—/Kuckuck)
Barbara Thompson, Lady Saxophone (—/TM Records)

Art Hodes

Chicagoan pianist Art Hodes was a member of 'The White School' who remained faithful to the tenets of New Orleans, playing an exuberant brand of Dixieland music well into the 1940s.

Influenced by Jelly Roll Morton, Hodes plays fine blues piano, though his most typical work is to be found away from the solo spotlight as a group player. Along with trumpeter Max Kaminsky, and various personnel, Rod Cless, Mezz Mezzrow, Vic Dickenson, Edmond Hall, Omer Simeon and Danny Alvin, Hodes led several excellent sessions for Blue Note between 1944 and 1945.

Albums:
Original Blue Note Jazz, Vol 1 (Blue Note/Blue Note)

The Funky Piano Of Art Hodes
(Blue Note/Blue Note)
Sittin' In (Blue Note/Blue Note)
Sidney Bechet (Blue Note/Blue Note)
South Side Memories (Sackville/—)

Jazz Classics—The Funky Piano Of Art Hodes (courtesy Blue Note).

Johnny Hodges

One of jazz's greatest solo instrumentalists, and without question one of the three most important alto saxophonists in the history of the music, John Cornelius 'Rabbit' Hodges (born Cambridge, Massachusetts, 1906) was a supreme individualist whose playing (especially his vibrato) was reminiscent only of Sidney Bechet, his sole admitted influence. (Not surprisingly, Hodges' involvement with the soprano sax, an instrument he played during the 1930s, was an even more perfect corollary to Bechet.)

Hodges was probably the greatest of the many extraordinarily gifted soloists to grace the ranks of the Duke Ellington Orchestra. Although he had previously played with several different bands, including shortish spells with Willie 'The Lion' Smith, Chick Webb, and Luckey Roberts, it was not until Hodges joined Ellington, in May 1928, that he found the most ravishing saxophone tone to be heard thus far in the jazz world.

Hodges, who had studied for a time with his idol, Bechet, (he is also reported to have actually played live dates with Bechet, in 1925) contributed an unbelievably large number of classic alto sax solos to the Ellington discography. His matchless tone, together with powerful yet always subtle approach to the rhythmic aspect of his art, and a passionate though never histrionic way of conveying emotion, soon established him as the major voice on his premier instrument. A situation which lasted until the emergence of the genius of Charlie Parker at the beginning of 1940s, and despite periodic challenges from Benny Carter, Pete Brown and Willie Smith.

During the last period of his association with Ellington, 1955-70, Hodges often affected a seemingly total disinterest in his solos during concert performances; and his recordings with the band during this period tended to range from absolutely brilliant **(The Far East Suite, Duke Ellington's 70th Birthday Concert** and **... And His Mother Called Him Bill)** to the merely average. In many cases, the best work Hodges recorded during latter part of his career took place within the context of the kind of smallgroup settings that had further helped him sustain his reputation during late-1930s/early-1940s **(Hodge Podge** and **The Works Of Duke, Vols 12, 16/17)**.

Whatever the company, Hodges — like all truly great performers — inevitably stood out. Thus he contributed handsomely to sessions involving Billie Holiday **(The Golden Years, Vol 2** and **The Original Recordings)**; Teddy Wilson **(The Teddy Wilson** and **Teddy Wilson & His All Stars)**; Earl Hines **(Stride Right)**; Shelly Manne **(Shelly Manne & Co.)** and Gerry Mulligan **(Gerry Mulligan Meets The Sax Giants, Vols 1-3)**. Of even more importance—and achieving even greater artistic and musical success—was a rare session with Billy Strayhorn as leader **(Cue For Saxophone)**. Although, for contractual reasons, Hodges masqueraded under the pseudonym of 'Cue Porter', there was no chance of mistaking his glorious sound. Of special interest was a highly memorable record date **(The Charlie Parker Sides/The Parker Jam Session)** wherein Hodges locked altos with his two major rivals, Parker and Carter. Major triumph of organization for producer Norman Granz

Granz put together another remarkable studio session, this one involving Hodges, his then boss Ellington at the piano, Harry Edison trumpet, and a rhythm section which included Jo Jones. Hodges' contributions were little short of magnificent — glorious, soaring alto which breathed freshness and vitality into fine old warhorses such as **Loveless Love, Weary Blues, Wabash Blues** and **Beale Street Blues (Blues Summit/Back To Back — Side By Side)**.

Hodges' equally beguiling work on soprano sax is **Good Gal Blues, Jeep's Blues, Empty Ballroom Blues, Wanderlust** (all **Hodge Podge); Harmony In Harlem (The Ellington Era, Vol 1); Dear Old Southland (The Works Of Duke, Vol 8); Live & Love Tonight (The Works of Duke, Vol 9)** and also **Blue Goose (The Works Of Duke, Vol 10)**.

Apart from brief spells away from Ellington band during the last portion of his career, Hodges' only lengthy absence was between 1951-55 when he left to form own band. Personnel included, at various times, Lawrence Brown (who left Ellington same time as Hodges, and Sonny Greer, Ellington's drummer), Emmett Berry, and, for a while, a youthful John Coltrane **(The Jeep Is Jumpin')**.

John Cornelius Hodges was indeed one of jazz's great irreplaceables, a fact which became stark reality when he died suddenly, following a heart attack, in May 1970.

Albums:

Duke Ellington, The Beginning (1926-1928) (Decca/MCA—Germany)
Duke Ellington, Hot In Harlem (1928-1929) (Decca/MCA—Germany)
Duke Ellington, Rockin' In Rhythm (1929-1931) (Decca/MCA—Germany)
Duke Ellington, The Works Of Duke Ellington, Vols 2-18 (RCA Victor—France)
The Complete Duke Ellington, Vols 1-7 (CBS—France)
Duke Ellington, In A Mellotone (RCA Victor/RCA Victor—France)
Duke Ellington, Black, Brown & Beige (Ariston—Italy)
Duke Ellington, Such Sweet Thunder (Columbia/CBS—Realm)
Duke Ellington, Ellington At Newport (Columbia)
Duke Ellington, The Far East Suite (RCA Victor/RCA Victor)
Duke Ellington, ... And His Mother Called Him Bill (RCA Victor/RCA Victor)
Duke Ellington's 70th Birthday Concert (Solid State/United Artists)
Duke Ellington, Souvenirs (Reprise)
Johnny Hodges, Hodge Podge (CBS—Realm)
Johnny Hodges, Ellingtonia '56 (Norgran/Columbia—Clef)
Johnny Hodges, Duke's In Bed (Verve)/ Johnny Hodges & The Ellington All Stars (Columbia—Clef)
Johnny Hodges & The Ellington All Stars (—/Verve)
Johnny Hodges (Verve/—)
Everybody Knows Johnny Hodges (Impulse/Impulse)
Earl Hines/Johnny Hodges, Stride Right (Verve/Verve)
Billy Strayhorn, Cue For Saxophone (Master Jazz Recordings/Vocalion)
Billie Holiday, The Golden Years, Vol 2 (Columbia/CBS)
Billie Holiday: The Original Recordings (Columbia/CBS)
Gerry Mulligan Meets The Sax Giants, Vols 1-3 (—/Verve)
The Teddy Wilson (CBS/Sony—Japan)
Teddy Wilson & His All-Stars (Columbia/CBS)
Johnny Hodges, The Jeep Is Jumpin' (—/Verve)

Below: John Cornelius 'Rabbit' Hodges, peerless altoist and arguably the finest soloist from the ranks of Ellingtonia of any era.

Jay Hoggard

Since the late '70s, Jay Hoggard has become one of the most popular of the new generation of vibes-players. Hoggard's style deftly brings together influences from all corners of the world and all spheres of the music.

Born in Washington, DC, on September 28, 1954, Hoggard was raised in Mount Vernon, New York. He studied piano from age 4, taking up alto sax at 10 and vibes at 16. While majoring in ethnomusicology at Wesleyan University in Connecticut, Hoggard received instruction, as well as inspiration, from such luminaries as Sam Rivers, Jimmy Garrison and Clifford Thornton (it was Thornton who gave Hoggard his first professional gigs). In '74, Hoggard received a grant to travel to Tanzania to study East African xylophone music — an experience which was greatly to influence his future direction as a composer and performer.

A year of teaching followed graduation and in '77 he returned to New York. In a short time he was to work with some of America's most vital new voices of the music — Chico Freeman **(Kings Of Mali; No Time Left; Peaceful Heart, Gentle Spirit)**, Anthony Davis **(Song For The Old World)**, Sam Rivers, Michael Gregory Jackson **(Gifts)**, Cecil Taylor, the Art Ensemble of Chicago, Ahmed Abdullah **(Life's Force)**, Muhal Richard Abrams and Henry Threadgill, as well as poets Ntozake Shange, Alexis De Veaux and Amiri Baraka.

Since '79, Hoggard has led his own groups **(Solo Vibraphone; Days Like These; Mystic Winds, Tropic Breezes)**, while a European tour in '80 — in duo with pianist Anthony Davis — produced the well-received **Under The Double Moon**. Hoggard's **Rain Forest** album of '81, drawing on popular African, Caribbean, Latin and Afro-American influences, brought him considerable commercial recognition internationally.

Albums:

Solo Vibraphone (India Navigation/—)
Days Like These (Arista-GRP/Arista-GRP)
Jay Hoggard-Anthony Davis, Under The Double Moon (—/MPS—Germany)
Rain Forest (Contemporary/Contemporary)
Mystic Winds, Tropic Breezes (India Navigation/—)
Chico Freeman, The Search (India Navigation/—)

Vibist Jay Hoggard, Rain Forest (courtesy Contemporary).

Billie Holiday

The Voice Of Jazz proclaims the title of a series of her recordings. For Billie Holiday (born Baltimore, Maryland, 1915) *was* (and most certainly on record remains) the voice of jazz. Apart from Louis Armstrong, and with the possible exception of Sarah Vaughan, there never has been a jazz vocalist whose unique abilities have approached those of Billie Holiday. Her timing, for example, was as impeccable as the finest jazz instrumental players (many of whom she worked with during her career). She phrased in a definitely instrumental fashion, although her instrumental-like, horn-influenced singing never was less than music, distorting neither melodic line nor interfering with the matchless way in which she lived a lyric. The feeling she communicated through a song, whether live or on record, could be devastating.

At the time when Billie's talent was emerging —during early 1930s — it was fashionable often for black singers to sound white, to appeal to a wider audience. Billie Holiday always was a black singer; curiously, she ended up probably appealing more to a white audience. Holiday was not a blues singer per se, using comparatively few actual blues items in her repertoire. Yet everything she sang was tinged with a blues feel — even pop banalities (viz **These 'N' That 'N' Those, Your Mother's Son-In-Law, Yankee Doodle Never Went To Town** and **Under A Jungle Moon**).

Born of unmarried teenage parents, Sadie Fagan and Clarence Holiday, the latter guitarist and banjoist who worked with Fletcher Henderson, McKinney's Cotton Pickers, etc; was raped at 10, and went into prostitution a couple of years later. Apart from experiencing more than a fair share of racialist problems, she later sought solace in alcohol, marijuana, then finally, heroin. In fact, she died in hospital, under police guard, where she was incarcerated on what now seems to have been a trumped-up charge of narcotics possession.

After moving from Baltimore to New York with her mother in 1929, commenced singing engagements in Harlem clubs. At one of these, was heard by John Hammond who tried, unsuccessfully, to persuade Benny Goodman to sign her as singer with his band. Goodman did play at her initial record dates (in November, December '33), sessions that produced just two Holiday items; **Your Mother's Son-In-Law** and **Riffin' The Scotch (The Billie Holiday Story, Vol 1)**. Even at this time it was obvious that a teenage Billie Holiday had both style and sound all her own, even though singing itself was raw and lacked later confidence.

In between her début record dates and the next occasion she was to appear inside a studio came an unexpected chance to appear, briefly, in film featuring Duke Ellington Orchestra: *Symphony In Black*. She sang **Big City Blues (Saddest Tale)** with astonishing maturity, looking stunningly beautiful. Next recording date, organized by pianist Teddy Wilson (for several years he became Holiday's A&R man, bandleader, arranger) took place in July 1935. Session also involved Roy Eldridge, Ben Webster. Recordings from this date finally established her reputation amongst jazz aficionados. Both singing and instrumental work were given equal prominence, a procedure that was to continue until the 1940s.

Billie Holiday recording sessions became almost legendary events during 1930s, involving always the cream of musicians of the day, especially those featured with bands of Ellington, Fletcher Henderson, Benny Goodman, Chick Webb, John Kirby and Count Basie. It was in company with various members of latter band that Billie Holiday made many of the sides which rank with her very best — musicians like Freddie Green, Walter Page, Jo Jones, and of even more importance, Buck Clayton and Lester Young. With Young, she established almost unbelievable rapport, the tenorist providing sublime intros, obbligatos, as well as solos of superlative quality, each complementing, enhancing vocal lines to perfection.

Between 1937-40, typical examples of the kind of music produced by this unsurpassed partnership can be found on tracks like **This Year's Kisses, Why Was I Born?, I Must Have That Man, Mean To Me, Fooling Myself, Easy Living, Me, Myself & I, A Sailboat In The Moonlight** (all **The Lester Young Story, Vol 1**); **He's Funny That Way, My First Impression Of You, Now They Call It Swing** (all **The Golden Years, Vol 2**); **Getting Some Fun Out Of Life, If Dreams Come True, On The Sentimental Side, When A Woman Loves A Man** (all **The Golden Years, Vol 1**). And those items cover just one year: 1937. Other Holiday-Young masterpieces include: **Back In Your Own Backyard, The Very Thought Of You (The Billie Holiday Story, Vol 1); The Man I Love, All Of Me (The Original Recordings)**.

Billie Holiday's role as singer with big bands was limited, although she did work with Count Basie for just over a year (1937-38). Due to contractual reasons, she never did get a chance to record with Basie, although three fine airshot performances of the singer in this setting **Swing! Brother, Swing!, They Can't Take That Away From Me** (both datelined 30/6/37), and **I Can't Get Started** (3/11/37) subsequently have come to light, courtesy John Hammond **(Billie Holiday, Vol 2)**. Billie also worked with Artie Shaw for nine months (1938). Again, her opportunity to record was negated by her Brunswick contract. She made just one side, **Any Old Time**, with Shaw **(Concerto For Clarinet)** but originally this was withdrawn because of objections by the label to which she was signed.

She broadcast — apparently once only — with Benny Goodman band in 1939; **I Cried For You (BG. His Stars & His Guests)** certainly was a superior example of her rhythmic powers.

For the rest of her career, she was usually to be found in small-combo setting—the kind of situation in which invariably she was to be found at her best—although she did make isolated bigband appearances as, for instance, with Duke Ellington **(Concert At Carnegie Hall)**. After leaving Shaw, the Holiday solo career blossomed when she became resident singer at New York's Café Society, accompanied by Frankie Newton's orchestra. During same year, together with Newton and band, recorded for Milt Gabler's Commodore label, a session that produced three numbers which forever thereafter were to be identified with Billie Holiday alone; the macabre **Strange Fruit** (with lyric by poet Lewis Allan), terrifyingly sad **Yesterday's**, and a magnificent (and rare) blues performance and composition called **Fine & Mellow** (written by Holiday) **(Strange Fruit/ The Commodore Years)**. From around that time, Billie Holiday's recordings, whilst still featuring solos and obbligatos from top jazzmen like Eldridge and Young, tended to become more arranged, less spontaneous.

But the 1940s arrived, with Billie Holiday singing as well as (sometimes even better than) before. There were more superb vocals to be found within recordings of **Georgia On My Mind, Body & Soul, Solitude, Jim** and **God Bless The Child** (all **God Bless The Child**); last-named the most familiar of Billie Holiday's own lyrics and probably the best. There was also the suicidal **Gloomy Sunday (The Golden Years, Vol 1)** sung inimitably by Holiday. Further sessions with Commodore followed the termination of her association with Vocalion label.

By mid-1940s, she had moved on to Decca where strings, reeds, et al, were utilized on her records, presumably to make her art accessible to a wider audience. Very first Decca title — a poignant version of **Lover Man** (written by jazz pianist-organist Ram Ramirez) — became another of her most famous songs. **Don't Explain**, from the third session, was blessed with another sensitive Holiday lyric. **Porgy**, from two years later, received definitive reading; **Ain't Nobody's Business** (1949) was a rare, but satisfying, blues performance (all Decca titles mentioned—**The Billie Holiday Story**).

Already, though, there were tell-tale signs of ennui creeping into Billie Holiday's work, and by 1950s it was obvious too that her personal excesses were beginning to take their toll of what writer-broadcaster Charles Fox once called 'a certain neutrality of timbre'. During the last period of her lifetime, she recorded extensively for various Norman Granz-owned labels **(The Voice Of Jazz, Vols 1-10)**. Singing ranged from very good to pitifully inadequate, the latter exemplified in two live recordings, from 1946 **(Vol 1)** and 1957 **(Vol 9)**. But there were times, especially when she was accompanied by old friends like Ben Webster, Harry Edison, Benny Carter, Charlie Shavers, and younger musicians like Oscar Peterson, Barney Kessel, and Tony Scott, when temporarily she all but scaled previous peaks of performance.

One of the comparatively few occasions (on record at least) when she recaptured some of the magic of the past occurred during a four-session record project which took place in January 1957 **(Vols 7-9)**. With admirable assistance from Edison, Webster, Kessel et al she imbued standard songs like **Just One Of Those Things, Day In, Day Out, Comes Love**, and **One For My Baby**, with a depth and meaning they have not received, before or since.

Not surprisingly, her in-person appearances tended to become even more erratic than her records. Again, though, there were those times when the adrenalin flowed as of old — or almost. Typical of the happier occasions are **The Lady Lives, Radio & TV Broadcasts, Vol 2, 1953-1956** and **The Real Lady Sings The Blues**. There is more fine singing to be found from recordings emanating from a season at Storyville Club, Boston, in 1951 **(Gallant Lady** and **Billie Holiday)**, the latter having additional interest with the presence of Stan Getz, a disciple of Billie's erstwhile partner, Lester Young.

Appeared on special CBS/TV programme, *The World of Jazz*, in 1957, singing a painful, moving version of **Fine & Mellow (Billie Holiday, Vol 1)** accompanied by a truly all-star band including Young, Coleman Hawkins, Eldridge, Gerry Mulligan and Vic Dickenson. Holiday's penultimate studio album **Lady In Satin** harrowingly encapsulates the last tragic years of her life, with all its inherent bitterness and despair. By which time (1958), her voice was but a rasping parody of her peak years; but the mood and depth she sustains throughout (never better illustrated than on the prophetic **For All We Know)** rarely, if ever, has been surpassed — even by Billie Holiday herself.

Billie Holiday, who previously had served prison sentence for a narcotics offence (1948), and had been acquitted on a similar charge (also '48), died at Metropolitan Hospital, New York City, July 1959, where she was detained, prior to her being charged with possession of drugs.

During her career she appeared in the following movies: *Symphony In Black* (1935), *New Orleans* (1947 — with Louis Armstrong All Stars, Woody Herman Orchestra), plus superior film short with Count Basie Sextet (1950) *(Hot Jazz On Film, Vol 2)*.

Winner of various readers'/critics' jazz polls, she wrote (in collaboration with William Dufty) *Lady Sings The Blues*, her autobiography. *Billie's Blues*, biography by John Chilton, has been published in more recent times (1975), and there is an illuminating chapter on the singer in Ralph J. Gleason's *Celebrating the Duke & Louis, Bessie, Billie, Bird, Carmen, Miles, Dizzy & Other Heroes* (1975). Despite fine acting-singing performance by Diana Ross, the 1973 movie, *Lady Sings The Blues*, purporting to be based on Billie Holiday's life story, was nothing more than a travesty. A more reliable — not to say more realistic — film account of Billie Holiday's life, with its emphasis on the immeasurable value of her work, can be found in John Jeremy's '85 documentary *The Long Night of Lady Day*.

In April '85, Baltimore — Billie Holiday's hometown — belatedly honored her with the unveiling of an 8 foot-plus high statue of Lady Day, on the corner of Pennsylvania and Lafayette Avenues.

As long ago as '81, jazz critic — and long-time friend of Billie Holiday — Leonard Feather started a campaign to raise money so a 'Billie Holiday' star could be placed on Hollywood's 'Walk of Fame'. Feather and Ron Berinstein (owner of the Vine Street Bar & Grill) organized a fund-raising event. Among those artists who paid tribute to Holiday that memorable night were Jimmy Rowles and daughter Stacey, Ella

Below: The immortal Billie Holiday, seen here with Jimmy Davis, co-composer of the classic Lover Man. Billie was the most gifted of all jazz vocalists.

Mae Morse, Carmen McRae, Marlena Shaw, Jimmy Witherspoon, Gerald Wiggins' trio, Herb Ellis, Dick Berk, Lorraine Feather, Charlotte Crossley, Artie Shaw, Johnny Ray, Dolly Dawn, Ernie Andrews, Dave Frishberg, Maxine Andrews, Margie Evans, Ruth Price and Bill Henderson, with Henry Mancini offering to make up the short-fall on the $3000 needed. The installation of the Billie Holiday star finally took place on April 7, 1986 (it would have been her 71st birthday) — as Leonard Feather said, better late than never.

Billie Holiday, The Golden Years (courtesy CBS).

Albums:
The Billie Holiday Story, Vol 1 (Columbia/CBS)
Billie Holiday, God Bless The Child (Columbia/CBS)
Billie Holiday: The Original Recordings (Columbia/CBS)
Billie Holiday, The Golden Years, Vols 1, 2 (Columbia/CBS)
Billie Holiday, Strange Fruit (Atlantic)/ The 'Commodore' Days (Ace of Hearts)
Billie Holiday, The Real Lady Sings The Blues (—/Boulevard)
The Billie Holiday Story (Decca/MCA—Germany)
The 'Real' Lady Sings The Blues (—/Coral)
Billie Holiday, Vols 1-3 (—/Saga)
Billie Holiday, Gallant Lady (Monmouth—Evergreen/One-Up)
Various (Including Billie Holiday), The First Esquire Concert, Vol 1 (—/Saga)
The Teddy Wilson (CBS/Sony—Japan)
Teddy Wilson & His All Stars (Columbia/CBS)
The Lester Young Story, Vols 1-3 (Columbia/CBS)
Billie Holiday, The Voice Of Jazz, Vols 1-10 (—/Verve)
Various (Including Billie Holiday), Jazz At The Philharmonic: The Historic Recordings (Verve/—)
Billie Holiday, The First Verve Sessions (Verve/—)
Billie Holiday, Lady In Satin (Columbia/CBS—Realm)
Artie Shaw, Concerto For Clarinet (RCA Victor/RCA Victor)
Benny Goodman, BG, His Stars & His Guests (Queen Disc—Italy)
Various (Including Billie Holiday), Concert At Carnegie Hall (DJM)
For A Lady Named Billie (Giants of Jazz)
The Essential Billie Holiday, Carnegie Hall Concert (Verve/Verve)
Lady Day (Verve/Verve)
The Billie Holiday Song Book (Verve/Verve)

Dave Holland

Whether playing bass or cello, Britain's Dave Holland stands out as one of the most advanced and versatile musicians in contemporary music. His wealth of experience ranges from British bebop and the avant-garde to Miles Davis' far-reaching, late '60s-early '70s electric experiments.

Born in Wolverhampton in 1948, Holland taught himself the barest essentials of guitar-playing at age 10, then switched to electric bass, moving to the upright model at 15. Within a couple of years, Holland was working regularly in London with such British stalwarts as John Surman, Tubby Hayes, Ronnie Scott and South Africa's Chris McGregor and, by the late '60s, had joined drummer John Stevens in the pioneering freedoms of the Spontaneous Music Ensemble.

Holland made an international breakthrough in '68 when Miles Davis heard him playing at Ronnie Scott's Club in London. He subsequently joined Miles' band in the States (contributing to **In A Silent Way, Filles De Kilimanjaro, Bitches Brew, Miles At Fillmore).** Leaving Miles, he joined Chick Corea's acoustic trio including drummer Barry Altschul **(The Song of Singing, A.R.C.).** With the addition of multi-reeds-player Anthony Braxton, the band evolved into the influential Circle **(Paris Concert).** When Circle split up, Altschul and Braxton, plus Sam Rivers, joined Holland for his quartet recording of **Conference Of The Birds.** The Holland-Rivers association was renewed later in Rivers' avant-garde trio **(Contrasts).**

Holland made his first solo-bass album in '77—**Emerald Tears;** another lone effort, the '83 album **Life Cycle,** finds Holland in mesmerizing form on cello—an extraordinary solo *tour de force*.

Dave Holland's multi-faceted bass-playing has been heard with a diversity of artists, notably on ECM — with Barre Phillips (the highly acclaimed duo album **Music From Two Basses),** in duo with Derek Bailey **(Improvisations For Cello And Guitar),** Collin Walcott **(Cloud Dance),** Tomasz Stanko **(Balladyna),** Kenny Wheeler **(Deer Wan, Gnu High),** as part of the Gateway Trio with drummer Jack De Johnette and guitarist John Abercrombie **(Gateway, Gateway 2)** and with George Adams **(Sound Suggestions).** Holland's inspirational bass is also applied with good effect to Carla Bley's enduring **Tropic Appetites.**

In the mid-'80s, Holland toured and recorded with his own quintet (trumpeter Kenny Wheeler, trombonist Julian Priester, saxophonist Steve Coleman and drummer Marvin 'Smitty' Smith) resulting in the lively, improvisational **Seeds Of Time.** Well towards the '90s, the multi-dimensional Dave Holland promises to continue as one of Britain's most valuable exports.

Albums:
Miles Davis, Bitches Brew (Columbia/CBS)
Barre Phillips-Dave Holland, Music From Two Basses (ECM/ECM)
Dave Holland-Derek Bailey, Improvisations For Cello and Guitar (ECM/ECM)
Circle, Paris Concert (ECM/ECM)
Emerald Tears (ECM/ECM)
Conference Of The Birds (ECM/ECM)
Jumpin' In (ECM/ECM)
Life Cycle (ECM/ECM)
Kenny Wheeler, Double, Double You (ECM/ECM)
Seeds Of Time (ECM/ECM)

Below: British bass-player Dave Holland—also a brilliant cellist. His solo album Life Cycle of 1983 finds him in mesmerizing form on cello.

John Lee Hooker

Bluesman John Lee Hooker was born in Clarksdale, Mississippi in 1917, and in common with most post-war blues recording artists, soon learned to adapt to the amplified urban sound. Like most Delta bluesmen, Hooker's city style is merely an intensification of the drones, moans, repetitions and raw power of the original.

Based in Detroit, he began recording in 1948 and sold phenomenally well in the R&B market, **Boogie Chillen'** selling a million copies. His voice has a menacing weight, heavy and bruising, the lyrics often violent and obsessive. The chopping of word-endings carries a primitive dramatic charge which is hammered home by the guitar in rhythmic unison. Hooker's guitar technique is functional, making the most of a rudimentary stock of devices.

A more restricted artist than Lightnin' Hopkins, Hooker nevertheless triumphs in terms of impact. Moving between R&B and the more purist blues, his main audience today is the generation of young whites who first heard the blues secondhand from the Rolling Stones.

Hooker's informal appearance in John Landis' *The Blues Brothers* ('80) is just one of that film's many memorable moments. In the '80s, many of Hooker's enduring earlier sides, recorded for the American Vee-Jay label, have enjoyed a massive re-issue program courtesy of Britain's Charly Records.

Albums:
The Blues (Crown/—)
Slim's Stomp (—/Polydor—Juke Blues)
House Of The Blues (Chess/Marble Arch)
How Long Blues (Riverside/Fontana)
I Want To Shout The Blues (Vee-Jay/Stateside)
Don't Turn Me From Your Door/Drifting Blues (Atco/Atlantic)
This Is Hip (—/Charly)
Everybody Rockin' (—/Charly)
Moanin' The Blues (—/Charly)
Solid Sender (—/Charly)

Elmo Hope

Born 1923, Hope was dismissed at the outset as a Bud Powell imitator, though in fact his piano style developed a quirky, elusive quality that was all his own. His move to the West Coast shunted his career up the siding of public disinterest: back East, fashion decreed, was where the vigor and pace-setting occurred. Hope had proved himself in a hard bop blowing context **(All Star Session)** with John Coltrane and Hank Mobley, though the trio section of the album gives him more room to show the startling elasticity of his concept. Notes are held until their edges puddle like spilled ink; bright treble runs hunch and buckle into dissonance. Scurry, tremolo, blur — time seems to stretch at his bidding. The definitive trio album is **Elmo Hope** with the perfect West Coast drummer, Frank Butler, whose inventiveness matches his own. Other sympathetic interpreters of his compositions are tenorist Harold Land **(The Fox)** and the Curtis Counce Quintet **(Exploring The Future),** both albums fueled by Butler. There is a quiet, off-centre lyricism in Elmo Hope's work **(Barfly, Eejah, Eyes So Beautiful)** that is haunting.

Albums:
The All-Star Sessions (Milestone/Milestone)
Elmo Hope (Contemporary/Vocalion)
Harold Land, The Fox (Contemporary/Boplicity)
Curtis Counce, Exploring The Future (Dooto/Boplicity)

Elmo Hope, Hope-Full (courtesy Riverside)—a rare album.

Sam 'Lightnin' Hopkins

Born 1912, near Houston, Texas, Lightnin' Hopkins was one of the last of the old country bluesmen. He gained early experience with Blind Lemon Jefferson and with his cousin, Texas Alexander, acquiring his nickname through a partnership with barrelhouse pianist Thunder Smith.

His first recordings from 1946 made an immediate impact, revealing a major artist. Much of his best and freshest work was done for Bill Quinn's now rare Gold Star label; the voice harsh and direct, the guitar accompaniment quirkily irregular.

A uniquely subjective performer, Hopkins was usually at his most expressive when dealing with episodes from his own life but also invested that universal feature of the blues tradition with his own sense of immediacy and drama.

A prolific recording artist, Hopkins' talents often were in danger of over-exposure, though the mid-'50s saw a slump in the country blues market in favor of Chicago blues bands. In 1959, he found acceptance among the folk audiences of the concert hall and campus. Hopkins died in 1981, just prior to making a European tour.

Albums:

Lightnin' Hopkins Strums The Blues (Score/—)
Lightnin' Hopkins Early Recordings (Arhoolie/Fontana)
Lightnin' Hopkins Sings The Blues (Time/Realm)
Lightnin' Hopkins Sings Dirty House Blues (Time/Realm)
Sam Lightnin' Hopkins (—/77)
Autobiography In Blues (Tradition/—)
Country Blues (Tradition/—)
The Roots Of Lightnin' Hopkins (Verve—Forecast/Verve—Folkways)
Lightnin' Strikes (—/Stateside)
Lightnin' Hopkins, The Legacy Of The Blues, Vol 12 (Sonet/Sonet)
Various, The Blues Legend (—/Time Wind—Germany)

Below: Sam 'Lightnin' Hopkins—unequalled as a gifted blues singer and guitarist. An immortal figure in post-war blues.

Freddie Hubbard

Trumpeter Freddie Hubbard was born in Indianapolis in 1938 into a musical family, arriving in New York in 1958.

He built up considerable experience with J. J. Johnson's Sextet, Max Roach, Sonny Rollins and Slide Hampton, before getting an ideal showcase with Art Blakey's Messengers in 1961. With Wayne Shorter sharing the frontline, this was arguably Blakey's finest unit since the Horace Silver days, and Hubbard's playing and writing were generously featured **(Mosaic, Free For All, Buhaina's Delight** and **Thermo).** Sounding completely poised over the leader's furious drumming, the young trumpeter often recalled the warmth, strength and prettiness of Clifford Brown, an early influence.

The same period saw Hubbard as a sideplayer on numerous Blue Note dates with Dexter Gordon, Herbie Hancock, Jackie McLean and Wayne Shorter, as well as heading his own series of albums **(Open Sesame, Ready For Freddie** and **Breaking Point).** His romantic, rich approach to the ballad is well illustrated on **I Wish I Knew (Goin' Up)** and **But Beautiful (Open Sesame),** while the schizophrenic approach, some chord change material, some free jazz, was exemplified on the album **Breaking Point.** Hubbard was flexible enough to play free with Ornette Coleman **(Free Jazz)** and with Dolphy **(Out To Lunch)** but his long, legato phrases and orthodox delivery made him better suited to an harmonic base. Vibrato, half-valve effects and growls played a very sparing role in his improvisation, which has a classic purity.

Having been hailed by some critics as the successor to Clifford Brown, and winning the *Downbeat* New Star Award in 1961, Hubbard's subsequent work for Atlantic began to show commercial tendencies. The début album **Backlash** features a couple of soul tracks, the title track and **The Return Of The Prodigal Son,** while a later release, **High Blues Pressure,** showed a backbeat and riff on **Can't Let Her Go** that was more than a nod towards Lee Morgan's hit, **The Sidewinder.** On the jazz credit side, the two tracks fueled by master drummer Louis Hayes, **True Colors** and **Fox B.P.,** are excellent examples of Hubbard's clean articulation at speed. The anti-war concept album composed by Ilhan Mimaroglu **(Sing Me A Song Of Songmy)** featured the lyrical, emotional trumpet.

In 1971 Hubbard signed to CTI, a label that had popularized the Creed Taylor A&R approach, and produced a series of big-selling albums **(Red Clay, Straight Life, First Light, Sky Dive** and **Polar Arc)** in which few chances are taken, or surprises sprung, and the emphasis is on the seamless and the glossy. He signed to Columbia, where his output moved from disco material, choirs, violins and a regular amplified thud of drums **(Windjammer)** to the regular jazz setting again **(Super Blue).**

In the late '70s, Freddie Hubbard recorded and toured with Herbie Hancock, Wayne Shorter, Tony Williams and Ron Carter in the much-vaunted VSOP group. Throughout the '80s, Hubbard has been a regular and reliable favorite on the international festival circuit — his blistering, live performances probably captured nowhere better than **Freddie Hubbard Live At The North Sea Festival, The Hague, Holland, 1980.** Apart from some remarkable playing throughout, this double album is memorable for his particularly hair-raising interpretation of John Coltrane's **Impressions.**

Hubbard's festival appearances have become regular and reliable crowd-pullers. In '86, he was a great attraction touring with pianist McCoy Tyner as a 'special guest' alongside Joe Henderson and follow trumpeter Woody Shaw.

Albums:

Art Blakey's Jazz Messengers: Mosaic (Blue Note/Blue Note)
Free For All (Blue Note/Blue Note)
Buhaina's Delight (Blue Note/Blue Note)
Thermo (Milestone/Milestone)
Open Sesame (Blue Note/Blue Note)
Ready For Freddie (Blue Note/Blue Note)
Breaking Point (Blue Note/Blue Note)
Goin' Up (Blue Note/Blue Note)
Here To Stay (Blue Note/Blue Note)
Backlash (Atlantic/Atlantic)
High Blues Pressure (Atlantic/Atlantic)
Sing Me A Song Of Songmy (Atlantic/Atlantic)
Red Clay (CTI/CTI)
Straight Life (CTI/CTI)
First Light (CTI/CTI)
Sky Dive (CTI/CTI)
Polar Arc (CTI/CTI)
Windjammer (Columbia/CBS)
Super Blue (Columbia/CBS)
VSOP, VSOP (Columbia/CBS)
VSOP, The Quintet/VSOP Live (Columbia/CBS)
Skagly (Columbia/CBS)
Freddie Hubbard Live At The North Sea Jazz Festival, The Hague, Holland, 1980 (Pablo/Pablo)
Ride Like The Wind (Elektra Musician/Elektra Musician)
Hub Cap (Blue Note/Blue Note)
Hub Tones (Blue Note/Blue Note)
Outpost (—/Enja—Germany)

Right: The kids are always Ready For Freddie. Trumpeter Freddie Hubbard has become a reliable attraction at any time on the festival circuit.

Bobby Hutcherson

Vibraphone player Bobby Hutcherson was born in Los Angeles in 1941, playing with Curtis Amy and Charles Lloyd on the West Coast before moving to New York in 1961.

Usually associated with the Blue Note school of experimentation — musicians like Andrew Hill, Anthony Williams, Herbie Hancock, fastidiously combining some of the freedoms of the New Thing within a basically harmonic outlook — Hutcherson's flexible approach to the vibraphone made him a useful voice in the more adventurous ensembles. His chiming, atmospheric sound graces the textures on many excellent sessions: Eric Dolphy's **Out To Lunch;** Andrew Hill's **Andrew** and **Judgement;** Anthony Williams' **Lifetime;** Jackie McLean's **One Step Beyond** and Grachan Moncur III's **Evolution.** A Newport performance by Archie Shepp, **Scag (New Thing At Newport),** has Hutcherson playing a mesmerizing vamp that exemplifies the prison of heroin addiction.

His own early Blue Note albums cover a wide variety of approaches from the delicacy of **Bouquet** to the expressionistic **The Omen (Happenings).** Using a larger group **(Components)** Hutcherson shares the composer's credits with Joe Chambers, his most compatible drummer. A funkier version of Ornette Coleman's **Una Muy Bonita** is to be found on what was arguably his last challenging album **(Stick-Up!).** His later work has been in line with Blue Note's more popular and commercial orientation **(Linger Lane** and **Natural Illusions),** though there were indications that he was returning to something like his old form **(The View From The Inside).**

Albums:

Dialogue (Blue Note/Blue Note)
Happenings (Blue Note/Blue Note)
Components (Blue Note/Blue Note)
San Francisco (Blue Note/Blue Note)
Stick-Up! (Blue Note/Blue Note)
The View From The Inside (Blue Note/Blue Note)
Solo/Quartet (Contemporary/Contemporary)
Total Eclipse (Blue Note/Blue Note)

Vibist Bobby Hutcherson, Components (courtesy Blue Note).

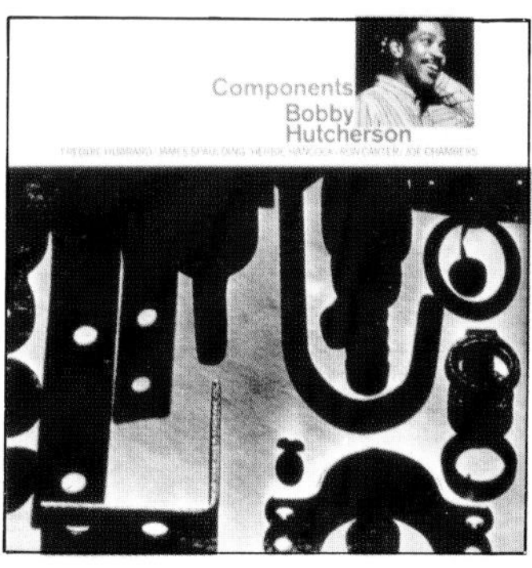

Abdullah Ibrahim

(Dollar Brand)

At a time when Afro-Americans were once more looking to Africa as their spiritual and cultural home, and the word 'Uhuru' began to appear on the album sleeves of post-'60s jazz, the genuine article erupted onto the music scene.

Pianist Abdullah Ibrahim (formerly known as Dollar Brand) is a South African Moslem for whom the function of music is both a celebration and a prayer; it has not lost its social role in Africa as it has in the West. A melange of influences runs through his playing — Ellington and Monk mix with mission hall hymns and zikr, the repetition of the holy attributes of Allah.

Born Adolph Johannes Brand in 1934, he started playing piano as a child, encouraged by his grandmother, a pianist in the local A.M.E. church. In '61, he formed the Jazz Epistles which included local luminaries Hugh Masekela and Kippy Moeketsi. In '62, Ibrahim and his wife, vocalist Sathima Bea Benjamin, left South Africa and its creativity-stifling apartheid system in search of new musical freedoms in Switzerland. Here, he was heard and recorded by Duke Ellington. In '65, he made his début in the United States, performing at the Newport Festival with Ellington's orchestra and subsequently solo at Carnegie Hall. Traveling the world as a soloist, and in trios, quartets and big bands, Ibrahim has written more than 700 pieces, ranging from folk songs to extended works for orchestra.

The early album **Anatomy Of A South African Village** covers a wider selection of material than is normally associated with him. Later releases **(African Piano, African Sketchbook** and **Ancient Africa)** convey the unique flavor of his playing in which originals like **Xaba** or **Bra Joe From Kilimanjaro** bed down into the mesmerizing fabric of his improvisation. His duo album with Argentinian tenorist, Leandro 'Gato' Barbieri **(Confluence)** has an overwhelming impact, a starkly religious atmosphere that is both measured and passionate.

A percussive, repetitive player, Ibrahim uses rumbling left-hand figures and a lot of pedal to sustain the dense, droning climate. It is almost as if he beats upon the piano to release its inner voicings, proceeding at the tempo of a stately cortège. His flute-playing, too, has a multi-vocal quality in which the piped notes mingle with the humming voice and the percussive poppings of his fingers on the holes.

Ibrahim's '83 album **Ekaya** is a South African word for 'home' and celebrates the spirit of his Africa, his roots.

Albums:

Anatomy Of A South African Village (—/Fontana)
The Dream (Black Lion/Black Lion)
Confluence/Hamba Khale (Black Lion/Affinity)
African Piano (Japo/Japo)
Ancient Africa (Japo/Japo)
African Portraits (Sackville/Sackville)
African Sketchbook (—/Enja)
African Space Programme (—/Enja)
Good News From Africa (—/Enja)
The Children Of Africa (—/Enja)
The Journey (—/Chiaroscuro)
Autobiography (—/Plainisphare)
Africa Tears And Laughter (—/Enja)
Echoes From Africa (—/Enja)
African Marketplace (Elektra/Elektra)
At Montreux (—/Enja)
South African Sunshine (—/Pläne)
Matsidiso (—/Pläne)
Duke's Memories (—/Enja)
African Dawn (—/Enja)
Zimbabwe (—/Enja)
Ekaya (—/Enja)

Abdullah Ibrahim (Dollar Brand), African Dawn (courtesy Enja).

The JCOA

see Carla Bley, Mike Mantler

Milt Jackson

see Modern Jazz Quartet

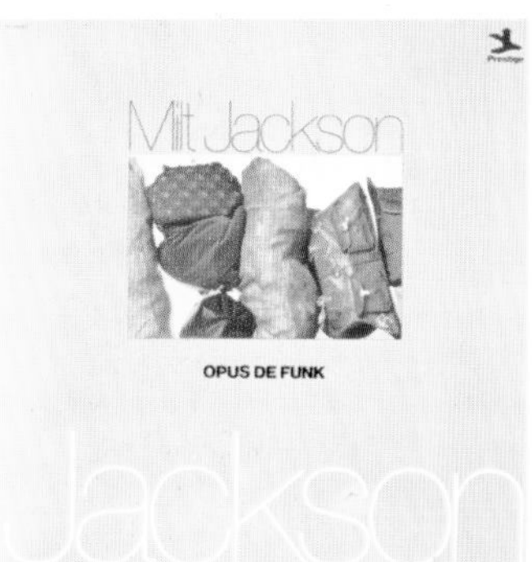

Milt Jackson, Opus De Funk (courtesy Prestige)—a classic.

Ronald Shannon Jackson

As leader of the Decoding Society—one of the most innovative groups to emerge in the early '80s — Ronald Shannon Jackson has been hailed as one of the most important drummers of the new age, making his name with Ornette Coleman and James Ulmer.

Born in Fort Worth, Texas, Jackson began playing piano at age 5, moving to drums at 8. Throughout high school, he played drums in the marching band and sang as lead tenor and soloist in the choir. Early experience was gained at 15, working with the local jazz and blues band James Clay and the Red Tops.

While at Lincoln University, Jackson performed with such luminaries as Lester Bowie, Julius Hemphill, Oliver Nelson and John Hicks. Moving to New York in '62, his first gig—with Albert Ayler — must have been something approaching a baptism of fire. His first recording date was with Charles Tyler in '66 and he was subsequently to work with Charles Mingus, Betty Carter, McCoy Tyner, Stanley Turrentine, Marion Brown, Julius Hemphill and Cecil Taylor.

Shannon's high-stepping drum technique (a blend of rock and funk with a lacing of the expansive two-beat percussion of New Orleans) has added an extra dimension to recordings by Weldon Irvine, Ray Bryant, Taruo Nakamura, Cecil Taylor, Ornette Coleman and James Blood Ulmer. The album with Ulmer **(Are You Glad To Be In America)** was largely responsible for raising Shannon's profile with European audiences.

Albums like **Eye On You, Mandance** and **Barbecue Dog** brought Jackson and his two-guitar line-up Decoding Society into the front line of a funk-based, hard-driving, demanding new-wave jazz in the '80s. With the Decoding Society, Jackson has strongly featured his own powerful compositions which he describes as 'Circadian, i.e. noting or pertaining to rhythmic biological cycles which recur at regular intervals'.

A later, digitally recorded album, **Pulse,** finds Jackson's unorthodox—at times, almost anarchistic — rhythms giving the words of Edgar Allan Poe, William Shakespeare *et al* an entirely new meaning.

Albums:

James Blood Ulmer, Are You Glad to Be In America (—/Rough Trade)
Eye On You (About Time/—)
Mandance (Antilles/Antilles)
Barbecue Dog (Antilles/Antilles)
Decode Yourself (Island/Island)
Bill Laswell, Baselines (Elektra Musician/Elektra Musician)
Pulse (Celluloid/Celluloid)

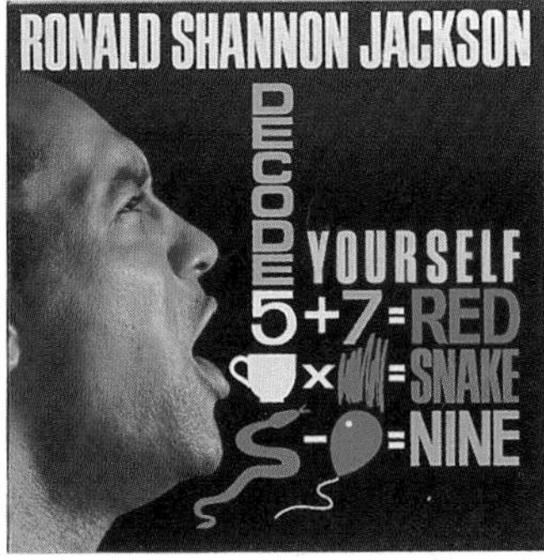

Ronald Shannon Jackson, Decode Yourself (courtesy Island Records).

Illinois Jacquet

Illinois Battiste Jacquet was born Broussard, Louisiana, 1922, but his father (bass player with railroad company band) moved family to Houston, Texas, before Illinois was one year.

Jacquet will be best remembered for the extraordinary potency of his swing—and an ability to build excitement in performance by use of freak high-note effects. But Jacquet is more than an eccentric, exhibitionist tenor saxophonist. He has successfully outlived his somewhat dubious reputation acquired with the wildly-swinging big band which Lionel Hampton put together when leaving Benny Goodman.

With Hampton, Jacquet was featured soloist, whose special feature was the immensely exciting and grossly over-used **Flying Home (The Best Of Lionel Hampton).** Jazz At The Philharmonic impresario Norman Granz also utilized Jacquet's ability to stir jazz audiences into the kind of frenzy pitch rock concerts have subsequently engendered **(Concert Contrasts/Jazz At The Philharmonic 1944-46).** And Jacquet's honking, booting tenor has been a welcome addition to organized studio jam sessions **(The Gillespie Jam Sessions)** where his playing generally has been, of necessity, free of gallery-fetching excesses with which he made his name in live performance.

He began on soprano and alto saxes, playing with territory R&B bands (including Lionel Proctor, Bob Cooper, Milton Larkins). Joined Hampton from Floyd Ray Orchestra, after which the little man with the huge tone enlivened the bands of Cab Calloway (1943-44), Count Basie (1945-46) and various JATP troupes. With Basie, his solo features included **Mutton Leg (One O'Clock Jump);** and **The King (Count Basie Classics).** During post-Basie period, Illinois Jacquet also led own bands, often including trumpet-playing brother Russell **(Illinois Jacquet**—*Epic* and **King Jacquet).**

Since then, he has toured with further outfits of which he has been leader, as well as with package shows such as Newport All Stars, or as featured soloist at concerts and in clubs, in the US and abroad. From the 1960s, Jacquet, who had concentrated almost exclusively on tenor sax during his halcyon big-band days, recommenced playing both alto and soprano sax. In addition, he added bassoon to his armory **The King!),** an instrument he plays with a fair degree of fluency and expertise.

During his career, Jacquet has locked horns with some of the greatest names in jazz. In 1944, for example, he was seen and heard in jazz movie *Jammin' the Blues* **(Jammin' With Lester)** together with Lester Young, one of his major influences, along with Coleman Hawkins and, most notably, Herschel Evans.

Outside of big-band set-up, he has worked with Count Basie **(Port Of Rico);** Edison **(Groovin' With Jacquet);** Nat Cole **(Nat Cole Meets The Master Saxes)** and Wynton Kelly **(The Blues: That's Me!).**

In more recent years, Jacquet's blistering tenor work often has been heard in friendly, mutually inspiring dialogue with drummer Jo Jones and organist Milt Buckner **(Genuis At Work!)** with trio sometimes effecting the powerhouse storm of an extrovert big band.

Jacquet's presence at all-star gatherings, like Newport Jazz Festival, gives more than adequate demonstrations of his undiminished blowing powers, and as an uplifting, fiery purveyor of ballads like **Misty (Newport In New York '72, Vol 3), The Man I Love (Newport in New York '72, Vol 5)** and **Stardust (Here Comes Freddy).**

Albums:

The Best Of Lionel Hampton (MCA—Coral—Germany)
Nat Cole Meets The Master Saxes (Including Illinois Jacquet) (Phoenix/Spotlite)
Lester Young, Jammin' With Lester (Jazz Archives/—)
Various (Including Illinois Jacquet), JATP New Volume Five-Concert Contrasts (Verve)/ Jazz At The Philharmonic 1944-46 (Verve)
Illinois Jacquet/Eddie 'Lockjaw' Davis, The Angry Tenors (Savoy/Realm)
Illinois Jacquet, Groovin' With Jacquet (Verve/Columbia—Clef)
Dizzy Gillespie, The Gillespie Jam Sessions (Verve)
Illinois Jacquet (Imperial)
Illinois Jacquet (Epic/Epic—Holland)
Illinois Jacquet, The King! (Prestige/—)
Illinois Jacquet, Bottoms Up (Prestige/—)
Illinois Jacquet, The Blues: That's Me (Prestige/—)
Illinois Jacquet/Arnett Cobb, Jazz At Town Hall, Vol 1 (JRC/—)
Various, Newport At New York '72, Vols 3, 5 (Atlantic/Atlantic)
Illinois Jacquet, Genius At Work (Black Lion/Black Lion)
Buddy Tate & His Buddies (Chiaroscuro/—)
Howard McGhee/Illinois Jacquet, Here Comes Freddy (—/Sonet)
Illinois Jacquet, King Jacquet (—/RCA—France)
Various (Including Illinois Jacquet), The Tenor Sax Album (Savoy/Savoy)
Various (Including Illinois Jacquet), The Changing Face Of Harlem, Vol 2 (Savoy/Savoy)
Illinois Flies Again (Argo/—)

Above: The Tearway of the Tenor Sax, Illinois Jacquet...a comprehensive swinger and archetypal Jazz At The Phil roof-raiser.

Bob James

In addition to his world-wide reputation as an arranger and conductor, pianist Bob James has become a top figure in fusion with his own successful recordings.

Born in Marshall, Missouri, on Christmas Day, 1939, James learned piano from age 4. His early inspiration was classical—Hindemith, before discovering the delights of jazz through Stan Kenton, Charlie Parker, Miles Davis, Chet Baker, Gerry Mulligan and Oscar Peterson.

In '62, James received a master's degree in composition from the University of Michigan and went on to establish his reputation as Sarah Vaughan's musical director and accompanist. In '68, he left Vaughan and became a top arranger in the soul field. In '73, Quincy Jones (who had spotted James in '62 at the Notre Dame Festival) introduced James to Creed Taylor. As a result, James became an arranger/producer for the CTI label.

From '74-'76, James released four successful solo albums **(One, Two, Three** and **Four).** In '76, James joined CBS as Director of Progressive A&R and, the following year, founded his own Tappen Zee label recording his own **Heads** and albums by Joanne Brackeen, Wilbert Longmire, Richard Tee, Mark Colby and Mongo Santamaria.

In '80, James decided to return to his own music-making and in '81 released one of his jazziest albums of late—the double **All Around The Town.** In the mid-'80s, another aspect of James' versatile musical character was revealed on **Rameau** for the CBS Masterworks classical label—a selection of pieces by 18th-century baroque composer Jean-Philippe Rameau, performed by James on a battery of synthesizers.

Further evidence of James' diversity of interests is shown in his musical scores (for Broadway's *The Selling of the President* and his arrangements for the *Serpico* film music). The definitive version of his popular theme **Angela** (which opens episodes of the TV series *Taxi*) is found on **Touchdown** ('78).

Albums:

New Jazz Conceptions (Mercury/Mercury)
Explosions (ESP/—)
One (CTI/CTI)
Two (CTI/CTI)
Three (CTI/CTI)
Four (CTI/CTI)
Heads (Tappen Zee-CBS/Tappen Zee-CBS)
Touchdown (Tappen Zee-CBS/Tappen Zee-CBS)
All Around The Town (Tappen Zee-CBS/Tappen Zee-CBS)
Bob James-Earl Klugh, Two Of A Kind (Tappen Zee-CBS/Tappen Zee-CBS)
Foxie (Tappen Zee-CBS/Tappen Zee-CBS)
Rameau (CBS Masterworks/CBS Masterworks)
12 (Tappen Zee-CBS/Tappen Zee-CBS)

Bob James, All Around The Town (courtesy CBS).

Above: Bob James—teamed up with Dave Sanborn in 1986 on Double Vision.

Harry James

Some jazz buffs never have forgiven Harry Haag James (born Albany, Georgia, 1916) for leaving Benny Goodman, starting his own big band and playing schmaltzy trumpet on tunes like **Ciribiribin, You Made Me Love You** and **Carnival In Venice.**

In spite of the obvious commercial slantings of bands James led, he continued to show, from time to time, that he could still play heated jazz with a technical expertise. Not to be forgotten, too, is the string of superbly executed solos James had taken as a principal soloist with the most famous of Benny Goodman bands.

James had joined the clarinettist in January 1937, remaining as No 1 trumpet soloist until December 1938. During which time, his—and Goodman's—reputation had been established worldwide, through his personal contributions to such Goodman favorites as **Make Believe (The Complete Benny Goodman, Vols 1-3/Benny Goodman, Vol 4); Sugar Foot Stomp, Big John's Special (The Complete Benny Goodman, Vols 1-3/Benny Goodman, Vol 5); Peckin'** and **Life Goes To A Party,** both composed-arranged by James **(The Complete Benny Goodman, Vols 1-3/Benny Goodman, Vol 7).** And, indeed, James' splendid blowing at the famous **1938 Carnegie Hall Jazz Concert** on numbers like **Sing, Sing, Sing, Blue Skies, Honeysuckle Rose** and, again, **Life Goes To A Party.**

James began on drums, then at ten took trumpet lessons from father. Family moved to Beaumont, Texas, and young James began working in various bands operating within that state. First major break came when he joined orchestra of Ben Pollack (1935-36) **(Harry James & His Orchestra 1936-1938).** During his time with Goodman, James participated in one of Teddy Wilson's studio get-togethers, including one date at which James and Wilson were joined by Red Norvo, xylophone, and John Simmons, bass. James' solos on **Ain't Misbehavin'** and **Just A Mood,** both from this session **(Teddy Wilson & His All Stars)** are as impeccable as those with Wilson at other similar occasions.

James fronted an impressive, hard-swinging nine-piece band inside recording studios in 1937 and 1938. The band, comprising seven members of the then Basie outfit, James and pianist Jess Stacy from Goodman, plus Basie's singer, Helen Humes, laid down some fine tracks, with James' trumpet sparkling throughout both sessions **(Harry James & His Orchestra 1936-1938).** Even more impressive — surprisingly so — was James' superb, crackling trumpet work on all four titles emanating from an early-1939 record date in company with boogie-woogie piano giants Albert Ammons and Pete Johnson (sharing two numbers apiece). James immersed himself into the boogie woogie idiom with commendable application, with immensely satisfying results **(Café Society Swing & The Boogie Woogie 1938-1940).** With his own big band he became a tremendous box-office success, including **Ciribiribin, You Made Me Love You, I've Heard That Song Before, I Had The Craziest Dream, I Don't Want To Walk Without You, I'm Beginning To See The Light, Music Makers,** etc. His popularity was enhanced by appearances in many Hollywood movies, including *Private Buckaroo, Syncopation, Springtime In The Rockies* and *If I'm Lucky.*

During late-1950s James invited top jazz writers like Ernie Wilkins and Neal Hefti to write a brand new library for the band. Jazz content was dramatically increased, and although the Harry James bands subequently closely mirrored the powerhouse sound and style of post-1950s Count Basie outfits **(The Big Band Sound Of Harry James, Vols 1-3),** the change was greeted with widespread approval.

With the band enjoying renewed success in the '60s, Harry James' trumpet flared more brightly than it had for 30 years, when the music had taken a middle-of-the-road approach. James, it seemed, had now returned to the jazz fold, reviving happy memories of the trumpeter's earlier excellence with Goodman. Fans everywhere welcomed this change in direction.

Even well into his 60s, James' trumpet-playing powers seemed as formidable as ever. Sadly, Harry James died in July '83 in a Los Angeles hospital from cancer. He was 67.

Albums:

The Complete Benny Goodman, Vols 1-3 (RCA)/ Benny Goodman, Vols 4-7 (RCA Victor—France)
Benny Goodman, 1938 Carnegie Hall Jazz Concert (Columbia/CBS)
Harry James & His Orchestra 1936-1938 (The Old Masters/—)
Teddy Wilson & His All Stars (Columbia/CBS)
Various (Including Harry James/Pete Johnson/Albert Ammons), Café Society Swing & The Boogie Woogie (1938-1940) (Swingfan—Germany)
Various (Including Harry James), Great Swing Jam Sessions, Vol 1 (—/Saga)
Swinging With Harry James (Joker—Italy)
The Big Band Sound Of Harry James, Vols 1-3 (—/Verve)
Harry James & His Orchestra Featuring Buddy Rich (CBS/Columbia)

Harry James And His New Swingin' Bands (courtesy MGM). The impact of the Basie band on James' outfit can be gauged from this album.

Joseph Jarman

see Art Ensemble of Chicago

Al Jarreau

Being a late-starter didn't prevent Al Jarreau from soaring to the top as one of America's most influential jazz vocalists. His multi-dimensional, acrobatic, scat-inspired vocals have earned him a world-wide following, notably at a time when jazz vocals had become almost unfashionable. Since the '80s, and the new wave of interest in jazz vocals, Jarreau stands as one of the most distinctive and popular voices in jazz.

Born into a musical family in Milwaukee, Wisconsin, on March 12, 1940, Jarreau was singing from age 4 (his first public concert was at 7). His earliest musical influences were big-band and bebop records belonging to his older brother and sisters. Graduating with a master's degree in psychology from the University of Iowa, he worked as a rehabilitation counselor until he was 28.

In '68, while singing in his spare time with a trio called the Indigos, Jarreau decided to turn professional. He worked with guitarist Julio Martinez in Sausolito, then moved to Los Angeles where he became a popular attraction around the clubs. He recorded his first album **(We Got By)** in early '75 and a two-month tour of Europe the following year brought him international acclaim. In '77, Jarreau won an American Grammy for Best Jazz Vocal Performance — the first of a string of subsequent similar accolades.

In recent years, Jarreau has also written much of his own material and, apart from his successful cross-over appeal, albums like **Breakin' Away** ('81) have produced his unforgettable and sparkling vocal interpretations of jazz 'standards' like Dave Brubeck's unlikely 'vocal' work **Blue Rondo A La Turk.**

The popular album **Live In London** — Al Jarreau performances (including **Let's Pretend**), recorded at the Wembley Arena in November '84 — was also captured on a special WEA Music Video.

Above: Al Jarreau—helped revive the public taste for jazz vocals.

Albums:

We Got By (Warner Brothers/Warner Brothers)
Glow (Warner Brothers/Warner Brothers)
All Fly Home (Warner Brothers/Warner Brothers)
Breakin' Away (Warner Brothers/Warner Brothers)
High Crime (Warner Brothers/Warner Brothers)
Jarreau (Warner Brothers/Warner Brothers)
Al Jarreau—Live In London (Warner Brothers/Warner Brothers)
L Is For Lover (Warner Brothers/Warner Brothers)

Keith Jarrett

The celebrated pianist Keith Jarrett first established his reputation in the popular Charles Lloyd group **(Dream Weaver)** where he proved himself to be a dazzlingly gifted player. A period with Miles Davis in the early '70s **(Live-Evil** and **At Fillmore)** did not lead — as with pianists Chick Corea, Joe Zawinul and Herbie Hancock — to subsequent formation of a jazz-rock outfit. Jarrett's career has been remarkably diverse.

Born Allentown, Pennsylvania, on May 8, 1945, Jarrett learned piano from age 3, exploring improvisation and composition as early as 7. At 15, he took formal lessons and by 16 was presenting program of his own work, even touring with Fred Waring's Pennsylvanians. In '63, he spent an eventful year on a scholarship to Berklee School of Music and built his early reputation on having been kicked out of Berklee.

After working around Boston, in '65 Jarrett moved to New York becoming an Art Blakey Jazz Messenger (for three months) and working with Roland Kirk. In February '66, Charles Lloyd found Jarrett playing as a cocktail-bar pianist and, over the next three years, Jarrett toured Europe six times with Lloyd, covering 18 countries including a trip to Moscow **(Charles Lloyd In The Soviet Union).**

In '69, Jarrett formed his own trio with bassist Charlie Haden and drummer Paul Motian, later adding ex-Ornette Coleman saxophonist Dewey Redman **(Byablue** etc.). With this group, Jarrett displayed his ensemble talents. The music is vigorous, driving and the interaction between the players — particularly between Haden and Jarrett — is phenomenal. There is a great variety of approach towards Jarrett's compositions, from the simultaneous soloing on **Great Bird,** the rapt duet for bass and piano on **Prayer (Death And The Flower)** to a tapestry of percussive effects on **Kuum (Backhand)** where all the musicians double on maracas, drums etc.

In '70, Miles Davis invited Jarrett to join his line-up. At first, Jarrett resisted because of his own commitments but eventually agreed and their resulting association is well documented.

In '71, Jarrett became committed to acoustic solo performance, recording **Facing You** for ECM, Manfred Eicher's quality label which has established new standards of freedom for the artist. Although Jarrett returned to group format for his classic and enduring **Belonging** (with saxophonist Jan Garbarek, bassist Palle Danielsson and drummer Jon Christensen), to say that Jarrett has recorded 'prolifically' as a soloist is almost understating the case. Few other musicians would have the clout, let alone the nerve, to release 20 sides of pure improvisation as *one* set **(Sun Bear Concerts).** Hours of live, unaccompanied acoustic piano **(The Köln Concert** and **Solo — Concerts, Bremen & Lausanne** etc) seemed, at their time of issue, a sure commercial disaster but **The Köln Concert** alone sold over one million copies for ECM. Jarrett's sheer approachability, romanticism and dedication to beauty have won him a popularity beyond that of a coterie jazz following.

Impossible to categorize, his rushing stream of improvisation ransacks the classical, baroque, gospel, country and boogie bags, rolling them all together over ostinato rhythms that hypnotize the senses. Not restricted to theme and variations, Jarrett's longer pieces, untitled, treat form as a verb rather than a noun. He has also produced several albums as an orchestral composer **(In The Light, Luminescence** and **Arbour Zena)** which have a brooding neo-classical feel. Saxophonist Jan Garbarek's contribution leavens the overall tristesse and dolorousness of the string section.

Jarrett's recorded projects are often a personal revelation — like his album dedicated to G. I. Gurdjieff **(Sacred Hymns).** Or just plain intriguing — like the digitally recorded double, **Invocations/The Moth And The Flame,** which finds Jarrett in the depths of Ottobeuren Abbey at the pipe organ and on soprano sax. Extraordinarily gothic, chillingly gloomy — but soul-stirring.

In the mid-'80s, Jarrett returned to the trio format in company with bassist Gary Peacock and drummer Jack De Johnette, producing the improvisational **Changes.** A surprising move, with this rhythm section, was Jarrett's return to a standards repertoire. The three **Standards** albums **(Volumes 1** and **2,** plus **Live)** include only one self-penned track **(So Tender** on Volume 2), all other material being old favorites, almost in the MOR mold but subjected to the 'Jarrett treatment' — **All The Things You Are, God Bless The Child, I Fall In Love Too Easily, Stella By Starlight, Falling In Love With Love** etc.

In '86, Jarrett confirmed his change of musical direction, touring with his trio (Peacock and De Johnette) and performing a standards repertoire.

Despite Jarrett's undeniably significant contribution to Miles Davis' ground-breaking electric-jazz period, Jarrett has since defended the acoustic piano as though the Fender Rhodes had never been invented. He has declared: 'I am, and have been, carrying on an anti-electric-music crusade...'.

While Jarrett's solo concert albums undoubtedly created a market for the sound of the grand piano again, his electric approach and lyrical gifts have converted many who were baffled by the dissonances of Cecil Taylor.

With Jarrett, you'll hear down-home blues right next to the European classical tradition as stated by Delius, Debussy or Satie; sedate lines of plainsong can crop up alongside the hot gospel; explorations of some ancient Moorish scale can suddenly give way to some raunchy rock & roll. Jarrett's music is primeval and futuristic at the same time. Not for nothing has Keith Jarrett been described as 'the most influential pianist since Monk'.

Below: The solo output of pianist Keith Jarrett has been prolific—who else would have the muscle to produce 20 record sides of pure improvisation as one set?

Albums:

Charles Lloyd, Dream Weaver (Atlantic/Atlantic)
Charles Lloyd, Forest Flower (Atlantic/Atlantic)
Miles Davis, Miles Davis At Fillmore (Columbia/CBS)
Miles Davis, Live-Evil (Columbia/CBS)
Somewhere Before (Atlantic-Jazzlore/Atlantic-Jazzlore)
Mourning Of A Star (Atlantic/Atlantic)
El Juicio (Atlantic/Atlantic)
Death And The Flower (Impulse/Impulse)
Backhand (Impulse/Impulse)
Mysteries (Impulse/Impulse)
Shades (Impulse/Impulse)
Fort Yawuh (Impulse/Impulse)
Impulsively (Impulse/Impulse)
Treasure Island (Impulse/Impulse)
Byablue (ABC/ABC)
Piano Giants (Prestige/Prestige)
Expectations (Columbia/CBS)
The Progressives (Columbia/CBS)
Facing You (ECM/ECM)
Ruta And Daitya (ECM/ECM)
In The Light (ECM/ECM)
Solo—Concerts, Bremen & Lausanne (ECM/ECM)
Luminescence (ECM/ECM)
Belonging (ECM/ECM)
The Köln Concert (ECM/ECM)
Arbour Zena (ECM/ECM)
The Survivors' Suite (ECM/ECM)
Hymns/Spheres (ECM/ECM)
Staircase (ECM/ECM)
Sun Bear Concerts (ECM/ECM)
My Song (ECM/ECM)
The Eyes Of Heart (ECM/ECM)
Nude Ants (ECM/ECM)
Sacred Hymns (ECM/ECM)
The Celestial Hawk (ECM/ECM)
Invocations/The Moth And The Flame (ECM/ECM)
Concerts (ECM/ECM)
Changes (ECM/ECM)
Standards Volumes 1 and 2 (ECM/ECM)
Standards Live (ECM/ECM)
Works (ECM/ECM)

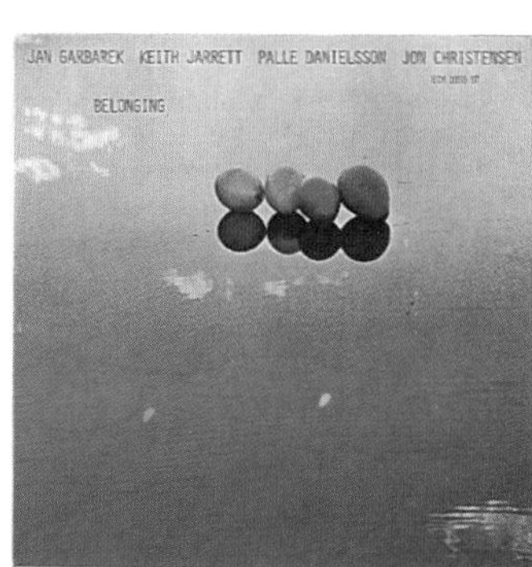

Keith Jarrett, Belonging (courtesy ECM)—quartet 'goes for bust'.

Jazz Messengers

see Art Blakey

Leroy Jenkins

Violinist Leroy Jenkins, born Chicago, 1932, was part of that city's AACM and involved in sessions with Muhal Richard Abrams **(Levels & Degrees Of Light)** and Anthony Braxton **(Three Compositions Of New Jazz** and **New York, Fall, 1974).** In 1970 he formed the Revolutionary Ensemble with bassist Sirone and percussionist Jerome Cooper. Their albums, the first three live, all embrace the collective principle. The impact of the first **(Vietnam)** is arguably the greatest, though the level of intensity is high throughout their output. Jenkins states that he is 'carrying on the tradition of Stuff Smith and Eddie South', though clearly with the vocabulary of today.

Classically trained, his work avoids tonal distortion and concentrates on a sinuous projection of melody. Sirone's bass lines plait with the violin, supplying textures, and on numbers like **New York (The People's Republic)** rising in arco duet. The music swirls and soars with a passion that is a far cry from chamber music, and through the use of gongs and voices, covers a wide spectrum. An extended work **(For Players Only)** uses the resources of an orchestra.

Albums:

Muhal Richard Abrams, Levels & Degrees Of Light (Delmark/Delmark)
Anthony Braxton, Three Compositions Of New Jazz (Delmark/Delmark)
New York, Fall, 1974 (Arista/Arista)
Revolutionary Ensemble, Vietnam (ESP/ESP)
Manhattan Cycles (India Navigation/—)
The Psyche (RE Records/—)
The People's Republic (A&M/A&M)
Leroy Jenkins, For Players Only (JCOA/JCOA—Virgin)
Swift Are The Winds Of Life (Survival/—)
Solo Concert (India Navigation)
The Legend Of Ai Glatsen (Black Saint/Black Saint)
Mixed Quintet (Black Saint/Black Saint)

J. J. Johnson

The J. J. Johnson style of trombone-playing dominated the 1940s and '50s. Dispensing with the growls and slurs of swing and dixieland players, Johnson used the instrument to play the fast, agile lines of the bebop saxophonists, concentrating on its linear possibilities rather than old-style — and currently, new style — brass-band expressionism.

Technically perfect, Johnson's work within the idiom has never been equaled. As a sideman with Sonny Stitt's group **(Genesis)**, he contributed three fine originals, **Blue Mode, Teapot** and **Elora**, as well as displaying a rare melodic gift on John Lewis' **Afternoon In Paris**. Leading a sextet that included the great trumpeter Clifford Brown, Johnson cut an album that was virtually a definition of bebop trombone, the tone consistent, the turn of speed on numbers like **Get Happy** phenomenal **(The Eminent J. J. Johnson)**.

In 1954 he teamed up with fellow trombonist Kai Winding, while a meeting with tenorist Sonny Rollins **(Sonny Rollins, Volume 2)** resulted in some of the most exciting trombone on record, the lines complex, poised yet driving. Another off-the-cuff meeting with a tenorist, Stan Getz **(Getz & J.J. 'Live')** finds Johnson in peak form, matching the lyrical Getz on the ballad features, and producing a magnificent **Yesterdays** and **I Waited For You**.

Increasingly, he concentrated on writing works like **El Camino Real, Sketch For Trombone & Orchestra** and the six-part

Above: Leroy Jenkins, one of the avant-garde's foremost violinists and founder member of The Revolutionary Ensemble.

composition, **Perceptions**, for Gunther Schuller's Third Stream orchestra, which attempted a marriage between jazz and classical music. Three pieces for this orchestra by John Lewis, Jimmy Giuffre and J. J. Johnson **(Music For Brass)** use classical forms such as the fugue in Johnson's **Poem For Brass**.

In later years, he has settled into film and studio work, making welcome appearances on the festival circuit with all-star line-ups.

In the '80s, Johnson's recordings for Pablo include his dynamic collaboration with fellow trombonist Al Grey **(Things Are Getting Better All The Time)**.

Albums:

Sonny Stitt, Genesis (Prestige/Prestige)
The Eminent J. J. Johnson (Blue Note/Blue Note)
Miles Davis (Blue Note/Blue Note)
Sonny Rollins, Volume 2 (Blue Note/Blue Note)
Getz & J. J. 'Live' (Verve/Verve)
Music For Brass (Columbia/—)
J. J. Johnson, Kai Winding, Bennie Green, Willie Dennis, Four Trombones... The Début Recordings (Prestige/Prestige)
Pinnacles (Milestone/Milestone)
Concepts In Blue (Pablo/Pablo)
Things Are Getting Better All The Time (Pablo/Pablo)
J. J. Johnson, Milt Jackson and Ray Brown, Jackson, Johnson, Brown & Company (Pablo/Pablo)
Joe Pass-J. J. Johnson, We'll Be Together Again (Pablo/Pablo)

James P. Johnson

James Price 'James P.' Johnson (born Brunswick, New Jersey, 1891) was a well-nigh perfect link between ragtime and early jazz Moreover, he was the finest musician to emerge from the so-called stride school of piano-players — pianists with large hands and powerful wrists whose exciting, percussive style depended as much on physical strength and endurance as technical skills.

Johnson, though, was, like his pupil Thomas 'Fats' Waller, a notch above the rest of the stride pianists in that he possessed a fine all-round technique, no doubt a legacy of his youth, when his mother and an Italian piano teacher ensured he received a thorough schooling in classical keyboard techniques.

The combination of several important musical influences — ragtime, blues, classical — resulted in jazz playing that was to give Johnson a position of omnipotence amongst early-jazz pianists before the arrival of the 1920s. The Johnson family moved to Jersey, then to New York (the home of stride piano — or, to be more specific, Harlem in New York).

His first public appearances were at numerous of the celebrated rent parties, before he was 21. In 1912, he played first professional gigs at Coney Island, after which he became a familiar figure, playing solo in clubs in New York and Atlantic City. Toured Southern vaudeville circuit, then back to New York for further seasons in a variety of clubs. Made a series of piano rolls for Aeolian Co, then ORS **(James P. Johnson 1917-21)** and in 1921 made début on records.

Played with James Europe's Hell Fighters Band (1920-21), fronted a band onstage during a Broadway show, also working in two revues, *Black Sensations* and *Smart Set*. Played with Harmony Seven band in New York (1922). Composed music for *Plantation Days*, which Johnson took to UK in 1923.

During 1920s he became a highly successful composer of songs which long since have become standards, in both jazz and pop worlds. Amongst his most popular numbers are **If I Could Be With You (One Hour Tonight), Charleston, Runnin' Wild, Old Fashioned Love, A Porter's Love Song.** In 1925, he orchestrated own *Running Wild* revue, and three years later **Yamecraw,** an extended composition, received its première at Carnegie Hall. Johnson's most famous piano piece, **Carolina Shout,** received first recording by its composer in 1921 **(James P. Johnson: Piano Solos).** Other Johnson solo recordings of the 1920s, all of which demonstrate his all-round superiority as Harlem-style pianist, include **Arkansas Blues, Eccentricity** (both 1921), **Ole Miss Blues** (1922), a four-song **Runnin' Wild** medley (including **Old Fashioned Love, Charleston**) (1924), and **Sugar** and **Harlem Choc'late Babies On Parade** (both 1926) (all **James P. Johnson: Piano Solos).**

Further proof of his superb adaptability is contained in recordings he made (1927, 1929) with blues singer Bessie Smith. His superbly confident, yet totally sympathetic accompaniments for Smith on tracks like **Backwater Blues (Nobody's Blues But Mine); Blue Spirit Blues, Wasted Life Blues** and **Worn Out Papa Blues (Any Woman's Blues)** could not have been bettered. And just how good a band pianist he was, all through his career, can be judged from records by Mezz Mezzrow **(The Complete Ladnier-Mezzrow-Bechet),** Frankie Newton **(The Big Apple),** Pee Wee Russell **(Jack Teagarden/Pee Wee Russell),** Edmond Hall **(Edmond Hall's Blue Note Jazzmen)** and Eddie Condon **(The Eddie Condon Concerts, Vol 2).**

In this context can be cited records made by Johnson himself, best of which was 1939 date, with Red Allen, J. C. Higginbotham, Big Sid Catlett and others **(Father Of The Stride Piano** and **Swing Combos 1935-1941).** In 1932 he wrote four-movement *Symphony Harlem*, presented onstage as ballet music. During 1930s concentrated on composing, and also collaborated with poet Langston Hughes on one-act *De Organizer*, although he continued to record and play live gigs.

Apart from illness in 1940, he continued to work regularly, with own bands and others. Suffered a stroke in 1946, but was playing again following year. In 1949, he took part in production of his *Sugar Hill* revue. Suffered severe stroke on return to New York (1951), which left him bedridden and unable to speak until he died, in New York City, 1955.

Albums:

Various (Including James P. Johnson), Rare Piano Rags 1920-23 (Jazz Anthology—France)
James P. Johnson, 1917-21 (Biograph/—)
James P. Johnson: Piano Solos (Joker—Italy)
Bessie Smith, Nobody's Blues But Mine (Columbia/CBS)
Bessie Smith, Any Woman's Blues (Columbia/CBS)
Various (Including James P. Johnson), The Complete Ladnier-Mezzrow-Bechet (RCA Victor—France)
(Mezz Mezzrow)/Frankie Newton, The Big Apple (RCA Victor—France)
Jack Teagarden/Pee Wee Russell (Byg—France)
Edmond Hall's Blue Note Jazzmen (Blue Note/—)
The Eddie Condon Concerts, Vol 2 (Chiaroscuro/—)
Various (Including James P. Johnson), 'This Is Jazz', Vols 1, 2 (Rarities/—)
James P. Johnson, Father Of The Stride Piano (Columbia/—)
Various (Including James P. Johnson), Swing Combos 1935-1941 (Swingfan—Germany)
James P. Johnson, Fats & Me (1944) (MCA—Germany)
James P. Johnson (—/Xtra)

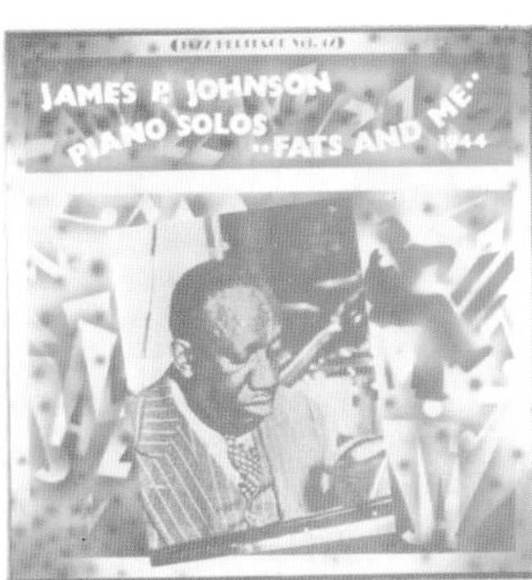

James P. Johnson piano solos, Fats And Me (courtesy MCA).

Lonnie Johnson

Alonzo 'Lonnie' Johnson (born New Orleans, Louisiana, around 1889) was an exceptionally gifted and certainly most versatile bluesman, one who seemed as happy singing or playing pop ballads as more profound, moving blues. One of the most technically assured of all blues guitarists, and a wholly individualistic performer, Johnson nevertheless seldom lacked the essential blues feel. Less impressive, at times, as a singer, occasionally lapsing into excesses of sentimentality. Little doubt, though, he could sing blues — it was when he featured pop-type ballads that he was less effective.

Played both violin and piano in New Orleans before going to London to various revues (1917), returning to New Orleans c. 1921-22. Moved to St Louis beginning of 1920s. Played with bands like those of Charlie Creath, Fate Marable (again, using mostly violin, piano), and worked in a foundry for two years, playing only part-time. As result of winning Okeh Records talent contest, commenced lengthy association with label in 1925. Recorded with Louis Armstrong Hot Five in December 1927, producing typically fine solos on **Savoy Blues, I'm Not Rough,** and providing superb rhythmic support for Armstrong scat vocal on **Hotter Than That (V.S.O.P. (Very Special Old Phonography, 1927-1928), Vols 3 & 4).**

In 1928, recorded with Duke Ellington Orchestra — one of comparatively rare examples of guest soloists featured with Ellington. As with Hot Five recordings, Johnson adapted himself with skill and taste to this context. With Ellington, featured on **The Mooche, Hot & Bothered (The Ellington Era, Vol 1/The Ellington Era, Vol 1 — Part 1)** and **Move Over, Misty Morning (The Ellington Era, Vol 2).** Also in '28, recorded blues guitar solos, **Playing With The Strings, Stompin' 'Em Along Slow, Away Down The Alley, Blues,** and **Blues In G**.

Same year, the extraordinary two-guitar partnership of Johnson and Eddie Lang entered recording studios for first time. The total empathy between the pair never was anything less than exceptional, at times achieving the musically sublime, as with **Bull**

Above: The individualistic guitarist Lonnie Johnson—whether alone or with long-time partner Eddie Lang, Duke or Louis, one of the giants of the blues.

Frog Moan, A Handful Of Riffs, Two Tone Stomp, and **Guitar Blues (The Golden Days Of Jazz: Eddie Lang & Joe Venuti — Stringing The Blues).** Duo also provided sympathetic accompaniment for blues singer Texas Alexander and cornettist King Oliver. Johnson, alone, also soloed most efficiently with **The Chocolate Dandies** and, during late-1920s and early-1930s played guitar with, and occasionally supplied extra vocals for, singers Texas Alexander, Victoria Spivey, Katherine Baker, etc **(Mr Johnson's Blues).**

Going to Cleveland in 1932, he worked for Putney Dandridge, also did much radio work. Went to Chicago, 1937, becoming resident at Three Deuces (including work with Johnny Dodds) until 1939. During 1940s, concentrated mostly on singing, playing amplified guitar in accompaniment. Went to Britain in 1952, for concert, then back to US to live in Cincinatti; then, to Philadelphia (1958-62), where he worked as chef in leading hotel. Toured Europe in blues package show in 1963. From mid-1960s, was heard mostly in Toronto, Canada. Suffered stroke, after serious accident in '69. During '63 European tour recorded in Copenhagen, in company with pianist Otis Spann **(See See Rider),** playing, singing, almost as brilliantly as during his earlier peak years, including excellent guitar on **Swingin' With Lonnie,** and fine re-working of **Tomorrow Night,** original version of which resulted in huge-selling single disc (1948).

Of other records made in last 10-15 years of his life, probably best are **Lonnie Johnson**** and parts of **Blues By Lonnie Johnson.** Aficionados, however, probably would prefer his earlier work with Lang and Armstrong, including his superb solo on 1929 **Mahogany Hall Stomp (V.S.O.P. (Very Special Old Phonography, 1928-1930), Vols 5 & 6),** the Johnson solos mentioned above, plus 'mid-period' recordings like **Lonnie Johnson*** and **Bluebird Blues.**

Lonnie Johnson died in 1970.

Albums:

Louis Armstrong, V.S.O.P. (Very Special Old Phonography, 1927-1928), Vols 3 & 4) (CBS—France)
Louis Armstrong, V.S.O.P. (Very Special Old Phonography, 1928-1930), Vols 5 & 6 (CBS—France)
Duke Ellington, The Ellington Era (1927-1940), Vol 1 (Columbia)
The Ellington Era (1927-1940), Vol 1 — Part 1 (CBS)
Duke Ellington, The Ellington Era (1927-1940), Vol 2 (Columbia/—)
The Golden Days Of Jazz: Eddie Lang & Joe Venuti — Stringing The Blues (CBS)
The Chocolate Dandies (—/Parlophone)
Lonnie Johnson, Mr Johnson's Blues (Mamlish/—)
Lonnie Johnson* (—/Brunswick—Germany)
Lonnie Johnson** (—/Xtra)
Various (Including Lonnie Johnson), Bluebird Blues (RCA Victor/RCA Victor)
Blues By Lonnie Johnson (Prestige—Bluesville/—)
Lonnie Johnson, See See Rider (—/Storyville)
*and **two separate different recordings.

Pete Johnson

During a career which lasted 45 years, Pete Johnson (born 1904) established an enviable reputation as a superior two-handed pianist whose basic style encompassed blues, jazz, barrelhouse and boogie woogie. Kansas City (his birthplace) and New York were the two most important cities in respect of geographical location of his peak musical achievements.

He started his professional career in Kansas (in 1926), where he had spent part of his childhood in an orphanage; then worked initially as drummer (1922-26), accompanying various piano-players. After taking piano lessons, switched from drums to keyboard, full-time in '26. Soon, his reputation as a powerful exponent of rolling blues was established in the Kansas City area. Johnson was to spend the next 12 years in Kansas City as a solo performer.

During this time, he met blues singer Joe Turner, working as bartender at Piney Brown's Sunset Cafe, and pair played occasional gigs together. Combination of singer and pianist was to re-appear on numerous occasions throughout next 30-odd years. In 1938 they were invited to New York to appear on Benny Goodman radio show as well as at Apollo, Harlem. After returning to KC, duo was recalled by John Hammond to appear at his December '38 Spirituals To Swing concert **(John Hammond's Spirituals To Swing).**

Johnson stayed on in New York, teamed up with fellow pianists Meade Lux Lewis, Albert Ammons, at times augmented by voice of Turner and became a seminal participant in widespread popularity of boogie-woogie. Focal point of impact was Café Society where all three played long residencies, from 1939 until early-1940s. Three recorded together extensively (again, with Turner adding his own unique brand of blues vocalism). And like Ammons, Johnson collaborated on record with Harry James in strictly boogie-woogie vein, most successfully on **Café Society Swing & The Boogie Woogie.** Later same year (1939), he also successfully integrated his piano style with trumpet of Hot Lips Page and own Boogie Woogie Boys at record date. Also recorded extensively in solo capacity: fine Blue Note date **(Pete Johnson)** gives ample evidence of his capabilities when left to his own devices, notably on **Barrelhouse Breakdown** and **You Don't Know My Mind.**

Following split between Lewis and Turner, Ammons and Johnson stayed on together at Café Society. Johnson also took part in film, *Boogie Woogie Dream.* During 1940s, continued to make appearances throughout US, and to record at fairly frequent intervals **(Pete Johnson: Master Of Blues & Boogie Woogie, Vols 1, 2),** either alone or as part of a quartet, or with additional instrumentalists, like Hot Lips Page, Budd Johnson, Clyde Bernhardt. Perhaps his finest recorded work during this decade was in 1944 **(Vol 1)** when he cut eight titles for Brunswick, of which **Dive Bomber, Zero Hour** (an especially potent example of his blues-playing technique), **Rock It Boogie** and **Rock & Roll Boogie** are exceptional.

Johnson-Ammons recorded again in 1949 **(Boogie Woogie Man)** but then they, too, parted company. Three trips to California in 1947 resulted in further fine Johnson recordings. In 1949 he appeared at one of the Blues Jubilee concerts promoted by Gene Norman and Frank Bull **(Vol 1)** but by this time the pianist's repertoire tended to drop in quality (viz **Swanee River Boogie).** Active 1949-52, playing major US cities. In latter year took part (with Erroll Garner, Art Tatum) in Piano Parade tour. At conclusion of tour, Johnson lost part of his little finger, whilst changing car tire—a loss which, curiously, he shared with erstwhile keyboard companion, Ammons.

Was forced to leave music business full-time in 1953, playing only at week-ends. By following year, was employed as janitor. Was invited, in 1955, to take part in recording session, featuring singer Jimmy Rushing **(Listen To The Blues)** proving he had lost little of his old skills. Better still was 1956 date reuniting Johnson with old friend Joe Turner **(Boss Of The Blues).** Two had last recorded together in late-1940s, but the '56 get-together sparked both men into producing their best. Of particular potency—vocally and instrumentally—is comprehensive work-out on **Roll 'Em Pete,** Johnson's most famous composition. (Johnson had previously worked, briefly, as accompanist to Turner, in 1955; he performed in similar capacity for Rushing.)

Toured Europe in 1958, as member of JATP (with Turner), played Newport Jazz Festival, but was stricken with serious illness towards end of year. Was to suffer from recurring ill-health for rest of his life, working and recording infrequently. Made poignant appearance at Carnegie Hall, as member of Joe Turner's Café Society All Stars **(Spirituals To Swing-1967)** just before he died in 1967, although it was obvious by his appearance that he was gravely ill.

Much interesting information is to be found in *The Pete Johnson Story,* compiled and edited by Hans J. Mauerer.

Pete Johnson, Master Of Blues And Boogie Woogie (courtesy Oldie Blues-Holland).

Albums:

Various, John Hammond's Spirituals To Swing (Vanguard/Vogue)
Various, Café Society Swing & Boogie Woogie (Swingfan—German)
Meade Lux Lewis/Albert Ammons/Pete Johnson, The Complete Library of Congress Boogie Woogie Recordings (Jazz Piano/—)
Meade Lux Lewis/Albert Ammons/Pete Johnson, Giants Of Boogie Woogie (Storyville)
Pete Johnson (Blue Note)
Pete Johnson/Albert Ammons/Jimmy Yancey (Boogie Woogie Man) (RCA Victor—France)
Various, 29 Boogie Woogie Originaux (RCA Victor—France)
Pete Johnson, Master Of Blues & Boogie Woogie 1904-1967, Vols 1, 2 (Oldie Blues—Holland)
Jumpin' With Pete Johnson (Riverside/London)
Have No Fear, Big Joe Turner Is Here (Savoy/Savoy)
Various (Including Pete Johnson), Barrelhouse, Boogie Woogie & Blues (—/Fontana)
Joe Turner & Pete Johnson (EmArcy/—)
Jimmy Rushing, The Essential Jimmy Rushing (—/Vogue)
Joe Turner, Boss Of The Blues (Atlantic/Atlantic)
Various (Including Pete Johnson/Joe Turner), Spirituals To Swing-1967 (Columbia/—)

Robert Johnson

Robert Johnson (born near Clarksdale, Mississippi, c. 1913) died at a tragically young age—he was not quite 24 years old when he was poisoned in a San Antonio, Texas, hotel by, it is said, a jealous girlfriend. Robert Johnson's death was tragic insofar as his was one of the most extraordinary talents to emerge from any era of the history of the blues.

Johnson, in a period of only a few years, established a powerful reputation as a bluesman whose music often was terrifyingly real and unbearably intense. The Johnson legend has been maintained in the years following his death, in 1937, with the fairly frequent reappearance of the 30-plus discs he cut between 1936-37. Not too much is known about his background but he seems to have been something of a schizophrenic, a condition worsened by his persistent hard drinking. Said by some to be extremely shy, by all accounts he was far from being introverted or retiring in company of women. Certainly, women figured prominently in many of his blues—like **Kindhearted Women Blues,** whose two separate takes make intriguing contrast **(King Of The Delta Blues Singers, Vol 1** and **King Of The Delta Blues Singers, Vol 2)** and **Walking Blues (Vol 1),** which finds him in inconsolable mood, after being ripped off by a woman.

Other recordings, such as **Hellhound On My Trail, Preaching Blues, Me & The Devil** (all **Vol 1),** are formidable demonstrations of his preoccupation with inner nightmares and fantasies of terror, no doubt induced by his alcoholic extravagances. Often, his vocals—sometimes using falsetto to a maximum dramatic effect—were imbued with a genuinely frightening intensity. Johnson ranks with the greatest of all blues poetry—aforementioned items typify his best work. Other classics include **Phonograph Blues, Drunken Hearted Man, Rambling On My Mind (Vol 2)** and **Crossroads Blues, Walkin' Blues, Come On In My Kitchen (Vol 1).** And Johnson's pungent guitar lines, executed with the same passion as his singing, were the perfect corollary to his lyrics and their vocal projection. As a guitarist, Johnson was also influential—his unique walking bass line was copied by numerous other bluesmen (including many latter-day blues-conscious rock guitarists); similarly, his bottleneck playing was exceptional.

Albums:

King Of The Delta Blues Singers, Vol 1 (Columbia/CBS)
King Of The Delta Blues Singers, Vol 2 (Columbia/CBS)

Elvin Jones

Best known for his classic partnership with John Coltrane, Elvin Jones is one of the major innovators on drums. Born 1927 (in Pontiac, Michigan), brother to trumpeter Thad and pianist Hank, Elvin Jones' conception of a freer accompaniment was a logical extension of post-bop drumming. Breaking away from the regular cymbal beat, he launched a barrage of accents and rhythmic patterns that offered endless possibilities to the soloist. An early example of his polyrhythmic accompaniment can be found with the classic Sonny Rollins trio **(A Night At The Village Vanguard)** where the concepts of drummer and tenorist, though not always compatible, strike sparks.

Coltrane's legato attack, the longer lines, was eminently suited to Jones' multiple pulse which moved out into freer areas as the solo developed. Any of the many Coltrane Impulse albums illustrate the partnership at work, the two men stretched to the utmost and transcending the traditional idea of solo and accompaniment. **The Drum Thing (Crescent)** is a fine example of Jones' solo strength and ability to combine complexity with forward momentum, while **Africa (Africa Brass)** is structured from thematic elements. **Chasin' The Trane,** a classic headlong tenor solo, fuels on the drummer's endless strength **(Live At The Village Vanguard)** while the addition of drummer Rashied Ali, an extremely loose worker, marked the beginning of the dissolution of the partnership **(Meditations).**

Jones' own groups, though lacking the front-line distinction of a Coltrane, have been characterized by fine musicianship and great drumming. The first trios with saxophonist Joe Farrell and bassist Jimmy Garrison **(The Ultimate** and **Puttin' It Together)** are beautifully paced and show Jones' ability to vary the intensity of his work to complement the soloist.

Albums:

Sonny Rollins, A Night At The Village Vanguard (Blue Note/Blue Note)
John Coltrane, Crescent (Impulse, Impulse)
John Coltrane, Africa Brass (Impulse, Impulse)
John Coltrane, Live At The Village Vanguard (Impulse, Impulse)
John Coltrane, Meditations (Impulse, Impulse)
The Ultimate (Blue Note/Blue Note)
Putting' It Together (Blue Note/Blue Note)
Heavy Sounds (Impulse/Impulse)
Live At The Vanguard (Enja/Enja)
The Prime Element (Blue Note/Blue Note)
Poly-currents (Blue Note/Blue Note)
Earth Jones (Palo Alto/Palo Alto)

Hank Jones

Henry ('Hank') Jones (born Pontiac, Michigan, 1918), the eldest of three noted jazz brothers—Thad Jones and Elvin Jones are the other two—has worked with practically all the major jazz figureheads (pre-avant garde) of the past 30-odd years, including Coleman Hawkins **(The High & Mighty Hawk)**, Stan Getz **(Opus De Bop/The Savoy Sessions)**, Charlie Parker **(The Definitive Charlie Parker, Vols 1-3, 6)**, Milt Jackson **(Second Nature/The Savoy Sessions)** and Lester Young **(Lester Swings)**. Reasons for his popularity as a pianist are obvious: a wholly distinctive touch—delicate, yet firm; his sensitivity as accompanist; his beautifully understated invention and constant rhythmic approach as soloist; and a brand of rare all-round musicianship that is without equal.

Jones, who as a youth studied with Carlotta Franzell, has worked with singers of the calibre of Ella Fitzgerald and Billy Eckstine. His innate musical catholicity, coupled with a rare ability to operate within practically any given jazz framework, made him an obvious selection for numerous Jazz At The Philharmonic concert tours **(Norman Granz' JATP—Carnegie Hall Concert 1952,** Record 3).

During 1950s Jones featured on literally hundreds of album dates, mostly for Savoy for whom he became, together with drummer Kenny Clarke and bassist Wendell Marshall, a member of house rhythm section. Jones recorded for Savoy alone (**Have You Met Hank Jones?**—one of his finest personal recorded statements).

Jones also worked many times in a quartet setting (together with bassist Milt Hinton, drummer Osie Johnson and guitarist Barry Galbraith), providing ideal backings for further top-class instrumentalists.

His style might be described as basically mainstream-modern, with influences of Art Tatum, Teddy Wilson, Al Haig, Bud Powell, and Nat Cole being clearly discernible. Not all the albums made under his own name have done his talents full justice. But the two Savoy albums cited above, plus **Keeping Up With The Joneses**—a 1958 date with brothers Thad and Elvin and bassist Eddie Jones—

Below: Elvin Jones, the master drummer who fuelled Coltrane's finest flights. A percussionist of limitless inspiration.

contain much excellent piano playing.

Earliest portion of Jones' career found him working mainly in Ohio and Michigan, before he moved to New York (1944). There, he worked with such as Hot Lips Page, John Kirby, Coleman Hawkins and Howard McGee. Was accompanist for Ella Fitzgerald between 1948 and 1953 (including a European tour). Has worked for Benny Goodman on several occasions (first time, 1956).

Albums:
Stan Getz Opus De Bop/The Savoy Sessions (Savoy)
Norman Granz' JATP—Carnegie Concert 1952 (Gene Krupa Trio), Record 3 (Clef/Columbia—Clef)
Milt Jackson, Second Nature/The Savoy Sessions (Savoy)
Donald Byrd, Long Green/The Savoy Sessions (Savoy)
Ernie Wilkins, Top Brass (Savoy/London)
Milt Jackson, Big Band Bags (Milestone)
The Definitive Charlie Parker, Vols 1-3, 6 (Verve/Verve)
Coleman Hawkins, The High & Mighty Hawk (Felsted/Vocalion)
Flip Phillips, Flip (—/Verve)
Lester Young, Lester Swings (—/Verve)
Lucky Thompson, Lucky Strikes (Prestige/—)
Kenny Dorham, But Beautiful (Milestone)
Ray Brown/Milt Jackson, Much In Common (Verve/Verve)
The Jones Bros, Keeping Up With The Joneses (MetroJazz)
Have You Met Hank Jones? (Savoy/London)
Hank Jones/Kenny Clark/Wendell Marshall, The Trio (Savoy/London)

Above: Hank—eldest of the Jones boys (brother of Thad and Elvin). A rare, all-round brand of musicianship—an inventive soloist and sensitive accompanist.

Quincy Jones

An important and familiar figure in recent fusion, Quincy Jones' success with pop artists like the Brothers Johnson and Michael Jackson often tends to overshadow his significant contribution to earlier jazz history. Jones was one of the youngest and most brilliant arrangers-composers to make an impact in the '50s. In spite of financial disasters in the '60s and serious illness in the '70s, Jones' immeasurable talent and drive has seen him through one of the most remarkable and colorful lives in jazz—an exceptional career which has bristled with achievement and creaks under the weight of awards and accolades.

Composer, trumpeter, pianist, band-leader Quincy Delight Jones Jr was born in Chicago, Illinois, on March 14, 1933. He moved to Seattle at age 10 and sang in the local church choir, taking up trumpet in '47. At 14, he formed a band with Ray Charles, working around the Seattle clubs. At 15, Jones would eagerly have joined Lionel Hampton's big band permanently except Hampton's wife insisted that the boy went back to his schooling and, in '51, he took up a scholarship at Schillinger House, Boston (later known as the Berklee School of Music).

At 17, Jones went to New York, gaining a reputation for writing arrangements for musicians like bassist Oscar Pettiford. Eventually he did join Hampton's band and, later, Dizzie Gillespie's. (Jones' first composition on record was **Kingfish**, recorded by Lionel Hampton and featuring one of Jones' rare trumpet solos.)

In the '50s, Jones worked in Paris as music director for Barclay Records, while studying classical composition with Nadia Boulanger. By the late '50s, Jones was leading a superb all-star, 18-piece band—it was a creative success but a financial disaster and he returned to the States in '61, heavily in debt.

Back home, his reputation had gone before him; his career took an upward turn with his appointment as a vice-president at Mercury Records (the first black person ever to hold such a position in a white corporation), producing and arranging hundreds of pop sessions resulting in a host of chart hits. Jones also branched out into producing some memorable film scores (including *The Pawnbroker, In the Heat of the Night, John and Mary, Bob and Carol and Ted and Alice)* and popular television programme themes *(Ironside, The Bill Cosby Show, Roots etc)*.

In the late '60s, Jones signed with A&M, producing spectacular hit albums like his **Walking In Space, Gula Matari, Smackwater Jack** etc. In '71, Jones and long-time friend Ray Charles were able to collaborate on a vast and important historic work. Their *Black Requiem*, documenting the black people's struggle in the United States from slavery to the present day, was performed by Charles with the Houston Symphony and an 80-voice choir.

In '74, the year his magnificant **Body Heat** album went gold, Jones suffered two brain aneurisms. But Jones characteristically refused to capitulate and, after two serious operations, returned in '76 with the Brothers Johnson under his wing, the first of his numerous protégés. Since the late '70s, his many successes include scoring the film music for *The Wiz*, 'discovering' Randy Crawford, and producing-arranging Michael Jackson's mega-hit album **Off The Wall** in '79 and, of course, the unprecedently popular **Thriller** album and video in '82.

In the '80s, there was a renewed appreciation of Jones' excellent work from the '60s with albums like **Big Band Bossa Nova** being re-issued to great public interest, and **Q** ('82) remains a useful compilation of some of his notable later solo work. The illustrious, multi-faceted career of this extraordinary man and musician continues to prosper with each passing year. Quincy Jones is assured a special place in jazz history as one of the music's supreme catalysts.

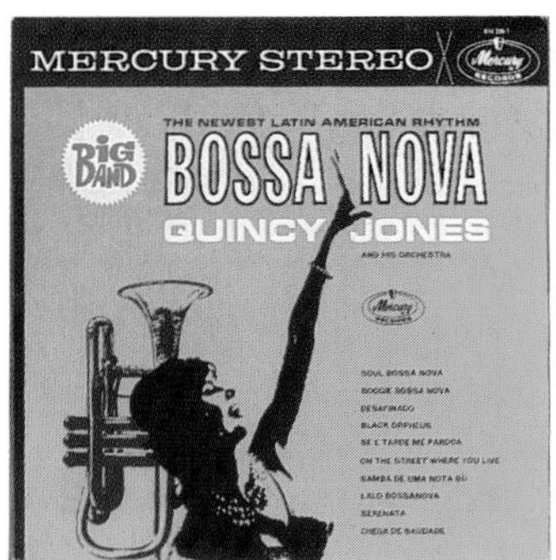

Quincy Jones, Big Band Bossa Nova (courtesy Mercury)—1963 classic.

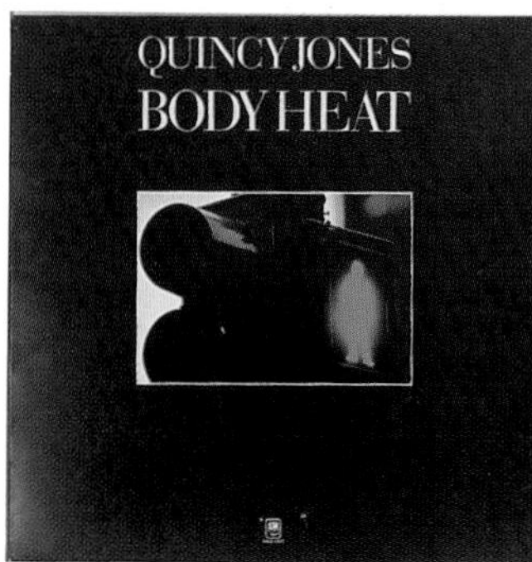

Body Heat (courtesy A&M)—features Everything Must Change, 1974.

Albums:
Quincy Jones (Impulse/Impulse)
The Quintessence (Impulse/Impulse)
Big Band Bossa Nova (Mercury/Mercury)
Take Five (—/Happy Bird)
Great Wide World (Trip/—)
Live at Newport 1961 (Trip/—)
Mode (ABC/—)
Walking In Space (A&M/A&M)
Gula Matari (A&M/A&M)
Smackwater Jack (A&M/A&M)
You've Got It Bad, Girl (A&M/A&M)
Body Heat (A&M/A&M)
Yellow Madness (A&M/A&M)
I Heard That!! (A&M/A&M)
Roots (A&M/A&M)
Sounds And Stuff Like That (A&M/A&M)
The Dude (A&M/A&M)
Q (A&M/A&M)

Thad Jones

Right: Ex-Basie trumpeter Thad Jones went on to co-lead the Thad Jones-Mel Lewis Big Band—universally acclaimed as one of the best large ensembles in jazz. He worked with brothers Elvin and Hank in the late 1930s.

One of the famous Jones brothers—drummer Elvin, pianist Hank—Thad was born in 1923 in Michigan. His initial impact as trumpeter with the Basie band in 1954 was considerable but it was his own Blue Note releases which established his reputation. His attack and accuracy at tempo, his hot, blatant tone balanced by a concept of musical architecture that is both weird and logical, made Jones a man to watch in the hard bop '50s. His performance of **April In Paris**, a frequent ballad choice, illustrates his horn-playing virtues **(The Magnificant Thad Jones)**.

A meeting with Thelonious Monk struck creative sparks, both men highly individual in their use of intervals and far-fetched figures **(Brilliance)**, while an album with baritonist Pepper Adams **(Mean What You Say)** has the two men making intelligent use of the new harmonic freedom. With the fine drummer, Mel Lewis, Jones formed a big band in the mid-'60s, and a series of hard-swinging, straight-ahead albums followed, featuring the leader's trumpet, cornet and flugelhorn. Consistent musically, there is little to choose between their albums.

Albums:
The Magnificent Thad Jones (Blue Note/Blue Note)
Thelonious Monk, Brilliance (Milestone/Milestone)
Thad Jones-Pepper Adams, Mean What You Say (Milestone/Milestone)
Thad Jones & Mel Lewis: Monday Night At The Village Vanguard (Solid State/—)
Central Park North (Solid State/—)
Consummation (Blue Note/Blue Note)
Potpourri (Philadelphia International/—)
Thad Jones-Mel Lewis (Blue Note/Blue Note)
Suite For Pops (Horizon/A&M Horizon)
New Life (Horizon/A&M Horizon)

Scott Joplin

Ragtime pianist-composer Scott Joplin was born in 1868 in Texarkana, the son of an ex-slave, and died in a mental institution in 1917.

The great pioneers Joseph Lamb, Tom Turpin, James Scott and Louis Chauvin established the form but Joplin's genius stretched it to its limits. He dreamed of moving ragtime from the saloons and sporting houses of St Louis into the concert halls, and his finest compositions aspire to the stature of Chopin or Strauss. Tragically, Joplin's dream of a respectable Afro-American art form was ignored, and his rags became the diversion of the hour. His opera, **Treemonisha**, an extended work dealing with the black predicament, was a failure and Joplin sank into a depression which led to the final insanity.

There is a charming insouciance and primness about his best work, an avoidance of the robust displays of technique associated with ragtime. 'Do Not Play Fast' is the habitual instruction on the sheet music. His earliest compositions, **Original Rags** and **The Favorite**, are fairly thin in comparison with the late masterpieces like **Magnetic Rag**. His most popular number, **Maple Leaf Rag**, bought by music publisher John Stark, established Joplin as 'King of Ragtime' from 1899, though he benefited little from the later ragtime boom-period with its commercial dilution and Tin Pan Alley exploitation. Among his large output of 50 or so rags, **The Entertainer, Elite Syncopations, Weeping Willow, Palm Leaf Rag, The Chrysanthemun, The Cascade,**

The Sycamore, Nonpareil, Gladiolus and **Rose Leaf Rag** are outstanding in their combination of strains, melody and harmony cohering exquisitely.

Joplin influenced Jelly Roll Morton and the Harlem Stride School of Fats Waller, James P. Johnson and Willie 'The Lion' Smith, and ragtime in general has enjoyed resurgences of popularity in the '40s and '70s, the most recent attributable to the movie, *The Sting.* The best book on the subject remains *They All Played Ragtime* by Rudi Blesh and Harriet Janis. The feature film *Scott Joplin*—directed by Jeremy Paul Kagan ('76), with superstar Billy Dee Williams in the title role—was a glossy dramatization of the pianist's eventful story (Dick Hyman doing an excellent job arranging the music). Amelia Anderson's brief documentary, *Scott Joplin, King of Ragtime Composers* ('77), tightly charts Joplin's life. Both films, interestingly, include contributions from the late Eubie Blake and Taj Mahal.

Best-selling versions of Joplin favorites have been recorded by Joshua Rifkin **(The Scott Joplin Golden Gift Box)**; these are distinguished by his authentic and scholarly approach. There are numerous piano rolls on record, though the sound quality is often poor, an enduring reminder of his legacy.

Albums:

The Scott Joplin Golden Gift Box (Nonesuch/Nonesuch)
Keith Nichols Plays Scott Joplin & The Classic Rag Masters (—/One-Up)
Heliotrope Bouquet, William Bolcom (Nonesuch/Nonesuch)
Ragtime Piano Roll Classics (—/BYG)

Scott Joplin Rags (courtesy Sonet) —a colorful Joplin bouquet.

Louis Jordan

Louis Jordan (born Brinkley, Arkansas, 1908) is best remembered as leader of an R&B-based jazz combo which achieved considerable popularity throughout most of the 1940s, playing before large audiences and selling impressive quantities of records. Its leader played basically swinging alto sax and sang in blues-inflected style; both Jordan's playing and singing, like music produced by his Tympany Five, reflected his appealing sense of humour and immense vitality. Jordan & His Tympany Five recorded prolifically for Decca between 1938-55, during which time it notched up a string of hit records, including **Knock Me A Kiss, Choo Choo Ch'Boogie, Caldonia, Beware, Brother Beware, Saturday Night Fish Fry** and **Let The Good Times Roll** (all **The Best of Louis Jordan**). During this period, Jordan also recorded with Louis Armstrong, Bing Crosby, Ella Fitzgerald. Repertoire of Tympany Five comprised mostly blues, R&B, jazz, and pops of the day—for millions, the combination was irresistible.

However, Jordan's career did not begin with his highly successful Tympany five. Originally he had studied clarinet and started professional career (in 1929) with Jimmy Pryor's Imperial Serenaders. Worked through various bands between 1930-36, latter year joining orchestra of Chick Webb, playing alto and soprano sax, and taking occassional vocals. During his two years with Webb, Jordan's solo opportunities tended to be limited.

On break-up of Tympany Five, Jordan signed as solo artist with Mercury. Not surprisingly, company asked him to re-record some of the old hits, like **Caldonia, Choo Choo Ch'Boggie, I'm Gonna Move To The Outskirts Of Town, Is You Is Or Is You Ain't My Baby?** and **Let The Good Times Roll (Choo Choo Ch'Boogie)**. With arrangements by Quincy Jones, and with pick-up band including such as Budd Johnson, Ernie Royal, Sam 'The Man' Taylor, and Jimmy Cleveland, results were better than comparable 'revival' records, with Jordan instrumentally and vocally, as irrepressible as ever.

Tried his hand at leading big band in 1951 **(Silver Star Swing Series Presents Louis Jordan & His Orchestra)** and although the music was fine, it lacked a disinctive sound of its own. After a couple of years touring and recording, Jordan disbanded the larger unit and reverted to Tympany Five format. During early-1950s, suffered several bouts of ill-health, often preferring to stay in his Phoenix Arizona home. Moved to Los Angeles in early-1960s, after making something of a comeback during late-1950s. Visited UK in 1962, signed with Ray Charles' Tangerine label in '64 (after one LP, unsuccessful sales-wise, association was terminated), and toured Asia in two consecutive years (1967-68).

Formed own label, Pzazz in '68, making at least one fine album, with big band conducted-arranged by tenorist Teddy Edwards **(Santa 'Claus, Santa Claus/Sakatumi)**. Recorded also in 1960s, with Chris Barber Band **(Louis Jordan Swings)**, although generally results were less than inspiring.

Much more successful was **Great Rhythm & Blues Oldies, Vol 1** with Jordan, once again, revisiting trusted-and-true repertoire of the past, this time in company with Shuggie Otis (guitar, bass, piano, organ), Johnny Otis (drums, piano), and others. Recorded in 1974, year before his death, it is a healthy reminder of just how appealing—and vital—Louis Jordan and his music remained until the very end of a successful and colorful career.

Interest in Jordan's irrepressible jump-blues style surged again in the '80s, especially in the United Kingdom prompted by pop-artist Joe Jackson's lively **Jumpin' Jive** album ('81). Joe Jackson (whose pre-pop credits include a spell with the National Youth Jazz Orchestra as pianist *Dave* Jackson) revived some classics of jump, jive and swing—songs by Cab Calloway, Lester YoungKing Pleasure **(Symphony Sid)**, Glenn Miller and (as Jackson explained) 'our main inspiration, Louis Jordan, the King of the Juke Boxes, who influenced so many but is acknowledged by so few. Like us, he didn't aim at purists, or even jazz fans—just anyone who wanted to listen and enjoy...'.

Singing and playing vibes, Jackson chose some of Britain's top young jazz musicians to help him recreate Jordan's infectious 'hep-music' era including altoist Pete Thomas, tenorist Dave Bitelli, trumpeter Raul Oliviera and pianist Nick Weldon.

Pete Thomas (who had also filled the vacant Rudi Pompilli spot with Bill Haley for a time) was subsequently to perpetuate the Jordan-inspired legacy with his roof-raising Deep Sea Jivers to the extent of touring with the Lindyhop Jivers' dance troupe. Others in the '80s—like The Chevalier Brothers, Rent Party, Ian Stewart's Rocket 88 and the Big Town Playboys—have also discovered that the Louis Jordan spirit and magic still holds good 40 years on.

Albums:

Chick Webb, King Of The Savoy (1937-1939) (Decca/MCA—Germany)
Chick Webb, Strictly Jive (1936-1938) (Decca/MCA—Germany)
Louis Jordan, Let The Good Times Roll (Decca/—)
Louis Jordan, The Best Of... (—/MCA)
Louis Jordan, Choo Choo Ch'Boogie (Philips Internationaly)
Silver Star Series Presents Louis Jordan & His Orchestra (MCA/Coral—Germany)
Louis Jordan/Chris Barber, Louis Jordan Swings (Black Lion)
Louis Jordan, Santa Claus, Santa Claus/ Sakatumi (Pzazz/—)
Louis Jordan, Prime Cuts (Swing House/—)
Look Out! (—/Charly)

Louis Jordan, Choo Choo Ch'Boogie (courtesy Philips International).

Stanley Jordan

Regarded as the most innovative guitarist since Jimi Hendrix, Stanley Jordan has laid claim to new territory for the instrument in the '80s. His revolutionary, two-handed 'tapping' technique has opened up a wealth of new possibilities for guitarists. He uses almost no strumming or picking and, rather than anchoring his right hand in the conventional way, both Jordan's hands roam the fretboard with equal freedom, achieving multi-textured contrapuntal lines without resorting to a battery of FX. His developments have enabled him to create a level of musical and orchestral complexity previously possible only on keyboard instruments.

From Palo Alto in California, Stanley Jordan was born in 1960. His piano training from age 6 was to influence greatly his later innovations on guitar. At 11, he became interested in the instrument, inspired by the late Jimi Hendrix. From 11 to 14, he listened to rock, blues and pop; then guitarists like John McLaughlin, Larry Coryell, George Benson, Wes Montgomery, Barney Kessell and Kenny Burrell, eventually moving on to keyboard-players like Herbie Hancock, Art Tatum and Keith Jarrett.

Frustrated by the limitations of the standard guitar instrument, he experimented with unorthodox tunings and made a significant breakthrough when he tuned his Travis Bean guitar in fourths. This simplified the fretboard, enabling him to expand his chordal vocabulary almost in a pianistic manner. By 16, he was developing his unique two-handed tapping technique—a method which took him nine years to perfect.

Above: Guitar revolutionary Stanley Jordan—from scratching for cents on the sidewalks to festival superstar in 1984 (photo: Allan Titmuss).

In '77, he went to Princeton University, graduating four years later with a degree in music. Soon, he was selling his first album—**Touch Sensitive** (recorded on his own label)—at his gigs.

In the spring of '84, he moved in on New York, although had such a hard time getting auditions for the clubs he played for pennies on the sidewalks, notably outside music stores like Manny's and Sam Asch on 48th Street, and even on Wall Street. Jordan's unannounced début at the '84 Kool Jazz Festival brought a phenomenal reaction, receiving similarly enthusiastic ovations at the Montreux Festival. That year, Jordan became the first new artist to be signed by Bruce Lundvall to the rejuvenated Blue Note label.

Jordan has kept detailed notes of his experiments over the years and has written a book about his innovatory technique for 21st Century Music Productions in New Jersey. Future possibilities include applying his technique to a classical project like Bach's Goldberg Variations. Aware that his technique is so unusual, Jordan feels that he has a responsibility to play in a diversity of styles, almost as though he's 'teaching' a new way of playing. Jordan's '84 Blue Note début, **Magic Touch**, demonstrates a cross-section of these styles.

On **Magic Touch** he plays blues (Miles Davis' **Freddie Freeloader**), ballads (Thad Jones' **A Child Is Born**), rock and pop (Lennon-McCartney's **Eleanor Rigby**, Jimi Hendrix's **Angel**, Rod Temperton's **The Lady In My Life**), jazz classics (Thelonious Monk's **Round Midnight**), plus his own improvisational compositions like the African-inspired **Return Expedition**. Produced by guitarist Al Di Meola, Jordan's **Magic Touch** presents an interesting showcase for the limitless possibilities of his innovative technique.

Jordan's appearance on the video *One Night With Blue Note—Preserved Volume One* (recorded February 22, '85) will, in time, become an important document of his early work. Much is promised by this exceptional young guitar pioneer as the years unfold. His development will be interesting.

Albums:
Touch Sensitive (Tangent Records/—)
Magic Touch (Blue Note/Blue Note)
Various, One Night With Blue Note Volume One (Blue Note/Blue Note)

Stanley Jordan's international début, Magic Touch (courtesy Blue Note).

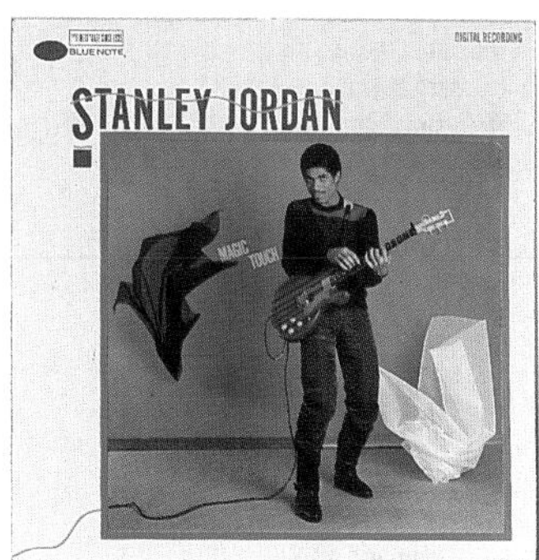

Stan Kenton

Band-leader Stanley Newcomb Kenton was born in Kansas in 1912, forming his first band in 1940 with a thirteen-piece group to play a residency at the Rendezvous Restaurant in Balbao, California. This was the jitterbug era, and Kenton's predilection for experimental classical music had to be tempered by the more straightforward demands of his audience. Although Kenton is usually associated with grandiose cathedrals of sound, he always played a varied book; dance music, pop, jazz and neo-classical. **Opus In Pastels (Artistry In Rhythm)**, arranged and composed by the leader in 1941, gives a fair idea of his aspirations, while **Artistry in Rhythm** from 1943 has a strong flavor of the movie concerto, with romantic Kenton piano, punching brass, thumping drums.

Numbers like **Eager Beaver, Painted Rhythm** and the June Christy vocal on **Tampico** are typical early '40s Kenton, and went out over the airwaves three times a week, gaining him a considerable following.

In 1945, arranger Pete Rugolo started working for the band, contributing numbers like the impressionistic **Interlude, Unison Riff (Greatest Hits)**; the Stravinsky-influenced **Artistry in Percussion** and the Ravel-influenced **Artistry In Bolero (Artistry In Rhythm)**, while Kenton wrote **Intermission Riff, Artistry In Rhythm** and **Eager Beaver**.

In 1947 Kenton organized his second orchestra with musicians like drummer Shelly Manne, guitarist Laurindo Almeido, tenorist Bob Cooper and trombonist Milt Bernhardt. Playing 'Progressive Jazz', which utilized dissonance and atonality, Kenton drew on the composing and arranging talents of Bob Graettinger, Neil Hefti, Gene Roland and Shorty Rogers. The sheer volume of the music, the screaming trumpet section, immensely structured works that slam in by section on schedule, intimidated the critics who declared Kenton's music empty and pretentious. Nevertheless, the Kenton Orchestra played the most upmarket venues, the classical concert halls and colleges.

His interest in Latin American music gave him his biggest hit of the period in **The Peanut Vendor (Greatest Hits)**. During 1950-51 he gave a series of concerts under the heading **Innovations In Modern Music** using a 43-piece orchestra including strings and woodwinds, and concentrating on neo-classical works like Graettinger's **City Of Glass**. In the early '50s the orchestra reverted to a jazz policy, employing a host of excellent soloists like altoist Art Pepper on **Blues In Riff**, altoist Lee Konitz on **Of All Things**, trumpeter Shorty Rogers on **Riff Rhapsody (Artistry In Jazz)**.

The list of talent that has been through the Kenton ranks is staggering—Vido Musso, Boots Mussulli, Jimmy Guiffre, Eddie Safranski, Frank Rosolino, Stan Getz, Bud Shank, Richie Kamuca, Bill Perkins, Charlie Mariano, Pepper Adams, Lennie Niehaus, Stan Levey etc. The economics of maintaining a big band for nearly 40 years without pandering to fashion indicated Stan Kenton's great organizational skills, as well as great artistic conviction. Throughout the '60s and '70s, orchestra succeeded orchestra—the Mellophonium Orchestra, the Neophonic Orchestra—and their output can be sampled via a late Kenton compilation, **Artistry In Jazz**, as well as on Kenton's own Creative World label.

Kenton's career was interrupted several times by poor health but he remained active and influential till his death in New York on August 28, 1979. His records are still eagerly sought by collectors.

Band-leader Stan Kenton's Greatest Hits (courtesy Capitol).

Albums:
Stan Kenton's Greatest Hits (Capitol/Capitol)
Artistry In Rhythm (Capitol/—)
Artistry In Jazz (Capitol/—)
Live At Redlands University (Creative World/—)
Adventures In Jazz (Creative World/—)
Kenton/Wagner (Creative World/—)
National Anthems Of The World (Creative World/—)
Viva Kenton (Creative World/—)
7.5 On The Richter Scale (Creative World/—)
Stan Kenton Today (London/Decca)
Stan Kenton Live In Europe (London/Decca)

Barney Kessel

A prolific recording artist, guitarist Barney Kessel, born 1923 in Muskogee, Oklahoma, was originally influenced by Charlie Christian. During the '40s, he played with both Charlie Parker **(Charlie Parker On Dial, Volume Three)** and Lester Young **(Jammin' With Lester)**.

The self-taught Kessel was based in Los Angeles in the '40s and '50s, cutting an excellent, swinging series of albums for the West Coast Contemporary label in company with Ray Brown and Shelly Manne **(The Pollwinners** and **Pollwinners Three)**. Oscar Peterson chose him for his JATP trio with bassist Ray Brown **(In Concert)**, a demanding role for an accompanist. Kessel subsequently worked in Hollywood, re-emerging from time to time to cut a jazz album.

Using a British rhythm section of Brian Lemon, piano, Kenny Baldock, bass, and Johnny Richardson, drums, Kessel played an excellent set at the 1973 Montreux Jazz Festival **(Summertime In Montreux)**, with the outstanding numbers being the phenomenally dexterous **Laura** and the unaccompanied Lennon-McCartney **Yesterday**. Again using a British rhythm section, Kessel recorded the beautiful **Autumn Leaves** and the roisteringly bluesy **Watch The Birds Go By (Swinging Easy)**. Barney Kessel is obviously an artist of broad tastes, capable of playing in most idioms from rock 'n' roll, **One Mint Julep (Slow Burn)**, to the modern musical *Hair*, **Frank Mills (Blue Soul)**.

Albums:
Charlie Parker On Dial, Volume Three (Spotlite/Spotlite)
Lester Young, Jammin' With Lester (Jazz Archives/—)
The Pollwinners (Contemporary/—)
Pollwinners Three (Contemporary/—)
Oscar Peterson In Concert (Verve/Verve)
Summertime In Montreux (Black Lion/Black Lion)
Swinging Easy (Black Lion/Black Lion)
Slow Burn (Phil Spector/Phil Spector)

Above: The Artist in Rhythm at work—Stan Kenton coaxes up a crescendo. His opuses gave rise to Progressive Jazz.

Left: Barney Kessel—he provided the guitar accompaniment for Julie London's Cry Me A River in the rock and roll movie The Girl Can't Help It.

Blue Soul (Black Lion/Black Lion)
The Poll Winners: Exploring The Scene (Contemporary/Contemporary
Just Friends (Sonet/Sonet)
Barney Kessel-Red Mitchell, Two Way Conversation (Sonet/Sonet)
Barney Plays Kessel (Concord/Concord)
Soaring (Concord/Concord)
Jelly Beans (Concord/Concord)
Barney Kessel-Charlie Byrd-Herb Ellis, Great Guitars At Charlie's, Georgetown (Concord/Concord)
Solo (Concord/Concord)

B.B. King

Together with Sam (Lightnin') Hopkins, John Lee Hooker and Muddy Waters, Riley 'B.B.' King remains the most important post-war blues guitar player. Certainly, from an all-round standpoint, he is the most gifted blues guitarist extant. Which makes it no surprise at all to learn that his basic influences include guitarists Django Reinhardt, Elmore James, Charlie Christian, Oscar Moore, Johnny Moore and T-Bone Walker.

King, and his beloved guitar 'Lucille', have, in turn, exerted tremendous influence on other players since the early 1950s—from blues, R&B, jazz, rock; even C&W.

In more recent years, B.B. ('Blues Boy') King (born Itta Bena, Mississippi, 1925) has tended often to alarm blues purists by straying outside a more or less defined blues bag; although blues remains King's most important love, he has been interested in many forms of music, right from a very early age. His singing, for instance, shows an obvious respect for and knowledge of the Big Joe Turner, Jimmy Witherspoon and Jimmy Rushing style of hard-shouting blues vocalism. In 1966, he recorded items from blues-shouters' repertoire like **Confessin' The Blues, Cherry Red, Please Send Me Someone To Love, I'm Gonna Move To The Outskirts Of Town, Goin' To Chicago Blues** (all on **Confessin' The Blues**). King regularly includes in his concert repertoire the Count Basie-Joe Williams hit, **Every Day I Have The Blues**, a number which he recorded in 1959 with Basie band **(B.B. King's Greatest Hits)**. And his most familiar single recording, **The Thrill Is Gone (Completely Well),** found the guitar and voice of King within unusual context (for blues performances) of strings, et al—a combination which worked admirably. First recordings, in 1949, were for Nashville label, Bullet (including **Miss Martha King),** with a 17 year-old Phineas Newborn on piano. King, cousin of another famous bluesman, Bukka White, had left his home town two years before for Memphis where he became, for three years, a resident disc jockey, following meeting with Sonny Boy Williamson II. In 1950, he commenced recording for Modern's RPM label—King's **Three O'Clock Blues**, for RPM, first major hit. This, and other subsequent recordings like **Woke Up This Morning** and **Sweet Little Angel** figured high on US R&B charts.

In 1961 he was signed by ABC-Paramount, commencing lengthy relationship between artist and company. With ABC, genuine excitement engendered at typical King live performances recaptured on record in superb albums like—**Live At The Regal, Live In Cook County Jail** and one side of **Live & Well**. King with rockers like Hugh McCracken, Al Kooper (who both appear on the other—non-live—side of **Live & Well**); Carole King and Leon Russell (both featured on **Indianola Mississippi)** and Pete Green, Stevie Marriott **(B.B. King In London)**.

Away from his usual concert and recording ventures—wherein King's abiding love for big-band jazz finds him supported by solid-swinging bands—B.B. King's instrumental luminosity occasionally turns up, delightfully if a trifle unexpectedly, in somewhat out-of-the-ordinary places. One such rare event took place at 1972 Newport/New York Jazz Festival **(Newport In New York '72: The Jimmy Smith Jam, Vol 5)** during which time the contrasting guitar virtuosity of King and Kenny Burrell produced mutually stimulating music during an all-star jam session performance of Percy Mayfield's **Please Send Me Someone To Love**.

Riley 'B.B.' King, Completely Well (courtesy ABC-Bluesway).

Albums:
Confessin' The Blues (ABC—Paramount/HMV)
The B.B.King Story, Chapter Two (—/Blue Horizon)
B.B. King, 1949-1950 (Kent/—)
B.B. King Sings Spirituals (Crown/—)
Blues In My Heart (Crown/—)
The Jungle (Kent/—)
B.B. King's Greatest Hits (America—France)

To Know You Is To Love You (ABC—Paramount/Probe)
The Best Of B.B. King (ABC/—)
Completely Well (ABC—Bluesway/Stateside)
Live At The Regal (ABC/HMV)
Live & Well (ABC/Stateside)
Live In Cook County Jail (ABC/Probe)
Indianola Mississippi Seeds (ABC/Probe)
Guess Who (ABC/Probe)
B.B. King/Bobby Bland, Together, Live... For The First Time (ABC—Impulse/ABC—Impulse
Various, Newport In New York '72: The Jimmy Smith Jam, Vol 5 (Atlantic/Atlantic)

Above: Blues luminary B.B. King—an enduring influence on guitarists from Buddy Guy and Luther Allison to Jimi Hendrix and Eric Clapton.

Rahsaan Roland Kirk

Born 1936 in Ohio, Rahsaan Roland Kirk was playing with R&B bands at 11, and fronting his own unit at 14. His talents as a performer were extravagant: not only could he play three horns at once but the result was usually creative music rather than vaudeville; not only could he blow continuously throughout a number (many instrumentalists can hold a note) but he could move all over the horn. In fact, he developed a method of changing his airstream, so that simultaneous inhalation and exhalation took place, **Saxophone Concerto (Prepare Thyself To Deal With A Miracle)**. His aim was to produce an unbroken carpet of sound, to 'catch the sound of the sun'. Basically a tenorist, his armory of outlandish instruments included the stritch, manzello, flute, nose flute, clarinet, police whistle and siren. He wore the lot on a complex network of straps and adhesive tape while performing, a street player's image.

Rahsaan's early association with Charlie Mingus **(Oh Yeah)** reinforced his own sense of tradition, for both men paid musical respects to New Orleans and figures like Duke Ellington and Fats Waller—**Eat That Chicken (Oh Yeah)** and subsequent dedications on Rahsaan's own albums **Creole Love Call, The Seeker (The Art Of Rahsaan Roland Kirk)**. His clarinet approached the genuine sound of New Orleans, but his flute-playing—a mixture of humming, gasping and note-production—was all his own and has been widely imitated: **You Did It, You Did It (We Free Kings)**.

Fine examples of his multiple horn-playing are scattered throughout his albums, most notably on **A Sack Full Of Soul (We Free Kings); The Inflated Tear (The Inflated Tear)**. A fairly comprehensive idea of his range is caught live in a club on a double album **(Bright Moments)**. Critics usually put him down as an eclectic, an arid judgement on a man whose creativity ransacked black music to such good purpose.

A jam session reunion with Mingus **(Mingus At Carnegie Hall)** saw Rahsaan picking up the challenge of the formidable tenorist, George Adams, and producing solos of superhuman drive.

During his 40-year lifetime, Rahsaan Roland Kirk became the world's most celebrated multi-instrumentalist, while his personal eccentricities became legendary. He had been born *Ronald* Kirk but changed his name to Roland and added the 'Rahsaan' in the late '60s after spirits visited him in a dream and 'told him to'. Accidentally blinded as a baby, Kirk grew up in a dark world filled with those spirits' voices. There was no end to his quest for new sounds and, if the instrument didn't exist to reproduce what he heard in his head, he invented it. Even at age 6, he was found trying to get music out of a garden hose. He progressed to the bugle and trumpet until a doctor advised him that the forceful blowing required for trumpet could make his eyes worse, so he switched to clarinet and saxophone.

His experiments with playing two instruments simultaneously started about '51. He tried all the reed instruments at a local music-store unsatisfied until the long-suffering owner dragged up a couple of oddities from the basement. Thus began Kirk's fruitful relationship with the soprano-like manzello and alto-sounding stritch.

In '65, he produced one of his most influential multi-instrumental albums, **Rip Rig & Panic**, using tenor, manzello, stritch, electronic effects and a siren, even breaking glass. The glass was a throwback to when, aged 17, he had played a certain harmonic causing a glass vase to fall from the shelf. **The Inflated Tear** album of '68 stands as a moving and anguishing insight into his personal tragedy, the title track being a painful journey back to childhood—to that irreversible moment when he'd been blinded: 'I went through years', he explained, 'where my eyes used to run and hurt and be nothing but *tears*....

Apart from his musical genius, he looked so startling. He was well-built and packed his stocky frame into a one-piece jumpsuit long before they were required stage-wear. The dozens of instruments would hang from his neck, clanking from side to side in rhythm as he leapt up and down in full solo flight. He also did crazy, unpredictable things which all helped build the legend of 'Kirk the Eccentric'. Tales of his antics abound, one favorite story being the occasion Kirk asked a club-owner for his money in advance—then sat down onstage and started to eat it...

Kirk's musical influences were many and wide-ranging—from the New Orleans' tradition to the jazz of Mingus, Waller and Coltrane, even classical composers like Stockhausen and Varèse.

Kirk was a complete original, reaching out in all directions for his inspiration. He passionately believed that his music was 'black classical music' and, as such, never lost touch with his blues roots. 'People talk about freedom', he said, 'but the *blues* is *still* one of the freest things you can play...' (evidence his excursion on nose flute, **Fly Town Nose Blues** from **Bright Moments**). Occasionally—and because he knew it was expected of him—he would pull out one of his famous party-pieces, like holding one note for a full 20 minutes demonstrating his astounding circular-breathing technique. He would even play two different tunes at once like the mind-boggling 'duet for one' with Ellington's classic **Sentimental Journey** vying with Dvorak's classical **Going Home (The Vibration Continues)**.

In 1976, he experienced a stroke, continued to perform one-handed, and recaptured his old facility. During his illness, he was showered with messages from all over the world, a tribute to his immense popularity. When Rahsaan Roland Kirk died on December 6, 1977, the music lost one of its greatest originals. but his spirit lives on through his recorded legacy and legend.

Rahsaan Roland Kirk, We Free Kings (courtesy Mercury).

Albums:
Charles Mingus, Oh Yeah (Atlantic/Atlantic)
We Free Kings (Trip/Mercury)
The Inflated Tear (Atlantic/Atlantic)
The Art Of Rahsaan Roland Kirk (Atlantic/Atlantic)
Bright Moments (Atlantic/Atlantic)
Prepare Thyself To Deal With A Miracle (Atlantic/Atlantic)
Mingus At Carnegie Hall (Atlantic/Atlantic)
Rip Rig & Panic (Limelight/Limelight)
Now Please Don't You Cry Beautiful Edith (Verve/Verve)
The Vibration Continues (Atlantic/Atlantic)

John Klemmer

A composer-arranger and multi-reeds-player (tenor, soprano and clarinet plus piano), John Klemmer became influential in the mid-'70s working with the Don Ellis Big Band—a period during which he became fascinated by applying electronics to the saxophone.

Born in Chicago, Illinois (July 3, 1946), Klemmer played guitar from 5 and alto at 11, moving to tenor in his teens. At school, he led concert and stage bands, and studied theory and arranging—jazz and classical—tenor sax, clarinet and flute. He cites his early jazz influences as Sonny Rollins, John Coltrane, Miles Davis and Bill Evans and declares an admiration for classical composers like Ravel, Debussy and Stravinsky.

From '60-'65, Klemmer took part in Stan Kenton clinics and in '67 was making bebop records for the Chess label. In late '68, he toured West Africa among the Oliver Nelson line-up, and from '70 took another direction—spending four years learning film scoring with Albert Harris. In the mid-'70s, he became a great attraction with Don Ellis' far-sighted and eclectic big band, his developments with Echoplex and phase-shifter devices bringing him much acclaim.

Since the early '70s, Klemmer has toured and recorded with his own groups which have included pianists Milcho Leviev and Russell Ferrante on keyboards, acoustic guitarist Oscar Castro-Neves, bassist Bob Magnusson and percussionists Roy McCurdy, Ray Armando and Steve Forman.

Multi-reeds-player John Klemmer, Finesse (courtesy Elektra Musician).

Albums:
Oliver Nelson, Black, Brown And Beautiful (Flying Dutchman/—)
Don Ellis, Autumn (Columbia/CBS)
Don Ellis, The Band Goes Underground (Columbia/CBS)
Don Ellis, Don Eillis At The Fillmore (Columbia/CBS)
John Lee Hooker, Born In Mississippi, Raised Up In Tennessee (ABC/—)
Involvement (Cadet/—)
Blowin' Gold (Cadet/—)
Eruptions (Cadet Concept/—)
Constant Throb (Impulse/Impulse)
Magic And Movement (Impulse/Impulse)
Fresh Feathers (ABC/—)
Touch (ABC/—)
Barefoot Ballet (ABC/—)
Finesse (Elektra Musician/Elektra Musician)

Earl Klugh

Creating a new audience for the acoustic instrument in the electronically dominated 1970s, Earl Klugh has described himself as an 'unorthodox guitarist', preferring to rest the guitar on his right knee rather than more conventionally on the left.

Born in Detroit, Michigan, on September 16, 1953, Klugh moved to gut-string guitar at age 10 after studying piano. Although primarily self-taught (his early inspirations included Chet Atkins, George Van Eps and Laurindo Almeida), by 16 he was giving guitar lessons at a local music store. His first break was being hired by Yusef Lateef. Then, at just 17, Klugh gained considerable learning experience joining George Benson's group, before going on to work with Chick Corea's Return To Forever for a couple of months. In '74, Klugh received the accolade of being chosen to tour with George Shearing, following in the footsteps of numerous famous guitarist predecessors.

Since '75, Klugh has enjoyed immense popularity as a solo performer refusing, in spite of his success in the more electronically oriented cross-over field, to surrender his subtle touch on acoustic guitar to the amplified instrument.

Guitarist Earl Klugh, Low Ride (courtesy Capitol)—creating a new interest for the acoustic instrument in an age dominated by electronic sound.

Albums:
George Benson, White Rabbit (CTI/CTI)
George Benson, Body Talk (CTI/CTI)
Flora Purim, Stories To Tell
(Milestone/Milestone)
McCoy Tyner, Inner Voices
(Milestone/Milestone)
Earl Klugh (Blue Note/Blue Note)
Living Inside Your Love (Blue Note/
Blue Note)
Finger Painting (Blue Note/Blue Note)
Dreams Come True
(United Artists/United Artists)
Late Night Guitar
(United Artists/United Artists)
Crazy For You (Liberty/Liberty)
Earl Klugh-Bob James, One On One
(Columbia/CBS)
Earl Klugh-Bob James, Two Of A Kind
(Columbia/CBS)
Low Ride (Capitol/Capitol)

Lee Konitz

Born 1927 in Chicago, altoist Lee Konitz is the most famous disciple of pianist-teacher Lennie Tristano, and the only one—apart from bassist Peter Ind—to play with musicians outside the 'Cool School' coterie. The long, thin-spun and serpentine lines of his alto mesh with those of tenorist Warne Marsh on Tristano's historic Capitol album **(Crosscurrents)**; baroque counterpoint quite at variance to the prevailing emotionalism of bebop. An album from 1949 **(Subconscious-Lee)** shows all the typical Tristano school characteristics, and on **Rebecca** Konitz duets with guitarist Billy Bauer.

His work with Claude Thornhill's orchestra, which used Gil Evans' arrangements, led to his inclusion in Miles Davis' classic sonnet **(Birth Of The Cool)** and Konitz solos on several tracks, most notably **Move** and **Israel**. Miles and Konitz, sharing similar emotional terrain, again worked together on **Ezz-thetic!** which featured two of George Russell's compositions, **Ezz-thetic** and **Odjenar**, avant-garde and less successful than **Yesterdays** and **Hi Beck** which are moving performances of great unity.

In 1952, Konitz joined Stan Kenton's orchestra, an unlikely environment for the introverted stylist, but one which stripped away much of the ethereal quality in his tone, and strengthened his attack. His collaboration with baritonist Gerry Mulligan the following year **(Gerry Mulligan-Lee Konitz)** showed how far he had developed, and **Too Marvelous For Words** is a classic performance. A Lennie Tristano album from 1955 **(Lines)** features a masterly live club date with Konitz, the altoist positively robust on **All The things You Are**. Relaxation and swing are characteristics of Konitz's reunion with Warne Marsh **(Lee Konitz & Warne Marsh)** fueled by the driving rhythm section of Oscar Pettiford and Kenny Clarke.

Much of Konitz's best work is from the late '50s **(The Real Lee Konitz, Very Cool** and **Inside Hi Fi)**, the latter showing a surprisingly rugged Konitz on tenor, the Mr Hyde within the fastidious Dr Jekyll. In 1961, the altoist startled the jazz world by recording a trio album with drummer Elvin Jones, a freer and more tigerish player than the usual Tristanoite choice of timekeeper **(Motion)**. Clearly, Konitz's horizons had widened considerably, for the teaming produce some of his most driving and emotional work.

The late '60s saw a revival of interest in the great original, and a Milestone contract. Characteristically, Konitz has explored the contemporary avant-garde, finding some of it incompatible and some—the pianists Bill Evans, Paul Bley and Andrew Hill—rewarding. **Invitation**, a duet by Hill and Konitz **(Spiral)** shows their spontaneous, one-take rapport.

Konitz's own albums cover a variety of settings, from the alto and bass duo **(I Concentrate On You)** to a series of duos with guitarist Jim Hall, tenors Richie Kamuca and Joe Henderson and trombonist Marshall Brown **(The Lee Konitz Duets)**, to a solo album **(Lone-Lee)**. More conventional groups elicit excellent playing—**Spirits, Satori** and **Oleo**—and show a growing interest in the soprano saxophone.

Lee Konitz is one of the greatest stylists in jazz. All stages of his development are unique from the airy lyricism and icily etched tone of his late '40s work to the fully rounded musical architecture of his maturity.

Albums:
Lennie Tristano, Crosscurrents
(Capitol/Capitol)
Subsconscious-Lee (Prestige/—)
Miles Davis, Birth Of The Cool
(Capitol/Capitol)
Ezz-thetic! (Prestige/—)
Gerry Mulligan-Lee Konitz
(Blue Note/Blue Note)
Lennis Tristano, Lines (Atlantic/Atlantic)
Lee Konitz & Warne Marsh (Atlantic/—)
Notion (Verve/Verve)
Andrew Hill, Spiral
(Arista Freedom/Arista Freedom)
I Concentrate On You
(Steeplechase/Steeplechase)
The Lee Konitz Duets (Milestone/Milestone)
Spirits (Milestone/Milestone)
Satori (Milestone/Milestone)
Oleo (Sonet/Sonet)
Lone-Lee (Steeplechase/Steeplechase)
Live At Laren (Soul Note/Soul Note)
Wild As Springtime (—/GFM)
Lee Konitz-Harold Danko-Jay Leonhart,
Dovetail (Sunnyside/—)
Dedicated To Lee (—/Dragon—Sweden)

Alexis Korner

On New Year's Day, 1984, the death of blues musician and catalyst Alexis Korner struck a hard blow to the British music scene. Korner had justifiably been hailed the 'Father of British Blues' having exerted an enduring influence on the blues scene in the United Kingdom and Europe from the '50s.

His first musical interests were jazz and he retained his passion for jazz till the end. But it's as a disciple of the blues that Korner will most lovingly be remembered—a form of music which he brought to Britain with an almost missionary zeal.

Born in Paris in 1928 (of a Turkish-Greek mother and an Austrian cavalry officer father), Korner settled in Britain during World War II. He had classical piano training from age 5 but in '40, at 12, he heard Jimmy Yancy and blues and jazz became his obsession.

Korner was instrumental in launching the all-acoustic skiffle boom in Britain with Chris Barber and Ken Colyer in the '50s. By the late '50s, Korner had teamed up with the gifted harmonica-player Cyril Davies and on May 3, '62—inspired by Muddy Waters' electric Chicago blues—Alexis Korner's Blues Incorporated made their national début at the Marquee Club in London. A couple of months later, the British blues boom was made official country-wide by the release of Korner's **R&B From The Marquee** . Edging out the national fervor for traditional Dixieland jazz, Blues Incorporated paved the way for the new rock era and heroes like the Rolling Stones, the Animals, Manfred Mann, Long John Baldry, the Yardbirds, Cream, Free and Led Zeppelin. Through the ranks of BI were to pass a host of jazz talents, too—Graham Bond, Phil Seaman, John McLaughlin, John Surman *et al.*

Through BI, Korner brought together a diversity of musical inspirations—Bessie Smith's **Yellow Dog Blues** sat alongside pieces by Charles Mingus, George Russell and Ornette Coleman. He had extraordinary musical vision, early recognizing the importance of Coleman when the critics and public were decrying him and, although a non-religious man, he loved gospel music.

During '68, Korner formed New Church with Danish singer Peter Thorup, daughter Sappho Korner and bassist Colin Hodgkinson (Hodgkinson later to co-found Back Door). In '71, Thorup

Below: Alexis Korner—an irreplaceable musician: British blues pioneer, band-leader and an immortal musical evangelist through his regular BBC radio show.

and Korner formed the immensely successful studio big band CCS (Collective Consciousness Society), scoring commercial hits with **Whole Lotta Love, Walking** and **Tap Turns On The Water**. At the end of the '70s, Korner often performed with the big blues band Rocket 88 and, in the '80s, was in great demand working in a duo with the phenomenally talented bassist Colin Hodgkinson.

But it was, without doubt, through his popular and influential weekly BBC radio show that Korner was able to touch so many hearts at once. Always a delight, and often a relevation, Korner would do a fast fade from recordings of native African drummers into the marvelous mayhem of Mingus' **Hog Callin' Blues**; the Staples Singers' harmonies would melt into Ry Cooder's slide guitar; a nomadic Arab's wail would blossom as the melodic tones of Bonnie Raitt; Sweet Honey In The Rock's gospel would be chased by a Sun House blues. Alexis Korner's musical perception was as all-embracing as his friendly, ever-open mind and personality.

As a musician, and a messenger of the music, Korner broke down the barriers that other (closed) minds had erected. Alexis Korner will be remembered as the man who built bridges enabling so many others to cross.

Albums:

The Legendary Cyril Davies With Alexis Korner's Breakdown Group And The Roundhouse Jug Four (—/Folkways)
R&B From The Marquee (—/Ace of Clubs)
Alexis Korner's Blues Incorporated (—/Ace of Clubs)
Alexis Korner And New Church—Both Sides (—/Metronome—Europe)
Accidentally Born In New Orleans (—/Transatlantic)
Get Off My Cloud (Columbia/CBS)
Bootleg Him (—/Rak)
Alexis Korner's Blues Incorporated (—/Teldec—Germany)

Gene Krupa

Gene Krupa (born Chicago, Illinois, 1909) was the archetypal showman-drummer, the man who brought the drummer to the public's notice in a way which hitherto had not been accomplished. Krupa, though, was not the best drummer —in terms of showmanship or otherwise. His basic style was an exciting one, with an accent on supplying non-stop powerful beat, using all the tricks of the drummer's trade to do so. But, for all his undoubted skills and ability to lift a band, Krupa was hardly the equal of drummers like Big Sid Catlett, Jo Jones, or his own percussion idol, Chick Webb. Nor did he possess, even during his peak years (1935-45), the speed of Buddy Rich, or the subtlety of Davey Tough; no matter.

Whilst an integral member of the Benny Goodman Orchestra (and sundry small groups), from 1934-38, Krupa made the jazz drummer into a real front-row personality. Better drummers there might have been during the period, and his drumming tended to sound a trifle heavy-handed and flashy with the trio and quartet, but the Goodman big band sounded better for his presence **(Benny Goodman, Vols 4-11)**. Krupa's specialty number with Goodman was **Sing, Sing, Sing (Benny Goodman, Vol 8)**, which hundreds of would-be Krupas attempted (unsuccessfully) to emulate. The gum-chewing, wisecracking Krupa reprised and extended **Sing, Sing, Sing** devastatingly during the legendary **1938 Carnegie Hall Jazz Concert** with an enraptured audience applauding his every break.

Krupa, a jazz enthusiast from a very youthful age, had spent nearly all the 1920s in his home town playing drums with as many of the leading Chicago jazzmen as possible. Indeed, he had participated at an important Chicago record date (1927), featuring McKenzie & Condon's Chicagoans **(That Toddlin' Town—Chicago 1926-28)** which first brought his name to the attention of record-buyers. In 1929 he moved to New York, spending most of next two years in various bands (including theater bands) fronted by Red Nichols, and recording with cornettist's Five Pennies **(J.T.)**. Played with mostly pop dance bands during early-1930s, although he managed to make jazz record dates at frequent intervals. Recorded with Goodman and Jack Teagarden in 1933 **(Benny Goodman & The Giants Of Swing/Jazz In The Thirties)** and with Goodman again in the following year **(Recordings Made Between 1930 & 1941)**.

After joining Goodman (in December '34), occasionally recorded in other company, as with New Orleans Rhythm Kings **(Kings Of Jazz)**—in February '35. Drummed especially well at Chicago record session under own name **(Gene Krupa & His Chicagoans)**, using personnel from Goodman band (including leader); also rhythm section colleagues Jess Stacy and Israel Crosby on further three titles **(Benny Goodman & The Giants Of Swing/ Jazz In The Thirties** and **Swing Classics, 1935/Jazz In The Thirties)**. Gene Krupa's Swing Band produced superb recorded jazz early in 1936 **(Benny Goodman, Vol 4, 1935-1939)**.

Left Goodman to start own big band, a venture which proved most successful until forced to disband, for personal reasons, in 1943. The 1938-41 unit was first-class. Additional plus factors were Roy Eldridge and singer Anita O'Day. **Drummin' Man** was a hit for the band; **Rockin' Chair,** thanks to Eldridge, was a popular favorite with fans; and Eldridge and O'Day were jointly featured on **Let Me Off Uptown,** another successful number (all **Drummin' Man)**. Krupa returned to Goodman during part of 1943, moving on to Tommy Dorsey (1943-44).

Own big band, again, from 1944-51, with Krupa sympathetic to the newer jazz sounds to emerge from bebop revolution (although Krupa himself did not make the transition from swing to bop). **Disc Jockey Jump** (composed and arranged by youthful Gerry Mulligan who also produced numerous other superior charts for band), **Leave Us Leap, How High The Moon, Lemon Drop** and **Stardust** (all **Drummin' Man)** were representative of the band's high-quality output.

Disbanding in '51, Krupa joined Jazz At The Philharmonic, sometimes featuring own trio **(Norman Granz' JATP Carnegie Hall Concert 1952** and **J.A.T.P. in Tokyo)** and often pitching Krupa and Buddy Rich into crowd-baiting gladiatorial situations. When not touring with JATP, led own trios. Started drum school, with Cozy Cole, in '54. Played on soundtrack of movie *The Gene Krupa Story* (alleged to be biography), in 1959. Active through 1960s, although laid off through heart problems on at least one occasion. Died of leukemia, in October, 1973.

Albums:

Various (Including McKenzie & Condon's Chicagoans), That Toddlin' Town—Chicago (1926-1928) (—/Parlophone)
Red Nichols/Jack Teagarden, 'JT' (Ace of Hearts)
Benny Goodman & The Giants Of Swing (Prestige)/Jazz In The Thirties (World Records)
Various (Including Benny Goodman), Recordings Made Between 1930 & 1941 (CBS—France)
Various (Including New Orleans Rhythm Kings), Kings Of Jazz (Swaggie—Australia)
Various (Including Jess Stacy), Swing Classics, 1935 (Prestige)/Jazz In The Thirties (World Records)
Benny Goodman, Vols 4-11 (RCA Victor—Records)
Benny Goodman, 1938 Carnegie Hall Jazz Concert (Columbia/CBS)
Gene Krupa, Drummin' Man (Columbia/CBS)
The Big Band Sound Of Gene Krupa (—/Verve)
Various (Including Gene Krupa), Norman Granz' Jazz At The Philharmonic Carnegie Hall Concert 1952, Record 3 (Verve/Columbia—Clef)
Various (Including Gene Krupa), J.A.T.P. In Tokyo (Pablo Live/Pablo Live)
The Exciting Gene Krupa (Verve—Germany)

Above: Steve Lacy—pioneer of soprano saxophone in post-bop jazz The most significant voice on soprano since Bechet, Lacy was Coltrane's inspiration.

Steve Lacy

Ironically, Steve Lacy who has pioneered the use of the soprano saxophone in modern music —the man who showed Coltrane the way and thus caused its mass acceptance—remains largely unrewarded and underrated.

Born in New York in 1934, Lacy was originally inspired by the great Sidney Bechet, and continued to play in the New Orleans-Dixieland tradition until he met Cecil Taylor. He played on and off with the avant-garde pianist over the next six years, more or less by-passing the complex harmonies of bebop. **Cecil Taylor & Donald Byrd At Newport** and **New York City R&B** are examples of his sheer intelligence in dealing with the new music. Happily Blue Note have re-issued some early Lacy **(In Transition/Cecil Taylor)** which shows him wisely avoiding that pianistic volcano with his long, tonally pure notes.

After Taylor, he fell under the influence of another piano giant, Thelonious Monk, and spent 12 years concentrating on the Monk repertoire. He formed a quartet with another ex-Dixielander, trombonist Roswell Rudd, and together they explored those angular harmonies and rhythms **(School Days)**. In the early '60s, arranger Gil Evans made frequent use of the soprano in his orchestral voicings, giving Lacy a chance to show his paces in performances like **Straight No Chaser (Pacific Standard Time)**.

In 1965, Lacy went to Europe, falling in with the US new music expatriates there, and showing up on various sessions with Don Cherry. Based in Paris for some years, he gradually put together a group of like-minded players, bassist Kent Carter, for example, and established his own music.

Following a totally free and themeless period of improvisation, Lacy has returned to using tunes that restrict him to given areas of exploration. For instance, **The New Duke** from a solo album **(Steve Lacy Solo)** uses a controlled farmyard squawk as its point of departure, while **Stations** uses a randomly selected radio station as inspiration.

His soprano covers an astonishing four octaves, and his tone in all registers is an ice maiden of purity. His approach over the years has been towards essences, so that his recent work has a concentration and rigor miles removed from the crop of dervish dancers.

In recent years, Lacy has built several groups round altoist Steve Potts and vocalist Irene Aebi, one particularly interesting project being his 'casebook cantata' **Tips** based on painter Georges Braque's written advice to artists.

Albums:

In Transition/Cecil Taylor (Blue Note/Blue Note)
School Days (Emanem/Emanem)
Pacific Standard Time, Gil Evans (Blue Note/Blue Note)
Steve Lacy Solo (Emanem/Emanem)
The Crust (Emanem/Emanem)
Saxophone Special (Emanem/Emanem)

Trickles (—/Black Saint)
Flakes (—/Vista)
Tips (—/hat Art)
For Example (—/FMP)
The Flame (Soul Note/Soul Note)
Two, Five And Six: Blinks (—/hat Art)
Misha Mengelberg-Steve Lacy-George Lewis-Arjen Gorter-Han Bennink, Change of Season (Soul Note/Soul Note)
Futurities (—/hat Art)
The Straight Horn Of Steve Lacy (Candid/Candid)

Tommy Ladnier

Thomas 'Tommy' Ladnier (born Mandeville, Louisiana, 1900) was one of jazz's all-time great blues instrumentalists. Blessed with only average technique, Ladnier made up for mechanical deficiencies by the moving quality of his playing, especially in respect of blues, a genre of which he was a master. In this respect, he was an obvious (and ideal) choice to support singers Ma Rainey **(Mother Of The Blues, Vol 1)**; Bessie Smith **(The Empress)**; and Ida Cox **(Ida Cox, Vols 1, 2)**, his work with the latter artist being exceptional. As member of Lovie Austin's Blues Serenaders **(Lovie Austin & Her Blues Serenaders)**, Ladnier's cornet was at its most beseeching, exemplified best of all on **Steppin' On The Blues, Charleston, South Carolina, Peepin' Blues** and **Mojo Blues**.

After moving to Chicago (before 1920) he worked with numerous name bands, including Charlie Creath, Ollie Powers **(Blues & Stomps, Vol 1)**, Fate Marable, King Oliver and Sam Wooding. With Wooding, visited Europe in 1925 and left band in Germany, going on to Poland with touring Louis Douglas revue (1926). Joined Fletcher Henderson (late '26), with whom he recorded several fine solos, including **Snag It, The Chant, Henderson Stomp (The Fletcher Henderson Story, Vol 1)**; and **St Louis Shuffle, I'm Coming Virginia** and **Goose Pimples (The Fletcher Henderson Story, Vol 2)**.

To Europe in 1928, again with Sam Wooding, followed by further tour of continent (after leaving Wooding in France) with Benton E. Peyton. Played in Spain and France (again, this time with own band), and worked in Paris and London with Noble Sissle Orchestra. With Sidney Bechet, formed New Orleans Feetwarmers. Combination of Bechet's totally uninhibited soprano sax, clarinet and Ladnier's more restrained passion resulted in glorious music, immortalized in recordings like **Maple Leaf Rag, Sweetie Dear, Shag** and **I've Found A New Baby** (all **Sidney Bechet, Vol 2**); and **Lay Your Racket** and **I Want You Tonight** (both **Sidney Becket, Vol 1**).

Tommy Ladnier's most powerful, poignant playing (on record at least) was produced in the year before he died (1938). At famous record sessions organized by French jazz critic Hugues Panassie **(The Complete Ladnier-Mezzrow-Bechet)** Ladnier's blues playing reached its peak of expression, gloriously so on **Revolutionary Blues, Weary Blues, Really The Blues** and **If You See Me Comin'**. During same month as final Panassie session, Bechet and Ladnier reprised **Weary Blues** at John Hammond-promoted concert at Carnegie Hall **(John Hammond's Spirituals To Swing)** supported powerfully by James P. Johnson and Basie-ites Jo Jones, Walter Page and Dan Minor. Suffered illness after this, and in June 1939, died from a heart attack in New York.

Albums:
Ma Rainey, Mother Of The Blues, Vol 1 (Riverside)
Tommy Ladnier, Blues & Stomps, Vol 1 (Riverside/London)
Ida Cox, Vols 1, 2 (—/Fountain)
Bessie Smith, The Empress (Columbia/CBS)
Lovie Austin & Her Blues Serenaders (Riverside/Fountain)
The Fletcher Henderson Story, Vols 1, 2 (CBS)
Sidney Bechet, Vols 1, 2 (RCA Victor—France)
The Complete Ladnier-Mezzrow-Bechet (RCA Victor—France)
Various (Including Sidney Bechet/Tommy Ladnier), John Hammond's Spirituals To Swing (Vanguard/Vanguard)

Bireli Lagrene

In danger of being saddled with the 'child-wonder' tag, guitarist Bireli Lagrene emerged — still in his early teens — as a remarkable individual talent in the 1980s. As early as 13, his exceptional technical facility on guitar, recreating the spirit of the immortal Django Reinhardt, was documented on disc **(Routes To Django**, '79). The tendency to regard Lagrene as purely 'a Reinhardt imitator' detracts from his own distinctive voice and versatility — his music incorporates a diversity of elements including Brazilian rhythms, blues, even funk-inspired fusion and he often drops in quotes from jazz standards like **St Thomas** and **Seven Come Eleven**. (His album **Back In Town**, recorded in '83, shows just how far Lagrene's musical directions had advanced in four years.)

Born on the German-French border in Alsace on September 4, 1966, Lagrene (like Reinhardt) comes from pure gypsy stock. Picking up the fundamentals of guitar at age 5 from his father Fiso (an established guitarist in France in the '30s and '40s), Lagrene is self-taught on guitar, bass, violin and zither, although he can't read or write music.

Lagrene came to attention at 12 in '78 winning a prize at the Strasbourg Festival. The following year, his appearance at a televised gypsy festival in Darmstadt brought him national recognition and, in '80, he was invited to play with Reinhardt-associate Stephane Grappelli and bassist Niels-Henning. More recently, he has performed with Larry Coryell and Philip Catherine and toured with the guitar trio of Al Di Meola, Paco De Lucia and John McLaughlin.

Lagrene lists his favorite guitarists as Joe Pass, Pat Martino, B. B. King, Wes Montgomery and Charlie Christian. His more recent influences include Joe Zawinul, Jaco Pastorius, Pat Metheny and Al Jarreau — perhaps a clue to his future development.

Albums:
Routes To Django (Antilles/Jazzpoint—Germany)
Bireli Swing '81 (—/Jazzpoint—Germany)
Bireli Lagrene 15 (Antilles/Antilles)
Down In Town (Antilles/Antilles)

Bireli Lagrene, Down In Town (courtesy Antilles)—prodigiously accomplished guitarist in the Reinhardt tradition with a developing, individual style.

Cleo Laine

see Johnny Dankworth & Cleo Laine

Lambert Hendricks & Ross

Originally formed as a vocal trio to record the one-off **Sing A Song Of Basie** in 1959, Lambert Hendricks & Ross created a wider audience for the vocalese style initially developed by the late Eddie Jefferson on **Moody's Mood For Love** (based on James Moody's solo on **I'm In The Mood For Love**), subsequently immortalized by Clarence 'King Pleasure' Beeks.

Dave Lambert (born in Boston, Massachusetts, in 1917) — an ex-drummer and former tree surgeon — had no formal music training. In '45, he and Buddy Stewart with the Gene Krupa band recorded **What's This**, credited as the first vocal bop record.

Jon Hendricks (born Newark, Ohio, 1921) had sung since childhood. A drummer like Lambert (he reads no music), he moved to New York as a songwriter (his instrumental, **Minor Catastrophe**, was recorded by the Art Pepper-Jimmy Knepper Quintet). In '57, he collaborated with Lambert on a vocalization of Jimmy Giuffre's **Four Brothers**.

Annie Ross (born Surrey, England, 1930) was raised in California. Her imaginative interpretation of **Twisted** in '52, on which she deftly vocalized Wardell Gray's tenor solo, brought her a wealth of admirers.

Together, Lambert Hendricks & Ross wrapped their gymnastic vocal style round instrumentals like Neil Hefti's **Li'l Darlin'** and Horace Silver's **Doodlin'**, Jon Hendricks setting lyrics, complete with space for individual vocalizations of the original instrumental solos. They subsequently appeared live to great acclaim, with a celebrated appearance at the '59 Jazz For Moderns tour. In '62, the Ceylon-born singer Yolande Bavan replaced Annie Ross until the group disbanded in '64. Dave Lambert was killed in a road accident two years later.

The innovations of Lambert Hendricks & Ross have had an enduring influence, particularly from the late '70s-early '80s in the vocal styles of Al Jarreau, Manhatten Transfer, Bobby McFerrin and Michael Franks.

Albums:
Sing A Song Of Basie (ABC-Paramount/ABC-Paramount)
Sing Along With Basie (Roulette/Roulette)
The Swingers (Pacific Jazz/Affinity)
Hottest New Group In Jazz (Columbia/CBS)
Havin' A Ball At The Village Gate (RCA/RCA)

Classic Lambert Hendricks & Ross, The Swingers (courtesy Affinity).

Harold Land

Born Houston, Texas, 1928, tenorist Harold De Vance Land got his first major break with the Max Roach-Clifford Brown group in 1954, staying two years and improving immensely in terms of dramatic power **(I Remember Clifford).**

Initially influenced by Coleman Hawkins, Lucky Thompson and Charlie Parker, he gradually developed an extremely individual approach to rhythm, and his solos with the excellent Curtis Counce Group have a real sense of the shaping mind. Solos like **Sarah** or **Landslide (Landslide)** grow in a serpentine fashion before the logical arrival at long-held notes. His warm, round sound is well illustrated by the ballad, **I Can't Get Started (Carl's Blues),** a sinuous mixture of the oblique and the declamatory.

Land cut two albums under his own name, collaborating fruitfully with pianist-composer Elmo Hope **(Harold In The Land Of Jazz** and **The Fox),** the latter being a classic. The title track is taken at a great clip but Land still shows his habitual mastery of tenor saxophone dynamics and structure.

A meeting with Thelonious Monk **(In Person)** resulted in some unusually committed examination of Monk's themes, and **Round Midnight** shows Land playing comfortably within this demanding field. Subsequent collaboration with vibes player, Bobby Hutcherson **(San Francisco, Total Eclipse** and **Now!)** showed Land's increasing allegiance to the Coltrane sound.

Albums:
Max Roach-Clifford Brown, Remember Clifford (Trip/Mercury)
Curtis Counce, Landslide (Contemporary/Contemporary)
Curtis Counce, Counceltation (Contemporary/Contemporary)
Curtis Counce, Carl's Blues (Contemporary/Contemporary)
Curtis Counce, Exploring The Future (Dooto/Boplicity)
Harold In The Land Of Jazz (Contemporary/Contemporary)
The Fox (Contemporary/Contemporary)
Thelonious Monk, In Person (Milestone/Milestone)
Bobby Hutcherson, San Francisco (Blue Note/Blue Note)
Bobby Hutcherson, Total Eclipse (Blue Note/Blue Note)
Bobby Hutcherson, Now! (Blue Note/Blue Note)
Dolo Coker, Dolo! (Xanadu/Xanadu)
Jon Faddis, Legacy (Concord/Concord)

Harold Land, The Fox (courtesy Contemporary)—re-issued via Boplicity.

Jazz In The Thirties (courtesy World Records)—features classic Eddie Lang alongside his old boyhood friend and long-time partner Joe Venuti.

Eddie Lang

Eddie Lang (born Philadelphia, Pennsylvania, 1904; real name Salvatore Massaro) was jazz's first real virtuoso guitar performer. His elegantly picked single-string work complemented by precise, warm chord patterns, and effortlessly rhythmic playing made him much in demand from early-1920s until his untimely death (complications resulting from tonsillectomy) in 1933.

During his all-too-short playing career he recorded prodigiously: consistency on record, whether solo or as accompanist, is testimony to his greatness. He possessed an extraordinarily keen ear and seemingly unlimited powers of invention. Studied violin from seven and at 13 met Joe Venuti, then aged 12, whilst both were in grade school. Had to read music for school concerts but had no need to read music for guitar or banjo (which he played at the beginning of his career in music) — his keen ear took care of that 'deficiency'. Played banjo, then guitar, on first professional engagement with Venuti in 1921, after previously making début at L'Aiglon Restaurant, Philadelphia, using violin, followed by short spell with Charlie Kerr Orchestra, this time using banjo. Continued to work prolifically with Venuti, the pair playing residencies in Atlantic City. After working with Billy Lustig's Scranton Sirens, became member of Mound City Blue Blowers, in '24, visiting London with the band (1924-25).

Settled in New York from mid-1920s, becoming involved with session work (ie radio, records). Worked with Roger Wolfe Kahn Orchestra (Venuti also in line-up) (1926-27), as well as in big band fronted by Adrian Rollini. Spent year with Paul Whiteman Orchestra (1929-30); again, Venuti was at his elbow. Appeared in Whiteman movie *The King of Jazz*, then back again with Roger Wolfe Kahn (1932). During year before he died, was employed as personal accompanist to Bing Crosby, whose admiration for Eddie Lang's guitar playing bordered on the idolatrous.

Recorded with Red Nichols **(Red Nichols & His Five Pennies, 1926-9)** soloing expressively on **That's No Bargain.** Played both banjo and guitar on classic Bix Beiderbecke recording **Singin' The Blues,** and assumed important role in intriguing versions of **For No Reason At All In C** and **Wringin' & Twistin',** as part of Frankie Trumbauer-Beiderbecke-Lang trio (all **The Golden Days Of Jazz: Bix Beiderbecke).** Had shared solo duties with Beiderbecke on 1927 recording of **Clementine (The Bix Beiderbecke Legend)** when both were members of Jean Goldkette Orchestra. And it was Lang who laid down an elegant rhythmic texture behind some of Tommy Dorsey's finest trumpet playing **(Tommy, Jimmy & Eddie, 1928-29).**

Lang was one-half of two of the most famous jazz partnerships. With boyhood friend Venuti, there is scarcely one Lang solo during any one of their impressively large number of recordings which is not of an impeccable standard. Lang's partnership with fellow guitarist Lonnie Johnson was, if anything, even more en rapport than that with Venuti.

The sheer beauty of the Johnson-Lang duo on such as **Midnight Call Blues, Blue Guitars, Blues In G, Hot Fingers (Blue Guitars);** and **Two Tone Stomp, Bull Frog Moan** and **Perfect (Blue Guitars, Vol II)** is unsurpassed in the field of jazz guitar. **Church Street Sobbin' Blues (Blue Guitars, Vol II, The Golden Age of Jazz: Eddie Lang-Joe Venuti/Stringing The Blues)** emphasizes that Lonnie Johnson was a far more natural blues player than Lang. Yet his solo on **In The Bottle Blues (The Golden Age Of Jazz: Eddie Lang-Joe Venuti/Stringing The Blues)** is masterful; something which can also be said for his contribution to **Knockin' A Jug (Blue Guitars)** in company, this time, with Jack Teagarden and Louis Armstrong. With Venuti, the Teagarden brothers, and Benny Goodman in support, Lang's playing on a 1931 record date by Eddie Lang-Joe Venuti All Star Orchestra **(Nothing But Notes)** was especially fluent, and fierier than usual. At a Venuti-Lang Blue Five session the month before he died, Eddie Lang played as superbly as always **(Ridin' In Rhythm).**

Albums:
Red Nichols & His Five Pennies (MCA-Coral—Germany)
The Golden Days Of Jazz: Bix Beiderbecke (CBS)
The Golden Days Of Jazz: Eddie Lang-Joe Venuti/Stringing The Blues (CBS)
The Bix Beiderbecke Legend (RCA Victor—France)
Tommy Dorsey/Jimmy Dorsey/Eddie Lang, Tommy, Jimmy & Eddie 1928-29 (—/Parlophone)
Joe Venuti/Eddie Lang, Venuti-Lang 1927-8 (—/Parlophone)
Joe Venuti/Eddie Lang, The Sounds Of New York, Vol 2: 'Hot Strings' (RCA Victor—France)
Blue Guitars, Vols 1, 2 (—/Parlophone)
Joe Venuti (Including Eddie Lang), Nothing But Notes (MCA Coral—Germany)
Various, Ridin' In Rhythm (—/World Records)

Yusef Lateef

Born Bill Evans, 1921, in Chattanooga, Tennessee, multi-instrumentalist Yusef Lateef was one of the first jazz musicians to incorporate Middle Eastern and Asian influences into his work. His early infatuation for the East led him to take up instruments like the argol and various ethnic flutes, pre-dating the general jazz interest by a decade or more.

A Detroit musician, many of his early groups included fellow citizens like Donald Byrd and Barry Harris. Lateef is featured on tenor, flute and oboe on an excellent album **(Eastern**

Sounds) which has the bass player Ernie Farrow doubling on the rabat. **Blues For The Orient** is an outstanding display of oboe, while a later album **(The Golden Flute)** shows his sensitivity as a composer and flautist.

Exoticism aside, Lateef is an excellent tenor-player, with a hard driving tone and a strong sense of the blues. **Rosetta** is a booting performance **(The Golden Flute)** and so is **Goin' Home**, despite tambourine and arco bass opening **(The Many Faces Of Yusef Lateef)**. Two albums recorded live **(Live At Pep's** and **Club Date)** catch the player at his peak with a fine quintet including the excellent trumpeter, Richard Williams.

Lateef has recorded very little as a sideman, and the period with Cannonball Adderley proved that he was rather more intense than his employer **(The Japanese Concerts)**.

The Many Faces Of Yusef Lateef (courtesy Milestone).

Albums:
Eastern Sounds (Prestige/—)
The Golden Flute (Impulse)
The Many Faces Of Yusef Lateef (Milestone/Milestone)
Live At Pep's (Impulse/Impulse)
Club Date (Impulse/Impulse)

Left: Multi-instrumentalist Yusef Lateef—his experiments with Eastern instruments pre-date 1960s' universalism.

Ronnie Laws

In 1976, saxophonist and flute-player Ronnie Laws earned himself the distinction of becoming the Blue Note label's biggest-selling début artist.

Born in Houston, Texas, on October 3, 1950, Laws comes from a musical family (his grandfather was a harmonica-player and virtually a one-man band; his mother, a gospel pianist; his older brother is flute-player Hubert; and his two sisters, Eloise and Debbie, are both singers). Playing from the age of 12, Laws grew up with the musicians who were later to form the Crusaders and while still at high school, Laws worked with his own group, the Lightmen.

After majoring in flute at Stephen F. Austin State University, at 21 he moved to Los Angeles where he played with rock band Von Ryan's Express, Quincy Jones and Walter Bishop. He became a member of Earth Wind & Fire for 18 months **(Last Days In Time)** and worked with Hugh Masekela, Los Angeles-based group Ujima and his brother Hubert.

Laws' first album—**Pressure Sensitive**, which scored such a success for the pre-Bruce Lundvall Blue Note label—was produced by fellow Texan and former Crusaders trombonist Wayne Henderson. Since that initial success, Laws has consistently produced winning albums and has carved out a niche for himself as a popular cross-over vocalist.

Albums:
Pressure Sensitive (Blue Note/Blue Note)
Fever (Blue Note/Blue Note)
Friends & Strangers (Blue Note/Blue Note)
Flame (United Artists/United Artists)
Every Generation (Blue Note/Blue Note)
Solid Ground (EMI-Liberty/EMI-Liberty)
Mr Nice Guy (EMI-Liberty/EMI-Liberty)

Huddie 'Leadbelly' Ledbetter

Bluesman Huddie Ledbetter was born in Louisiana in 1885, spending much of his youth there and in Texas, though his musical influences pre-date the regional blues.

A great maverick artist, Leadbelly's songs include folk material, reels, cowboy songs, spirituals and prison songs. He served two lengthy jail sentences for murder and intent to murder, and was discovered by the Lomax father-and-son team who were collecting recordings of folk music for the Library of Congress, and recorded at the Angola Penitentiary.

An indispensable repository of the vanishing musical heritage, Leadbelly traveled with the Lomaxes on their field-recording expeditions, and established himself as a night-club and concert-hall performer. His powerful voice and driving accompaniment on 12-string guitar produced many classic interpretations, **Good Night Irene, Rock Island Line, John Henry, Good Morning Blues** and **Ella Speed** being among the best-known. Since his death in 1949, his reputation has fluctuated. A legend to the white folklorists, his music was seldom popular among the black community.

Albums:
Leadbelly: The Library Of Congress Recordings (Elektra/Elektra)
Leadbelly's Legacy (Folkways/—)
The Leadbelly Box (—/Xtra)
Leadbelly (Stinson/Melodisc)
Leadbelly Sings & Plays (—/Saga)
Blues Songs By The Lonesome Blues Singer (Royale/—)
Good Morning Blues (—/RCA Victor)
Leadbelly, His Guitar, His Voice, His Piano (Capitol/Capitol)
Leadbelly—Keep Your Hands Off Her (Verve—Forecast/Verve—Folkways)
Take This Hammer (Verve—Forecast/Verve—Folkways)
Rock Island Line (Folkways/—)
Leadbelly—Last Session (Folkways/—)
Various, The Blues Legend (—/Time Wind)

Above: Huddie 'Leadbelly' Ledbetter—one of the most influential and colorful figures in the blues. His music encompassed blues and folk.

Peggy Lee

Peggy Lee (real name: Norma Deloris Egstrom, born Jamestown, North Dakota, 1922) is superbly representative of the kind of vocalist who, whilst operating in a basically pop field (Mel Torme is another) most definitely is strongly influenced by jazz

She came from a family of six children, began singing at 14 with semi-professional bands (broadcasting over local radio station), finally joining up with a vocal-instrumental outift called The Four Of Us. Benny Goodman caught the group in Chicago, and asked her to join his band (as replacement for Helen Forrest). He also gave her a new, professional name: Peggy Lee. Commercial success came with a July 1942 recording of **Why Don't You Do Right?** (arranged by band's pianist Mel Powell).

Made several record dates for Capitol, in 1946 winning as top female singer in that year's *Down Beat* readers' poll.

Became a successful single act, with hit recordings like **Manana, It's A Good Day, Don't Smoke In Bed** then later, **Mr Wonderful Fever** (a marvelous example of her rhythmic abilities with instrumental support consummately provided by just two jazz musicians, Shelly Manne, drums, and Joe Mondragon, bass), and **Is That All There Is?**

From a more basic jazz standpoint a 1953 album date, **Black Coffee**, in company with trumpeter Pate Candoli, drummer Ed Shaughnessy, pianist Jimmy Rowles and bassist Max Wayne, produced superlative jazz singing on titles like **Easy Living** (much influenced by Billie Holiday's version), **Love Me Or Leave Me, I Didn't Know What Time It Was**, and a whirlwind **My Heart Belongs To Daddy**; it is representative of her best work.

Other notable jazz-based recordings include sessions with Quincy Jones **(Blues Cross Country)**, Benny Carter, Max Bennett and Jack Sheldon (as featured trumpet soloist) **(Mink Jazz)** and a live recording, in company with George Shearing Quintet **(Beauty & The Beat)**.

Peggy Lee has appeared in a handful of films—*Mr Music* (1950), *The Jazz Singer* (1953), and *Pete Kelly's Blues* **(Pete Kelly's Blues)**, last-named for which she was nominated for Academy Award as best supporting actress.

Talented songwriter, she has written lyrics for successful full-length Walt Disney movie *Lady & The Tramp* (she also did soundtrack vocals), as well as a string of first-rate pop songs, including **It's A Good Day, What More Can A Woman Do, I Don't Know Enough About You, Where Can I Go Without You?, I'm Gonna Get It, There'll Be Another Spring, Then Was Then (And Now Is Now)**.

Albums:
We'll Meet Again (Hallmark)
The Very Best Of Peggy Lee (—/Capitol)
Black Coffee (MCA/Coral)
Bewitching-Lee (Capitol/Capitol)
Blues Cross Country (Capitol/Capitol)
Things Are Swingin' (Capitol/Capitol)
Mink Jazz (Capitol/Capitol)
Peggy Lee/George Shearing, Beauty & The Beat (Capitol/Capitol)
If You Go (Capitol/World Record Club)
Peggy (Polydor/Polydor)

George Lewis

George Lewis (born New Orleans, 1900) remains, for many purists, the archetypal New Orleans clarinettist. Self-taught, Lewis possessed all the customary attributes of the classic New Orleans players (other than a disconcerting habit of going out of tune, frequently, during his solos): a tremendous feeling for blues; warm, mahogany tone; ample use of both lower and upper registers of his instrument; and a typical New Orleansian basic rhythmic concept.

As a boy, Lewis' involvement with music began with his learning to play a toy fife, acquiring his first clarinet at 16. Outside New

George Lewis and his New Orleans All Starts, live in concert, King Of New Orleans (courtesy Telefunken).

Orleans, Lewis was not a household word until invited to take part in recordings by Bunk Johnson in '42, recordings usually credited with being in the vanguard of the great traditional jazz revival of 1940s. His singing and passionate playing alongside Johnson was a prime reason for the success of the trumpeter's American Music discs of the period.

Between 1917-23, he worked with many legendary New Orleans names, including Buddie Petit, Henry 'Kid' Rena, Kid Ory, Chris Kelly. After leading own band in 1923 (Henry 'Red' Allen played trumpet), joined Eureka Brass Band, working with them for several years. Joined Evan Thomas Band in 1932, based in Crowley, Louisiana (Bunk Johnson also worked in same band). Worked as stevedore in New Orleans, plus regular work as member of Eureka Brass Band. During a season at Harmony Inn, New Orleans, he played more alto sax than clarinet.

After Johnson-American Music recording sessions, returned to New Orleans for work with own bands. To New York with Bunk Johnson Band (1945-46), then back to New Orleans where he continued his band-leading activities. Worked in San Francisco with singer Lizzie Miles (1952), after which embarked on regular tours with own band (occasionally also as soloist). Visited Europe in 1957, 1959, to rapturous applause from fans—even though the playing of Lewis and fellow New Orleans veterans tended to be erratic. Received even wilder acclamation in Japan (1964) **(King Of New Orleans: George Lewis & His New Orleans All Stars Live In Concert)** with one of his best post-1940s bands, including 'Kid Punch' Miller, Louis 'Big Eye' Nelson and Joe Robichaux.

During his career, Lewis made other classic recordings, including the results of a 1943 date which contains superb Lewis clarinet on **See See Rider Blues, Lord, Lord You Sure Been Good To Me (George Lewis & His New Orleans Stompers, Vol 1)**; and **Just A Closer Walk With Thee, Deep Bayou Blues** and **Two Jim Blues (George Lewis & His New Orleans Stompers, Vol 2)** last-named title constituting realization of a totally supreme blues performance.

Lewis (real name: George Louis Francis Zeno) had to contend with continued poor health during his final years. Died in 1968, fittingly in the city whose music he had helped perpetuate so movingly, for so long.

Albums:
Bunk Johnson's Band 1944 (Storyville/Storyville)
Bunk Johnson & His New Orleans Band (Commodore/Melodisc)
George Lewis (American Music/American Music)
George Lewis & His New Orleans Stompers, Vols 1, 2 (Blue Note/Blue Note)
George Lewis: Classic New Orleans Traditions (Riverside/Riverside)
George Lewis With Kid Shots (American Music/—)
George Lewis Jam Session 1950 (Alamac/—)
George Lewis, On Parade (Delmark/Delmark)
George Lewis Memorial Album (Delmark/Delmark)
George Lewis Jam Session (Jazz Unlimited/—)

John Lewis

see Modern Jazz Quartet

Meade Lux Lewis

Meade 'Lux' Anderson Lewis (born Chicago, Illinois, 1905) spent part of his childhood in Louisville, Kentucky, where he learned to play violin, before turning to piano. Established reputation in and around Chicago as fine blues-player who could also adapt himself to play in several styles. Lewis (nickname 'Lux' apparently derived from fact that as a child he was often called Duke of Luxembourg) recorded a remarkable train blues for Paramount Records, in 1929; **Honky Tonk Train Blues** was later to become one of the most familiar tunes during late-1930s/early-1940s boogie-woogie craze. But during early-1930s, Lewis found work in music hard to find, working as taxi driver, member of a shovel gang, and carwash attendant. It was while working in latter capacity that John Hammond discovered him, late in 1935. And it was Hammond who persuaded Lewis to re-record **Honky Tonk Train Blues**, specially for release in Britain **(Ridin' In Rhythm)**; by following year Lewis was again involved with music, leading own band in Chicago and by end of 1936 had recorded **Honky Tonk Train Blues** on two further occasions.

After moving to New York, teamed up with Albert Ammons and Pete Johnson to form formidable boogie-woogie trio. Apart from recording as a threesome **(Café Society Swing & The Boogie Woogie** and **The Complete Library Of Congress Boogie Woogie Recordings)** and a live **Boogie Woogie Trio**, all three recorded in solo capacity. Lewis laid down a series of sparkling tracks for Decca **(Kings & Queens Of Ivory, 1935-1940)**, and for Victor **(29 Boogie Woogie Originaux)**. Also recorded for Blue Note **(Blue Note's Three Decades Of Jazz—1939-1949, Vol 1)** as solo pianist; as member of Edmond Hall's Celeste Quartet **(Celestial Express)**; and with Sidney Bechet **(Sidney Bechet Jass Classics, Vol 1)** to whom he gave sensitive support, on celeste, during the sopranoist's classic version of **Summertime**.

Lewis, whilst not as mightily percussive as his two boogie-woogie associates, was a more elegant pianist. Split from Ammons and Johnson in 1941, leaving New York, too, to settle on West Coast (Los Angeles). From whence he continued to tour, as solo act, and to record for a variety of labels. Apart from a live date for Norman Granz's Clef label in 1946 **(Boogie At The Philharmonic)** and a further studio session for same label in 1954 **(Yancey's Last Ride)** Lewis' playing was heard on Tops **(Barrel House Piano)**, Verve (again, for Granz) **(Cat House Piano)** and Stinson **(Meade Lux Lewis)**.

As well as with Bechet and Hall, Lewis used celeste on at least one other occasion, with delightful results. This was his own recording date **(Piano Jazz—Boogie Woogie Style)** which produced an eloquent **I'm In The Mood For Love** and **Celeste Blues**. However, his final recordings tended to sound clichéd; the boogie-woogie fad had, of course, long since expired, probably the victim of overexposure. Still, it was a sad occasion indeed when Lewis was killed in car crash in 1964 when returning from a gig in Minneapolis.

Meade Lux Lewis included on Ridin' In Rhythm (courtesy World Records).

Albums:
Various, John Hammond's Spirituals To Swing (Vanguard/Vanguard)
Various, Kings & Queens Of Ivory (1935-1940) (MCA—Germany)
Meade Lux Lewis/Albert Ammons/Pete Johnson, the Complete Library Of Congress Boogie Woogie Recordings (Jazz Piano/—)
Various (Including Meade Lux Lewis) Ridin' In Rhythm (World Records)
Various, Blue Note's Three Decades Of Jazz —1939-1949, Vol 1 (Blue Note)
Various, 29 Boogie Woogie Originaux (RCA Victor—France)
Various, Café Society Swing & The Boogie Woogie (Swingfan—Germany)
Various, Honky Tonk Train (Riverside/—)
Meade Lux Lewis/Albert Ammons/Pete Johnson, Boogie Woogie Trio (—/Storyville)
Meade Lux Lewis (Stinson/—)
Meade Lux Lewis, Boogie At The Philharmonic (Clef/Columbia—Clef)
Meade Lux Lewis, Yancey's Last Ride (Verve/Columbia—Clef)
Meade Lux Lewis, Piano Jazz—Boogie Woogie Style (Swaggie—Australia)
Various, Giants Of Boogie Woogie (Riverside/—)
Meade Lux Lewis, Barrel House Piano (Tops/Storyville—Denmark)
Meade Lux Lewis, Cat House Piano (Verve/—)

Ramsey Lewis

Ramsey E. Lewis, Jr (born Chicago, Illinois, 1935) has been one of the most successful cross-over artists to have risen to international prominence since the tail end of 1950s.

A pianist, composer and leader, his approach to conventional jazz gradually became synthesized with various other musical elements: soul, R&B, gospel, pop—even classical. Various Lewis-led combos (mostly trios) attained popularity starting with mid 1960s No 1 hit disc, **The In Crowd (Solid Ivory)** followed by other successful single releases, like **Hang On, Sloopy, Wade In The Water**, and **Uptight** (all on **Solid Ivory**).

He put together the first of his piano trios in '56 (with Eldee Young, bass, and Red Holt, drums). Combo gigged in and around Chicago until 1958, during which time Lewis also recorded with other jazz musicians (Clark Terry, Max Roach). First trio lasted ten years. Young and Holt eventually left to form Young-Holt Unlimited, replaced by Maurice White (later to found Earth Wind & Fire) and Cleveland Eaton. Since then Lewis-led small combos—their basic sound and concept pivoting on the leader's funky approach to piano—have continued to attract widespread attention from a majority audience, especially by way of their string of album releases, such as **Down To Earth, Back To The Roots, Tobacco Road, Upendo Ni Pamoja, Funky Serenity, Sun Goddess, Salongo** and **Love Notes**. Since 1976, Lewis has often worked with six-piece band (including flute, clarinet, guitar, vocals).

Albums:
Down To Earth (EmArcy/Fontana)
Tobacco Road (Chess/Checker)
The Groover (Chess/Checker)
Solid Ivory (Chess/Checker)
Back to The Roots (Chess/Checker)
Upendo Ni Pamoja (Columbia/CBS)
Funky Serenity (Columbia/CBS)
Sun Goddess (Columbia/CBS)
Salongo (Columbia/CBS)
Love Notes (Columbia/CBS)
The Best Of Ramsey Lewis (Columbia/CBS)

Booker Little

Born 1938, Tennessee, Booker Little died of uraemia at the age of 23 in 1961, another of jazz's tragically short-lived trumpet giants. His early promise was clear enough for Max Roach to hire him in 1958, along with his Memphis blowing partner, tenorist George Coleman **(Deeds Not Words)**. The association continued through Roach's magnificent political albums, with Little excellent on **Tears for Johannesburg (We Insist!—Freedom Now Suite)** and **Garvey's Ghost** and **Praise**

For A Martyr (Percussion Bitter Sweet).

Like Eric Dolphy, with whom Little produced much of his best work, the trumpeter was constantly searching beyond the chord changes: 'The more dissonance, the bigger the sound'. In fact, it is Little's lyricism that strikes the listener, the clean, sweet trumpet lines of **Ode To Charlie Parker (Far Cry)** or the soaring accuracy of **Life's A Little Blue** with Scott La Faro's brilliant bass below **(The Legendary Quartet Album)** while **The Grand Valse** invites comparison with the Roach-Clifford Brown waltzes. The collaboration with Dolphy is illustrated by the mammoth recording session from New York's Five Spot **(The Great Concert Of Eric Dolphy)**, both players hitting a peak on **The Prophet** and **Fire Waltz**. Little's arranging skills are prominent on singer Abbey Lincoln's album **Straight Ahead** and the rare Candid **Out Front**.

Albums:

Max Roach: Deeds Not Words (Riverside/Riverside)
We Insist! Freedom Now Suite (Candid/—)
Percussion Bitter Sweet (Impulse/Impulse)
Eric Dolphy: Far Cry (Prestige New Jazz/—)
The Great Concert of Eric Dolphy (Prestige/—)
Abbey Lincoln, Straight Ahead (Candid/—)
Out Front (Candid/—)
The Lengendary Quartet Album (Island/Island)
Victory & Sorrow (Bethlehem/—)

Booker Little, The Legendary Quartet Album (courtesy Island).

Charles Lloyd's widely awaited comeback album, Montreux 82 (courtesy Elektra Musician)—features Michel Petrucciani on piano and morale-raising.

Charles Lloyd

After a 10-year sabbatical, the reappearance in the 1980s of multi-reeds-player Charles Lloyd —one of the most popular and colorful figures of the late '60s—was an unexpected surprise and delight.

Born in Memphis, Tennessee, on March 15, 1938, Lloyd was given his first saxophone at age 9. He played with R&B bands while still at high school, led by such luminaries as B.B. King and Bobby 'Blue' Bland. He graduated from the University of Southern California in '60 with a master's degree in music.

Lloyd first came to prominence as musical director of the Chico Hamilton Quintet in 1960, taking over Eric Dolphy's place in the group. Both editions can be heard on one album **(Chico Hamilton)**, the later unit dispensing with the cello, and tracks like **Sun Yen Sen** putting the Rollins-Coltrane influenced Lloyd tenor through its paces.

Following a period with the Cannonball Adderley Sextet, Lloyd branched out as a leader. With guitarist Gabor Szabo and Miles Davis' rhythm section of Ron Carter and Tony Williams, he showed his range from the Coltrane-derived **Apex** to the prettily piping flute on the Giuffre-ish composition **Of Course, Of Course** (on album of same name).

An eclectic performer, Lloyd's commercial success led swiftly to formula. In 1966, he took his group to Europe on three rapturously received tours.

That period is typified by music from the catchiness of **Sombrero Sam** to the exoticism of **Dream Weaver**. With pianist Keith Jarrett's flashy facility and the excellent Jack De Johnette on drums (the whole group colorfully kitted out in beads and kaftans) Charles Lloyd was a festival favorite **(Forest Flower)**. With this excellent outfit, Lloyd was the first jazz musician to play San Francisco's Fillmore West—an indication of his all-embracing appeal and popularity. Around '69, however, he withdrew from music to embark on a long, inward, personal journey, meditating quietly on Malibu beach. He moved to California and out of this period came his association with the Beach Boys' Mike Love, forming the mid-'70s record company Lovesongs.

Afer 10 years of relative inactivity, Lloyd's sudden return to jazz in the early '80s was one of *the* events of the decade. His auspicious comeback is documented on **Montreux '82**. This live album shows Lloyd in great form with renewed energy in the remarkable company of 18-year-old French pianist Michel Petrucciani (responsible for persuading Lloyd to take to the road again), bassist Palle Danielsson and percussionist Son Ship Theus. Lloyd is also captured live with this excellent line-up, plus vocalist Bobby McFerrin, at the '83 Copenhagen Jazz Festival **(One Night In Copenhagen)** released in '85 on the rejuvenated Blue Note label.

Albums:

Chico Hamilton, Chico Hamilton (Atlantic/Atlantic)
Discovery (Columbia/CBS)
Of Course, Of Course (Columbia/CBS)
Dream Weaver (Atlantic/Atlantic)
Forest Flower (Atlantic/Atlantic)
Nirvana (Columbia/CBS)
Charles Lloyd In The Soviet Union (Atco/Atlantic)
Moon Man (Kapp/—)
Waves (A&M/A&M)
Geeta (A&M/A&M)
Weavings (Pacific Arts/—)
Big Sur Tapestry (Pacific Arts/—)
Pathless Path (Unity/—)
Autumn In New York (Destiny/—)
Montreux '82 (Elektra Musician/Elektra Musician)
One Night In Copenhagen (Blue Note/Blue Note)
One Night With Blue Note Preserved Volume 4 (Blue Note/Blue Note)

Loose Tubes

Since the Johnny Dankworth and Ted Heath bands of the 1950s, or the large Tubby Hayes unit of the '60s, Britain has lacked the luxury of a regular, extended, all-star 'pro' unit like America's Thad Jones-Mel Lewis Orchestra to provide an incubator for embryo talent. This function has largely been left to the National Youth Jazz Orchestra, under its dedicated director Bill Ashton, which has virtually singlehandedly — and on a regular basis — supplied the early training ground for many of today's young British musicians.

As a result, the 21-piece Loose Tubes has been hailed as one of the most important bands to appear on the British jazz scene, evolving in the mid-'80s from a rehearsal band originally instigated by composer and band-leader Graham Collier.

Loose Tubes has subsequently built up a unique organization of young, burgeoning talents, with a couple of 'older hands' (ie trumpeter Dave DeFries and tenorist Tim Whitehead) for good measure. Loose Tubes has included such gifted young musicians as pianist Django Bates; bassist Steve Berry; saxophonists Iain Ballamy, Steve Buckley, Mark Lockhart, Julian Arguelles; clarinettist Dai Pritchard; flute-player Eddie Parker; trumpeters John Eacott, Chris Batchelor, Lance Kelly; trombonists John Harborne, Steve Day, Richard Pywell, Ashley Slater; tuba-player Dave Powell; electric guitarist John Parricelli; and percussionists Nic France and Steve Arguelles.

Although a co-operative, Bates, Berry, Batchelor, Eacott and Parker write most of the arrangements. The band's individual brand of contemporary orchestration incorporates a welcome humor (often lacking in such weighty aggregations), drawing on a diversity of sources — minimalism, spacey ECM-inspired balladry, funky blues, Latin, swing, even Carla Bley-like passages — in all, a combination of cool precision and collective pandemonium, performed with a persuasive *joie de vivre*. The '85 album **Loose Tubes** and the '86 **Loose Tubes Too** (distributed by the London-based Import Music Service division of Polygram) combine into an excellent two-part catalog of a wealth of inspiration.

Loose Tubes has enjoyed considerable media attention, playing from cramped, local clubs to major national festivals including a performance in Green Park Station (one of Brunel's monumental edifices for the Great Western Railway) at the '86 Bath Festival.

Loose Tubes deserve to develop and, unlike others before them, not fall victim to the sad

Loose Tubes (courtesy Loose Tubes Records)—the cream of a rising generation of young British luminaries, including pianist Django Bates.

realities of big-band economics. Loose Tubes — with its cream of the rising generation — will go down in history as making a distinctly 1980s British music out of jazz

Albums:
Loose Tubes (—/Loose Tubes)
Loose Tubes Too)—/Loose Tubes)

Frank Lowe

Memphis-born tenorist Frank Lowe was influenced by Stax Soul as well as the more usual idols like John Coltrane. His early involvement with Sun Ra in 1966, and his studies in San Francisco with Donald Garrett and Sonny Simmonds, resulted in enormously strong, assured playing.

His work with ex-Coltrane drummer, Rashied Ali, in the exposed duo situation **(Duo Exchange)** is wildly exciting, screams, overblowings and honks used to devastating effect. Less coherent is the meeting with AACM saxophonist Joseph Jarman **(Black Beings)** which tends towards the unrelieved energy blast. His contribution to a Don Cherry album **(Don Cherry)** adds short, fiery dabs to the transcendental atmosphere.

His work with trombonist Joseph Bowie and trumpeter Leo Smith **(The Flam)** is a major achievement of group playing, showing Lowe's promise of becoming a major voice. Much more spacious and occasionally desultory, is the treatment of Monk themes, **Epistrophy** and **Mysterioso (Fresh)** while **Chu's Blues** has Lowe accompanied to good effect by the Memphis Four.

Albums:
Rashied Ali-Frank Lowe, Duo Exchange (Survival/—)
Black Beings (ESP/ESP)
Don Cherry (A&M/A&M)
The Flam (Black Saint—Italy)
Fresh (Arista—Freedom/Arista—Freedom)
Doctor Too Much (Kharma/—)
Exotic Heartbreak (Soul Note/Soul Note)
Decision In Paradise (Soul Note/Soul Note)

Tenorist Frank Lowe, The Flam (courtesy Black Saint—Italy)

Rashied Ali and Frank Lowe, Duo Exchange (courtesy Survival).

Above: Jimmie Lunceford. A perfectionist, for 20 years he fronted an exciting, superbly drilled orchestra—rival bands called them the 'trained seals'.

Below: Frank Lowe (right) with drummer Rashied Ali—they spurred each other on to even greater heights in a wildly exciting musical exchange.

Jimmie Lunceford

Jimmie Lunceford's orchestra was, along with Duke Ellington's and Count Basie's, one of the greatest of the 1930s. Less emotionally expressive than Ellington's, less unswervingly dedicated to swing than Basie's, it was superior to either in terms of virtuosity.

Lunceford's band was a great dance band; it was a visual treat, with the musicians wearing different uniforms for each show, sections standing up to point their trumpets at the ceiling, or rotating the trombones in circles, an expert showmanship that Glenn Miller copied; above all, it was a high-precision jazz outfit executing wildly original charts, and earning the description, 'the trained seals'.

Lunceford was born in 1902 in Missouri, receiving musical tuition from Paul Whiteman's father and going on to get a BA from Fisk University in 1926. His orchestra opened at Harlem's Cotton Club in 1933. The distinctive character came mainly from Sy Oliver's arrangements which were brilliantly unpredictable and showed a great feeling for dramatic contrast and dynamics. His range of approach — the simplicity of **Dream Of You** or **On The Beach At Bali-Bali**; the startling complexity of the section work on **My Blue Heaven**; the inspired absurdities of **Organ Grinder Swing**; the tongue-in-cheek deployment of sentimental vocals amid instrumental *tours de force* like Dan Grissom on **Charmaine** — shows that Oliver was one of the greatest arrangers in jazz history **(Harlem Shout, Harlem Express** and **For Dancers Only)**. His scores for **Swinging Uptown, Annie Laurie, Swanee River (Jimmie Lunceford), Muddy Water, Slumming On Park Avenue** and **Stomp It Off (Rhythm Is Our Business)** are classics, and when Oliver left to join Tommy Dorsey in 1939, he achieved the same miraculous blend of the straightforward and the staggering. Other Lunceford arrangers like pianist Ed Wilcox or altoist Willie Smith contributed fine scores, most notably for the unrivaled sax section which was dominated by the exuberant lead alto of Smith. **Sleepy Time Gal (For Dancers Only)** or **I'm Nuts About Screwy Music (Jimmie Lunceford)** show Wilcox's skill, while the sheer punch of guitarist Eddie Durham's **Harlem Shout** and **Avalon** rival the impact of Basie **(Harlem Shout)**.

Lunceford had two major soloists in Smith and trombonist Trummy Young, who joined in 1937, but tenorist Joe Thomas, trumpeter Eddie Tomkins and Durham all made significant contributions. The rhythm section, with the resourceful Jimmy Crawford on drums, functioned mainly in a two-beat style, a decision of Sy Oliver's which was hotly disputed by other members of the band, but which lends the band a distinctive springiness. Humor was a strong feature of the vocals, with Dan Grissom, Sy Oliver or the vocal trio featuring a light-hearted nod to commercial viability.

The peak years were 1933-43, with low salaries a big factor in the band's decline. The genius of Lunceford's arrangers elevated the slightest material into great music.

Albums:
Harlem Shout (MCA/MCA)
Harlem Express (—/Coral)
For Dancers Only (Decca/Brunswick)
Jimmie Lunceford (—/Brunswick)
Rhythm Is Our Business (—/Ace of Hearts)
Lunceford Special (Columbia/Philips)
Lunceford Special (Columbia/Realm)
Jimmie Lunceford & His Orchestra (—/DJM)
Blues In The Night (MCA/MCA)
Jimmie's Legacy (MCA/MCA)
The Last Sparks (MCA/MCA)

Humphrey Lyttelton

Since the mid-1940s, Humphrey Lyttelton (born Windsor, England) has been a catalytic figure on the British jazz scene, as a trumpet player (and occasionally clarinettist), bandleader, broadcaster and writer.

At the beginning of his career, Lyttelton was a staunch traditionalist, his own playing showing obvious affection for Louis Armstrong. With George Webb's Dixielanders, Lyttelton became a focal point in the great interest in traditional jazz in UK which followed World War II.

The ex-public schoolboy assembled first band in 1948, containing other bastions of traditional jazz in Britain, including Webb, clarinettist Wally Fawkes, joined later by brothers Keith Christie, trombone, and Ian Christie, clarinet. Music produced by these early Lyttelton bands tried faithfully to recapture that of famous US bands within the genre. It was not always the best kind of jazz to be heard and there were times when comparisons between the originals and the efforts of Lyttelton & Co were decidedly in favor of the former. But some of the band's recordings, including **Careless Love, Trouble In Mind, Trog's Blues** and **Original Jelly-Roll Blues** (all **The Best Of Humph 1949-56)** register with moderate conviction even today. And a 1956 recording of Lyttelton's own **Bad Penny Blues (The Best Of Humph 1949-56)** reached the Top Twenty of UK pop charts. Other Lyttelton recordings (from 1950-51) which bring back fond memories for British fans are **Tom Cat Blues, Get Out Of Here** and **Cake Walkin' Babies Back Home** (all **Humphrey Lyttelton Jazz Concert**).

Lyttelton's jazz horizons broadened during 1950s, music of his band moving more into a 'mainstream' groove. At the same time, Lyttelton's trumpet-playing evoked Buck Clayton as much as Armstrong. The presence of saxophonist/clarinettist Bruce Turner was significant in overall change in policy at this time. Other musicians to work with Lyttelton during '50s were saxist-clarinettist Tony Coe, tenorist Kathleen Stobart, baritonist Joe Temperley. Temperley, Coe and Jimmy Skidmore, tenor sax, worked with Lyttelton when **Triple Exposure** was recorded, in 1959; likewise, with **Blues In The Night** from following year.

Lyttleton band's repertoire on latter album was interesting: included were **Creole Love Call, Blues In Thirds** and **The Champ**. Buck Clayton recorded with Lyttelton band for first time in Switzerland, '63, and his presence inspired the band to give of its collective best **(Me & Buck)**. Clayton recorded on two further occasions with the band **(Le Vrai Buck Clayton** and **Le Vrai Buck Clayton, Vol 2)** with mutually rewarding results.

Just how much musical progress (in the best sense) Humphrey Lyttelton made in over 30 years as a jazz musician can be found within the grooves of **Duke Ellington Classics** with Lyttelton's trumpet most impressive as part of superb nine-piece band, including Ray Warleigh, alto sax, flute; Temperley; and John Surman. Lyttelton has recorded live on several occasions, probably best of all at London's Queen Elizabeth Hall, in '73 **(South Bank Swing Session)** which includes a Turner-Lyttleton clarinet duet **(Blues At Dawn)** rather in the manner of Mezzrow-Bechet. And Lyttelton's trumpet work during 1975-recorded **Take It From The Top** was as good as at any other time of his career.

Lyttleton, perennial catalyst, retains the ability to lift proceedings during someone else's gig, as he did, as guest, during an early-1970s concert by Alex Welsh Band **(An Evening With Alex Welsh, Parts 1, 2)**. A witty, perceptive writer, Lyttelton has also authored books: *I Play As I Please, Second Chorus* and *Take It From The Top*. The Humphrey Lyttelton Band made its first visit to US in 1959.

Above: (L. to r.) Humphrey Lyttelton—a catalyst on the British jazz scene, with Joe Temperley and blues singer Big Joe Turner.

Albums:

Humphrey Lyttelton, The Best of Humph 1949-1956 (—/Parlophone)
Humphrey Lyttelton Jazz Concert (—/Parlophone)
Humphrey Lyttelton, Triple Exposure (—/Parlophone)
Buck Clayton/Humphrey Lyttelton, Me & Buck (—/World Record Club)
Buck Clayton/Humphrey Lyttelton, Le Vrai Buck Clayton (—/77)
Buck Clayton/Humphrey Lyttelton, Le Vrai Buck Clayton, Vol 2 (—/77)
Humphrey Lyttelton, Duke Ellington Classics (Black Lion/—)
Humphrey Lyttelton, South Bank Swing (Black Lion/—)
Humphrey Lyttelton, Take It From The Top (Black Lion/—)
Various (Including Humphrey Lyttelton), An Evening With Alex Welsh, Parts 1, 2 (Black Lion/—)

Bobby McFerrin

Astounding audiences with his unaccompanied — ie voice *only* — 'orchestral' performances in the 1980s, the description of 'a rhythmic one-man orchestra' sounds incredible but, as far as the remarkable Bobby McFerrin is concerned, hearing is believing.

He was born in New York on March 11, 1950, into a distinguished family of vocalists (his father, Robert McFerrin, provided Sidney Poitier's rich singing voice in the film *Porgy and Bess*; his mother, Sara McFerrin — a soprano, chairs the Voice Department at Fullerton College). Bobby McFerrin composed his first 'song' at age 2 and from 5, studied theory at Juilliard, composing on piano, while taking lessons on clarinet, flute and piano. Moving to Hollywood in '58, McFerrin formed the Bobby Mac Jazz Quartet in his last year of high school, doing covers of Sergio Mendes and Henry Mancini tunes. In '70, Miles Davis' **Bitches Brew** opened McFerrin's ears to jazz Hearing Miles' group the following year, he was particularly impressed by pianist Keith Jarrett's solo improvisations — a musician who has remained one of his major inspirations (along with Jon Hendricks, Charles Ives and Fred Astaire).

After studies at Sacramento State University and Cerritos College, Norwalk (where he wrote arrangements for the school's big band), he made an unremarkable début with Shipstad & Johnson Ice Follies as a keyboard-player. In '77, what he describes as a 'voice' told him to become a vocalist and he initially worked the piano bars, the following year moving to New Orleans and joining the Astral Project. In '79, he came to wider attention singing with Jon Hendricks in New York and the following year appeared at the '80 Playboy Festival. But it was the '81 Kool Jazz Festival which was to bring overnight acclaim for McFerrin's wordless vocal improvisations.

Below: Bobby McFerrin—'the Voice'. An extraordinary, vocal one-man-band, his solo performances are enthralling and entertaining simultaneously.

His first album, **Bobby McFerrin**, is an introduction to the range of his vocal gymnastics (which span Charlie Parker to John Coltrane and Bach to James Brown, with just about everything in between) and includes an extraordinary interpretation of Van Morrison's enduring **Moondance. The Voice** (his follow-up album) comes closer to capturing the indescribable magic of McFerrin's live performance **(A-Train, Blackbird, I'm My Own Walkman** etc).

McFerrin has also toured and recorded with saxophonist Chico Freeman and has worked with Vocal Summit alongside vocalist Lauren Newton, Urszula Dudziak, Jeanne Lee and Jay Clayton.

Albums:
Bobby McFerrin
(Elektra Musician/Elektra Musician)
The Voice (Elektra Musician/Elektra Musician)
Chico Freeman, Tangents
(Elektra Musician/Elektra Musician)
Vocal Summit, Sorrow Is Not Forever—Love Is
(—/Moers)
Weather Report, Sporting Life (Columbia/CBS)
Joe Zawinul, Dialects (Columbia/CBS)

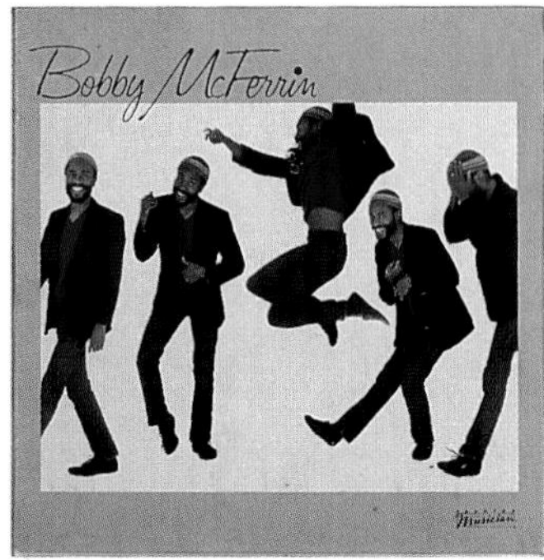

Bobby McFerrin (courtesy Elektra Musician)—'the Voice's' début album.

Chris McGregor

At a time when political developments in America lent an added significance to the African heritage of jazz, there emerged from South Africa a band that combined cultures in a natural, unselfconscious way.

Chris McGregor's Blue Notes — a racially mixed unit and therefore subject to apartheid laws — played at the Antibes Jazz Festival and then, through the good offices of South African pianist Abdullah Ibrahim (Dollar Brand), settled to regular gigs in Switzerland before reaching London in 1965. Their impact on the British scene was enormous, a force of nature.

The leader's antecedents place him uniquely at the roots of jazz — the son of a Scottish mission teacher, raised in South Africa, McGregor soaked up both the tin-roof Moody & Sankey hymnal and the music of Xhosan tribesmen. At the Capetown College of Music he fell under the influence of Schoenberg, Bartok and Webern but spent his evenings improvising in the native township bands. The Blue Notes — Dudu Pukwana, alto; Montezi Feza, trumpet; Johnny Dyani, bass; and Louis Moholo, drums — moved away from their highly original version of hard bop, into freer areas following a residency at Copenhagen's Montmartre, scene of recent gigs by Cecil Taylor, Albert Ayler and Don Cherry.

In 1970, McGregor organized the Brotherhood of Breath, a big band that moved easily between kwela, New Orleans, swing and the new wave. The proportion of writing to improvising is blurred, and a wild, often ragged ensemble fever will abruptly sweep the band. Moholo is a great big-band drummer, playing with an iron and irreducable simplicity, and there is no shortage of fine soloists, many of whom lead their own units. Dudu Pukwana's alto has the temperament of a burst fire hydrant and his own albums **(In The Townships** and **Flute Music)** are both explosive and danceable. Mongezi Feza, who died in 1975, was a rapidly developing trumpeter, moving away from the early Don Cherry influence into a personal style **(Music For Xaba)**. Harry Miller's unit, Isipingo, shows his lyrical writing and fine bass-playing.

In the '70s, McGregor settled in the French countryside and a new incarnation of the Brotherhood of Breath made its début at the Angoulême Festival in May '81 **(Yes Please)**, with a return to touring. In '84, the band toured Mozambique, inspiring a new McGregor project with singers and dancers.

Albums:
Blue Notes For Mongezi (—/Ogun)
Brotherhood Of Breath (—/RCA Victor)
Brotherhood Of Breath Live At Willisau
(—/Ogun)
Dudu Pukwana & Spear, In The Townships
(—/Caroline)
Dudu Pukwana & Spear, Flute Music
(—/Caroline)
Mongezi Feza, Music For Xaba (Sonet/Sonet)
Blue Notes For Mongezi (—/Ogun)
Procession (—/Ogun)
Piano Song, Volumes 1 & 2 (—/Musica)
In His Good Time (—/Ogun)
Brotherhood Of Breath, Yes Please
(—/In and Out)

Below: Chris McGregor, South African pianist, whose Brotherhood of Breath contributed so much to jazz in the United Kingdom in the 1960s and '70s.

John McLaughlin

With his revolutionary Mahavishnu Orchestra, John McLaughlin became one of *the* most influential and individual fusion guitarists of the 1970s. His awesome, soaring, seemingly ever-ascending guitar lines — exploding in increasingly mind-bending time signatures — test the limits of human endurance for both player and listener (for the partisan listener, though, McLaughlin's excesses of technique are almost exquisitely unbearable).

Born in Yorkshire, England, on January 4, 1942, McLaughlin was encouraged to learn piano from age 9 by his mother, an amateur violinist. All his brothers were musical and, two

Chris McGregor's Brotherhood of Breath, Brotherhood (courtesy RCA Victor).

years later, hearing an older brother playing the blues of Bill Broonzy, Muddy Waters and Leadbelly, McLaughlin knew his destiny was to be a guitarist.

Essentially self-taught, McLaughlin's earliest influence outside blues was flamenco music at 14; later, Django Reinhardt, Tal Farlow, Jim Hall, Barney Kessel, Miles Davis, John Coltrane, Cannonball Adderley, Bartok and Debussy were all to make a lasting impression. In the '60s, McLaughlin contributed to the British blues revival with Alexis Korner, Georgie Fame, Graham Bond and Brian Auger. He then entered into a period of experimentation with free music in company with baritonist John Surman and bassist Dave Holland **(When Fortune Smiles)**. In '68, he took part in pianist Gordon Beck's **Experiments With Pops**; in '69, the magnificent McLaughlin-Surman collaboration **Extrapolation** (with bassist Brian Odges and drummer Tony Oxley) produced some of the most exciting, free-ranging exploration heard in jazz at that time.

In '69, McLaughlin crossed the Atlantic and joined Miles Davis' drummer, Anthony Williams, in his new Lifetime unit. Through Williams, he was included on Miles Davis' influential new direction album **(In A Silent Way)** and the association continued with McLaughlin growing in confidence and a new economy **(Bitches Brew)**.

McLaughlin's **My Goal's Beyond** (early '70s, re-issued '82) has his solo 'duets' on jazz classics like Mingus' **Goodbye Pork Pie Hat** and Miles' **Blue In Green**, while the ensemble side featured Dave Liebman, Charlie Haden and Airto.

In 1971, the guitarist, by now a disciple of Sri Chinmoy, and deeply inspired by meditation, formed the Mahavishnu Orchestra with bassist Rick Laird, keyboard-player Jan Hammer, violinist Jerry Goodman and drummer Billy Cobham. Mountains of equipment appeared on stage to project the colossal volume, and the eclecticism of approach ransacked the globe. Playing a double-barreled guitar, McLaughlin's demanding rhythmic playing is usually closer to a fusion of Indian music and rock, and the group's impetus is based upon lengthy riff-figures, often used in multiples. The first orchestra **(Inner Mounting Flame, Birds Of Fire, Between Nothingness & Eternity)** was characterized by non-stop virtuosity by all members, and occasionally consequent confusion as to who was doing what. **Between Nothingness & Eternity** (recorded in concert in Central Park, New York) at times exposes the internal chaos McLaughlin's challenging charts created for the group, although allowance must be made for the 'liveness' of this performance. The collective dynamics of the long **Dreams** section (all side two) is considered by Mahavishnu devotees as the band's *pièce de résistance*, notable for the spectacular and staggering duet passages between McLaughlin and drummer Cobham.

Clash of egos resulted in the break-up of the orchestra, members like Cobham and Hammer making their own bids for stardom. The second Mahavishnu Orchestra launched out with electric violinist Jean-Luc Ponty and the London Symphony Orchestra **(Apocalypse)** in 1974, followed by a return to the earlier format **(Visions Of The Emerald Beyond)**. A meeting with fellow Chinmoy-disciple Carlos Santana resulted in disappointing **Love Devotion Surrender**.

In the mid-'70s, McLaughlin went deeper into Indian music with his quartet Shakti **(Shakti)** featuring an Indian line-up, L. Shankar on violin, Zakir Hussain, tabla, T. H. Vinayakram on percussion. With the all-acoustic Shakti, McLaughlin played a specially designed Gibson, its raised frets allowing for easier string-bending, enabling him to create 'drone-like' effects, simulating an authentic sitar sound. Early in '78, McLaughlin replaced Shakti with a short-lived electric group — the One Truth Band which included keyboardist Stu Goldberg, bassist Tom (T.M.) Stevens, violinist L. Shankar and drummer Son Ship Theus (later to work with Charles Lloyd).

In '78, McLaughlin took another direction, joining forces with Paco De Lucia and Larry Coryell, touring as a virtuosi acoustic guitar trio (Coryell being replaced in '80 by Al Di Meola — **Friday Night In San Francisco**). After two solo projects **(Belo Horizonte, Music Spoken Here)**, McLaughlin took the daring step of re-forming the Mahavishnu Orchestra **(Mahavishnu)** in '85 with Billy Cobham and a completely new line-up, this time minus a violinist but, instead, featuring the dynamic improvisations of saxophonist Bill Evans (formerly with Miles Davis). In '86, with new keyboardist Jim Beard, the Mahavishnu toured internationally, including an appearance at the André Previn Festival in London. In spite of an updated, mid-'80s sound, the Mahavishnu's original musical elements remain the same — the guitar mastery of John McLaughlin still takes the breath away.

Albums:
Miles Davis, In A Silent Way (Columbia/CBS)
Miles Davis, Bitches Brew (Columbia/CBS)
Miles Davis, Jack Johnson (Columbia/CBS)
Tony Williams' Lifetime, Emergency (Polydor/Polydor)
Tony Williams' Lifetime, Turn It Over (Polydor/Polydor)
John McLaughlin-John Surman, Extrapolation (Polydor/Polydor)
John Surman, Where Fortune Smiles (Pye/Pye)
Devotion (Celluloid/Celluloid)
My Goal's Beyond (Elektra Musician/Elektra Musician)
Mahavishnu Orchestra, Inner Mounting Flame (Columbia/CBS)
Mahavishnu Orchestra, Birds Of Fire (Columbia/CBS)
Mahavishnu Orchestra, Between Nothingness & Eternity (Columbia/CBS)
Mahavishnu Orchestra, Apocalypse (Columbia/CBS)
Mahavishnu Orchestra, Visions Of The Emerald Beyond (Columbia/CBS)
Mahavishnu Orchestra, Inner Worlds (Columbia/CBS)
Shakti With John McLaughlin (Columbia/CBS)
Shakti, Natural Elements (Columbia/CBS)
John McLaughlin-Carlos Santana, Love Devotion Surrender (Columbia/CBS)
Johnny McLaughlin, Electric Guitarist (Columbia/CBS)
John McLaughlin-Paco De Lucia-Al Di Meola, Friday Night In San Francisco (Warner Brothers/Warner Brothers)
Belo Horizonte (Warner Brothers/Warner Brothers)
Music Spoken Here (Warner Brothers/Warner Brothers)
Mahavishnu Orchestra, Mahavishnu (Warner Brothers/Warner Brothers)
Miles Davis, You're Under Arrest (Columbia/CBS)

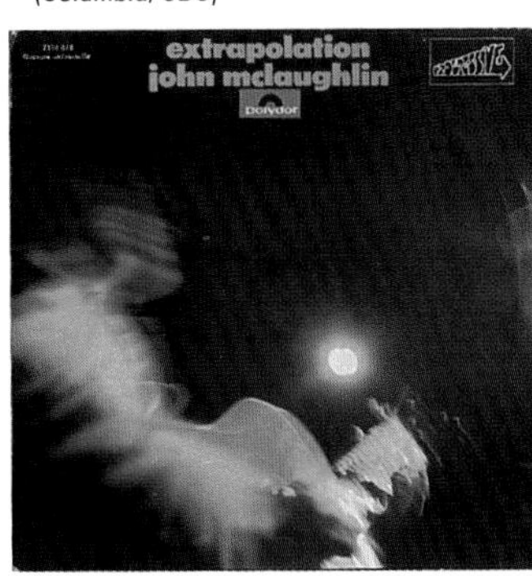

McLaughlin-Surman, Extrapolation (courtesy Polydor): a British classic.

Above: The uniquely gifted and innovative British guitarist-composer 'Mahavishnu' John McLaughlin has established an international reputation and influence.

Jackie McLean

Born 1931, altoist Jackie McLean had the early advantage of 'keepin' heavy company'. At 17, he was playing with giants like Charlie Parker, Bud Powell and Thelonious Monk, bebop's toughest forcing house. His earliest recordings with Miles Davis **(Dig)** catch both McLean and a young Sonny Rollins still under the Parker influence. A period with Charlie Mingus developed his tonal strength and exposed him to a freer climate in expressionist pieces like **Pithecanthropus Erectus (Pithecanthropus Erectus)** and raging gospel-inspired blues numbers like **Moanin' (Blues & Roots)**.

He spend nearly three years with Art Blakey's Jazz Messengers in the mid-'50s, sharing the front line with trumpeter Bill Hardman, and adding a sharp cutting edge to the unit which has subsequently utilized the beefier attack of tenor-players. McLean's work on **Little Melonae** and **Stanley's Stiff Chickens** shows how successfully he could ride the leader's furious battery.

Numerous hard bop sessions of the middle and late '50s feature the altoist **(House Of Byrd)** but it is with Blue Note's series under his own name that his full maturity blossomed. McLean's development had been steady, his tone becoming more expressive of emotional extremes—harsh, strident, relentless. His phrasing was angular and often unpredictable in its side-saddle relationship to the beat. No longer at pains to deliver the multi-note passages of a Parker, McLean's work was stark and economic.

All these characteristics cohere around the turn of the decade **(Swing Swang Swingin', Bluesnik, Capuchin Swing, New Soil** and **A Fickle Sonance)**. **Bluesnik** contains a bursting solo, massive drive with passages of wildly effective tonal distortion. **Francisco (Capuchin Swing)** is searing in its intensity. All his best work is driven by great drumming: Pete La Rocca, Art Taylor, Billy Higgins; the atmosphere at its most demanding.

The New York staging of the Jack Gelber play, *The Connection*, featured McLean as an actor as well as within the band, and the music is recreated on an excellent Freddie Redd album **(The Connection)**.

In 1963, influenced by free music developments from Ornette Coleman and John Coltrane, McLean announced a change of direction: 'the search is on'. The first album to display his freer approach **(Let Freedom Ring)** had all the old qualities of drive and inventiveness plus a more intensely vocalized sound ranging from oboe-like low notes to a high, searing whistle. Collaboration with the Blue Note school of young experimenters—Grachan Moncur III, Anthony Williams and Bobby Hutcherson—produced several excellent albums **(Destination Out, One Step Beyond** and **Evolution)**. 'The new breed has inspired me all over again', wrote McLean, and formed a band with the talented young trumpeter, Charles Tolliver, which was distinguished by fine writing from both of them **(Action, It's Time** and **Jacknife)**.

A meeting in 1967 with Ornette Coleman, featured on trumpet, showed that McLean's new direction was less radical and more rooted in conventional harmony than his iconoclastic sideman's, but that both men could work together fruitfully **(New And Old Gospel)**. The altoist's work for Steeplechase with veteran tenorist Dexter Gordon **(The Meeting)** and with fellow alto Gary Bartz **(Ode To Super)** find him in inventive form, and, in company with The Cosmic Brotherhood, sharing the front line with his son Rene **(New York Calling)**.

With the interest in hard bop running so high in the '80s, the UK-based Boplicity label's re-issues of McLean classics like **Swing Swang Swingin'** and **The Music From The Connection** have found a new and captive audience.

Albums:
Miles Davis, Dig (Prestige/Prestige)
Charlie Mingus: Pithecanthropus Erectus (Atlantic/Atlantic)
Blues & Roots (Atlantic/Atlantic)
Art Blakey & The Jazz Messengers (CBS-France)
Donald Byrd, House Of Byrd (Prestige/Prestige)
Swing, Swang, Swingin' (Blue Note/Boplicity)
Bluesnik (Blue Note/Blue Note)
Capuchin Swing (Blue Note/Blue Note)
New Soil (Blue Note/Blue Note)
A Fickle Sonance (Blue Note/Blue Note)
Freddie Redd, The Connection (Blue Note/Boplicity)
Let Freedom Ring (Blue Note/Blue Note)
Destination Out (Blue Note/Blue Note)
One Step Beyond (Blue Note/Blue Note)
Grachan Moncur III, Evolution (Blue Note/Blue Note)

Altoist Jackie McLean, Swing, Swang, Swingin' (courtesy Boplicity). The McLean classic, re-issued in the 1980s on the wave of revival of hard-bop.

Action (Blue Note/Blue Note)
It's Time (Blue Note/Blue Note)
Jacknife (Blue Note/Blue Note)
New And Old Gospel (Blue Note/Blue Note)
The Meeting (Steeplechase/Steeplechase)
Ode To Super (Steeplechase/Steeplechase)
New York Calling
(Steeplechase/Steeplechase)

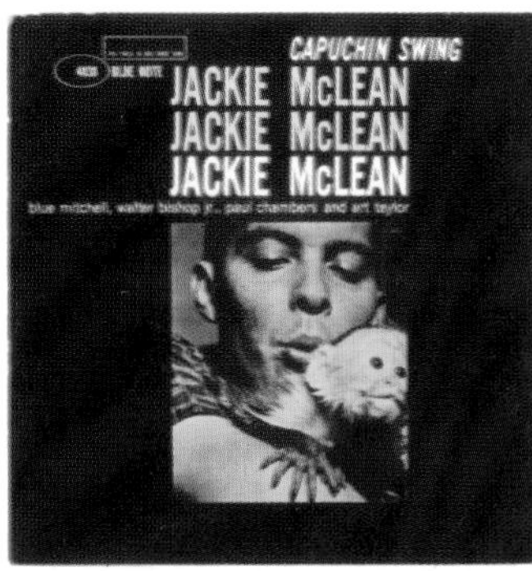

Altoist Jackie McLean, Capuchin Swing (courtesy Blue Note).

Joe McPhee

Trumpet and tenorist Joe McPhee is an interesting avant-garde musician, pretty on his first instrument (his father was a trumpeter, too) and darkly turbulent on the tenor. Both can be heard within one number, **Scorpio's Dance (Nation Time)** the character of the piece changing radically with the different horns. The title track, dedicated to playwright and poet LeRoi Jones (Amiri Baraka), is a long, churning free outing fueled by two drummers, Bruce Thompson and Ernest Bostic. **Shakey Jake** is probably the most approachable track, with attractive counterpoint and a danceable rhythm.

An earlier album **(Underground Railroad)** takes its title from the routes used by runaway slaves, and opens with a long drum solo—Bostic again—before the horns take over, McPhee on trumpet, Reggie Marks tenor, then the leader for a blistering tenor solo. Based mainly in the Poughkeepsie area, McPhee has played in New York with Dewey Redman and Clifford Thornton, and teaches at Vassar College.

Albums:
Nation Time (CJR/—)
Underground Railroad (CJR/—)
Trinity (CJR/—)
Pieces Of Light (CJR/—)

Jay McShann

Jay McShann (born Muskogee, Oklahoma, 1909) is an accomplished blues pianist with a reputation for leading a variety of blues-based bands, large and small. From late 1930s until comparatively recent times, McShann has continued to lead a variety of bands, each representative of what usually is known as 'Kansas City jazz'. It was after he commenced working in that city (mid-1930s) that his reputation was established, both as pianist and leader. By 1937, he had played and toured with various bands.

Same year, put together first combo (quintet), including bassist Gene Ramey and altoist Charlie Parker.

By 1940 the band had increased to eight pieces and was touring and broadcasting regularly, building up a healthy reputation. Parker, together with leader, was star soloist **(Early Bird)**. McShann Orchestra made first records in 1941 **(The Jumping Blues)**, by which time it was of big-band size. Blues shouter Walter Brown, an average vocalist, appeared on many of initial sides, but there was always room for solos by Parker, McShann, trumpeters Orville Minor, Bernard 'Buddy' Anderson, lead altoist John Jackson. Discs like **Swingmatism, Hootie Blues** (co-authored by Parker, McShann) and **One Woman's Man** achieved some degree of real popularity—**Confessin' The Blues**, written by Brown, probably was most popular of all. In 1942, the band became more widely respected, thanks in part to records like **The Jumpin' Blues, Get Me On Your Mind** (vocal, Al Hibbler), **Sepian Bounce** (all **The Jumping Blues)** but by 1943, Parker, its principal soloist, had left.

Following the band's New York début, McShann was called up for army service (1943). A year later, though, he re-formed, with subsequent McShann combos being seven or eight strong then spent 1945 and 1946 based in Kansas City, leading own combos.

Recorded for Swing Time (1947-1949), with sidemen such as trumpeter Art Farmer, guitarists Louis Speiginer or Tiny Webb, tenorists Maxwell Davis, Pete Peterson or Charles Thomas. There were generally superior blues vocals, especially those by Jimmy Witherspoon, and solid instrumentals **(The Band That Jumps The Blues!** and **Ain't Nobody's Business!)**. In 1957, McShann assembled two all-star bands to support his ex-singer Witherspoon for Victor sessions, which produced mostly first-rate music, vocally as well as instrumentally—**Blue Moods In The Shade Of Kansas City** and **A Spoonful Of Blues**. In 1969, McShann made his first European trip, appearing at Jazz Expo festival, London. Since then, has continued to tour, mostly as soloist, and been recorded at fairly frequent intervals. One such latter occasion took place during 1975 Montreux Jazz Festival **(Vine Street Boogie)** where McShann's solidly swinging piano-playing (and, on occasion, vocals) created a favourable impression, with McShann saluting Ellington on **I'm Beginning To See The Light** and **Satin Doll**, recalling personal successes of the past on **Hootie Blues** and **Confessin' The Blues**, and paying respects to his most famous band alumnus on **Yardbird Waltz.**

In 1976 Sam Charters selected McShann to play piano at recording date **(Kansas City Joys)**, co-starring Buddy Tate, Paul Quinichette (another former McShann sideman) and Claude Williams on violin, during which the spirit of KC jazz was evoked, superbly and rewardingly.

Albums:
Jay McShann/Charlie Parker, Early Bird (1940-1943) (—/Spotlite)
Jay McShann, New York—1208 Miles (Decca)/ The Jumpin Blues (Coral)
Various (Including Jay McShann), History Of Jazz, Vols 3, 4 (Capitol/Capitol)
Count Basie/Jimmy Witherspoon, Blue Moods In The Shade Of Kansas City (RCA Victor—France)
Jimmy Witherspoon, A Spoonful Of Blues (RCA Victor—France)
Jay McShann, Vine Street Boogie (Black Lion)
Buddy Tate/Paul Quinichette/Jay McShann, Kansas City Joys (—/Sonet)
Jimmy Witherspoon/Jay McShann, The Band That Jumps The Blues! (Black Lion)
Just A Lucky So-And-So (Sackville/—)

Left: The magnificent Jay McShann—his name is synonymous with Kansas City jazz His late 1930s band gave Charlie Parker his start.

Jay McShann and band, The Jumping Blues (courtesy Coral-Decca), 1941.

Mahavishnu Orchestra

see John McLaughlin

Mike Mainieri

As early as 1964, vibraphonist Mike Mainieri was path-finding the electronic potential for extending the instrument's sound. His subsequent five-octave 'synthi-vibe' (an ingenious synthesizer with a vibes keyboard) enabled him to bring 'the vibes out of the closet'.

Born into a vaudeville family in the Bronx, New York, on July 24, 1938, Mainieri took up vibes at age 10, inspired by Lionel Hampton's masterful concert performance. After a period at Juilliard, he joined the Paul Whiteman band and, in the '60s, spent six years with drummer Buddy Rich before turning almost exclusively to session work. He formed the much-vaunted 16-piece rock big band White Elephant and the quartet L'Image with Steve Gadd, Tony Levin and Warren Bernhardt.

His most successful group commercially has been Steps (a 'contemporary bebop band', formed '79) which has a particularly devoted following in Japan. Steps has included saxophonist Mike Brecker, drummer Pete Erskine, bassist Eddie Gomez and pianist Don Grolnick and was responsible for introducing the exceptional, if under-rated Brazilian keyboard-player Eliane Elias **(Steps Ahead)**.

Despite his youthful looks, Mainieri's career has been long and diverse, working with a variety of artists like Charlie Shavers, Roy Eldridge, Coleman Hawkins, Eddie Vinson, Benny Goodman, Chico Hamilton, Sonny Stitt, Billie Holiday, Philly Joe Jones, Elvin Jones, Paul Desmond, Bob James, Art Farmer-Jim Hall, Laura Nyro, Tim Hardin and Carly Simon.

Albums:
Blues On The Other Side (Argo/—)
White Elephant (Just Sunshine/—)
Love Play (Artista/Artista)
Journey Through An Electric Tube (Solid State/—)
Insight (Solid State/—)
Wanderlust (Warner Brothers/Warner Brothers)
Steps, Steps Ahead (Elektra Musician/Elektra Musician)
Steps, Modern Times (Elektra/Elektra)
Steps, Magnetic (Elektra/Elektra)

Above: Innovative vibist Mike Mainieri—since the late 1970s he has led his commercially successful 'contemporary bebop band' Steps.

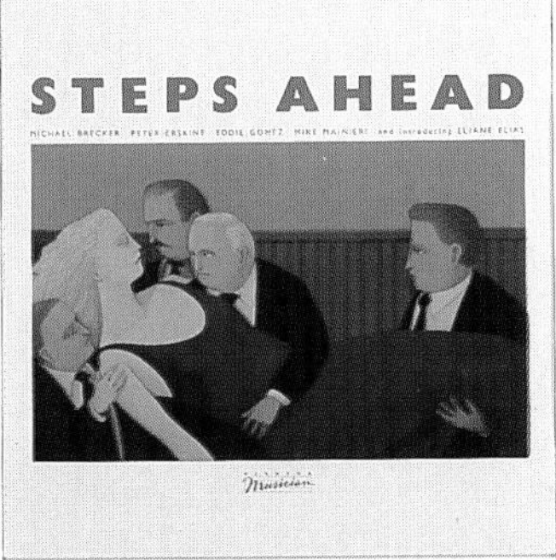

Mike Mainieri, Steps Ahead (courtesy Elektra Musician) with Elaine Elias.

Major Surgery

Affectionately remembered seminal British jazz-rock group formed in early 1970s by one of the country's most formidable and respected tenorists, Don Weller.

Weller—born in Thornton Heath, Surrey, on December 19, 1940—was playing award-winning clarinet from age 14 with the Croydon Youth Orchestra, before moving on to become one of Britain's most in-demand tenor-players (he also plays soprano with equal facility). His earliest jazz influence was Benny Goodman followed by Coltrane **(Blue Train)**, Hank Mobley and Dexter Gordon.

In the early '70s he worked with rock band East of Eden and the ground-breaking jazz-rock group Boris which included ace improvisers East of Eden/Colosseum blues guitarist Jimmy Roche, plus Jamie Muir and Jamie Peters. Out of Boris came the adventurous Major Surgery (Weller on tenor with guitarist Roche, bassist Bruce Colcutt, drummer Tony Marsh, pianists Gordon Beck and Pete Jacobsen). Playing Weller's idiosyncratic, definitive original compositions **(Foul Group Practices, Jubileevit, Fruit Salad (='Ballad'), The Deb** etc)—many written in collaboration with guitarist Roche—Major Surgery built up a loyal following. A particularly famous (or, perhaps, infamous) residency at Croydon's Dog & Bull public house inspired their Major Surgery 'classic' **Dog And Bull Fight**. Before Major Surgery disbanded in '79, they had sadly recorded only one album **(The First Cut** in '77), now a collector's item.

Since the demise of Major Surgery, Weller has been a regular member of Stan Tracey's Octet and co-led the Weller-Spring Quartet (with dynamic drummer Bryan Spring and pianist Martin Blackwell—**Commit No Nuisance)**. He is also a featured soloist with the Gil Evans Orchestra, has toured with trumpeters Hannibal Marvin Peterson and Ted Curson, and worked with Ian Stewart's big blues band Rocket 88.

It's Weller's distinctive horn which can be heard to such good, booting effect on Gil Evans' soundtrack for Julien Temple's ambitious *Absolute Beginners* (in the score, Weller's tenor represents the film's leading character).

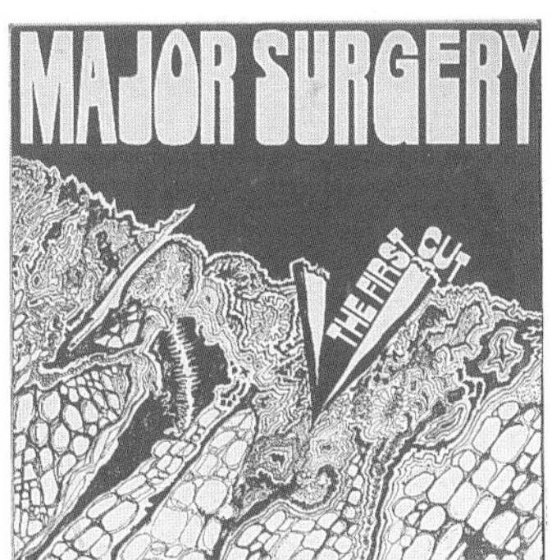

Don Weller's Major Surgery, The First Cut (courtesy Next): a British classic.

Albums:
Major Surgery, The First Cut (—/Next)
Mike Garrick, You've Changed (—/Hep)
Weller-Spring Quartet, Commit No Nuisance (—/Affinity)
Stan Tracey, The Bracknell Connection (—/Seam)
Gil Evans, The Gil Evans British Orchestra (—/Mole Jazz)
Stan Tracey, Stan Tracey Now (—/Steam)
Hannibal Marvin Peterson, Ben Song (—/Mole Jazz)

Manhattan Transfer

Formed in New York in 1972, Manhattan Transfer's distinctive four-part harmonies and multi-directional vocal style have created a wide international following, a broad appeal underlined by their regular receipt of awards in both 'jazz' and 'pop' categories.

Since their début, Manhattan Transfer—Tim Hauser, Janis Siegel, Alan Paul and Cheryl Bentyne—have been influential in reviving what had been waning interest in the jazz vocal tradition, notably through their now-classic interpretation (arranged by Janis Siegel) of Joe Zawinul's Weather Report *tour de force* **Birdland** and their skilful and extremely effective sorties into vocalese (à la Lambert, Hendricks & Ross).

After the success of their '84 **Bodies And Souls** album, which included a tribute to pianist Thelonious Monk, their thoughts turned to making a totally *jazz* album the following year. It was to be Manhattan Transfer's contribution to the 'acoustic revival'.

Their '85 album, called **Vocalese**, attracted such diverse jazz support as the Count Basie Orchestra, Dizzy Gillespie, Richie Cole, Grady Tate, Ron Carter, McCoy Tyner, Walter Davis Jr, Ray Brown, Jon Hendricks, Bobby McFerrin and the Four Freshmen. The album showcased Manhattan Transfer's jazz mastery with the memorable **Another Night In Tunisia; Sing Joy Spring; Meet Benny Bailey; That's Killer Joe; Airegin;** and **Oh Yes, I Remember Clifford**.

In the '86 Grammy awards, the Vocalese album scooped 'Best Jazz Vocal Performance: Group', with the track **Another Night In Tunisia** winning 'Best Vocal Arrangement for Two or More Voices' (Bentyne and McFerrin), and 'Best Jazz Vocal Performance: Guest Vocalists' (Hendricks and McFerrin).

Albums:
Manhattan Transfer (Atlantic/Atlantic)
Coming Out (Atlantic/Atlantic)
Pastiche (Atlantic/Atlantic)
Mecca For Moderns (Atlantic/Atlantic)
Bodies And Souls (Atlantic/Atlantic)
Vocalese (Atlantic/Atlantic)

Herbie Mann

For 13 years, Herbie Mann reigned supreme as *Down Beat* readers' choice of favorite flute-player in their yearly polls—a position unchallenged from 1959 to '71 when Hubert Laws narrowly edged him out of top spot. As a result, Mann's influence on flute has been all-pervading throughout a variety of styles from post-bebop to fusion.

Mann—born in Brooklyn, New York, on April 16, 1930—was playing clarinet at age 9. He also became a proficient tenor saxophonist before deciding to specialize in flute, then an under-used instrument in jazz

While posted to Trieste during his army days, Mann had three years in which to hone his exceptional technique while playing with a service band. During the early '50s, he worked and recorded with the Mat Mathews Quintet before joining Pete Rugolo's dynamic octet. In '56, he found his compositional talents much in demand writing and directing music for television. In '59, he also formed his Afro Jazz Sextet and went on a musically broadening, six-month tour of Africa. As the '60s unfolded, Mann's music was to incorporate many different elements—African, Latin, Brazilian, even Arabian, Jewish and Turkish, and in the '70s Mann eagerly embraced the potentially lucrative rock market.

Herbie Mann has often displayed a gift for adding an extra dimension to any musical setting. An example is the exceptional **Nirvana** album with Bill Evans' trio (including Chuck Israels on bass and Paul Motian, drums). The album featured standards like **Willow Weep For Me** and **Lover Man**, contrasting with Erik Satie's beautiful **Gymnopedie**, while Mann's own directions were revealed by his **Nirvana** and **Cashmere**.

In the late '70s, Mann's eclectic group was to provide a launching pad for the solo career of young vibrist Roy Ayres—one of his most celebrated protégés. Since the '80s, Mann's groups (including the aptly named Family of Mann) have been popular inclusions on the international festival circuit.

Albums:
The Evolution Of Mann (Atlantic/Atlantic)
Herbie Mann-Bill Evans, Nirvana (Atlantic/Atlantic)
Impressions Of The Middle East (Atlantic/Atlantic)
Waterbed (Atlantic/Atlantic)
Push Push (Embryo/—)
Windows Opened (Atlantic/Atlantic)
Memphis Underground (Atlantic/Atlantic)
Muscle Shoals Nitty Gritty (Atlantic/Atlantic)

Below: The multi-talented vocal four-piece Manhattan Transfer—their Vocalese album was an offering to the 'acoustic jazz' revival of the mid-1980s.

Mike Mantler

Composer Mike Mantler, married to Carla Bley, established his reputation with the avant-garde of the 1960s both musically and as a moving force behind the Jazz Composers Orchestra Association which produces its own albums and pools its musical resources.

Mantler's writing is chiefly structured to highlight the soloist, and he is brillantly served by Don Cherry, Gato Barbieri, Roswell Rudd, Pharoah Sanders and Cecil Taylor on a series of **Communications (Jazz Composers Orchestra)**. The characteristically slow, even swell of orchestral harmonies tends to evoke a sombre mood, and subsequent works based on the Samuel Becket monolog, **How It Is (No Answer)**; Edward Gorey's writing and drawing **(The Hapless Child)**; or Harold Pinter **(Silence)** are increasingly bleak. A competent trumpeter, he turns up on several JCOA productions.

Albums:
Jazz Composers Orchestra (JCOA/JCOA—Virgin)
No Answer (Watt/Watt)
The Hapless Child (Watt/Watt)
Silence (Watt/Watt)
Mike Mantler & Carla Bley 13 & 3/4 (Watt/Watt)
Something There (Watt/Watt)
Alien (Watt/Watt)

Mike Mantler and The Jazz Composer's Orchestra (courtesy JCOA-Virgin).

Charlie Mariano

The career of the eclectic Charlie Mariano has been interestingly diverse. One of the most important post-Parker alto-players, Mariano has developed an ever-broadening range with a variety of woodwind instruments like flutes and recorders, notably using the Italian nagaswarum (an unlikely 'jazz' instrument with which Mariano has opened up new musical dimensions).

Born Carmine Ugo Mariano in Boston, Massachusetts, on November 12, 1923, the alto and soprano saxophonist put in three years of study at Boston's Schillinger House (later called Berklee School of Music—he was to return here as a teacher in '75). By the late '40s, Mariano was exchanging musical ideas with Quincy Jones and Sam Rivers. Entering the ranks of Stan Kenton's progressive and exciting band **(Contemporary Concepts)** brought Mariano wider national attention between '53 and '55. He subsequently joined Shelly Manne's band in Los Angeles, returning to Boston to work with Herb Pomeroy. In '59, he rejoined Kenton briefly and in '62 was working with Charles Mingus. In the early '60s, he formed a band with pianist-composer Toshiko Akiyoshi (to whom, at that time he was married).

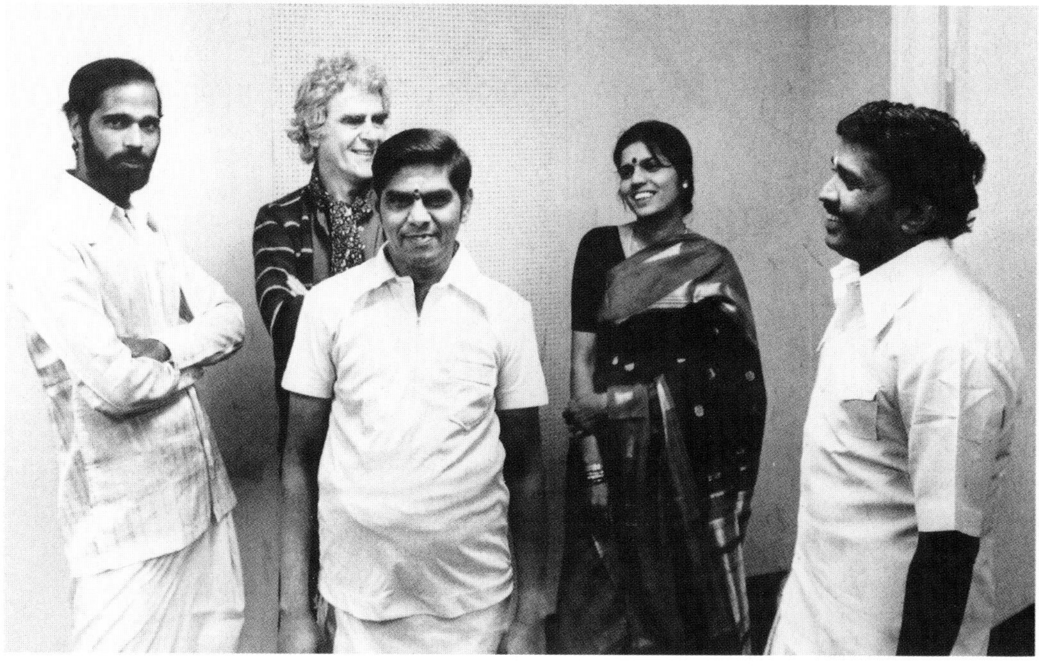

Above: Multi-reeds virtuoso Charlie Mariano—an inspired collaboration with the Karnataka College of Percussion in 1982.

During the '60s and '70s, Mariano was to combine his bebop experience with a more modern modal and Eastern-influenced meditative playing. In '71, he moved to Europe, working with Dutch keyboardist Jasper van't Hof and the English-born but Belgian-raised guitarist Philip Catherine, forming the group Pork Pie. Mariano has also been a vital contributor to bassist Eberhard Weber's Colours and works regularly with the much-vaunted German-based United Jazz+Rock Ensemble, the 'oldest member' of this 'Band of Band-leaders'.

Mariano's exploration of Indian instruments and modes (particularly on the decidedly odd-sounding nagaswarum) resulted from a trip to Malaysia and India in the late '60s. In the '80s, Mariano has continued to extend his musical experience. In '82, he traveled to Bangalore to work with the Indian musicians of the Karnataka College of Percussion. Their fascinating collaboration is documented on **Jyothi**.

Charlie Mariano-College of Karnataka, Jyothi (courtesy ECM).

Albums:
Stan Kenton, Contemporary Concepts (Capitol/Capitol)
Jerry Dodgion-Charlie Mariano, Beauties Of 1918 (World Pacific/—)
Alto Sax For Young Moderns (Bethlehem/Affinity)
Charlie Mariano-Jasper van't Hof-Philip Catherine, Sleep My Love (—/CMP)
Eberhard Weber, Touch (ECM/ECM)
Eberhard Weber, Eyes That Can See In The Dark (ECM/ECM)
Eberhard Weber, Little Movements (ECM/ECM)
United Jazz+Rock Ensemble, United Live Opus Sechs (—/Mood)
Charlie Mariano-Karnataka College of Percussion, Jyothi (ECM/ECM)

Branford Marsalis

An exceptionally versatile multi-reeds-player to emerge from the 1980s' new generation, Branford Marsalis was born on August 26, 1960, into one of New Orleans' most formidable musical families. His father is pianist, teacher and band-leader Ellis Marsalis, and he has equally accomplished brothers—Wynton plays trumpet; Delfeayo is a trombonist and Jason, a percussionist.

Although Branford's first instrument was piano at age 4, he was playing clarinet at 6. At 15, he characteristically opted for alto saxophone as his main instrument when his father said it was the hardest of the saxophone range to play. He took lessons briefly but fruitfully with Florence Bowser (a teacher he especially credits because of her all-round musical vision and support). In '78, he enroled at the Southern University at Baton Rouge, studying with clarinettist Alvin Batiste.

From '79-'81, Marsalis sharpened his musical skills at Berklee. During this time his remarkable versatility was becoming evident. He toured Europe as a baritone-player with Art Blakey's big band and played tenor on a creatively rewarding, if unfortunately short-lived, gig with Lionel Hampton, working with Clark Terry in '81. By now, his early high-school inspirations (Charlie Parker and Cannonball Adderley) were obviously broadening out to include Wayne Shorter (his hero), Sonny Rollins, Ornette Coleman, Joe Henderson and John Coltrane.

He went to New York where work was initially hard to find until eventually being faced with the unenviable choice of gigs with Elvin Jones or the chance to rejoin Blakey. He chose to go with Blakey, alongside his younger brother Wynton. In '82, Branford worked with Wynton's quintet on tour and in the studio, both touring internationally to great acclaim as part of Herbie Hancock's VSOP II.

The following year, Branford made his début album as leader, **Scenes In The City**—his arrangement and interpretation of the classic Mingus work. The album also gave full rein to his individuality as a player and a composer featuring a number of his own compositions like **No Backstage Pass, Solstice** and **Waiting For Tain.**

Refusing to limit himself, the eclectic and open-minded Branford Marsalis has also contributed reeds to some wide-ranging musical stylists including trumpeter Dizzy Gillespie, pianist Andy Jaffe, guitarist Kevin Eubanks and even with rock singer Sting.

Marsalis worked on Sting's album **The Dream Of The Blue Turtles** and appeared in the singer's '85 film *Bring On The Night*, interesting for the rehearsals of their first concert. Marsalis made his classical début in '86—**Romances For Saxophone** with the English Chamber Orchestra (CBS Masterworks).

Albums:
Fathers And Sons (Columbia/CBS)
Wynton Marsalis, Wynton Marsalis, (Columbia/CBS)
Wynton Marsalis, Think Of One (Columbia/CBS)
Wynton Marsalis, Hot House Flowers (Columbia/CBS)
Wynton Marsalis, Black Codes (From The Underground) (Columbia/CBS)
Art Blakey, Keystone 3 (Concord/Concord)
Kevin Eubanks, Opening Nights (GRP/GRP)
Dizzy Gillespie, New Faces (GRP/GRP)
Dizzy Gillespie, Closer To The Source (Atlantic/Atlantic)
Andy Jaffe, Manhattan Projections (Stash/Stash)
Scenes In The City (Columbia/CBS)

Branford Marsalis, Scenes In The City (courtesy CBS)—his solo début.

Wynton Marsalis

When the prodigiously talented trumpeter Wynton Marsalis arrived on the scene in 1980, just 19 years old, he was proclaimed as 'a symbol for the new decade'. Overnight, he leapt from exceptionally gifted teenager to one of jazz's hottest properties. The excitement and media attention was intense. By the time his first album as leader **(Wynton Marsalis)** appeared two years later, this undeniably technically brilliant musician had become a standard-bearer for his generation.

Born in New Orleans on October 18, 1961 (one of six brothers), his father Ellis Marsalis named him Wynton in honor of pianist Wynton Kelly. (Wynton, tenorist brother Branford and pianist Ellis can be heard together on **Fathers And Sons**).

At age 6, Wynton received his first trumpet courtesy of family friend and Ellis Marsalis-associate Al Hirt. But it wasn't until Wynton was 12 that he began taking his studies at all seriously when the teaching of John Longo instiled in him a love for playing, both jazz and classical. Wynton became a classical student of Norman Smith, principal trumpeter in the New Orleans Philharmonic, from whom he learned tonguing and phrasing, and the challenges of the piccolo trumpet. He also took lessons with Longo's old teacher—the veteran George Jensen (one of the few white players who were prepared to teach black musicians in the days of segregation). When Wynton was 12, he heard the formidable Maurice André and was inspired to study classical music even harder. By 14, he was playing solo on Haydn's Trumpet Concerto with the New Orleans Symphony.

At 17, Wynton arrived in New York with a full scholarship to Juilliard, ekeing out his allowance by playing in *Sweeny Todd* on Broadway. Then came his fortuitous meeting with Art Blakey who instantly recognized Wynton's potential (in spite of a disastrous—for Wynton—audition). So, he became a Jazz Messenger—another in a long line of trumpet geniuses like Kenny Dorham, Clifford Brown, Lee Morgan and Freddie Hubbard. After a few months with Blakey, George Butler sent Herbie Hancock a tape of Wynton's playing. As a result, Wynton substituted for Freddie Hubbard in Hancock's quartet on the eve of a tour, this experience leading to his début as a band leader on his first album **Wynton Marsalis** (produced by Hancock).

In '83, he toured internationally with Hancock's VSOP II line-up, alongside his older brother Branford. The same year, two Wynton Marsalis albums were released simultaneously, each to individual acclaim—the jazz project, **Think Of One**, and his classical début, **Trumpet Concertos**. In '84, his **Hot House Flowers** album showed a change of course featuring strings and his dynamic new arrangements of standards as well as his originals.

Also in '84, his **Black Codes (From The Underground)**—was his strongest personal statement yet: 'The overall quality of every true artist's work is a rebellion against black codes ... (a reference to the 19th-century slave laws). The album's musicians included brother Branford Marsalis (soprano and tenor), pianist Kenny Kirkland, bassist Charnett Moffett, Jeff 'Tain' Watts on drums and bassist Ron Carter on one track **(Aural Oasis)**.

A testimony to the respect and influence Wynton Marsalis subsequently commanded is contained in Burrill Crohn's film documentary *Trumpet Kings* ('85)—a profile of the instrument's most celebrated exponents including Louis Armstrong, Bunny Berigan, Roy Eldridge, Dizzy Gillespie, Freddie Hubbard and—in case anyone was still in *any* doubt—Wynton Marsalis.

Wynton Marsalis regards himself, his music and his various groups as the end product of a long tradition and has declared a commitment to uphold to standards of that tradition—an uncompromising artistry. This striving for individualism—'I do not entertain and I will not...I am a jazz musician...I play jazz'—has characterized the early days of his already distinguished career and has helped set Wynton Marsalis apart from the common herd.

Above: Trumpeter Wynton Marsalis, upholder of 'the tradition of uncompromising artistry'—so gifted, he was hailed as 'a symbol for the new decade' in 1980.

Below: An eclectic, open-minded and adaptable saxophonist, Branford Marsalis stands tall as one of the new 'young lions' of the music in the 1980s.

Albums:

Art Blakey And The Jazz Messengers, Live At Bubba's (—/Kingdom Jazz)
Art Blakey And The Jazz Messengers, Keystone 3 (Concord/Concord)
First Recordings (—/Kingdom Jazz)
Wynton Marsalis (Columbia/CBS)
Fathers And Sons (Columbia/CBS)
Think Of One (Columbia/CBS)
Trumpet Concertos (CBS Masterworks/CBS Masterworks)
Hot House Flowers (Columbia/CBS)
Black Codes (From The Underground) (Columbia/CBS)

Wynton Marsalis, Hot House Flowers (courtesy CBS).

Warne Marsh

Born 1927 in Los Angeles, tenorist Warne Marsh is a disciple of Lennie Tristano's 'Cool School'. Making his début with altoist Lee Konitz and leader Tristano on the celebrated Capitol session of 1949 **(Crosscurrents)**.

Marsh's work is characterized by great rhythmic subtlety, a pale sound and long, looping lines that plait with those of Konitz For many years, he recorded solely with other Tristanoites, preferring — like his mentor — to perfect his playing in isolation rather than compromise with the commercial world of the jazz club. A session from 1955 finds him sharing a recording with Konitz **(Lee Konitz & Warne Marsh)** in which counterpoint and the interplay of serpentine lines generate considerable heat and tension. This is Baroque music, full of odd accents and unpredictable shapes. Marsh's work with fellow tenor, Ted Brown, and alto Art Pepper is found on **Jazz Of Two Cities** and **Free Wheeling** and Art Pepper's belated release **(The Way It Was!)** catches the two men in a homage to their main influence, Lester Young, on **Tickle Toe**.

Marsh and pianist Joe Albany got together informally for a classic one-off session **(The Right Combination)** which contradicted all the critical brickbats about the tenorist's frigidity. **All The Things You Are** shows a rare melodic imagination at work while Marsh cooks like a peat fire. Bassist Peter Ind's British Wave label has examples of the mature Marsh **(Release Record – Send Tape** and **Jazz From The East Village)** which show that he is one of the most original players around.

Warne Marsh has only recently received the recognition he deserves. In 1969 he led a quartet of second generation Tristano followers through the familiar steeplechase tempos of **Lennie's Pennies** and **Subconscious-Lee (Ne Plus Ultra)**. In 1976 he went to Europe, teaming up again after 10 years with Konitz and the resulting music was a triumph of integrity, and a vindication of 25 years of obscurity **(The London Concert)**.

Albums:
Lennie Tristano, Crosscurrents (Capitol/Capitol)
Lee Konitz & Warne Marsh (Atlantic/—)
Art Pepper, The Way It Was! (Contemporary/Contemporary)
Joe Albany, The Right Combination (Riverside/—)
Release Record—Send Tape (Wave/Wave)
Jazz From The East Village (Wave/Wave)
Ne Plus Ultra (Revelation/—)
Lee Konitz+Warne Marsh, The London Concert (—/Wave)
A Ballad Album (Criss Cross Jazz/—)

Tenorist Warne Marsh, Jazz From The East Village (courtesy Wave).

Above: Hugh Masekela—1967 footage of the trumpeter in performance can be seen by re-running the movie Monterey Pop.

Hugh Masekela

In the mid-1980s, South African trumpeter Hugh Masekela enjoyed a new wave of success, particularly in Britain where the interest in Africa's musical tradition burgeoned.

Masekela was born in the coal-mining town of Witbank on April 4, 1939. From age 6 he was singing street songs, immersing himself in a strong, local church tradition and playing piano. Appaled at the injustices of the apartheid system, he realized that music was his only way out of South Africa. His early jazz education was listening to the records of Duke Ellington, Glenn Miller, Louis Jordan and Count Basie. His musical aspirations were encouraged at school by its enlightened chaplain, Father Huddlestone, who got him a trumpet.

In '55 Masekela formed the bebop-inspired Merry Makers of Spring with trombonist Jonas Gwanga. At 19, Masekela was a star trumpeter with Alfred Herbert's African Jazz Revue (the first black show which the authorities allowed whites and mixed races to view). Leaving the Revue, Masekela and Gwanga formed the Jazz Epistles with Dollar Brand (later Abdullah Ibrahim). As the political situation worsened in the early '60s, Masekela and Brand contrived to leave. John Dankworth and Harry Belafonte procured a passport for Masekela and a place at the Guildhall, London. He transferred to the Manhattan School of Music a few months later and eventually settled in California.

In the '70s, he toured Nigeria and Ghana with Fela Ransome Kuti's Africa 70, before putting his indelible stamp on the Hedzollah Soundz band. Back in California, he worked briefly with Dollar Brand-protégé pianist Cecil Barnard and saxophonist Rennie McLean (Jackie McLean's son) before returning to Africa in '80 — first to Zimbabwe, then Botswana.

With his Kalahari Band in '84, including top South African session musicians plus a quartet of women vocalists, he recorded **Technobush** (a eulogy to his roots) with Masekela classics like **Grazing In The Grass, African Secret Society** and **It's Raining**. The '80s have reconfirmed Hugh Masekela's status as an acknowledged master of African jazz.

Albums:
Trumpet African (Mercury/Mercury)
The Americanization Of Ooga Booga (MGM/MGM)
The Emancipation Of Hugh Masekela (Chisa/—)
Promise Of A Future (Chisa/—)
Reconstruction (Chisa/—)
Home Is Where The Music Is (Chisa/—)
Hedzollah Soundz, Colonial Man (Chisa/—)
Main Event (A&M/A&M)
Herb Alpert-Hugh Masekela, Herb Alpert/Hugh Masekela (A&M/A&M)
Kalahari Band, Technobush (—/Jive Africa)

George Melly

George Melly, author, art expert, film and television critic, cartoon collaborator and entertainer is a difficult man to classify. Influenced by Bessie Smith, Melly first came to prominence as a singer during the British trad boom of the early 1950s. His re-emergence in 1974 with John Chilton's Feetwarmers has proved immensely successful, and although he is an all-round entertainer rather than a blues singer, he has feeling for the form.

Albums:
Nuts (Warner/Warner)
Son Of Nuts (Warner/Warner)
It's George (Warner/Warner)
At It Again (Reprise/Reprise)

Memphis Slim

Memphis Slim (real name: Peter Chatman), born Memphis, Tennessee, 1915, has become, since the 1950s, one of the most popular of all blues performers. He has a fine vocal style — rarely intense or chilling like, say, Blind Lemon Jefferson, or profound like Big Bill Broonzy — but convincing nevertheless. His rolling piano-playing is proof of continued validity of the barrelhouse-cum-boogie-woogie school. Compositionally, too, is one of the most accomplished writers. His most famous number, **Every Day I Have The Blues** — indeed a modern blues standard — achieved international acclaim following recording by singer Joe Williams and orchestra of Count Basie **(Count Basie Swings, Joe Williams Sings)**. Same combination brought Slim's **The Comeback** before a wide audience.

Memphis Slim began his career in 1934, deputizing for one of his early blues idols, Roosevelt Sykes. It really began, though, after moving to Chicago in 1939. He jammed with top artists there, including Sonny Boy Williamson, Big Bill Broonzy, Washboard Sam. Became regular pianist for Broonzy following year. Also in 1940 made record début for Bluebird. Slim's humorous **Beer Drinking Woman (Memphis Slim)** helped establish his name almost immediately. Other fine early-Slim recordings (1940-41)—**Grinder Man Blues, You Didn't Mean Me No Good, Maybe I'll Lend You A Dime, Two Of A Kind, I Believe I'll Settle Down** (all **Memphis Slim**). Accompanied Broonzy on record **(Big Bill's Blues)** — but left to go solo in 1944, forming own accompanying unit, the House Rockers. For some years worked mainly in Chicago. After prestigious appearances at Carnegie Hall and Newport Jazz Festival (both '59), moved to Paris two years later.

Toured Europe extensively on numerous occasions, with occasional trips back home. Since 1950s, has recorded prolifically. Played piano behind Washboard Sam, Broonzy, in 1953 **(Genesis: The Beginnings Of Rock)** — and cut numerous records under own name, with or without House Rockers **(The Real Boogie Woogie, Memphis Slim & The Real Honky Tonk)** or with bassist Willie Dixon **(The Blues Every Which Way)**. Year prior to becoming Parisian citizen, recorded in London for first time **(Chicago Boogie)**.

Although not all subsequent recordings have been comparable to his greatest work inside studio, there have been other occasions when his talents have been heard at, or near to, his best. Such examples include **Memphis Slim — Matthew Murphy; The Legacy Of The Blues, Vol 7: Memphis Slim; No Strain; Rock Me Baby!** and **Raining The Blues**.

Like B. B. King, Memphis Slim has tended to irritate blues purists by his periodic forays outside the basic blues field.

Albums:
Memphis Slim (RCA Victor/Bluebird—France)
Big Bill Broonzy, Big Bill's Blues (—/CBS—Realm)
Various (Including Memphis Slim), Genesis: The Beginnings Of Rock Vol 1 (Chess/Chess)
Traveling With The Blues (—/Storyville)
Bad Luck & Troubles (Barnaby/—)
The Real Boogie Woogie (Folkways/—)
The Blues Every Which Way (Verve/—)
'Frisco Bay Blues (—/Fontana)
Matt Murphy, Memphis Slim-Matthew Murphy (Black & White—France)
All Them Blues (DJM)
The Legacy Of The Blues: Vol 7 (—/Sonet)
Raining The Blues (Fantasy/—)
Chicago Boogie (Black Lion/Black Lion)
Various (Including Memphis Slim), Barrelhouse Blues & Boogie Woogie, Vol 1 (Storyville)
Rock Me Baby (Black Lion/Black Lion)
No Strain (Prestige—Blues/Fontana)
Memphis Slim & The Real Honky Tonk (Folkways/—)

Pat Metheny

As a virtuoso musician, a multi-dimensional composer and guitar-synthesizer pioneer, the influential Pat Metheny has been described as 'the guitarist's guitarist'. In the late 1970s, Metheny quickly established one of the most distinctive and distinguished voices on the guitar.

Born in Lee's Summit, Missouri, on August 12, 1954, Metheny played guitar from age 14, initially inspired by the Beatles before discovering the untold delights of Miles Davis, John Coltrane and Sonny Rollins. On leaving school, he taught guitar at the University of Miami and Berklee College, coming to international attention and acclaim when, at 19, he joined Gary Burton's group for three years.

With his own groups — notably in a mutually inspiring partnership with keyboardist Lyle Mays — Metheny has produced a string of magnificent albums (**American Garage; As Falls Wichita, So Falls Wichita Falls; Offramp; Travels** etc). His developments in the '80s with the Synclavier guitar-synthesizer (heard to good effect on the '82 **Offramp)** have elevated him to the ranks of significant musical innovators.

In addition to his electric group success, '80 revealed another aspect of his explorative character with **80/81** — four sizzling sides of spontaneous combustion with such established jazz 'heavyweights' as saxophonists Mike Brecker and Dewey Redman, acoustic bassist Charlie Haden and drummer Jack De Johnette. In '83, he further surprised his jazz-rock following with a trio album — the improvisational **Rejoicing**, in the company of ex-Ornette Coleman cohorts bassist Charlie Haden and drummer Billy Higgins, including his individual arrangements of Horace Silver's **Lonely Woman** and Ornette Coleman's **Tears Inside, Humpty Dumpty** and **Rejoicing**. (Interestingly, though, **Rejoicing** sold as many copies as his follow-up electric group album, **First Circle.)**

Although it was not realized at the time, **Rejoicing** was a pointer to Metheny's subsequent, unexpected partnership with pioneer free-saxophonist Coleman. Their **Song X** was recorded 'live' in three days and released in '86, initially to some consternation. With Metheny responding so enthusiastically to the challenges aimed at him by Coleman, **Song X** provided an interesting link between two musicians of completely different generations and directions. The collaboration wasn't, perhaps, so surprising considering that Metheny once described himself as 'basically an Ornette Coleman-styled player'. In any event, the Metheny-Coleman association will go down as one of *the* events of the '80s.

A good cross-section of Metheny's ECM recordings is contained in the limited-edition **Works** compilation. The double **Travels** — recorded live in concert with percussionist Nana Vasconcelos and a brilliant performance from keyboardist Lyle Mays — stands out as one of Metheny's finest electric group recordings from its lyrical and haunting opening **Are You Going With Me?** to the Latin romp through **Straight On Red**.

Above: Guitarist Pat Metheny—one of jazz's biggest-sellers, whether playing in improvisational style or straight-ahead jazz-rock (photo: Allan Titmuss).

Albums:
Gary Burton, Ring (ECM/ECM)
Gary Burton, Dreams So Real (ECM/ECM)
Gary Burton, Passengers (ECM/ECM)
Bright Life Size (ECM/ECM)
Watercolors (ECM/ECM)
Pat Metheny Group (ECM/ECM)
New Chautauqua (ECM/ECM)
American Garage (ECM/ECM)
80/81 (ECM/ECM)
As Falls Wichita, So Falls Wichita Falls (ECM/ECM)
Offramp (ECM/ECM)
Travels (ECM/ECM)
Rejoicing (ECM/ECM)
First Circle (ECM/ECM)
Works (ECM/ECM)
Song X (Geffen/Geffen)

Metheny-Mays, As Falls Wichita, So Falls Wichita Falls (courtesy ECM).

Pat Metheny, Travels (courtesy ECM)—live in concert.

Below: Memphis Slim—his forays outside the blues field have demonstrated his ability to relate to more than one area of music.

Mezzoforte

Iceland seemed an unlikely spawning ground for one of Europe's top jazz-funk bands but, since 1981, Mezzoforte have become one of that country's most important exports. By the first half of '85, Mezzoforte had performed in front of more than 400,000 European fans (more than *twice* the population of Iceland).

Influenced by American jazz fusion, Mezzoforte — keyboardist Eythor Gunnarsson, guitarist Fridrik Karlsson, drummer Gunnlaugur Briem and bassist Johann Asmundsson — formed in '78 when their ages ranged from 15 to 17, an immediate success around the Reykjavik jazz circuit.

The high standard of material and performance on their album **I Hakanum** — which included the contribution of Back Door saxophonist Ron Aspery — created enormous interest in the UK in '82 (quite an achievement considering its baffling and impenetrable Icelandic sleeve-notes, a DJ's nightmare).

Subsequently, working with vocalists Chris Cameron and the superb Noel McCalla (ex-Moon, Jody Street, Mike Rutherford and Morrissey-Mullen), Mezzoforte have become unprecedently successful across Europe. In '86, they toured internationally on the festival circuit with long-time associate, saxophonist Kristinn Svavarsson.

Albums:
Mezzoforte (—/Steinar—Iceland)
I Hakanum (—/Steinar)
Thvilikt Og Annadeins (—/Steinar—Iceland)
Surprise Surprise (Steinar/Steinar)
Observations (Steinar/Steinar)
Catching Up With Mezzoforte (—/Steinar)
Rising (—/Steinar)
Sprellifandi (—/Steinar)
The Saga So Far (—/Steinar)

Mezzoforte, I Hakanum (courtesy Steinar)—The Icelandic original.

Bubber Miley

James 'Bubber' Miley (born Aiken, South Carolina, 1903) was perhaps the first trumpet-player to gain widespread acclaim — within the context of a big band — for his adroit use of trumpet and mute. Miley specialized in 'growl' solos, moving plunger mute in and out of the bell of the instrument with left hand while depressing the trumpet's valves, in normal fashion, with the other. Miley was not, however, the first trumpeter/cornetist to use mutes in successful, individual manner but was one of the earliest examples of American jazz instrumental playing at its most basic and expressive.

Coming from a musical family, Miley served 18 months with US navy before entering music, as trumpeter first, with Carolina Five, then successively with Willie Gant, Mamie Smith, Elmer Snowden before Snowden's Washingtonians were taken over by Duke Ellington. In between two spells with Mamie Smith, also toured as part of *Sunny South* revue, as well as undertaking cabaret and dance band work in New York. Left Ellington in 1929, visited Paris with Noble Sissle, then back to New York for various jobs, including leading own band (1931) which appeared in *Sweet & Low* revue. Band project was, however, short-lived. Miley contracted tuberculosis and died in hospital in 1932. Miley's major contributions are all too little documented on record. He recorded, briefly, with Jelly Roll Morton **(Jelly Roll Morton & His Red Hot Peppers, Vol 1, 1927-1930)** and, interestingly, alongside another of the great trumpet stylists of the 1920s, Bix Beiderbecke, as member of Hoagy Carmichael's Orchestra, in 1930 **(The Bix Beiderbecke Legend)**.

But Miley will be best remembered for his solo work with Ellington. Classic, biting offerings like those on **Black & Tan Fantasy, East St Louis Toddle-oo** (Miley was co-author of this, Ellington's first signature tune), **Tishomingo Blues, Immigration Blues, Yellow Dog Blues** (all **The Beginning 1926-1928); The Mooche, Louisiana (Hot In Harlem 1928-1929); Bandanna Babies, I Must Have That Man, St Louis Blues (The Works Of Duke, Vol 2); Creole Love Call, East St Louis Toodle-oo** (different version from before), **Black & Tan Fantasy** (ditto) **(The Works Of Duke, Vol 1)** and **Take It Easy, Hot & Bothered, Blues With A Feeling (The Ellington Era, 1927-1940, Vol 1)**.

Miley's immediate post-Ellington work is documented intriguingly on **Bubber Miley & His Friends 1929-1931** through recordings of his playing with his own Mileage Makers as well as with orchestra of Joe Steele, Leo Reisman, and King Oliver. It is especially interesting to hear him alongside King Oliver (already in decline), on **St James Infirmary** and **When You're Smiling**.

Albums:
Duke Ellington In Harlem (Jazz Panorama/—)
Duke Ellington, Toodle-oo (—/Vocalion)
Duke Ellington, The Works Of Duke, Vols 1, 2 (RCA Victor—France)
Duke Ellington, The Beginning 1926-1928 (MCA—Germany)
Duke Ellington, The Ellington Era, 1927-1940, Vol 1 (Columbia/CBS)
Duke Ellington, Hot In Harlem (1928-1929) (MCA—Germany)
Jelly Roll Morton & His Red Hot Peppers, Vol 1 (1927-1930) (RCA Victor—France)
The Bix Beiderbecke Legend (RCA Victor—France)
Bubber Miley & His Friends (1929-1931) (RCA Victor—France)

Harry Miller

The inventive, ever open-minded bassist-composer and eclectic band-leader Harry Miller was born in Johannesburg, South Africa, on April 25, 1941. He arrived in London in '61, heralding an exodus of similarly gifted musicians from South Africa.

The first band he joined in London was the Group Sounds Five, led by West Indian drummer Don Brown (later to commit suicide). Alan 'A. J.' Jackson took his place in the drum-chair and the Miller-Jackson rhythm section lasted seven years, before Miller formed his creative partnership with Louis Moholo, another South African-in-exile.

Miller worked with the cream of British improvisers — John Stevens, Elton Dean, Nick Evans, Keith Tippett, Mike Osborne, John Surman, Mike Westbrook and fellow South African Chris McGregor (notably with McGregor's big band Brotherhood of Breath). While Miller's African roots surfaced distinctively in his own work, he wasn't a musician to distinguish between musical categories, playing with equal commitment in the King Crimson line-up and collaborating with Bob Downes on a score for the London Contemporary Dance Company.

In '73, Miller and his wife Hazel founded Ogun — a record label which was to be of untold significance in documenting the developing music of the '70s and early '80s.

In the mid-'70s, Miller often toured with his band Isipingo (early versions of which included Mike Osborne, Louis Moholo and elfin-like South African trumpeter Mongezi Feza who died in '75). In '77, Miller moved to Europe — first to Berlin (working with saxophonist Peter Brotzmann), then to Holland (joining Leo Cuypers and Van Manen).

In '83, Harry Miller with trumpeter Jeff Reynolds and trombonist Joe Maessen were involved in a car crash in Holland (November 27). The two other musicians were killed instantly and Miller sustained injuries from which he was to die just before Christmas. His body was flown to South Africa so that he could be buried in his home-town of Johannesburg.

The album **Down South**, recorded in March '83, was released posthumously. The magnificent music it contains stands as a lasting testimony to the catalytic effect he had on other musicians and is a tribute to a strikingly original and individual musician. His death was another great loss.

Albums:
John Surman, John Surman (—/Deram)
Mike Westbrook, Celebration (—/Deram)
Mike Westbrook, Metropolis (RCA/RCA)
Children At Play (—/Ogun)
Ninesense, Oh! For The Edge (—/Ogun)
Isipingo, Family Affair (—/Ogun)
In Conference (—/Ogun)
Leo Cuypers, Zeeland Suite (—/BvHaast)
Berlin Bones (—/FMP)
Down South (—/Vara Jazz)

Lucky Millinder

What Lucky Millinder lacked in the ability to play an instrument, he compensated for with his charm, charisma and shrewd organizational prowess. During the 1940s, this imposing yet non-playing (occasionally singing) band-leader gave a start to countless future luminaries. Henry Red Allen, Charlie Shavers, Harry Edison, J. C. Higginbotham, Wilbur De Paris, Buster Bailey, Dizzy Gillespie, Tab Smith, Paul Quinichette, Ike Quebec, Sam 'The Man' Taylor, Lucky Thompson, Don Byas, Frank Wess, Bull Moose Jackson, Sir Charles Thompson, Joe Guy, Eddie 'Lockjaw' Davis, Bill Doggett, George Duvivier, Al McGibbon, Panama Francis, Sister Rosetta Tharpe and Wynonie Harris all appeared in his line-ups at some time.

Born Lucius Miller in Anniston, Alabama, on August 8, 1900, Millinder was raised in Chicago. His diverse career was to include Chicago ballroom MC, disc-jockey, publicist and even fortune-teller. He fronted his first band aged 31, touring the RKO circuit, and the following year ('32), he became leader of the 'Doc' Crawford big band at Harlem's Uproar House. In '34, took over Irving Mills' Blue Rhythm Boys which, eventually, became Lucky Millinder and His Orchestra. During the '30s, he made a number of three-minute 'soundies' with his orchestra and vocalists like Sister Rosetta Tharpe, Mamie Smith and Annisteen Allen.

In the late '30s, his band career teetered on the brink for a while (he was actually declared bankrupt in '39). But in '40, he bounced back, characteristically undaunted, secured a successful Decca contract and cut more than 40 sides for the label between '41 and '47. The band continued into the '50s becoming one of Harlem's most popular dance line-ups but Millinder gradually phased himself out of the band business, working as a DJ then an agent. Lucky Millinder died in New York on September 28, 1966.

Albums:
Mills Blue Rhythm Band, Lucky Days 1941-45 (MCA/MCA)
Keep The Rhythm Going (Jazz Archives/—)
Apollo Jump (—/Affinity)

Charles Mingus

Born Arizona, 1922, and raised in Los Angeles, bassist Charles Mingus started in the bands of Louis Armstrong and Kid Ory and later Lionel Hampton but by 1953 was firmly in the modernists' camp, as the Massey Hall concert with Charlie Parker, Dizzy Gillespie, Bud Powell, Mingus and Max Roach shows **(The Quintet Of The Year)**. In fact, Mingus' career always transcended categories, and his work as a bandleader-composer shows him to be one of the great innovators of jazz. Mingus workshops from the early '50s reveal, in rather academic terms, his embryonic interest in variable tempos, counterpoint and collective improvisation **(Jazz Composers' Workshop No 1)**.

By 1955 he had made strides towards a more organic form of composition, and early drafts of **Love Chant** and **Foggy Day** with side-players trombonist Eddie Bert and tenorist George Barrow are more than merely historically interesting. A duet with drummer Max Roach, **Percussion Discussion**, is very free and melodic **(Charles Mingus)**. Successful, and highly influential, performances of his **Pithecanthropus Erectus** and **Foggy Day** make use of expressionistic devices and both horn men, Jackie McLean and J. R. Monterose, are driven into the extremes of register and pitch **(Pithecanthropus Erectus)**.

In 1956 Mingus was joined by Dannie Richmond, the ideal drummer for his music, and the association lasted over 20 years. The following year saw the first great plateau of achievement with a series of albums featuring the great trumpeter Clarence Shaw in performances like **Duke's Choice (Duke's Choice)** and exciting work from saxophonist Shafti Hadi and trombonist Jimmy Knepper. Both here and on a superior album **(Reincarnation Of A Lovebird)** Mingus uses a narrator in his compositions; the title track, based on fragments of Parker solos, and **Haitian Fight Song**, a more complex and developed version than on the **Charles Mingus** album, are outstanding tracks. A musical portrayal of a border town **(Tijuana Moods)** is a classic, with **Ysabel's Table Dance** raunchy and explosive, and **Tijuana Gift Shop** a masterpiece of texture.

Mingus' method of working without scores, rehearsing his team from the piano, shouting instructions during performances and allowing the soloists to develop the compositions in flight, accounted for the exhilarating sense of spontaneity. Unlike most composers, Mingus seldom had difficulty in reconciling the writing with the improvisation. Simultaneous soloing, cross riffs, collective playing and savage changes in tempo, stop-time, double-time, shaped the composition in the unique mold of this tempestuous leader. Volcanic climaxes erupted from his music, which, in its techniques and emotional climate, anticipated many of the features of the New Thing. Mingus had a great respect for tradition, for the music of Fats Waller, **Eat That Chicken (Mingus Oh Yeah)**; for gospel, **Wednesday Night Prayer Meeting, Moanin' (Blues And Roots)**; for Lester Young, **Goodbye Pork Pie Hat (Mingus Ah-Um** and **The Great Concert Of Charles Mingus)**; and Ellington on all of his longer works.

Brilliantly served by musicians like tenorist Booker Ervin, trombonist Knepper and the preternaturally alert Dannie Richmond, Mingus' late '50s-early '60s output is crowded with fine solos. Multi-instrumentalist Roland Kirk's wild gifts find a compatible environment on **Hog Calling Blues (Mingus Oh Yeah)** while another great multi-instrumentalist, Eric Dolphy, pushes his bass clarinet technique to its limits in an expressionistic duet — a musical recreation of a quarrel — with the leader, **What Love (Charles Mingus Presents Charles Mingus)**.

In the '60s, Mingus experimented with orchestral settings, using a 22-piece band **(Mingus Re-visited)** on several Ellingtonian pieces, and saw further compositions sabotaged by poor recording and incorrect juxtaposition **(Town Hall Concert)**. Two ambitious masterpieces **(Mingus Mingus Mingus Mingus Mingus** and **The Black Saint &**

Above: The innovative and influential Charles Mingus in action, Holland, 1977. A brilliant bassist and composer, master of the molten ensemble.

The Sinner Lady) are extended compositions of great complexity, built in layers of overlapping textures and using the talents of his regular team as well as brilliant contributions from altoist Charlie Mariano.

A concert in Paris in 1964 **(The Great Concert Of Charles Mingus)** was captured on a three-album set, with superb playing by the quartet, Dolphy, tenorist Clifford Jordan, Mingus and Richmond in lengthy performances of the leader's compositions. The next period is badly represented on record, but Mingus surfaced again in the '70s with a great group including the dynamic tenorist George Adams, and the virtuoso pianist Don Pullen **(Mingus Moves, Changes One** and **Changes Two)**. A concert at Carnegie Hall in 1974 assembles Mingus, Richmond, Pullen, Adams, altoist Charles McPherson, trumpeter Jon Faddis, baritone saxist Hamiet Bluiett and the astoundingly extroverted Roland Kirk for a blowing session on **C Jam Blues** and **Perdido**.

Mingus wrote a brilliantly evocative score for the John Cassavetes film *Shadows* in the '50s, and an autobiography, *Beneath The Underdog*. He died in January 1979.

Albums:
The Quintet Of The Year (Debut/Vogue)
Jazz Composers Workshop, No 1 (Savoy/—)
Charles Mingus (Prestige/Prestige)
Pithecanthropus Erectus (Atlantic/—)
Duke's Choice (Bethlehem/Polydor)
Re-incarnation Of A Lovebird (Bethlehem/Polydor)
East Coasting (Bethlehem/Polydor)
Tonight At Noon (Atlantic/Atlantic)
Tijuana Moods (RCA/RCA)
Mingus Oh Yeah (Atlantic/Atlantic)
Blues & Roots (Atlantic/Atlantic)
Mingus Ah-Um (Columbia/CBS Realm)
Mingus Dynasty (Columbia/CBS)
Charles Mingus Presents Charles Mingus (Barnaby CBS/Barnaby CBS)
Charles Mingus (Barnaby CBS/Barnaby CBS)
Mingus Re-Visited (Trip/—)
Town Hall Concert (United Artists/—)
Mingus Mingus Mingus Mingus Mingus (Impulse/Impulse)
The Black Saint & The Sinner Lady (Impulse/Impulse)
Mingus At Monterey (Fantasy/—)
The Great Concert Of Charles Mingus (Prestige/America)
Mingus Moves (Atlantic/Atlantic)
Changes One (Atlantic/Atlantic)
Changes Two (Atlantic/Atlantic)
Mingus At Carnegie Hall (Atlantic/Atlantic)
Cumbia & Jazz Fusion (Atlantic/Atlantic)
Concertgebouw Amsterdam April 10th 1964 (—/Ulysse Musique)
Abstractions (Bethlehem/Affinity)

Charles Mingus Presents Charles Mingus (courtesy Candid). A showcase for the bass clarinet technique of Eric Dolphy.

Roscoe Mitchell

see Art Ensemble of Chicago

Hank Mobley

Tenorist Hank Mobley, born 1930 in Georgia, is one of jazz's more under-rated figures, possibly because his great gifts ran counter to the prevailing climate.

At the height of the hard bop era. with the declamatory approach at a premium, Mobley's tone was comparatively soft, a round sound capable of great subtlety. An early album **(Hank Mobley & His All Stars)** illustrates the problem, with Mobley's own contributions overshadowed by the more obviously driving work of Milt Jackson, Horace Silver and Art Blakey. His playing on the blues, **Lower Stratosphere**, is funky in a more relaxed and unpredictable way.

After stints with Max Roach and Dizzy Gillespie, Mobley was in at the start of the Jazz Messengers in 1955. **Creepin' In (Horace Silver & The Jazz Messengers)** featured his best solo work to date, illustrating his unique, oblique rhythmic sense and complex ideas.

Ballad features like **Alone Together (The Jazz Messengers At The Cafe Bohemia)** or **Silver's Blue (Silver's Blue)** are tinged with melancholia. The typical hard-driving cutting contest **(Blowing Sessions)** with the supercharged Johnny Griffin and John Coltrane were not his forte, leaving no room for his thoughtful, restrained constructiveness.

By 1960, Mobley's own Blue Note albums had achieved a balance of his unfashionable qualities, and the lyricism of **The More I See You (Roll Call)**, and the elaborate attack of **This I Dig Of You (Soul Station)** represent a peak in his creativity.

A period with Miles Davis, replacing Coltrane in the quintet, produced the beautiful **I Thought About You (Someday My Prince Will Come)**, the imaginative **No Blues (Miles Davis At The Carnegie Hall)** and excellent, quirkily melodic solos on **Oleo** and **So What (Friday & Saturday Nights At The Blackhawk)**.

With the mid-'80s 'rediscovery' of the hard-bop era's heroes, Mobley's big tenor sound enjoyed a revival of interest (the reactivated Blue Note label re-issuing Mobley classics like **Soul Station, Far Away Lands, Another Workout** and **Hi Voltage)**.

Prior to a much-vaunted European tour, Hank Mobley died on May 30, 1986, from double pneumonia. He was 55.

Albums:
Hank Mobley & His All Stars (Blue Note/Blue Note)
Horace Silver & The Jazz Messengers (Blue Note/Blue Note)
The Jazz Messengers At The Cafe Bohemia (Blue Note/Blue Note)
Horace Silver, Silver's Blue (—/Epic CBS)
Blowing Sessions (Blue Note/Blue Note)
Roll Call (Blue Note/Blue Note)
Soul Station (Blue Note/Blue Note)
No Room For Squares (Blue Note/Blue Note)
Miles Davis: Someday My Prince Will Come (Columbia/CBS)
At The Carnegie Hall (Columbia/CBS)
Friday & Saturday Nights At The Blackhawk (Columbia/CBS)
Far Away Lands (Blue Note/Blue Note)
Another Workout (Blue Note/Blue Note)
Hi Voltage (Blue Note/Blue Note)

Tenorist Hank Mobley and his All Stars (courtesy Blue Note).

The Modern Jazz Quartet

The MJQ's musical director, John Lewis, was born in Illinois, 1920, studying music and anthropology at the University of New Mexico.

His early work as a pianist in the bebop '40s is usually forgotten, though he accompanied Charlie Parker on several sessions **(The Savoy Sessions** and **The Definitive Charlie Parker, Vol 5)**, played and arranged for Dizzy Gillespie's big band **(In The Beginning** and **The Greatest Of Dizzy Gillespie)** and contributed the beautiful composition **Afternoon In Paris** to the Sonny Stitt-J. J. Johnson date

(Genesis). His keyboard touch was extemely distinctive and, balancing his fastidious sense of structure, was the convincing emotionalism of his blues. The earliest quartet with Milt Jackson **(Milt Jackson)** from 1952 shows Lewis very much the accompanist, though by the time the group adopted its new collective name, he had taken over the direction.

Milt Jackson was born 1923, Detroit, and by 1945 was established as the pioneer bebop vibraphone player. His early work with Dizzy Gillespie's small combos was badly recorded, the instrument sounding like a row of milk-bottles, but his mastery of the new idiom comes through loud and clear **(The Greatest Of Dizzy Gillespie** and **In The Beginning)**. Sessions with Thelonious Monk show him to be one of the few great interpreters of that idiosyncratic genius's music, **Genius Of Modern Music, Eronel** and **Criss Cross** being particularly good, and **I Mean You** a masterpiece.

As the Modern Jazz Quartet (John Lewis, Milt Jackson, bassist Percy Heath and, initially, Kenny Clarke on drums), the group specialized in collective improvisation, fragmenting the melodies and reworking them in flexible interplay between the instruments. Lewis was the guiding hand, elegant and precise, vastly knowledgeable about European musical forms, preoccupied above all things with form.

Most of the criticisms leveled at the MJQ centre on Lewis as too classical, not virile, miniaturist and effete, a straitjacket of respectability on the funky talents of Jackson etc. In fact, during their 22 years together, the group achieved much of lasting merit, and comparison with a comparable chamber-jazz outfit, Chick Corea's Return To Forever, will show just how superior the MJQ were in exploiting a mood or combining swing and delicacy. The development of black militancy tended to negate the MJQ's breakthrough in putting jazz into the establishment's concert halls, the dark suits, sober manner, seriousness of presentation.

With the replacement of Clark by the quieter Connie Kay, a percussionist more than a drummer, specializing in brushwork, tiny pinpoint cymbal sounds, the MJQ assumed its final form. Playing several versions of Lewis' compositions, fugues like **Vendome, Concorde** or the wonderfully structured **Django, Milano, Fontessa** and **Sun Dance**, the MJQ also extensively reworked standards like **Softly As In A Morning Sunrise, Night In Tunisia** and **How High The Moon**.

Over the years, as technique and empathy developed, their repertoire has been presented in increasingly polished form. More space has been given to Percy Heath as his tone has strengthened, while the effectiveness of Connie Kay is best judged in the ensemble rather than by brush features like **La Ronde** and **Drums (Night In Tunisia)**. The moving **Cortège (One Never Knows)** rises to its emotional peak on Kay's splendid command of dynamics, bursting in a shower of cymbals under Jackson's measured row of sombre chords; in fact, the entire album is a masterpiece of evocation and was written by Lewis for the Venice-based movie, *Sait-On Jamais*. **The Golden Striker** is a classic, while **Three Windows**, a triple fugue, works like a Swiss watch. Jackson's writing is best represented by **Bag's Groove (Modern Jazz Quartet, Night In Tunisia** and **The Last Concert)** and, outside the MJQ, with Miles Davis, Jackson and Monk **(Tallest Trees)**; while **The Martyr** shows his lyrical gifts at slow tempo **(The Legendary Profile)**. In 1974, the vibesman's departure brought the group's first period to an end, commemorated by one of their finest albums, which is in effect a summation of their achievements **(The Last Concert)**.

When the MJQ went their separate ways, it seemed like the end of a cherished era. John Lewis took a sabbatical, returned to writing and jazz education, appearing as a revered solo pianist. In '86, Lewis was appointed conductor and director of Cooper Union's American Jazz Orchestra.

Milt Jackson returned to solo touring, recording prolifically for Norman Granz's Pablo label. In '86, Jackson toured with the Ray Brown-Milt Jackson Quartet including pianist Cedar Walton, drummer Mickey Roker and tenorist Stanley Turrentine.

Drummer Connie Kay worked with all-star Dixieland line-ups, touring as one of Doc Cheatham's band legends in '86. Percy Heath, meanwhile, went on to enjoy unprecedented success with the Heath Brothers.

In '81, the MJQ members were finally persuaded to reunite to play at the Newport Jazz Festival. Their return to the international festival circuit the following year was extraordinary. Undiminished in form, content and performance — and in spite of the exhausting demands of summer festival touring — it was like turning the clock back 30 years.

The Modern Jazz Quartet's marvelous music has stood the test of time, and remains as fresh and adventurous as ever.

The Modern Jazz Quartet, The Last Concert (courtesy Atlantic).

Albums

John Lewis, Charlie Parker: The Savoy Sessions (Savoy/Savoy)
The Definitive Charlie Parker, Vol 5 (Verve/Metro)
John Lewis, Dizzy Gillespie: In The Beginning (Prestige/Prestige)
The Greatest Of Dizzy Gillespie (RCA/RCA)
John Lewis, Sonny Stitt: Genesis (Prestige/Prestige)
Improvised Meditations (Atlantic/Atlantic)
Music For Brass (Columbia/—)
Milt Jackson: Milt Jackson (Blue Note/Blue Note)
Theolonious Monk, Genius Of Modern Music (Blue Note/Blue Note)
Miles Davis, Tallest Trees (Prestige/Prestige)
Second Nature (Savoy/Savoy)
Opus De Funk (Prestige/Prestige)
Plenty, Plenty Soul (Atlantic/Atlantic)
The Art Of Milt Jackson (Atlantic/Atlantic)
Big Band Bags (Milestone/Milestone)
Big 4 At Montreux (Pablo/Pablo)
Big 3 (Pablo/Pablo)
Modern Jazz Quartet:
First Recordings (Prestige/—)
Fontessa (Atlantic/Atlantic)
Pyramid (Atlantic/Atlantic)
One Never Knows (Atlantic/Atlantic)
Lonely Woman (Atlantic/Atlantic)
Night In Tunisia (Atlantic/Atlantic)
At Music Inn (Atlantic/Atlantic)
Blues At Carnegie Hall (Atlantic/Atlantic)
Sheriff (Atlantic/Atlantic)
The Legendary Profile (Atlantic/Atlantic)
Modern Jazz Quartet (Atlantic/Atlantic)
The Art Of The Modern Jazz Quartet (Atlantic/Atlantic)
The Best Of The Modern Jazz Quartet (Atlantic/Atlantic)
The Last Concert (Atlantic/Atlantic)
John Lewis, The Modern Jazz Society Presents A Concert Of Contemporary Music (Verve/Verve)
Milt Jackson, Soul Route (Pablo/Pablo)
Milt Jackson-J. J. Johnson-Ray Brown, Jackson, Johnson, Brown & Company (Pablo/Pablo)
Milt Jackson-Ray Brown, It Don't Mean A Thing If You Can't Tap Your Foot To It (Pablo/Pablo)

Miff Mole

Irving Milfred 'Miff' Mole (born Roosevelt, Long Island, New York, 1898) was one of the major influences on trombone during 1920s. Mole's was a major advance, in terms of sheer technical dexterity—less emphatic than some other trombonists, but superior to most in elegance of phrase and delivery.

He started on violin, age 11, studying that instrument for three years. Also played piano—first public performances were as accompanist to silent movies.

First professional gig on trombone with Charlie Randall (with whom Mole studied). After two years with Randall, joined Original Memphis Five. Recorded with 'Ladd's Black Aces' **(Ladd's Black Aces, Vols 1-3)** between 1921-22. Ladd's Black Aces was a pseudonym, used by OMF for recordings. Mole's playing on LBA titles like **Sister Kate, Two-Time Dan** and **All Wrong** demonstrates his all-round excellence and his ability to lift this and other bands. (OMF also recorded under other names, including Tennessee Tooters, Original Tampa 5.) Mole left OMF temporarily, working with Abe Lyman Orchestra on West Coast, but rejoined former band for further period.

After work with various other bands, became closely associated with cornettist Red Nichols. Contributed significantly to music produced by Nichols' Five Pennies **(Red Nichols & His Five Pennies 1926-1928)** and to yet another band which existed only inside a recording studio and of which both Nichols and Mole were seminal members **(The Charleston Chasers 1925-1928)**. Mole-Nichols partnership was heard at its best during 1928 recording by Miff Mole & His Little Molers **(That Toddlin' Town—Chicago 1926-28)**. Mole worked with Roger Wolfe Kahn (1926-27), became staff trombonist with studio band at station WOR, then spent next nine years as session musician at NBC.

Joined Paul Whiteman Orchestra, 1938, staying two years. Recorded with Eddie Condon in '40 **(Jam Sessions At Commodore)** and his fine playing during four-part **A Good Man Is Hard To Find** proved his long involvement with session work had not taken the edge from his jazz-abilities. Left Whiteman due to ill heath, worked again for NBC, then became member of Benny Goodman Orchestra (1942-43). Participated in numerous Condon Town Hall concerts **(The Eddie Condon Concerts Town Hall 1944-45 Featuring Pee Wee Russell)** and recorded with his own Nicksieland Band **(Trombone Scene)** in '44; it transferred to Nick's, New York jazz spot, where Mole worked for four years (1943-47).

Spent several years in Chicago, underwent surgery on more than one occasion. Miff Mole, who died in New York in 1961, spent most of the last years of his life in non-music activities.

Albums:

Various (Including Miff Mole), Treasaurus Of Classics, Vol 2 (Columbia/CBS)
Ladd's Black Aces, Vols 1-3 (—/Fountain)
Red Nichols & His Five Pennies (1926-1928) (MCA Coral—Germany)
The Charleston Chasers (1925-1928) (—/VJM)
Various (Including Miff Mole), That Toddlin' Town—Chicago (1926-28) (—/Parlophone)
Eddie Condon, Jam Sessions At Commodore (Commodore/Ace of Hearts)
The Eddie Condon Concerts Town Hall 1944-45 Featuring Pee Wee Russell (Chiaroscuro/—)

Grachan Moncur III

Born in New York in 1937, Grachan Moncur III is the son of the bassist with the Savoy Sultans. After stints with Ray Charles and the Art Farmer -Benny Golson Jazztet, Moncur joined Jackie McLean, appearing on his change of direction album **(One Step Beyond)**. Associated with the Blue Note school of young, second generation New Thing players, he turns up with Herbie Hancock **(My Point Of View)**, taking a trenchant solo on **King Cobra**.

His own album **(Evolution)** has a compatible band of McLean, Lee Morgan, Bobby Hutcherson and Anthony Williams, and the numbers—all by Moncur—cover a wide spectrum of approaches from the free and doomy title track to the more conventional **Monk In Wonderland**.

He played a second trombone line with Roswell Rudd in Archie Shepp's combo in the late '60s, and was clearly more traditional than Rudd. Moncur's next album **(New Africa)** was strongly melodic, and the composition **When**, fueled by the amazing drumming of Andrew Cyrille, was a minor jazz hit. His later work with the Jazz Composers' Orchestra **(Echoes Of Prayers)** is a requiem for Luther King, Medger Evers and Marcus Garvey, the atmosphere dark and the riffs overlapping. There are several movements, including a near-township section and a chanted vocal. Moncur's trombone struts starkly at the beginning and end of this effective and homogeneous work.

Albums:

Evolution (Blue Note/Blue Note)
New Africa (—/Affinity)
Echoes Of Prayers (JCOA/JCOA Virgin)

Thelonious Monk

The pioneering pianist and composer Thelonious Sphere Monk (born in Rocky Mount, North Carolina, on October 10, 1920) remains one of the greatest seminal figures of modern jazz — and yet somehow at a tangent to every school. Along with Parker, Gillespie, Powell, Christian and Clarke, Monk was one of the pioneers of bebop but his originality was such that each new generation of musicians has found a different challenge in his concept of harmony, rhythm and structure.

A reputation for eccentricity and a seemingly home-made keyboard technique kept him in comparative obscurity until the '50s, when the hard bop movement discovered the exacting logic beneath the outlandish hats and deceptive hammerings. His angular, dissonant piano-style omitted the obvious and, like a scalpel, exposed basic structures. On a standard like **Sweet And Lovely (Thelonious Monk)** he sent up the sentimentality by introducing the sub-theme of **Tea For Two**, butting the tempo up and down, and plunging the close into a travesty of the romantic concerto as he searched for that final chord.

Sardonic towards the sugary, Monk's own compositions are virtually impregnable. Cunningly knotted, already stripped to essentials,

Above: Trombonist Grachan Moncur III, a significant musician among the second generation of 'New Thing' players.

they are an obstacle course to test the imagination and resourcefulness of the improviser. **Mysterioso** has the air of a walking bass line but transposed for piano which makes it a very different animal. Interpretation of Monk's themes requires a thematic approach and few musicians have succeeded. Drummer Art Blakey and vibraphonist Milt Jackson are two of the earliest and most sympathetic sideplayers **(Genius Of Modern Music)**. Tenorist Sonny Rollins shares Monk's sense of humor, and thinks architecturally, so that their collaborations **(Brilliance** and **Sonny Rollins, Vol 2)** have a weight and unequivocal strength that Johnny Griffin's freewheeling encounter lacks **(Thelonious In Action).**

During the '50s, Monk was signed to the Riverside label and recorded prolifically. There are scores of versions of his **Epistrophy, Round Midnight, Blue Monk, Monk's Mood, Little Rootie Tootie, I Mean You** and **Off Minor** ranging from solo piano to big band. The Town Hall concert **(In Person)** features a 10-piece band handling the almost accidental harmonies in unison, and swinging like a trunk-to-tail Hannibal caravan. The solitary, unadorned artist can be found on **Pure Monk**.

Other notable encounters were with John Coltrane **(Thelonious Monk & John Coltrane)**, a stretching experience for the growing tenorist and with Art Blakey's driving unit **(Art Blakey's Jazz Messengers With Thelonious Monk)**, where the shifting meters and accents of the pianist find their perfect complement.

In the late '50s, Monk formed a steady working quartet with Charlie Rouse on tenor, but the finest albums came with the addition of guest stars like Harold Land **(In Person)** and Thad Jones **(Brillance)**. Over-exposure tended to sap the impact of Monk's music, but he was by no means a spent force, as the '70s recordings prove **(Something In Blue** and **The Man I Love)**.

During the '70s, Monk toured infrequently. One of his last major tours included a memorable appearance with the Newport Festival All-Stars at London's New Victoria Theatre in '72. Plagued by health problems in his last years, he withdrew from the public eye. When Monk died on February 17, 1982—from a stroke at Englewood, New Jersey, aged 64—he hadn't performed for six years. He was survived by his wife (whose companionship he had so beautifully celebrated on his enduring **Crepuscule With Nellie)** and his funk musician son, T.S. Monk Jr.

His influence on fellow pianists has been enormous—Randy Weston, Cecil Taylor, Stan Tracey—and shows no sign of diminishing. The jazz world mourned Monk's death universally, prompting a wave of musical tributes from other artists who had been touched by his magic: eg Charlie Rouse, Ben Riley, Buster Williams and Kenny Barron (collectively as Sphere)—**Four In One**; Chick Corea—**Trio Music**; Arthur Blythe—**Light Blue**...

In '84, perhaps the most unlikely memorial album appeared in the form of A&M's remarkable **That's The Way I Feel Now—A Tribute To Thelonious Monk** on which an extraordinarily diverse selection of musicians paid homage to one of the modern music's founding fathers. (To its credit, the album includes a reasonable list of recommended original Monk recordings.) Contributions included Terry Adams, Mark Bingham, Carla Bley, Bob Dorough, Dr John, Gil Evans, Donald Fagen, Bruce Fowler, Peter Frampton, Sharon Freeman, Johnny Griffin, Barry Harris, Joe Jackson, Elvin Jones, Steve Khan, Steve Lacy, Bobby McFerrin, Charlie Rouse, Todd Rundgren, Shockabilly, Steve Slagle, Chris Spedding, Was (Not Was), Randy Weston, Gary Windo and John Zorn. You just can't help wondering *what* Monk would have made of it.

The magic of Monk's music is so enduring it will last for ever.

Albums:

Genious Of Modern Music (Blue Note/Blue Note)
Thelonious Monk (Prestige/Prestige)
Pure Monk (Milestone/Milestone)
Thelonious Monk & John Coltrane (Milestone/Milestone)
Art Blakey's Jazz Messengers With Thelonious Monk (Atlantic/Atlantic)
In Person (Milestone/Milestone)
Brilliance (Milestone/Milestone)
Something In Blue (Black Lion/Black Lion)
The Man I Love (Black Lion/Black Lion)
Dizzy Gillespie, Thelonious Monk, Kai Winding, Sonny Stitt, Al McKibbon, Art Blakey, Giants Of Jazz (George Wein Collection/George Wein Collection)

J.R. Monterose

Tenorist J.R. Monterose, born Detroit 1927, gained experience with Charles Mingus, Kenny Dorham and Horace Silver but headed only three albums in 28 years. **Straight Ahead** is his best and a magnificent achievement by any standards.

Monterose's family had settled in New York in '28 and he studied clarinet at age 13, before taking up the tenor saxophone two years later.

Basically a Rollins-derived hard-bopper, Monterose comes across from the opening notes of the title track with great authority, building to a climax with controled power, and returning after Tommy Flanagan's piano solo for exchanges with the brilliant drummer, Pete La Roca. **Chafic**, a waltz, shows the leader's thrusting, angular figures intensifying over a call-and-response pattern, while **Green Street Scene** has him chopping away over a rocking rhythm section. Domiciled in Belgium, Monterose has added the guitar to his sax and clarinet skills.

Albums:

Straight Ahead (Xanadu/—)

Below: Thelonious Sphere Monk, among the founders of bebop and one of jazz's greatest, most influential composers and piano stylists.

Wes Montgomery

Born Indianapolis 1925, guitarist Wes Montgomery didn't leave his home town until age 34, when the success of his brothers Buddy and Monk, the Mastersounds, led him to enter the lists. Montgomery established his reputation from the first albums, which were rapturously received by the critics as the greatest guitar since Charlie Christian.

The early, and best work **(Beginnings)** shows all the hallmarks of his style, the octave-doubling runs on the amazing **Finger Pickin'**, the lyrical gifts allied to that glowing, bronze tone on **Old Folks**. Montgomery was unusual in that he didn't use a pick, preferring the tone he got with his thumb.

Thanks to the enthusiasm of Cannonball Adderley, Montgomery secured a contract with Riverside, and much of his finest work was recorded for that label. Many of his solos pursue a similar strategy in which single note runs build to chunky chord and octave passages that judder and crouch like a cavalry charge, **Airgun, Four On Six (While We're Young)**. The unaccompanied title track is sumptuous, the rich, shot-silk tone at its most beautiful. Like most 'natural' musicians, the blues was his element, and he had a seemingly inexhaustible capacity for permutating the obvious cadences in fresh ways, startling the expectations with an abruptly splayed chord. Later albums teamed the guitarist with Milt Jackson, George Shearing **(Wes & Friends)** to good effect, and with Johnny Griffin for a hard-driving blowing-session **(Movin')**.

Wes Montgomery's contract with Verve proved disastrous from the jazz point of view, featuring the guitarist in lush settings with strings, and removing him from the challenging small group context necessary to his most committed work. He died in 1968 at the age of 43.

Montgomery's influence can still be heard in a new generation of guitarists from George Benson to Emily Remler.

Wes Montgomery, Wes and Friends (courtesy Riverside)—Cannonball Adderley's chance discovery of the guitarist led to the Riverside contract and success.

Albums:
Boss Guitar (Riverside/Riverside)
Beginnings (Blue Note/Blue Note)
While We're Young (Milestone/Milestone)
Wes & Friends (Milestone/Milestone)
Movin' (Milestone/Milestone)
Movin' Wes (Verve/Verve)
Midnight Guitarist
(—/Jazz Masterworks—Italy)
West Montgomery Trio
(OJC—RCA/OJC—RCA)
The Incredible Jazz Guitar
(OJC—RCA/OJC—RCA)

Below: The influential Wes Montgomery—he didn't start playing guitar until he was 19, influenced by the recordings of Charlie Christian.

James Moody

Born 1925, the multi-instrumentalist's recording début was with the Dizzy Gillespie big band. A reliable side-musician throughout the bebop era, Moody played with many of the giants, including Tadd Dameron, Al Haig, Howard McGhee and Milt Jackson, though in fact his playing has a straight ahead swing typical of an earlier period. In 1949, vocalist King Pleasure cut a version of his tenor solo on **I'm In The Mood For Love**, which turned out to be a hit, and Eddie Jefferson sang **Moody's Workshop** and **I've Got The Blues**.

Moody's history after that became picaresque; a lengthy sojourn in Europe; a physical collapse; a painful struggle back to professionalism with—along the way—expertise on alto and flute. By 1963, he was back with Gillespie.

Never less than professional, Moody is a swinger on tenor and alto saxophones, and a fleet, sweet flautist — no mumbles, no phlegmy stunts.

In '86, he proved he was still a dynamic challenger, engaging in tough-tenor battles with Johnny Griffin to the delight of audiences on the international festival circuit.

Below: James Moody—a total professional on flute and reeds.

Albums:
James Moody (Prestige/Prestige)
Moody's Workshop (Prestige/Xtra)
The Beginning & End Of Bop
(Blue Note/Blue Note)
Dizzy Gillespie, Trumpet Masters (—/Vogue)
Dizzy Gillespie, Something Old, Something New
(—/Philips)
James Moody, Group Therapy (—/DJM)
Brass Figures (Milestone/Milestone)
Easy Living (Chess/Chess)

James Moody, Brass Figures (courtesy Milestone)—orchestra and quartet.

Airto Moreira

Brazilian percussionist-extraordinaire Airto Moreira showed—especially through his association with Miles Davis in the early '70s—that a battery of Latin rhythm instruments could provide a bank of upfront sound rather than just supplying 'background' effects.

Born in Itaiopolis, Southern Brazil, on August 5, 1941, Airto grew up in the small village of Curitiba. A genuinely instinctive musician (he had no early, formal music training), he was making music at age 3; at 5, he was even playing and singing on the local radio station. At 16, he went to Sao Paulo, playing drums in local clubs and, in the early '60s, moved closer to the centre of Brazilian music, Rio de Janeiro, working with Quarteto Novo. But, even here, he found the local music scene too restricting for his wider horizons.

In '68, he moved to the United States, studying with Moacir Santos in Los Angeles, before heading east. The most important connection Airto made in New York was with trumpeter Miles Davis who, by '70, had made big inroads into electric jazz-rock. With Miles strengthening the non-Western elements of his music, his choice of Airto—a musician steeped in Brazilian folk forms—was significant **(Big Fun, Bitches Brew, Miles At The Fillmore, On The Corner, Live-Evil)**.

In '72, Airto worked with Weather Report **(Weather Report)** and Chick Corea's Return To Forever. With RTF, he was featured on a conventional drum-kit as well as Latin percussion **(Return To Forever, Light As A Feather)**, his creative playing adding just the right joyful Latin-American feel Corea required (eg **La Fiesta**).

During the '70s, Airto turned up as a supersession studio musician with a diversity of artists—George Benson **(White Rabbit, Bad Benson)**, John McLaughlin **(My Goal's Beyond)**, Stan Getz **(Captain Marvel)**, Cannonball Adderley **(Happy People)**, Santana **(Welcome)**, Wayne Shorter **(Super Nova, Native Dancer)**, Joe Zawinul **(Zawinul)**.... It was a short step to becoming an arranger and producer himself. Apart from recording his own successful solo albums, since '73 he has also helped make some fine albums for his wife, vocalist Flora Purim, as well as producing groups like George and Hugo

Above: Brazil's Airto, a superlative and inventive percussionist, a modern Latin luminary—wowing 'em in London in 1986 (photo: Allan Titmuss).

Fattoruso's OPA **(Golden Wings)**.

With the mid-'80s revival of awareness in Latin music worldwide, Airto and Flora Purim toured internationally in '86 hailed as honored 'veteran' Latin luminaries, making their first visit to the UK. Their '85 album, **Humble People**, is a Latin feast spiced up by keyboardist Jorge Dalto, saxophonists Joe Farrell and Dave Sanborn, guitarists José Neto and David Zeheir, and a battery of Brazilian percussionists in the tradition.

Albums:
Essential (Buddah/—)
Identity (Arista/Arista)
I'm Fine, How Are You (Warner Brothers/
Warner Brothers)
In Concert (CTI/CTI)
Promises Of The Sun (Arista/Arista)
Seeds On The Ground (Buddah/—)
Free (CTI/CTI)
Virgin Land (CTI/CTI)
Flora Purim, Butterfly Dreams
(Milestone/Milestone)
Flora Purim, Open Your Eyes You Can Fly
(Milestone/Milestone)
Flora Purim, Nothing Will Be As It Was...
Tomorrow (Warner Brothers/
Warner Brothers)
Airto Moreira-Flora Purim, Humble People
(George Wein Collection/
George Wein Collection)

Lee Morgan

Born 1938, Philadelphia, trumpeter Lee Morgan was shot and killed outside Slugs, where he was working, in 1972, thus robbing jazz of one of its most delightful performers.

Morgan turned professional before his 15th birthday, joining the Dizzy Gillespie big band at 17. His early albums for Blue Note show tremendous verve and high-spirited fireworks without a greal deal of attention to structure. A session with John Coltrane from 1957 **(Blue Train)** shows his wildly spontaneous spirit and, on **I'm Old Fashioned**, indications of the deeper emotional impact to be created through restraint. In 1958, he joined Art Blakey's Jazz Messengers, remaining until 1961 and making great strides in that forcing house of talents.

His breadth of tonal variety, the vocalized half-valve effects and slurs, is shown on **It's Only A Paper Moon**, and his accuracy in the top register on **Lester Left Town (The Big Beat)**. The search for concision continued through a series of excellent albums as leader and side-player with Jackie McLean **(Leeway)** and Wayne Shorter **(Search For The New Land)**, all characterized by his bubbling wit and enthusiasm.

In 1963 he made the charts **(The Sidewinder)** with the title track, a 24-bar blues that drives along on the drumming of Billy Higgins. In fact, every track packs a colossal rhythmic punch, with Morgan's solo on **Totem Pole** his all-time best. Heading a quintet with multi-reeds-player Bennie Maupin **(Live At The Lighthouse)**, he showed that constant growth was more important to him than repeating the commercial success of **The Sidewinder**, and over the four lengthy tracks displays his controled inventiveness.

The following year, another double album, with Billy Harper and Grachan Moncur III **(Lee Morgan)**, showed considerable group organization with no loss of spontaneity in the solos, and an atmosphere of experimentation.

In spite of his early demise,Morgan—along with other hard-bop protagonists—has been the subject of a new wave of interest in the mid-'80s. In UK jazz discos, particularly, identifying correctly the solos of respective Art Blakey

Below: Lee Morgan—bright young trumpet star brutally murdered in 1972.

trumpet-prodigies has become a national sport. Morgan's '63 **Sidewinder** became a 'hit' again, this time for a generation of fans who hadn't even been born when the album was originally recorded.

Albums:
John Coltrane, Blue Train (Blue Note/Blue Note)
The Jazz Messengers, The Bigbeat (Blue Note/Blue Note)
The Jazz Messengers, The Freedom Rider (Blue Note/Blue Note)
Leeway (Blue Note/Blue Note)
Search For The New Land (Blue Note/Blue Note)
The Sidewinder (Blue Note/Blue Note)
Live At The Lighthouse (Blue Note/Blue Note)
Lee Morgan (Blue Note/Blue Note)
Lee Morgan (DJM/DJM)
Delightfulee (Blue Note/Blue Note)
The Rajah (Blue Note/Blue Note)
The Gigolo (Blue Note/Blue Note)
The Rumproller (Blue Note/Blue Note)
Expoobident (Vee-Jay/Affinity)

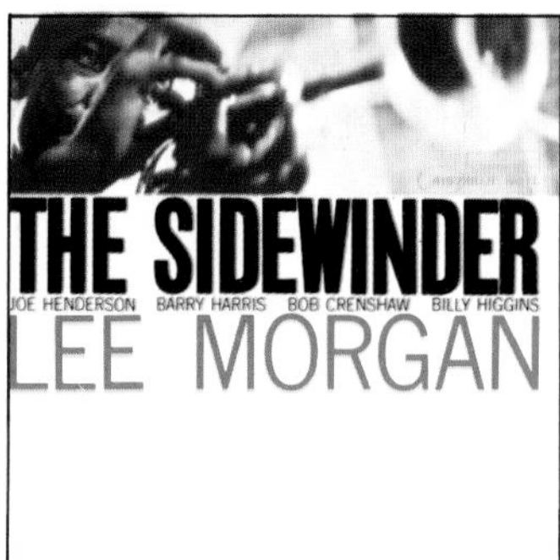

Lee Morgan, The Sidewinder (courtesy Blue Note): a hit again in the 1980s.

Above: Guitarist Jim Mullen and saxophonist Dick Morrissey—one of Britain's finest fusion units.

Morrissey-Mullen

The dynamic combination of English tenorist Dick Morrissey and Scottish guitarist Jim Mullen began not in Britain but in New York in the mid-1970s, while working with Herbie Mann and the Average White Band. Fired by the explosive fusion made by Tee, Gale, Gadd & Co in Stuff, the two Britons returned to England and formed Morrissey-Mullen—a group which was to reach dizzy heights in popularity and herald the early '80s British jazz-funk boom.

Jim Mullen, whose reputation as a guitarist is formidable, originally played double-bass which helps explain his famous thumb-style guitar technique. In '63, he formed Jim Mullen & Co in Scotland which included two future members of AWB. In '69, he arrived in London becoming a blues-guitar attraction with such diverse artists as Brian Auger's Oblivion Express ('71-'73), Vinegar Joe ('73) and the unsurpassed vocal group Kokomo ('73-'75) before going to work in the States.

As a 16-year-old clarinettist, Dick Morrissey had been inspired by British trad-jazz heroes like Chris Barber and Ken Colyer until his Latin classics teacher also pointed him in the direction of King Oliver, Louis Armstrong and Johnny Dodds. One of Britain's most sought-after 'tough tenors' on the mainstream/hard-bop circuit, he also formed the early jazz-rock band If with guitarist Terry Smith (finding himself, with If, an unlikely opener for Black Sabbath and The Faces at Fillmore East).

The original Morrissey-Mullen group included the electric-keyboard versatility of Martin Blackwell and the staggering virtuosity of electric bassist John Mole. Subsequent line-ups featured pianists John Critchenson, Pete Jacobsen, Geoff Castle and Dave McCrae, and bassists Clive Charman, Mark Smith and Trevor Barry.

Morrissey-Mullen created some of the most vibrant, spontaneous music heard in Britain, whipping up a fever-pitch in live performance where (like their inspiration, Stuff) they gave unreservedly of their best. It was a dismal day when, in '86—after a decade of creative music-making together — Morrissey-Mullen disbanded with no successors in sight.

Albums:
Up (Atlantic/Atlantic)
Cape Wrath (—/EMI)
Badness (Beggars Banquet/Beggars Banquet)
Life On the Wire (Beggars Banquet/Beggars Banquet)
It's About Time (Beggars Banquet/Beggars Banquet)
This Must Be The Place (Coda/Coda)

Benny Morton

During a professional career which began in 1924 (with Billy Fowler's Orchestra), Benny Morton earned and sustained a reputation as one of the most consistent of trombone soloists in jazz

Henry Sterling 'Benny' Morton (born New York City, 1907) first played trombone with school friends. After leaving Fowler he joined Fletcher Henderson in 1926. Solo on **Jackass Blues**, 1926 **(The Fletcher Henderson Story/The Fletcher Henderson Story, Vol 1)** is not typical of his work in general (certainly not in later years): blustery, hard-hitting, with no frills.

He worked with Chick Webb (1930-31) but returned to Henderson in 1931. By this time, Morton's style had taken shape, as evinced in solos like **Clarinet Marmalade** and **Sugarfoot Stomp (The Fletcher Henderson Story/The Fletcher Henderson Story, Vol 3)**. Joined Don Redman Orchestra, remaining from 1932-37. His development as a soloist of real stature took place during this period.

Whilst a regular with Redman, he also recorded with Ben Pollack **(Ben Pollack & His Orchestra 1933-1934)**; Coleman Hawkins and Red Allen **(Recordings Made Between 1930 & 1941)**; and Benny Carter, **(Benny Carter, 1933/Ridin' In Rhythm)**; next, with Count Basie (1937-40).

He also appeared at some of the classic Billie Holiday sessions arranged by Teddy Wilson **(The Golden Years, Vols 1, 2)** and

Above: Benny Morton, acclaimed as a gifted and consistent soloist yet remaining one of jazz's most under-appreciated trombonists.

other similar Wilson-led dates (sans Holiday) **(Teddy Wilson & His All Stars)** demonstrating unusual consistency during solos.

Joined jumping Joe Sullivan Café Society band (1940), moving on to Teddy Wilson for longer spell (1940-43). Appeared at Condon's Town Hall concerts during World War II. With Edmond Hall after leaving Wilson, before assembling own band which lasted two years (1944-46). Also worked with Raymond Scott orchestra at CBS, and in pit bands of several well-known Broadway musicals (including *Guys & Dolls*, *Silk Stockings* and *Jamaica)*. Constantly in demand for session work during 1950s and 1960s with time off for jazz gigs and recordings. In latter category, he produced what was his best-ever ballad performance **(I Can't Get Started)** at a mid-1950s record date **(Buck Clayton's Band)**.

Toured Europe late-1960s as member of all-star 'Top Brass' package. During 1968 worked often with Wild Bill Davison, also participating in excellent recording date with Davison outift **(The Jazz Giants)**, producing exquisite variations on **I Surrender, Dear**. He continued to be active throughout the 1970s, including memorable gigs with Bobby Hackett (1970), Roy Eldridge, and World's Greatest Jazz Band.

Benny Morton's death—from pneumonia in New York on December 28, 1985—ended a distinguished jazz career in which his all-round consistency had served him admirably.

Albums:

The Fletcher Henderson Story (Columbia)/ The Fletcher Henderson Story, Vols 1, 3 (CBS)
Don Redman (—/CBS—Realm)
Ben Pollack & His Orchestra 1933-1934 (—/VJM)
Coleman Hawkins, Recordings Made Between 1930 & 1941 (CBS—France)
Benny Carter, 1933 (Prestige)/ Various (Including Benny Carter), Ridin' In Rhythm (World Records)
Count Basie, The Best Of Basie (Decca/MCA—Germany)
Billie Holiday, The Golden Years, Vols 1, 2 (Columbia/CBS)
Teddy Wilson & His All Stars (Columbia/CBS)
Various (Including Benny Morton), Blue Note's Three Decades Of Jazz, Vol 1 (1939-1949) (Blue Note/—)
Various (Including Red Allen), Harlem On Saturday Night (—/Ace Of Hearts)
Eddie Condon, Jam Sessions At Commodore (Decca/Ace of Hearts)
Various (Including Hot Lips Page), Swing Classics, Vol 2 (Polydor/Polydor)
Buck Clayton's Band (Vanguard/Vanguard)
Fletcher Henderson All-Star Reunion Band, The Big Reunion (Jazztone/—)
Roy Eldridge, The Nifty Cat (Master Jazz Recordings/—)
Wild Bill Davison, The Jazz Giants (Sackville/Sackville)

Jelly Roll Morton 1923/24 (courtesy Classic Jazz). This great pianist-composer's earliest band recordings. One of the great originals.

Jelly Roll Morton

Pianist-composer Jelly Roll (Ferdinand Joseph La Menthe) Morton, 1885-1941, was one of the great originals of jazz His work is unclassifiable, combining ragtime, blues, opera, New Orleans Brass Band, Spanish and folksong.

Influenced by Scott Joplin, Morton's compositions are multi-thematic, developing two or three melodies within a number, but his approach differs in important respects. Morton's use of harmony is subtler, more complex, the rhythm surging over the mechanical stop-go patterns of ragtime. The interplay between the hands is very different, the left-hand in particular anticipating the beat and releasing octave runs of 16 notes.

The methods by which Morton transformed ragtime into jazz is well illustrated on a late recording from 1939 on which he plays a selection of Joplin's Original Rags **(New Orleans Memories)**. The reverse side contains five classic blues, **Mamie's Blues, Michigan Water Blues, Don't You Leave Me Here, Buddy Bolden's Blues** and **Winin' Boy Blues**.

Morton's early experience playing in the Storyville sporting houses brought him into contact with the great piano 'professors' around the turn of the century. Some of his first recordings recall the tunes of that era, **Jelly Roll Blues, Big Fat Ham, New Orleans Joys, Perfect Rag (Jelly Roll Morton)**. The 13 classic solos cut at the Gennett studios in 1923 and 1924 are included here, the version of 'King Porter' later taken up by Benny Goodman and turned into a swing era hit. Two devices originating with Morton, the break and the riff, became important features of big-band swing: 'If you can't have a decent break you haven't got a jazz band and you can't even play jazz Without a break you have nothin'.' Morton consciously set out to increase the scope of the piano, using its voicings in ways suggestive of an orchestra: 'The piano should always be an imitation of a jazz band'.

In 1926, the pianist fronted the Red Hot Peppers, a small group including trumpeter George Mitchell and clarinettist Omer Simeon, and their recordings remain classics of New Orleans style. Morton's deployment of the three-horn front line, trumpet, clarinet and trombone, the polyphonic and the solo voice, the lithe rhythmic variety and the natural blending of improvisation and score show that Morton was a great composer. Versions of **Black Bottom Stomp, The Chant, Grandpa's Spells, Doctor Jazz** or **Jelly Roll Blues (King Of New Orleans Jazz)** include contributions from side-musicians like Kid Ory, John St Cyr, while **Steamboat Stomp** and **Sidewalk Blues** add Darnell Howard and Barney Bigard to the unit. Apart from his work with the Red Hot Peppers, Morton recorded duo performances with cornettist King Oliver, **King Porter Stomp** and **Tom Cat Blues** in 1924, inspiring the later collaboration of Louis Armstrong and Earl Hines **(Louis Armstrong & King Oliver)**. A collection by the New Orleans Rhythm Kings from 1923 has Morton on several tracks including **Clarinet Marmalade, Mr Jelly Lord, London Blues** and **Milenburg Joys**. A trio performance **Mournful Serenade**, with Morton, Simeon and trombonist Geechy Fields, is a masterpiece of pastel lyricism, and contrasts with the lusty trio on **Shreveport Stomp (Stomps & Joys** and **King Of New Orleans Jazz**.

With the onset of the Depression, Morton went to New York, touring for a while before finally fetching up in penury in a Washington club. Alan Lomax, who was collecting folk material for the Library of Congress archive, found him in 1938, and encouraged him to commit his reminiscences, verbal and musical, to record. Twelve albums **(The Library Of Congress Recordings)** contain Morton's often boastful version of jazz history, and examples of scat singing, blues singing, cabaret material and piano styles. His personality comes across forcefully; Jelly Roll Morton was a great dandy, a great pool-player and womanizer, but, above all, a great musician. A fascinating album of piano rolls **(Jelly Roll Morton)** dating from 1924, captures the flavor of his compositions.

Jelly Roll Morton, Mr Jelly (courtesy Maestri del Jazz-Italy).

Albums:

New Orleans Memories (Commodore/Fontana)
Jelly Roll Morton (Milestone/Milestone)
King Of New Orleans Jazz (RCA Victor/RCA Victor)
Louis Armstrong & King Oliver (Milestone/Milestone)
New Orleans Rhythm Kings (Milestone/Milestone)
Stomps & Joys (RCA Victor/—)
The Library Of Congress Recordings (Classic Jazz Masters/Classic Jazz Masters)
Jelly Roll Morton (—/DJM)

Morton, Library of Congress Recordings (courtesy Classic Jazz Masters).

Bennie Moten

Bennie Moten (born Kansas City, Missouri, 1894) started on piano, switched to baritone horn and, by 12, was playing latter instrument in youth brass band. After reverting to keyboard, he started working in local Kansas City bands, before putting together own quintet—a unit which had become six-piecer for its first records—**Elephant's Wobble, Crawdad Blues,** both Moten compositions **(Bennie Moten Kansas City Orchestra 1923-25).**

Apart from the leader's ragtime-influenced piano, Moten Sextet members included cornettist lammar Wright, clarinettist Herman 'Woody' Walder, trombonist Thamon Hayes. Amongst the band's recordings—most numbers composed by Moten—were fine sides like **Tulsa Blues, Vine Street Blues, Sister Honky Tonk** and **South**, last-named destined to become a jazz standard.

By the time Moten band commenced recording for Victor (in 1926), its numbers had increased to 10 (personnel included saxists Harland Leonard, later to lead own fine jump band, Jack Washington, and trumpeter Paul Webster). **White Lightin' Blues, Midnight Mama, Ding Dong Blues** and **Moten Stomp** (all **Bennie Moten's Kansas City Orchestra, Vol 1)** are fine examples of the Moten band during 1926-27. Nephew Ira ('Buster') Moten (1904-65) worked with band from around 1929, playing accordian and doubling on piano. Most important personnel arrival, also in '29, was pianist William 'Count' Basie; guitarist-trombonist-composer-arranger Eddie Durham was another important addition to the aggregation (both on **Bennie Moten's Kansas City Orchestra, Vol 3 (1929): Moten's Blues)**.

Subsequent key figures to join (both in '30): trumpeter Oran 'Hot Lips' Page, singer Jimmy Rushing (both on **Bennie Moten's Kansas City Orchestra, Vol 4 (1929-1930); New Moten Stomp)**. By the time the band made its final recordings (1932), notable newcomers included tenorist Ben Webster, trombonist Dan Minor, saxist-clarinettist Eddie Barefield, bassist Walter Page.

Bennie Moten Band, always improving, continued to spread the message of big-band KC jazz music until the leader's death in 1935, even though, by 1932, it had begun to feel the effects of the Depression. First Count Basie

Orchestra comprised, in the main, remnants of the final Bennie Moten organization.

Albums:
Bennie Moten's Kansas City Orchestra 1923-1925 (—/Parlophone)
Bennie Moten's Kansas City Orchestra, Vols 1-5 (RCA Victor—France)

Alphonse Mouzon

The multi-dimensional drum technique of Alphonse Mouzon made him one of the most successful artists in late 1970s funk but it was in the more improvisational context with pianist McCoy Tyner in the early '70s which consolidated his reputation as one of jazz's most creative and dynamic percussionists.

Born in Charleston, South Carolina, on November 21, 1948, Mouzon was playing 'drums' improvised from boxes and cans at age 5. At Charleston's Bonds-Wilson High School he played in the band, directed by Lonnie Hamilton. At school, he achieved top academic grades but had to turn down scholarships because of his family's financial hardship. One of his first professional gigs was 10 days with Chubby 'The Twist' Checker in '65 and the following year he went to New York, initially studying medicine while playing with the Ross Carnegie Big Band in his spare time.

He attended New York's City College for a while and worked in the orchestra in the Broadway show *Promises, Promises.* In '70, he spent a year with vibist Roy Ayres, joining Weather Report the following year. But it was with McCoy Tyner in '72 which brought accolades for his multi-faceted drumming—the experience clearly inspired Mouzon to even greater technique on Tyner's enduring epic **Sahara** and subsequent albums like **Song Of The New World** and **Enlightenment**.

From '73-'75, he worked with Larry Coryell in his Eleventh House and, as a solo in the early '70s, became one of Blue Note's most successful artists. With his lively funk line-ups, Mouzon has evolved into one of the '80s' biggest-selling artists with exceptional albums like **By All Means, Morning Sun** and **Step Into The Funk**.

Albums:
Gil Evans, Gil Evans (Ampex/—)
Weather Report, Weather Report (Columbia/CBS)
Eleventh House, Introducing The Eleventh House (Vanguard/Vanguard)
MyCoy Tyner, Sahara (Milestone/Milestone)
MyCoy Tyner, Song Of The New World (Milestone/Milestone)
The Drums (Impluse/Impulse)
The Essence Of Mystery (Blue Note/Blue Note)
Funky Snakefoot (Blue Note/Blue Note)
Mind Transplant (Blue Note/Blue Note)
Man Incognito (Blue Note/Blue Note)
Alphonse Mouzon-Larry Coryell, Back Together Again (Atlantic/Atlantic)
Virtue (—/MPS)
In Search Of A Dream (—/MPS)
Baby Come Back (—/Metronome)
By All Means (Decca/Excalibur)
Morning Sun (Decca/London)
Step Into The Funk (—/Metronome)

Alphonse Mouzon, Step Into The Funk (courtesy Metronome-West Germany)—the drummer's earlier work with McCoy Tyner made his reputation.

Gerry Mulligan

Baritone saxophonist Gerry Mulligan was born in Long Island, 1927, and was writing arrangements for big bands like Elliot Lawrence, Claude Thornhill and Gene Krupa while still in his teens.

He contributed tunes like **Jeru, Rocker** and **Venus De Milo**, as well as taking several good baritone solos, to the influential Miles Davis band of 1948 **(Birth Of The Cool)**. 1951 saw him recording some of his finest compositions like **Bweebida Bobbida** and **Funhouse** with a tentet which included two baritones, George Wallington on piano and tenorist Allen Eager **(Gerry Mulligan & Chet Baker)**.

In 1952, his famous piano-less quartet with trumpeter Chet Baker, bassist Carson Smith and drummer Chico Hamilton made its début in Los Angeles. The lack of chord commentary from the piano gave the soloists great melodic freedom, and Mulligan and Baker played backing lines for each other. Interweaving counterpoint over a surging rhythm section gave the group an identifiable sound, and many of its characteristics were copied on the West Coast. In 1952, they recorded much of their standard repertoire for Prestige, including Mulligan compositions like **Line For Lyons, Bark For Barksdale, Turnstile** as well as re-arrangements of standards like **Carioca, The Lady Is A Tramp** and their biggest hit, **My Funny Valentine (Gerry Mulligan & Chet Baker)**.

Above: Another superb solo from Gerry Mulligan, titan of the baritone sax, at the Newport Jazz Festival, 1958 (from the movie Jazz On A Summer's Day).

The following year, Mulligan added altoist Lee Konitz to the group for a classic version of **Too Marvelous For Words (Revelation)**, and also led a tentet for a Capitol recording session which features some of Mulligan's arranger's piano, most of the solo work divided between the leader and Baker, and the odd instrumentation of two baritones, tuba and French horn **(Walking Shoes)**. In 1954, with trombonist Bob Brookmeyer replacing Baker, the quartet made a triumphant appearance at Salle Pleyel in Paris. Brookmeyer, like Mulligan, is a traditionalist despite great harmonic sophistication, and the two men made a highly compatible front line, with the great Red Mitchell bass and Frank Isola drums **(The Fabulous Gerry Mulligan Quartet)**. Various personnel changes occurred—Jon Eardlay on trumpet replacing Brookmeyer, Brookmeyer back with Zoot Sims added, and in 1957 Mulligan led an octet with Konitz, Sims, Al Cohn and Allen Eager through a set of Bill Holman arrangements **(Revelation)**.

In '58, the baritonist featured in the movie *I Want To Live* (he also turns up in *The Subterraneans*, '60, in the role of 'the friendly neighborhood clergyman'). Several of the Johnny Mandel compositions from the *I Want To Live* score, including a great Mulligan solo on the theme, are included on the album made by his Concert Jazz Band **(Gerry Mulligan & The Concert Jazz Band Live)**. Two versions of the ballad **Come Rain Or Come Shine** are presented, contrasting exercises in lyricism by Mulligan and Sims. Fueled by drummer Mel Lewis, the band belts along, and **Blueport** has some of the most swinging Mulligan on record, especially in the exchange of fours and eights with Clark Terry.

A musician who loves to jam, Mulligan made numerous albums with Stan Getz, Paul Desmond and Thelonious Monk.

Contemporary Mulligan is best represented by an A&M album **(The Age Of Steam)**, which bears a photo of the one-time prototypical modernist (crew-cut, shades) with long hair and a beard.

In the '80s, Mulligan leads a 15-piece orchestra,mostly devoted to playing his own charts, and occasionally doubles on soprano saxophone. A gruff, laconic player, Gerry Mulligan is the essence of relaxed swing. An album like **Little Big Horn** in the '80s—all original compositions, featuring such fusion favorites as Richard Tee and Dave Grusin on keyboards, and saxophonist Mike Brecker—is an indication of how willing Gerry Mulligan has been is to move with the times.

The Fabulous Gerry Mulligan Quartet (courtesy Vogue), recorded live at Salle Pleyel, Paris 1954.

Albums:
Miles Davis, Birth Of The Cool (Capitol/Capitol)
Gerry Mulligan & Chet Baker (Prestige/Prestige)
Gerry Mulligan & Lee Konitz, Revelation (Blue Note/Blue Note)
The Gerry Mulligan Tentette, Walking Shoes (Capitol/—)
The Fabulous Gerry Mulligan Quartet (—/Vogue)
The Age Of Steam (A&M/A&M)
Little Big Horn (GRP/GRP)
My Funny Valentine (CBS/CBS)
Gerry Mulligan-Scott Hamilton, Soft Lights And Sweet Music (Concord/Concord)

David Murray

Originally from the West Coast, the gifted young saxophonist David Murray emerged from New York's loft scene in the early 1970s as a major new voice on tenor.

Murray (born in Berkeley, California, in 1955) learned piano as a child, playing saxophone at 9, responding to a family musical tradition (his father was a guitarist; his mother, a revered pianist with the Sanctified Church). Murray's first interest was in R&B at 12, leading his own blues bands while still in his teens. A meeting with poet, writer and educator Stanley Crouch opened up Murray's interest in jazz Through Crouch, Murray joined Bobby Bradford and Arthur Blythe in the Black Music Infinity Band.

In '75, he moved to New York, originally intending just to complete his college saxophone thesis. Here, he soon became a talking point sitting in with the new improvisers of the age, experimentalists like Cecil Taylor, Don Cherry, Anthony Braxton, Sunny Murray, Philip Wilson, Don Pullen, Olu Dara and Fred Hopkins. In '77, Murray became the youngest member of the formidable and unique World Saxophone Quartet alongside Hamiet Bluiett, Julius Hemphill and Oliver Lake — bringing a wealth of musical ideas to a group which managed to combine the avant-garde with an Ellingtonian power and lyricism.

A player in the explorative Albert Ayler tradition, Murray paid an enduring tribute to that great individualist on his first, highly rated album **Flowers For Albert**. With an equal facility on both tenor and bass clarinet, some of Murray's most compeling performances have been with his octet in the '80s. This has included such challenging company as altoist Henry Threadgill, trumpeters Olu Dara, Butch Morris and Bobby Bradford, trombonists Craig Harris and George Lewis, pianists Curtis Clark and Anthony Davis, bassist Wilber Morris and percussionist Steve McCall (**Home** and **Murray's Steps**).

In '86, David Murray toured on the international festival circuit with his own group (pianist John Hicks, bassist Ray Drummond, drummer Ed Blackwell and guest saxophonist Hamiet Bluiett) and appeared with the World Saxophone Quartet. That summer he received the North Sea Jazz Festival's 'Bird Winner' prize — an accolade, named in honor of Charlie Parker, and awarded to musicians who have made notable contributions to jazz over the previous decade.

Albums:
Flowers For Albert (India Navigation/—)
Low Class Conspiracy (Adelphi/—)
Wildflowers (Douglas/—)
London Concerts (—/Cadillac)
Ming (Black Saint/Black Saint)
Home (Black Saint/Black Saint)
Murray's Steps (Black Saint/Black Saint)
Moring Song (Black Saint/Black Saint)
Live At 'Sweet Basil' (Black Saint/Black Saint)
World Saxophone Quartet, Point Of No Return (—/Moers Music)
World Saxophone Quartet, Live In Zurich (Black Saint/Black Saint)
Clarinet Summit, Clarinet Summit: In Concert At The Public Theater (India Navigation/India Navigation)

Below: Saxophonist David Murray—awarded the North Sea Jazz Festival's 'Bird' prize, 1986, for contribution to jazz over previous decade.

David Murray's Octet, Murray's Steps (courtesy Black Saint-Italy).

Above: Drummer Sunny Murray—meeting the demands of Ayler and Taylor.

Sunny Murray

Free drummer Sunny Murray was born in Oklahoma, and gradually evolved a style of drumming to meet the needs of avant-garde leaders like Albert Ayler and Cecil Taylor. Using a very basic kit, cymbals, snare, bass drum and hi-hat, Murray avoided regular time-keeping duties altogether, building up layers of rhythm that ebbed and flowed dramatically between the continuous cymbal and the tripping snare runs. Masterpieces like Ayler's ESP **(Spiritual Unity)** or Taylor's marathon **D. Trad That's What (Live At The Café Montmartre)** owe much to the drummer's unconfining momentum.

Albums under his own name revealed a gift for composition that incorporated characteristics of his former leaders, along with an advance and recede development that springs from his own style of playing. A great, original group player, he seldom solos, preferring to control the climate and dynamics of his bands within the ensemble. His first album **(Sunny Murray)** shows the rapport that existed with bassist Alan Silva, whose arco work in the upper register was equally pioneering. A session with Ayler and Don Cherry includes a LeRoi Jones poetry reading, **Black Art**, and a long Murray composition, **Justice (Sunny's Time Now)**.

In 1968 he left for France, recording three albums the following year with French and

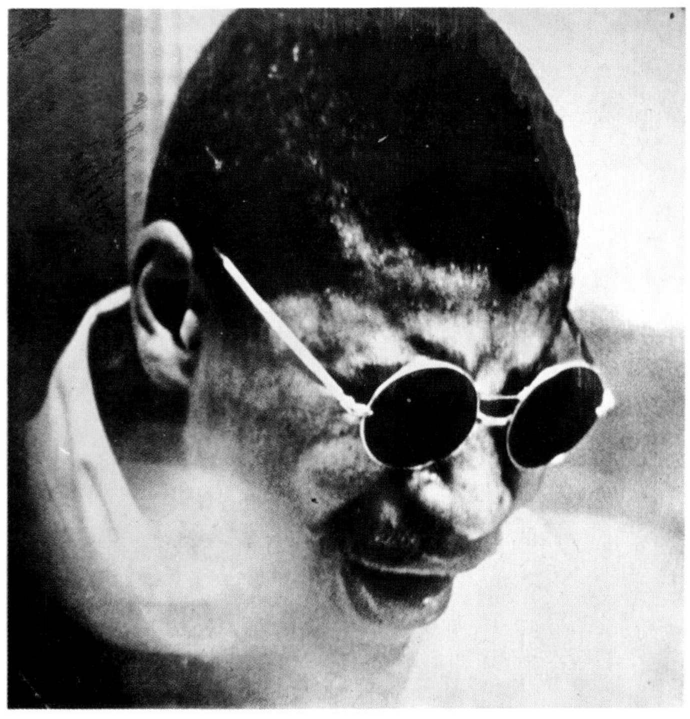

Sunny Murray (courtesy ESP)—pioneer of free drumming, his first outing as leader with a quintet which included bassist Alan Silva.

Amina Claudine Myers Salutes Bessie Smith (courtesy Leo Records) in the company of drummer Jimmy Lovelace and bassist Cecil McBee, 1980.

American musicians. Using a septet, Murray's keening themes, like the outstanding **Angel Son**, owe much to the prescience of Alan Silva's violin **(Big Chief)**. A long composition, **Suns Of Africa (Homage To Africa)** again uses dense ensemble textures and the large unit includes Archie Shepp, Lester Bowie, Roscoe Mitchell and Grachan Moncur III. A quartet **(An Even Break)** marked a return to comparatively straightforward performances, and has Murray reading his own poetry.

Albums:

Albert Ayler:
- Spiritual Unity (ESP/ESP)
- Prophecy (ESP/ESP)
- Vibrations (Arista—Freedom/Arista—Freedom)
- Witches & Devils (Arista—Freedom/Arista—Freedom)
- Spirits Rejoice (ESP/ESP)
- Bells (ESP/ESP)
- New York Eye & Ear Control (ESP/ESP)

Cecil Taylor:
- Into The Hot (Impulse/Impulse)
- Live At The Café Montmartre (Fantasy/—)
- Nefertiti (Arista—Freedom/Arista—Freedom)

Sunny Murray (ESP/ESP)
Sunny's Time Now (Jihad/—)
Big Chief (Pathé—France)
Homage To Africa (BYG/BYG)
An Even Break (BYG/BYG)
Wild Flowers, The New York Loft Sessions (Douglas/—)

Amina Claudine Myers

Pianist, organist, composer and vocalist Amina Claudine Myers came to prominence in the '60s through Chicago's progressive AACM and has subsequently been hailed as a musician whose influence in the '80s and '90s could be as profound as that of Mary Lou Williams in the '30s and '40s.

Born in Arkansas, Myers was singing and playing piano from age 4, arranging and writing music for church choirs at 11. In her early career, she worked and recorded with gospel groups and blues artists like Little Milton and Fontella Bass. But it was Chicago's AACM (Association for the Advancement of Creative Musicians) in the '60s which provided a suitably open environment in which she was able to explore, experiment and develop her unique style.

In the late '70s, she moved to New York where she consolidated her reputation as a solo performer. The many musicians who have benefited from Myers' expressive keyboard-style and emotional vocals include some of the most significant improvisers of the age — Muhal Richard Abrams, Joseph Jarman, Leroy Jenkins, Lester Bowie, Henry Threadgill, Frank Lowe... There is seemingly no limit to her versatility. In '79, for instance, she performed her dynamic improvisational *Suite for Chorus, Pipe Organ and Percussion* with a 19-piece ensemble; in '80, she filled 'Duke's seat' at the piano in the Kool Jazz Festival's tribute to Ellington.

On **Song For Mother E** — an Amina Myers album from '79 — she played both piano and organ (she was voted 'Talent Deserving Wider Recognition on Organ' in *Down Beat* magazine's critics' poll in '80). Myers' **Poems For Piano** features her own interpretations of Marion Brown's compositions for keyboard.

Apart from the respect she has won as a highly individual pianist-composer and organist, Myers' blues roots and gospel background are given vocal rein, particularly on her superb **Salutes Bessie Smith** which must be one of the finest modern interpretations of the Empress of the Blues' classics.

Albums:

Maurice McIntyre (Kalaparusha), Humility In The Light Of The Creator (Delmark/Delmark)
Muhal Richard Abrams, Lifea Blinec (Arista/Arista)
Henry Threadgill, X-75 Volume I (Arista/Arista)
Song For Mother E (—/Leo Records)
Poems For Piano (Sweet Earth/—)
Amina Claudine Myers Salutes Bessie Smith (—/Leo Records)
Frank Lowe, Exotic Heartbreak (Soul Note/Soul Note)
Jumping In The Sugar Bowl (—/Minor Music)

Zbigniew Namyslowski

Principally an alto-player, Warsaw-born Zbigniew Namyslowski has become one of Poland's leading musicians and a major voice in European jazz-rock.

Namyslowski's early career (he plays alto and sopranino saxophones, flute, cello and piano) was spent sharpening his technique on Poland's traditional jazz circuit. Even before completing his bachelor's degree course at Warsaw's Academy of Music he was hailed as one of Poland's most talented young musicians.

Concentrating on alto since the early '60s, Namyslowski came to wider attention when he received Best Soloist award at the '64 Prague Festival. He subsequently developed a melodic and lively brand of jazz-rock with a subtle hint of the Polish folk form — a style which allows adequate space for his improvisational skills. His recordings with Polish compatriots violinist Michael Urbaniak and vocalist Urszula Dudziak show he's no slouch as a sympathetic accompanist, either.

His American début album, the oddly spelt **Namyslovski**, was released to great interest, while his UK release **Air Condition** provided a minor hit in the early '80s jazz discos, and encouraged a British tour.

Zbigniew Namyslowski, Air Condition (courtesy Affinity-DeKael).

Albums:

Live At Jazz Jamboree (—/Muza)
Lola (—/Decca)
Jazz Greetings From The East (—/Fontana)
Namymanu (WEA/WEA)
Namyslovski (Inner City/Inner City)
Jasmine Lady (—/Vinyl)
Michael Urbaniak, Urbaniak (Inner City/Inner City)
Air Condition (—/Affinity—DeKael)

Ray Nance

Raymond Willis Nance (born Chicago, 1913) was a multi-talented performer. Primarily, he was a first-class Armstrong-influenced trumpet player. In addition, Nance had one of the most distinctive sounds on jazz violin — a somewhat curious hybrid of North American jazz and European gypsy-like music.

Nance, who died in 1976, started his career in music with college band, following tuition on piano, violin and trumpet. In 1932 he played and sang in Chicago nightclubs, fronted own sextet, and gigged outside the Windy City. Joined Earl Hines big band (1937), staying for almost two years. Next came a period of just over one year (1939-40) with Horace Henderson, followed by short interlude prior to joining Duke Ellington (end of 1940). First recorded solo in January, '41 (although track remained unissued until more recently) when Ellington band recorded what was to become its longest-serving theme, **Take The 'A' Train**. (Version of the number which did get released on original 78rpm disc was recorded a month after the first.) At this second date, Nance's violin was heard for the first time with Ellington (on Juan Tizol's **Bakiff**).

Nance was to become one of Ellington's most prolific, priceless and popular front-line soloists throughout the next 23 years (except for odd instances of absence from band, in 1944, 1945, 1961).

Whilst in Ellington band first time round, Nance, with Ellington and singer Kay Davis, toured British variety halls, in 1948. In 1966 he toured Europe as solo act, and a year later worked in Switzerland with band of Henri Chaix.

During years 1966-69, teamed up at regular intervals with clarinettist Sol Yaged.

Nance's violin playing figured interestingly on such diverse non-Ellington recordings as **Jazz For A Sunday Afternoon, Vol 1** in company with Dizzy Gillespie, Elvin Jones, Chick Corea — **Duke Ellington Jazz Violin Session** — pitting Nance's individualism against that of Stephane Grappelli and Svend Asmussen; and **Body & Soul**, probably the finest, certainly most comprehensive, of Ray Nance's jazz fiddle on record, this one under his own name.

Elsewhere, both trumpet and violin were utilized at sessions involving musicians like Shelly Manne **(Shelly Manne & Co)**, Paul Gonsalves, Harold Ashby **(Ellingtonians Play A Tribute To Duke Ellington)**, with Nance also playing trumpet but not violin, on tracks by Harry Carney; and Coleman Hawkins **(Duke Ellington Meets Coleman Hawkins)**.

Albums:

Ray Nance, Body & Soul (Solid State/—)
Ray Nance, Huffin' & Puffin' (—/MPS/BASF)
Ray Nance/Stephane Grappelli/Svend Asmussen, Duke Ellington's Jazz Violin Session (Atlantic/—)
Various (Including Ray Nance), Jazz For A Sunday Afternoon, Vol 1 (Solid State/Solid State)
Everybody Knows Johnny Hodges (Impulse/Impulse)
Duke Ellington Meets Coleman Hawkins (Impulse/Impulse)
Earl Hines, Once Upon A Time (Impulse/Impulse)
Various, Great Ellingtonians Play A Tribute To Duke Ellington (—/Double-Up)
Johnny Hodges, Ellingtonia '56 (Norgran/Columbia—Clef)
Shelly Manne & Co. (Flying Dutchman/—)
Duke Ellington:
The Duke 1940 (Jazz Society/—)
The Works Of Duke Vols 14-20 (RCA Victor—France)
His Most Important Second War Concert (—/Saga)
Ellington '55 (Capitol)/Toast To The Duke (World Record Club)
Historically Speaking, The Duke (Bethlehem)/ Stomp, Look & Listen (Ember)
Midnight In Paris (Columbia/CBS)
Such Sweet Thunder (Columbia/CBS—Realm)
Pretty Woman (RCA Victor/RCA Victor)
We Love You Madly (Capitol—Pickwick)
Duke Ellington Vol 2 (—/Saga) (Peer Gynt Suites Nos 1, 2)/ Suite Thursday (Columbia/CBS)
Ellington Indigos (Columbia/—)
The Golden Duke (Prestige/Prestige)
Souvenirs (Reprise—France)

Joseph 'Tricky Sam' Nanton

Together with trumpeter Bubber Miley, trombonist Joe Nanton provided Duke Ellington Orchestra with its first individual purveyors of the so-called 'jungle style' which Ellington pioneered in 1920s and thereafter.

Nanton's ability in projecting a blues-filled, often poignant humanized 'cry', via trombone and plunger-mute, has never been surpassed. Nanton's wah-wah plungering was an integral ingredient of numerous Ellington recordings of **Black & Tan Fantasy** (where his trombone eccentricities provided its own totally individual evocation of the funereal atmosphere of an exceptional piece of Ellington creation), including the very first **(The Beginning).** Nanton was one of most important individual contributors to work with Ellington from mid-1920s until mid-1940s.

Superb as his playing was during his early days with the band, he was especially rewarding during the last decade of his lifetime. His were classic solos to add to the luster of acknowledged Ellington masterpieces during early 1940s, one of his most creative periods; **Ko Ko, A Portrait Of Bert Williams, Jack The Bear, Stompy Jones** and **Harlem Airshaft**.

Joe Nanton (born New York, 1904, of West Indian parentage) began his professional career with stride pianist Cliff Jackson (1921), then spent two years with Earl Frazier's Harmony Five (1923-25), before rejoining Jackson ('25). Prior to joining Ellington, he worked with Elmer Snowden.

Suffered a stroke in 1945, but recovered to resume work with the band following year. Collapsed and died during band's 1946 West Coast tour. His nickname of 'Tricky Sam' was bestowed by fellow Ellingtonian Otto 'Toby' Hardwicke.

Albums:

The Complete Duke Ellington (1928-1937), Vols 1-7 (CBS—France)
The Works Of Duke Ellington, Vols 1-17 (RCA Victor—France)
Duke Ellington:
Masterpieces (1928-1930) (RCA Victor—France)
Jungle Jamboree (—/Parlophone)
The Beginning (1926-1928) (Decca/MCA—Germany)
Hot In Harlem (1928-1929) (Decca/MCA—Germany)
Rockin' In Rhythm (1929-1931) (Decca/MCA—Germany)
At The Cotton Club, 1938, Vols 1, 2 (Jazz Archives/—)
Black, Brown & Beige (Aristan—Italy)
His Most Important Second War Concert (—/Saga)
The Jimmy Blanton Years (Queen Disc—Italy)

Fats Navarro

Born Key West, Florida, 1923, Theodore 'Fats' Navarro was bebop's most perfect trumpeter. Never flamboyant like Dizzy Gillespie, Navarro's playing has a classical perfection and balance, the tone true and brassy, the articulation accurate at even the fastest tempos. Though he died of TB and addiction at the age of 26, his influence on later generations of trumpeters — Clifford Brown, Kenny Dorham, Lee Morgan — was paramount.

Although Navarro played trumpet from age 13, he had little formal tuition. He also played tenor sax for a while.

Following experience with the big bands of Snookum Russell and Andy Kirk, he took over Dizzy Gillespie's chair in the legendary Billy Eckstine band from 1945, soloing brilliantly on **Long Long Journey** and **Tell Me Pretty Baby (Mister B & The Band)**. Small group sessions for Savoy featured Navarro with baritonist Leo Parker, **Fat Girl, Ice Freezes Red**; with altoist Sonny Stitt and fellow trumpeter Kenny Dorham, **Boppin' A Riff**; with tenorist Eddie 'Lockjaw' Davis, **Calling Dr. Jazz** and, with pianist-composer Tadd Dameron's group, including Dexter Gordon and altoist Ernie Henry, **Bebop Caroll** and **Tadd Walk (Fat Girl)**.

The association with Dameron proved ideal, with the pianist's lyrical compositions providing a perfect setting for Navarro's beautiful sound and vaulting imagination. **Our Delight, The Squirrel, The Chase, Lady Bird, Dameronia, Jahbero** and **Symphonette (Prime Source)** show his poise at a variety of tempos, his harmonic ideas as sophisticated as Charlie Parker's and his improvisations as finished as if they had been scored. Swapping choruses with trumpeter Howard McGhee on numbers like **Boperation, Double Talk** and **The Skunk** conveys the soaring exhilaration of young musicians matching their gifts. The tracks with Bud Powell and a youthful Sonny Rollins, **52nd Street Theme, Dance Of The Infidels, Wail** and **Bounding With Bud** show that no matter how turbulent the relationship between the trumpeter and the pianist, their music was a meeting of genius.

The Dameron band which was resident at The Royal Roost in 1948, including Navarro, tenor-player Allen Eager and altoist Rudy Williams, made a stunning version of **Good Bait**, a headlong *tour de force* for the trumpeter **(Good Bait)**, who somehow contrived to sound as relaxed as the laconic Eager. Recordings from Café Society with Charlie Parker and Bud Powell in the year of Navarro's death, 1950, proved a meeting of equals, the trumpeter's solos on **Street Beat, Ornithology** or **Move** hardly confirming the stories of physical deterioration.

Albums:

Billy Eckstine, Mister B. & The Band (Savoy/Savoy)
Fat Girl (Savoy/Savoy)
Prime Source (Blue Note/Blue Note)
Tadd Dameron, Fats Navarro, Good Bait (Riverside/—)
Saturday Night Swing Session (—/GI Records)
Charlie Parker Historical Masterpieces (Le Jazz Cool/—)
Fats Navarro (Milestone/Milestone)
The Fabulous Fats Navarro Vols 1 & 2 (Blue Note/Blue Note)

Below: The multi-talented Ray Nance—violinist, trumpeter and singer. One of Duke Ellington's most rewarding soloists.

Fats Navarro-Tadd Dameron, Good Bait (courtesy Riverside).

Oliver Nelson

Before disappearing into Hollywood, Oliver Nelson — like Quincy Jones, Lalo Schifrin, Shorty Rogers — was an excellent jazz arranger and good saxophonist.

A major suite in seven parts **(Afro-American Sketches)** uses a big band including cellos, French horns, a tuba and four rhythm for an imaginative re-working of ethnic sources. Typically here, as elsewhere, Nelson's alto is cast in the lead because of the purity and cutting edge of his upper register work. A lengthy collaboration with multi-instrumentalist Eric Dolphy resulted in some of Nelson's best work as arranger for combo and instrumentalist **(Images)**. Some of his best known compositions like **Stolen Moments** and **Hoe-Down** came from the classic session with Dolphy, Freddie Hubbard and Bill Evans **(Blues & The Abstract Truth)**. A big-band session from 1967 **(Live From Los Angeles)**, and a Montreux performance of his **Swiss Suite**, featuring Gato Barbieri and altoist Eddie 'Cleanhead' Vinson, prove that Nelson has the ability to give the most ad-hoc assembly a collective identity. Born 1932, St Louis, Nelson is also an expert in embalming and taxidermy.

Albums:
Afro-American Sketches (Prestige/—)
Images (Prestiges/Prestige)
Blues & The Abstract Truth (Impulse/Impulse)
Live From Los Angeles (Impulse/Impulse)
Swiss Suite (Flying Dutchman/Philips)

Oliver Nelson telling The Blues And The Abstract Truth (courtesy Impulse).

Albert Nicholas

Albert Nicholas (born New Orleans, Louisiana, 1900) was an archetypal New Orleans clarinettist—warm, liquid tone, supple phrasing, attractive vibrato, subtle swing, blues-orientated.

The nephew of cornettist/clarinettist Wooden Joe Nicholas, Albert Nicholas took lessons from legendary Lorenzo Tio Jr, later playing with some of the other great New Orleans names: Buddie Petit, Manuel Perez, Kid Ory, King Oliver.

Worked with various bands (including Perez) before fronting own band, in New Orleans (1923-24). In 1924, toured with King Oliver, leaving after two months to resume previous own gig **(King Oliver's Dixie Syncopators)**. Returned with Oliver, staying this time almost two years (1924-26).

Joined orchestra of Luis Russell (1928), staying over five years. With Russell, attained (at last) featured-soloist status, making memorable contributions to **Panama, Saratoga Shout** and others **(Luis Russell & His Louisiana Swing Orchestra/Luis Russell Story)**. With Jelly Roll Morton in '39, Nicholas produced beautifully posed solos on **Climax Rag, Ballin' The Jack** and **West End Blues (Jelly Roll Morton, Vol 2)**.

Nicholas also worked with Chick Webb, Sam Wooding Orchestra and Bernard Addison. Nicholas' contributions to a series of recordings from 1935, involving bands led by Addison, Freddie Jenkins, Ward Pinkett **(Adrian Rollini & His Friends, Vol 1)** were wholly delightful, as demonstrated especially on **Tap-Room Special**. As with his stint with Addison band, Nicholas played Adrian Rollini's Tap Room with John Kirby and own group. Worked with band accompanying Louis Armstrong (1937-39), then with Zutty Singleton, for eight months (1939-40).

On record with Bechet in '46 **(Sidney Bechet Jazz Classics, Vols 1, 2)**, Nicholas seemed better than before. The rapport between the pair on **Weary Way Blues, Blame It On The Blues** and **Old Stack O'Lee Blues** is masterful, and these sensitive, deeply felt performances have been elevated to the greatest in record jazz Nicholas' work with Wild Bill Davison & His Commodores, recorded one month before Bechet date **(The Davison-Brunis Sessions, Vol 3)** is not as emotionally involved but produces fine clarinet solos nevertheless.

After working on West Coast with Kid Ory, Nicholas started lengthy residency, with own trio, at Jimmy Ryan's, New York. Based mainly in Los Angeles and district, 1949-53, and after working season with Rex Stewart, went to live in France (1953). Recorded during final portion of his career, **Let Me Tell You** is a delightful retrospective survey by this Creole clarinettist of his career in music, with Nicholas' own reminiscences along the way.

Apart from the Nicholas-Bechet classics on Blue Note, probably the best example of Nicholas' recorded work in the 1940s is to be found within **Creole Reeds**, with top-form clarinet on **Buddy Bolden's Blues** and **Albert's Blues**, supported only by Baby Dodds and Don Ewell, from 1946.

Albert Nicholas died in Basle, Switzerland, in 1973, a much-loved and highly respected musical personality.

Albums:
King Oliver's Dixie Syncopators (MCA Coral—Germany)
Luis Russell & His Louisiana Swing Orchestra (Columbia/—)
The Luis Russell Story (—/Parlophone)
Jelly Roll Morton, Vol 2 (RCA Victor—France)
Adrian Rollini & His Friends, Vol 1 (RCA Victor—France)
Sidney Bechet Jazz Orchestra, Vols 1, 2 (Blue Note/—)
(Sidney Bechet)/Albert Nicholas, Creole (Riverside/London)
Various (Including Wild Bill Davison), The Davison-Brunis Sessions, Vol 3 (—/London)
Albert Nicholas Quartet (Delmark/Esquire)
Albert Nicholas, Albert's Blues (—/77)
Albert Nicholas, Let Me Tell You (—/Double-Up)

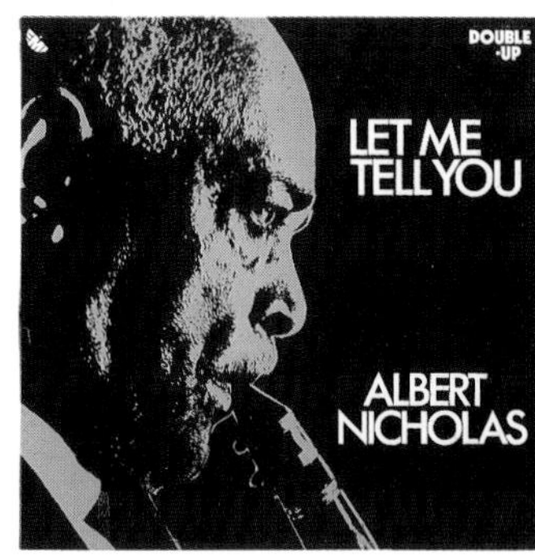

Albert Nicholas, Let Me Tell You (courtesy Double-Up/EMI)—in his own words.

Below: Albert Nicholas, one of the classic New Orleans clarinet stylists—a featured soloist with Luis Russell band from the late 1920s.

Wooden Joe Nicholas

Uncle of clarinettist Albert Nicholas, 'Wooden Joe' Nicholas (born New Orleans, 1883) was said by William Russell, New Orleans historian, to have been 'the most powerful cornettist since King Bolden'. And much like Buddy Bolden, Nicholas was something of a legend as a superior horn-player. For Wooden Joe made but a handful of records — and these give but a hint of his full capabilities during his peak years.

Of available recordings — all made in Crescent City for American Music — earliest (1945) are best, especially from a solo standpoint. Nicholas' timing and strength are, even at 63, admirable, most notably on **Lead Me On, Eh-La-Bas, Shake It & Break It**. His ensemble playing is admirably evidenced on **Tiger Rag, Up Jumped The Devil**. Latter is trio number, with Nicholas receiving superb support from clarinettist Albert Burbank and banjoist Lawrence Marrero.

On remainder of the '45 tracks, the additional presence of trombonist Jim Robinson and drummer Josiah Frazier completes well-nigh classic New Orleans ensemble. Of two sides from '49, Nicholas joins Burbank on clarinet in one passage (Wooden Joe first worked with King Oliver in Storyville, circa 1917, as clarinettist, switching to cornet after practicing with Oliver's instrument). And on **The Lord Will Make A Way Somehow**, playing both open and with plunger mute, Nicholas complements Ann Cook's vocal with tenderness and underlying strength — and good taste.

After working with Oliver, led own band (1918), known variously as Wooden Joe's Band or the Camelia Band. During Depression days, played only occasionally, concentrating on teaching music. Apart from American Music recordings (1945, 1949), Nicholas also recorded (in '44) with Creole Stompers.

Albums:
Wooden Joe's New Orleans Band (American Music/—)
Wooden Joe's New Orleans Band (—/Storyville)

Herbie Nichols

The most moving study in A. B. Spellman's *Four Lives in the Bebop Business*, composer-pianist Herbie Nichols' career in jazz was destroyed by public indifference.

Born 1919, New York, his style shows a Monk influence but overlaps most categories. All that remained in the catalog for many years was a double album of trio performances with either Art Blakey or Max Roach on drums from 1955 and 1956, which happily represents his finest work. His evocative compositions, **House Party Starting, Chit-Chatting**, the justly famous **Lady Sings The Blues** which Billie Holiday picked up on, **(The Third World)**, reveal an encyclopedic knowledge of jazz history from stride through bop to the New Thing, and a rhythmic conception that demands considerable interaction with the drums. How his compositions would have sounded with a fuller instrumentation remains tragically unanswered. He died in 1963 at the age of 44.

Albums:
The Third World (Blue Note/Blue Note)

HERBIE NICHOLS TRIO
HERBIE NICHOLS TRIO
HERBIE NICHOLS TRIO
HERBIE NICHOLS TRIO
HERBIE NICHOLS TRIO
HERBIE NICHOLS TRIO
HERBIE NICHOLS TRIO

Herbie Nichols Trio (courtesy Blue Note)—tragically under-rated pianist.

Red Nichols

Between 1925-30, Ernest Loring 'Red' Nichols (born Ogden, Utah, 1905) was classified by many as being the closest rival to Bix Beiderbecke amongst white cornet/trumpet players of the period. Which was rather a presumption in that Nichols had not the sensitivity, flair, or the superbly logical flow to his playing that was Beiderbecke's. In any case, Nichols' more-than-adequate playing followed a different pathway from Beiderbecke's. Nichols was much involved in jazz which centered on New York during 1925-30.

He recorded prolifically with bands sporting colorful names like Arkansas Travellers, Red Heads, Louisiana Rhythm Kings, Charleston Chasers *et al*. His most famous name-association was with innumerable versions of his own Red Nichols & His Five Pennies (containing, invariably, more members than its title designated). Miff Mole, Benny Goodman, Jack Teagarden, Jimmy Dorsey, Fud Livingston, Pee Wee Russell, Eddie Lang and Vic Berton were amongst those who played with Five Pennies of 1920s vintage.

Personnel from Pennies' first record date (1926) did comprise five players: Nichols, Dorsey, Berton, Lang, Arthur Schutt. From that session came **Washboard Blues** and **That's No Bargain (Red Nichols & His Five Pennies 1926-1928)**, two perennial Five Pennies favorites. Trombonist Miff Mole, added for second session, gave the group extra dimension in overall ensemble sound as well as an additional and distinctive solo voice.

Nichols became director of Charleston Chasers in 1927. Basically, it comprised same (or similar) personnel as previously noted Five Pennies line-up **(The Charleston Chasers 1925-1928)**.

Nichols' personal involvement with music began at 12, when he played cornet with family musical act, as well as father's brass band. At Culver Military Academy ('19) he played cornet, violin and piano, before eventually heading for New York.

From 1924-27, played with Sam Lanin, Bennie Kreuger, Vincent Lopez, California Ramblers, Paul Whiteman. Fronted various bands for next two years. Continued to be active as bandleader during 1930s.

Retired from music in 1942, moved to California, and took employment as shipyard worker. Back to playing, with five months as member of Casa Loma Orchestra (1944). Therafter, continued to lead own Five Pennies bands.

During 1950s, resided and played on West Coast (mostly). Also during this decade, film purporting to be based on Nichols' career was made: *The Five Pennies* **(Meet The Five Pennies/Masters Of Dixieland, Vol 5: Red Nichols & The Five Pennies)**. Nichols appeared in another jazz biopic: *The Gene Krupa Story* **(Drum Crazy)**. Interest engendered by *Five Pennies* movie enabled Nichols to take further bands of same name on tour, including two overseas trips (1960, 1964).

Ernest Loring 'Red' Nichols died, of a heart attack, in 1966 — affectionately remembered as a musician who had contributed to some of the best white jazz to emanate from New York in the late '20s and early '30s.

Albums:
Jack Teagarden/Red Nichols, J.T. (Ace of Hearts)
Benny Goodman, A Jazz Holiday (Decca/MCA)
Red Nichols & His Five Pennies 1926-1928 (MCA Coral—Germany)
The Charleston Chasers (—/VJM)
Meet The Five Pennies (Capitol)/Masters Of Dixieland, Vol 5: Red Nichols & The Five Pennies (Capitol Electrola—Germany)

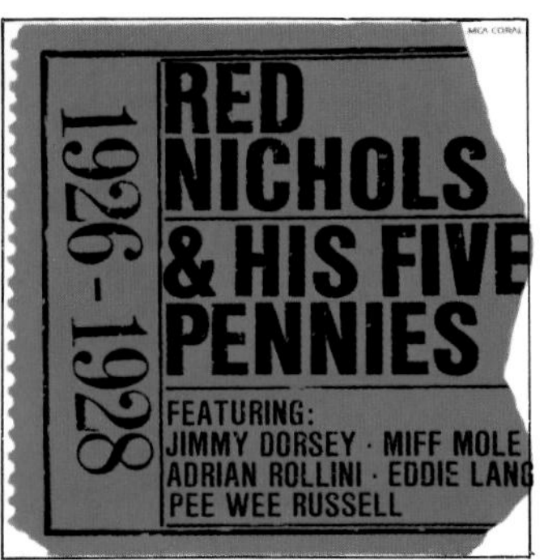

Red Nichols & His Five Pennies, 1926-28 (courtesy MCA Coral).

Jimmie Noone

One of the classic jazz clarinettists, Jimmie Noone (born Cutt-Off, Louisiana, 1895) first played guitar, switching to clarinet at 15. Tutored by Sidney Bechet, he first worked for trumpeter Freddie Keppard.

Together with Buddie Petit he assembled Young Olympia Band. Also worked with Papa Celestin, Kid Ory. In 1917, he went to Chicago for début on record and to work with Keppard again. Following year, back to New Orleans — returning to Chicago for gigs with, amongst others, King Oliver **(West End Blues)**. First recorded solo on **Play That Thing** with Tommy Ladnier **(Blues & Stomps)**. With orchestra of Doc Cook (1920-26), played clarinet and soprano.

Fronted own combo at Chicago's Apex Club (1926-28), a superior little band which included pianist Earl Hines, altoist Joe Poston (no trumpet, trombone in front line). Noone Apex Club Orchestra produced a series of classic recordings, including **Sweet Lorraine, I Know That You Know, Four Or Five Times, Apex Blues, My Monday Date** and **Blues My Naughty Sweetie Gives To Me** (all Jimmie Noone & Earl Hines **At The Apex Club, Vol 1 (1928)**) with Hines' forward-looking orchestral piano solos and accompaniments providing perfect complementary voice to Noone's limpid, warm, springy clarinet contributions. Even with eventual loss of Hines (replaced by Zinky Cohn), Noone's fine band continued to turn out exquisite jazz discs, including **Delta Bound, I'd Do Anything For You, Liza** (all **Jimmie Noone 1931-1940**).

Noone recorded with Louis Armstrong and singer Lillie Delk Christian — **(Armstrong & Hines, 1928)** — but here his quiet artistry has to take second place to Armstrong's incandescent brilliance. From 1928-31 he continued to front own groups in Chicago, where he remained until 1935, except for season at Savoy Ballroom, NYC (1931). In 1935 he went to NYC, once more, for short residency before returning to Chicago. In 1938 he toured US, fronted (for radio) big band. Continued touring and recording: in 1940, for instance, he recorded with pick-up band that included among others Lonnie Johnson, Richard M. Jones, Preston Jackson, Natty Dominique **(Jimmie Noone 1937-41)**.

In 1943 he returned to California, where he resided for rest of his life. Died of a heart attack in Los Angeles, 1944, having influenced many other first-rate players, including Irving Fazola, Benny Goodman, Jimmy Dorsey, Omer Simeon, Darnell Howard.

Albums:
Various (Including Tommy Ladnier), Blues & Stomps (Riverside/London)
King Oliver, West End Blues (CBS—France)
Jimmie Noone & Earl Hines: At The Apex Club, Vol 1 (1928) (Decca/—)
At The Apex Club (1928) (MCA—Germany)
Jimmie Noone, 1931-1940 (Queen-Disc—Italy)
Jimmie Noone/Johnny Dodds, Battle Of Jazz, Vol 8 (Brunswick/Vogue—Coral)
Louis Armstrong/Earl Hines, Armstrong & Hines, 1928 (Smithsonian Collection/—)
Kimmie Noone 1937-1941 (Collector's Classics—Denmark)
Various (Including Jimmie Noone), New Orleans, Vol 3 (RCA Victor—France)
Kid Ory & Jimmie Noone (—/Avenue—International)

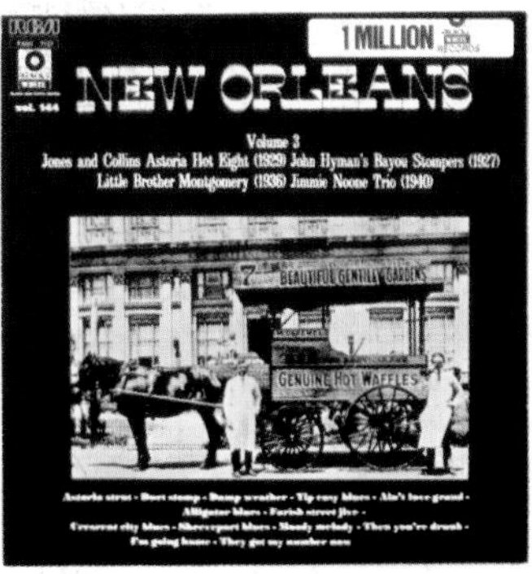

Jimmie Noone, 1937-41, New Orleans Volume 3 (courtesy Collector's Classics).

Red Norvo

Red Norvo (real name: Kenneth Norville) single-handedly made the xylophone into a valid, respectable solo jazz instrument, one which could safely take its place alongside sundry horns, keyboards, guitars/etc. Studied xylophone as a youth but it was with the wooden marimba that Norvo made his first musical tour, in 1925 with The Collegians. Left band in Chicago, enroled as mining student at University of Missouri (1926-27), then returned to music.

Worked with own band at Station KSTP and with Victor Young Orchestra. Moved on to Paul Whiteman, where he met his future wife, Mildred Bailey (they were married 1933-45). Left Whiteman to settle in New York.

Fronted an intriguing piano-less octet, with advanced-sounding arrangements by Eddie Sauter. Enlarged band to dozen, employing Mildred Bailey as singer, and with Sauter as principal arranger. Records made by band **(Red Norvo & His All Stars)** are much sought after by aficionados of the period and of subtle, out-of-the-ordinary chamber-type music.

Worked regularly with various bands at all kinds of venues (mostly in New York), from 1935-44. Switched finally, in 1943, from xylophone to vibraphone. On latter instrument, basic Red Norvo style became even more apparent; little or no vibrato, subtle swing and fast technique (achieved by holding mallets close to the instrument). In 1944 became member of Benny Goodman aggregation **(Benny Goodman 1945)** and in June 1945, whilst still with Goodman, fronted nine-piece band at special New York concert **(Town Hall Concert, Vol 1)**.

Joined Woody Herman in 1946 and although his mid-period playing might have appeared at variance with the forward-looking Herd, his solos sounded fresh and hardly at all out of place **(The Thundering Herds)**. Moved to California with second wife (Eva Rogers, sister of ex-Herman colleague Shorty Rogers), worked in freelance capacity and with own bands until returning to New York (1949) with sextet. Disbanded in '50, to front a vibes-guitar-bass trio which achieved some popularity. (Tal Farlow, Charles Mingus were in first line-up; Jimmy Raney, Red Mitchell, their replacements.) Red Norvo Trio **(The Red Norvo Trio/ The Savoy Sessions)** produced consistently fine music, the interplay between the respective musicians being the most notable attribute.

Without ever changing his style, Norvo was very warmly disposed towards bebop. In 1945, for example, he led an all-star sextet (including Charlie Parker and Dizzy Gillespie) through a generally satisfactory mainstream-bop record date **(Fabulous Jam Session)**. For several years after, he was often found with young bop-type musicians (Gerry Mulligan Tentet: **Walking Shoes (Plus Red Norvo & Stan Hasselgard)**) and during 1950s his combos tended to reflect much of the cool West Coast sounds **(Ad Lib)**.

Red Norvo Quintet was incorporated by Benny Goodman within a 10-piece band which toured Europe in '59. Subsequently has spent most of his time in California (often working with Frank Sinatra).

Norvo's playing during a 1969 tour of Europe, as member of Newport All Stars, is documented on **Tribute To Duke**, as is his appearance at a 1970 University of Pasadena concert **(The Complete 1970 Pasadena Jazz Party)**.

In '81 and '82, the celebrated reunion of Red Norvo with that incomparable and influential guitarist Tal Farlow was definitely one of *the* high-spots on the international touring circuit.

Albums:
Red Norvo & His All Stars (Epic/Philips)
Mildred Bailey: Her Greatest Performances (1929-1946), Vols 1-3 (Columbia/CBS)

National Youth Jazz Orchestra, NYJO Down Under (courtesy NYJO Records)—Bill Ashton's widely travelled British young luminaries.

Above: Veteran vibraphonist Red Norvo—his first trio included the formidable talents of Charles Mingus on bass and Tal Farlow on guitar. Memorable.

Benny Goodman 1945 (CBS—Holland)
Woody Herman, The Thundering Herds (Columbia)
Various (Including Red Norvo), The Herdsmen (Mercury)
Red Norvo, Town Hall Concert, Vol 1 (London)
The Red Norvo Trio/The Savoy Sessions (Savoy/—)
Gerry Mulligan Tentette: Walking Shoes (Plus Red Norvo & Stan Hasselgard) (Capitol/Capitol—Holland)
Red Norvo, Ad Lib (Liberty/London)
Red Norvo, The Greatest Of The Small Bands, Vol 1 (RCA Victor—France)
Various (Including Red Norvo), Tribute to Duke (MPS)
Various (Including Red Norvo), The Complete 1970 Pasadena Jazz Party (Blue Angel Jazz Club Presents/—)
Red Norvo's Fabulous Jam Session (Spotlite/Spotlite)

NYJO

Britain's National Youth Jazz Orchestra (NYJO) was founded in 1965 by Lancashire-born saxophonist and schoolteacher Bill Ashton, now its enthusiastic and dedicated musical director. Originally the 'London Schools Jazz Orchestra', the band's reputation as a useful training ground attracted country-wide young talent, and NYJO was born. Since NYJO's first major concert tour in '74, it has been a professional orchestra.

The average age of the musicians tends to be 18-19, with the oldest in their early 20s and the youngest 10 or even younger. NYJO's exceptional standard of musicianship, performance and lively, original charts have made the band a popular choice for national concerts, major festivals and international tours. They are a favorite UK touring band with visiting American artists like Shorty Rogers, Clark Terry, Joe Newman and Mel Torme.

A multitude of today's most formidably gifted British instrumentalists and vocalists has risen through NYJO's ranks to become nationally and internationally acclaimed. A random selection would include Steve Arguelles, John Barclay, Guy Barker, Pete Beachill, Chris Biscoe, Richard Burgess, Geoff Castle, Paul Hart, Nigel Hitchcock, Chris Hunter, Dave 'Joe' Jackson, Laurence Juber, Carol Kenyon, Chris Laurence, Kim Lesley, Andy Mackintosh, Steve Melling, Paul Morgan, Nigel Nash, Andy Pask, Dick Pearce, Frank Ricotti, Steve Sidwell, Stan Sulzmann, Jamie Talbot, Rick Taylor, Phil Todd and Alan Wakeman...

Albums:
National Youth Jazz Orchestra (—/Philips)
NYJO (—/Charisma)
11+—NYJO Live At LWT (—/RCA)
Return Trip (—/RCA)
In Camra (—/RCA)
To Russia With Jazz (—/NYJO)
Mary Rose (—/Pye)
Sherwood Forest Suite (—/NYJO)
NYJO Down Under (—/NYJO)
NYJO Playing Turkey (—/NYJO)
Who Don't They Write Songs Like This Any More? (—/NYJO)
Concrete Cows (—/NYJO)

Laura Nyro

Singer-songwriter Laura Nyro came to attention in the late 1960s as a writer of other people's hits. However, by the time of her first CBS album, the quality of her own unique interpretations was established.

She was born in The Bronx, New York, in 1947, into a musical environment (her father was a jazz trumpeter) and was writing songs as early as age 8. Her later vocals and songwriting revealed substantial jazz, blues and soul roots. As a teenager, Nyro had listened endlessly to John Coltrane records; songs from **Eli And The Thirteenth Confession** such as **Lonely Women** (featuring saxophonist Zoot Sims) and **December's Boudoir** clearly reveal her love for jazz

The songs and performances of her next album, **New York Tendaberry** (less heavily arranged than the previous), have tremendous power and range, carrying a deep emotional impact. **Christmas And The Beads Of Sweat** found her in the company of such alumni as Richard Davis, Alice Coltrane and Joe Farrell, producing music of great refinement. In '72 her **Gonna Take A Miracle** — cover versions of '60s soul hits—was hailed as a masterpiece. Then, Nyro married and largely withdrew from public commitments.

Smile in '76 was her first release to contain new material for five years. It showed a marked change in lyric content and musical approach. She accompanied herself on guitar instead of piano. Two long jazz improvisations were included — **Money** and **I Am The Blues**. A new maturity replaced the tremendous spirit and power of her early songs.

In '84, Nyro produced one of her best albums, **Mother's Spiritual**, with beautifully crafted and delivered songs and sensitive musical accompaniment. Clearly, Nyro's career will remain stimulating.

Albums:
First Songs (Columbia/CBS)
Eli And The Thirteenth Confession (Columbia/CBS)
New York Tendaberry (Columbia/CBS)
Christmas And The Beads Of Sweat (Columbia/CBS)
Gonna Take A Miracle (Columbia/CBS)
Smile (Columbia/CBS)
Seasons Of Light (Columbia/CBS)
Nested (Columbia/CBS)
Mother's Spiritual (Columbia/CBS)

Anita O'Day

The impact of Anita O'Day's inventive, individual and imposing vocal artistry in the 1940s was immeasurable, having a profound influence on June Christy (her successor with Stan Kenton), Chris Connor and countless others.

Born in Chicago on December 18, 1919, the professional career of Anita O'Day began unpromisingly working as a dancethon contestant during the Depression. At 19, she worked as a singing waitress and dice-girl until her singing career started in earnest in '39 with the Max Miller combo at Chicago's Three Deuces. In '41, at 22, she replaced Irene Daye in Gene Krupa's popular band — her features on numbers like **Let Me Off Uptown** (with Roy Eldridge) and **That's What You Think** becoming a special attraction.

Between '44-'45 she received further acclaim as the vocalist with Stan Kenton's orchestra — her inimitable interpretation of songs like **And Her Tears Flowed Like Wine** have never been surpassed. Her early vocal inspirations were Mildred Bailey, Billie Holiday, Ella Fitzgerald and Martha Raye but O'Day was no copyist. She created a unique style — instinc-

Above: Anita O'Day—an enduring image of the late 1950s on film in Jazz On A Summer's Day.

tive and uncommonly inventive, able to sing all the quarter-notes as written, yet a formidable improviser. Her solo career was beset by personal and health problems although she made a celebrated comeback in later years.

In '58, an extraordinary O'Day *pièce de résistance* was immortalized in the film *Jazz On A Summer's Day* at the Newport Festival — O'Day (complete in hobble skirt, *très à la mode*) singing a unique version of *Sweet Georgia Brown*, her voice snaking out slyly from under an outrageous picture-hat.

The double album **Anita O'Day/The Big Band Sessions** brings together some of her finest work from '59-'61 with the Gary McFarlane, Johnny Mandel, Jimmy Giuffre and Billy May bands. It's a document of her incomparable skill as a vocal interpreter of such classics as **Boogie Blues, The Ballad Of The Sad Young Man** and **I Hear Music**.

Albums:

Gene Krupa, Drummer Man (Verve/Verve)
Stan Kenton, Kenton Era (Capitol/Capitol)
Anita Sings (Verve/Verve)
Pick Yourself Up (Verve/Verve)
Lady Is A Tramp (Verve/Verve)
An Evening With Anita O'Day (Verve/Verve)
At Mr Kelly's (Verve/Verve)
Swings Cole Porter (Verve/Verve)
Trav'lin' Light (Verve/Verve)
Anita Sings The Winners (Verve/Verve)
Anita O'Day/The Big Band Sessions (Verve/Verve)

The influential Anita O'Day, Trav'lin' Light, 1961 (courtesy Verve).

King Oliver

Cornet-player Joe 'King' Oliver was born in 1885, joining Kid Ory's Brownskin Babies in 1914 or 1915, and developing great expressive skills in the use of mutes.

Oliver, like many New Orleans musicians, left for Chicago after the closure of Storyville in 1918, forming his own band, King Oliver's Creole Jazz Band. Clarinettist Johnny Dodds eventually replaced Jimmie Noone, Lil Hardin took over piano from Lottie Taylor and Baby Dodds on drums replaced Minor Hall. In 1922, Oliver further cemented his dominance of the Chicago music scene by sending for the young Louis Armstrong, already a powerful contender for the cornet crown.

In 1923, the Creole Jazz Band became the first to record in the New Orleans style, establishing a standard never to be surpassed. The loose counterpoint of the melody instruments — cornets balanced by trombone, clarinet weaving supple patterns between the brass — remains a model of symmetry. The intuitive understanding between the cornets in their brilliant breaks, the leader's mastery of the mute on the famous **Dippermouth Blues**, Armstrong's historic first recorded solo on **Riverside Blues**, all contribute to jazz's cornerstone collection **(Louis Armstrong & King Oliver** and **King Oliver's Jazz Band)**. The former album also contains two duets between Oliver and Jelly Roll Morton, **King Porter Stomp** and **Tom Cat Blues**.

The strains of touring broke up the band by 1924, with Armstrong marrying Lil Hardin and the Dodds brothers and trombonist Honore Dutrey quitting. The following year Oliver formed the Dixie Syncopators, usually a ten-piece band with three saxophones and tuba. Playing for dancers at the Plantation Cafe in Chicago between 1925-27, the band was commercially successful, and numbers like **Someday Sweetheart** and **Dead Man Blues** became King Oliver's best-selling records **(King Oliver's Dixie Syncopators)**. Also included is Oliver's version of a number associated with Armstrong, **West End Blues**, a less dramatic rendering. From 1927 until his death in 1938, Oliver's decline was shown among scratch bands; pyorrhoea made playing an agony, and his attempts to adapt to the changing musical climate were often ill-considered.

Pianist Clarence Williams used him on a fairly routine session with his Novelty Four in 1928, and Oliver plays well on **Blue Blood Blues** and **Jet Black Blues** the following year in an Eddie Lang group, Blind Willie Dunn's Gin Bottle Four **(Classic Jazz Masters: King Oliver)**. Occasional felicities are to be found among his late recordings for Victor **(King Oliver & His Orchestra** and **King Oliver In New York)**. At his death in 1938, he was working as a janitor.

Albums:

Louis Armstrong & King Oliver (Milestone/Milestone)
King Oliver's Jazz Band (—/Parlophone)
King Oliver's Dixie Syncopators, Vols 1 & 2 (—/Ace of Hearts)
Classic Jazz Masters: King Oliver (Philips/Philips)
King Oliver & His Orchestra (—/RCA Victor—France)
King Oliver In New York (RCA Victor/—)

King Oliver's Jazz Band, The Complete 1923 OKehs (courtesy EMI).

Oregon

The multi-dimensional music of Oregon created one of the most rewarding collective sounds in folk-inspired jazz They reached into every corner of world music for their inspiration, becoming one of the most eclectic and explorative musical travelers of the 1970s.

Oregon was formed in '72 (from the Paul Winter Group) by Ralph Towner, Paul McCandless, Glen Moore and Collin Walcott. All four musicians were prodigiously accomplished: Towner on 12-string and classical guitars, piano, French horn, trumpet; McCandless—oboe, bass-clarinet, English horn, wooden flutes; Glen Moore—bass, violin, flute, piano; Collin Walcott—tabla, sitar, assorted percussion, clarinet.

During their long association, Oregon were to pool widely acquired musical experience. Towner had become one of the world's most advanced acoustic guitarists (an instrument he didn't take up till he was 23); he studied with Karl Scheit in Vienna and worked with Astrud Gilberto, Airto Moreira, Miroslav Vitous, Dave Holland, Jeremy Steig and Jimmy Garrison. McCandless had a classical background, standing out as one of the oboe's few champions outside that field—his experience took in the music of Annette Peacock, Cyrus Faryar and Paul Stookey. Glen Moore studied bass with Gary Karr and James Harnett, working with Steve Reich-pianist Larry Karush, Jan Hammer and the Paul Bley-Annette Peacock Synthesizer Show. Walcott—a Buddhist—had studied sitar with Ravi Shankar and tabla with Ustad Alla Rakha, working with Miles Davis **(On The Corner)**, Don Cherry (notably, in Codona) and performance-artist/composer Meredith Monk. In the early days, Walcott's contribution, particularly, had helped to define Oregon's unique sound.

In November '84, Oregon's 12-year musical journey together was tragically brought to a halt. Collin Walcott and road manager Jo Härting were killed when the Oregon tour-bus crashed in Berlin. Walcott was too individual a musician to be replaced.

Albums:

Music Of Another Present Era (Vanguard/Vanguard)
Oregon/Elvin Jones Together (Vanguard/Vanguard)
Distant Hills (Vanguard/Vanguard)
Winter Light (Vanguard/Vanguard)
In Concert (Vanguard/Vanguard)
Friends (Vanguard/Vanguard)
Out Of The Woods (Elektra-Asylum/Elektra-Asylum)
Oregon (ECM/ECM)
Crossing (ECM/ECM)

Towner, McCandless, Moore & Walcott, Oregon, 1983 (courtesy ECM).

Original Dixieland Jazz Band

The Original Dixieland Jazz (originally spelled 'Jass') Band is of immense historical importance. For it was probably responsible for first recordings to be made by what was truly a *jazz* band—**Darktown Strutters' Ball, Indiana**, recorded January 1917. ODJB's next studio date (after being signed by Victor) produced **Livery Stable Blues** and **Original Dixieland One-Step**—which jointly became jazz's first big-selling disc.

ODJB's live appearances as well as its records did more than any other one band or musician to spread the jazz word—first, in the US, thence to Europe and to other parts of the globe.

Earliest ODJB comprised Dominic James ('Nick') La Rocca, cornet; Alcide Nunez, clarinet; 'Eddie' Edwards (Edwin Bransford), trombone; Henry Ragas, piano; Johnny Stein, drums. This quintet made its first live appearance at Schiller's Café, Chicago, in 1916. By the time the band was making initial records, Nunez had been fired and replaced by Chicagoan Larry Shields (by consensus, ODJB's best soloist), and New Orleansian Tony Sbarbaro (Spargo) had joined in place of Stein. This personnel comprised line-up with which ODJB, for almost a decade, was to find fame and fortune.

Band was given special boost by Al Jolson, whose influence helped obtain prestigious gig at plush Reisenweber's, NYC (1917). ODJB's tremendous success here, celebrated by the band with its Aeolian recording of **Reisenweber Rag (ODJB/Louisiana Five)**, led to a trip to UK where the band appeared for London Palladium season and—privately—for members of British Royal Family, by which time J. Russel Robinson had replaced Ragas (who died in 1918).

Band recorded for Columbia whilst in London. Continued to record for Victor on return to States. But by the 1920s its popularity began to wane—ODJB disbanded in 1925, Shields having left in 1921.

A revived ODJB recorded again in '35; the following year, Victor recorded **Nick La Rocca & His Original Dixieland Band**—this line-up included Sbarbaro and Robinson from ODJB's halcyon days in an otherwise ordinary-sounding big-band setting of a dozen ODJB titles. La Rocca, Shields, Sbarbaro, Robinson and Edwards made final ODJB recordings in 1936—again, efforts to rekindle the spirit of earlier times resulted in music barely memorable.

Finally, a six-piece outfit directed by Edwards recorded for Bluebird in 1938—this time, only Shields, Sbarbaro remained of former ODJB colleagues. Later, in 1945 and 1946, Edwards recorded with his own Original Dixieland Jazz Band **(Eddie Edwards & His Original Dixieland Jazz Band)** for Commodore. Once more drummer Sbarbaro was present as representative of the past. Other musicians who took part included trumpeters Maz Kaminsky, Wild Bill Davison, clarinettist Brad Gowans, guitarist Eddie Condon, and pianists Gene Schroeder and Teddy Roy. Ironically, these sides are far superior to efforts by the original band, certainly in terms of rhythmic flexibility and superior all-round solos (including those by ODJB veteran Edwards).

Amongst ODJB's most popular recordings from 1917-24 are **Livery Stables Blues, Original Dixieland One-Step, At The Jazz Band Ball, Ostrich Walk, Tiger Rag, Sensation, Skeleton Jangle, Clarinet Marmalade** (composed jointly by Ragas and Shields: all on **Original Dixieland Jazz Band**). From a purely musical standpoint, the ODJB scarcely compares with classic black combos of early jazz—nor, indeed, with many of the superior white outfits like Original Memphis Five, McKenzie-Condon Chicagoans or those fronted by Miff Mole. Eddie Lang and Joe Venuti.

Historically, however, the Original Dixieland Jazz Band was a first—and an important one. For literary reference, see *The Story of The Original Dixieland Jazz Band*, by H.O. Brunn.

Albums:
Original Dixieland Jazz Band
(RCA Victor—France)
ODJB/Louisiana Five (—/Fountain)
Eddie Edwards & His Original Dixieland Jazz Band (London/London)

Kid Ory

Edward 'Kid' Ory's major claim to jazz immortality was in his enormously powerful and uplifting ensemble playing, especially in classic New Orleans format, with extensive use of glissandi, making him the king of so-called 'tailgate' trombone players of early jazz During a career which spanned over 50 years (*c.* 1910-71), Ory also played clarinet, drums, string bass, cornet, alto sax (briefly, with King Oliver in 1926), valve trombone and banjo (his first instrument which he played from 10).

Ory (born La Place, Louisiana, 1886) moved to New Orleans around 1912, staying seven years before, for health reasons, he moved to California. Invited several New Orleans musicians to join him on West Coast in new band. In addition, it became first black small combo to make records (1922).

Gave up leadership of band in 1925 to record with Armstrong in Chicago. Results of first and subsequent Hot Five sessions resulted in truly classic jazz, with Ory's driving trombone standing out in ensembles, especially in numbers like **Muskrat Ramble, Skid-Da-De-Dat, Gut Bucket Blues (The Louis Armstrong Legend)**. Even better, though, was Ory's playing on recordings from 1926 by his and Johnny Dodds' New Orleans Wanderers and Bootblacks **(Johnny Dodds & Kid Ory)**. And his contributions to Jelly Roll Morton's **Doctor Jazz, Black Bottom Stomp** and **Grandpa's Spells (Jelly Roll Morton & His Red Hot Peppers, Vol 3)** helped to make these, and other Morton tracks on which he appeared, assume similar classic proportions. With King Oliver (1925-27) he performed a similar role in admirable fashion **(King Oliver's Dixie Syncopators 1926-1928)**.

Before returning to Los Angeles in 1930, Ory had spent previous two years playing in both Chicago and New York. After gigging with several West Coast bands and touring with Leon Rene Orchestra, left music to help brother on a chicken farm (1933). Resumed playing career during early 1940s and between 1943-44 played mostly bass or saxophone.

After widespread acclaim following appearance on Orson Welles radio show (1944) put together own Kid Ory's Creole Jazz Band. With a rejuvenated Ory roaring away in ensembles/solos, it became the finest band he was to lead, as indicated via its 1944-45 recordings, including **Tailgate! (Kid Ory's Creole Jazz Band)**. Continued to lead own bands during 1940s through early 1950s. Disbanded in 1955 because of health problems but recovered to tour abroad on several occasions. **Muskrat Ramble**, his most famous composition, became pop smash-hit in 1954 after it had been given lyrics.

Had acting and playing role in film *The Benny Goodman Story* in '55, after previously appearing in *New Orleans* and, together with own band, in *Crossfire, Mahogany Magic* and *Disneyland After Dawn*. Regular performer at own club On The Levee, San Francisco, between early 1950s and 1961. After recurring ill health, settled in Hawaii, playing occasional gigs in Honolulu. His final trip to Europe had taken place in 1959.

Kid Ory died at the beginning of 1973, of pneumonia and heart failure after a career which encompassed much of the jazz era.

Albums:
The Louis Armstrong Legend (World Records)
King Oliver's Dixie Syncopators
(MCA Coral—Germany)
Johnny Dodds & King Ory (Columbia/—)
Tailgate! Kid Ory's Creole Jazz Band
(Good Time Jazz/Good Time Jazz)
Kid Ory, When The Saints
(Good Time Jazz/Good Time Jazz)
Various (Including Kid Ory), New Orleans Memories (Ace of Hearts)
Jelly Roll Morton & His Red Hot Peppers, Vol 3 (RCA Victor—France)

Mike Osborne

Considered by many as the finest alto saxophonist outside America, Britain's Mike Osborne plays with an intensity that slices deep into the emotions.

Below: Kid Ory—the man who virtually single-handedly invented the jazz phrase 'tailgate trombone'.

Above: Two of the United Kingdom's finest altoists, Mike Osborne (right) and South African-in-exile Dudu Pukwana.

From an early Jackie McLean influence, he added the freedoms of Ornette Coleman, and gradually emerged with a style all his own. His tonal range covers the oboe-like lower register and the squalling upper, and his frame of reference covers bop classics, folk songs and a near-medieval estampe.

A volcanic player—indeed, there seems no distance between the sound and the emotion behind it—his best work has been with players of equal stature, bassist Harry Miller and the mighty Louis Moholo on drums (**Border Crossing** and **All Night Long**) or in duet with pianist Stan Tracey (**Original** and **Tandem**) and in the all-saxophone trio with John Surman and Alan Skidmore (**SOS**), contributing brilliantly to music for the ballet *Sablier Prison* performed by SOS in Paris in '74. Osborne has also been featured soloist in the big bands of Mike Westbrook and Chris McGregor.

Albums:
Mike Osborne Trio, Border Crossing (—/Ogun)
Mike Osborne Trio, All Night Long (—/Ogun)
Mike Osborne-Stan Tracey, Original (—/Cadillac)
Mike Osborne-Stan Tracey, Tandem (—/Ogun)
Osborne-Surman-Skidmore, SOS (—/Ogun)
Mike Westbrook, Metropolis (—/RCA Neon)
Brotherhood Of Breath, Live At Willisau (—/Ogun)

All Night Long (courtesy Ogun)—Mike Osborne in searing form.

Out Of The Blue

As one of the first new signings to the reactivated Blue Note label in the mid 1980s, Out Of The Blue—in spite of being in their early 20s—are very much in that record company's classic hard-bop tradition. Their lively, uncompromising music could easily have come out of any one of Blue Note's studios of the late '50s-early '60s.

Each member of O.T.B. comes with an impressive former track-record...

Drummer Ralph Peterson Jr, a Rutgers graduate, has performed with the Terence Blanchard-Donald Harrison and Jon Faddis quintets.

Pianist Harry Pickens was featured, at 19, with Jackie McLean, Dizzy Gillespie and later the Johnny Griffin group.

Trumpeter Philip Mossman has a formidable classical-music reputation; his jazz experience includes lead trumpet with Machito's orchestra, working with the Count Basie and Lionel Hampton line-ups, plus touring with Anthony Braxton's Creative Orchestra.

Bassist Bob Hurst was working with trumpeter Marcus Belgrave at 15, subsequently with Hank Jones, Tommy Flanagan, Barry Harris and Freddie Hubbard.

Altoist Kenny Garrett has contributed to the big bands of Mercer Ellington, Mel Lewis, Lionel Hampton and David Murray, plus Dannie Richmond's quintet and Woody Shaw's sextet.

Tenorist Ralph Bowen studied with Pat LaBarbara and David Baker, joining Baker's Twentyfirst Century Bebop Band and later the Latin-inspired Manteca.

On the overwhelming evidence of their first album, with its Blue Note seal-of-approval, the durability of **Out Of The Blue** looks as though it comes complete with a cast-iron guarantee. In common with quite a few of their generation, Out Of The Blue have avoided 'fusion' and chosen to enlist in the 'new guard' of hard bop, albeit from another age.

Albums:
O.T.B. (Blue Note/Blue Note)

Hot Lips Page

Oran Thaddeus 'Hot Lips' Page (born Dallas, Texas, 1908) ranks with the greatest blues-players—vocally as well as instrumentally—jazz has produced.

Page took up trumpet after abortive earlier efforts to master clarinet and alto sax. (At various times throughout his career he also played mellophone. Started music career proper as member of blues singer Ma Rainey's accompanying band. Also accompanied Bessie Smith and Ida Cox. Joined Walter Page's Blue Devils (1928), leaving in 1930 to work with Bennie Moten. Following Moten's death, fronted own quintet in Kansas City. Worked with Count Basie at Reno Club, KC, in '36.

Moved to New York and assembled own big band (1937) which lasted about one year. It was a healthy-sounding outfit with an admirable regard for blues but resting on the horn and voice of Page—the former passionate and strong on **Skull Duggery, Feelin' High & Happy**; the latter featured warmly and humorously on **Small Fry, I'm Gonna Lock My Heart (And Throw Away The Key)** (all **Feelin' High & Happy/Big Sound Trumpets**).

Toured with Bud Freeman, Joe Marsala, then reunited, briefly, with own big band, worked with small combo on 52nd Street, before joining Artie Shaw Orchestra for five months (1941-42).

Left Shaw in January '42 to resume touring with own big band but by mid-1943 was back to smaller size. Between 1943-49, played major cities with mostly small combos, although did increase for specific engagements. Recorded prolifically for Commodore label in early-1940s, with Albert Ammons (**Commodore Jazz, Vol 1**) and own bands (**Sax Scene**). Also worked with Don Redman (1945) and backed Ethel Waters during New York engagement (1946). Although choice of Page for Mezzrow-Bechet Septet dates in '45 (**The Prodigious Sidney Bechet Quintet & Septet** and **Sidney Bechet-Mezz Mezzrow**) was obvious, the relaxation that marked his best work was missing for most part.

Visited Europe for the first time in 1949, scoring heavy applause at Paris Jazz Festival. Same year, record by Page and Pearl Bailey (**Baby, It's Cold Outside**) appeared in pop charts. Made four-month European tour (1951), then back to US for touring and concerts etc. Went to Europe, again, in '52. Before his death in November 1954, following a heart attack, Page had continued to work at frequent intervals.

Albums:
Bennie Moten's Kansas City Orchestra, Moten's Swing, Vol 5 (1929-1932) (RCA Victor—France)
Hot Lips Page/(Louis Jordan), Jumpin' Stuff (Rarities/—)
Hot Lips Page, Feelin' High & Happy (RCA Victor)/
The Big Sound Trumpets (RCA Victor—France)
Artie Shaw, Concerto For Clarinet (RCA Victor/—)
Artie Shaw & His Orchestra, Vol 2 (RCA Victor/—)
Various (Including Albert Ammons), Commodore Jazz, Vol 1 (—/London)
Various (Including Hot Lips Page) Sax Scene (—/London)
Chu Berry, Chu (Epic—France)
Sidney Bechet-Mezz Mezzrow (Concert Hall/—)
The Prodigious Sidney Bechet Quintet & Septet (—/Festival—France)
Various (Including Hot Lips Page), Swing Classics, Vols 1, 2 (—/Polydor)

Hot Lips Page, Feelin' High & Happy (courtesy RCA Victor).

Below: Hard-boppers, 1980s—Out of the Blue—(l. to r.) Kenny Garrett, Ralph Peterson, Ralph Bowen, Harry Pickens, Michael Philip Mossman and Bob Hurst.

Charlie Parker

Charlie Parker was born in Kansas City in 1920 and died in the apartment of Baroness Nica de Koenigswarter in 1955, prematurely worn out by narcotics and alcohol.

The key figure in the bebop revolution of the 1940s, and—with Louis Armstrong—jazz's greatest soloist, Parker's innovations still determine much of the course of jazz today.

The impetus of Kansas City and the Southwest had congealed by the mid-40s, and Parker – nicknamed 'Bird' or 'Yardbird' – sought alternative musical directions. His earliest recordings with Jay McShann's Orchestra in 1940 show a debt to tenorist Lester Young on numbers like **Lady Be Good**, and great technical fluency on up-tempo features like **Honeysuckle Rose (Early Bird). Hootie Blues** and **The Jumpin' Blues** find the young altoist further into complex harmonic changes, grace notes, and an oblique relationship to the beat: 'I kept thinking there's bound to be something else, I could hear it sometimes but I couldn't play it.'

His experiments provoked mockery and abuse among the older generation but young musicians were spellbound. Parker's concept was radical, affecting every aspect of the music. Harmonically, he pointed the way out of the diatonic log-jam into the wider field of chromaticism, using progressions that were new to jazz and sounded angular and unsettled to contemporary ears. In fact, without commensurate breadth of imagination, a musician could run himself ragged among that plethora of choice like a rat in a maze.

Rhythmically, too, Parker was the most imaginative player that jazz has known, accents falling on heavy, weak and between the beats, yet still making the line swing. He cut clean across the old four and eight bar divisions, moving in an up-rush of semi-quavers that would abruptly skid back into line with a simple and perfect phrase. He brought a harder edge to the music, an emotional force and passion that held his super-technical dexterity in subordination and revealed the man. His sound on alto is unforgettable.

In New York, Parker found a handful of musicians who were working along similar lines—men like Dizzy Gillespie, Thelonious Monk, Charlie Christian and drummer Kenny Clarke who congregated at the after-hours clubs like Minton's Playhouse and Monroes. Parker's first small-group recordings in 1944 found him in mixed company with swing players like guitarist Tiny Grimes and his solos on **Red Cross** and **Tiny's Tempo** sit oddly amidst the chugging jollity **(The Savoy Sessions)**.

The Parker-Gillespie combo made its début on record, unfortunately saddled with swing drummers like Cozy Cole and Big Sid Catlett, playing their own material like **Dizzy Atmosphere, Groovin' High, Salt Peanuts** and **Shaw 'Nuff** which, for speed and complexity and imagination, stand as a manifesto of modern music **(In The Beginning)**.

In 1945, the definitive bebop group recorded for Savoy. Parker, Gillespie, a young Miles Davis, pianist Argonne Thornton, bassist Curley Russell and drummer Max Roach laid down a series of masterpieces like **Now's The Time, Ko Ko** and **Billie's Bounce (The Savoy Sessions)**. The altoist's three choruses on **Now's The Time** are a model of modern blues playing, the swoops and descents in the line touching subtly on the notes of the chord, the shape of the solo infinitely elastic, accommodating double-tempo runs and unfamiliar chords like the augmented 2nd and minor 7th. *Down Beat* magazine failed to recognize its quality, awarding the track a no-star rating. Over the next three years, Parker added **Cheryl, Buzzy, Bird Gets The Worm, Blue Bird, Another Hairdo, Barbados, Parker's Mood** and **Constellation** to his Savoy classics—quintet performances with Miles Davis, Bud Powell or John Lewis or Duke Jordan on piano, Russell or Tommy Potter on bass, and Max Roach on drums.

The Immortal Charlie Parker (courtesy London)—perhaps no single figure, before or after, has had quite the same impact as Charlie 'Bird' Parker.

In 1945, Parker went with the Gillespie Sextet to California for an engagement at Billy Berg's club, staying on when the rest of the group returned to New York in 1946. Playing at the Finale Club with the young West Coast beboppers, he turned Los Angeles into a second center for the new music. He signed a contract with Ross Russell for Dial, cutting six incredible albums over seven sessions **(Charlie Parker On Dial)**. The first date produced **Ornithology, Moose The Mooche** (dedicated to Emry Byrd, Parker's pusher), **Yardbird Suite** and **A Night In Tunisia**, but the second, four months later, found the genius in a desperate mental and physical condition. Ross Russell's book, *Bird Lives*, gives a detailed account of the session which produced the nightmarish beauty of **Loverman,** stark, strident and unparalleled in its exposure of the artist's emotional depths.

Following **Bebop**, where Parker was too sick to play, the altoist returned to his hotel, somehow set his bed on fire, and was confined in Camarillo State Hospital for the next six months. Following his release, he recorded some sides with singer Earl Coleman, **Dark Shadows, This Is Always** and splendid instrumentals like **Cool Blues** and **Bird's Nest**.

Subsequent classic performances include **Relaxin' At Camarillo, Cheers, Carvin' The Bird, Stupendous, Home Cooking, Dexterity, Bongo Bop, Dewey Square, The Hymn, Bird Of Paradise, Embraceable You, Drifting On A Reed, Quasimodo, Charlie's Wig, Bongo Beep, Crazeology, How Deep Is The Ocean, Bird Feathers, Klactoveesedstene, Scrapple From The Apple, My Old Flame, Out Of Nowhere** and **Don't Blame Me**, following Parker's return to New York. Most of these are quintet performances with Davis, Jordan, Potter and Roach, the band that Parker was using around 52nd Street at clubs like the Three Deuces.

Illegally recording for Savoy as well as Norman Granz's label, Parker showed an Olympian disregard for the niceties of business, as did the scores of amateur recordists who taped broadcasts, club performances and concerts. Away from the studios, Parker's work often rises to greater heights of imagination and daring: the meeting with Woody Herman's band **(Bird Flies With The Herd)**; the extended blowing session with Chet Baker and altoist Sonny Criss **(Bird On The Coast)**; the pairings with Navarro **(Historical Masterpieces)** and Gillespie **(Diz 'n' Bird In Concert** and **The Quintet Of The Year)**.

In 1949, Parker brought his quintet to Paris; Kenny Dorham, Al Haig, Potter and Roach **(Bird In Paris)**, visiting Sweden the following year and playing with local musicians **(Bird In Sweden)**. Back home, signed to Granz's Mercury label, Parker appeared in a great variety of contexts. He had already toured with Jazz At The Phil, playing with altoist Willie Smith and tenorists Lester Young and Coleman Hawkins **(Jazz At The Philharmonic, 1946, Vol 2)**, an idea which later produced the historic jam session with Parker, Johnny Hodges and Benny Carter, three great alto-players together on **Funky Blues (The Parker Jam Session)**.

With an assortment of woodwinds and singers, Parker recorded the brilliant **Old Folks**, while a session with Machito's Afro-Cuban band produced **Mango Mangue** and **Okiedoke. Just Friends**, from an album with strings, is a classic performance, the contrast between the conservative and romantic setting and the passionate alto curiously moving. The best tracks are to be found in the small combo setting, **Now's The Time, Confirmation, I Remember You, Kin, Chi Chi, Cosmic Rays, Star Eyes, Si Si, Swedish Schnapps, Au Privave, She Rote, KC Blues (The Definitive Charlie Parker)**. A 1950 reunion with Gillespie, Monk and Russell, and the unsuitable Buddy Rich on drums, produced **Bloomdido, Mohawk** and **Leapfrog**. For Prestige, Parker cut several tracks on tenor with Sonny Rollins and Miles Davis, using the pseudonym Charlie Chan **(Collectors Items)**.

With the advent of bebop, jazz lost much of its audience, leaving Parker in the limbo between pop and art. His music reflects his predicament, alternately wooing and defiant, sardonic and anguished: without the sounding board of an audience, he anatomizes himself. Parker's blues were an anthem for the dispossessed, celebrations of the fleeing moment, and one of the most revealing portraits of our times.

Charlie Parker was to die aged just 35 on March 12, 1955. In his brief but so brilliant career, Parker had exerted an unparalleled influence on his contemporaries, on the music and musicians to come for successive generations.

Albums:

Early Bird (Spotlite/Spotlite)
Jay McShann, Kansas City Memories (Decca/Brunswick)
The Savoy Sessions (Savoy/Savoy)
Alternative Takes (Savoy/Savoy)
Dizzy Gillespie, In The Beginning (Prestige/Prestige)
Charlie Parker On Dial, Vols 1-6 (Spotlite/Spotlite)
Anthropology (Spotlite/Spotlite)
Bird Flies With The Herd (Main-Man/Main-Man)
Bird On The Coast (Jazz Showcase/Jazz Showcase)
Bird On The Road (Jazz Showcase/Jazz Showcase)
Historical Masterpieces (Le Jazz Cool/MGM)
Bird On 52nd Street/Bird At St Nick's (Prestige/Prestige)
Hi Hat Broadcasts 1953 (Phoenix/Phoenix)
Charlie Parker (Queen-Disc/Queen-Disc)
Diz 'N' Bird In Concert (—/Saga)
The Quintet Of The Year (Debut/Vogue)
Lullaby In Rhythm (Spotlite/Spotlite)
Bird In Paris (Spotlite/Spotlite)
Bird In Sweden (Spotlite/Spotlite)
Jazz At The Philharmonic 1946, Vol 2 (Verve/Verve)
The Parker Jam Session (Verve/Verve)
The Definitive Charlie Parker, Vols 1-4 (Verve/Metro)
Miles Davis, Collectors' Items (Prestige/Prestige)
Birds Nest (—/Vogue)
Collections (Japanese Odeon)
One Night In Washington (Elektra Musician/Elektra Musician)
The Cole Porter Songbook (Verve/Verve)
Charlie Parker At Storyville (Blue Note/Blue Note)
Charlie Parker With Strings (Verve/Verve)
Machito: Afro-Cuban Jazz/Machito Jazz With Flip And Bird (Verve/Verve)
The Magnificent Charlie Parker (Verve/Verve)
Charlie Parker—South Of The Border (Verve/Verve)
Charlie Parker Big Band (Verve/Verve)
West Coast Time (Charlie Parker Records/Charlie Parker Records)
Birdology (Charlie Parker Records/Charlie Parker Records)
Jazz At Massey Hall (Fantasy/Fantasy)

Charlie Parker On Dial (courtesy Spotlite)—cornerstones in jazz

Evan Parker

Saxophonist Evan Parker is—along with Phil Seamen, Stan Tracey, John Surman and Derek Bailey—one of the most original jazz musicians Britain has ever produced. A leading figure in the European free-music field, he has worked with Alexander von Schlippenbach's Quartet and the Globe Unity Orchestra, as well as the comparatively orthodox Brotherhood Of Breadth.

Associated in the '60s with John Stevens' Spontaneous Music Ensemble, Parker formed a duo with percussionist Paul Lytton in 1970 **(Collective Calls** and **Evan Parker & Paul Lytton At The Unity Theatre)** in which the two musicians extend sonic barriers and produce some inventive lines and textures. The Music Improvisation Company—with Parker, Bailey, Hugh Davies and Jamie Muir—proved to be another fertile arena for free playing **(Music Improvisation Company)**, while the saxophonist's collaboration with guitarist Baily has produced some of the most adventurous music of the decade **(The Topography Of The Lungs** and **London Concert)**.

Parker's style, taking Coltrane and Pharoah Sanders as a starting point, has evolved over the years into a tonally rich and intensely emotional vehicle for his essentially logical imagination, the furiously scribbled lines contributing to a musical shape of great originality. A demonstration of his skills on soprano saxophone reveals total command of free-music techniques **(Saxophone Solos)**, circular breathing, slaps, snorts and overblowing used to symmetrical ends.

Involvement in Company, a pool of international free musicians, demonstrates his ability for concentrated listening and response to the collective situation **(Company 1)**.

In '85, Parker contributed to a special festival in London to celebrate 16 creative years of the Incus label founded in '69 by Parker, Derek Bailey and Tony Oxley as the first musician-run independent record company in Britain.

Albums:
Collective Calls (—/Incus)
Music Improvisation Company (—/Incus)
The Topography Of The Lungs (—/Incus)
London Concert (—/Incus)
Saxophone Solos (—/Incus)
Company 1 (—/Incus)
Globe Unity 73, Live In Wuppertal (—/FMP)
Manfred Schoof, European Echoes (—/FMP)
Peter Brotzmann, Machine Gun (—/FMP)
Monocerous (—/Incus)
Company 2 (—/Incus)
The Longest Night (—/Ogun)
The Snake Decides (—/Incus)
Schlippenbach-Parker-Lovens, Detto Fra Di Noi (—/PoTorch)

Leo Parker

Originally a bebopper, Washington baritone saxophonist Leo Parker was a featured sideplayer with Fats Navarro, **Ice Freezes Red (Fats Navarro Memorial)** and Dexter Gordon, **Settin' The Pace (Long Tall Dexter)**. Usually a driving, bellowing player, his sensitive side is shown on **Solitude (The Foremost!)**.

Born in 1925, Parker began on alto, switching to the bigger horn for the Billy Eckstine band as Charlie Parker had the alto chair **(Mr B & The Band)**. His work with Gene Ammons **(Red Top)** shows the honking influence of Illinois Jacquet—in fact, Jacquet once warned him off his stylistic territory. After a long period with R&B bands, Parker made a short-lived comeback for Blue Note **(Let Me Tell You 'Bout It)** and died in 1962.

Albums:
Fats Navarro Memorial (Savoy/—)
Dexter Gordon, Long Tall Dexter (Savoy/Savoy)
The Foremost! (Onyx/Polydor)
Billy Eckstine, Mr B & The Band (Savoy/Savoy)
Gene Ammons, Red Top (Savoy/Savoy)
Leo Parker, Let Me Tell You 'Bout It (Blue Note/—)

Leo Parker, Let Me Tell You 'Bout It (courtesy Blue Note).

Joe Pass

Guitarist Joe Pass has been on the scene since the 1940s, achieving widespread recognition in the '70s due to shrewd management by Norman Granz

A veteran of countless sessions with a wide selection of musicians—Chet Baker, Bud Shank, Gerald Wilson, Les McCann, Earl Bostic and Duke Ellington—Pass is a complete professional. Since signing to Pablo, he made triumphant appearances at the Montreux Festival **(Joe Pass At Montreux)** and JATP tours with Oscar Peterson, Zoot Sims etc. A sensitive, lyrical soloist with a warm and sonorous tone, Pass can also sound like a full rhythm section in accompaniment.

An album with another veteran guitarist, Herb Ellis, finds the two men plaiting melody and counter-melody, and showing great empathy in interplay on numbers like **Cherokee (Two For The Road)**. A duet with Ella Fitzgerald **(Ella Fitzgerald & Joe Pass)** is relaxed and melodic, while the collaboration with Oscar Peterson reaches a more demanding artistic peak **(Oscar Peterson Et Joe Pass A Salle Pleyel)** with both players at full stretch. A pretty album with Peterson on clavichord **(Porgy & Bess)** has Pass dispatching rhythm duties until his solo outing on **They Pass By Singing**. In later years, the guitarist has expressed a preference for solo performance, with two of his finest albums, **Joe Pass, Virtuoso 1 & 2**.

Albums:
Joe Pass At Montreux (Pablo/Pablo)
Herb Ellis-Joe Pass, Two For The Road (Pablo/Pablo)
Portraits Of Duke Ellington (Pablo/Pablo)
Ella Fitzgerald & Joe Pass (Pablo/Pablo)
Oscar Peterson Et Joe Pass A Salle Pleyel (Pablo/Pablo)
Porgy & Bess (Pablo/Pablo)
Virtuoso 1 & 2 (Pablo/Pablo)
Joe Pass-J.J. Johnson, We'll Be Together Again (Pablo/Pablo)
Live At Long Beach City College (Pablo/Pablo)

Ira, George and Joe: Joe Pass Loves Gershwin (courtesy Pablo).

Jaco Pastorius

Through his contribution to Weather Report, Jaco Pastorius emerged as one of the most individualistic and influential electric bassists during the late 1970s. His first solo album **(Jaco Pastorius)** provided inspiration and encouragement for a generation of bass-players to come, even guitarists were intrigued by his use of harmonics on his **Portrait of Tracy**.

Pastorius was born in Norristown, Pennsylvania, on December 1, 1951, but was raised in Florida. His earliest musical influence came from his father—a drummer and singer; then from the music he heard in Florida (mostly on radio), from steel bands to the Beatles. He taught for a while at the University of Miami and wrote for the university's big band. He also provided charts for Baker's Dozen (led by multi-instrumentalist Ira Sullivan—a musician who was to have an enduring influence on Pastorius) and bass trombonist Peter Graves' big band.

Pastorius' extraordinary bass technique and sound received international acclaim when he replaced Alfonso Johnson in Weather Report in '76 and his dynamic contribution to Joni Mitchell's eclectic **Hejira** and **Mingus** albums helped point scores of rock fans in the direction of the late Charles Mingus' music.

Since leaving Weather Report, Pastorius has occasionally toured with his Word of Mouth band in which there is strong evidence of his early big-band experience—eg **Liberty City** on **Word Of Mouth**. From that album, his imaginative arrangement of Lennon-McCartney's **Blackbird** remains as one of his most remarkable musical achievements.

Albums:
Ira Sullivan, Ira Sullivan (Horizon/Horizon)
Weather Report, Heavy Weather (Columbia/CBS)
Weather Report, Black Market (Columbia/CBS)
Joni Mitchell, Hejira (Asylum/Asylum)
Pet Metheny, Bright Life Size (ECM/ECM)
Jaco Pastorius (Epic/Epic)
Word Of Mouth (Warner Brothers/Warner Brothers)

Jaco Pastorius as leader, Word Of Mouth (courtesy Warner Brothers).

Paz

Led by vibist Dick Crouch, Paz has become one of Britain's favorite and longest-lived Latin fusion bands on the club circuit. Their 1983 **Look Inside** (issued on a small, under-resourced independent label) sold 2000 copies in its first week of issue—an indication of the group's popularity.

Crouch—heavily influenced by Miles Davis, Sonny Rollins and Wes Montgomery—formed Paz in '72, having previously worked with Ginger Johnson's African Drummers. Crouch describes Paz's music as 'today's form of bebop' and has consistently recruited top-class musicians—their first saxophonist was the eclectic Lol Coxhill, followed by Brian Smith and Ray Warleigh. Over the years, Paz's line-up has boasted such British-scene stalwarts as keyboardist Geoff Castle; guitarists Phil Lee and Jim Mullen; bassists Ron Mathewson, Henry Thomas and Martin York; drummers Dave Sheen, Dave Early and Mike Bradley; percussionists Simon Morton, Joao Bosco de Oliviera, Roberto Pla and Danny Cummins.

With a book of lively original charts written by either Crouch, Castle or Lee (Crouch's **AC/DC** has become a Paz *tour de force*), they have maintained a loyal following and have influenced many of the Latin-inspired groups which proliferated in the UK during the '80s.

The lively response to Paz's club performances confirms their popularity.

Above: Vibist Dick Crouch (far right) leader of influential and popular British Latin-fusion band Paz.

Albums:
Kandeen Love Song (—/Spotlite)
Paz Are Back (—/Spotlite)
Look Inside (—/Paladin)
Always There (—/Coda)

Paz, Look Inside (courtesy Paladin)—featuring guitarist Jim Mullen.

Annette Peacock

One of the most gifted composers to emerge from the mid-1960s jazz scene, Annette Peacock has remained an enigma mainly as a result of an erratic pattern of record releases.

At age 19, this extraordinary and unconventional musician-composer eloped to New York with bassist Gary Peacock. Soon after, she became associated with Timothy Leary's new psychedelic community at Millbrook. She came to wide attention in '66 as a contributor of expressive compositions to Paul Bley's albums—pieces like **Albert's Love Theme, Touching, Gary, Gesture Without Plot** and **Nothing Ever Was, Anyway**.
In '68, inventor R.A. Moog presented her with one of the first modular synthesizers. She formed one of the first electronic improvising jazz groups with Paul Bley, Han Bennink, Barry Altschul and Robert Wyatt, devising ways of processing vocals through a synthesizer.

Her first album as leader, **Revenge**, and the follow-up, **I'm The One**, found her incorporating this new electronic language into her earlier acoustic approach. In '74, she left the United States and settled in England. Her long-awaited **X-Dreams** ('78) and **The Perfect Release** ('79) were mostly built around straightforward rock structures—a seeming break from her former dualism.

The subsequent release of three powerful and unified albums on her own Ironic Records label have revealed a marked return to form and creative improvisation, featuring previously undocumented material alongside new compositions. In the '80s, Peacock was heard working with inventive improvising percussionist Roger Turner. This collaboration is found on **Been In The Streets Too Long** (released '83)—an album which also features Peacock with saxophonist Evan Parker, guitarist Dave Terry, drummer Bill Bruford, bassist Steve Cook, guitarists Chris Spedding and Brian Godding, and percussionist Sol Nastasi.

Albums:
Paul Bley, Improvisie (America/—)
Paul Bley, Dual Unity (Freedom/—)
Revenge (Polydor/Polydor)
I'm The One (RCA/RCA)
X-Dreams (Aura/Aura)
The Perfect Release (Aura/Aura)
Sky-skating (—/Ironic Records)
Been In The Streets Too Long (—/Ironic Records)
I Have No Feelings (—/Ironic Records)

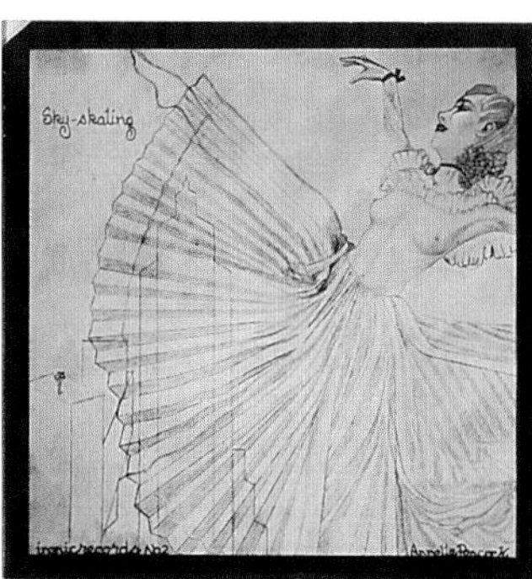

Annette Peacock, Sky-skating (courtesy Ironic): cover artwork by Ms Peacock.

Right: The gifted and unconventional Annette Peacock—composer, vocalist and synthesizer pioneer.

Niels-Henning Ørsted Pedersen

The undeniably virtuoso acoustic bass-playing of Demark's Neils-Henning Ørsted Pedersen has brought him an international reputation since the 1960s.

Born in Osted, Denmark, Niels-Henning spent six years studying the piano before moving on to classical bass studies. By 14, he was already playing in top Danish jazz groups and one of his first professional dates was at 16 accompanying pianist Bud Powell. His reputation soon extended outside Europe and he turned down an invitation to work with Count Basie Orchestra in the United States, preferring to stay in Denmark. Being based in Europe, he was a favorite choice as accompanist for such visiting American luminaries as Dexter Gordon, Ben Webster, Albert Ayler, Roland Kirk, Kenny Drew and Sonny Rollins.

Niels-Henning became the regular bassist with pianist Oscar Peterson's trio in the early '70s, with whom he has toured widely and recorded frequently. In the '80s, Niels-Henning came to even wider attention in the UK through the TV series *Jazz At The Gateway* which featured him as a genial presenter and a gifted player (with pianist Gordon Beck, guitarist Philip Catherine and drummer Jon Christensen).

Albums:
Oscar Peterson, Live At The North Sea Jazz Festival, The Hague, Holland, 1980 (Pablo/Pablo)
Oscar Peterson, A Tribute To My Friends (Pablo/Pablo)
Dexter Gordon, Billie's Bounce (Steeplechase/Steeplechase)
Neils-Henning-Rune Gustafsson, Just The Way You Are (Sonet/Sonet)
The Viking (Pablo/Pablo)

Niels-Henning and Rune Gustafsson, Just The Way You Are (courtesy Sonet).

Art Pepper

Born 1925, Los Angeles, Art Pepper was one of the greatest altoists in post-bebop jazz, ranking with Lee Konitz or Eric Dolphy but less well known for a variety of extra-musical factors.

Influenced by Lester Young, Parker, Konitz and Zoot Sims, Pepper's best work was poised on the knife edge between raw emotion and form. His early work with Stan Kenton and Shorty Rogers **(Artistry In Jazz, Blues Express)** and with his own West Coast groups from the early '50s **(Discoveries)** showed great technical fluency and the makings of an original style. 1956 found him in great form with tenorist Warne Marsh on numbers like Lester Young's **Tickle Toe (The Way It Was!)** while a group with vibraphonist Red Norvo featured his own Zootish tenor on **Tenor**

Above: The virtuoso bass technique of Denmark's Niels-Henning Ørsted Pedersen found an international showcase with pianist Oscar Peterson.

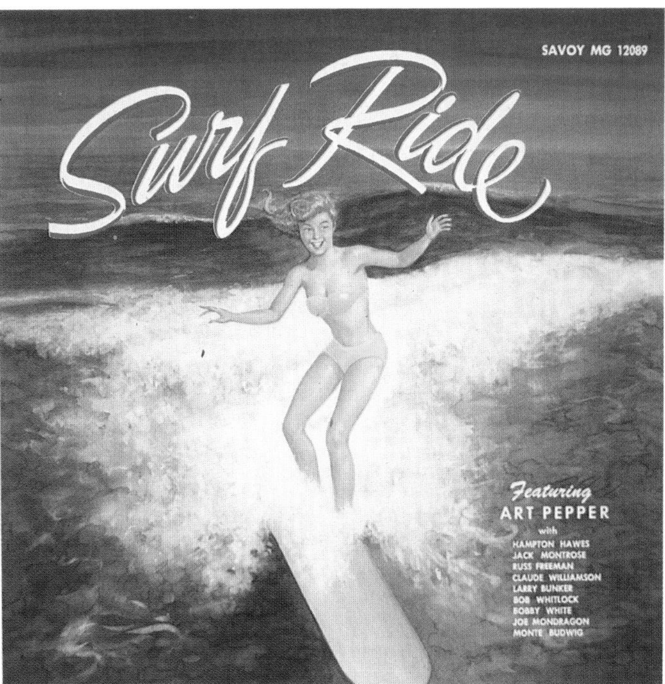

Art Pepper and friends, Surf Ride (courtesy Savoy)—the infamous cover is a 'collectible' example of West Coast kitsch.

Living Legend (courtesy Contemporary) —Pepper's 'comeback' in 1975.

Roadgame (courtesy Galaxy): one of his last, recorded on a 'full-moon night'.

Blooz, and with pianist Russ Freeman for numbers like **Mambo De La Pinta** dedicated to the various prisons to which his addiction had introduced him **(Early Act)**.

Pepper's life—narcotics, ill-health, prison—was similar to Chet Baker's, and the survival of his talent was miraculous. In 1957, he made an album with Miles Davis' rhythm section of Red Garland, Paul Chambers and Philly Joe Jones; the results made nonsense of much of the critical comparisons between East and West Coast. **Jazz Me Blues**, a Dixieland classic, showed the altoist's freedom from musical snobbery, while **Star Eyes** was a searingly emotional statement **(Art Pepper Meets The Rhythm Section)**. A later session with another Davis rhythm section **(Gettin' Together)** was even better, with Pepper's rhythmic mastery feeding on Thelonious Monk's **Rhythm-a-ning**, and his passionate lyrical gifts in full spate on **Whims Of Chambers, Bijou The Poodle** and **Softly As In A Morning Sunrise**. A late-'70s issued obscurity featured Pepper and the great pianist Carl Perkins in almost an hour of magnificent invention **(The Omega Man)**. **I Can't Believe That You're In Love With Me** showed all the characteristics of Pepper's style—the clear, concise articulation, the pure tone, the increasingly fragmented melody stretched tight over an alternating pattern of rests and squeezed notes until it yielded up a deeper, more anguished emotion.

Between 1957 and 1961 Pepper cut a series of classic albums for Contemporary **(Art Pepper Meets The Rhythm Section, Gettin' Together** and **Modern Jazz Classics)** which used an 11-piece band and Marty Paich's arrangements of numbers like **Walkin'**, a great Pepper tenor outing, and a clarinet version of **Anthropology**.

Two further albums made with the perfect rhythm team of Jimmy Bond, bass, and Frank Butler, drums, were even better. Ornette Coleman's **Tears Inside** proved a fine vehicle for the altoist's own brand of tonal variations **(Smack Up)**, while a program of ballads like **Long Ago & Far Away** and **Too Close For Comfort (Intensity)** resulted in moving interpretations.

Most of the '60s were a wasteland of imprisonment and illness but an album from 1975 **(Living Legend)** found Pepper with an ideal rhythm section, Hampton Hawes, piano; Charlie Haden, bass; Shelly Manne, drums; all in peak form. An original, **Lost Life**, remains an overwhelming experience comparable with Billie Holiday's **For All We Know**.

In '79, Pepper's biography *Straight Life* (co-written by his wife Laurie) was a catalog — often in graphic and harrowing terms — of his life, times and music (published by Shirmer Books in New York and Macmillan, London). He was to make his last international tour in '81, creating indescribable magic on countless festival stages across the world. On the evidence of these blistering performances, Pepper seemed the ever-indestructible survivor. But the following year, on June 9, 1982, Pepper was admitted to Kaiser Hospital, Panorama City, in a coma following a brain hemorrhage. Art Pepper never regained consciousness and died on June 16, aged 56.

A musician with a unique charisma and one of the most individual voices on alto sax, Art Pepper was irreplaceable. The power of the emotionalism his later playing could create is illustrated, perhaps nowhere better, through his lament to his 'lost daughter' **Patricia (Art Pepper Today)**. A poignant performance of **Patricia** can also be heard in Don McGlynn's exceptional documentary film *Art Pepper: Notes From A Jazz Survivor*, completed just three months before Pepper's death.

Albums:
Stan Kenton, Artistry In Jazz (Capitol/—)
Shorty Rogers, Blues Express (RCA/RCA—France)
Art Pepper, Discoveries (Savoy/Savoy)
The Way It Was! (Contemporary/Contemporary)
Early Art (Blue Note/Blue Note)
Art Pepper Meets The Rhythm Section (Contemporary/Boplicity)
The Omega Man (Onyx/—)
Art Pepper Plus 11, Modern Jazz Classics (Contemporary/Boplicity)
Smack Up (Contemporary/Contemporary)
Intensity (Contemporary/Boplicity)
Living Legend (Contemporary/Boplicity)
The Early Show (Xanadu/Xanadu)
Dolo Coker, California Hard (Xanadu/—)
The Late Show (Xanadu/Xanadu)
On The Road (Contemporary/Boplicity)
Friday Night At The Village Vanguard (Contemporary/Contemporary)
Saturday Night At The Village Vanguard (Contemporary/Contemporary)
Art Pepper Today (Galaxy/Galaxy)
New York Album (Galaxy/Galaxy)
Artworks (Galaxy/Galaxy)
Milcho Leviev, Blues For The Fisherman (—/Mole Jazz)
Milcho Leviev, True Blues (—/Mole Jazz)
Winter Moon (Galaxy/Galaxy)
One September Afternoon (Galaxy/Galaxy)
Roadgame (Galaxy/Galaxy)

Carl Perkins

Born Indiana, 1928, pianist Carl Perkins was self-taught and used an unorthodox technique with his left forearm parallel to the keyboard.

Centered in Los Angeles, Perkins was one of the finest pianists of the '50s — direct, sinewy and totally convincing as a blues performer. His one featured album **(Introducing Carl Perkins)** shows a Bud Powell influence and a very personal emotionalism on ballads like **You Don't Know What Love Is**. He turns up on another Dooto album **(Dexter Blows Hot & Cool)** as a virile accompanist for the driving tenor of Dexter Gordon. His work with the Curtis Counce group **(Landslide, Counceltation** and **Carl's Blues)** featured some of his writing **(Mia, Carl's Blues)** and much of his finest playing. An album by practically the same personnel under Harold Land's leadership **(Harold In The Land Of Jazz)** contains Perkins' **Grooveyard**, a performance steeped in the blues tradition. Sadly, it was his swansong, for he died the same year, 1958.

Albums:
Introducing Carl Perkins (Dooto/Boplicity)
Dexter Gordon, Dexter Blows Hot & Cool (Dooto/Boplicity)
Curtis Counce, Counceltation (Contemporary/Contemporary)
Curtis Counce, Landslide

(Contemporary/Contemporary)
Curtis Counce, Carl's Blues
(Contemporary/Contemporary)
Harold Land, Harold In The Land Of Jazz
(Contemporary/Boplicity)

Introducing...Carl Perkins (courtesy Dooto): re-issued by Boplicity, 1980s.

Hannibal Marvin Peterson

One of the most eclectic and accomplished young trumpeters of the 1980s, Hannibal Marvin Peterson steamed to international attention as an expressive soloist with the Gil Evans Orchestra in the early '70s.

Born on a farm in Smithville, Texas, on November 11, 1948, Peterson was still at school when he first caught the ear of multi-instrumentalist Roland Kirk. Kirk presented the young trumpeter with a copy of Miles Davis' **In A Silent Way** and eventually took him into his band. Work with Thad Jones-Mel Lewis, Roy Haynes, McCoy Tyner, Pharoah Sanders and Elvin Jones soon followed but the most significant boost to his growing reputation came as featured soloist with Gil Evans' line-up.

A widely inspired, open-minded musician (he numbers among his influences John Coltrane, Duke Ellington, Janacek, B. B. King and T-Bone Walker), Peterson has toured widely with his own groups including his quintet and Sunrise Orchestra. In the mid-'70s, his travels took him to Kenya to study East African music.

His interesting and broad-based musical career has included touring as group-leader with Bobby 'Blue' Bland and T-Bone Walker, performing solo in St Peter's Cathedral ('70), producing his *Suite de Mémoir* (In memory of Mahatma Ghandi) ('73), and writing his *Flames For South Africa* ('77) for the Hanover Radio Symphony Orchestra.

Peterson's first major orchestral presentation was his **Children Of The Fire** in '74 (dedicated to the children of Vietnam) — an ambitious five-movement work for strings, percussion, trumpet and voice (the voice being provided by 9-year-old Waheeda Massey).

In the early '80s, Peterson toured widely as a soloist — notably, to much acclaim, in the UK with the Weller-Spring Quartet (tenorist Don Weller, drummer Bryan Spring, pianist Martin Blackwell and bassist Dave Green). Their dynamic collaboration was captured live in '81 at London's 100 Club on **Poem Song**.

Albums:
Roy Haynes, Roy Haynes Hip Ensemble
(Mainstream/—)
Gil Evans, Gil Evans (Impulse/Impulse)
Gil Evans, Svengali (Atlantic/Atlantic)
Gil Evans, Gil Evans Plays Hendrix (RCA/RCA)
Pharoak Sanders, Black Unity
(Impulse/Impulse)
Children Of The Fire (Sunrise/—)
Hannibal (—/MPS)
Live In Berlin (—/MPS)
Live In Lausanne (—/RCA—Japan)
The Light (—/RCA—Japan)
Poem Song (—/Mole Jazz)

Below: Hannibal Marvin Peterson stepped out of the Gil Evans' line-up to become a solo success.

Oscar Peterson

Oscar Peterson was born in Montreal, 1925 and taken up by promoter Norman Granz in 1949 to make a startling début at the Carnegie Hall Jazz At The Phil concert.

Tatum-influenced, Peterson is a virtuoso pianist with an overwhelming command of everything from up-tempo numbers to ballads, great harmonic insight and a monumental swing. Not an innovator in the Bud Powell or Cecil Taylor sense, Peterson's style is securely anchored in the mainstream-modern tradition.

Oscar Peterson, The History Of An Artist (courtesy Pablo): one of jazz's most prolific and accomplished pianists in a variety of trio settings.

A long-running favorite of JATP audiences, Peterson has worked with almost everybody throughout his career, contributing to the success of numerous Verve albums in the '50s **(Sittin' In, Soulville** and **The Parker Jam Session)** as well as heading his own groups.

Starting as a duo with bassist Ray Brown, he added guitarists Barney Kessel and Herb Ellis to form the famous trio, dropping the guitar in 1959 to take on a succession of drummers like Ed Thigpen, Louis Hayes and Bobby Durham. Two excellent albums map out his achievement in this area, one **(In Concert)** collecting highlights from 1950, including the famous **Tenderly** and **C-Jam Blues** and closing with the superb set from the 1956 Shakespeare Festival; the other **(History Of An Artist)** is a series of reunions with past sidemen, recorded in the '70s.

Peterson's reputation, for years under attack as flashy, eclectic and mechanical, reached a turning point with an undeniably great series of albums recorded at the home of a German recording engineer **(Exclusively For My Friends)**. All four albums display his total commitment to the material, with the lengthy **I'm In The Mood For Love (Girl Talk); Satin Doll (The Way I Really Play); At Long Last Love (Action)**; and the unaccompanied **Perdido (My Favorite Instrument)** outstanding.

His recordings for Granz's Pablo label in the '70s have set the final seal on his emergence as a great solo performer, summoning vast orchestral textures from the piano. Two classic double albums of solo, duo and trio concert performances capture Peterson at his peak, with **Just Friends** a staggering display of artistic resources **(In Russia)** and the unaccompanied fireworks of **Indiana** and **Sweet Georgia Brown** rivaled only by the chases with guitarist Joe Pass on **Honeysuckle Rose (A Salle Pleyel)**.

Five encounters with great trumpeters displayed Peterson's gifts as an accompanist, capable of varying his manner from stride for the older players **(Oscar Peterson & Roy Eldridge, Oscar Peterson & Clark Terry** and **Oscar Peterson & Harry Edison)** to the more harmonically complex backing on **Dizzy Atmosphere (Oscar Peterson & Dizzy Gillespie)** or waltz-time for **Take The 'A' Train (Oscar Peterson & Jon Faddis)**. An album on clavichord with Joe Pass **(Porgy & Bess)** shows the same craftsmanship and lyrical imagination as his work on the piano. A meeting with Count Basie works splendidly, the two dissimilar styles — Basie economic, Peterson multi-fingered — respectfully deployed **(Satch & Josh)**.

Due to well-managed TV and concert appearances, Oscar Peterson is one of the best-known jazz names in the world today, and players like Joe Pass or bassist Niels-Henning Ørsted Pedersen have achieved due recognition by association with him in the trio.

Albums:
Sonny Stitt, Sittin' In (Verve/Verve)
Ben Webster, Soulville (Verve/Verve)
Charlie Parker, The Parker Jam Session (Verve/Verve)
The George Gershwin Song Book (Verve/Verve)
In Concert (Verve/Verve)
History Of An Artist (Pablo/Pablo)
Exclusively For My Friends (BASF/Polydor)
In Russia (Pablo/Pablo)
A Salle Pleyel (Pablo/Pablo)
Oscar Peterson & Roy Eldridge (Pablo/Pablo)
Oscar Peterson & Clark Terry (Pablo/Pablo)
Oscar Peterson & Harry Edison (Pablo/Pablo)
Oscar Peterson & Dizzy Gillespie (Pablo/Pablo)
Oscar Peterson & Jon Faddis (Pablo/Pablo)
Porgy & Bess (Pablo/Pablo)
Satch & Josh (Pablo/Pablo)
Peterson 6 (Pablo/Pablo)
Live At The North Sea Jazz Festival, The Hague, Holland, 1980 (Pablo/Pablo)
A Tribute To My Friends (Pablo/Pablo)
If You Could See Me Now (Pablo/Pablo)

Michel Petrucciani

The prodigiously gifted Michel Petrucciani will go down in jazz history as the unknown 18-year-old pianist whose dazzling technique inspired, and finally persuaded, saxophonist Charles Lloyd to come out of retirement in the early 1980s. Petrucciani — like Keith Jarrett before him — received well-deserved international exposure through Lloyd's group.

Born in Orange, France, on December 28, 1962, Petrucciani entered a musical family — his Italian father Tony and brother Philippe were guitarists and his brother Louis, a bassist. Michel started on drums but when at the age of 4, he saw Duke Ellington on TV, he demanded a piano. From the age of 10, Bill Evans' playing was to have an enduring effect on him. Before he was 16, he worked with trumpeter Clark Terry and performed with his own trio.

At 18, Petrucciani traveled to Big Sur in California where he persuaded Charles Lloyd to play again after the saxophonist's indefinite sabbatical. This auspicious collaboration was documented on Lloyd's celebrated comeback album **Montreux 82**, and Petrucciani's international reputation was well established. In '82, he won the Prix Django Reinhardt as French Jazz Musician of the Year and the following year the cultural department of the Italian government voted him Best European Jazz Musician. He has since worked in a duo with bassist Charlie Haden and in '84 astounded all at the summer jazz festivals with Freddie Hubbard's All Stars. In '86, Petrucciani toured the international festival circuit again in a spectacular collaboration with guitarist Jim Hall.

Some of Petrucciani's finest performances can be heard in the company of his own trio — bassist Palle Danielsson and drummer Eliot Zigmund **(Live At The Village Vanguard**, a double, was released in '84).

Michel Petrucciani is undoubtedly one of the most exciting young European musicians to emerge in the '80s. His progress will be viewed with increasing interest.

Albums:
Michel Petrucciani (—/Owl)
Oracle's Destiny (—/Owl)
Lee Konitz, Toot Sweet (—/Owl)
Charles Lloyd, Montreux 82 (Elektra Musician/Elektra Musician)
Charles Lloyd, A Night In Copenhagen (Blue Note/Blue Note)
The Michel Petrucciani Trio Live At The Village Vanguard (George Wein Collection/George Wein Collection)

Below: France's gifted Michel Petrucciani—he inspired Charles Lloyd to tour again. Albums under his own leadership reveal a unique keyboard talent.

Above: Flip Phillips, tenor-sax star of the first Herman Herd and perennial Jazz At The Phil favorite who never fails to swing.

Flip Phillips

'Flip' Phillips (real name Joseph Edward Filipelli, born Brooklyn, New York, 1915) was one of the leading lights in the trail-blazing Woody Herman First Herd from 1944-46.

Originally, Phillips studied clarinet. As clarinettist, worked mainly at Schneider's Lobster House, Brooklyn, occasionally on alto sax.

Joined Frankie Newton on 52nd Street (1940), playing clarinet; with same band at Lake George (1941). Switched to tenor sax in '42 to work with Larry Bennett, in New York. Brief period with Benny Goodman, then with Wingy Manone, Red Norvo, before joining Herman. With latter he established an enviable reputation as warm ballad player on **With Someone New** (a Phillips original), **I Wonder, I Surrender Dear**, and perpetrator of exciting, hard-swinging tenor solos on flagwavers like **Caldonia, Apple Honey, Northwest Passage** (all **The Thundering Herds**).

Phillips also recorded with colleagues Chubby Jackson and Bill Harris on separate occasions during 1945 **(The Herdsmen)**. There was much fine music heard, too, when Phillips, Jackson, Denzil Best, drums, and Lennie Tristano joined Harris for a typical 1947 New York club performance **(A Knight In The Village)**.

Phillips' peak of popularity came with his joining JATP. His roof-raising version (Illinois Jacquet-style) of **Perdido** (which for years he had to repeat ad nauseam) was the one number which brought Phillips his widespread following **(JATP: New Vol 6—Midnight At Carnegie Hall)**.

As exciting as Phillips' performances were in this context, a better idea of his real abilities can be found in **Flip** with Phillips leading bands of varying sizes. Even though Phillips never crossed over into bebop field, it is rewarding to hear him inspire, and be inspired by, boppers like Howard McGhee, Max Roach and Sonny Criss. Likewise, his playing on own 1950-51 tracks and others by an all-star Ralph Burns unit **(Kings Of Swing, Vol 2)** shows him in a more productive vein. Phillips was also to give a good account of himself at the legendary **The Charlie Parker Sides/The Parker Jam Session**, although not in the same league as participants such as Johnny Hodges, Charlie Parker, Benny Carter and Ben Webster. Was member of Gene Krupa Trio in 1952.

During late-1950s, settled in Florida and co-led band with Bill Harris. Came out to tour Europe with Benny Goodman (1959). During **The Complete 1970 Pasadena Jazz Party** his tenor appeared to have become more spring-heeled on the up-tempo numbers than in 25 years. **USA Jazz Live** recorded in the Grand Ballroom, Broadmoor Hotel, Colorado Springs, as part of Dick Gibson's 1971 Colorado Jazz Party, finds him in equally fetching form, especially when paired with Clark Terry.

Albums:
Woody Herman, The Thundering Herds (Columbia)
Woody Herman At Carnegie Hall (Verve/Verve)
One Night Stand With Woody Herman (Joyce/—)
Various (Including Chubby Jackson/Bill Harris), The Herdsmen (—/Mercury)
Bill Harris, A Knight In The Village (Jazz Showcase/—)
Various (Including Flip Phillips), JATP: New Vol 6—Midnight At Carnegie Hall (Verve/Columbia—Clef)
Various (Including Flip Phillips), Norman Granz' Jazz At The Philharmonic — Carnegie Hall Concert, 1952, Vols 1-3 (Verve/Columbia—Clef)
Various (Including Flip Phillips), JATP In Tokyo (Pablo Live/Pablo Live)
Flip Phillips, Flip (—/Verve)
Various (Including Flip Phillips), Kings Of Swing, Vol 2 (—/Verve)
Various (Including Flip Phillips), The Charlie Parker Sides (Verve)/
The Parker Jam Session (Verve)
Various (Including Flip Phillips), The Complete 1970 Pasadena Jazz Party (Blue Angel Jazz Club Presents/—)
Various (Including Flip Phillips), USA Jazz Live (MPS—Germany)

Courtney Pine

The uncompromisingly dedicated Courtney Pine has appeared in the 1980s as one of Britain's most promising new young voices on tenor saxophone, having worked hard — unaided — to develop his volcanic saxophone technique.

Born in London in 1965 to Jamaican parents, Pine grew up in Paddington. He attained high grades as a clarinettist before turning to the saxophone (most recently, he has also taken up bass clarinet). Initially, he played sax with reggae and funk bands before discovering the possibilities of jazz through Sonny Rollins' **Way Out West** album. Rollins led him to John Coltrane and then Lester Young, Sidney Bechet and Albert Ayler. Against the advice of his reggae colleagues, Pine put in eight hours of practice a day, in a concerted effort for self-improvement. He worked with drummer John Stevens' Freebop group and the Charlie Watts Big Band, all the while consolidating his formidable reputation as a tenorist.

In '84, at the age of 19, he formed The Abibi Jazz Arts as a rallying point for young black British musicians aspiring to play jazz, or what Pine defines as 'Afro-classical music'. From the ranks of TAJA, his much-vaunted 19-piece Jazz Warriors was drawn. He also leads and composes for his all-saxophone quartet (The World's First Saxophone Posse) and his quintet. Pine is confident that the UK is on the threshold of a new black British style of jazz — a new music which will incorporate various elements of West Indian culture like reggae, calypso, the local Baptist Church and ska.

Since attracting so much attention locally, Pine has toured in the UK with the George Russell Orchestra and sat in with Art Blakey and the Jazz Messengers. A jam with Elvin Jones resulted in an offer to tour with Jones' combo, finishing up in Japan for a John Coltrane Memorial Concert. Meanwhile, Pine's first album was released in '86 on Island Records.

Considerable interest is assured for Courtney Pine's every musical advance and achievement.

Above: Saxophonist Courtney Pine—a new voice in raising the consciousness and profile of young black musicians in the United Kingdom.

Albums:
Journey To The Urge Within (Island/Island)

King Pleasure

Born Clarence Beeks, 1922, King Pleasure was one of the first vocalists to fit words to famous instrumental solos. Similar artists have been Eddie Jefferson, Lambert, Hendicks & Ross.

His biggest hits were **I'm In The Mood For Love** based on James Moody's tenor solo: **Parker's Mood, Little Boy, Don't Get Scared** from Stan Getz, **Sometimes I'm Happy** from Lester Young. His popularity lasted from 1952-56 with a comeback album in 1960 **(Golden Days)**.

Beeks died from a heart attach in 1981, just as a new generation was re-discovering the delights of his early works.

Albums:
The Source (Prestige/Prestige)
Golden Days (HiFi/Vogue)

Jean-Luc Ponty

Born in a Normandy village, violinist Jean-Luc Ponty was the son of a violin professor, putting in six hours practice a day at the age of 13. A phenomenal technician, Ponty toured the United States in 1969, making a greater impact than most European jazzmen. A double-album from this period, with George Duke on keyboards **(Cantaloupe Island)** and a meeting of four of the foremost violinists, Stuff Smith, Svend Asmunssen, Stephane Grappelli and Ponty **(Violin Summit)** contains a good example of his earlier jazz output.

In the early '70s, Ponty made a dramatic change in musical direction and joined the jazz-rock revolution in the company of Frank Zappa's Mothers of Invention **(Overnight Sensation)** and John McLaughlin's Mahavishnu Orchestra **(Visions Of The Emerald Beyond)**. In '70, he recorded **King Kong**, one of his finest albums to date — an imaginative collaboration with Frank Zappa. The project included an extended orchestral Zappa *pièce de résistance* entitled **Music For Electric Violin And Low Budget Orchestra** (so called, apparently, because the producer unreasonably refused Zappa's request for a 97-piece ensemble). Next, Ponty joined forces with guitarist John McLaughlin's Mahavishnu; in '74, Ponty and the entire London Symphony Orchestra assembled to record McLaughlin's *magnum opus* **Apocalypse**.

Since the late '70s, Jean-Luc Ponty has toured and recorded as a successful solo artist with his own groups. Playing mainly electric violin these days. Ponty's music has a romantic, often raga-like feel.

Albums:
Jean-Luc Ponty Jazz Long Playing (Philips/Philips)
More Than Meets The Ear (World Pacific Jazz/World Pacific Jazz)
King Kong (World Pacific Jazz/World Pacific Jazz)
Various, Violin Summit (BASF/BASF)
Open Strings (—/MPS)
Upon The Wings Of Music (Atlantic/Atlantic)
Aurora (Atlantic/Atlantic)
Imaginary Voyage (Atlantic/Atlantic)
Enigmatic Ocean (Atlantic/Atlantic)
Mystical Adventures (Atlantic/Atlantic)

Violinist Jean-Luc Ponty, Mystical Adventures (courtesy Atlantic).

Bud Powell

Between 1947-53, Bud Powell was the most overwhelmingly creative piano player in the hot-house of bebop. His drive — like Charlie Parker's — was a monstrous horsepower that shook the chassis apart. Powell is emotion in spate: ecstatic.

The first piano album **(The Bud Powell Trio)** was a perfect translation of the Parker style onto the keyboard — up-tempo numbers like **Bud's Bubble** or **Indiana** show a speed of imagination and rhythm that rival Tatum.

The two Blue Note albums **(The Amazing Bud Powell)** give a broader picture of his genius. **Glass Enclosure** is a Powell composition in four distinct movements, opening ceremonially and quickly becoming angular and ominous before swerving again into the more familiar attack. It never settles for long on any mood and its bewildering transpositions leave behind an impression of stasis. On bumpy, bebop warhorses like **Ornithology** and **Reets & I**, the vertiginous flow of single-note, right-hand figures tugs solid chords from the left. Counterpoint and tension underpin the most fevered flights of imagination. Horn-like blast-offs abound in up-tempo numbers like **I Want To Be Happy**, the sudden dip followed by the plunging, high-velocity run in which every note is cleanly articulated.

In Powell's music, off the ground and moving, the moment is everything. His treatment of ballads is deeply affecting, from the sombre, glowing **Polka Dots And Moonbeams** to the scampering **Somewhere Over The Rainbow**. The tracks with trumpeter Fats Navarro and tenorist Sonny Rollins, **Dance Of The Infidels, 52nd Street Theme, Wail** and **Bouncing With Bud** are classics of combo jazz

Bud Powell's work with Charlie Parker is a meeting of giants and the Massey Hall concert from 1953 **(The Quintet Of The Year)** has the unbeatable line-up of Parker, Dizzy Gillespie, Powell, Charlie Mingus and Max Roach, while the Café Society broadcasts find Parker and Powell joined by Fats Navarro **(Charlie Parker Historical Masterpieces)**.

A meeting with Sonny Stitt **(Genesis)** found Powell at the height of his powers, sweeping through the session like a cavalry charge. From 1954 on, following a breakdown, Powell's work became inconsistent. Conflicting moods, misfingerings and loss of speed mark some of his playing but the emotional and imaginative content remained unique. His interpretation of Thelonious Monk's **Round Midnight (Ups 'N' Downs)** is strangely disturbing in its massive chords and oblique timing, while a Blue Note date **(The Scene Changes)** finds him in good humor, funky on **Duid Deed**, simple and affecting on **Borderick** and confident on the up-tempo **Crossin' The Channel**.

In 1959 Powell settled in Paris, cutting an album with tenorist Dexter Gordon **(Our Man In Paris)** and with Coleman Hawkins **(Hawk In Germany)** both of which offer fine piano-playing in accompaniment and solo. A meeting with the dynamic tenorist Johnny Griffin **(Hot House)** produced wildly exciting music, with **Straight No Chaser** outstanding. A trio album from the same year, 1964, has the ultra-fast **Little Willie Leaps** and the moving slow blues title track **(Blues For Bouffemont)**. Great bebop standards receive classic treatment on a live session from Paris' Blue Note Club **(Earl Bud Powell)**.

Powell returned to his home-town, New York, and died shortly afterwards in 1966. One of the most affecting players in all of jazz, comparable to Billie Holiday in terms of emotional impact, Bud Powell's technical innovations form the basis of modern jazz piano.

Above: The late, great Bud Powell—bebop's foremost pianist. One of the most creative and inspiring players in the history of the music.

The Amazing Bud Powell (courtesy Blue Note)—broad picture of this genius.

Albums:
The Bud Powell Trio (Roost/Vocalion)
The Vintage Years (Verve/Verve)
The Amazing Bud Powell, Volumes 1 & 2 (Blue Note/Blue Note)
The Quintet Of The Year (Debut/Vocalion)
Charlie Parker Historical Masterpieces (Le Jazz Cool—France)
Sonny Stitt, Genesis (Prestige/Prestige)
Ups 'N' Downs (Mainstream/Mainstream)
The Scene Changes (Blue Note/Blue Note)
Dexter Gordon, Our Man In Paris (Blue Note/Blue Note)
Coleman Hawkins, Hawk In Germany (Black Lion/Black Lion)
Hot House (—/Fontana)
Blues For Bouffemont (—/Fontana)
Earl Bud Powell (ESP/Fontana)
Inner Fires (Elektra Musician/Elektra Musician)
Alternate Takes (Blue Note/Blue Note)

Don Pullen

Avant-garde pianist Don Pullen's début was with the Giuseppi Logan Quartet, where he and drummer Milford Graves supplied most of the interest. Their partnership continued through two duo albums recorded at Yale University in 1966 **(Nomo** and **In Concert)** which are something of a classic in free music. Their improvisations intersect and diverge in an ever-changing flow, the pianist's variety of keyboard device staggering in its complexity and inventiveness. Dissonant, scattering handfuls of tone clusters, the texture of Pullen's music is similar to Cecil Taylor's, but less abrupt and dramatic.

In '66, Pullen and Milford Graves set an astute, if brave, example forming their SRP mail-order label with the intention of making their acclaimed Yale University concert album more widely available.

Having established a near-legendary reputation, Pullen disappeared for a decade into the anonymity of the accompanist, playing behind singers Arthur Prysock and Nina Simone. A period with the Charles Mingus Quartet revealed hitherto unimagined facility within the traditional forms. On **Black Bats And Poles**, his solo moves from fleet, boppish, single-note runs into harmonic areas and back into a funky vamp, while on **Free Cell Block F, 'Tis Nazi USA** his playing is rhapsodic. Mingus' sense of tradition breaks down most of the artificial classifications and Pullen's work within the group showed a mastery of varied idioms **(Changes One** and **Changes Two)**.

1975-76 was a productive period, with Pullen recording with Sam Rivers **(Capricorn Rising)** and ex-Mingus colleague George Adams **(Don Pullen, George Adams** and **Suite For Swingers)** as well as three solo albums. **Pain Inside** shows his sensitive and effective use of the inside of the piano and a delicate lyricism, while **Tracey's Blues (Healing Force)** and **Big Alice (Solo Piano Album)** move the funkiest blues in and out of tonality without ever losing the emotion.

In the '80s, Pullen continued to make excellent albums for the Italy-based Black Saint label, like the highly acclaimed solo **Evidence Of Things Unseen** and **The Sixth Sense** with his quintet; **Decisions**, meanwhile, found him again in a dynamic collaboration with George Adams.

Albums:
Don Pullen & Milford Graves:
Nomo (SRP/—)
In Concert (SRP/—)
Charles Mingus:
Changes One (Atlantic/Atlantic)
Changes Two (Atlantic/Atlantic)
George Adams:
George Adams (Horo—Italy)
Suite For Swingers (Horo—Italy)
Capricorn Rising (Black Saint/—)
Don Pullen (Horo—Italy)
Five To Go (Horo—Italy)
Solo Piano Album (Sackville/—)
Healing Force (Black Saint/—)
Warriors (—/Black Saint)
Montreux Concert (Atlantic/Atlantic)
Evidence Of Things Unseen (Black Saint/Black Saint)
The Sixth Sense (Black Saint/Black Saint)
George Adams-Don Pullen Quartet, Decisions (Timeless/Timeless)

Don Pullen solo, Healing Force (courtesy Black Saint).

Flora Purim

Moving to the United States from her native Rio in the late 1960s, Flora Purim's distinctive wordless vocal style, improvised around basic Latin rhythms and melodies, became influential internationally.

Born in Rio de Janeiro, Brazil, on March 6, 1942, Purim was listening to a wide range of music from an early age; her Rumanian-born father and Brazilian mother were both classical musicians and interested in jazz As she grew up, the local music of Brazil was also to have a profound effect on her. From age 6, she studied piano and, at 12, switched to acoustic guitar. By 17, she was singing with Rio's Quarteto Novo which also included Airto Moreira (later to be her husband) and Hermeto Pascoal. In '68, she went to the States, initially to study with Moacir Santos. She graduated with a music degree from the California State University and also studied drama in Los Angeles.

In the late '60s, she established her reputation in New York working with Duke Pearson **(How Insensitive, It Could Only Happen With You)**, Stan Getz and Gil Evans, joining Chick Corea's Return To Forever along with Airto in '71 **(Return To Forever, Light As A Feather)**. Since the mid-'70s, Purim has worked almost exclusively with Airto and her own groups, occasionally contributing her unique vocals to other artists' projects (Hermeto Pascoal's **Slave Mass**, Santana's **Welcome,** George Duke's **A Brazilian Love Affair)**.

In the mid-'80s, Flora Purim and Airto made a celebrated return on the crest of a new wave of interest in Latin music, releasing the much-vaunted **Humble People**, and performing in the UK for the first time.

Albums:
Airto, Identity (Arista/Arista)
Airto, I'm Fine How Are You (Warner Brothers/Warner Brothers)
George Duke, A Brazilian Love Affair (Epic/Epic)
Butterfly Dreams (Milestone/Milestone)
Open Your Eyes You Can Fly (Milestone/Milestone)
Nothing Will Be As It Was... Tomorrow (Warner Brothers/Warner Brothers)
That's What She Said (Milestone/Milestone)
Everyday, Every Night (Milestone/Milestone)
Humble People (George Wein Collection/ George Wein Collection)

Below: Individualistic Brazilian vocalist Flora Purim with percussionist Airto Moreira—internationally influential, a dynamic and unequalled partnership.

Magnificent Ma Rainey (courtesy Milestone)—influential 'Mother of the Blues', classic tracks.

Ma Rainey

If Bessie Smith was the Empress of the Blues, then certainly Ma Rainey was the Mother of the Blues, for Rainey's long list of protegées reads like a Who's Who of classic female blues singers and, indeed, included the remarkable Bessie Smith.

Rainey (real name Gertrude Malissa Pridgett, born Columbus, Ohio, 1886) made her first public appearance at 12 in a vaudeville show, *A Bunch of Blackberries*, in Columbus.

At 18, she married William 'Pa' Rainey — a dancer, singer and comedian. Couple toured with Rabbit Foot Minstrels show, also with Tolliver's Circus & Musical Extravaganza (1914-16), billed as Rainey & Rainey, Assassinators of the Blues. Her first recordings were for Paramount label in December 1923, aged 37. Whether material was pure blues or vaudevillia did not matter; Ma Rainey's majestic vocal powers always were equal to the occasion. And only Bessie Smith could surpass that extraordinary Rainey vibrancy. Over the years, her accompaniments varied. The backgrounds provided by 'Georgia Tom' Dorsey and Tampa Red left much to be desired (in terms of overall singer-band rapport) during magnificent examples of blues vocalism to be found on 1928-recorded titles like **Hear Me Talking To You, Deep Moanin' Blues, Sweet Rough Man, Tough Luck Blues** and **Leavin' This Morning** (all on **Ma Rainey**).

Better, by far, were backings from earlier sessions (1924, 1925) which featured such as Coleman Hawkins, Joe Smith, Louis Armstrong, Fletcher Henderson, Kaiser Marshall, Charlie Green. Armstrong's cornet was, as always, a major asset on **Jelly Bean Blues, See See Rider, Countin' The Blues** (all **Ma Rainey)** — and Smith, also playing cornet, was equally prominent on **Titanic Man Blues, Stack O' Lee** (both **Ma Rainey, Vol 3); Wringin' & Twistin' Blues, Chain Gang Blues, Bessemer Bound Blues** (all on **Ma Rainey)**. Tommy Ladnier was equally complementary to the Rainey declamatory style on other recordings, like **Ma Rainey's Mystery Record, Cell Bound Blues (Ma Rainey, Vol 1)**. Even more basic accompaniments are provided for **Dead Drunk Blues** (Claude Hopkins), **Mountain Jack Blues** (Jimmy Blythe), **Trust No Man** (Lil Henderson) (all on **Ma Rainey)** — each having piano as sole support. Rainey's humor **(Ma Rainey's Black Bottom** on **Ma Rainey)** contrasts splendidly with the despair of tracks like **Wringin' & Twistin' Blues, Deep Moanin' Blues** and **Daddy, Goodbye Blues**, or the sensuality of **Slow Driving Moan** (all on **Ma Rainey)** — and the classic **Shave 'Em Dry Blues (Ma Rainey, Vol 1)**.

Toured tent-show and theatre circuits during 1920s, fronted own show *Arkansas Swift Foot* in 1930. Latter fell apart whilst Rainey was on the road and she became one of Boise De Legge's 'Bandana Babies' for three years. In 1933, Ma Rainey's sister and mother died, so she retired to Rome, Georgia, where she also ran two theaters. Ma Rainey died in 1939, in the town of her birth and where she had spent the last years of her life. Much interesting background material on Ma Rainey and those she influenced is to be found within *Ma Rainey & The Classic Blues Singers*, by Derrick Stewart-Baxter (see companion record below).

Albums:
Ma Rainey (Milestone)
Ma Rainey, Vols 1-8 (—/Rarities)
Various, Ma Rainey & The Classic Blues Singers (—/CBS)

Jimmy Raney

Born 1927, guitarist Jimmy Raney is a master of that cool brand of bebop that falls halfway between Lester Young and Charlie Christian. An infrequent visitor to the recording studios, his best-known work remains the sides he cut with Stan Getz in 1951 **(At Storyville)**. In the passages of counterpoint with the tenorist and on solos like **Move, Parker 51** and **The Song Is You**, he shows his subtle melodic invention, the unemphatic surface with the muscular strength below.

Collaborations with fellow guitarist Jim Hall have been long out of print but a concert appearance found him playing two-part Bach contentions with his guitarist son, Chuck.

A couple of albums for Don Schlitten's Xanadu label **(Live In Tokyo** and **Influence)** with Sam Jones on bass and either Billy Higgins or Leroy Williams on drums, find the guitarist in great form, rocketing through **Anthropology** and **Cherokee** and producing, in his judgment, his best ever solo on **Darn That Dream**. Another album finds him reunited with ex-Getz pianist, Al Haig, an ideal partner of similar temperament **(Special Brew)**.

Albums:
Stan Getz At Storyville (Prestige/—)
Live In Tokyo (Xanadu/—)
Influence (Xanadu/—)
Special Brew (Spotlite/Spotlite)
Jimmy Raney-Doug Raney, Nardis (Steeplechase)

Dewey Redman

Born Fort Worth, Texas, 1931, tenorist Dewey Redman cut his début album, **Look For The Black Star**, in 1966, which showed him to be one of the more conservative avant-garde players.

In 1968 he joined Ornette Coleman, where his strong regional feeling (both men are from Texas) and his stylistic similarity to Ornette's tenor playing made him a compatible member of that demanding group. Redman takes good solos on several albums **(Ornette At 12, New York Is Now, Love Call, Crisis** and **Science Fiction)**, showing considerable development so that by the time **Trouble In The East** was recorded **(Crisis)** Redman was confident enough to handle the free collective performance. A light-toned player, Redman literally vocalizes through his horn, moaning and exhorting down the mouthpiece in tandem with his playing. Subsequent albums made under his own name invariably work best on blues material; **Lop-O-Lop**, a trio performance with the great Ed Blackwell on drums and Malachi Favors on bass **(Tarik)**; **Boody**, with the great bass support of Sirone **(The Ear Of The Behearer)** and **Qow (Coincide)**. Whooping and moaning, Redman seems to reach all the way back to the field holler. He was also a member of pianist Keith Jarrett's group, along with Charlie Haden on bass and Paul Motian drums, where his taste for exotic instruments — musette, maracas — formed a part of the ensemble texture. Tenor solos like **Rotation** are well controled and close to the orthodox **(Mysteries)** while **Inflight (Backhand)** motors along comparatively evenly over a surging groundswell of percussive effects.

Albums:
Ornette Coleman, Ornette At 12 (Impulse/Impulse)
Ornette Coleman, New York Is Now (Blue Note/Blue Note)
Ornette Coleman, Love Call (Blue Note/Blue Note)
Ornette Coleman, Crisis (Impulse/Impulse)
Ornette Coleman, Science Fiction (Columbia/CBS)
Ornette Coleman, Look For The Black Star (Arista—Freedom/—)
Ornette Coleman, The Ear Of The Behearer (Impulse/Impulse)
Ornette Coleman, Coincide (Impulse/Impulse)
Keith Jarrett, Birth (Atlantic/Atlantic)
Keith Jarrett, El Juicio (Atlantic/Atlantic)
Keith Jarrett, Death & The Flower (Impulse/Impulse)
Keith Jarrett, Mysteries (Impulse/Impulse)
Keith Jarrett, Backhand (Impulse/Impulse)
Keith Jarrett, Shades (Impulse/Impulse)
Tarik (—/Affinity)
The Struggle Continues (ECM/ECM)
Dewey Redman-Ed Blackwell, In Willisau (Black Saint/Black Saint)

Right: Texan tenorist Dewey Redman —his combination of voice and horn comes on like the most down-home Delta blues. He indulged his taste for exotic instruments working with Keith Jarrett.

Don Redman

Arranger Don Redman was the pioneer of big-band jazz and his innovations determined the course of the '30s, establishing the size and relationship of brass, reed and rhythm sections. Even reading techniques followed the Redman pattern, departing from legitimate methods to get that swing.

Born in 1900 in Piedmont, West Virginia, Redman was an infant prodigy, playing cornet, piano, trombone and violin before settling for alto saxophone. He was conservatoire trained, arranging for Billy Paige's band in 1922, and then working for Fletcher Henderson from 1923-27. Aiming at a blend of writing and improvisation, Redman's writing improved as the band's soloists became more flexible but the great leap forward came with the arrival of Louis Armstrong in the ranks in 1924.

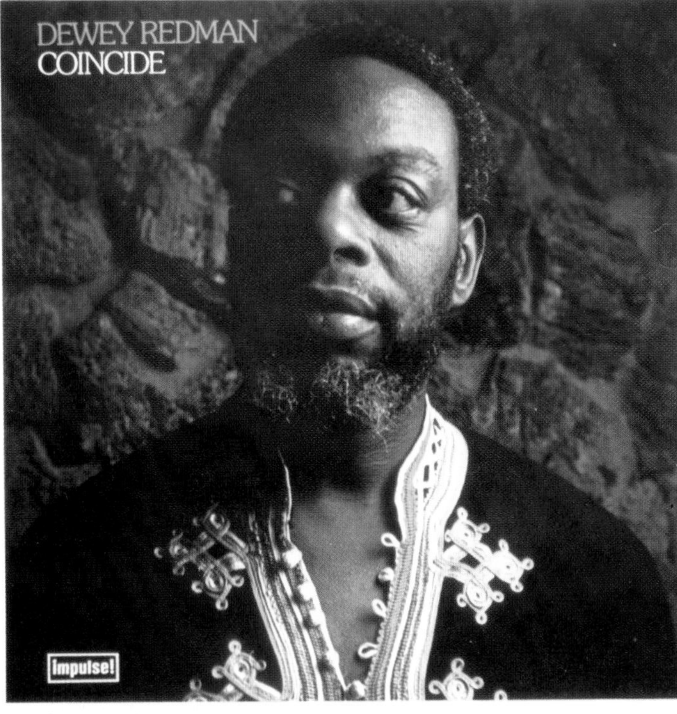

Dewey Redman, Coincide (courtesy Impulse)—the tenorist offers an update of the blues all the way back to the field-holler.

The New Orleans influence was dominant, and a great source of inspiration to Redman in its use of riffs, blues feeling and elastic but precise ensemble playing. **Sugar Foot Stomp**, a re-working of the King Oliver-Louis Armstong classic, **Dippermouth Blues**, features Armstrong over an eleven-man band, as does **Copenhagen (The Fletcher Henderson Story)**, while on **Words** Redman uses sustained chords from the three-man sax section under the trumpet. The pioneering use of saxophones playing together in harmony was a constant feature of Redman's writing, as was the clarinet trio on **Alabamy Bound**.

By 1925, with musicians like trombonist Charlie Green, tenorist Coleman Hawkins and clarinettist Buster Bailey (Armstrong was replaced by Tommy Ladnier in 1926) the Fletcher Henderson band was equal to Redman's increasingly sophisticated use of sectional counterpoint, advanced harmonies and abrupt changes of rhythm. **Henderson Stomp** and **Whiteman Stomp**—also recorded by Paul Whiteman—are very advanced pieces **(Smack** and **The Fletcher Henderson Story)**.

In 1927 Redman left to take over McKinney's Cotton Pickers, a novelty band until he took over the book. He built up the sax section into a formidable unit by the following year, contrasting their sweetness with other voicings in a growing preoccupation with texture. Vocal routines like **If I Could Be With You One Hour, Rocky Road (McKinney's Cotton Pickers)** and **Gee Baby, Ain't I Good To You** brought the band considerable success, which enabled Redman to recruit Joe Smith, Coleman Hawkins and Benny Carter from the Henderson band.

In 1931 he took over the Horace Henderson band. With soloists like trombonist Benny Morton and clarinettist Edward Inge, Redman's first recording session saw the unveiling of masterpieces like **Shakin, The African** and **Chant Of The Weed (Harlem Jazz)**, and some fine arrangements like **Got The Jitters**, while **Sophisticated Lady** gives an example of Redman's clarinet, and **Tea For Two** of his soprano **(Don Redman)**. His use of a swing choir, much imitated, in which the band sing a unison counter-melody to the lyrics, is shown on **Exactly Like You** and **Sunny Side Of The Street. Sweet Sue** is the best of late Redman.

In '33, he orchestrated the Betty Boop cartoon, *I Heard* (including **Chant Of The Weed)**, while interesting film of his '34 band was captured on the Vitaphone short *Don Redman and His Orchestra.*

In 1940 he gave up band-leading to free-lance as an arranger, **Five O'Clock Whistle** for Count Basie, **Deep Purple** for Jimmy Dorsey, and numerous scores for Harry James, Jimmy Lunceford, Charlie Barnet, Ella Fitzgerald and Pearl Bailey. He took a big band overseas on a continental tour immediately after World War II, and briefly directed Jay McShann's band in 1941. Don Redman died in 1964, one of jazz's most influential arrangers.

Albums:
The Fletcher Henderson Story (Columbia/CBS)
Smack (—/Ace of Hearts)
Fletcher Henderson & His Orchestra (—/Fountain)
McKinney's Cotton Pickers (—/RCA Victor—France)
The Chocolate Dandies (—/Parlophone)
Master Of The Big Band (RCA Victor/RCA Victor)
Harlem Jazz (Brunswick/Brunswick)
Don Redman (—/Realm)
Louis Armstrong, V.S.O.P., Vol 5 (Columbia/CBS)
Bessie Smith (Columbia/CBS)

Django Reinhardt

One of jazz's most exotic legends, guitarist Django Reinhardt was the first non-American jazzman of originality.

Born 1910 in a caravan in Belguim, Reinhardt was a gypsy, and his playing was a fusion of jazz and tzigane traditions. Forced to give up the violin after a caravan fire had mutilated his left hand (he retained the effective use of only two fingers) he concentrated on guitar and developed a highly individual technique.

His most famous unit, the all-string Quintet of the Hot Club de France, was founded in 1934 with Reinhardt and violinist Stephane Grappelli improvising over a rhythm section of two guitars and a string bass. Most of the interest centers around Reinhardt's lyrical and baroque contributions, his glittering single-string runs and occasional octave passages. The Quintet broke up in 1939 with the outbreak of war, leaving a legacy of fine recordings **(Django** and **Reindhart-Stephane Grappelli)**.

Between 1935-39, the guitarist recorded with many of America's giants on tour in Europe, including Rex Stewart, Dicky Wells, Coleman Hawkins, Benny Carter, Barney Bigard, Eddie South and Bill Coleman **(Django Reinhardt & His American Friends, Vols 1 & 2)**.

Undeterred by the Occupation, Reinhardt soon recruited a new quintet using a different instrumentation of clarinet and drums along with the second guitar and bass. The leader himself switched to amplified guitar, cutting down on his use of chords. A pair of albums from 1947 reflects the influence of bebop on tracks like **Moppin' The Bride** and **Babik (Django Reinhardt)** though the habitual romanticism is evident on numbers like **Vendredi 13**. His inventiveness at tempo is illustrated by performances like **Lover** or **Apple Honey** which feature him with big bands, or by **Crazy Rhythm** with the reunited Hot Club from 1947 **(Django Reinhardt)**. His best work tended to be at slow tempo, like the melancholy **Nuages** or **Crepuscule (Django Reinhardt)**.

Stories about Django Reinhardt are legion—his obsession with billiards, his obliviousness to time which led him to be late for one Carnegie Hall concert with Duke Ellington in 1946, and to miss the second; his restlessness, inability to read music, lavish spending. He died suddenly in 1953, a standard influence on subsequent guitarists.

Albums:
Django (—/Oriole)
Django Reinhardt-Stephane Grapelly (—/Ace of Clubs)
Django Reinhardt & His American Friends (—/HMV)
Django Reinhardt (Everest/Xtra)
Django Reinhardt (—/DJM)
Django Reinhardt (—/Vogue)

Django Reinhardt (courtesy RCA)—the guitarist's unique enchantment.

Emily Remler

The exceptional guitar technique of Emily Remler has taken her from the category of 'talent deserving wider recognition' in the early '80s to a top place among America's most respected and individual guitar-players.

Born in Manhattan, New York, on September 18, 1957, Remler was raised in Englewood Cliffs by 'totally non-musician' parents. Playing guitar from age 8, her early love of folk music was supplemented by the rock of the Rolling Stones and blues of Jimi Hendrix. She subsequently became intrigued by Ravi Shankar's complex sitar technique and memorized his records. In time, she also added jazz guitarists like Wes Montgomery and Pat Martino to her prime inspirations.

At 18, Remler took a two-year degree course at Berklee College of Music. Moving to New Orleans, she became house guitarist at a local club. In New Orleans, a meeting with Herb Ellis resulted in her guest appearance at the Concord Jazz Festival alongside 'her jazz-guitar heroes' Ellis, Charlie Byrd, Tal Farlow and Barney Kessel.

She returned to New York in '79, working with Nancy Wilson and Astrud Gilberto before recording her highly acclaimed début album as leader for the guitar-oriented Concord label. **Firefly** revealed that Remler could play from the Montgomery tradition **(Movin' Along)** to Ellington **(In A Sentimental Mood)** and post-bop (McCoy Tyner's **Inception**), as well as write lively blues-inspired originals like **Perk's Blues** and **The Firefly**.

An inventive and inspirational player, subsequent Remler albums—**Take Two, Transitions** and **Catwalk**—have combined to confirm her advance as one of the most gifted young guitarists to emerge in the '80s.

In '85, Remler toured in a creative musical duo collaboration with fellow guitarist Larry Coryell. Their contrasting but complementary styles and individual commands of jazz guitar technique are documented on their '85 album **Together**.

Emily Remler, Firefly (courtesy Concord) —the guitarist's solo début.

Albums:

Clayton Brothers, It's All In The Family (Concord/Concord)
Firefly (Concord/Concord)
Take Two (Concord/Concord)
Transitions (Concord/Concord)
Catwalk (Concord/Concord)
Emily Remler-Larry Coryell, Together (Concord/Concord)

Return To Forever

see Chick Corea

Buddy Rich

Born in New York, 1917, drummer Buddy Rich began in vaudeville at the age of 18 months, earning the nickname 'Baby Traps' by the time he was seven.

He worked with the bands of Bunny Berigan, Artie Shaw and Tommy Dorsey, developing into one of the best big-band drummers of the swing period. In 1946, he formed his own big band with financial help from Frank Sinatra, with whom the belligerent drummer had had stormy relations since their Dorsey days.

With the decline of big bands, Rich joined Norman Granz's Jazz At The Phil unit and features on numerous albums from the tours **(Jazz At The Philharmonic, Vol 2)**. The competitive, flamboyant atmosphere suited him well, better than the bebop combo context with Charlie Parker, Dizzy Gillespie, Thelonious Monk and Curley Russell **(The Definitive Charlie Parker, Vol 2)**. A typical Granz session pitted Rich against fellow drummer Gene Krupa, with the bristling Rich grabbing all the honors on **Bernie's Tune, The Drum Battle** and **Perdido (Drum Battle)**.

One of his best albums from the '50s remains the live session with Flip Phillips **(The Monster)** where his drumming combines with Peter Ind's masterly bass to drive the tenorist into some of his best performances. In 1966, Rich returned to fronting his own bands, with excellent arrangements but usually devoid of colorful soloists, apart from Rich. Two albums from 1968 represent the band's best work **(Take It Away** and **Mercy, Mercy)** the second including altoist Art Pepper.

In 1971, Rich signed with RCA and recorded in the jazz-rock vein using an increased rhythm section **(A Different Drummer)**.

In '74, Rich took time off briefly from his big band forming a small group with Sal Nistico, Sonny Fortune, Joe Romano, Jack Wilkins, Kenny Barron and John Bunch to play at his New York club, Buddy's Place.

Returning to big-band life, Rich suffered a serious heart attack in January '83, necessitating open-heart surgery but, after less than two months' convalescence, the irrepressible Rich was back on the road, raring to take his orchestra on a UK tour. In the '80s, his band has toured with the extraordinary tenorist Steve Marcus as a featured front-line soloist and occasionally the band has appeared with the four-piece vocal group Zee which includes Rich's daughter Cathy.

Buddy Rich is a controversial figure. Some rate him as the greatest drummer of all time, others as insensitive and flashy. Technically, he is phenomenal; fast, accurate and endlessly driving.

Below: Emily Remler—inventive and inspirational, she has emerged as one of the most gifted jazz guitarists of her generation.

Albums:

Jazz At The Philharmonic, Vol 2 (Verve/Verve)
The Definitive Charlie Parker, Vol 2 (Verve/Metro)
Drum Battle (Verve/Verve)
The Monster (Verve/Verve)
Take It Away (Liberty/Liberty)
Mercy, Mercy (Liberty/Liberty)
A Different Drummer (RCA/RCA)
Stick It (RCA/RCA)
The Roar Of '74 (Groove Merchant/Mooncrest)
Buddy Rich At Ronnie Scott's (RCA/RCA)
Lionel Hampton Presents Buddy Rich (—/Kingdom Jazz)
Buddy Rich—The Man From Planet Jazz (—/Ronnie Scott Records)

Drum Battle (courtesy Verve): Rich and Krupa, seconds out to Round One...

Lee Ritenour

The instantly recognizable style and sound of Lee Ritenour has elevated him to one of the most distinctive and internationally influential guitarists in jazz fusion. In the mid-1970s, he emerged from unknown super-session musician to become universally acclaimed as 'Captain Fingers'.

Born in Los Angeles on January 11, 1952, Ritenour took up guitar at age 6, although formal studies didn't start until he was 10. His first inspiration was Wes Montgomery and, later, George Benson, B.B. King, John McLaughlin, Howard Roberts, Joe Pass and Barney Kessel. He attended the University of Southern California where he studied classical guitar with Christopher Parkening. He also took a master class with Joe Pass and learned about studio techniques with Howard Roberts.

In '74, he toured Brazil with the Sergio Mendes band and the music of that country was to have an enduring influence on his future compositions and performances. Returning to California, Ritenour became one of Los Angeles' most coveted session guitarists contributing to more than 2000 studio dates for artists like Steely Dan, Herbie Hancock, Stanley Clarke, Flora Purim and Patrice Rushen. His appearance at the Montreux Jazz Festival's Guitar Summit in '74 was to bring him overwhelming international acclaim as a solo performer.

He launched a solo career with Friendship—a superb group including bassist Abraham Laboriel, keyboardist Don Grusin, reeds-player Ernie Watts, drummer Alex Acuna and percussionist Steve Forman. Exceptional albums like **The Captain's Journey, Feel The Night** and **Rit** established his considerable ability as a writer and arranger as well as showcasing the Gibson 335 guitar-style for which Ritenour has became famous.

A joint venture with Dave Grusin in the mid-'80s produced the excellent **Harlequin**, rooted in Brazilian music, and confirmed Ritenour's status as one of contemporary music's master guitarists.

Albums:

First Course (Epic/Epic)
Guitar Player (MCA/MCA)
Captain Fingers (Epic/Epic)
The Captain's Journey (Elektra-Asylum/Elektra-Asylum)
Feel The Night (Elektra-Asylum/Elektra-Asylum)
Friendship (Elektra-Asylum/Elektra-Asylum)
Rit (Elektra-Asylum/Elektra-Asylum)
Rio (Elektra Musician/Elektra Musician)
Rit 2 (Elektra-Asylum/Elektra-Asylum)
On The Line (Elektra Musician/Elektra Musician)
Banded Together (Elektra-Asylum/Elektra-Asylum)
Dave Grusin-Lee Ritenour, Harlequin (GRP/GRP)

Lee Ritenour, Rit (courtesy Elektra-Asylum)—a modern master.

Above: Lee Ritenour—from super-session guitarist to leader of Friendship and creator of one of the most widely imitated styles in modern music.

Below: Multi-instrumentalist Sam Rivers—his Studio Rivbea was to become vital as one of the power-houses of experimental contemporary music.

Sam Rivers

Multi-reeds player Sam Rivers was born in Oklahoma, 1930, of musical parents.

Over the years, Rivers has developed fluency on six instruments; tenor, soprano, bass clarinet, flute, piano and viola, playing the latter at the Boston Conservatory of Music where he studied composition. In Boston he met drummer Anthony Williams who recommended him to Miles Davis, and Rivers went with Miles' group on the Japanese tour in 1964 **(Miles In Tokyo)** but left, finding the atmosphere too conservative.

Together with his tenor replacement, Wayne Shorter, he appeared on Anthony Williams' date **(Spring)** and proved himself to be a dramatically powerful and original soloist; in fact, his work dominates this and the earlier Williams' session **(Life Time)**.

His own albums for Blue Note **(Fuchsia Swing Song, Contours** and **A New Conception)** proclaim the essential logic behind his avant-garde stand. His compositions, like his playing, reflect a sense of jazz's continuing tradition, so that his forays into noise effects and sound clusters are never alien graftings. Unlike many of the Blue Note experimenters, Rivers stayed with it because it was a natural arena for his creativity. A performance like **Dance Of The Tripedal (Contours)** hangs together mainly due to the velocity of attack which effectively dismantles the theme.

As a member of the Jazz Composers Guild, he came to the attention of Cecil Taylor, accompanying him to Europe **(Nuits De La Fondation Maeght)** and subsequently landing a contract with Impulse. At the Montreux Jazz Festival in 1973, Rivers led his trio, Cecil McBee, bass, and Norman Connors, drums, through an astonishing 50 minutes of music **(Streams)** playing tenor, flute, piano and soprano and sustaining the interest throughout the extended work. A collection of short pieces by the trio **(Hues)** was recorded the same year, and a big-band album showcasing his unique writing talents **(Crystals)** followed.

Sam Rivers' development has been consistent, never aridly doctrinaire, always committed. He ran the Studio Rivbea for some years on a policy of open-house for experimentation, and is an established force on the New York scene. In the '80s, this powerful multi-instrumentalist has worked extensively with an extended line-up—Sam Rivers' Winds of Manhattan—which has included young altoist Bobby Watson.

Albums

Miles Davis, Miles In Tokyo (CBS-Sony—Japan)
Anthony Williams, Spring (Blue Note/Blue Note)
Anthony Williams, Life Time (Blue Note/Blue Note)
Fuchsia Swing Song (Blue Note/Blue Note)
Contours (Blue Note/Blue Note)
A New Conception (Blue Note/Blue Note)
Involution (Blue Note/Blue Note)
Cecil Taylor, Nuits De La Fondation Maeght (Shandar/Shandar)
Streams (Impulse/Impulse)
Hues (Impulse/Impulse)
Crystals (Impulse/Impulse)
Sizzle (Impulse/Impulse)
Wildflowers, The New York Loft Sessions (Douglas/—)
Essence (—/Circle Records)
Black Africa (—/Horo)
Dave Holland-Sam Rivers (Improvising Artists Inc/—)
Sam Rivers' Winds Of Manhattan, Colours (Black Saint/Black Saint)

Max Roach

Drummer Max Roach was born in 1925 in New York, and first came to prominence as Charlie Parker's drummer between 1946-48. Extending Kenny Clarke's concept of polyrhythmic accompaniment, Roach carried the beat on the cymbal and used the rest of the trap set for subsidiary rhythms which allowed greater mobility for the soloist. The Parker Savoys and some of the Dials furnish excellent examples of Roach's work **(The Savoy Recordings** and **On Dial, Vol 4)**. Roach has recorded with most modernists of importance, including Thelonious Monk, Dizzy Gillespie and Bud Powell.

In 1954 Roach assembled a classic quintet with the great trumpeter Clifford Brown and Harold Land or Sonny Rollins on tenor. Every album made by this unit represents an unbeatable peak within the hard bop idiom **(The Best Of Max Roach & Clifford Brown In Concert, At Basin Street, Study In Brown, Remember Clifford** and **Dahoud)**. Sonny Rollins' **Valse Hot** was the first modern jazz composition in 3/4 time, and marks the beginning of Roach's interest in metric experiments **(Three Giants)**.

In 1956, Brown and the group's pianist, Richie Powell, were killed in a car crash, and although Roach continued with Kenny Dorham and Ray Bryant, the unit eventually began to drift. Two good albums were produced; **Jazz In 3/4 Time** which includes an up-tempo and superior version of **Valse Hot**; and **Dr Free-Zee**, which is a drum solo supplemented through multi-tracking with tympani **(Max Roach + 4)**.

In 1958, Roach was joined by another phenomenal young trumpeter, Booker Little, whose rhythmic confidence matched his own, and the collaboration produced some excellent albums. Dispensing with the piano, Roach's new instrumentation featured Little, George Coleman, tenor, and Ray Draper on tuba. At the same time, Max Roach's commitment to the growing movement towards racial equality gave a political significance to much of his writing, a fact which goes far in explaining the five-year blacklist from the studios in the '60s.

The first of these albums **(We Insist! Freedom Now Suite)** was the result of a collaboration with songwriter Oscar Brown Jr and features singer Abbey Lincoln. **Driva Man** opens starkly and violently with voice over tambourine, the lyrics describing the brutality of plantation life and giving way to a driving tenor solo by Coleman Hawkins. **Freedom Day** is fast and intense, while **Tears For Johannesburg** has a wordless vocal and a magnificent solo by Booker Little.

Roach's drumming style had undergone major alterations, and in place of the former crowded surface was a heightened and more ascetic style in which bar length was determined by the phrase. The finest album from this period, **Percussion Bitter Sweet**, featured Abbey Lincoln, Little and Eric Dolphy. Roach's playing here is very free and, as shown on **Mendacity**, carefully structured. **Tender Warriors** combines 3/4 and 6/8. Multiple meters and voices combine splendidly on **It's Time**, and an album from 1966, **Drums Unlimited**, has three solo drum tracks which display the breadth and logic of Roach's conception. **In The Red** has the leader playing very freely, and an excellent solo by James Spaulding on alto.

A live album with tenorist Clifford Jordan, **Speak, Brother, Speak**, is one of the most exciting performances of later years. In the early '80s, **Speak Brother, Speak** (recorded in '62) was coupled with **Deeds Not Words** (from '58) and released as the double **Conversations**. In '84, Roach's momentous meeting

Above: Max Roach—indestructible after 40 years, still one of jazz's most influential drummers and an inspiration to a new generation avid to learn from him.

in '79 with pianist Cecil Taylor (at columbia University's McMillin Theater, New York) finally saw the light of day—courtesy of the Italy-based Soul Note Label—as **Historic Concerts**.

The mid-'80s have found Roach taking a variety of paths... writing music for three Sam Shepard plays (*Shepardsets*); working with rap-artists and break-dancers at The Kitchen; providing a score for a TV documentary on Martin Luther King; not to mention an extraordinary and visually fascinating collaboration with video artist Kit Fitzgerald.

In May '86, Roach premiered his Double Quartet—his regular hard-bop cohorts Cecil Bridgewater, Odean Pope and Tyrone Brown combined with the Uptown String Quartet (daughter Maxine Roach, Diane Monroe and Lesa Terry on violins, together with Zela Terry on cello).

A musician who has never stood still, Roach is prepared to move where and when the music, mood and moment take him. Max Roach is among the greatest drummers in modern music; not surprisingly, his style and spirit have been phenomenally instructive and influential.

Albums:

Charlie Parker, The Savoy Recordings (Savoy/Savoy)
Charlie Parket, On Dial, Vol 4 (Spotlite/Spotlite)
The Best Of Max Roach & Clifford Brown in Concert (GNP/—)
At Basin Street (EmArcy/Mercury)
Study In Brown (EmArcy/Mercury)
Remember Clifford (EmArcy/Mercury)
Dahoud (Mainstream/Mainstream)
Sonny Rollins, Three Giants (Prestige/—)
Jazz In 3/4 Time (EmArcy/Mercury)
Maz Roach + 4 (Trip/—)
Deeds Not Words (Riverside/—)
We Insist! Freedom Now Suite (Candid/—)
Percussion Bitter Sweet (Impulse/Impulse)
It's Time (Impulse/Impulse)
Drums Unlimited (Atlantic/Atlantic)
Speak, Brother, Speak (Fantasy/America-France)
Graz 1963 Concert (—/Jazz Connoisseur)
The Loadstar (—/Horo)
Anthony Braxton-Max Roach, Duo (—/Black Saint)
Clifford Brown-Max Roach, Pure Genius Volume One (Elektra Musician/Elektra Musician)
Max Roach Again (—/Affinity)
Conversations (Milestone/Milestone)
Max Roach-Cecil Taylor, Historic Concerts (Soul Note/Soul Note)
Long As You're Living (—/Enja—Germany)
Survivors (Soul Note/Soul Note)
Scott Free (Soul Note/Soul Note)

Speak, Brother, Speak! (courtesy America-France)—the master at work.

Rocket 88

The powerful big-band blues sound of Britain's Rocket 88—with its lively trombone-saxophone front-line—evolved into a popular circuit attraction in the early 1980s.

Formed in '79 as an 'occasional' band, Rocket 88's first line-up included Alexis Korner, Charlie Watts and Jack Bruce (the original Blues Incorporated rhythm section) plus pianists Ian Stewart, Bob Hall and George Green, trombonist John Picard, saxophonists Dick Morrissey and Don Weller, trumpeter Colin Smith and later guitarist Danny Adler.

Ian Stewart's affection for the blues reinforced his determination to perpetuate the music through Rocket 88 (he had named the band after the Jackie Brenston-Ike Turner hit of '51). Stewart put the band on a more permanent footing, subject to his commitments with the Rolling Stones. Stewart had been at the birth of British R&B, working with early Blues Incorporated line-ups and becoming the Stones' pianist. His subsequent backstage role as their tour manager earned him the often uncomfortable sobriquet, the 'Sixth Stone'; as a result, Stewart's contribution as a British R&B pioneer was often underestimated.

With a regular and committed line-up of pianist Stewart, drummer Charlie Watts, trombonists John Picard and Mike Hogh, saxophonists Olaf Vas and Willie Garnett, guitarist Jimmy Roche and bassist-vocalist Roger Sutton, Rocket 88 also called on a float of all-star deps like saxophonist Don Weller, bassist Colin Hodgkinson, and drummers Mickey Waller and Clive Thacker. Favorite Rocket 88 show-stoppers like Sutton's vocal features on *The Outskirts Of Town*, Stewart's *Walkin' & Talkin'*, Roche's searing T-Bone Walker-style guitar solos and Garnett's saxophone *tour de force* on *Willie's Trip* helped make Rocket 88 into a popular festival band nationally.

Ian Stewart's sudden death from a heart attack on December 12, 1985, aged just 47, left the future of Rocket 88 in doubt and robbed British music of an individual pianist and life-long champion of the blues.

Albums:

Rocket 88 (Atlantic/Atlantic)

Red Rodney

Trumpeter Red Rodney—born Robert Chudnick, 1927, Philadephia—worked extensively with the big bands of the '40s, including Jimmy Dorsey, Gene Krupa, Claude Thornhill and Woody Herman. Conversion to bebop led him to association with the other modernists in Herman's Second Herd, most notably with baritonist Serge Chaloff **(Brother & Other Mothers)**.

In 1949, his worship of Charlie Parker was rewarded by an offer to join the quintet. Ross Russell's book, *Bird Lives*, describes how Bird beat the bigots by billing Rodney as Albino Red for a tour of the Southern States. He was an ideal foil for Parker and in his eight-month stay recorded several excellent solos **Si Si, Swedish Schnapps, Back Home Blues (The Definitive Charlie Parker, Vol 5)** and showed the same confidence and attack on the live sessions **(Bird At St Nick's)**.

After Bird, he played with Charlie Ventura but much of the '50s was written off to narcotics problems. In recent years, Rodney has made a convincing comeback, having lost none of his old bubbling vivacity and big sound. While based in Denmark, he cut an excellent album with the Scandinavians, altoist Arne Domnerus and pianist Bengt Hallberg **(Yard's Pad)** with driving trumpet on the title track and **Red Rod** and mutued lyricism on **Informality**. During a British tour, Rodney recorded with the highly compatible Bebop Preservation Society, including altoist Pete King, trumpeter Hank Shaw and Bill Le Sage piano, a session which he declared his easiest and happiest ever **(Red Rodney With The Bebop Preservation Society)**.

In the '80s, Rodney toured internationally in a dynamic partnership with multi-instrumentalist Ira Sullivan (another Parker-inspired musician). Their rewarding quintet collaboration is documented live on the '82 album **Sprint**.

Albums:

Brothers & Other Mothers (Savoy/Savoy)
The Definitive Charlie Parker, Vol 5 (Verve/Metro)
Bird On 52nd Street, Bird At St Nick's (Prestige/Prestige)
Yard's Pad (Sonet/Sonet)
Red Rodney With The Bebop Preservation Society (Spotlite/Spotlite)
Red Rodney-Ira Sullivan, Sprint (Elektra Musician/Elektra Musician)

Red Rodney, Yard's Pad (courtesy Sonet)—driving trumpet.

Shorty Rogers

Born 1924 in Massachusetts as Milton M. Rajonsky, Shorty Rogers worked with Red Norvo and—most significantly—with the big bands of Woody Herman and Stan Kenton as an arranger-composer-trumpeter.

Leading his own groups from '51 in the Los Angeles area, Rogers became the leader of the much-maligned West Coast movement. Critics have found the music rigid, emotionless and over-written but the best of Rogers' work still sounds fresh decades later. His 17-piece big-band boasted men like Art Pepper, Bob Cooper, Jimmy Giuffre, Bud Shank and Shelly Manne and at least four tracks, the stomping **Short Stop**, the tenor-French horn chase **Coop De Graas, Sweetheart Of Sigmund Freud** and the moody **Infinity Promenade** are classics **(Blues Express)**.

The original 10-inch album, **Cool & Crazy**, was a prized collectors' item fetching enormous prices, and the re-release has four extra tracks by a later outfit including Harry Edison. For sheer brass punch, the Rogers trumpet section with Maynard Ferguson screaming an octave above takes some beating.

His small-group work with Giuffre, pianist Peter Jolly, bassist Curtis Counce and the driving drummer, Shelly Manne produced the fine **Not Really The Blues (West Coast Jazz)**.

In complete contrast to all this West Coast 'cool', of interest are some extraordinary, rip-roaring—barn-storming, even—R&B sessions Rogers did in '52 with Bud Shank, Jimmy Giuffre and Gerry Mulligan hiding (perhaps understandably) behind the unlikely name of

'Boots Brown and His Blockbusters'. Superb stuff.

Rogers has been largely inactive since the mid-'60s but in later years, he has frequently toured as a celebrated single and worked with Bud Shank. His UK appearances in the '80s with NYJO have produced some memorable music and performances. Rogers remains one of the great originals.

Albums:
Blues Express (RCA—France)
West Coast Jazz (Atlantic/Atlantic)
Clickin' With Clax (Atlantic/Atlantic)
Jam Session No 100 (Jam Session/—)
Shorty Rogers-Bud Shank-Vic Lewis, Back Again (Concept/—)
Shorty Rogers-Bud Shank, Yesterday, Today And Forever (Concord/Concord)

Cool And Crazy (courtesy HMV), Shorty Rogers and his Orchestra featuring the Giants—a big-band classic which still sounds fresh.

Adrian Rollini

Adrian Rollini (born New York City, 1904) was one of the most in-demand musicians during 1920s-'30s—not surprising, as he was an immensely gifted multi-instrumentalist, who could produce superior solos on bass sax, vibraphone, xylophone, piano, drums, as well as two instruments he devised himself; a 'hot fountain pen' (miniature clarinet) and goofus (adapted from harmonica). Brother of saxist-clarinettist Arthur Rollini, Adrian Rollini was a child prodigy on piano, giving Chopin recital at four, at Waldorf-Astoria, New York.

First professional work, in 1921, was playing xylophone in a New York club. Joined California Ramblers, switching to bass sax. Used this instrument in most intelligent fashion within ensembles of a variety of bands with which he was associated, from California Ramblers until he gave up playing bass sax during 1930s. He became the only jazz musician to master this cumbersome instrument and convert it into a convincing solo voice. Made notable solo contributions to recordings by Miff Mole **(Thesaurus Of Classic Jazz, Vol 2)**; Red Nichols **(Red Nichols & His Five Pennies 1926-1928)**; Bix Beiderbecke **(The Golden Days of Jazz; Bix Beiderbecke** and **The Early BG)**; Jack Purvis **(Recordings Made Between 1930 & 1941)**; and a myriad of recordings featuring Joe Venuti or Venuti and Eddie Lang and others. With Nichols, Rollini, mostly on bass sax, was the driving force behind recording band Goofus Five **(The Goofus Five 1925-1926)** which produced charming, if lightweight, chamber-style jazz of the period.

Rollini was an average vibes player, accomplished technically, but rhythmically rather stilted. **Vibraphonia (Benny Goodman & The Giants Of Swing/Jazz In The Thirties)** and **Vibraphonia No 2 (Nothing But Not s)** give adequate definitions of his style on this instrument. An average piano soloist, Rollini was an even better drummer, his crisp, tasteful brushwork on recordings by Freddie Jenkins and Bernard Addison **(Adrian Rollini & His Friends, Vol 1: 'Tap Room Special')** being most impressive. Rollini managed to attract the interest of some of the best musicians available for his own record sessions, including Benny Goodman, Bunny Berigan, and brother Arthur, all of whom worked in studio under his leadership during 1933-34 **(Adrian Rollini & His Orchestra 1933-34)**. Even better were recordings by Adrian's Tap Room Gang (musically documenting own club he organized in 1935 at Hotel President, New York).

Moved to Florida in '50s, opening own hotel. Last-known job as musician was in Miami, in 1955. Died Homestead, Florida, 1956.

Albums:
Miff Mole, Thesaurus Of Jazz, Vol 2 (Columbia/Philips)
Red Nichols & His Five Pennies 1926-1928 (MCA Coral—Germany)
The Golden Days Of Jazz: Bix Beiderbecke (CBS—Germany)
The Golden Days Of Jazz: Eddie Lang-Joe Venuti (CBS)
Benny Goodman, The Early B.G. (—/Vocalion)
Coleman Hawkins/Jack Purvis, Recordings Made Between 1930 & 1941 (CBS—France)
Various (Including Joe Venuti/Adrian Rollini), Benny Goodman & The Giants Of Swing (Prestige)/Jazz In The Thirties (World Records)
The Goofus Five 1925-1926 (—/Parlophone)
Joe Venuti, Nothing But Notes (MCA Coral—Germany)
Adrian Rollini & His Friends, Vol 1: 'Tap Room Special' (RCA Victor—France)
Adrian Rollini & His Orchestra 1933-34 (Sunbeam/—)

Adrian Rollini & Friends: Tap Room Special (courtesy RCA Victor-France).

Sonny Rollins

Tenorist Sonny Rollins was born in New York, 1930, of a musical family. Coleman Hawkins was his first influence, although most of his direct acquaintances in the neighborhood, Thelonious Monk, Bud Powell, Jackie McLean, were beboppers.

His earliest recorded gigs were with scat-singer Babs Gonzales **(Strictly Bebop)** and the Bud Powell-Fats Navarro combo **(The Amazing Bud Powell)**, both from 1949 and revealing a strong Parker influence, ambitious but beset by technical lapses. Most of his pre-1954 work is like this, daring, driving, but the grand conception just out of reach. Early Rollins can be found in company with Miles Davis and Charlie Parker **(Collector's Items)** and on **Vierd Blues** he shows that his method of improvising was strongly based on thematic material, rather than merely running the chord changes.

With the release of a 1954 album **(Moving Out)** Rollins gives notice of his arrival in the major league, charging through numbers like **Swinging For Bumsy** and **Solid** with massive confidence and vigor. Between 1956-57, he worked in the Max Roach-Clifford Brown unit, rising to the challenge of Roach's front-line drumming and unusual time signatures like the waltz-time **Valse Hot (3 Giants)**.

The fertile relationship with the drummer continued throughout Rollins' next albums, including his masterpiece **Saxophone Colossus**. Here, the tenorist's sense of architecture produced the great **Blue 7**, his improvised structure as formally perfect as a composition, yet losing none of the heat and immediacy of the moment. His tonal strength, muscular, declamatory, bites like an axe on a frosty morning and his rhythmic mastery on his own calypso, **St Thomas**, is swaggeringly evident. Musicologist Gunther Schüller's analysis of the **Blue 7** performance probed so deeply into Rollins' creative processes that he vowed never to read the critics again.

His output throughout 1957-58 showed that **Saxophone Colossus** had not been a fluke and even a trio session with unfamiliar musicians on the West Coast, bassist Ray Brown and drummer Shelly Manne **(Way Out West)**, resulted in the magnificent **Come Gone** as well as demonstrating Rollins' penchant for odd material in **Wagon Wheels** and **I'm An Old Cowhand**.

A session with drummer Philly Jo Jones produced the incredible tenor-drums duo version of **The Surrey With The Fringe On Top (Newk's Time)** while a completely solo **Body & Soul** was intended as a homage to Coleman Hawkins who had cut the definitive version in 1939 **(Meets The Big Brass)**.

Various sessions with Thelonious Monk **(Brilliance** and **Sonny Rollins, Vol 2)** showed the similarity of approach in structure. A live session with a trio, including the polyrhythmic drumming of Elvin Jones—subsequently Coltrane's partner—caught the tenorist in peak form on numbers like **Sonnymoon For Two (Live At The Village Vanguard** and **More From The Vanguard)**.

In 1958 Rollins produced an extended composition of nineteen minutes, with a dedication to the cause of Afro-American equality **(The Freedom Suite)**, one of the earliest instances of the politico-musical statement that was to explode so forcefully in the '60s. Clearly a hot potato, for the record company deleted the dedication and re-issued it as **The Shadow Waltz**, the title of a short, noodling track on the

Way Out West (courtesy Contemporary): East Coast meets West in a masterpiece—Rollins as the original urban cowboy.

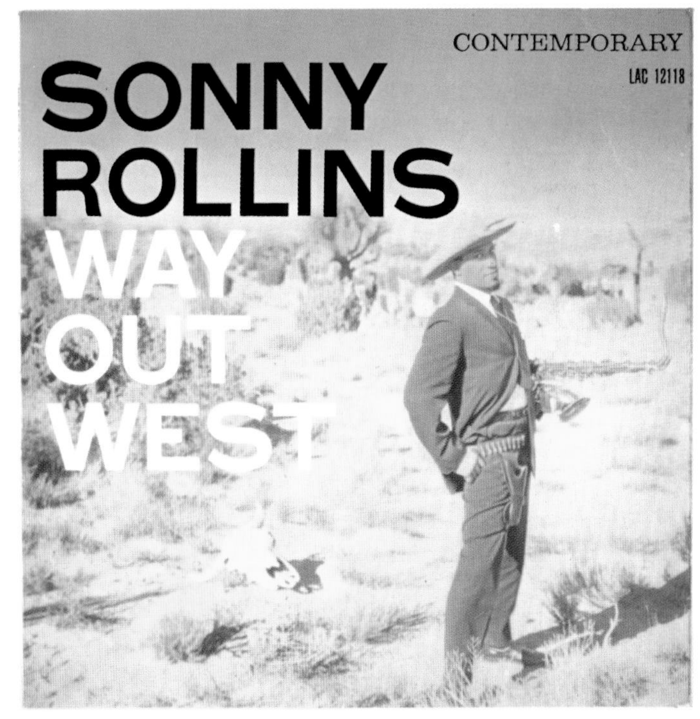

reverse. There are superb performances by Rollins, bassist Oscar Pettiford and Max Roach, the interaction of the trio an outstanding feature.

In 1959, established as a jazz master, Rollins retired from public performance for two years. He needed time to re-think his playing in the light of new developments pioneered by John Coltrane, Ornette Coleman and Cecil Taylor, and he needed time to develop himself spiritually. A fan reported that Rollins had been seen playing high on the catwalk over the East River on the Williamsburg Bridge, and indeed his first album following the sabbatical takes its name from these al fresco sessions **(The Bridge)**. Rollins stated that he made the album because he needed the money for dental work but the partnership with guitarist Jim Hall resulted in fine music, though little different from the pre-retirement period.

The next album, apart from a couple of jolly bossa nova numbers, **Don't Stop The Carnival, Brownskin Girl**, does show some startling developments in tonal manipulation on **Jungoso** with the tenorist stuttering out the components of the theme in shifting accents, clipping notes, slurring, honking and sustaining notes for bar upon bar as he alters the pitching **(What's New)**.

The long-awaited meeting with the New Thing occurred on his next album **(Our Man In Jazz)** with Don Cherry, bassist Bob Cranshaw and drummer Billy Higgins. Performances like **Oleo** illustrate that the great tenorist had a good deal in common with the younger musicians, for he had never belonged to the hard bop orthodoxy and many of his innovations—the tonal distortions, freedom from harmonic restriction, concern with sound as an expressive force—foreshadowed their revolution.

His experiments continued throughout the '60s. Rollins moved around as he played, angling his horn at the walls and ceiling, probing the environment for resonances. He worked out of doors, playing to streams and bluebell woods, and it came as a surprise to discover that he had recorded the soundtrack for that secular movie, *Alfie*.

Three Little Words (On Impulse), Four (Now's The Time) and **Blessing In Disguise (East Broadway Rundown)** show that the master was still at the height of his powers, though the oddly inconclusive treatment of **East Broadway Rundown** indicates deep-seated problems, and following this, he once again retired, this time for five years.

His output since his return has shown all his old supremacy of the tenor but less of that intensity of spirit that characterized his work in the late '50s. His series of albums for Milestone is mainly very good; full of charging elation and beautifully played ballads like **To A Wild Rose (The Cutting Edge)** or **Skylark**, while **Poinciana** showcases his soprano sax **(Next Album)**. Performances like **Playin' In The Yard** or **Swing Low, Sweet Chariot** with Rufus Harley on bagpipes are high-calibre funk **(Next Album** and **The Cutting Edge)** and subsequent releases show Rollins finding energy in electric soulbeat contexts **(Nucleus** and **The Way I Feel)**.

In later years, Rollins has preferred to produce his own recorded output, assisted by his wife Lucille. After a period of experimentation with electronic gadgets, like the lyricon, Rollins returned to tenor sax—the instrument on which he has become one of jazz's most celebrated voices. Frans Boelen's excellent, if all-too-short, film *Sonny Rollins Live At Laren* captured treasured footage of the tenorist in peak performance in the '70s at a Dutch jazz festival. In the '80s, Rollins found an eager audience on college campuses in the States while making infrequent appearances at clubs.

Rollins' latter-day burst of creativity included a widely-publicized European tour in '85. He was welcomed like a lost legend, performing with a band which included ex-Weather Report bassist Victor Bailey, keyboardist Mark Soskin, drummer Tommy Campbell and much-vaunted guitarist Bobby Broom. The tour coincided with the release of **Sunny Days—Starry Nights**, a new album for Milestone, hailed as his best for a decade.

Ablums:
Strictly Bebop (Capitol/Capitol)
The Amazing Bud Powell
(Blue Note/Blue Note)
Miles Davis, Collector's Items
(Prestige/Prestige)
Moving Out (Prestige/—)
Sonny Rollins (Prestige/Prestige)
3 Giants (Prestige/—)
Saxophone Colossus (Prestige/Prestige)
Way Out West (Contemporary/Boplicity)
Newk's Time (Blue Note/Blue Note)
Sonny Rollins, Vols 1 & 2
(Blue Note/Blue Note)
Live At The Village Vanguard
(Blue Note/Blue Note)
More From The Vanguard
(Blue Note/Blue Note)
Meets The Big Brass (MGM/—)
Thelonious Monk, Brilliance
(Milestone/Milestone)
The Freedom Suite (Milestone/Milestone)
The Bridge (RCA/RCA)
What's New (RCA/RCA)
Our Man In Jazz (RCA/RCA)
On Impulse (Impulse/Jasmine)
Now's The Time (RCA/RCA)
East Broadway Rundown (Impulse/Impulse)
Alfie (Impulse/Impulse)
Next Album (Milestone/Milestone)
Horn Culture (Milestone/Milestone)
The Cutting Edge (Milestone/Milestone)
Nucleus (Milestone/Milestone)
The Way I Feel (Milestone/Milestone)
Stuttgart 1963 Concert (—/Jazz Connoisseur)
Graz 1963 Concert (—/Jazz Connoisseur)
Don't Stop The Carnival (Milestone/—)
Sonny Rollins Brass (Verve/Verve)
St Thomas—In Stockholm 1959
(—/Dragon—Sweden)
Don't Ask (Milestone/Milestone)
No Problem (Milestone/Milestone)
Love At First Sight (Milestone/Milestone)
Sunny Days—Starry Nights
(Milestone/Milestone)

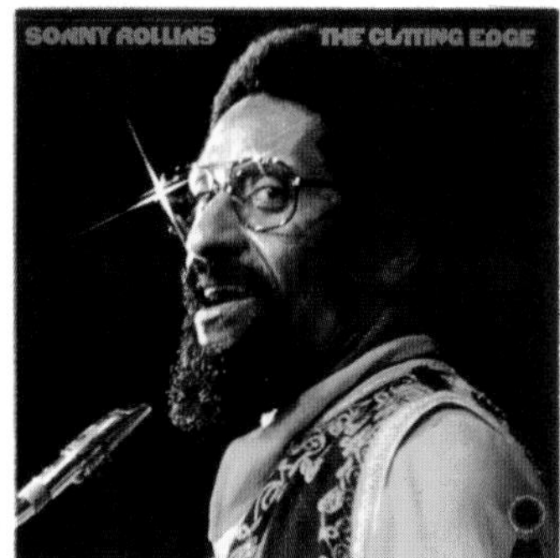

Sonny Rollins, The Cutting Edge (courtesy Milestone).

Annie Ross

British-born singer, songwriter and vocalese pioneer Annie Ross was born in Surrey, England, on July 25, 1930. She went to Los Angeles at the age of 3 where she was raised by her aunt, Ella Logan. In the '40s she began her acting career and subsequently studied dramatic art in New York before returning to England for a while.

ence, working with Lionel Hampton and Jack Parnell in the '50s. Most usually associated with vocalese (fitting words to a jazz musician's solo, a technique pioneered by King Pleasure), Annie Ross recorded her interpretations of tenorist Wardell Gray's **Twisted** and **Farmer's Market** in 1952 **(Annie Ross Sings)**.

As part of the vocal trio Lambert Hendricks & Ross, she appears on a couple of albums devoted to the Count Basie classics. The first of these **(Sing A Song Of Basie)** uses multi-taping to reproduce the sound of the entire band, with Miss Ross covering the trumpet section. Her version of Buck Clayton's **Fiesta In Blue** solo or **One O'Clock Jump** are gymnastic in the extreme, and later versions of **Jumpin' At The Woodside, Let Me See** and **Swingin' The Blues** show her phenomenal range and control **(Sing Along With Basie)**.

Returning to England again, she concentrated on stage revues and cabaret and found herself in demand as an actress, especially on television. In '81, she contributed magnificent vocal work **(Hong Kong Blues, My Resistance Is Low** being particularly memorable) to Georgie Fame's excellent **In Hoagland 1981**. Instigated by Fame as an affectionate and respectful tribute to Hoagy Carmichael for his 81st birthday, the project also included a strong line-up of British luminaries including altoist Pete King, tenorist Dick Morrissey, trumpeter Ian Hamer, trombonist Chris Pyne and keyboardist Geoff Castle, with superb arrangements by Fame and Harry South.

In '84, Ross returned to New York, finally moving back to Los Angeles in '86 with the intention of singing occasionally while continuing her acting career.

Album:
Annie Ross Sings (Prestige/—)
Lambert Hendricks & Ross, Sing A Song Of Basie (Impulse/HMV)
Lambert Hendricks & Ross, Sing Along With Basie (Impulse/HMV)
Lambert Hendricks & Ross, The Swingers (Pacific Jazz/Affinity)
Georgie Fame, In Hoagland 1981
(—/Bald Eagle)

Roswell Rudd

One of the finest trombonists of the New Thing, Roswell Rudd reintroduced many of the tonal qualities of that instrument which had been sacrificed for mobility during the bebop period. Rudd's early background in Dixieland with Eddie Condon and subsequent move into the avant-garde meant that he bypassed the pervading J.J. Johnson influence, playing, as one critic remarked, 'tailgate on a spaceship'.

With the short-lived New York Art Quartet, which he co-led with altoist John Tchichai **(New York Art Quartet** and **Mohawk)**, all his characteristic brass, vocalized efforts are deployed in the interplay with the jagged, angular alto. **Rosmosis,** his finest performance with the group, utilizes plunger mute and long slurring lines that recall both the traditional blues and free music. With Milford Graves on drums, the music interweaves in a loose counterpoint, free yet disciplined.

A period with tenorist Archie Shepp followed, starting with a sextet **(Four For Trane)**. Subsequent albums **(Live In San Francisco** and **Three For A Quarter, One For A Dime)** gave more space to Rudd as a soloist and in duet with the leader, their declamatory styles well suited. Shepp's interest in brass bands led to performances like **King Cotton (Mama Too Tight)** and textures for Rudd's trombone and Howard Johnson's tuba. **One For The Trane (Live At The Donaueschingen Festival)** added a second trombone, Grachan Moncur III.

Rudd's finest work is found on **Communications No. 10 (The Jazz Composers Orchestra)** where Michael Mantler's writing and Rudd's explosive, emotional playing reached a classic peak. Rudd's own album with the JCOA **(Numatik Swing Band)** shows his concern for textures, French horns rising over drum beat, piano and basses in unison, the scampering piccolo. Rudd himself plays well but the star of the session is drummer Beaver Harris, tirelessly inventive.

Albums:
New York Art Quartet (ESP/ESP)
Mohawk (—/Fontana)
Archie Shepp: Four For Trane
(Impulse/Impulse)
Live In San Francisco (Impulse/Impulse)
Three For A Quarter, One For A Dime
(Impulse/Impulse)
Mama Too Tight (Impulse/Impulse)
Live At The Donaueschingen Festival
(BASF/Saba)
The Jazz Composers Orchestra
(JCOA/JCOA—Virgin)
Numatik Swing Band
(JCOA/JCOA—Virgin)
The New Village On The Left (—/Black Saint)
Trickles (—/Black Saint)

Right: Roswell Rudd, the trombonist who moved the instrument away from glibness and back-line brass section truculence.

Patrice Rushen

The multi-talented Patrice Rushen—keyboardist, vocalist, composer, arranger and producer—was one of the first women instrumentalists to receive major recognitiion in the late '70s fusion field. While her, admittedly, exceptional vocal performance has tended to dominate her later career, Rushen's ability as a fine jazz pianist—featured in some of her earlier work—has suffered from under-exposure.

Born in Los Angeles on September 30, 1954, Rushen's musical talent showed up unusually early and as young as 3, she attended a program for young gifted children at the University of Southern California. By the time she was 10, she was able to write out her own compositions (earlier work, composed before she had learned to notate, was transcribed from tapes which her parents had the foresight to record). By junior high school, she had also become proficient on flute. She majored at USC in music education and studied orchestration privately with Dr Albert Harris.

One of her first professional appearances was in her early teens with trombonist Melba Liston's orchestra, subsequently working with Abbey Lincoln and Hubert Laws. As a session musician, she also appears with Jean-Luc Ponty **(Upon The Wings Of Music),** Flora Purim **(Nothing Will Be As It Was... Tomorrow)**, Harvey Mason **(Earth Mover)**, Donald Byrd **(Caricatures)**, Sonny Rollins **(That's The Way I Feel)**, Eddie Henderson **(Heritage),** and John McLaughlin **(Electric Guitarist)**.

Before she was 20, Rushen had established a successful solo career with albums like **Preclusion, Before The Dawn** and **Shout It Out**. Several of Rushen's albums found her providing most of the instrumental input, including some of the bass-playing parts. The inspiration of Bill Evans is clearly evident in her straight-ahead acoustic piano-playing although this, regrettably, has taken second place to her featured vocals and electric keyboard.

Albums:
Preclusion (Prestige/Prestige)
Before The Dawn (Prestige/Prestige)
Shout It Out (Elektra/Elektra)
Patrice (Elektra/Elektra)
Pizzazz (Elektra/Elektra)
Posh (Elektra/Elektra)
Now (Elektra/Elektra)

Multi-instrumentalist Patrice Rushen, Now (courtesy Elektra). Featured vocals obscure a fine jazz talent.

Jimmy Rushing

James Andrew 'Jimmy' Rushing (born Oklahoma City, Oklahoma, 1903) was, together with Joe Turner and Jimmy Witherspoon, probably the finest of the urban blues 'shouters'.

Rushing began to make a name with Walter Page's Blue Devils (1927). But it was with the orchestra of Bennie Morten that he grew in stature. Remained with Morten 1929-35. His earliest recordings with Moten show a not yet fully developed singer, although Rushing sings well on average-to-good material.

On Moten's death, in 1935, Rushing sang briefly with brother Buster Moten, before joining newly formed Count Basie band in Kansas City (1935). Was to remain as Basie's principal singer until 1948. During his long tenure with Basie, Rushing was involved with some of the band's most popular items. Included in lengthy list are the following: **Sent For You Yesterday & Here You Come Today, Good Morning Blues, Blues In The Dark, The Blues I Like To Hear, Do You Wanna Jump Children?, Don't You Miss Your Baby, Evil Blues** (all **Blues I Love To Sing**); **Harvard Blues, Take Me Back, Baby, Blues (I Still Think Of Her), Nobody Knows, How Long Blues** (all **Blues By Basie**); and **Jimmy's Blues, Rusty Dusty Blues (Basie's Best)**.

From 1948 worked as solo act. Put together own septet to accompany him on gigs and for touring purposes: Rushing with former colleagues comprising most famous of all Basie rhythm sections; Freddie Green, Walter Page, Jo Jones.

His third album, dating from late-1956 **(The Odyssey Of James Rushing, Esq)** sustained the high level of its predecessors with more fine singing and playing, particularly from Tate, again, and two other Basie alumni, Buck Clayton, Vic Dickenson.

Visited Europe in 1957, same year as he was reunited with Basie band (plus former colleagues Young, Illinois Jacquet, Jones) for rousing reworkings of old Basie-Rushing favorites at Newport Jazz Festival **(The Newport Years, Vol 6)**. Worked with Benny Goodman at Brussels World Fair ('58), and back for more extensive European tour with Clayton All Stars following year.

Final album date was, vocally, both excellent and sad in equal proportions. Rarely has Rushing evinced the kind of poignancy which permeates **The You & Me That Used To Be** but, sadly, the seemingly indestructible vocal cords could not reproduce another of jazz's inimitable sounds anywhere near as emphatically as before. Same year—1971—suffered heart attack, and in June 1972, James Rushing, Esq, died in Flower Fifth Avenue Hospital, NYC, of leukemia.

Albums:
Bennie Moten's Kansas City Orchestra: 'New Moten Stomp', Vol 4 (1929-1930) (RCA Victor—France)
Bennie Moten's Kansas City Orchestra: 'Moten's Swing', Vol 5 (1929-1932) (RCA Victor—France)
Jimmy Rushing/Count Basie, The Blues I Like To Sing (Decca/Ace of Hearts)
Count Basie, Blues By Basie (Columbia/Philips)
Count Basie, Basie's Best (CBS—France)
Count Basie, Basie Live (Trip/DJM)
Going To Chicago (Vanguard)/Listen To The Blues (Vanguard)/The Essential Jimmy Rushing (Vogue)
The Odyssey Of James Rushing, Esq (Columbia/Philips)
Count Basie, The Newport Years, Vol 6 (Verve/—)
Five Feet of Soul (Colpix/Pye)

Below: Singer Jimmy Rushing—'Mr Five By Five'—one of the finest of the urban blues-shouters and a forceful feature with the Basie band.

Who Was It Sang That Song?
(Master Jazz Recordings/—)
The You & Me That Used To Be
(RCA Victor/RCA Victor)
Little Jimmy Rushing And The Big Brass
(Columbia/CBS)

Jimmy Rushing, Blues I Love To Sing (courtesy Ace of Hearts).

George Russell

Composer-pianist George Russell has a formidable reuptation as a theorist, based on his massive work, *The Lydian Chromatic Concept of Tonal Organization*, which was published in 1953. Devising a system of shifting key centers, Russell's theory extends the innovations of bebop rather than by-passing them, as with the New Thing.

Born 1923, the son of a music professor, Russell started out as a drummer with Benny Carter, even being offered a gig with Charlie Parker which he turned down through ill health. Early compositions like **Cubano Be, Cupano Bop** for the Dizzy Gillespie Big Band **(The Greatest Of Dizzy Gillespie)** and **Ezz-thetic** and **Odjenar**, recorded by Lee Konitz **(Ezz-thetic!)** established him in the avant-garde of his contemporaries, and a piece like **A Bird In Igor's Yard** which combined the concepts of Parker and Stravinsky, was so far ahead that it waited years for release **(Crosscurrents)**.

A brilliant album from 1956, **The Jazz Workshop**, gives an idea of the breadth of his vision, particularly in the dazzling **Round Johnny Rondo**. A later album from 1960, **Jazz In The Space Age**, uses a larger ensemble, including piano duets by Paul Bley and Bill Evans. At the same time, Russell established his own working unit with ex-students of his, including Dave Baker, trombone and Don Ellis, trumpet. A compilation of his early **Riversides (Outer Thoughts)** also includes Eric Dolphy, outstanding on Thelonious Monk's **Round Midnight**, and singer Sheila Jordan on the classic arrangement of **You Are My Sunshine**. Russell left for Scandinavia in the mid-'60s and experimented with electronic music **(Living Time** and **Sonata For Souls)**.

In '69, Russell returned to America to teach at the New England Conservatory in Cambridge, Massachusetts. From '72-'79, he stopped composing to produce the second volume of his *Lydian Chromatic Concept* theory. During this period his **Listen To The Silence** ('a mass for our times') was recorded in Kongsberg Church, Norway, in June '71 (although not released until '83). In '78, he assembled his sensational New York Big Band **(New York Big Band)**, a unit revived in the '80s on his expansive **Live In An American Time Spiral**.

In '83, Russell's impressionistic tone-poem on the evolution of humanity in the African cradle **(The African Game)** was recorded with a 26-piece orchestra in Boston's Emmanuel Church and released as one of the first issues of the reactivated Blue Note label.

Above: The outstanding composer-pianist George Russell, creator of 'The Lydian Chromatic Concept of Tonal Organization'—ahead of this time since the 1940s.

Scaling down to a 13-piece, Russell's Living Time Orchestra toured widely. In '86, Russell made his first tour of Britain with a 14-piece Anglo-American orchestra (including American drummer Keith Copeland plus British luminaries trumpeter Kenny Wheeler, saxophonists Chris Biscoe and Courtney Pine, and pianist Django Bates).

Russell's work grows ever more inspiring—his *Vertical Form* rhythmic concept has become a focal point of his later works.

Albums:
The Greatest Of Dizzy Gillespie (RCA/RCA)
Ezz-thetic! (Prestige/—)
Lennie Tristano-Buddy De Franco, Crosscurrents (Capitol/Capitol)
Jazz In The Space Age (MCA/—)
Live At Beethoven Hall (BASF/BASF)
Outer Thoughts (Milestone/Milestone)
Living Time (Columbia/CBS)
Electronic Sonata For Souls Loved By Nature (Strata-East/—)
Listen To The Silence (Soul Note/Soul Note)
New York Big Band (Soul Note/Soul Note)
Live In An American Time Spiral (Soul Note/Soul Note)
The African Game (Blue Note/Blue Note)

George Russell, Live In An American Time Spiral (courtesy Soul Note).

Pee Wee Russell

Charles Ellsworth 'Pee Wee' Russell (born St Louis, Missouri, 1906) had a way of playing clarinet which was unique. The croaky, strangulated tone which was Russell's had a kind of slightly abrasive beauty enhanced by his ability to communicate deep emotion, particularly when playing blues. Russell's technique, although influenced in part by Frank Teschemacher and Johnny Dodds, bore no resemblance to that of any other jazz clarinettist.

For most of his playing career—starting with Perkins Brothers Band, near Muskogee, before 1920, and ending with his death in Alexandria, Virginia, in 1969—Russell was more or less pigeon-holed as a typical member of the white Dixieland school of jazz

From early-1930s right up until his last years, he worked with the likes of Bud Freeman **(Home Cooking** and **Chicagoans In New York)**; Georg Brunis **(The Davison-Brunis Sessions, Vol 1** and **Trombone Scene)** and, especially, the ubiquitous Eddie Condon **(Commodore Condon, Vol 1** and **The Commodore Years)**. And Russell was a 'regular' at Condon's renowned World War II organized jam sessions **(The Eddie Condon Concerts: Town Hall 1944-45 Featuring Pee Wee Russell** and **The Eddie Condon Concerts, Vol 2)**.

Pee Wee Russell's playing tended to be at its most interesting outside a basic two-beat setting, although the clarinet legend seemed unusually subdued as guest in a typical Teddy Wilson all-star date for **Don't Be That Way** in '38 **(Teddy Wilson & His All Stars)**.

Late in his career, 1962, he was persuaded, temporarily at least, to give the old Dixie warhorses a rest and tackle 'foreign' material: John Coltrane's **Red Planet,** Thelonious Monk's **Round Midnight** and Tadd Dameron's **Good Bait,** could be said to have been successful **(New Groove)**. Certainly, the more contemporary bass-drums rhythm section seemed to help give his playing a lift. (Far from being successful, though, were the record dates which matched Russell's delightful eccentricities with Monk's equally individualistic approach and Jimmy Guiffre's strictly academic clarinet playing.)

Apart from the Condon Town Hall concerts, the clarinettist seemed sublimely happy throughout **(Jam Session At Commodore, Condon A La Carte** and **Chicago & All That Jazz!)**. With superb support from Jess Stacy, quartet of 1944 tracks recorded by Russell's Hot Four **(Swingin' Clarinets)** contain playing by the leader that he rarely produced, before or later, including exquisite blues-playing on his own **D.A. Blues**.

Russell's early career was as colorful as his clarinet playing. After taking lessons on violin, piano and drums, did likewise with clarinet. After introduction to music business, worked for a short time on Arkansas riverboat. Enroled at Western Military Academy, Alton, Illinois (1920-21), also attended University of Missouri. Played with a bewildering variety of bands during early-1920s, including work with legendary pianist Peck Kelley, in Houston. With Frankie Trumbauer Orchestra in St. Louis, in 1925, and after working with Jean Goldkette, joined Red Nichols. Recorded with Nichols' variously titled bands, including **The Charleston Chasers 1925-1928** and **Red Nichols & His Five Pennies 1926-1928** and Louisiana Rhythm Kings **('JT')**.

Made superb contribution to 1929 recording by Mound City Blue Blowers of **If I Could Be With You One Hour Tonight (Body & Soul)** and his clarinet is at its most biting and exciting during the semi-legendary '32 recordings under singer Billy Banks' name **(Billy Banks & His Rhythm-makers)** during which he also provided that he was a tenor saxophonist of limited capabilities. During 1930s, he continued to work in all manner of settings (often in company with Bobby Hackett, with nationwide exposure as member of trumpeter Louis Prima's combo (1935-37).

Played with Bud Freeman's Summa Cum Laude Orchestra, also with Bobby Hackett big band, then became more or less regular at Nick's, NYC. Worked reguarly during World War II, member of Condon band of '46, and for the rest of 1940s spent most of his playing time either in New York or Chicago.

Major operation end of 1950, after moving to San Francisco earlier that year. Back in New York in 1951, playing irregularly until 1951-52. Resident at Eddie Condon Club (1955-56). During late-1950s and through 1960s, played major jazz festivals, toured Europe with Newport All Stars (1961) **(Midnight In Paris)** then fronted clarinet-valve trombone-bass-drums quartet which recorded the **New Groove** album and played gigs in UK and Canada. To Australasia and Japan in 1964 with Condon and Britain in different setting same year. Topped bill at special 1968 New York concert, at Town Hall.

Several times Pee Wee Russell was called 'The Poet of the Clarinet'. There seems no better epitaph to his uniqueness. Pee Wee Russell died in 1969.

Albums:
The Bix Beiderbecke Legend (RCA Victor—France)
The Charleston Chasers (1925-1928) (—/VJM)
Red Nichols & His Five Pennies (1926-1928) (MCA Coral—Germany)
Coleman Hawkins (Including Mound City Blue Blowers) Body & Soul (RCA Victor/—)
Jack Teagarden (Including Red Nichols), 'JT' (Ace of Hearts)
Billy Banks & His Rhythm-makers (CBS-Realm)
Bud Freeman, Home Cooking (Tax—Sweden)

Bud Freeman, Chicagoans In New York (Dawn Club/—)
The Davison-Brunis Sessions, Vol 1 (—/London)
Various (Including Georg Brunis), Trombone Scene (—/London)
Eddie Condon/Bud Freeman, The Commodore Years (Atlantic/—)
Eddie Condon, Commodore Condon, Vol 1 (—/London)
The Eddie Condon Concerts: Town Hall 1944-45, Featuring Pee Wee Russell (Chiaroscuro/—)
The Eddie Condon Concerts, Vol 2 (Chiaroscuro/—)
Eddie Condon, Condon A La Carte (—/London)
Eddie Condon, Chicago & All That Jazz! (—/Verve)
(Jack Teagarden)/Pee Wee Russell (Byg-France)
Teddy Wilson & His All Stars (Columbia/CBS)
The Pee Wee Russell Memorial Album (Prestige)/Swinging' With Pee Wee (Transatlantic)
Various (Including Pee Wee Russell), Jam Session At Swingville (Prestige/Prestige)
Pee Wee Russell, New Groove (Columbia/CBS)
Various (Including Pee Wee Russell), Swingin' Clarinets (—/London)
Pee Wee Russell, Portrait Of Pee Wee (Counterpoint/Society)

David Sanborn

The raunchy, R&B-influenced alto saxophone of David Sanborn came to wide attention through his tenure with the Gil Evans Orchestra. An accomplished and inspired soloist, his soaring and blues-wailing improvisations — like on **Short Visit** (from Gil Evans' **Priestess**) — remain memorable.

Suffering from polio as a child, Sanborn took up saxophone initially as a lung-strengthening exercise. Greatly influenced by Ray Charles and Hank Crawford, by 14 Sanborn was gigging around his native St Louis with blues artists like Albert King and Little Milton. After formal studies at Northwestern University, in '67 he joined Paul Butterfield's Blues Band in San Francisco.

After several years working with rock artists — including Stevie Wonder, James Taylor (Sanborn's lilting sax is heard on **How Sweet It Is**), David Bowie (**Young Americans**), James Brown *et al*, Sanborn struck out as a solo artist in '75 with **Taking Off.** Subsequent albums like **Sanborn, Heart To Heart, Hideaway** and **Voyeur** have brought him a wide, commercially-based fusion following. But don't be fooled — in live performance, few saxophonists can turn it on in quite such scintillating style as the dynamic Dave Sanborn.

Above: David Sanborn—unusual for a contemporary saxophonist, he came to jazz via R&B. His career includes memorable moments with Gil Evans' band.

Below: The distinguished Pee Wee Russell—once dubbed 'Poet of the Clarinet'. Played with an extraordinarily varied number of bands from the early 1920s.

Albums:
Gil Evans, Priestess (Antilles/Antilles)
Taking Off (Warner Brothers/Warner Brothers)
Sanborn (Warner Brothers/Warner Brothers)
Promise Me The Moon (Warner Brothers/Warner Brothers)
Heart To Heart (Warner Brothers/Warner Brothers)
Hideaway (Warner Brothers/Warner Brothers)
Voyeur (Warner Brothers/Warner Brothers)
As We Speak (Warner Brothers/Warner Brothers)
Backstreet (Warner Brothers/Warner Brothers)
Straight To The Heart (Warner Brothers/Warner Brothers)
Ed Palermo, Ed Palermo (Vile Heifer/—)
John Scofield, Electric Outlet (Gramavision/Gramavision)

Pharoah Sanders

One of the second wave of New Thing tenor-players — along with Shepp, Ayler — Sanders' recording début was on the courageous ESP label (**Pharoah Sanders**) and showed a style that was composed entirely of extremes: overblowing, screaming out clusters of notes, the line a furious supersonic scribbling.

He next appears with John Coltrane, chosen for his strength and spirit to remain the multi-directional impetus of that legendary unit, and his work here is probably his best. The wild collective session of 1965 (**Ascension**), including Coltrane, Sanders and Shepp, heralded a new direction for Coltrane's music and the end of the great quartet. As a foil for the leader's heavy, majestic passion, Sanders' raggedly scribbled outbursts offered the wildest contrast in trajectory; a writhing, tattooed Queequeg to the leader's iron-prowed obsession. **Meditations** remains the best album, the two horns plaiting and jostling over the dense rhythmic groundswell. On all albums, there are moments of incoherence, which is probably the price tag on free polyphony. Only **Naima (John Coltrane Live At The Village Vanguard Again)** catches Sanders in formal mood, the extremes of pitch and phrase pressed into service to tell a story, a twisted, volatile language of hieroglyphic and morse which nevertheless has its own symmetry.

Pharoah Sanders proved an excellent side-musician, thus his work with trumpeter Don Cherry (**Symphony for Improvisers** and **Where Is Brooklyn**) or set against the massive orchestration of Michael Mantler's **Preview (Jazz Composers Orchestra)**, where he turns and twists through the pile-driving forest of chords, includes his best work.

His début for Impulse (**Tauhid**) is interesting but contains the seeds of later shortcomings, for example, the short weight tenor exposure. **Upper And Lower Egypt** takes for ever to establish a climate for one of his Behemoth entrances, and the long haul — all ebb and flow and percussive textures — isn't greatly grabbing until the montuna section which triggers the Sanders blast off. A fatal liking for the Om-type mantra begins to take the foreground, with a romantic, anonymous lyricism. The best feature of his next album (**Jewels Of Thought**) is the incredible double bass duet between Cecil McBee and Richard Davis. Subsequent albums (**Karma, Thembi** and **Wisdom Through Music**) are endless chanting, rippling and swirling, music as embroidered as a matador's costume, with — very occasionally —the entrance of the bull.

Pharoah Sanders, Jewels Of Thought (courtesy Impulse).

Above: The supersonic tenor of Pharoah Sanders, ex-Coltrane musician capable of a formidable attack, in performance with bass-player Richard Davis.

Albums:
Pharoah Sanders (ESP/ESP)
John Coltrane, Ascension (Impulse/Impulse)
John Coltrane, Meditations (Impulse/Impulse)
John Coltrane, Live At The Village Vanguard Again (Impulse/Impulse)
John Coltrane, Live In Seattle (Impulse/Impulse)
Don Cherry, Symphony For Improvisers (Blue Note/Blue Note)
Don Cherry, Where Is Brooklyn (Blue Note/Blue Note)
Michael Mantler, The Jazz Composers Orchestra (JCOA/Virgin)
Tauhid (Impulse/Impulse)
Jewels Of Thought (Impulse/Impulse)
Pharoah (India Navigation/—)

Mongo Santamaria

Cuban drumming has often fascinated jazz musicians like Dizzy Gillespie, who experimented with the genre in his Afro-Cuban big band recordings. Conga, bongo and percussion player Mongo Santamaria came up through the more commercial Cuban bands like Perez Prado and Tito Puento, before joining Cal Tjader.

Much of his own output features a dense polyrhythmic surface supplemented by timbale and cowbell players of whom Willie Bobo is the best known. One of Santamaria's compositions, **Afro-Blue**, has been frequently recorded by jazz musicians. Very much in the tradition of Gillespie's orginal Cuban conga player, Chano Pozo, he dedicated a composition to him **(Afro-Roots)**.

Albums:
Afro Roots (Prestige/Prestige)
Skins (Milestone/Milestone)
Watermelon Man (Milestone/Milestone)
Greatest Hits (Columbia/—)
Dizzy Gillespie-Mongo Santamaria, Summertime (Pablo/Pablo)

John Scofield

Apart from virtuoso guitarist John Scofield's widely publicized connection with the Miles Davis group in the early 1980s, he already had a history of keeping exalted company dating back to the mid-1970s.

Born in Ohio on December 26, 1951, Scofield was raised in Connecticut. Learning guitar at age 12, he played in rock bands till discovering the urban blues of Muddy Waters, Jimmy Reed, Otis Rush and B. B. King, then the jazz delights of Jim Hall, Pat Martino, George Benson and John McLaughlin. Between '70 and '73, he studied at Berklee College. In '74, recommended by Berklee luminary Mick Goodrick, Scofield's first major gig was a significant start — with Chet Baker and Gerry Mulligan at their much-vaunted Carnegie Hall reunion.

Scofield then worked with Billy Cobham for two years (replacing John Abercrombie) and later with Cobham-George Duke's project. From '77-'78, Scofield took the chair vacated by guitarist Pat Metheny in vibist Gary Burton's band. Subsequently, he worked with a diversity of artists including Charles Mingus **(Three Or Four Shades Of Blue)**, Ron Carter, Jay McShann, Lee Konitz, Zbigniew Seifert, Niels-Henning and Dave Liebman.

In '77, he made his first outing as leader on **John Scofield Live** (the beginning of a creative association with the German-based Enja label), followed by **Rough House, Shinola** and **Out Like A Light**, plus **More Sightings** (with tenorist George Adams, trumpeter Hannibal Marvin Peterson and pianist Ron Burton) — all on Enja.

In '82, Scofield's performances with Miles Davis' two-guitar line-up (alongside Mike Stern) were highly acclaimed **(Star People, Decoy** and **You're Under Arrest)**. Back in the studio with his own group (this time including trombonist Ray Anderson and altoist Dave Sanborn), he made his début for Gramavision **(Electric Outlet). Still Warm** ('86) found him in the equally inspirational quartet setting of keyboardist Don Grolnick, bassist Darryl 'The Munch' Jones and percussionist Omar Hakim (the connection with Hakim leading to work with Weather Report).

In '86, Scofield toured the international festival circuit with a new line-up including keyboardist Mark Cohen, drummer Ricky Sebastian and bassist Gary Grainger.

Albums:
Billy Cobham, The Funky Thide Of Sings (Atlantic/Atlantic)
Chet Baker, You Can't Go Home Again (A&M Horizon/A&M Horizon)
John Scofield Live (—/Enja)
Rough House (—/Enja)
Hal Galper, Ivory Forest (—/Enja)
Shinola (—/Enja)
Out Like A Light (—/Enja)
Who's Who (Arista/Arista)
Bar Talk (Arista-Novus/Arista-Novus)
Miles Davis, Star People (Columbia/CBS)
Miles Davis, Decoy (Columbia/CBS)
Miles Davis, You're Under Arrest (Columbia/CBS)
John Scofield-John Abercrombie, Solar (Palo Alto/Palo Alto)
Marc Johnson, Bass Desires (ECM/ECM)
Electric Outlet (Gramavision/Gramavision)
Still Warm (Gramavision/Gramavision)

John Scofield Trio, Out Like A Light (courtesy Enja).

Ronnie Scott

Tenorist Ronnie Scott was born in London, 1927, working with the bands of Ambrose, Tito Burns, Cab Kaye, Ted Heath and Jack Parnell before forming his own band in 1952.

Belonging to that generation of British jazz musicians who worked on the liners crossing the Atlantic for a chance to hear the bebop revolution for themselves, Scott remains true to the chord changes, although his style has kept abreast of the newer developments, due to his ownership of an internationally renowned jazz club since 1959. Zoot Sims, Stan Getz, Hank Mobley and Sonny Rollins — all featured at his club — have had an influence on his playing over the years. The early Scott band can be heard on **Great Scott**.

With tenorist Tubby Hayes, he co-led the driving Jazz Couriers **(The Jazz Couriers)** 1957-9, was a featured soloist with the Kenny Clarke-Francy Boland band **(At Her Majesty's Pleasure)** and led a young band of New Thing players including John Surman and drummer Tony Oxley **(Ronnie Scott & The Band)**.

In more recent years, Scott's exceptional tenor-playing has been heard in a challenging quintet including brilliant guitarist Louis Stewart, and more latterly, young trumpeter Dick Pearce, bassist Ron Mathewson, drummer Martin Drew and pianist John Critchinson.

A much-loved and influential figure in British jazz, Scott is equally famous for his jokes, usually pithy one-liners (favorites include

Above: Phil Seamen as we remember him—a legend in his own time. One of the most powerful and original drummers Britain has produced.

'You've made a happy man very old...', 'Ah yes, I remember my youth...whatever happened to him?' and, in reply to a customer's telephone inquiry as to what time his show starts: '...What time can you get here?').

Scott's tenor and jazz club have been a major force on the British jazz scene for decades (his club celebrated its 25th anniversary in '84) and his contribution to the music earned him an O.B.E. honor in '81. The life and times of Ronnie Scott are amusingly recounted in two illuminating and entertaining books — *Some of My Best Friends are Blues* (by Scott with Mike Hennessey, '76, W. H. Allen) and *Let's Join Hands and Contact the Living* (by John Fordham, '86, Elm Tree).

Albums:
Great Scott (—/Esquire)
The Jazz Couriers (Jazzland/Jazzland)
Ronnie Scott & The Band (Columbia/CBS Realm)
Scott At Ronnie's (RCA/RCA)
The Kenny Clarke-Francy Boland Big Band, At Her Majesty's Pleasure (Black Lion/Black Lion)
Serious Gold (—/Pye)

Phil Seamen

British drummer Phil Seamen, who died in 1972, was a legend in his own lifetime, both as a world-class musician and as a personality. He came up through the big bands in the late '40s — Nat Gonella, Jack Parnell — and became a convert to bebop.

Frequently described as Britain's greatest big-band drummer, his work with small combos is equally distinguished, often anticipating developments that later occurred in America. His driving, aggressive playing can be heard behind the two-tenor Jazz Couriers **(The Message From Britain)** while his gift for timbre and imaginative melodic improvisation within a free context is represented with altoist Joe Harriott **(Free Form)**. A meeting with Bill Evans' bassist, Eddie Gomez, further illustrates his openness and adaptability.

Drum battles, starting with Jack Parnell, continued throughout his career, contestants including Vic Feldman, Ginger Baker (a student of his), and John Stevens. A tribute album **(The Phil Seamen Story)** includes his work with American blues singer, Jimmy Witherspoon, and great blues tenorist, Dick Morrissey.

Albums:
Jazz Couriers, The Message From Britain (Jazzland/—)
Joe Harriott, Free Form (Jazzland/—)
Phil Seamen Meets Eddie Gomez (—/Saga)
The Phil Seamen Story (—/Decibel)
A Jam Session At The Hide-Away (—/77 Jazz)

Bud Shank

Multi-reeds-player Bud Shank (born Ohio, 1926) worked mainly on the West Coast, playing in the big bands of Stan Kenton and Shorty Rogers, as well as numerous Californian combos.

An excellent alto, heavily influenced by Art Pepper, he was also a sensitive flautist and a proficient tenor and baritone. Along with Brazilian guitarist Laurindo Almeida, he pioneered the Latin American and jazz fusion in the mid-'50s, eight years before Stan Getz's trend-setting **Jazz Samba** album. Performances like **Acertate Mas (Laurindo Almeida Quartet)** combine swing and lightness of touch. Shank's later work showed an increasing power, and solos like **Walkin'** or **Bag of Blues (Bud Shank Quartet)** and the later **White Lightnin' (New Groove)** catch him at his peak. After several years of commercial work, Shank has surfaced again **(Sunshine Express)**.

In more recent years, Shank has renewed his earlier association with guitarist Almeida as part of the L. A. Four.

Albums:
Laurindo Almeida Quartet (Pacific Jazz/—)
Bud Shank Quartet (Pacific Jazz/—)
New Groove (Pacific Jazz/—)
Sunshine Express (Concord/—)
Laurindo Almeida-Bud Shank, Selected Works For Guitar And Flute (Concord/Concord)
The L. A. Four Scores (Concord/Concord)
The L. A. Four Live At Montreux—Summer 79 (Concord/Concord)
L. A. Four, Just Friends (Concord/Concord)
Bud Shank-Shorty Rogers-Vic Lewis, Back Again (Concept/—)
Live At 'The Haig' (Concept/Concept)
This Bud's For You (Muse/Muse)

Artie Shaw

Artie Shaw (born New York City, 1910) brought to jazz one of the finest clarinet techniques. He swung in a subtle and effortless way (although not as emphatically as Benny Goodman, for years his great rival, both as bandleader and clarinettist). That Shaw could play jazz with body, as well as great technical expertise, is evident in his solo from a recording by Billie Holiday of her own **Billie's Blues (Lady Day/ Billie Holiday's Greatest Hits)** during which Shaw plays a remarkably authentic blues solo.

Raised in New Haven, Connecticut, Shaw (real name Arthur Jacob Arshawsky) played saxophone in local high school band. After gigging locally with quartet, made professional début with Johnny Cavallaro, as saxophonist and clarinettist. Resident for three years in Cleveland, playing with various bands (including Irvin Aaronson's Commanders — this time featured on tenor sax). Moved to New York, freelanced for CBS and on record; then, in 1934, left music completely for a year.

Returned to New York and music the following year, appearing in concert with clarinet-and-strings quintet. Recorded with Billie Holiday in 1936 and Bunny Berigan, taking part in a session which produced Berigan's first version of **I Can't Get Started With You (Bunny Berigan & His Boys)**, then put together first (and short-lived) big band with string section.

Formed second, more conventional, big band (1937) which soon became one of the most popular outfits during swing era. Band had tremendous hit with its recording of **Begin The Beguine (The Complete Artie Shaw/ Concerto For Clarinet)** and its popularity became too much for its leader, who disbanded in December, '39, and lived for two months in Mexico. Re-formed mid-1940, and before joining US Navy (1942), had disbanded at least once, and toured with large band containing sizeable string section. Fronted Naval Band which toured Pacific area (1943-44).

Medically discharged in February 1944, formed another (civilian) band later that year, which included Roy Eldridge as star soloist, and youngsters like Dodo Marmarosa, Herbie Steward, and Barney Kessel **(The Complete Artie Shaw/Concerto For Clarinet, Artie Shaw & His Orchestra, Vol 2)**.

Often an outspoken critic of commercial exploitation of music, Shaw disbanded orchestra for the last time and retired to become a writer. (His autobiography, *The Trouble With Cinderella*, caused much comment when first published in 1952.) Periodically, from late-1940s until late-1953, led small groups. Final band was an updated version of his Gramercy Five, his band-within-a-band of the peak years of popularity. Much of the basic jazz content of Shaw's music came from Gramercy Five, which first recorded in 1940 **(Artie Shaw & His Gramercy Five)** with fine solos from Billy Butterfield, pianist Johnny Guarnieri (who also played harpsichord), and Shaw himself. Even here, though, jazz was, like that emanating from the larger outfit, of low-key variety. Best of Gramercy Five tracks probably were **Special Delivery Stomp, Summit Ridge Drive** (recording of which sold over a million), **My Blue Heaven** and **The Grabtown Grapple** (from later Gramercy Five and featuring Eldridge).

Shaw and his '40 orchestra are featured in the movie *Second Chorus* with Fred Astaire as an aspiring trumpet star.

Retired to run dairy farm, then to live in Spain (1955-60). Subsequently moving back to the United States, Shaw took up writing and adapting for the theater.

Artie Shaw and his Gramercy Five (courtesy RCA)—Shaw and some of his finest soloists at their best.

Albums:
Bunny Berigan, Take It, Bunny! (Epic/Philips)
Billie Holiday, Lady Day (Columbia)/
Billie Holiday's Greatest Hits (CBS—Italy)
The Complete Artie Shaw, Vols 1, 2 (Bluebird)/
Concerto For Clarinet (RCA Victor)/
Artie Shaw & His Orchestra, Vol 2
(RCA Victor)
Artie Shaw & His Orchestra (1937-1938), Vols 1-3 (First Time Records/—)
Artie Shaw & His Gramercy Five (RCA Victor)
Artie Shaw Featuring Roy Eldridge
(RCA Victor/—)
Artie Shaw, Melody In Madness, Vols 1, 2
(Jazz Guild/—)
Dance To Artie Shaw (Coral)
Artie Shaw & His Gramercy Five
(Clef/Columbia—Clef)

Archie Shepp

Above: Archie Shepp, one of the most expressive saxophone voices in jazz. An emotionally overwhelming musician.

Tenorist Archie Shepp was born in Florida, 1937, and made his earliest recordings with Cecil Taylor (**Air** and **Into The Hot**), sounding at that time, 1960, like an amalgam of Rollins and Coltrane.

By 1962 he had emerged as a highly original voice and his quartet with trumpeter Bill Dixon produced a classic solo on **Trio (Bill Dixon-Archie Shepp Quartet)**.

With the New York Contemporary Five of the following year, Shepp picked up ideas about group voicings **(Archie Shepp & The New York Contemporary Five)** and although the free drumming of J. C. Moses suited him less well than Don Cherry or John Tchicai, the lessons of the NYC5 were fruitfully continued in a Shepp studio band with Tchicai, trumpeter Alan Shorter and trombonist Roswell Rudd **(Four For Trane)**. His arrangement of Coltrane's **Syeeda's Song Flute** is excellent small group writing.

The links with Coltrane were reinforced on the massive collective work **Ascension** in 1965, featuring many of the New Thing musicians, including Shepp. The most readily approachable of that group, Shepp's tone is a fiercely exciting blend of hoarse cries, rasps, loose vibrato and cutting clarity, his dramatic control of dynamics similar to Ben Webster's. His feeling for the blues is intensely emotional, while his ballad playing — **In A Sentimental Mood (On This Night** and **Live In San Francisco)** or **Prelude To A Kiss (Fire Music** and **Mama Too Tight)** — is robustly romantic.

Shepp's second major involvement in group writing **(Fire Music)** produced two magnificent works, **Hambone** and **Los Olvidados**, and a deeply moving trio performance, **Malcolm, Malcolm — Semper Malcolm** on which the tenorist reads his own poem to Malcolm X. Shepp's poetry, *The Wedding* **(Live In San Francisco)**, *Scag* **(New Thing At Newport)** or his later albums like **Things Have Got To Change** and **Attica Blues**, are aspects of his fervent political beliefs: 'I play of the death of me by you'.

A period with vibraphonist Bobby Hutcherson in the group **(On This Night** and **New Thing At Newport)** gave way to the collaborations with trombonists like Roswell Rudd **(Live In San Francisco** and **Three For A Quarter)** and later, additionally, Grachan Moncur III **(One For The Trane** and **Mama Too Tight)**.

1966-67 saw Shepp experimenting with dense counterpoint, savage collective playing and straight-faced Sousa marches, the lengthy **Portrait Of Robert Johnson (Mama Too Tight)** being a fine example. The title track, an explosive tenor solo over a ragged R&B riff, is a genre in which Shepp reigns supreme, while **Damn If I Know (The Way Ahead)** follows a similar pattern. Eighteen minutes of tenor over assorted percussion **(The Magic Of Ju-Ju)** is either boring or mesmerizing depending on the listener's stamina but the unaccompanied **Rain Forest** made during Shepp's stay in France, 1969-70, is an unqualified masterpiece, spine-chillingly brutal and tender by turns **(Poem For Malcolm)**. A great deal of recording went on in 1969 as Paris was seething with expatriate New Thingers like the Art Ensemble Of Chicago and Sunny Murray, and most of the albums for BYG (more recently re-issued through Affinity) featured extensive sitting-in. Malachi Favors and Philly Joe Jones back the tenorist, as well as two bluesy harmonica players, on an album featuring the singer Jeanne Lee **(Blase)**, while Lester Bowie, Roscoe Mitchell, Hank Mobley, Leroy Jenkins, Anthony Braxton, Noah Howard, Clifford Thornton and Sunny Murray turn up variously on several excellent Shepp dates **(Yasmina, A Black Woman, Black Gipsy, Archie Shepp & Philly Joe Jones** and **Coral Rock)** and during an Algerian festival which also includes Tuareg musicians **(Live At The Panafrican Festival)**.

Returning to America in 1971, Shepp worked with singer Joe Lee Wilson **(Things Have Got To Change** and **Attica Blues)** using some of the practices of Tamla Motown to achieve a broad image of black culture. Later Shepp releases from Europe revealed him to be in great form, and his group — Charles Greenlea trombone, Dave Burrell piano, Cameron Brown bass and the habitual Beaver Harris on drums — played a magnificent set at the Massy Festival **(Shepp A Massy)**. Archie Shepp's piano playing is interesting, his soprano leaner than his tenor, which remains one of the most commanding sounds in jazz

An historic, influential and outspoken avant-garde pioneer, Shepp's forays into more 'bebop' stylistic forms in his later playing didn't please all of his earlier fans. Shepp eschews the term 'bebop', preferring to call it the 'baroque period of Afro-American music'. He explains: 'Each time a new white performer emulates an earlier negro performer with success they are acclaimed. They're given money. But when blacks attempt to recreate their own forms they are castigated and criticised as being old-fashioned and so on. There is not only discrimination in this but it represents a subtly disguised way of stealing the negro's music...'. As Shepp says, when an artist is involved in a creative quest, at some point he or she re-examines the most classical elements of the form in order to redefine technique — this is merely what Shepp has been doing.

Albums:
Cecil Taylor, Air (CBS Barnaby/CBS Barnaby)
Cecil Taylor, Into The Hot (Impulse/Impulse)
Bill Dixon-Archie Shepp Quartet (Savoy/—)
Archie Shepp & The New York Contemporary Five (Sonet/Polydor)
Archie Shepp, Four For Trane
(Impulse/Impulse)
John Coltrane, Ascension (Impulse/Impulse)
On This Night (Impulse/Impulse)
Live In San Francisco (Impulse/Impulse)
Fire Music (Impulse/Impulse)
Mama Too Tight (Impulse/Impulse)
New Thing At Newport (Impulse/Impulse)
Three For A Quarter (Impulse/Impulse)
The Way Ahead (Impulse/Impulse)
The Magic Of Ju-Ju (Impulse/Impulse)
One For The Trane (BASF/Saba)
Poem For Malcolm (—/Affinity)
Live At The Panafrican Festival (—/Affinity)
Black Gipsy (Prestige/America)
Archie Shepp & Philly Joe Jones
(Fantasy/America)
Coral Rock (Prestige/America)
Things Have Got To Change (Impulse/Impulse)
Attica Blues (Impulse/Impulse)
Shepp A Massy (—/Uniteledis—France)
Archie Shepp (—/Horo—Italy)
Steam (—/Enja—Germany)
A Sea Of Faces (Black Saint/Black Saint)
There's A Trumpet In My Soul
(Arista Freedom/Arista Freedom)
Live At Montreux
(Arista Freedom/Arista Freedom)
Body & Soul (—/Horo)
Archie Shepp-Lars Gullin, The House I Live In
(Steeplechase/Steeplechase)
Archie Shepp-Niels-Henning Ørsted Pedersen, Looking At Bird
(Steeplechase/Steeplechase)
My Man (Ispre/Ispre)
I Know About The Life (Sackville/Sackville)
Soul Song (—/Enja—Germany)
The Good Life (Varrick/Varrick)
New York Contemporary Five, Consequences
(Fontata/Fontata)
John Tchicai-Archie Shepp, Rufus
(Fontata/Fontata)
Down Home New York (Soul Note/Soul Note)

Live At The Pan-African Festival (courtesy BYG): re-issued, Affinity, 1979.

Wayne Shorter

see Weather Report

Ben Sidran

A talented jazz pianist, Ben Sidran has made a name for himself as a modern-day writer of contemporary lyrics to classic jazz instrumentals. Although lacking the vocal dexterity of Jon Hendricks, the technique of Mark Murphy or the intuitive feel of Georgie Fame, Sidran's vocal work does have a certain charm.

Raised in Racine, Wisconsin, Sidran played piano from age 7, working in local bands while still at high school. At 17, a meeting at the University of Wisconsin with rock singers Steve Miller and Boz Scaggs led to Sidran joining their group the Ardells. While studying for his PhD at Sussex University in England, his doctoral thesis was eventually to become his book, *Black Talk*, published in '71.

In the early '70s, albums like **I Lead A Life, Puttin' In Time On Planet Earth** (featuring ex-Stan Kenton band-members Frank Rosolino and Bill Perkins) and **Don't Let Go** all followed a similar jazz-fusion format. In the late '70s, starting with **The Doctor Is In** ('77), Sidran revealed a preference for more traditional jazz content (Mingus' **Goodbye Pork Pie Hat** and Horace Silver's **Silver's Serenade**).

Subsequent albums continued with a strong bop influence, interpreting more jazz classics —**A Little Kiss In The Night** ('78) featured Blue Mitchell and Phil Woods and included the Sidran-Jon Hendricks version of Charlie Parker's **Moose The Mooch**.

On his **Bop City ('83)**, Miles Davis' **Solar** and **Nardis**, Thelonious Monk's **Monk's Mood**, Freddie Hubbard's **Up Jumped Spring**, John Coltrane's **Big Nick** and Charlie Rouse's **Little Sherry** were all given the Sidran treatment in the company of vibist Mike Mainieri, guitarist Steve Khan and bassist Eddie Gomez While his **Monk's Mood** was a vocal disappointment, he fared much better with his rather appealing version of **Nardis** (which—interestingly—is, of course, 'Sidran' spelled backwards).

Later work has found Sidran exploring more modern fusion through a bank of electric keyboards.

Albums:
Feel Your Groove (Capitol/Capitol)
I Lead A Life (Blue Thumb/Blue Thumb)
Puttin' In Time On Planet Earth (Blue Thumb/Blue Thumb)
Don't Let Go (Blue Thumb/Blue Thumb)
Free In America (Arista/Arista)
A Little Kiss In The Night (Arista/Arista)
Old Songs For The New Depression (Antilles/Antilles)
Bop City (Antilles/Antilles

Horace Silver

Born in Norwalk, Connecticut, in 1928, the pianist-composer started out as a Bud Powell disciple like many of his generation and, following a stint with the Stan Getz Quartet, began to develop into an influential stylist in his own right.

With drummer Art Blakey, he co-founded the Jazz Messengers, which was—with its fire and brimstone attack—the most typical hard bop unit in the '50s. Silver's playing became increasingly percussive, so that accompaniment for the soloist—caught between the drums and piano, and forced to raise his game—was a barrage of rhythmic riffs, goadings and peremptory proddings.

Silver's themes for the Jazz Messengers, **Quicksilver, Doodlin'**, and particularly **The Preacher**, set the pattern for much of the next decade. The fact that **The Preacher** started the trend for 'soul', a back-to-the-roots mixture of gospel and blues over a simple backbeat, often featuring call-and-response patterns along the lines of the preacher and congregation, obscures the fact that the composer was responsible for many innovations. All the Messengers' albums from the early period are excellent **(A Night At Birdland, At The Cafe Bohemia** and **Horace Silver & The Jazz Messengers)** but Silver left in 1956 to form his own quintet.

Personnel over the years included tenorists Junior Cook, Hank Mobley, Joe Henderson, trumpeters Joe Gordon, Carmell Jones, Woody Shaw, Blue Mitchell and Art Farmer, and drummers Louis Hayes, Roy Brooks and Roger Humphries. Silver's arrangements for the unit are seldom complex but never predictable either. The horns state the theme—often a mixture of blues, gospel and Latin influences, multi-layered, choppy and chock-a-block with contrasts—and the leader's piano figures slide slyly sideways as if begging to differ. Bars come in an odd assortment of remnant lengths and alternative melodies emerge as the piece gets under way. Funky blues, **Home Cookin' (The Stylings Of Silver), Sweet Sweetie Dee** and **Let's Get To The Nitty Gritty (Silver's Serenade)**; hard-driving blues, **Filthy McNasty (Doin' The Thing)**; exotic blues, **Senor Blues (Six Pieces Of Silver), The Cape Verdean Blues (The Cape Verdean Blues), Song For My Father (Song For My Father)**; and hauntingly beautiful ballads like **Calcutta Cutie (Song For My Father)** seem to pour from Silver's fertile imagination.

His later output for Blue Note showed an attempt to broaden his palette **(Silver & Wood)** and write for larger ensembles but the quintet remained the heart of his music.

As a pianist, he has stripped away much of the multi-note complexity of bop in favor of a more direct, blues-based, percussive approach. Boogie figures rumble from the left hand, single note on the beat phrases alternating with locked hands chordal hammerings, the style seemingly simple but in fact inimitable. The cheeky quotes and immediately attractive lines generate a friendliness that has communicated itself to a wide and appreciative audience over two decades.

Albums:
The Jazz Messengers, A Night At Birdland (Blue Note/Blue Note)
The Jazz Messangers, At The Cafe Bohemia (Blue Note/Blue Note)
Horace Silver & The Jazz Messengers (Blue Note/Blue Note)
The Stylings Of Silver (Blue Note/Blue Note)
Silver's Serenade (Blue Note/Blue Note)
Doin' The Thing (Blue Note/Blue Note)
Six Pieces Of Silver (Blue Note/Blue Note)
Song For My Father (Blue Note/Blue Note)
The Cape Verdean Blues (Blue Note/Blue Note)
Silver & Wood (Blue Note/Blue Note)
Blowin' The Blues Away (Blue Note/Blue Note)
Finger Poppin' (Blue Note/Blue Note)

Nina Simone

Strongly associated with black civil rights issues since the 1970s, Nina Simone's music —often a stark, outline drawing in realism with a sharp, provocative lyricism—pricked the conscience of a white, middle-cass audience with whom, ironically, she still remains a favorite.

Born Eunice Waymon in North Carolina in 1933, Simone was self-taught on piano and organ by age 7, singing in the local church choir—indeed, her later music revealed an edgy, gospel intensity. She studied music formally at high school in Asheville, then at Juilliard in New York and Philadelphia's Curtis Institute where she also taught piano. Working in a club in Atlantic City brought Simone a record deal with the Bethlehem label and her first major hit, **I Loves You, Porgy** in '59.

Throughout the '60s, success followed success from Screaming Jay Hawkins' **I Put A Spell On You** to **Ain't Got No—I Got Life**. Her involvement in the black civil rights movement produced enduring, thought-provoking classics like **Mississippi Goddam**. Taking inspiration from black poets, she put music to Paul Dunbar's **Compensation** and Langston Hughes' **The Backlash Blues** and the perennial **To Be Young, Gifted And Black**, while her own **Four Women** was a blistering vocal indictment of the stereotypes inflicted on black American women.

An unusual video *Nina Simone At Ronnie Scott's, London*, in the mid-'80s featuring performances and a rare interview was the first ever jazz video to reach the UK Top 20. Highly strung and emotionally unpredictable, Simone's later performances have tended to be brief and occasionally disruptive, recording infrequently in recent years—a tragedy because the undeniable genius of Nina Simone still commands a unique place in modern music and a loyal, affectionate audience wherever she goes.

Albums:
Baltimore (CTI/CTI)
Here Comes The Sun (RCA/RCA)
It's Finished (RCA/—)
Pure Gold (—/RCA)
The Best Of Nina Simone (Philips/—)
Nina Simone Sings The Blues (RCA/RCA)
The Most Beautiful Songs Of...Nina Simone (—/RCA)
Nina's Back (VPI Records/—)

Below: Pianist and 'soul jazz' survivor Horace Silver. A musician with a taste for Home Cookin', he created wide acceptance for the word 'funk'.

Zoot Sims

Tenorist Zoot Sims was one of the most consistent musicians in jazz, unfailingly swinging and inventive on ballads and blues.

Born in California, 1925, he joined Benny Goodman in the mid-40s, and then Woody Herman's Second Herd, where he made up the famous 'Four Brothers' saxophone line with Stan Getz, Herbie Steward and Serge Chaloff **(The Best Of Woody Herman)**. Stylistically Sims derived from Lester Young, but incorporated the wider harmonic practices of the early modernists. He stayed two years with Herman, 1947-49, before moving back to the West Coast where he gigged with a wide variety of accomplished players like Clifford Brown and Chet Baker.

He joined Stan Kenton in 1953 and the Gerry Mulligan Sextet in 1955, and recorded later with Mulligan's Concert Jazz Band. **Red Door, Apple Core** and **Come Rain Or Come Shine** are outstanding performances, well worth tracking down **(Gerry Mulligan & The Concert Jazz Band Live)**.

In '50, Sims recorded Prestige's first long-playing album, taking advantage of the room to stretch out on **Zoot Swings The Blues (Zootcase)**. The compilation also includes fine sessions from the early '50s with George Wallington and Al Cohn, a favorite blowing partner from the Herman days. Sims and Cohn cut several albums together **(Body & Soul)** including the lyrical dove-tailing on **Emily (Motoring Along** and **You 'N' Me)** with their compatibility illustrated by the remarkable **Improvisation For Unaccompanied Saxophones**.

Another great partnership occurred with veteran violinist, Joe Venuti **(Joe & Zoot)** and numbers like **I Got Rhythm** are the epitome of swing. One of the best Sims albums is **Jive At Five**, from 1960 and subsequent years saw a flood of Sims albums for Norman Granz. They are all excellent, and show his mature style with its warm, Ben Websterish tone **(Basie & Zoot, Zoot Sims & The Gershwin Brothers** and **Hawthorne Nights)** with a large ensemble and arrangements by Bill Holman, and an album featuring Sims playing airy and elegant soprano saxophone **(Soprano Sax)**.

Even in the '80s, albums like **I Wish I Were Twins** confirm that Sims was one of jazz's most outstanding stylists.

Zoot Sims died in 1985, aged 59, being elected to *Downbeat* magazine's Hall of Fame in that year's Critics' Poll in recognition of his inestimable contribution to jazz

Albums:

The Best Of Woody Herman (Columbia/CBS)
Gerry Mulligan & The Concert Jazz Band Live (Verve/Verve)
Zootcase (Prestige/Prestige)
Body & Soul (Muse/—)
Motoring Along (Sonet/Sonet)
You 'N' Me (Mercury/Mercury)
Joe & Zoot (Chiaroscuro/Vogue)
Basie & Zoot (Pablo/Pablo)
Zoot Sims & The Gershwin Brothers (Pablo/Pablo)
Hawthorne Nights (Pablo/Pablo)
Soprano Sax (Pablo/Pablo)
Dream Dancing (Choice/DJM)
If I'm Lucky (Pablo/Pablo)
Down Home (Bethlehem/Affinity)
Rune Gustafsson-Zoot Sims, The Sweetest Sounds (Sonet/Sonet)
The Swinger (Pablo/Pablo)
I Wish I Were Twins (Pablo/Pablo)
Quitely There/Zoot Sims Plays Johnny Mandel (Pablo/Pablo)
In A Sentimental Mood (Sonet/Sonet)

Bessie Smith

The Empress of the Blues, Bessie Smith, was born in Chattanooga, Tennessee, at a date variously given as 1894 or 1898. Her voice, ringing and declamatory, retained the early influence of the black churches and by the age of 14 she had become the protégé of blues singer Ma Rainey, touring with her Rabbit Foot Minstrels on the tent show circuit and learning the craft.

Like Ma Rainey, she based her interpretations around secure center tones, returning to them time and again to produce a stark, incantatory effect, utilizing key changes to vary the impact. More sophisticated than her mentor, Bessie Smith's dramatic delivery employs bent notes, slurs and a rhythmically adventurous use of rests, which tends to place her stylistically at a midpoint between the rural blues and instrumental jazz.

Despite the blues vogue opened up by Mamie Smith's hit record, **Crazy Blues**, Bessie was passed over by the record companies as too rough-hewn until 1923, when she cut two commercially successful sides, **Down Hearted Blues** and **Gulf Coast Blues**, for Columbia. These performances can be found on the first of a five-volume set **(The World's Greatest Blues Singer)** in a format which groups early and late recording sessions. Clarence Williams' piano accompaniment is easily outclassed by the Fletcher Henderson sides, while the singer's swan-song, **Do Your Duty, Gimme A Pigfoot, Take Me For A Buggy Ride** and **Down In The Dumps** use a swing era instrumentation of Frankie Newton, Jack Teagarden, Benny Goodman and Chu Berry.

Bessie Smith, The World's Greatest Blues Singer (courtesy CBS). When she sang about the Empty Bed Blues, you immediately understood.

Below: Zoot Sims—during his lifetime, a guarantee of taste, drive and imagination, notably when teamed with favorite blowing partner Al Cohn.

The second volume **(Any Woman's Blues)** is a mixed bag, offering popular and vaudeville material on **Sam Jones Blues** and **My Sweetie Went Away**, duets with the rival blues singer, Clara Smith, **Far Away Blues** and **I'm Going Back To My Used To Be**, the classic **Nobody Knows You When You're Down And Out** from 1929 and the magnificent partnership with pianist James P. Johnson. The third and fourth volumes contain examples of the singer with her ideal accompanists, trombonist Charlie Green and cornettist Joe Smith, the latter a simple and affecting foil on the great **Weeping Willow Blues**, while the trombonist provides a humorous commentary on **Empty Bed Blues (Empty Bed Blues)**. Both men with Fletcher Henderson on piano and a youthful Coleman Hawkins on tenor add greatly to the excitement on **Cake Walkin' Babies** and **Yellow Dog Blues**, while Louis Armstrong plays classic obbligatos on **St Louis Blues, Reckless Blues** and **Cold In Hand Blues (The Empress)**.

The final volume, **Nobody's Blues But Mine**, covers 1925-27, arguably her finest period, before drink and declining popularity overcame her talents. Competition from singer Ethel Waters and public boredom with the more elemental blues forced Bessie to include material like **Alexander's Ragtime Band** and **After You've Gone** along with the more appropriate and magnificent **Back Water Blues** and **Preachin' The Blues**.

The Depression saw the long decline of Bessie Smith, and her tragic death in a car accident in 1937. She had taken the blues from the tent shows and vaudeville circuits into the Northern theaters, and given the form its most majestic expression. Her power and emotional integrity transcended the often trivial lyrics, paring away prettiness to reveal an irreducible structure. Her dramatic gifts found an outlet in revues like *Harlem Frolics, The Midnight Steppers* and the two-reel movie, *St Louis Blues*.

In '70, the great Bessie Smith was still lying in an unmarked grave at Mount Lawn Cemetery, Sharon Hill, Pennsylvania. Learning of this, rock singer Janis Joplin—greatly influenced by Bessie (and herself to die in unhappy circumstances less than two months later)—contributed towards the cost of a headstone. On August 7—34 years after Smith's death—the headstone was unveiled. The inscription read: *The Greatest Blues Singer In The World Will Never Stop Singing—Bessie Smith—1895-1937.*

The definitive biography, *Bessie*, by Chris Albertson, clears away many of the baseless legends and rumors that have surrounded her turbulent life and death.

Bessie Smith (a portrait by Elaine Feinstein, '85) was included in Penguin Books' 'Lives of Modern Women' series alongside other significant 20th-century women whose lives, ideas, struggles, creative talent and courage had contributed something new to a world in transition.

Ablums:

The World's Greatest Blues Singer (Columbia/CBS)
Any Woman's Blues (Columbia/CBS)
Empty Bed Blues (Columbia/CBS)
The Empress (Columbia/CBS)
Nobody's Blues But Mine (Columbia/CBS)

Jimmy Smith

Organist Jimmy Smith was responsible for transforming that much-reviled instrument into the ubiquitous and popular seller of the 1960s.

Born in Philadelphia, 1925, he started out as a pianist, formally training as a bassist after service in the navy. In the early '50s, he switched to organ, forming his first trio in 1955 and his early output for Blue Note remains the best.

Adapting the hard bop style to the organ, and influenced by pianists Horace Silver and Bud Powell, Smith brought a crispness and speed of attack which effectively removed all associations with skating rinks. Supplying his own bass line, the virtuoso spun endless variations; fast, single-note runs and sustained chords around which he embroidered his

Above: 'Organ-grinder' Jimmy Smith—he produced huge hits with The Sermon, A Walk On The Wild Side, Got My Mojo Working and Slaughter On Tenth Avenue.

supercharged improvisations. By 1956, he was hailed as Metronome's New Star.

Two volumes with Art Blakey **(The Incredible Jimmy Smith)** show what a dazzling performer he was, from the wildly exciting duet for drums and organ, **The Duel**, to the blues **All Day Long** or **Plum Nellie**. His endless inventiveness around the blues is well illustrated on Silver's hit, **The Preacher (At Club 'Baby Grand')**. A series of blowing sessions produced the expected tear-up, and also showed Smith's gifts as an accompanist **(Open House, The Sermon** and **A Date With Jimmy Smith)** to players like Hank Mobley, Jackie McLean, Ike Quebec and Lou Donaldson.

Mid-period Smith tended to reflect the great popularity of **Midnight Special** and, with Stanley Turrentine or Lou Donaldson, he recorded a string of medium tempo funky blues **(Back At The Chicken Shack, Rockin' The Boat** and **Prayer Meetin')**. Two of the best albums from this period return to the trio format **(Softly As A Summer Breeze** and **Crazy! Baby)**.

Leaving Blue Note, he signed with Verve and increased his popularity with numbers like **A Walk On The Wild Side (Bashin')** on which he fronts a big band, and **Goldfinger (Monster)**, an album which also contains the more interesting **Slaughter On Tenth Avenue** and **Bluesette**.

Success tended to produce formula playing and a rash of imitators like Jimmy McGriff and Jack McDuff, and the adoption of electric piano has seen the eclipse of the organ.

Albums:

The Incredible Jimmy Smith (Blue Note/Blue Note)
At Club 'Baby Grand' (Blue Note/Blue Note)
Open House (Blue Note/Blue Note)
The Sermon (Blue Note/Blue Note)
A Date With Jimmy Smith (Blue Note/Blue Note)
Midnight Special (Blue Note/Blue Note)
Back At The Chicken Shack (Blue Note/Blue Note)
Rockin' The Boat (Blue Note/Blue Note)
Prayer Meetin' (Blue Note/Blue Note)
Softly As A Summer Breeze (Blue Note/Blue Note)
Crazy! Baby (Blue Note/Blue Note)
Greatest Hits (Blue Note/Blue Note)
Bashin' (Verve/Verve)
The Monster (Verve/Verve)
Houseparty (Blue Note/Blue Note)
Got My Mojo Workin' (Verve/Verve)
Off The Top (Elektra Musician/Elektra Musician)
Keep On Comin' (Elektra Musician/Elektra Musician)

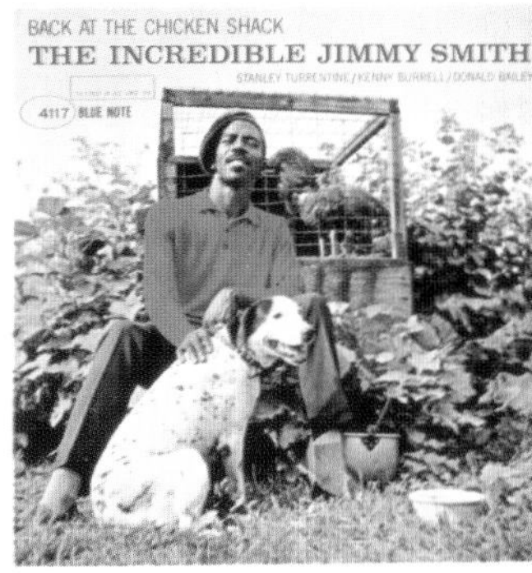

Back At The Chicken Shack, Jimmy Smith (courtesy Blue Note).

Stuff Smith

Hezekiah Leroy Gordon 'Stuff' Smith (born Portsmouth, Ohio, 1909) was, without doubt, the most basic jazz violinist of all. In many ways, he could well be termed the greatest jazz violinist.

He bowed his instrument with an unequaled ferocity and swung with tremendous unrelenting power. He had a genuine and readily communicated feeling for the blues. He was capable of the most astonishing flights of fancy, as his playing opposite another virtuoso, Dizzy Gillespie, during their second get-together on record **(Dizzy Gillespie & Stuff Smith)**, indicates superbly. And in company with fellow jazz violinists, there was little they could teach him in terms of technique and, of course, swing; illustrated graphically on **Violin Summit** where Smith is juxtaposed, in a concertized setting, with Jean-Luc Ponty, Stephane Grappelli and Svend Asmussen.

After Smith's father (himself a multi-instrumentalist) had made him his first violin at eight, he had an early introduction to playing music by appearing with his father's band, aged 12. Won musical scholarship to Johnson C. Smith University, North Carolina, but left in 1924 to tour with a revue band. Worked with Alphonse Trent (1926-29) except for a brief spell, in '27, as member of Jelly Roll Morton's band; he returned to Trent because the loudness of the rest of the band drowned out his acoustic violin.

Moving to Buffalo, he became a regular favorite in local clubs. Eventually he and small combo went to New York (1936).

Smith's reputation was established thereafter, mostly because of long residency at Onyx Club, on 52nd Street. Here Smith first used an amplified with his violin. Stuff Smith's became one of the most popular bands on 52nd Street, with the leader's violin and hoarse vocals complemented splendidly by trumpet (and sometimes additional vocals) of Jonah Jones and driving drumming of Cozy Cole. The music by Stuff Smith & His Onyx Club Orchestra was good, always, as recordings like **I Hope Gabriel Likes My Music, Tain't No Use, After You've Gone, Serenade For A Wealthy Widow** (all **Stuff Smith & His Onyx Club Orchestra)** and **Twilight In Turkey, Upstairs** and **Onyx Club Spree** (all **The Swinging Small Bands 1 — 1937-1939)** indicate delightfully. A single record by the band, **I'se A-Muggin'**, a piece of infectious musical hokum, became a hit. Smith & Co also proved popular during 1937-38 in California.

Smith took over leadership of Fats Waller's band on the pianist's death in 1943. After contracting pneumonia in Hollywood, Smith left. On recovery, put together own trio, playing regularly in Chicago where he settled for a while in 1940s. Spent most of 1950s on West Coast, mostly neglected by jazz buffs.

Recorded in 1957, in company with Oscar Peterson-led quartet **(Stuff Smith)**; created favorable impression all over again. Included in repertoire at this date were two fine Smith originals, **Desert Sands** and **Time & Again**. Two months later, recorded with Dizzy Gillespie. Recorded third album in '57 for same label as Peterson, Gillespie sessions, Verve, and the standard again was first rate **(Have Violin, Will Swing)**.

During rest of 1950s, and early-1960s, continued to lead own groups, as solo attraction, and with others (including highly successful season at Embers, New York, with Joe Bushkin Quartet, '64). Starting with a well-received season in London, Smith was more or less permanently based in Europe from 1965. Proved immensely popular, especially in Denmark, where he recorded, in '65, the remarkable **Swingin' Stuff**, producing searing solos of almost unbelievable intensity. One of his final recordings, before he died in 1967 (in Munich, Germany), was **One O'Clock Jump**, from same year. As with his first recordings, so with his last; Stuff Smith was in dazzling form and technically superb.

Albums:

Various (Including Stuff Smith), The Swinging Small Bands 1 (1937-1939) (MCA—Germany)
Stuff Smith & His Onyx Club Orchestra (Collector's/—)
Dizzy Gillespie, Dee Gee Days/The Savoy Sessions (Savoy/—)
Stuff Smith (Verve/Columbia—Clef)
Dizzy Gillespie & Stuff Smith (Verve/HMV)
Stuff Smith, Swingin' Stuff (EmArcy/Polydor)
Various (Including Stuff Smith), Violin Summit (Saba/Polydor)
Stuff Smith, One O'Clock Jump (Polydor)
Stuff Smith, Have Violin, Will Swing (Verve/—)
Herb Ellis/Stuff Smith, Together (Epic/—)

Tommy Smith

The extraordinarily mature style and technique of British saxophonist Tommy Smith attracted national attention when he was just 16, bringing him a scholarship to Berklee College in the United States the following year.

Born in Luton, England, on April 27, 1967, Smith's family moved to Edinburgh, Scotland, six months later. At age 9, he was playing recorder and cornet at school, taking up the saxophone at 12 because he 'liked its shape'. Just two years later, he won the Best Musician award in the Edinburgh Jazz Festival's youth band competition and in '83 contributed to the European Community Youth Jazz Orchestra in Brussels.

In December '82 — still only 15 — he made his stunning national UK television début (on *Jazz At The Gateway* with bassist Niels-Henning and pianist Gordon Beck). Smith's first album **Giant Strides** and the subsequent **Taking Off!** offered a further insight into his remarkable style and approach on tenor, soprano and flute.

Tapes and manuscripts of his compositions submitted to Berklee College in Boston brought the scholarship and the award of the Phil Woods saxophone prize. At Berklee, he has been heard regularly with vibist Gary Burton's band alongside young pianist Makoto Ozone. Performances with his own Forward Motion group, which includes other young Berklee luminaries **(The Berklee Tapes)**, find Smith engaging in far-ranging group improvisation moving towards a more multi-directional free-style area.

The future development of this gifted young tenorist will undoubtedly be followed with increasing interest from both sides of the Atlantic.

Albums:
Giant Strides (—/GFM)
Taking Off! (—/Head)
Forward Motion, The Berklee Tapes (Hep/Hep)

Giant Strides for Britain's saxophonist Tommy Smith (courtesy GFM).

Below: Willie 'The Lion' Smith—one of the legendary pioneers of Harlem stride from the 1920s and an enduring influence on Duke Ellington.

Willie 'The Lion' Smith

Born William Henry Joseph Bonaparte Bertholoff Smith in 1897, Willie The Lion was one of the New York pioneers who adapted ragtime to the needs of jazz piano, establishing the style known as Harlem stride.

The Harlem pianists of the '20s, James P. Johnson, Willie The Lion, Luckey Roberts, Duke Ellington, Fats Waller, engaged in piano cutting-contests, interacting creatively at rent parties and clubs like the Clef Club, the Rhythm Club, The Rock and Leroy's.

Willie The Lion, creator of scores of delicate, impressionistic melodies, is also an exciting performer with a rhythmically driving left hand and a jaunty and bombastic stage presence complete with bowler hat and cigar. Uneven on record, **Hallelujah (A Legend), Tango La Caprice** and **Relaxin'**, his own compositions **(Harlem Piano), Contrary Motion (Jazz Piano—A Musical Exchange), Portrait Of The Duke**, the teacher's response to his famous student's tribute, **Portrait Of The Lion (Memorial)**, and a keyboard partnership with Don Ewell **(Grand Piano)**, represent a cross-section of his best work.

Albums:
A Legend (Mainstream/Fontana)
Harlem Piano, Willie The Lion Smith & Luckey Roberts (Good Time Jazz/Good Time Jazz)
Jazz Piano—A Musical Exchange (RCA Victor/RCA Victor)
Memorial (—/Vogue)
Grand Piano, Willie The Lion Smith & Don Ewell (—/'77)

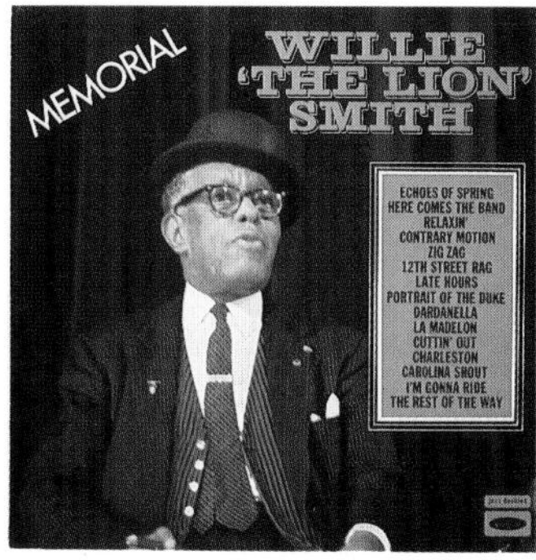

Willie 'The Lion' Smith, Memorial (courtesy Vogue).

Muggsy Spanier

Francis Joseph 'Muggsy' Spanier (born Chicago, Illinois, 1906) never claimed to have the best technique among trumpeters/cornettists to emerge from the beginning of 1920s. Always, though, until his death in the 1960s, he insisted on playing in a fiery, hard-hitting manner, reflecting a deep and abiding admiration for King Oliver and Louis Armstrong.

He started on drums, but at 13 had acquired a cornet. Played semi-professionally with Elmer Schoebel (1921), then with a succession of varied bands through 1920s, culminating in his joining Ted Lewis Orchestra in 1929 (he was to remain until 1936).

Made record début 1924 with Bucktown Five **(Muggsy Spanier 1924-1928)** with the 18-year-old cornettist acquitting himself well, particularly with his hot, rhythmic playing on **Darktown Strutters' Ball**.

Visited Europe with Lewis (1930). With Ben Pollack Orchestra (1936-38). Suffered complete physical collapse which proved almost fatal and was confined in Touro Infirmary, New Orleans. To commemorate the event — and his recovery — he composed blues **Relaxin' At Touro**, which, together with 15 other titles, he recorded in 1939 with his Ragtimers. **Touro**, with marvelous use of plunger-mute, illustrates his greatness as blues-player, and remains probably his finest recorded solo. The Ragtimers' tracks **(The Great 16)** collectively rank with finest-ever white Dixieland recordings, and his playing throughout impressive.

Spanier was back with Lewis (1939-40) for three months, later joining Bob Crosby Orchestra (1940-41). Left to put together own big band **(Muggsy Spanier)** (1941-43).

Led own groups and worked with other bands before rejoining Ted Lewis a second time (1944). Between 1944-48, mostly led own small combos at Nick's, NYC, and until joining Earl Hines in '51, had worked in other major US cities as band-leader. Stayed with Hines, on and off, until 1959; late-1959, continued to make appearances in various parts of the States, plus trip to Germany (1960). Appeared at 1964 Newport Jazz Festival but soon afterwards illness forced his retirement.

Spanier died in Sausalito, California (the state in which he had settled, in '57), early in 1967.

Albums:
Various (Including Bucktown Five), Bix Beiderbecke & The Chicago Cornets (Milestone)
Muggsy Spanier 1924-1928 (—/Fountain)
Various (Including Mound City Blue Blowers), Recordings Made Between 1930 & 1941 (CBS—France)
New Orleans Rhythm Kings (1934-1935) (MCA Coral—Germany)
Muggsy Spanier, The Great 16 RCA Victor/RCA Victor—France)
Sidney Bechet/Muggsy Spanier, Ragtime Jazz (Olympic)/Tribute To Bechet (Ember)
Muggsy Spanier (Ace of Hearts)
Muggsy Spanier & His Ragtimers (—/London)
'This Is Jazz': Muggsy Spanier (Jazzology/—)
The Genius Of Sidney Bechet (Jazzology/—)

The Great 16, Muggsy Spanier's Ragtime Band (courtesy RCA Victor).

Spirit Level

One of Britain's most enduring and original bands since the late 1970s, Spirit Level created a dynamic style which leaped uncompromisingly out of hard bop long before that particular idiom found renewed favor nationally and internationally in the mid-'80s.

Formed in Bristol in the West of England in '79, Spirit Level have evolved a distinctive collective voice and attack. One of their greatest assets is an extraordinarily compatible rhythm section of Paul Anstey on acoustic bass, Tony Orrell on drums and the unusually gifted, blues-inspired pianist-composer Tim Richards.

Their front-line features the unequivocal voice of formidable tenor saxophonist Paul Dunmall. Having spent three formative years working in the United States — notably with Johnny 'Guitar' Watson and Alice Coltrane — Dunmall's numerous accolades include 'best soloist' award at the '79 Dunkirk Jazz Festival. Spirit Level have also regularly featured trumpeter/flugelhorn-player Dave Holdsworth, a familiar figure on the British jazz circuit with such local luminaries as Mike Osborne, Chris McGregor, Mike Westbrook, Graham Collier and the London Jazz Composers Orchestra.

Spirit Level have produced two excellent albums — **Mice In The Wallet** ('82) and **Proud Owners** ('84) — and, in '86, toured the UK to great acclaim with former Mingus trumpeter Jack Walrath.

Albums:
Mice In The Wallet (—/Spotlite)
Proud Owners (—/Spotlite)

UK's Spirit Level, Mice In The Wallet (courtesy Spotlite—their début.

Spontaneous Music Ensemble

Britain's Spontaneous Music Ensemble has never been concerned with abstractions but rather with shapes, relationships and the organic growth of musical conversation.

Established in 1966 by drummer John Stevens and altoist Trevor Watts, SME has had a shifting personnel — Evan Parker, Kenny Wheeler, Paul Rutherford, Derek Bailey, Dave Holland — but since the music is based on collective principles, the texture remains the same.

There are no solos in SME music, yet it has attracted star soloists like Steve Lacy and Bobby Bradford **(Bobby Bradford + SME)** and, during SME's eight-year residency at the Little Theatre Club, avant-gardists like Don Cherry, Rashied Ali and Han Bennink sat in.

One of the finest free collectives in the world, its output reflects its steady growth **(Challenge, Karyöbin, Oliv, The Source, Birds Of A Feather, So What Do You Think** and **Face To Face)**. Trevor Watts' band Amalgam, with John Stevens on drums and various bassists, gives a more conventional setting to their talents and shows both men to be magnificently inventive swingers **(Prayer For Peace, Amalgam Play Blackwell & Higgins** and **Innovation)**.

Stevens has also led the jazz-rock-influenced Away and has worked more recently with his hard-hitting Freebop group; his album **Freebop** (recorded at a Bracknell Jazz Festival) is dedicated to the memory of the influential and under-sung British drummer Phil Seamen. Recent Stevens' projects have also included his nine-piece Folkus, a 27-piece dance orchestra and a collaboration with the Rolling Stones' drummer Charlie Watts. Trevor Watts has subsequently worked with a re-vamped Amalgam, while his formidable Moiré Music group is, without doubt, one of the most exciting and musically explorative bands to emerge in the UK in the '80s.

Albums:
Challenge (—/Eyemark)
Karyöbin (—/Island)
Oliv (—/Marmalade)
The Source (—/Tangent)
Birds Of A Feather (BYG/BYG)
So What Do You Think (—/Tangent)
Face To Face (Emanem/Emanem)
Amalgam, Prayer For Peace (—/Transatlantic)
John Stevens/Evan Parker, The Longest Night (—/Ogun)
Chemistry (—/Vinyl)
Amalgam—Deep (—/Vinyl)
SME, 1.2 Albert Ayler (—/Affinity)
SME, Biosystems (—/Incus)
John Stevens' Freebop (—/Affinity)
John Stevens' Folkus, The Life Of Riley (—/Affinity)

Spontaneous Music Ensemble, The Source—From And Towards (Tangent).

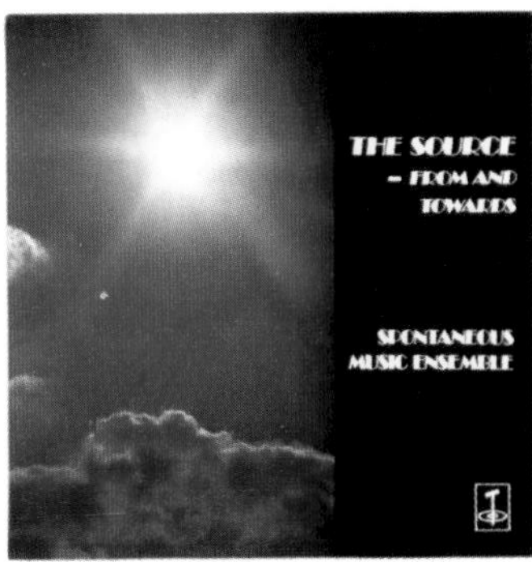

Above: Festival Favorites Spyro Gyra—'South America by way of New York City'. An enormously successful fusion band.

Spyro Gyra

The lively Latin-jazz and rock fusion of Spyro Gyra has been described as coming from 'South America by way of New York City'.

Formed in 1975 in Buffalo by saxophonist Jay Beckenstein and keyboard-player Jeremy Wall (originally as a bar-jam band), they entered into a creative partnership with producer Rich Calandra. Their first album, **Spyro Gyra**, was initially self-produced and self-distributed before Amherst Records picked them up. In '78, Spyro Gyra's **Shaker Song** single appeared in six different **Billboard** charts and *Record World* named them 'top new jazz group of the year'. Subsequently, the group has scored enormous successes with albums like **Morning Dance** and **Carnival**.

Since those early days, the group has also included keyboardist Thomas Schuman, guitarists Chet Catallo and Julio Fernandez, bassists Jim Kurzdorfer, Kim Stone and David Wofford, drummer Richie Morales, vibist Dave Samuels and percussionist Gerardo Velez.

A popular festival and concert band, Spyro Gyra are captured in live performance on **Access All Areas**.

Albums:
Morning Dance (MCA/MCA)
Catching The Sun (MCA/MCA)
Carnival (MCA/MCA)
Freetime (MCA/MCA)
Alternating Currents (MCA/MCA)
Access All Areas (MCA/MCA)

John Stevens

see Spontaneous Music Ensemble

Rex Stewart

Rex William Stewart (born Philadelphia, Pennsylvania, 1907) was one of the most expressive, and impressive, trumpeters/cornettists in the history of jazz music.

Established an impressive reputation as prominent soloist with Duke Ellington between 1934-45. Most distinctive quality was an ability to produce an instantly recognizable tonal effect by depressing valves of his instrument

Above: Rex Stewart—his half-valve skills and fierce blowing made him one of the great individualists of jazz cornet technique.

halfway (other trumpeters have attempted to reproduce this effect but only Clark Terry has succeeded in obtaining the kind of originality in approach which Stewart pioneered with total success). Nowhere else but within the framework of Ellingtonia did Stewart sound as compeling and fulfiling, nor did he ever achieve elsewhere the heights he scaled with, say, **Boy Meets Horn**, heard first in a studio recording **(The Ellington Era, 1927-1940, Vol 1)** and then in performance, **The Duke 1940**.

When Cootie Williams left Ellington for Benny Goodman, Stewart (until arrival of Ray Nance), shouldered the responsibility of taking the lion's share of trumpet solos.

With Fletcher Henderson, Stewart first established himself as a top-class soloist. With Henderson, he soloed impressively on **The Stampede (The Fletcher Henderson Story, Vol 1); Feeling Good, Old Black Joe Blues (Vol 2)**; and **Wang Wang Blues, Sugar Foot Stomp** and **Singin' The Blues (Vol 3)**. Most interesting of these is **Singin' The Blues** because it shows Stewart's obvious affection for and familiarity with Bix Beiderbecke's more famous solo on same.

First visit to New York in 1921, returning in 1925 to work with Elmer Snowden, Horace Henderson and others. Also worked with McKinney's Cotton Pickers (1931), Luis Russell (1934), and even led own big band in New York for over a year (1933-34). After leaving Ellington, fronted several small combos as well as guesting with others, including regular work, on and off, with Eddie Condon bands. Worked for radio stations as disc jockey and began to write regularly for leading jazz periodicals when he settled in California at end of 1950s. Worked sporadically during 1960s — including at least two trips to Europe — mostly as guest soloist, at jazz festivals and special events.

Probably his best work on record, outside of Ellington, came when he was reunited with former big-band colleagues Coleman Hawkins, Cootie Williams and others for a totally delightful **The Big Challenge**.

Made in 1960, **The Rex Stewart Memorial Album** contains much fine post-Ellington playing, but there are also occasions when his solos tend to become sloppy and uncreative, and his singing and kazoo-playing are of even less stature. A better picture of the true Rex Stewart, dating from 1934-39, and with numerous Ellington associates in support, is to be found within the grooves of **Rex Stewart Memorial**.

Albums:

Luis Russell & His Louisiana Swing Orchestra (Columbia/—)
The Fletcher Henderson Story (Columbia)/ The Fletcher Henderson Story, Vols 1, 2, 3 (CBS)
The Complete Duke Ellington, Vols 6,7 (CBS—France)
Duke Ellington, The Ellington Era, 1927-1940, Vols 1, 2 (Columbia/CBS)
Duke Ellington (Trip)/ All That Jazz: Duke Ellington (DJM)
If Dreams Come True: Duke Ellington—Cotton Club, 1938, Vol 1 (Jazz Archives)
The Works Of Duke, Vols 9-17 (RCA Victor—France)
Duke Ellington, Black, Brown & Beige (Ariston—Italy)
Duke Ellington 1943-1946 (Jazz Society/Jazz Society)
Django Reinhardt, Django & His American Friends, Vol 2 (—/HMV)
Various (Including Rex Stewart/Cootie Williams), The Big Challenge (Jazztone/Concert Hall)
Various, The Big Reunion (Jazztone/—)
Rex Stewart Memorial (—/CBS—Realm)
The Rex Stewart Memorial Album (Prestige/—)

Sonny Stitt

Born 1924 in Boston, saxophonist Sonny Stitt had the misfortune to come up with a sound and style similar to Charlie Parker's for, unlike the imitators, Stitt's had developed independently. To duck the Bird comparisons, he switched to tenor for a period after 1949 and he had equal facility on alto, tenor and baritone.

Like most of his generation, Stitt gained experience in the big bands, Tiny Bradshaw, Billy Eckstine, Dizzy Gillespie, and solos with a Gillespie small group on **Oo Bop Sh'Bam** and **That's Earl, Brother** in 1946 **(In The Beginning)**. He can be heard playing all three horns on a compilation of his own small groups, 1949-51, which included side-players like Bud Powell, John Lewis, J J Johnson, Gene Ammons, Max Roach and Art Blakey. Stitt stretched throughout and the result is arguably his best work, from the stomping **All God's Chillun Got Rhythm** to the unique voicings of **Afternoon In Paris (Genesis)**.

An unlikely pairing of Stitt and trumpeter Roy Eldridge takes off, with both musicians attacking the blues program with ferocity **(Sittin' In)**. The second album from this set features Stitt with Oscar Peterson and has excellent solos from the Stitt tenor on **Moten Swing, Blues For Pres, Sweets, Ben & All The Other Funky Ones** and **Easy Does It**. A meeting with fellow tenorist, Sonny Rollins, illustrates their different gifts — Rollins analytical and adventurous, Stitt lithe within the tradition **(Sonny Side Up)**.

He made scores of albums in later years, the best being in company with contemporaries like Gene Ammons, two-tenor stormers **(Soul Summit, Together Again For The Last Time)** or Art Blakey's Messengers **(In Walked Sonny)**, while a session from 1967 reunited him with bebop giants Howard McGhee and Kenny Clarke **(Night Work)**. In the '70s, he toured with the Giants of Jazz, in company with Gillespie, Monk, Blakey and Al McKibbon. In later years, Stitt also renewed an earlier acquaintance with another favorite musical sparring-partner, altoist-tenorist Red Holloway.

Stitt was taken ill in '82, shortly after having undertaken a tour of Japan. Sonny Stitt — that great individualist on tenor — died on July 22, 1982, from cancer.

Sonny Stitt with Blakey and the Jazz Messengers, In Walked Sonny (Sonet).

Albums:

Dizzy Gillespie, In The Beginning (Prestige/Prestige)
Genesis (Prestige/Prestige)
Sittin' In (Verve/Verve)
Sonny Stitt-Gene Ammons, Soul Summitt (Prestige/Transatlantic)
Sonny Stitt-Gene Ammons, Together Again For The Last Time (Prestige/—)
Sonny Stitt, Art Blakey, In Walked Sonny (Sonet/Sonet)

Above: Sonny Stitt, alto and tenor, even baritone on occasion. He always maintained he developed independently of Parker.

Night Work (Black Lion/Black Lion)
The Bop Session (Sonet/Sonet)
Sonny Stitt-Red Holloway, Just Friends (Catalyst/Affinity)
Sonny's Last Recordings (—/Kingdom Gate)
Various, Giants Of Jazz (George Wein Collection/George Wein Collection)
Constellation (Muse/Muse)

Billy Strayhorn

Even as a teenager, Billy Strayhorn (born Dayton, Ohio, 1915) was well developed as an impressionistic composer, orchestrator, lyricist, pianist. For a youngster, Strayhorn showed remarkable gifts of sophistication and maturity in writing complex melody for, and scholarly lyric to, songs like **Lush Life** — one of his finest songs.

Strayhorn (also known as 'Swee' Pea' or 'Strays') played classical music in school orchestra in Pittsburgh (his parents had moved to Pennsylvania, via Hillsboro, North Carolina), after he had received private tuition.

Submitted composition (1938) to Duke Ellington, who was impressed: **Something To Live For**, with vocal by Jean Eldridge and with Strayhorn at the piano, was the first of his compositions recorded by Ellington **(The Ellington Era, 1927-1940, Vol 2)** by which time he had been welcomed as part of Ellington entourage. Was to remain thus employed until his death 29 years later. From '37 onwards, Strayhorn was to become Ellington's closest collaborator, an inseparable companion and friend (one of Ellington's precious few confidants) and a second pianist — alone or in duet with Ellington — in both big-band and small-group settings. As a pianist, Strayhorn was best-known as sensitive accompanist; as soloist, his style was spare, economic, but not especially distinctive. There was, however, a certain similarity in approach to keyboard by Strayhorn and his employer. Even more pronouned was the closeness in the writing by the pair. So close, in fact, that where the two had collaborated, it is difficult to tell which had composed what portions, such as **Such Sweet Thunder, Toot Suite (Ellington Jazz Party), A Drum Is A Woman, The Far East Suite, The Queen's Suite (The Ellington Suites)** and **Suite Thursday**.

Strayhorn was responsible for **Take The 'A' Train** which, following its initial recordings **(The Works Of Duke, Vols 14, 15)**, was to become Ellington's longest-serving signature tune. Other Strayhorn creations which became part of the Ellington song book were: **I'm Checking Out, Goodbye**—feature for singer Ivie Anderson **(The Ellington Era, 1927-1940, Vol 2); Daydream** — first recorded by Ellington small group in 1940 **(The Works Of Duke, Vol 12); Rock Skippin' At The Blue Note (The World Of Duke Ellington, Vol 3/The World Of Duke Ellington, Vol 2); Johnny Come Lately (The Works Of Duke, Vol 18)**; and **Passin' Flower, Raincheck, Clementine, Chelsea Bridge, Love Like This Can't Last, After All** (all **The Works Of Duke, Vol 17)**. **Chelsea Bridge**, which has been compared — favorably — to Ravel's **Valses Nobles Et Sentimentales**, is a firm clue as to one of Strayhorn's premier musical influences and inspirations.

Outside of Ellington, Strayhorn's output on record never was a large one. Best of all was a 1959 date **(Cue For Saxophone)** with leader-for-the-day Strayhorn's compositions and arrangements resulting in exceptional music from a sextet including Johnny Hodges (for whom Strayhorn wrote and played piano on many occasions), Harold Baker and Strayhorn himself. Strayhorn also recorded several piano duets with his alma mater, best of which are divided between the 12 selections on **The**

Golden Duke, four of which are more or less a showcase for the cello artistry of Oscar Pettiford, then Ellington's bassist. Other albums that bear testimony to Strayhorn's musical sensitivity and eloquence include **Everybody Knows Johnny Hodges**; Ella Fitzgerald's **Ella At Duke's Place**; Hodges' **The Jeep Is Jumpin'** and... **And His Mother Called Him Bill**, last-named a deeply-felt salute by Ellington and his then (1967) orchestra, immediately following Strayhorn's death. There could be no more poignant tribute to Billy Strayhorn than the unaccompanied piano solo (featuring Strayhorn's **Sweet Lotus Blossom**), recorded by Ellington after the session officially had ended.

Albums:

Duke Ellington, The Ellington Era, 1927-1940, Vols 1, 2 (Columbia/CBS)
Duke Ellington, The Works Of Duke Vols 12-20 (RCA Victor—France)
Duke Ellington, The Golden Duke (Prestige/Prestige)
The World Of Duke Ellington, Vol 3 (Columbia)/The World Of Duke Ellington, Vol 2 (CBS)
Duke Ellington & The Ellingtonians (Vogue—France)
Duke Ellington, Such Sweet Thunder (Columbia/CBS-Realm)
Duke Ellington, Ellington Jazz Party (Columbia/Philips)
Duke Ellington, A Drum Is A Woman (Columbia/Philips)
Duke Ellington (Peer Gynt Suites, Nos 1 & 2)/ Suite Thursday (Columbia/CBS)
Duke Ellington, The Far East Suite (RCA Victor/RCA Victor)
Duke Ellington, The Ellington Suites (Pablo/Pablo)
Everybody Knows Johnny Hodges (Impulse/Impulse)
Ella Fitzgerald, Ella At Duke's Place (Verve/Verve)
Billy Strayhorn, Cue For Saxophone (Master Jazz Recordings/Vocalion)
Duke Ellington, ... And His Mother Called Him Bill (RCA Victor/RCA Victor)

Stuff

see Steve Gadd, Eric Gale

Maxine Sullivan

With a remarkably pure, non-abrasive singing voice, Maxine Sullivan (née Marietta Williams) began her career during early-1930s on radio stations in Pittsburgh (she was born in Homestead, Pittsburgh, 1911) before she was introduced to band-leader-pianist-writer Claude Thornhill.

Gained reputation with her fine singing at Onyx Club, New York, where she sang with musicians like John Kirby, Frankie Newton, Pete Brown and Buster Bailey. Thornhill took these, himself, and two others into the studios in 1937 to make a series of records on which singer and band interacted beautifully. Tonally and rhythmically, it is easy to understand why and how she influenced Ella Fitzgerald.

Amongst tracks recorded with Onyx Club musicians in August, '37, were two traditional Scottish airs, **Loch Lomond** and **Annie Laurie**. Recording of former became her first major hit record (and the biggest) **(Frankie Newton At The Onyx Club)**.

Worked regularly in California during late-1930s, then toured and recorded with Benny Carter Orchestra **(Benny Carter & His Orchestra 1940-41)**.

Retired to live in Philadelphia (1942), but made comeback during mid-1940s, playing clubs and occasional concerts. Visited Europe for first time in '48, returning six years later. Once again, left music business, only to make second comeback in 1958. This time she added to her vocal performances by playing either valve-trombone or miniature trumpet or flugelhorn, instruments she had learned to play — well — during her second 'retirement'.

Also worked in person/on record with pianist Earl Hines **(Earl Hines & Maxine Sullivan At The Overseas Press Club)** and, on more than one occasion, further enhanced concerts by World's Greatest Jazz Band **(The World's Greatest Jazz Band Of Yank Lawson & Bob Haggart In Concert, Vol 2: At Carnegie Hall)**. Typical latter-day Sullivan artistry is to be found within **Sullivan, Shakepeare, Hyman**, as she and pianist-arranger Dick Hyman work jazz-like wonders with Shakespearean lyrics to which Hyman set music.

Albums:

Frankie Newton At The Onyx Club (Tax—Sweden)
Benny Carter & His Orchestra (1940-41) (RCA Victor—France)
Maxine Sullivan/Bob Wlber, Close As Pages In A Book (Monmouth-Evergreen/Parlophone)
Maxine Sullivan/Bob Wilber, The Music Of Hoagy Carmichael (Monmouth-Evergreen/Parlophone)
Earl Hines & Maxine Sullivan Live At The Overseas Press Club (Chiaroscuro/—)
The World's Greatest Jazz Band Of Yank Lawson & Bob Haggart In Concert, Vol 2: At Carnegie Hall (World Jazz/—)
Maxine Sullivan/Dick Hyman, Sullivan, Shakespeare, Hyman (Monmouth-Evergreen)

Below: And His Mother Called Him Bill—'Swee' Pea' Billy Strayhorn. Until the day he died, Ellington's closest collaborator and inseparable companion.

Sun Ra

Band-leader Sun Ra was born Sonny Blount, 1928, and began as an arranger for Fletcher Henderson in the late '40s.

The earliest records of his own band **(Sun Song** and **Sound Of Joy)** give few hints of his subsequent and logical development into the avant-garde, although his preoccupation with percussive textures is shown in the gongs and organ of **Sun Song** and massed tympani of **Street Named Hell**. Musicians like baritonist Pat Patrick and tenorist John Gilmore, featured here, were to remain with him for two decades.

Based in Chicago, Sun Ra developed his ideas at a tangent to the prevailing hard bop idiom, exploring exotic voicings with his Solar Arkestra. A mystic, Sun Ra's image has always been other-wordly but his music, though startlingly original in its combination of naivety and prediction, is always approachable.

The great series of albums recorded on his own Saturn label — hand-painted, distributed by members of the Arkestra in their space-robes — were prized collectors' items throughout the '60s, and have since been re-issued. The Arkestra scarcely worked at all in this period, the bizarre pairings, maverick borrowings, dense collectives and massive strike-force of percussion being light-years ahead of the market.

In the aftermath of the New Thing, it was realized that Sun Ra had anticipated many of the new directions (Gilmore, in particular, having had an influence on John Coltrane), and the Arkestra's reputation moved from the underground into the mainstream. Atmospheric, often programmatic, his work on pieces like **Atlantis (Atlantis)** or **The Magic City (The Magic City), The Sun Myth** or **Cosmic Chaos (The Heliocentric Worlds Of Sun Ra)** offers an alternative to western methods of composition. In later years, Sun Ra added to his regular keyboards and sounds utterly unique on electric piano and Moog synthesizer **(The Solar-Myth Approach)** using the latter, that Fort Knox of sounds, to extend the textural variety of the Arkestra.

On stage, Sun Ra's Arkestra are overwhelming both musically and visually, the musicians dressed in weird costumes with light-up hats, back-projected film, dancers and fire-eaters. Soloists like Sun Ra himself, Gilmore, Patrick and altoist Marshall Allen are brilliant improvisers, though it is the ensembles, developing the composer's themes in layered counterpoint, that are the most breathtaking.

Albums:

Sun Song (Delmark/Delmark)
Sound Of Joy (Delmark/Delmark)
Angels & Demons At Play (Impulse/Impulse)
Astro-Black (Impulse/Impulse)
The Magic City (Impulse/Impulse)
Atlantis (Impulse/Impulse)
The Nubians Of Plutonia (Impulse/Impulse)
The Heliocentric Worlds Of Sun Ra, Volumes 1 & 2 (ESP/Fontana)
Pictures Of Infinity (Black Lion/Black Lion)
The Solar-Myth Approach, Volumes 1 & 2 (BYG/BYG)
Unity (—/Horo)
Other Voices, Other Times (—/Horo)
New Steps (—/Horo)
Sun Ra Solo Piano (Improvising Artists Inc/—)
Meets Salah Ragab In Egypt Plus The Cairo Jazz Band (Praxis/Praxis)
Live At Praxis '84, Vol. One (Praxis/Praxis)
Cosmo Sun Connection (Saturn/Saturn)
Children Of The Sun (Saturn/Saturn)
Hiroshima (Saturn/Saturn)
Nuits De La Fondation Maeght Vol. One (Recommended Records/Recommended Records)
Sunrise In Different Dimensions (HatArt/HatArt)
Strange Celestial Road (Y Records/Y Records)

The innovatory Sun Ra, Angels And Demons At Play (courtesy Impulse).

Above: **John Surman, virtuoso of the baritone sax. In the '80s, he has worked extensively with Norway's Karin Krog.**

John Surman

British-born baritone saxophonist, John Surman, is both a virtuoso and an innovator, extending the range of the big horn upwards into high harmonics, and freeing it of its lumbering tendencies while losing none of its weight.

John Surman's earliest involvement with jazz began in '58 in Plymouth, Devon. While still at school, he attended workshops organized by local luminary Mike Westbrook. In the early '60s, both Surman and Westbrook went to London where one of Surman's earliest gigs was with tenorist Ronnie Scott. By '68, Surman was leading his own groups which included trumpeter Harry Beckett, bassist Harry Miller and reeds-players Mike Osborne and Alan Skidmore.

A Coltrane-inspired saxophonist, Surman gained a wide reputation for his work, particularly on baritone, with the Mike Westbrook Orchestra, 1958-68. Over the years he has added soprano and bass clarinet. Some of his finest work with Westbrook **(Citadel/Room 315)** sees him rising like Krakatoa through the section on **Outgoing**, echo effects and overblowings running like seismic faults, and soaring lyrically on soprano on **Tender Love**. Surman's early explorations in free-blowing were to be extended with **Where Fortune Smiles** (alongside guitarist John McLaughlin and bassist Dave Holland). In '69, a celebrated collaboration with McLaughlin resulted in their ground-breaking **Extrapolation** — an album which was to provide a cornerstone in British jazz-rock fusion. In 1969, Surman established a trio with Americans Barre Phillips, bass, and Stu Martin, drums **(John Surman)** playing with a scope and authority that established him as the foremost baritonist in the history of that instrument. The unaccompanied section of **Caractacus**, for example, has a range, flexibility and grandeur that has never been equaled.

During a hiatus in trio work, Surman formed Morning Glory including Norwegian guitarist Terje Rypdal and British keyboards-player John Taylor, while a second formation of the trio evolved into the short-lived MUMPS with trombonist Albert Mangelsdorff **(A Matter Of Taste)**. In '70, Surman received worldwide acclaim touring as part of the Francy Boland Big Band. With his breathtaking performances at the World Exposition in Osaka, Japan, Surman became internationally recognized as the most important and innovative baritone-player of his time.

In 1973, Surman formed an all-saxophone trio (SOS) with altoist Mike Osborne and tenor-player Alan Skidmore, each horn in turn falling back to provide a rhythmic figure. The music is like a strange, barbaric maypole dance.

Surman worked infrequently in Britain during the '70s, finding constant work in Europe, but in '78 he returned to record **Sonatinas** with British pianist-composer Stan Tracey. In the '80s, Surman returned more frequently to his homeland, appearing notably with John Taylor and Norma Winstone in Azimuth (playing baritone, tenor and soprano). In '81, he premiered his vast Brass Project which included material from his *Wessex Collection* dating back to '68.

More recently, he has worked extensively in a duo with Norwegian vocalist Karin Krog **(Such Winters Of Memory)** and in '86 gave a unique and extraordinary musical performance with Krog, pianist John Taylor and the Cantamus Girls Choir. In the summer of that year, Surman renewed an earlier acquaintance with the Gil Evans Orchestra, touring internationally as one of Evans' indomitable front-line soloists.

Albums:
Mike Westbrook, Citadel/Room 315 (RCA/RCA)
How Many Clouds Can You See? (—/Deram)
Where Fortune Smiles (Pye/Pye)
Westering Home (Island/Island)
John Surman-John McLaughlin, Extrapolation (Polydor/Polydor)
John Surman (Vogue/Vogue)
The Trio (Dawn/Dawn)
Conflagration (Dawn/Dawn)
Morning Glory (Island/Island)
Barre Phillips, Mountainscapes (ECM/ECM)
SOS (—/Ogun)
Stan Tracey-John Surman, Sonatinas (—/Steam)
Mick Goodrick, In Pas(s)ing (ECM/ECM)
Upon Reflection (ECM/ECM)
Barre Phillips, Journal Violone II (ECM/ECM)
The Amazing Adventures Of Simon Simon (ECM/ECM)
John Surman-Karin Krog-Pierre Favre, Such Winters Of Memory (ECM/ECM)
Witholding Pattern (ECM/ECM)

John Surman solo, The Amazing Adventures Of Simon Simon (ECM).

Jamaaladeen Tacuma

The wide-ranging musical inspirations of Jamaaladeen Tacuma have contributed to making him one of the 1980s' most important and inspirational electric bassists. His studies have taken in everything from Ornette Coleman's new-age harmolodics to the possibilities of more primitive Eastern instruments like the oud, gamelan, koto and samisen.

Raised in Philadelphia (real name: Rudy McDaniel), Tacuma's earliest influences were local and visiting soul luminaries like James Brown, the Temptations and Stevie Wonder. His first professional gig was with organist Charles Earland. However, it was Ornette Coleman's rhythmic 'new wave-olodics' Prime Time band **(Dancing In Your Head**, '76; **Body Meta**, '78; **Of Human Feelings**, '79) which brought Tacuma international recognition as one of the music's brightest young improvisational bassists. Indeed, with Prime Time, Tacuma was often the leading soloist. In '78, he also joined the Colemans (Ornette and son Denardo) on James Blood Ulmer's explorations in 'guitar-olodics' on **The Tales Of Captain Black**.

An undeniably multi-directional musician, Tacuma has also been heard with his own units Cosmetic and Jamaal, and worked with Bill Laswell's Golden Palominos, Kip Hanrahan, Walt Dickerson and poet Jayne Cortez as well as Jeff Beck and son star Harold Melvin.

One of Tacuma's finest solo projects, **Renaissance Man** ('83-'84), finds him storming through some highly individualistic original material in the eclectic and exalted company of Ornette Coleman, Olu Dara, David Murray, Daniel Ponce and Bill Bruford. The album also includes Tacuma's extraordinary four-movement **The Battle Of Images** (for string quartet, tympani, percussion and electric fretless bass guitar).

In '81, Tacuma received the distinction of being awarded the highest number of votes for an electric bassist in *Downbeat* magazine's Critics' Poll for 'new talent deserving wider recognition'.

Albums:
Prime Time, Dancing In Your Head (A&M-Horizon/A&M-Horizon)
Prime Time, Body Meta (Artists House/—)
Prime Time, Of Human Feelings (Antilles/Antilles)
James Blood Ulmer, The Tales Of Captain Black (Artists House/—)
Golden Palominos (Celluloid/Celluloid)
Show Stopper (Gramavision/Gramavision)
Renaissance Man (Gramavision/Gramavision)

Renaissance Man, Jamaaladeen Tacuma (courtesy Gramavision).

Tania Maria

Brazilian-born pianist-composer Tania Maria became immensely popular in the 1980s with her boundlessly energetic, explosive piano-vocal style and dynamic live performances.

Tania Maria Reis was born in Sao Luis, Brazil, in 1948. Encouraged by her occasional-guitarist father, she learned piano from age 7, including several years of classical study. At 13, she was working with her own Brazilian ensemble — her main inspiration, at the time, being pianists Oscar Peterson and local luminaries Johnny Alf and Luiz Eça. Later — as a singer, pianist and composer — she would add other inspirations like Sarah Vaughan, Jackie Cain, Anita O'Day, McCoy Tyner, Keith Jarrett, Bill Evans, Antonio Carlos Jobim and Milton Nascimento.

As a woman, she found it hard trying to make a career in the male-dominated music scene of Brazil and 'escaped' to Paris in the '70s. A three-month visit became a seven-year stay and, using Paris as her home base, she toured widely. Bossa nova pioneer Charlie Byrd heard her in Australia and introduced her to Carl Jefferson of Concord Records in the United States. Her Concord début, **Piquant**, was a great success and brought a string of subsequent eagerly received albums, including **The Real Tania Maria: Wild!** live at the Great American Music Hall, '84.

Since receiving international recognition in the early '80s, Tania Maria's fire-ball concert style has been in great demand for festivals and clubs worldwide, receiving the ultimate accolade by being signed to the reactivated Blue Note label's roster of 'new artists' in '85.

Albums:
Tania Maria Live (—/Accord)
Piquant (Concord/Concord)
Taurus (Concord/Concord)
Come With Me (Concord/Concord)
Love Explosion (Concord/Concord)
The Real Tania Maria: Wild! (Concord/Concord)
Made In New York (Blue Note-Manhattan/Blue Note-Manhattan)

Tania Maria, Come With Me (Courtesy Concord—Ms Reis, 1982.

Wild! (courtesy Concord): Ms Reis live, 1984, with John Purcell on saxophones.

Buddy Tate

Born, 1915, mainstream tenorist Buddy Tate is part of that T-bone dynasty of Texas tenors — Illinois Jacquet, Arnett Cobb, Herschel Evans, Budd Johnson — characterized by a big, meaty sound.

He gained early experience in the territory bands, playing with Herschel Evans in Troy Floyd's band, then with Andy Kirk and Nat Towles. In 1939, he took over Evans' chair in the Basie band, and stayed until 1948, a featured soloist on '40s warhorses like **Rock-A-Bye Basie** and **Superchief**. Tate finally left the band and took up a 19-year incumbency at Harlem's Celebrity Club, fronting a fine septet. A straight-ahead swinger, beefily tender on ballads, Tate has been a thoroughly dependable recording artist and is usually at his best with fellow ex-Basieites. **Teeny Weeny** from an album which has one side of Tate with Buck Clayton, Dicky Wells and Jo Jones, is a good example of his tenor style **(Swinging Like Tate)**, while another session with Buck Clayton features his warm, relaxed clarinet on **Blue Creek (Kansas City Nights)**. Albums with Clark Terry **(Tate-a-Tate)** and with Paul Quinichette and Jay McShann **(Kansas City Joys)** abound with his robust sense of enjoyment.

Albums:
Swinging Like Tate (Felsted/Felsted)
Kansas City Nights (Prestige/Prestige)
Tate-a-Tate (Prestige-Swingsville/Prestige-Swingsville)
Kansas City Joys (Sonet/Sonet)
Groovin' With Buddy Tate (Prestige-Swingsville/Prestige-Swingsville)

Above: Buddy Tate, the 'Super Chief', himself. Texan tenorist of distinction, one of Basie's most distinguished soloists and leader of swinging combos.

Art Tatum

When Arthur 'Art' Tatum (born Toledo, Ohio, 1910) first paraded his technical piano skills, he amazed musicians and non-musicians alike.

They marveled at his dazzling right-hand runs (executed often at frightening speed), whilst an ever-active left hand pumped out what was his own refinement of a stride beat; his command of the keyboard was total. Harmonically, Tatum was advanced for the 1920s, indeed, despite subsequent technical developments, his harmonic sense was to cause a sense of wonderment amongst other pianists after his death in 1956. Tatum's predilection for sudden changes of key and tempo tended to baffle his listeners (even some musicians) but there was no denying his interest in retaining melodic interest in whatever he was playing. Classical piano virtuosi like Gieseking and Horowitz were seen in New York jazz clubs during late-1930s, 1940s, watching in apparent abject disbelief (and no little admiration) as Tatum unleashed his pyrotechnical skills.

Art Tatum was totally blind in one eye and suffered diminishing vision in the other. Started on piano at young age, taking violin and guitar lessons at 13 (whilst attending a Columbus, Ohio, school for the blind). Two years' study at Toledo School of Music, when he worked with own band in Toledo and district. Worked with band of Speed Webb prior to taking residency on local radio station (WSPD). After spending one-and-a-half years with Adelaide Hall, worked for a while in New York, before spending next two years in Cleveland and Chicago.

Moved to Hollywood in 1936 where he stayed for almost one year. Came to London in 1938 where he played at clubs and in variety. Back to California, where he worked for another period before returning to New York. After his first recording date, in 1933, Tatum continued to make discs (for Decca) which demonstrated, time and again, his highly developed artistry. Stand-out items from a batch of uniformly superb recordings—all solo—included **Get Happy, Tiger Rag, Indiana (Masterpieces/Art Of Tatum 2)** and **Gone With The Wind (Masterpieces/Art Of Tatum)**. There was fine Tatum, too, at a 1937 date with Tatum leading a six-piece band through a quartet of numbers, including a spirited **I've Got My Love To Keep Me Warm (Swing Combos 1935-1941)**.

Switched from solo to trio format in 1943 (with Tiny Grimes, guitar; Slam Stewart, bass). It worked well, in live performance and on record **(Masterpieces/Art Of Tatum, 1, 2)**, but by 1945 Tatum was again performing as solo artist. Remarkably fine concert performance taped by its promoter Gene Norman in 1949 **(Piano Starts Here/An Art Tatum Concert)** with Tatum, in joyous form throughout, showing incredible rhythmic flexibility on tracks like **The Man I Love** and **I Know That You Know**, and, on **Willow, Weep For Me**, evincing more feeling than was customary. Also in 1949, recorded three times for Capitol **Solo Piano)**. Starting December '53 (and probably completed the next April), Tatum recorded 125 titles for Norman Granz, 121 of which eventually appeared on **The Tatum Solo Piano Masterpieces**. The standard of performance throughout what were marathon sessions—over 70 titles were cut during first two sessions—is unbelievably high, with Tatum in incredible form: **The Man I Love, Jitterbug Waltz, Too Marvelous For Words, It's The Talk Of The Town, Stompin' At The Savoy, Caravan, You're Driving Me Crazy, This Can't Be Love, Fine & Dandy**, and **Ain't Misbehavin'**.

For Granz, Tatum also undertook interesting dates which placed him in company of first-rate musicians **(The Tatum Group Masterpieces)** like Roy Eldridge, Ben Webster and Lionel Hampton. Overall, the collaborations worked well, excepting that with Eldridge, the trumpeter sounding inhibited by the constant flurry of piano arpeggios Tatum furnished in accompaniment. Benny Carter, in particular, seemed to thrive on challenge; although rather emotionless, Buddy DeFranco's mercurial clarinet proved a perfect foil for Tatum's own pyrotechnics; Hampton and Buddy Rich weren't overawed by Tatum's reputation, and Tatum-Hampton-Rich Trio produced superlative music (especially **How High The Moon** and **Perdido**); and these three, together with Harry Edison, Barney Kessel and Red Callender, turned in similar results a month later. Tatum was the star soloist of latter date but meeting between pianist and Ben Webster, almost exactly a year later (1956), found Tatum, at times, having to take a back seat to the tenorist's matchless playing. To complete **The Tatum Group Masterpieces** Tatum achieved a wholly satisfactory trio date at beginning of '56 (with Callender and Jo Jones), repertoire including a convincing **Trio Blues**.

Tatum's final concert appearance was at Hollywood Bowl in August, '56. His last-known recordings, not too long before his death, in Los Angeles in November of same year, show no diminution of his immense talent. Indeed, there are tracks from these recordings **(Art Tatum In Person** and **Memories Of Art Tatum)** that rank with his finest.

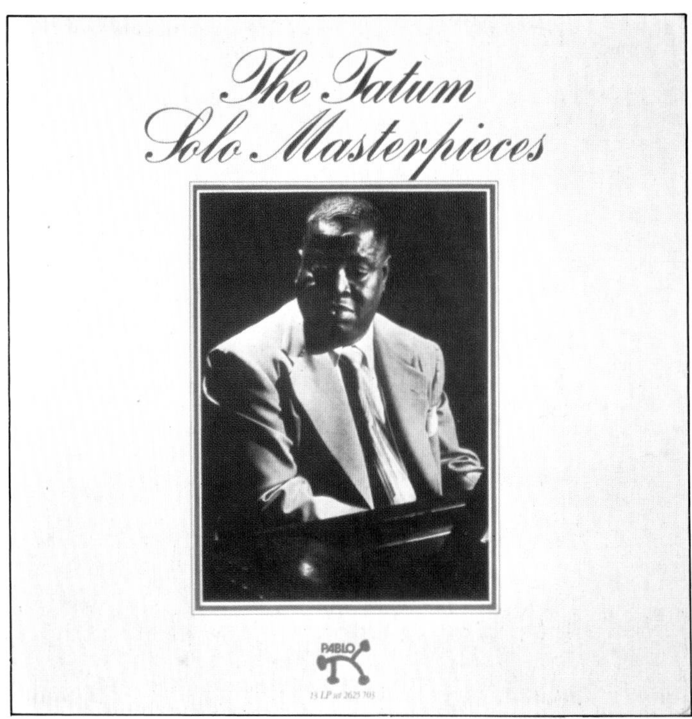

The Tatum Solo Masterpieces (courtesy Pablo): marathon sessions for Norman Granz by an inexhaustible Tatum in 1953-54—in incredible form.

Albums:
Art Tatum, Piano Starts Here (Columbia/—)
Art Tatum, Art Of Tatum (MCA-Germany)
Art Tatum Masterpieces (MCA/—)
Various, Swing Combos (Including Art Tatum) (Swingfan-Germany)
Various (Including Art Tatum) First Esquire Concert, Vols 1, 2 (—/Saga)
Various (Including Art Tatum) Second Esquire Concert, Vols 1, 2 (—/Saga)
Art Tatum, Solo Piano (Capitol/Capitol—Holland)
Art Tatum, Masters Of Jazz, Vol 3 (Capitol/Electrola—Germany)
Art Tatum, Song Of The Vagabonds (Black Lion/Black Lion)
Art Tatum, The Genius (Black Lion/Black Lion)
Art Tatum, Get Happy (Black Lion/Black Lion)
Art Tatum, God Is In The House (Onyx/Polydor)
Art Tatum, At The Piano, Vols 1, 2 (GNP-Crescendo/—)
The Tatum Solo Masterpieces (Pablo/Pablo)
The Tatum Group Masterpieces (Pablo/Pablo)
Art Tatum In Person (20th Fox/Ember)
Memories Of Art Tatum (20th Fox/Ember)
Strange As It Seems (Collectors Items/—)
Pure Genius (—/Affinity)
Pieces Of Eight (Smithsonian/—)
Piano Mastery (Shoestring/—)

Cecil Taylor

Born in 1933, the pianist Cecil Taylor was not only the first of the New Thing players to record but possessed such phenomenal technique that it was impossible for critics to dismiss him.

Taylor's first album **(Jazz Advance)** combines atonality with a deep and abiding respect for the jazz tradition, for Waller, Ellington, Monk and Powell. Accusations of classical borrowings—Bartok, Stravinsky—are irrelevant in the light of the pianist's belief that all Western music began in Africa. Taylor's lineage becomes clear on numbers like **Excursion On A Wobbly Rail (Looking Ahead)** which continues the fascination with train rhythms—Ellington's **Take The 'A' Train**, Monk's **Little Rootie Tootie**.

Taylor's music is overwhelming, so that the newcomer might like the toehold of a familiar standard to begin with. **This Nearly Was Mine** displays clearly the chalkmarks and pins of the pianist's alterations, and a subversion of the original mood of the piece through tempo changes à la Monk **(Air)**.

Naturally, the complexity of his music made it difficult for him to find suitable side musicians and steady employment. Sunny Murray's free drumming dove-tailed beautifully with the abrupt, percussive keyboard and altoist Jimmy Lyons proved one of the few who could rise to the challenge of such tireless energy. One of Taylor's finest achievements, **D Trad, That's What (Café Montmartre)** features the trio without a bassist. A larger unit, including tenorist Archie Shepp gives a less torrential workout to three of Talyor's compositions **(Into The Hot)** while a later composition, **Enter Evening (Unit Structures)**, explores gentler, more wistful moods than the New Thing usually gravitated towards.

On this album, and the next **(Conquistador)**, Taylor uses two bassists, including the pioneer of the bowed upper register, Alan Silva, and Andrew Cyrille, a drummer with a less melodramatic style than Murray, begins his long association with the pianist.

As Taylor's influence spread, he had the opportunity to record more frequently. The Jazz Composers' Orchestra, assembled by Mike Mantler, provides a massive backdrop for the virtuoso's headlong piano solo on **Communications 11**, which is literally overwhelming. Three albums resulted from an evening's recital in Europe **(Nuits De La Fondation Maeght)** by the regular trio, Taylor, Lyons, Cyrille, supplemented by multi-instrumentalist Sam Rivers.

While there are changes of mood and dynamic level in the music of Cecil Taylor, the impression of superhuman energy dominates. It can be tiring to listen to but it can be one of the most exhilarating and emotional experiences in all of jazz. It demands an open response and it imposes a total rhythm on audiences accustomed to more predictable patterns of tension and release that can be discharged through simple foot-tapping. Taylor's followers find catharsis by swaying the body back and forth in a variant of the Eastern chant.

Unrelentingly demanding within his groups, Taylor as a solo player **(Spring Of Two Blue J's, Silent Tongues** and **Indent)** proves a more tractable prospect to the average ear. He moves in and out of key register, ransacking past and future to feed his molten imagination. Arpeggios that sound as if he were zipping and unzipping the keyboard are abruptly countered by rumblings in the deep end. Dance and song are the disciplines behind his art, so there is—despite the avant-garde devices—a real sense of the Afro-American heritage.

Albums:
In Transition (Blue Note/Blue Note)
Looking Ahead (Contemporary/—)
Air (CBS Barnaby/CBS Barnaby)
Café Montmartre (Arista Freedom/Arista Freedom)
Into The Hot (Impulse/Impulse)
Unit Structures (Blue Note/Blue Note)
Conquistador (Blue Note/Blue Note)
Nuits De La Fondation Maeght (Shandar—France)
Spring Of Two Blue J's (Unit Core/—)
Silent Tongues (Arista Freedom/Arista Freedom)
Indent (Arista Freedom/Arista Freedom)
Dark To Themsleves (Enja/Enja)
Air Above... Mountains Below (—/Enja)
Student Studies (—/Affinity)
Garden (HatArt/HatArt)
Praxis (Praxis/Praxis)
Max Roach-Cecil Taylor, Historic Concerts (Soul Note/Soul Note)
The World Of Cecil Taylor (Candid/Candid)
Winged Serpent (Sliding Quadrants) (Soul Note/Soul Note)

Cecil Taylor, Nefertiti, The Beautiful One Has Come (courtesy Fontana).

Jack Teagarden

John Weldon 'Jack' Teagarden (born Vernon, Texas, 1905) could well turn out to be the greatest trombone soloist in jazz history. Particularly strong on blues and ballads, Teagarden further ranks with the greatest jazz vocalists—his mode of delivery and sound together were uncannily similar to his trombone-playing. Teagarden's role in steering the trombone away from the rigid format of the established 'tailgate' style is of major importance.

Came from a musical family, with brothers Charlie on trumpet and Clois on drums, and sister Norma on piano. Jack Teagarden began on piano, age 5, before he acquired a baritone horn. By 10 he was playing trombone and first playing experience in public came in 1918, after Teagarden family had moved to Chappell, Nebraska; together with his mother at the piano, he worked at local theaters.

Teagarden moved to Oklahoma City, then to San Angelo. There, he played with several local bands, also gigging in San Antonio and Shreveport. Worked with legendary Texan pianist Peck Kelley (1921-22). Then came work with a succession of bands including Doc Ross, Wingy Manone, and singers Willard Robison and Elizabeth Brice. Worked (during 1928)

Above: Cecil Taylor—the pianist at the vanguard of the New Thing. An immeasurably influential pioneer.

with bands of Billy Lustig, Tommy Gott, before joining Ben Pollack. Apart from brief periods away from his band, Teagarden remained with Pollack from 1928-33. Fine examples of Teagarden's trombone injecting a much-needed jazz boost into the Pollack organization can be found on **Futuristic Rhythm, Song Of The Blues** and **Keep Your Undershirt On** (all **Jack Teagarden, Vol 2 (1928-1957): 'Prince Of The Bone'**).

During his tenure with Pollack, Teagarden was involved in a large and varied number of recording dates, taking in the Mound City Blue Blowers, Eddie's (Condon) Hot Shots, commercial dance-band-leader Roger Wolfe Kahn (including magnificent Teagarden trombone on **She's A Great, Great Girl)** (all **Texas T. Party)**; Red Nichols (dozens of sides) **(J.T.** and **Jack Teagarden Classics)**; Jimmy McHugh's Bostonians, Mills' Merry Makers; and Cornell & His Orchestra (all **The Greatest Soloists Featuring Jack Teagarden)**. There was also much good jazz trombone in dates under his own name (including one with Fats Waller) **(King Of The Blues Trombone, Vols 1, 2)**. And Teagarden and Louis Armstrong proved that they were a great front-line partnership during a memorable 1929 recording of **Knockin' A Jug (V.S.O.P. (Very Special Old Phonography, 1928-1930), Vols 5 & 6)**.

Worked with Mal Hallet Orchestra during fall of 1933, then joined Paul Whiteman until 1938. To Whiteman's own brand of music, Teagarden added a definite warmth and some real jazz. His solos with Whiteman, like those on **Announcer's Blues** and **Ain't Misbehavin'** (vocal, too, on latter number) **(Paul Whiteman)**, are gems and emphasize strongly the gulf between 'real' jazz and something which was only a pastiche.

Teagarden recorded also with Paul Whiteman & His Swing **(Featuring Jack Teagarden)**. At various times of his stay with Whiteman the band contained musicians as talented as brother Charlie Teagarden, singer Johnny Mercer, George Wettling and Frankie Trumbauer **(Featuring Jack Teagarden, Jack Teagarden, Vol 2 (1928-1957): 'Prince Of The Bone'** and **Jack Teagarden -Frankie Trumbauer)**. Trumbauer and the Teagardens were also featured as the Three T's during special one-month engagement in New York, December 1936. Whilst with Whiteman, continued to record outside the band, a 1934 session with Adrian Rollini **(Featuring Jack Teagarden)** producing fine solos.

Between 1939 and 1947, Teagarden fronted a series of his own big bands. **Rompin' & Stompin', Jack Teagarden & His Orchestra 1944** and **It's Time For Teagarden** are representative of its basic swing-period sound and approach (with Dixieland influences). More of a compliment to Jack Teagarden's talents were record sessions like that by his Big Eight, in 1940 **(Jack Teagarden/Pee Wee Russell)** with the Texan stimulated by the presence of such as Ben Webster, Rex Stewart, Barney Bigard and Dave Tough.

Joined first of Louis Armstrong All Stars (1947-51) and the pair forged one of the great partnerhsips in jazz **(Satchmo At Symphony Hall** and **Louis Armstrong, Vols 1, 2)**. Probably the peak of the partnership was reached at celebrated 1947 New York concert **(Satchmo's Greatest, Vols 4, 5** and **Town Hall Concert: The Unissued Part)** with their rapport resulting in absolutely unforgettable jazz. Teagarden sings, plays gloriously on **St James Infirmary** (a Teagarden specialty), demonstrating another important facet of his playing, his deep and natural affinity with blues. There is also a sublime vocal duet between Armstrong and Teagarden on **Rockin' Chair**, another regular feature for Armstrong All Stars (even after Teagarden had left).

After leaving Armstrong, Teagarden formed own small combo with which he toured and recorded. Accepted invitation to play with Ben Pollack in 1956, then put together another band, this one with Earl Hines as co-leader. This all-star band visited Europe (1957) to widespread acclaim. Toured Asia (1958-59) with own band, with subsidy granted by the State Department.

Teagarden died from bronchial pneumonia in 1964. Of records on which he played during the last decade of his life, there were those that confirmed his stature as King of the Blues Trombone, including a brace of superb albums in company with Bobby Hackett **(Coast To Coast** and **Jazz Ultimate)**; and another with Teagarden reworking old favorites like **St James Infirmary, Lover, Stars Fell On Alabama** and **A Hundred Years From Today (T For Trombone)**. Even better were Teagarden's vocal-instrumental performances during a 1957 recording date featuring a reformed Bud Freeman-led Cum Laude Orchestra **(Jack Teagarden, Vols 1, 2)**.

During his career, Teagarden acted as well as played and sang in the movie *Birth of the Blues. Jack Teagarden*, a biography by Jay D. Smith & Len Gutteridge, first published 1960; *Jack Teagarden's Music*, by Howard J. Waters, Jr, first published in same year.

'J.T.' (courtesy Ace of Hearts)—the magnificent trombone of Teagarden.

Albums:

Benny Goodman, A Jazz Holiday (Decca-MCA/—)
Jack Teagarden, Texas T. Party (RCA Victor—France)
Jack Teagarden, Vol 2 (1928-1957): 'Prince Of The Bone' (RCA Victor—France)
Jack Teagarden/Red Nichols, 'JT' (Ace of Hearts)
The Great Soloists Featuring Jack Teagarden (Biograph/—)
Jack Teagarden Classics (Family—Italy)
Jack Teagarden, King Of The Blues Trombone, Vols 1-3 (Epic/Columbia)
Louis Armstrong, V.S.O.P. (Very Special Old Phonography, 1928-1930), Vols 5 & 6 (CBS—France)
Paul Whiteman (RCA Victor)
Featuring Jack Teagarden (—/MCA)
Jack Teagarden-Frankie Trumbauer (Totem—Canada)
Jack Teagarden & His Orchestra 1944 (Alamac/—)
Jack Teagarden, Rompin' & Stompin' (Swing Era/—)
Jack Teagarden, Sounds Of Swing (Sounds of Swing/—)
Jack Teagarden/(Pee Wee Russell) (BYG—France)
Louis Armstrong, Satchmo's Greatest, Vols 1, 2 (RCA Victor—France)
Louis Armstrong, Town Hall Concert (The Unissued Part) (RCA Victor—France)
Louis Armstrong, Satchmo At Symphony Hall, Vols 1, 2 (Decca/Coral)
The Legendary Jack Teagarden (Roulette)
Bobby Hackett/Jack Teagarden, Jazz Ultimate (Capitol/Capitol)
Bobby Hackett/Jack Teagarden, Coast To Coast (Capitol/Regal)
Jack Teagarden, T For Trombone (Jazztone/Society)

Jack Teagarden, Vol 2 (1928-1957) (courtesy RCA Victor-France).

Okay Temiz

With the compulsive 'folk-beat' of Oriental Wind, Turkish percussionist Okay (pronounced 'och-aye') Temiz has created one of the most adventurous and original improvisational groups to be heard in the West.

Born in Istanbul, Turkey, on February 11, 1939, Temiz learned his Turkish music skills from his mother Naciye Temiz, an accomplished musician. After studying classical percussion and tympani at Ankara Music Conservatory, he became a professional musician in '55.

Temiz toured Europe during '67-'68 with Ulvi Temel's Orchestra and his own Okay Sextet. An encounter with trumpeter Don Cherry in Sweden led to work in Cherry's trio along with South African bassist Johnny Dyani. In '71, Temiz joined trumpeter-pianist Maffy Falay's Turkish-Swedish group SEVDA, a band which was to have a profound influence on improvised music in Sweden. The following year, Temiz formed a trio with bassist Dyani and South African trumpeter Mongezi Feza, producing the enduring **Music For Xaba**.

Since '74, Temiz's own group Oriental Wind has included an interesting juxtaposition of Western and ethnic instruments—violin, saxophone, flute, clarinet and bass alongside Turkish instruments like the zurna, ney, sipsi, saz, gattam and bagpipes. Temiz's drum studies have taken him to South Africa and South America, and his battery of percussion includes talking drums, quicca, berimbau and finger-piano as well as an array of finely tuned hand-beaten copper Turkish drums.

One of his most interesting later projects has found him in collaboration with South India's classical Karnataka College of Percussion **(Sankirna)** in '84.

Above: Turkish percussionist Okay Temiz—coaxes a unique sound from hand-beaten copper drums.

Percussionist Okay Temiz. Turkish Folk Jazz (courtesy Sonet).

Okay Temiz and Oriental Wind, Chila Chila (courtesy Sonet).

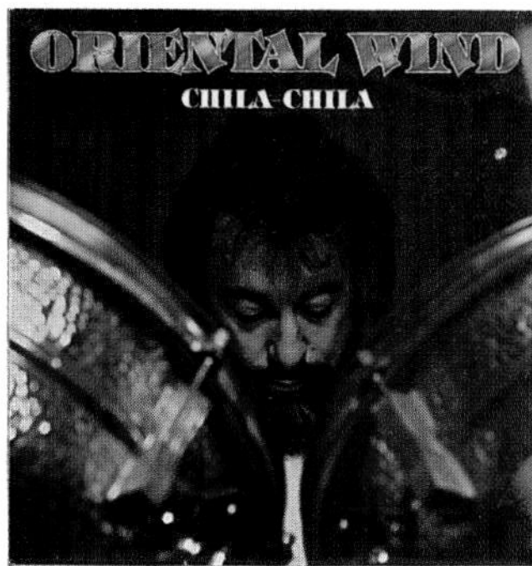

Albums:
Don Cherry, Live In Ankara (Sonet/Sonet)
Maffy Falay/SEVDA, Live At Fregatten (Sonet/Sonet)
Johnny Dyani-Okay Temiz-Mongezi Feza, Music For Xaba (Sonet/Sonet)
Turkish Folk Jazz (Sonet/Sonet)
Oriental Wind (Sonet/Sonet)
Chile Chile (Sonet/Sonet)
Zikir (Sun Records/Sun Records)
Live In Bremen (—/Jaro)
Oriental Wind-Karnataka College of Percussion, Sankirna (Sonet/Sonet)

Clark Terry

Trumpeter Clark Terry was born in St Louis in 1920, the home of many trumpeters, and gained experience with Charlie Barnet, Charlie Ventura and Eddie 'Cleanhead' Vinson before being taken on for a highly-educational three-year stint with the Count Basie orchestra.

He joined Duke Ellington in 1951 and stayed for eight years **(The World Of Duke Ellington, Vol 2)**. Probably his best known work for the Ellington orchestra was on **Up And Down, Up And Down** and **Lady Mac**, which Ellington wrote around his bubbling personality **(Such Sweet Thunder)**.

He spent the next few years as a staff musician with NBC, also co-leading a group with trombonist Bob Brookmeyer **(Terry-Brookmeyer Quintet)**. Numerous small group albums find Terry with Johnny Griffin and Thelonious Monk **(Cruisin')**; with Ben Webster **(The Happy Horns Of Clark Terry)** and with baritonist Cecil Payne in a set of bebop standards **(Cool Blues)**.

An exhilarating encounter between pianist Oscar Peterson and Terry **(Oscar Peterson Trio With Clark Terry)** which includes the trumpeter's hilarious brand of blues mumbling, is outstanding.

In later years, Clark Terry formed his own big band, a straight-ahead swinger using arrangements by Ernie Wilkins and Frank Wess **(Live On 57th Street)**.

A highly distinctive stylist on both trumpet and flugelhorn, Terry's work is witty and inventive, highly-colored with half-valve effects and clever use of a variety of mutes.

Albums:
The World Of Duke Ellington, Vol 2 (Columbia/CBS)
Duke Ellington, Such Sweet Thunder (Columbia/CBS)
The Terry-Brookmeyer Quintet (Mainstream/Mainstream)
Cruisin' (Milestone/Milestone)
Cool Blues (—/DJM)
Oscar Peterson Trio With Clark Terry (Mercury/Philips)
Clark Terry's Big Bad Band Live On 57th Street (—/Big Bear)
The Happy Horns Of Clark Terry (Impulse/Impulse)
Yes, The Blues (Pablo/Pablo)

Clark Terry's Big Bad Band Live On 57th Street (courtesy Big Bear).

Sonny Terry

'Sonny' Terry (real name: Saunders Terrell, born Durham, North Carolina, 1911) has few, if any, rivals as the most expressive blues harmonica practitioner of all. His great dexterity with the tiny instrument enabled him to produce an inimitable array of sounds; often as near to a human cry as seemed possible, sometimes of an inhuman variety. Terry could express grief, elation, misery, mirth...any kind of human emotion. As a singer, too, his gruff-voice style, whilst never approaching the electrifying quality of his 'mouth harp' work, often could be very effective.

Terry—blind in one eye from age 11 and totally blind five years following the accident which precipitated the loss of sight—teamed up with another sightlees blues exponent, singer-guitarist-composer Blind Boy Fuller. Terry was still in his teens. The pair recorded numerous classic blues performances **(Blind Boy Fuller With Sonny Terry & Bull City Red)**.

In 1939 (year after début on record with Fuller) he took part in John Hammond's *Spirituals To Swing* concert **(John Hammond's Spirituals To Swing)** using his falsetto whoops, eerie cries and extraordinary technique with harmonica to superb advantage on his own **Mountain Blues**; then, supported by Bull City Red, wailing through a fast version of **John Henry**.

In 1940, he first teamed up with guitarist-singer-composer Brownie McGhee—start of a most fruitful partnership. Previously, had recorded with Leadbelly **(Keep Your Hands Off Her)**. Also, during '40, made first records under own name **(History Of Jazz—The Blues)** including **Harmonica & Washboard Breakdown**. With McGhee, made countless recordings and toured extensively.

Alone, Terry's 'harp' has been heard to good advantage in front of washboard band **(Sonny Terry's Washboard Band)** together with guitarist-singer Alec Stewart **(Folk Blues)**—an album that includes the marvelously evocative **Fox Chase**; unaccompanied **(Harmonica Blues)**; and accompanied only by Sticks McGhee (Brownie's brother), guitar, and J.C. Burris (Terry's nephew), bones **(On The Road)**.

Of Terry-McGhee LPs, amongst best are **Sonny Is King, Sonny's Story, Where The Blues Begin, Whoopin' The Blues, A Long Way From Home** and **Blues From Everywhere,** last named with additional assistance from Sticks McGhee, Burris, and with Terry playing jawharp on some tracks (eg **Shortnin' Bread, Skip To My Lou).** Appeared on Broadway in production of musical *Finian's Rainbow* (mid-1940s) and toured (together with Brownie McGhee) in Broadway production of *Cat On A Hot Tin Roof* (1955-1957).

Albums:
Blind Boy Fuller With Sonny Terry & Bull City Red (Blues Classics/—)
Various (Including Sonny Terry), John Hammond's Spirituals To Swing (Vanguard/Vogue)
Leadbelly, Keep Your Hands Off Her (Verve-Forecast/Verve-Folkways)
Various (Including Sonny Terry), History Of Jazz —The Blues (Folkways/—)
Sonny Terry's Washboard Band (Folkways/—)
Folk Blues (Elektra/Vogue)
Harmonica Blues (Folkways/Topic)
On The Road (Folkways/Xtra)
Sonny Terry/Brownie McGhee, Sonny Is King (Prestige-Bluesville/—)
Sonny Terry/Brownie McGhee, Sonny's Story (Prestige-Bluesville/Xtra)
Sonny Terry/Brownie McGhee, Where The Blues Begin (Fontana)
Whoopin' The Blues (Capitol/Charly)
Sonny Terry/Brownie McGhee, At Sugar Hill (Fantasy/—)
The Best Of Sonny Terry & Brownie McGhee (Fantasy/—)
Sonny Terry/Brownie McGhee, Live! At The Fret (Fantasy/—)
Sonny Terry/Brownie McGhee, A Long Way From Home (ABC-Blues Way/Stateside)
Sonny Terry/Brownie McGhee, Blues From Everywhere (Folkways/Xtra)
Various (Including Sonny Terry), Penitentiary Blues (Fontana)
Sonny Terry - Johnny Winter - Willie Dixon, Whoopin' (Sonet/Sonet)

Toots Thielemans

Originally a guitarist, Toots Thielemans took that most earthy of folk-blues instruments—the harmonica—and gave it a distinctive bebop voice, creating one of the most identifiable sounds in jazz.

Jean-Baptiste 'Toots' Thielemans was born in Brussels on April 29, 1922. In '41, aged 19, Thielemans heard Django Reinhardt, won him-

Above: Sonny Terry—one of the most expressive harmonica-players in blues. Celebrated for a partnership with Brownie McGhee.

self a guitar in a bet and taught himself to play it while recovering from an illness. In the '50s, he settled in America, working as guitarist with the George Shearing Quintet **(In The Night)**. Subsequently working as a soloist, he also developed his extraordinary range on harmonica from brisk bebop standards like Sonny Rollins' **Tenor Madness** to beautiful ballads like Joanne Brackeen's **Images (Toots Thielemans 'Live')**.

In the '60s, he worked in Scandinavia with local musicians like guitarist Svend Asmussen **(Yesterday & Today)** and bassist Neils-Henning. In the mid-'60s, Thielemans was working as a staff musician with ABC Television in New York. During the next decade he became one of the busiest super-session musicians working with artists like Paul Simon and Quincy Jones. Working more recently with Jaco Pastorius, his contribution to the Lennon-McCartney **Blackbird** on Pastorius' **Word Of Mouth** is a *tour de force* in harmonica dynamics.

As well as writing film and TV scores, the instantly recognizable Thielemans harmonica can be heard in movies like *The Anderson Tapes, The Getaway, The Pawnbroker, Midnight Cowboy, The Sugarland Express,* even *The Wiz.* His own compositions include the enduring **Bluesette**.

In the mid-'80s, Thielemans' work with Swedish vocalist Sylvia Vrethammar and Brazilian guitarist Sivuca **(Toots & Sivuca)** inspired the hour-long film *Rendevous In Rio.*

Below: Toots Thielemans (left), Sylvia Vrethammar and guitarist-accordionist Sivuca. A fruitful collaboration.

Albums:
Too Much! Toots (Philips/Philips)
The Whistler And His Guitar (ABC Paramount/ABC Paramount)
Time Out For Toots (Decca/Decca)
Captured Alive (Choice/—)
Spotlight On Toots (Polydor/Polydor)
Toots Thielemans-Svend Asmussen, Yesterday & Today (Sonet/Sonet)
Toots Thielemans 'Live' (Sonet/Sonet)
Your Precious Love (Sonet/Sonet)
Toots & Sivuca (Sonet/Sonet)

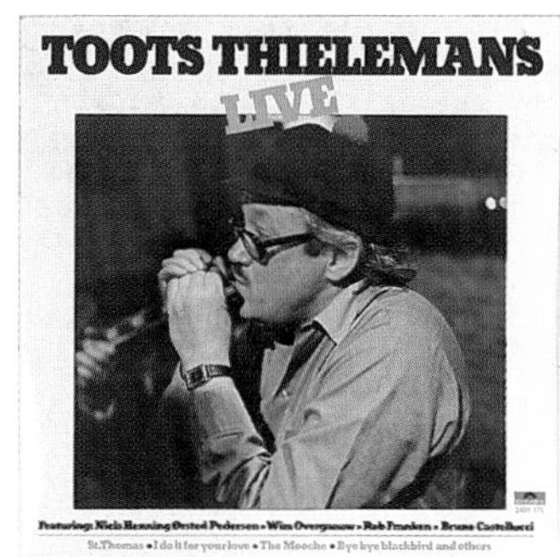

Harmonica-virtuoso Toots Thielemans Live (courtesy Sonet).

Barbara Thompson

The individual and accomplished British multi-instrumentalist and composer Barbara Thompson has been a major force on the local and European jazz-rock scene since the early 1970s, becoming one of the UK's most popular and enduring artists.

Born in Oxford, England, on July 27, 1944, Thompson achieved high honors on clarinet, flute, piano and in composition at the Royal College of Music, London. Simulaneously, she developed a formidable ability on soprano, tenor and baritone saxophones, as well as creating a distinctive and highly original voice on the unusual sopranino recorder.

In '65, she joined Neil Ardley's New Jazz

Above: Britain's extraordinarily talented Barbara Thompson—she plays all the reed instruments and is leader of jazz-rock group Paraphernalia.

Orchestra where she met her husband, drummer Jon Hiseman. Thompson has also worked with John Dankworth, Mike Gibbs, Wolfgang Dauner, Charlie Mariano, (she's an integral part of the European-based 'Band of Bandleaders', the United Jazz+Rock Ensemble) and Don Rendell. She has also contributed to projects by Andrew Lloyd Webber, notably in the West End show *Cats* and to his *Variations* and *Requiem*. Three major Thompson works for 20-piece orchestra have been recorded by the BBC, with *The Awakening* being performed at London's Round House.

Working with Paraphernalia (Thompson's generic name for a series of small groups she has led since '73), she has recorded and toured extensively throughout Europe. In '82, Thompson and Hiseman opened their own 24-track studio from which have emerged excellent albums like **Ghosts** (with keyboard-player Rod Argent), **Mother Earth** and **Pure Fantasy**. Much of the music for **Pure Fantasy** is drawn from her *In Search of Serendip*, deriving its inspiration from traditional folk songs of Sri Lanka, written for her 9-piece Serendipity.

Constantly in demand as a writer for TV and radio, tours with Paraphernalia and UJ+RE and studio projects, Thompson's hectic 'living and playing' schedule was revealed in BBC's '79 *Jazz, Rock and Marriage* documentary.

Barbara Thompson's long-awaited solo album, **Lady Saxophone**, was released in '86.

Albums:

Neil Ardley, Harmony Of The Spheres (Decca/Decca)
Don Rendell, Just Music (—/Spotlite)
Paraphernalia (MCA/MCA)
Wilde Tales (MCA/MCA)
Live In Concert (MCA/MCA)
Ghosts (MCA/MCA)
Mother Earth (—/TM Records)
Pure Fantasy (—/TM Records)
United Jazz+Rock Ensemble, 10 Years (—/Mood Records—Germany)
UJ+RE, United Live Opus Sechs (—/Mood Records—Germany)
Lady Saxophone (—/TM Records)

Barbara Thompson's Paraphernalia, Mother Earth (courtesy TM Records).

Charles Tolliver

The aim of trumpeter Charles Tolliver is to be abe to take any song for 25 or 50 choruses, and every one of them is a new song.

Born in Florida in 1942, an abiding influence has been Clifford Brown — in fact, Tolliver is remarkable for his orthodox values which place them squarely in the mainstream of modern jazz Like Woody Shaw, who shares his sense of tradition, he is a brilliant player capable of handling any tempo or mood. His début as a side-player with altoist Jackie McLean **(It's Time** and **Action)** featured some of his dramatic writing, **Plight**, as well as evocative ballads like **Truth**.

He spent two useful years with drummer Max Roach **(Members Don't Git Weary)** and dedicated a later number, **Grand Max**, to the master **(Live At The Loosdrechdt Jazz Festival)**.

In 1969, Tolliver established Music Inc with pianist Stanley Cowell, and their first recording was made on tour in Europe **(The Ringer)** featuring Tolliver compositions and excellent, lyrical, driving playing from the quartet. The finest single solo, **Drought**, was recorded by the trumpeter in 1973 **(Live In Tokya)**, and is on his own label, Strata-East, which he set up in the early '70s as 'a natural extension of wanting to be able to govern what I'm involved with'. Tolliver is one of the finest trumpeters on the scene today, and a practical businessman —a rare combination.

Albums:

Jackie McLean, It's Time (Blue Note/Blue Note)
Jackie McLean, Action (Blue Note/Blue Note)
Jackie McLean, Jacknife (Blue Note/Blue Note)
Max Roach, Members Don't Git Weary (Atlantic/Atlantic)
Live At The Loosdrechdt Jazz Festival (Strata-East/Black Lion)
The Ringer (Arista/Black Lion)
Live In Tokyo (Strata-East/Strata-East)
Live At Slugs (Strata-East/Strata-East)

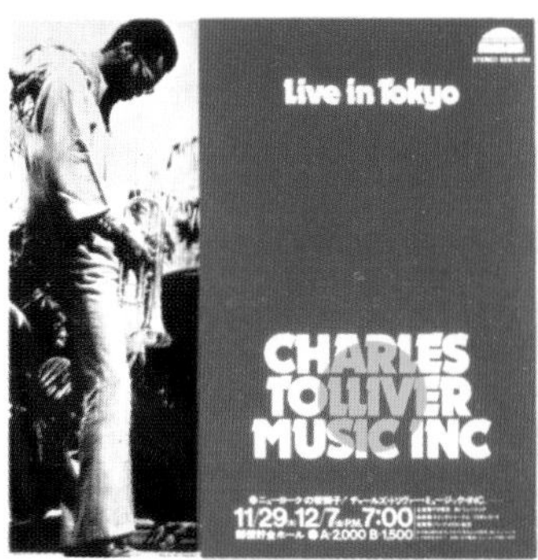

Charles Tolliver, Live In Tokyo (courtesy Strata-East).

Mel Tormé

Singer Mel Tormé, usually associated with the ritzier nightspot circuits, laid a series of classic jazz albums in the '50s. With his light voice and impeccable timing, he was *the* Cool School vocalist, approaching the material with all the lyricism and inventiveness of a Stan Getz

After paying dues with the Chico Marx Orchestra—Tormé's career began at the age of four—he collaborated with arranger Marty Paich, using his Dek-Tette to duplicate the sound of the Miles Davis 'Birth of the Cool' band. With Tormé singing definitive versions of the better popular songs, **Old Devil Moon, Too Darn Hot (Mel Tormé Swings Shubert Alley)** and **The Lady Is A Tramp (Lulu's Back In Town)** and soloists like Art Pepper, Bud Shank, Bill Perkins, most of the albums are collector's items. The 'Velvet Fog' is a fine scat singer and all-round musician.

Albums:

Mel Tormé-Marty Paich Dek-Tette, Lulu's Back In Town (Bethlehem/Affinity)
Mel Tormé-Marty Paich Dek-Tette, Tormé Sings Astaire (Bethlehem/Affinity)
Live At The Crescendo (Bethlehem/Affinity)
Mel Tormé Swings Shubert Alley (Verve/Verve)
The Duke Ellington & Count Basie Songbook (Verve/Verve)
Tormé/A New Album (Rhapsody/Rhapsody)
Mel Tormé-George Shearing, An Evening At Charlie's (Concord/Concord)
George Shearing-Mel Tormé, An Elegant Evening (Concord/Concord)

Mel Tormé Swings Shubert Alley (courtesy Verve).

Stan Tracey

The influential and pioneering British pianist-composer Stan Tracey has been a vital force since 1950, playing with Roy Fox, Laurie Morgan, Kenny Baker, Ronnie Scott, Tony Crombie and Ted Heath in his early career before his tenure as house pianist at Ronnie Scott's jazz club from 1960-68.

His original Duke Ellington-Thelonious Monk influence has borne fruit in a highly idiosyncratic style of writing and playing that seems to bring out the ibex in each new generation of musicians, including his fine drummer son Clark. Much of his earlier work is unavailable but his classic interpretations of Dylan Thomas **(Under Milk Wood)**, aided by the highly original Scottish tenorist Bobby Wellins, have been re-issued and remain a British classic.

Starless And Bible Black from **Milk Wood** is a haunting piece, rigorously pared to cast its somber mood. A master of harmony, Tracey has put himself out to explore those areas of freedom that most of his generation dismiss as noise and has been met halfway by the young musicians attracted to his structural wisdoms. His duets with altoist Mike Osborne **(Original** and **Tandem)** and his solo concert **(Alone At Wigmore Hall)** show how far he has incorporated New Thing techniques into his jolting, angular style.

His quartet **(Captain Adventure)** with the wildly imaginative tenor of Art Themen—a bone-surgeon by profession—the aggressively apt drummer Bryan Spring and the rock-steady bassist Dave Green, was one of the finest combos in Britain. Tracey's octet plays his quirky charts with punch, and features two-tenor chases between Themen and Don Weller.

Stan Tracey marked forty years in jazz in September 1983 with a memorable musical celebration in London. The concert looked back over an astonishingly creative career in which Tracey had consistently explored fresh areas of improvisation, written several outstanding major works (eg **Under Milk Wood, The Bracknell Connection, Salisbury Suite, South East Assignment, The Crompton Suite, The Poets' Suite**), started his own label Steam Records, toured opposite the Gil Evans Orchestra and toured South America and the Middle East.

The '83 anniversary concert brought together various Tracey ensembles supported by the cream of British jazz musicians—saxophonists Pete King, Art Themen, Tony Coe, Don Weller, Andy Mackintosh and Ronnie Scott; trumpeters Derek Watkins, Alan Downey, Henry Lowther and Harry Beckett; trombonists Malcolm Griffiths, Geoff Perkins and Chris Pyne; bassist Roy Babbington; and son Clark Tracey on drums. That night, many of the pianist's more recent achievements were paraded—Tracey's solo *pièce de résistance* **Now**; the stunning Tracey-Tony Coe duet conversation on **A Rose Without A Thorn**; the quartet's tribute to Thelonious Monk; the sextet (with saxophonists Themen, Coe and Weller); the octet (plus trumpeter Harry Beckett, trombonist Malcolm Griffiths and altoist Pete King); and, finally, the Stan Tracey Big Band.

In the climate of apathy towards British jazz that has pervaded the native scene, Stan Tracey's survival and continual growth is a tribute to his influence and integrity. In '84, Tracey received Honorary Membership of the Royal Academy of Music. For his inestimable contribution to British jazz, he was awarded the national honor of O.B.E. in 1986.

Albums:

Mike Osborne-Stan Tracey, Original (—/Cadillac)
Alone At Wigmore Hall (—/Cadillac)
Mike Osborne-Stan Tracey, Tandem—Live At The Bracknell Fest (—/Ogun)
Spectrum, Tribute To Monk (—/Switch)
Stan Tracey Quartet, Under Milk Wood (—/Steam)
Keith Tippett-Stan Tracey, T'N'T (—/Steam)
Stan Tracey Quartet, Captain Adventure (—/Steam)
Donald Houston-Stan Tracey Quartet, Under Milk Wood (—/Steam)
Stan Tracey Octet, The Bracknell Connection (—/Steam)
Stan Tracey Octet, Salisbury Suite (—/Steam)
John Surman-Stan Tracey, Sonatinas (—/Steam)
Hello, Old Adversary (—/Steam)
Stan Tracey Quartet, South East Assignment (—/Steam)
Stan Tracey Sextet, The Crompton Suite (—/Steam)
Stan Tracey Now (—/Steam)
Stan Tracey Quartet, The Poets' Suite (—/Steam)
Sal Nistico-Stan Tracey, Live In London (—/Steam)
Stan Tracey's Hexad, Live At Ronnie Scott's (—/Steam)

Stan Tracey Quartet, The Poets' Suite (courtesy Steam)—British pioneer.

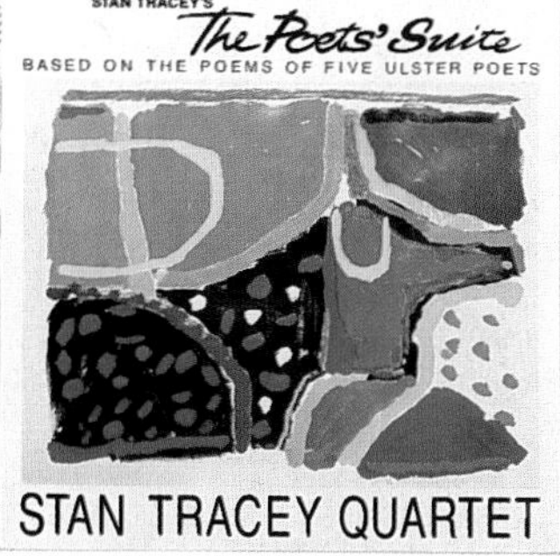

Lennie Tristano

Born 1919 in Chicago, blind pianist and teacher Lennie Tristano attracted a small dedicated group of disciples in the '40s and '50s for what was popularly called 'the Cool School'.

Running counter to the prevailing passion of bebop, Tristano experimented in linear improvisation, long, undulating Bach-like lines, counterpoint, atonality, a low decibel count and intense and subtle rhythmic complexity. An example of his playing in the mid-'40s **(Lennie Tristano/Red Rodney)** shows the piano lines interweaving with the guitar of Billy Bauer in an even flow. In 1949, the Lennie Tristano Sextet with altoist Lee Konitz, tenorist Warne Marsh, Billy Bauer, recorded a classic **(Crosscurrents)**. Over a steady rhythm, the players wove in and out of each other's lines lightly and precisely. **Intuition** from this session dispensed with an harmonic base and is arguably the starting point of the New Thing—certainly free collective improvisation has never sounded so seamlessly beautiful.

Though his detractors have accused Tristano of sounding bloodless and academic, Charlie Parker respected his music and the two men played together on the All Star Metronome broacast **(Anthropology)**. Tristano's moving blues for Bird, **Requiem (Lines)** proves that the cerebral approach need not preclude feeling. Multi-tracking on **Turkish Mambo** so that the three lines move in different times, **East 32nd Street** and **Line Up** caused a storm of controversy at the time, 1955, but would pass unnoticed in the technological '70s. In this case, the music justifies the means.

Always a recluse, the great pianist did not choose to record again until 1962 **(The New Tristano)**, which in terms of melodic invention, facility with complex time signatures and sheer technical mastery remains unsurpassed.

Albums:

Lennie Tristano/Red Rodney (Mercury/Mercury)
Crosscurrents (Capitol/Capitol)
Charlie Parker, Anthropology (Spotlite/Spotlite)
Lines (Atlantic/Atlantic)
The New Tristano (Atlantic/Atlantic)
New York Improvisations (Elektra Musician/Elektra Musician)

Bruce Turner

Britain's Bruce Turner (born Saltburn, Yorkshire, England 1922)—a confirmed 'mainstreamer' and influenced mostly by mid-period instrumentalists—spent his childhood in India. Served five years (1941-1946) in RAF. Worked with various bands on demobilization, including one bop-styled outfit. Played alto sax, clarinet with bands of Roy Vaughan, Freddy Randall (1948-50), then took job in a quartet making the trans-Atlantic trips on the liner *Queen Mary*. Eventually (together with QM colleagues pianist Ronnie Ball, bassist Peter Ind) took lessons in New York, first, from Lennie Tristano, then with Lee Konitz Worked with Ronnie Ball Quintet (1951), before rejoining Randall for two years. Accepted offer to work with Humphrey Lyttelton Band (in '53), playing clarinet, alto and, for a while, soprano sax.

Formed first of his celebrated Bruce Turner Jump Bands—small combos specializing in hard-swinging mainstream jazz—which lasted from 1957-65.

Spent four years as member of Acker Bilk's Paramount Jazz Band (1966-70). Since then, has gigged with various British bands (including Lyttelton) and has fronted a revived Turner Jump Band.

In '84, Turner published his autobiography, *Hot Air, Cool Music* (Quartet Books).

Albums:

Humphrey Lyttelton, The Best Of Humph 1949-56 (—/Parlophone)
Humphrey Lyttelton, Jazz Concert (—/Parlophone)
Humphrey Lyttelton, Humph At The Conway (—/Parlophone)
Accent On Swing (—/International Jazz Club)
Jumpin' For Joy, Nos 1, 2 (—/Philips) (EPs)
Goin' Places (—/Philips)
Wild Bill Davison With Freddy Randall & His Band (—/Black Lion)
Various (Including Bruce Turner), An Evening With Alex Welsh & His Friends, Parts 1, 2 (—/Black Lion)
Various (Including Alex Welsh/Bruce Turner), Salute To Satchmo (—/Black Lion)
Humphrey Lyttelton, South Bank Swing Session (—/Black Lion)
Humphrey Lyttelton, Take It From The Top (—/Black Lion)
Bud Freeman, Song Of The Tenor (—/Philips)
Bruce Turner/Johnny Barnes, Jazz Masters: Live At St Pancras Town Hall (—/Cadillac)
Humphrey Lyttelton, Hazy, Crazy & Blue (—/Black Lion)

Joe Turner

Joseph 'Big Joe' Turner (born 1911) started a long, impressive career by singing blues whilst doubling as bartender in a variety of clubs in his home town of Kansas City. It was at this time that Turner first worked together with pianist Pete Johnson. Couple stayed as a team in the city for several years before joint discovery by John Hammond resulted in sudden trip to New York to appear in a concert at Carnegie Hall.

After return trip to New York had gained Turner further recognition, he was featured in Duke Ellington revue, *Jump For Joy*, in Hollywood (1941). When show closed, Turner chose to work locally on West Coast, together with pianists Meade Lux Lewis and Joe Sullivan and others. Turner previously had worked with Sullivan, on record, in 1910 **(Café Society Swing & The Boogie Woogie)** and also with pianist, Art Tatum **(Swing Combos: 1935-1941** and **Swing Street, Vol 4)**. Each of these record dates found Turner singing at the top of his game—a veritable definition of 'blues shouting'.

During 1940s, Turner-Johnson partnership continued to flourish, in concert and/or on record, usually in company with dynamic, rocking little band; another pianist, Albert Ammons, also worked with Turner during this period.

Toured with Ammons and Johnson, 1944, and with Luis Russell, in 1945. Continued to record fairly frequently, including some electrifying sides for Arhoolie (Johnson, again, featured as pianist) **(Jumpin' The Blues)**. The 1950s found Turner attaining fresh popularity, mostly within an R&B framework.

His early-1950s recordings for Atlantic **(His Greatest Recordings)** were of great importance in the gradual emergence, then explosion, of rock and roll, not the least of which were **TV Mama, Sweet Sixteen, Honey Hush, Chains Of Love, Teenage Letter** and **Shake, Rattle & Roll**, latter soon to become principal breakthrough for rock and roll via bowdlerized version by Bill Haley & His Comets.

Perhaps Turner's single most impressive contribution to vocal blues recordings came in 1956 when, together with jazz instrumentalists of the calibre of Pete Brown, Lawrence Brown, Freddie Green and reunited with his oft-time musical associate and friend Pete Johnson, he laid down the tracks for what was to become probably the single most impressive definition of the urban blues shouter **(Boss Of The Blues)**. Turner sounded as indestructible as ever on 11 tried-and-trusted compositions of the genre (viz **Roll 'Em Pete, Cherry Red, How Long Blues, St Louis Blues, Wee Baby Blues)**.

During 1950s visited Europe on several occasions; in 1962, played residency at La Calvados, a Parisian club.

Turner continued to perform into the '80s in spite of advancing years and failing health (he was ill from diabetes for some time). One of his last recordings was in '85 at a 'blues summit' with fellow blues-singer Jimmy Witherspoon for Norman Granz's Pablo label. Big Joe Turner—one of jazz's most influential blues stylists—died from kidney failure and heart attack, following a stroke, in a Los Angeles hospital in November 1985. He was 74. On hearing of Turner's death, fellow singer Joe Williams acknowledged the enduring influence of 'the Boss of the Blues' (of whom he had been just one disciple)—'Without Joe Turner', he said, 'there wouldn't have been any Joe Williams singing the blues...'

Albums:

Various (Including Joe Turner), Café Society Swing & The Boogie Woogie 1938-1940 (Swingfan—Germany)
Various (Including Joe Turner), Swing Combos 1935-1941 (Swingfan—Germany)
Various (Including Joe Turner), Swing Street, Vol 4 (Epic/Columbia)
Joe Turner, Early Big Joe (1940-1944) (MCA—Germany)
Various (Including Joe Turner), John Hammond's Spirituals To Swing (Vanguard/Vogue)
Have No Fear, Big Joe Turner Is Here (Savoy/Savoy)
Joe Turner, Jumpin' The Blues (Arhoolie/Fontana)
Joe Turner, His Greatest Recordings (Atlantic)
Joe Turner, The Boss Of The Blues (Atlantic/Atlantic)
Joe Turner/Count Basie, The Bosses (Pablo/Pablo)
Joe Turner/T-Bone Walker/Eddie Vinson, Blues Rocks (Blues Time/RCA Victor)
The Trumpet Kings Meet Joe Turner (Pablo/Pablo)
Joe Turner, Nobody In Mind (Pablo/Pablo)
Joe Turner, In The Evening (Pablo/Pablo)
Various (Including Joe Turner), Spirituals To Swing—1967 (Columbia/—)
I Don't Dig It (Jukebox/—)

The late Joe Turner, The Boss Of The Blues (courtesy Atlantic)—undisputed.

McCoy Tyner

Born Philadelphia, 1938, pianist McCoy Tyner came from a musical background, consolidated

Above: Superlative pianist meets much admired altoist—McCoy Tyner and Jackie McLean together for the reactivated Blue Note label's It's About Time.

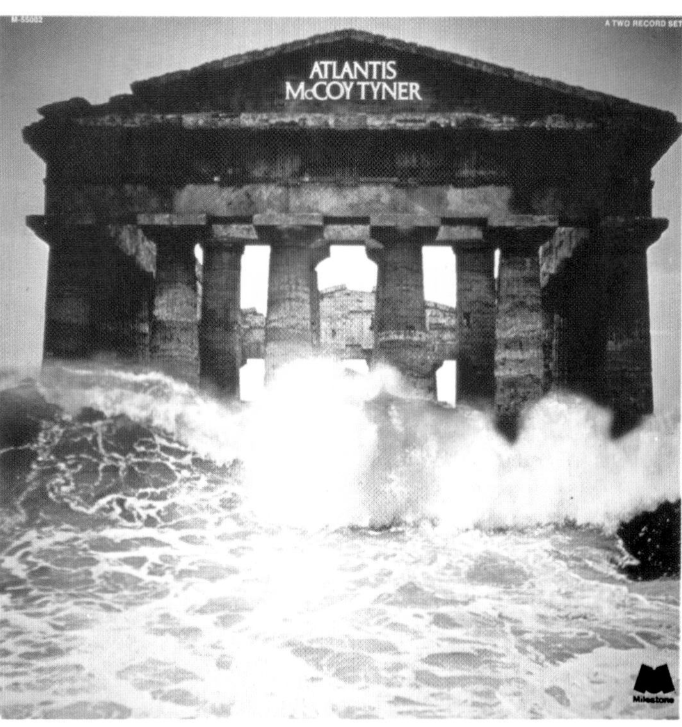

Atlantis (courtesy Milestone): pianist McCoy Tyner surmounting all obstacles. One of the most vital players in jazz, his entire output is excellent.

by later enrolment at music colleges.

In 1959, he was playing with the Jazztet, led by Art Farmer and Benny Golson, and in 1960 he joined the John Coltrane Quartet within a fortnight of its inception. He was with Coltrane for the next five years, an integral part of that classic, innovative group. He owes his tireless strength to that period, often laying a series of vamping figures that drove Coltrane in a modal, scalar direction away from conventional harmony. Tyner's later work was foreshadowed by the creative climate within the quartet — the intensity, the heightened rhythmic activity, the juggernaut drive. His keyboard style was largely formed in the '60s, fast, splashing arpeggios which leavened the sinew of percussive, massed chords.

Leaving Coltrane in 1965, Tyner had five bad years when work was scarce, even considering the alternative of taxi driving. Dissatisfied with his Impulse contract, he switched to Blue Note, working on other artists' sessions as well as heading his own. There is a remarkable consistency throughout Tyner's albums, and a direct line runs through the percussive themes of **African Village (Time For Tyner), Vision (Expansions), Message From The Nile (Extensions)** and on into his recent work for Milestone. His compositions reflect the universality of his — and Coltrane's — vision, drawing from ethnic origins other than the Afro-American, such as the rippling **Song Of Happiness (Expansions)** which is based upon Japanese scales.

Signing with Milestone in 1972, Tyner's career finally took off. The début album **(Sahara)** brought all the ingredients into focus — the sulfurous percussive climate established before the storming entry of the piano, the thumping, hypnotic chord structures, the sense of a series of triumphal entries into the Capitol. **Rebirth** showcases the pianist's incredible technique, while **Valley Of Life** has him trying the lighter voice of the koto; Tyner has experimented with various instruments, usually at the beginnings and ends of his compositions — harpsichord and celeste **(Trident)** — and dulcimer **(Focal Point)**. Subsequent albums testify to his unswerving sense of purpose, and his freedom from fashion's dictates: 'When you remove yourself and just become a vehicle, that's when those moments happen.' A Moslem since the age of 18, McCoy Tyner stands four-square in his creativity — as he says: 'I play what I live'.

The value of having a steady, working band is illustrated by the live double albums **Enlightenment** and **Atlantis,** all the players hitting an exhilarating level of intensity from the start and staying there. Tenor and soprano Azar Lawrence, bassist Joony Booth and Tyner himself are overwhelming, and Alphonse Mouzon on **Enlightenment** was a powerhouse of invention. Tyner made numerous changes in the drum department, kneading the difficult combination of fire and sensitivity to the dynamic level of acoustic piano. As if to temper the titanic breakers from keyboard and cymbals, he has added a free-ranging thread to the rhythmic fabric in the percussionist Guillerme Franco.

In a sincere and moving tribute to his late employer **(Echoes Of A Friend)**, Tyner recorded an album of unaccompanied piano, including some of Coltrane's most popular pieces, **Naima** and **My Favorite Things**. A trio album reunited him with Elvin Jones **(Trident)** and with Ron Carter on bass; this is a meeting of equals, a three-way exploration. Tyner's work with larger groups **(Sama Layuca, Song Of The New World** and **Fly With The Wind)**, the last two including strings and woodwinds, are romantic in the full-blooded sense, orchestral textures parting for the catapulting rush of the piano. Indeed, there is a touch of the tail-coated piano concerto manner about Tyner's grand entries, and his touch is unmistakable.

In the early '80s, Tyner toured with one of his finest units which included gifted violinist John Blake and saxophonist Joe Ford. Tyner's **4X4** album ('80) finds him in the mixed company of trumpeter Freddie Hubbard, altoist Arthur Blythe, vibist Bobby Hutcherson and guitarist John Abercrombie.

In '86, Tyner toured the international festival circuit with a superlative trio of bassist Avery Sharpe and drummer Louis Hayes plus three dynamic 'special guests' — tenorist Joe Henderson and trumpeters Freddie Hubbard and Woody Shaw.

McCoy Tyner remains one of the most vital and exciting creative forces on the jazz scene today.

Albums:

John Coltrane: A Love Supreme
(Impulse/Impulse)
Live At The Village Vanguard
(Impulse/Impulse)
Coltrane (Impulse/Impulse)
Meditations (Impulse/Impulse)
Reaching Fourth (Impulse/Impulse)
The Real McCoy (Blue Note/Blue Note)
Time For Tyner (Blue Note/Blue Note)
Extensions (Blue Note/Blue Note)
Asante (Blue Note/Blue Note)
Tender Moments (Blue Note/Blue Note)
McCoy Tyner-Jackie McLean, It's About Time
(Blue Note/Blue Note)
Sahara (Milestone/Milestone)
Trident (Milestone/Milestone)
Focal Point (Milestone/Milestone)
Enlightenment (Milestone/Milestone)
Atlantis (Milestone/Milestone)
Echoes Of A Friend (Milestone/Milestone)
Sama Layuca (Milestone/Milestone)
Song Of The New World (Milestone/Milestone)
Fly With The Wind (Milestone/Milestone)
The Greeting (Milestone/Milestone)
Passion Dance (Milestone/Milestone)
Together (Milestone/Milestone)
4 x 4 (Milestone/Milestone)
13th House (Milestone/Milestone)
Dimensions
(Elektra Musician/Elektra Musician)

James Blood Ulmer

Although a student of Ornette Coleman's harmolodics theory in the 1970s, guitarist James Blood Ulmer had been exploring on a similar scale as early as '68.

Born in St Matthews, South Carolina, on February 2, 1942, Ulmer sang with the Southern Sons gospel group from age 7 to 13. By 17, he was working in Pittsburgh with rock and roll bands. He spent 10 years playing in early jazz-funk line-ups and worked with organist Hank Marr in the mid-'60s **(Hank Marr In The Marketplace)**.

By '68, Ulmer was in Detroit and already experimenting with the innovative, if abrasive, style for which he would become noted in the '80s. Moving to New York in '71, his work with ex-Coltrane drummer Rashied Ali caught Ornette Coleman's ear. Coleman called Ulmer 'a natural harmolodic player' and thus began their decade-long association. During the '70s, Ulmer's work diversified. He performed in the Cal Massey-Archie Shepp musical *Lady Day* at Brooklyn Academy of Music, worked with Paul Bley, played at Carnegie Hall with Coleman, and recorded with Joe Henderson, Larry Young and Arthur Blythe.

In '78, Ulmer recorded his own, now-classic **Tales Of Captain Black** with Ornette and Denardo Coleman and 'upcoming' young bassist Jamaaladeen Tacuma. The album came ready packaged with a booklet detailing Ulmer's complex harmolodic guitar clef which many guitarists are still trying to fathom.

Ulmer was unknown to all but cognoscenti in Europe until the '80 release of his subsequently successful **Are You Glad To Be In America?** Here, Ulmer's heavy funk-based style collided with saxophonists David Murray and Oliver Lake, trumpeter Olu Dara, bassist Amin Ali and drummers Ronald Shannon Jackson and Calvin Weston but with no casualties. Since this significant breakthrough for Ulmer, his gritty vocals and even grittier guitar riffing have been heard on albums like **Freelancing** and **Part Time**, creating kinetic dance rhythms which are highly original and quite compulsive.

James Blood Ulmer, Tales Of Captain Black (courtesy Artists House).

Albums:
Hank Marr, Hank Marr In The Marketplace (King/—)
John Patton, Ascent Of The Blues (Blue Note/Blue Note)
Rashied Ali, The Rashied Ali Quintet (Survival/—)
Joe Henderson, Multiple (Milestone/Milestone)
Larry Young, Lawrence Of Newark (Perception/—)
Arthur Blythe, Lennox Avenue Breakdown (Columbia/CBS)
Tales Of Captain Black (Artists House/—)
Are You Glad To Be In America? (Rough Trade/Rough Trade)
Freelancing (Columbia/CBS)
Part Time (Rough Trade/Rough Trade)

Guitarist James Blood Ulmer, Freelancing (courtesy CBS).

Above: James Blood Ulmer—took his guitar, added harmolodics and came up with a heavy riff-based style which sounds like the James Brown band on acid.

United Jazz+Rock Ensemble

Justifiably described as the 'Band of Bandleaders', the United Jazz+Rock Ensemble has reigned supreme as Germany's most popular fusion band since the 1970s, with an equally enthusiastic following across Europe.

The group was formed in '75 by German keyboard-player Wolfgang Dauner, instigated by director Werner Schretzmeier who wanted a resident band for his young people's Sunday-night TV show. Schretzmeier's show became popular and the band soon gained a following. In January '77, the band toured Germany and received an unprecedented audience response. From that point, the United Jazz+Rock Ensemble became fixed—Dauner (keyboards), Eberhard Weber (bass), Volker Kriegel (guitar), Jon Hiseman (drums), Albert Mangelsdorff (trombone), Charlie Mariano and Barbara Thompson (reeds and flutes), Ack Van Rooyen and Ian Carr (trumpets) with trumpeter Kenny Wheeler joining in '79.

UJ+RE's début, **Live (Im Schützenhaus)**, became the best-selling German jazz record for decades. Subsequent albums **(Teamwork, Live In Berlin** etc) have all been received with equal enthusiasm.

UJ+RE's success in Germany has been phenomenal (at one sell-out concert in the '70s more than 1000 people had to be turned away). In '77, Dauner, Kriegel, Mangelsdorff, Van Rooyen and Schretzmeier decided to form their own company, Mood Records, and by the mid-'80s had sold over 150,000 albums. The UJ+RE has performed at major festivals and concert halls in Eastern and Western Europe and, in '84, made their first tour of the UK as part of the Arts Council of Great Britain's Contemporary Music Network.

To celebrate the UJ+RE's 10th anniversary in '85, a special box-set of the band's six albums was issued — within three months, it had sold 50,000 copies.

Albums:
Live (—/Mood Records)
Teamwork (—/Mood Records)
The Break Even Point (—/Mood Records)
Live In Berlin (—/Mood Records)
United Live Opus Sechs (—/Mood Records)
10 Years (—/Mood Records)

UJ + RE, United Live Opus Sechs (courtesy Mood Records-Germany).

Sarah Vaughan

Sarah Vaughan's highly individualistic vocal style was formed by her early association with bebop, singing with Billy Eckstine, Charlie Parker and Dizzy Gillespie in the Earl Hines and Billy Eckstine bands in the 1940s.

Born in Newark, New Jersey, in 1924, Vaughan studied piano from age 7 and was a church chorister and organist by 12. In '42, she accepted a dare and sang **Body and Soul** at an Apollo amateur contest. Eckstine recognized her unique vocal gift and recommended her to Earl Hines as co-vocalist and second pianist.

An early version of **Loverman** with Parker and Gillespie **(In The Beginning)** and **Everything I Have Is Yours** with Lennie Tristano **(Anthropology)** show the wide Eckstine-influenced vibrato and the bebop phrasing.

An album from 1954 with Clifford Brown, Paul Quinichette and Herbie Mann contains some of her finest work, including the seldom-used verse to **I'm Glad There Is You**, definitive versions of **Lullaby Of Birdland** and **April In Paris (Sarah Vaughan)**. Another session from the same year featured her trio, pianist Jimmy Jones, bassist Richard Davis and drummer Roy Haynes **(Swingin' Easy)**, and **Shulie A Bop** shows her mastery of scat singing, while **Loverman** is more mature and authoritative than the 1945 version.

A date with the Basie band, minus Basie, resulted in a fine, swinging album **(No Count Sarah)**. Always a superlative singer — whatever the context — Sarah Vaughan's almost 'operatic' vocal technique (a lesson in control and phrasing) is unrivaled.

Albums:
Dizzy Gillespie, In The Beginning (Prestige/Prestige)
Charlie Parker, Anthropology (Spotlite/Spotlite)
Sarah Vaughan (Trip/—)
Swingin' Easy (Trip/—)
No Count Sarah (Trip/—)
Sarah Vaughan Live (—/Pye)
Send In The Clowns (Pablo/Pablo)

Sarah Vaughan and Count Basie, Send In The Clowns (courtesy Pablo).

The 'divine Sarah' Vaughan, Live in Japan (courtesy Mainstream). As the years pass, her voice just gets better—an operatic technique and quality.

Joe Venuti

Giuseppe 'Joe' Venuti (born Lecco, near Milan, Italy, *c.* 1898/1903) was born just around the opening of 20th century and was a professional musician at start of 1920s. Venuti was a great jazz violinist, totally individual in approach, an improviser of originality, and one who believed in jazz that swung, always.

Raised by Italian immigrant parents in Philadelphia, he met guitarist Eddie Lang (*c.* 1920) and both worked in a small combo in Atlantic City in '21. Lang was to become an important influence on Venuti's continued progress as a jazz musician during 1920s. Worked with Red Nichols, Jean Goldkette, Roger Wolfe Kahn, Red McKenzie **(That Toddlin Town — Chicago 1926-28)**, Adrian Rollini and Lang in 1920s.

Lang-Venuti partnership was prolific on record—the pair made over 70 sides. Inspired by Lang's intuitive promptings and filigree guitar solos, Venuti's playing was particularly effective on **Beatin' The Dog, Wild Cat** (from first-ever Venuti-Lang session, playing as duo), **Goin' Places, Stringing The Blues, Dinah** and **Doin' Things** (all **Stringing The Blues); The Wild Dog** and remakes of **Doin' Things** and **Wild Cat** (all **The Sounds Of New York, Vol 2 (1927-1933): 'Hot Strings'**).

During 1920s, Venuti also recorded with Bix Beiderbecke and Frankie Trumbauer **(The Golden Days Of Jazz: Bix Beiderbecke)**. Joined Paul Whiteman in '29, staying until following spring (interrupted only by car crash mid-1929). With line-up including Benny Goodman, Jack Teagarden and Charlie Teagarden, Eddie Lang-Joe Venuti All Star Orchestra recorded some splendid music for American Decca in 1931 **(Nothing But Notes)** with Venuti's violin outstanding on **Farewell Blues** and **After You've Gone**. Recorded several titles for British market, with his Blue Five, Blue Six, and as members of Joe Venuti-Eddie Lang Blue Five **(Benny Goodman & The Giants of Swing/Jazz In The Thirties)** all vintage 1933.

Following year visited London, recording with local musicians and working with own band. Continued to work throughout US, until being called up for service in US Forces in 1943. After moving to West Coast, in 1944, started work as MGM studio musician.

Led own big band during mid-1940s, apparently without much success. Only recorded evidence **(Joe Venuti & His Big Band)** suggests its output was mediocre and, surprisingly, featured minuscule amount of Venuti's violin.

During 1950s-into-1960s, Venuti became unfashionable. His 'comeback' as special guest at Newport Jazz Festival of '68 astounded all. Venuti was also the most impressive soloist at Jazz Expo week in London (1969). Despite serious illness the following spring, Venuti's career during 1970s was a succession of triumphs **The Complete 1970 Pasadena Jazz Party, Tribute To Duke** and **The Dutch Swing College Band Meets Joe Venuti**.

The redoubtable Venuti's sudden death, in August 1978, remains one of the most tragic losses in jazz

Albums:
Various (Including Red McKenzie), That Toddlin' Town—Chicago 1926-28 (—/Parlophone)
Venuti-Lang 1927-8 (—/Parlophone)
The Golden Years Of Jazz: Eddie Lang-Joe Venuti/Stringing The Blues (CBS)
Eddie Lang/Joe Venuti, The Sounds Of New York, Vol 2 (1927-1933): 'Hot Strings' (RCA Victor—France)
The Golden Days Of Jazz: Bix Beiderbecke (CBS)
Joe Venuti, Nothing But Notes (MCA Coral—Germany)
Various (Including Joe Venuti), Benny Goodman & The Giants Of Swing (Prestige)/ Jazz In The Thirties (World Records)
Joe Venuti & His Big Band (Big Band Archives/—)
Newport All Stars (Including Joe Venuti), Tribute To Duke (MPS)
Various (Including Joe Venuti), The Complete 1970 Pasadena Jazz Party (Blue Angel Jazz Club Presents/—)
The Dutch Swing College Band Meets Joe Venuti (Parlophone)
The Jazz Violin Of Joe Venuti: Once More With Feeling (Ovation/—)
Joe Venuti/Zoot Sims, Joe & Zoot (Chiaroscuro)/The Joe Venuti Blue Four (Chiaroscuro)/Joe & Zoot (Vogue)
Joe Venuti & George Barns—Live At The Concord Summer Festival (Concord Jazz/—)

Venuti-Lang 1927-8 (courtesy Parlophone)—unparalleled teamwork.

Eddie Lang and Joe Venuti, Stringing The Blues (courtesy CBS). One of the most celebrated partnerships in jazz, forged in the Roaring Twenties.

Eddie 'Cleanhead' Vinson

Eddie ('Cleanhead') Vinson (born Houston, Texas, 1917) is a marvelously potent combination of primitive bluesman and sophisticated jazz musician. A vocal-instrumental performer who bridges crossover areas of jazz, blues, R&B, he manages to appeal to a wide (including rock) audience.

Prematurely bald (hence nickname), Vinson's first important engagement was as singer and instrumentalist with orchestra of Milt Larkins during 1930s. Then, he took his impassioned blues-based alto sax and raucous blues singing to band of Floyd Ray. In 1942 he went to New York, to join new Cootie Williams big band. Remained until call-up (1945) for US Army. With Williams, became a popular and familiar figure, both in jazz and R&B circles, a featured singer and instrumentalist with full band and sextet drawn from same.

Contributed numerous items to Williams' book, including **Floogie Boo** and **I Don't Know**, taking searing alto solos and humorous blues vocals on these and other numbers, like **Something's Gotta Go** (all **Cootie Williams Sextet & Orchestra**). On return from the Army, put together his own 16-strong band which attained national success with **Kidney Stew Blues** and **Juice Head Baby**. Played New York in 1947, then toured with same band the following two years. Cut back to six musicians because of economic situation re big bands at end of 1940s. Success came again with King recording of **Queen Bee Blues**. Disbanded early-1950s and became solo act. Rejoined Williams for few months in '54 **(Big Band Bounce)**. Co-leader, with tenorist Arnett Cobb, of hard-swinging combo based in Houston.

Widespread popularity eluded Vinson until 1969 when, thanks to bandleader-drummer Johnny Otis, he undertook European tour with Jay McShann. During same year, recorded for Flying Dutchman label **(The Original Cleanhead)**.

Vinson's re-emergence continued into 1970s, with ecstatically received performances at Montreux Jazz Festival, as leader of own combo **(You Can't Make Love Alone)** or as featured soloist with huge (26-piece) orchestra assembled by Oliver Nelson **(Swiss Suite)**. He also took part in all-star dates like **Blue Rocks** with Otis Spann, Joe Turner and T-Bone Walker.

In the '80s, the individualistic Vinson has remained a popular solo performer and a festival favorite. Vinson also toured internationally in the '80s with bassist Major Holley's memorable 'Tribute to Louis Jordan', stealing the show with his own **Cleanhead Blues**.

Eddie 'Cleanhead' Vinson, Jamming The Blues (courtesy Black Lion).

Albums:
Cootie Williams Sextet & Orchestra (Phoenix/—)
The Original Cleanhead (Flying Dutchman/Philips)
(Benny Carter)/Cootie Williams, Big Band Bounce (Capitol/Capitol—Holland)
Oliver Nelson, Swiss Suite (Flying Dutchman/Philips)
You Can't Make Love Alone (Mega/—)
Jamming The Blues (Black Lion/Black Lion)
Various (Including Eddie Vinson), Blue Rocks (Blues Time/RCA Victor)

Czechoslovakian bassist Miroslav Vitous, Journey's End (courtesy ECM).

Miroslav Vitous

Czechoslovakian-born Miroslav Vitous gained a daunting reputation outside his homeland as one of the new generation of technically brilliant and inventive bassist-composers.

Born in Prague on December 6, 1947, Vitous played violin at age 6, and piano and bass from 14. At the same time, he joined thousands of Europeans in listening to Willis Connover's *Voice of America Jazz Hour* — finding particular inspiration in Gary Peacock (with Paul Bley), Scott LaFaro (through Bill Evans) and Ron Carter (with Miles Davis). Studying bass at Prague Conservatory, he formed a trio with his brother Allan on drums and a young Jan Hammer on piano.

Vitous left Europe in '66 to take up a scholarship at Berklee College in Boston but, feeling restricted by the academic approach to improvising, he left to study on his own. In '67, he arrived in New York, working with a diversity of musicians including Walter Booker, Freddie Hubbard, Art Farmer, Bob Brookmeyer-Clark Terry. After a brief period with Miles Davis, he spent two years with Herbie Mann's group **(Windows Opened** and **Memphis Underground)**.

His first album as leader, **Infinite Search**, was originally issued on Embryo in '69 (reappearing in '72 as Atlantic's **Mountain In The Clouds)**. After contributing to Chick Corea's **Now He Sings, Now He Sobs** with Roy Haynes, Vitous became a founder-member of the influential Weather Report in '71 **(Weather Report, I Sing The Body Electric, Sweetnighter** and **Mysterious Traveller)**.

Since the late '70s, Vitous has recorded for the German-based ECM label and been able to renew his earlier association with Chick Corea and Roy Haynes in the '80s on their **Trio Music** an album of trio improvisations and Thelonius Monk classics.

Albums:
Mountain In The Clouds (Atlantic/Atlantic)
Purple (—/CBS Sony—Japan)
Magical Shepherd (Warner Brothers/Warner Brothers)
Majesty Music (Arista/Arista)
Miroslav (Arista-Freedom/Arista-Freedom)
First Meeting (ECM/ECM)
Miroslav Vitous Group (ECM/ECM)
Chick Corea, Trio Music (ECM/ECM)
Journey's End (ECM/ECM)

Mal Waldron

New York-born pianist Mal Waldron started in the mid-1950s as part of the house rhythm section — along with bassist Doug Watkins and drummer Art Taylor — for Prestige, accompanying musicians like Jackie McLean, Phil Woods and Donald Byrd. He was with Charles Mingus on one of his most expressionistic ventures **(Pithecanthropus Erectus)** and also with Max Roach **(Percussion Bitter Sweet)**.

He spent two-and-a-half years as Billie Holiday's accompanist, learning the use of space and shadings from her. His association with Eric Dolphy and Booker Little opened him to the new developments **(The Quest** and **At The Five Spot)** and **Fire Waltz** on the latter album is a typical Waldron composition.

Based in Europe for many years, Waldron keeps up a regular output of solo and trio albums and is a big jazz seller in Japan.

Albums:
Charles Mingus, Pithecanthropus Erectus (Atlantic/—)
Max Roach, Percussion Bitter Sweet (Impulse/Impulse)
Eric Dolphy, At The Five Spot (Prestige/Prestige)
The Quest (Prestige/—)
Black Glory (Enja/Enja)
Up Popped The Devil (Enja/Enja)
Free At Last (ECM/ECM)
The Call (JAPO/JAPO)
Mal Waldron Solo Piano (—/Horo)
A Touch Of The Blues (—/Enja)
One Upmanship (—/Enja)
Moods (—/Enja)
Mingus Lives (—/Enja)
What It Is (—/Enja)
One Entrance, Many Exits (Palo Alto/—)
Breaking New Ground (Baybridge Records/—)

Above: Aaron Thibaud 'T-Bone' Walker—a seminal figure in post-war blues as a singer, composer and guitarist.

T-Bone Walker

Aaron Thibaud 'T-Bone' Walker (born Linden, Texas, 1909) was, from the 1940s, a major influence on blues and R&B guitar. Inspired deeply by Blind Lemon Jefferson, Lonnie Johnson and Scrapper Blackwell, Walker evolved an individual style that, in turn, was to influence other guitarists.

Self-taught, he came to prominence through a Columbia disc cut in 1929 **(Trinity River Blues** and **Wichita Falls Blues)** released under pseudonym of 'Oak Cliff T-Bone'. Did not record again until a decade later. Toured with 16-piece band of Lawson Brooks, through Texas and Oklahoma. When Walker left, replacement was teenaged Charlie Christian. Moved to West Coast where he led own bands and his horn-like technique came into focus.

Worked with orchestra of Les Hite where his amplified guitar became a familiar sound — Walker claimed he was using an electric instrument as early as 1935. With Hite, recorded **T-Bone Blues**, his fist successful disc. Other successes on record during early-1940s included **Mean Bone Boogie** (1945 — with orchestra of Marl Young) and his most famous composition, **Call It Stormy Monday**. Also known as **Stormy Monday** and **Stormy Monday Blues**, this along with **T-Bone Shuffle, Hypin' Woman Blues, I Want A Little Girl, Lonesome Woman Blues**, remain among his most celebrated vocal-instrumental performances.

Walker's association with Imperial label produced **Strollin' With Bones, You Don't Love Me, Evil Hearted Woman** (all 1950); **Alimony Blues, I'm About To Lose My Mind, Blues Is A Woman** (all '51); **Blue Mood, Love Is A Gamble** ('52); and **Railroad Station Blues, Got No Use For You, Bye-Bye Baby** ('52 or '53).

During 1960s, and up to his death in 1975, he continued to make regular club and concert appearances. At concerts like a 1967 appearance for Norman Granz **(The Greatest Jazz Concert In The World)**, he sang and played in company with Oscar Peterson, Johnny Hodges, Clark Terry and Paul Gonsalves. He also recorded exceptional albums such as **Funky Town** (with Basie-type big band), and all-star sessions with bluesmen of the calibre of Joe Turner, Otis Spann **(Super Black Blues)**, Eddie Vinson, again with Spann and Turner **(Blue Rocks)**, and numerous top jazz instrumentalists like Gerry Mulligan, Dizzy Gillespie, Zoot Sims, Al Cohn and Wilton Felder **(Very Rare)**.

In the '80s, Walker's influence was celebrated by three excellent compilations issued by the UK-based Charly Records — **Jumps Again, Plain Ole Blues** and **The Natural Blues** with classic tracks from the early '40s to mid-'50s.

Albums:
The Blues Of T-Bone Walker (Capitol/Music For Pleasure)
Classics Of Modern Blues (Blue Note)
Feeling The Blues (Black & White—France)
Stormy Monday Blues (Blues Way/—)
Various (Including T-Bone Walker), Texas Guitar—From Dallas To LA (Atlantic/Atlantic)
Very Rare (Reprise/Reprise)
Various (Including T-Bone Walker), The Greatest Jazz Concert In The World (Pablo/Pablo)
Various (Including T-Bone Walker), Blue Rocks (Blues Time/RCA Victor)
Various (Including T-Bone Walker), Super Black Blues (Blues Time/Philips)
T-Bone Jumps Again (—/Charly)
Plain Ole Blues (—/Charly)
The Natural Blues (—/Charly)

Fats Waller

Thomas Wright 'Fats' Waller (born New York City, 1904) was one of jazz's most colorful personalities. A pianist, organist and songwriter of distinction, he was also an average singer who faced every performance with his own brand of irrepressible humor. As a songwriter his tunes (often with lyrics added by Andy Razaf) have become part of standard-pop history: **Honeysuckle Rose, Ain't Misbehavin', Keepin' Out Of Mischief Now, Black & Blue** and **Blue Turning Gray Over You**.

Waller's father was a church minister; his mother played both piano and organ. Waller also played pipe organ and his earliest jazz organ recordings are best **(Young Fats At The Organ (1926-1927), Vol 1)**.

Waller began on piano at six, receiving lessons from James P. Johnson, sometimes known as the King of the Stride Piano; he even took instruction from Cal Bohm and Leopold Godowsky. Began recording in 1922, cutting **Muscle Shoals Blues** and **Birmingham Blues (Fats Plays, Sings, Alone & With Various Groups)**, both unaccompanied solos. These tracks illustrate perfectly Waller jazz piano (his basic style already fully developed), a slightly more flexible version of stride epitomized by James P. Johnson.

Waller, regrettably, recorded comparatively few solo tracks, making **Young Fats Waller** a rarity and an album to treasure.

Waller is heard advantageously under leadership of Billy Banks **(Billy Banks & His Rhythmmakers)**, Jack Teagarden and Ted Lewis (both **Fats Plays, Sings, Alone & With Various Groups** and **The Chocolate Dandies)**. And in the distinguished company of Louis Armstrong, Teagarden and Bud Freeman **(Louis Armstrong/All That Jazz: Louis Armstrong)**, Waller tended to steal solo honors, as well as providing marvelous uplifting background support. He also recorded with Fletcher Henderson and McKinney's Cotton Pickers.

Waller's commercial success and international fame came in 1934 with the first of the Fats Waller & His Rhythm bands. The 'Rhythm' was a five-piece band with front-line of trumpet and saxophone (double clarinet). This format lasted until late-1930s and, although it provided much good-natured jazz and a perfect setting for the leader's singing, it all but stifled Waller's pianistic skills. Waller & Rhythm recorded prolifically **(Fats Waller Memorial, Nos 1, 2)**. Occasionally, performances were comparable to his pre-Rhythm days, as with **Fats On The Air, Vols 1, 2**, and mostly were solo piano performances. His attempts at leading own big band for touring and/or recording **(Fats Waller & His Big Band 1938-1942)** were not successful.

Ain't Misbehavin, The Story Of Fats Waller (a biography by his manager, Ed Kirkeby) was first published in 1966.

Albums:
Young Fats Waller (Joker—Italy)
Various, Fats Plays, Sings, Alone & With Various Groups (CBS—France)
Young Fats At The Organ (1926-1927), Vol 1 (RCA Victor—France)
Fats Waller Memorial, Vols 1, 2 (RCA Victor—France)
Jack Teagarden (RCA Victor/RCA Victor)
Louis Armstrong (Trip)/All That Jazz: Louis Armstrong (DJM)
Fats Waller, Ain't Misbehavin' (—/Music For Pleasure)
Fats Waller & His Big Band 1938-1942 (RCA Victor—Germany)
Billy Banks & His Rhythmmakers (CBS—Realm)
Fats Waller, Here 'Tis (Jazz Archives/—)
Fats Waller Memorial Album (—/Encore)
The Chocolate Dandies (—/Parlophone)
Thomas 'Fats' Waller (Biograph/—)

Fats Waller Memorial No. 2 (courtesy RCA Victor-France)—irreplaceable.

Above Saxophonist Grover Washington Jr stands tall as one of the most popular and successful artists on the scene today with a mellifluous sound and style.

Grover Washington Jr

With the unprecedented success of albums like **Mr Magic** in the 1970s and **Winelight** in the '80s, Grover Washington Jr has become one of fusion's most popular and biggest-selling saxophonists.

Washington was born in Buffalo, New York, on December 12, 1943, into a musical family—his mother was a church chorister and his father, an accomplished saxophonist. Playing saxophone from age 10, Washington was performing professionally at 12 with R&B groups but his first love was always jazz — Coleman Hawkins, Ben Webster, Lester Young, Charlie Parker and John Coltrane. At 16, he left Buffalo for Ohio working with the Four Clefs. After army service, he joined organist Charles Earland's band **(Living Black!)**.

Johnny 'Hammond' Smith's **Breakout** album of '70 established Washington as a major new voice on saxophone and led to Washington's first album as leader — his now-classic **Inner City Blues**. He also contributed to the success of other musicians' projects like Bob James' **Heads** etc, Randy Weston's **Blue Moses**, Eric Gale's Multiplication, Ralph McDonald's **Sound Of A Drum** and Dave Grusin's **One Of A Kind**.

In '85, Washington teamed with guitarist Kenny Burrell (plus bassist Ron Carter and percussionist Ralph McDonald) to record **Togethering** for the reactivated Blue Note label.

Albums:
Inner City Blues (Kudu/Kudu)
Reed Seed (Motown/Motown)
Paradise (Elektra/Elektra)
Winelight (Elektra/Elektra)
Kenny Burrell-Grover Washington, Togethering (Blue Note/Blue Note)

Muddy Waters

Muddy Waters (real name: McKinley Morganfield, born Rolling Fork, Mississippi, 1915) was the epitome of the electric post-war blues scene — indeed, its seminal figure. An immensely powerful, utterly compeling guitarist, he was a gifted harmonica player, a warm, convincing singer and a writer of stature and character.

Taught himself to play harmonica from age 10, but father gave him lessons on guitar. Mother died young so he was raised by grandmother on Stovall plantation near Clarksdale—she gave him the nickname Muddy Waters. From a youthful age, he became absorbed with Delta blues, deeply influenced by Robert Johnson and Son House, both acknowledged bottleneck-guitar masters. In time, Waters, too, was to be revered for his own use of the technique.

Began playing in early-1930s but first exposure outside Mississippi came when Alan Lomax from Library of Congress visited Stovall plantation to record Waters — alone and as member of Son Simms Four — in 1941 **(Down On Stovall's Plantation: The Celebrated 1941-42 Library Of Congress Recordings)**. Recordings showed Waters to be an impressive country-blues guitarist-singer, although barely hinting at later developments.

Moved to Chicago, 1943, worked in clubs and bars. Recorded for Aristocrat in fall of 1947, and second single **I Feel Like Going Home** and **I Can't B Satisfied (Genesis: The Beginnings Of Rock, Vol 1)** became a hit in 1948.

Success of the disc helped the amplified blues scene to break through in Chicago. As Aristocrat label became Chess, Waters was able to record full-time with classic line-up of harmonica, piano, drums, bass, rhythm guitar and Waters on lead guitar and vocals.

Side musicians to work in Muddy Waters blues bands from 1950s include: Little Walter, Walter Horton, James Cotton, Junior Wells — harmonica; Matt Murphy, Jimmy Rogers, Pat Hare, Buddy Guy, Sammy Lawhorn — guitar; Big Crawford, Willie Dixon, Luther Johnson, Luther Tucker — string bass or bass-guitar; Francey Clay, Fred Below, Clifton James — drums; and, most important, pianist-vocalist Otis Spann.

Waters also played guitar on records for Chess made by Jimmy Rogers and Little Walter (both **Genesis: The Beginnings Of Rock, Vols 1, 2**). Then came further hit records, **Louisiana Blues, Long Distance Call, Rollin' Stone, I'm Your Hoochie Coochie Man, I Want You To Love Me, I'm Ready, Just To Be With You, Got My Mojo Working**, and **Trouble No More**. The music of Muddy Waters had a profound effect on the development of popular music of 1950s/1960s, being crucial in the careers of Jimi Hendrix and Rolling Stones. Waters (and Cotton) appeared at Carnegie Hall in 1959, in band with Memphis Slim **(Folk Song Festival)**.

Muddy Waters Blues Band recorded for blues singer Victoria Spivey's label, with Spivey sitting in for two numbers. Made literally electrifying appearance at 1960 Newport Jazz Festival. A poll-winner in leading jazz/blues publications, Waters received Grammy awards for **They Call Me Muddy Waters, The London Muddy Waters Sessions** (recorded in company with top British rock stars including Rory Gallagher, Stevie Winwood, Mitch Mitchell) and received Grammy award nominations for others. Visited Europe in 1976 as part of package show which also included jazz instrumental giants Sonny Rollins and McCoy Tyner.

One of Waters' most memorable '70s performances was not in a blues context but in Martin Scorsese's film *The Last Waltz* at The Band's '76 farewell concert. Waters' hypnotic delivery of **Mannish Boy** was the movie's highspot, effortlessly upstaging even Bob Dylan and Van Morrison. In '78, Waters performed at President Carter's White House picnic as an honored guest. One of Waters' last trips to Europe was in '81, when he was to be seen whipping up audiences on George Wein's international festival circuit.

Waters' death in Chicago from a heart attack on April 30, 1983, aged 68, brought a classic era in post-war blues to an abrupt and untimely end. But, as the 'Father of Modern Chicago Blues', Muddy Waters remains immortal and his influence — like his music — endures.

Albums:
Afro-American Songs (Library of Congress/—)
Down On Stovall's Plantation: The Celebrated 1941-42 Library Of Congress Recordings (Testament/Bounty)
The Real Folk Blues (Chess/Chess)
After The Rain (Cadet/—)
Muddy Waters Sings 'Big Bill' (Chess/Pye)
Muddy Waters At Newport (Chess/Checker)

Above: Muddy Waters—probably the single most important figure in post-war Chicago blues. His Rollin' Stone blues inspired Mick Jagger & Co in the 1960s.

Muddy Waters In London (Chess/Chess)
McKinley Morganfield AKA Muddy Waters (Chess/—)
More Real Folk Blues (Chess/—)
Muddy Waters, Live At Mister Kelly's (Chess/—)
Can't Get No Grindin' (Chess/Chess)
Muddy Waters, Hard Again (Blue Sky/Blue Sky)
Various (Including Muddy Waters), Genesis: The Beginnings Of Rock, Vols 1, 3 (Chess/Chess)

The immortal Muddy Waters, Hard Again (courtesy Blue Sky).

Bobby Watson

The virtuosity of the multi-talented Bobby Watson has made him one of the most important young altoists to emerge in the 1980s, with his contributions to one of Art Blakey's youngest Jazz Messengers' line-ups bringing him international acclaim.

Born in Lawrence, Kansas, Watson first studied piano and clarinet before taking up tenor saxophone, then alto, in high school. After studying at the University of Miami, Watson graduated with a degree in music composition. In college, he met his wife Pamela who plays piano and sings on two of his earliest albums, **Estimated Time Of Arrival** and **All Because Of You**.

Arriving in New York in '76, one of his first gigs was with guitarist Roland Prince and drummer Billy Higgins. Watson's fiery alto soon caught the attention of drummer Art Blakey and, in '80, Watson began a four-and-a-half-year stay as a Jazz Messenger. Leaving Blakey, Watson formed a band with pianist Mulgrew Miller, bassist Curtis Lundy and drummer Kenny Washington, recording **Beatitudes**, their first album together, in '83. The quartet was extended to a sextet with vibist Steve Nelson and percussionist Dom Um Romao for the subsequent **Jewel**.

Watson's astonishing adaptability has been heard with a diversity of other ensembles, large and small. These cover an extraordinarily broad spectrum including the Angel Angelo-Jimmy Madison Orchestra, Charlie Persip's Superband, the adventurous and improvisational 29th Street Saxophone Quartet (an ex-busking band), tenorist George Coleman's hard-bop combo, even Panama Francis and the Savoy Sultans. In the '80s, Watson has also contributed alto/flute to Sam Rivers' multi-faceted, all-woodwind 11-piece Winds of Manhattan **(Colours)**.

Albums:

Art Blakey and the Jazz Messengers, Reflections In Blue (Timeless/Timeless)
Art Blakey and the Jazz Messengers, Recorded Live At Bubba's (—/Kingdom Jazz)
Panama Francis and the Savoy Sultans, Everything Swings (Stash/—)
Charlie Persip, In Case You Missed It (Soul Note/Soul Note)
Beatitudes (Hep/Hep)
Jewel (Amigo/—)
Advance (—/Enja—Germany)

Below: The adaptability of Mr Robert Watson has taken him from gusty blowing with Blakey & Jazz Messengers to being one of the gale-force Winds of Manhatten.

Trevor Watts

The multi-faceted saxophonist Trevor Watts' contribution to the development of contemporary jazz in Britain has been immeasurable. From his early involvement with the Spontaneous Music Ensemble in the 1960s, he has continued to break new ground in the '80s with his highly acclaimed 10-piece Moiré Music.

Watts, a founder-member of the New Jazz Orchestra in the '60s, also played saxophone with blues groups led by Sonny Boy Williamson, Long John Baldry and Rod Stewart. In '65, Watts co-founded SME with drummer John Stevens and trombonist Paul Rutherford, helping to pioneer free group-improvisation in Europe.

In '67, Watts formed Amalgam with the bassist Barry Guy and Paul Rutherford, initially to explore more conventional paths. A particularly productive period of Amalgam came with the empathetic line-up of progressive guitarist Keith Rowe (of AMM), invincible rock drummer Liam Genockey and young bass-guitarist Colin McKenzie **(Over The Rainbow**, '83).

In the '80s, Watts has also toured with his dynamic Drum Orchestra, inspired by the work of the Burundi drummers, featuring the percussion of Ghana's Nana Tsiboe and Sierra Leone's Mamadi Kamara. When Watts' introduced his ground-breaking Moiré Music at the Camden Festival, London, in March '82, its impact was unprecedented. Moiré Music's shifting textures and its exciting, rhythmic fusion of world music can be heard on the '86 **Trevor Watts' Moiré Music** with Lol Coxhill, Keith Beal, Simon Picard (saxes), Peter Knight, Steve Dunachie (violins), Veryan Weston (piano), Ernest Mothle (bass), Liam Genockey (drums) and Nana Tsiboe (percussion).

Watts has also worked with Archie Shepp, Don Cherry, Steve Lacy, Bobby Bradford, Rashied Ali, Dave Holland, Stan Tracey, Keith Tippett (Ark and Centipede), Pierre Favre and Irene Schweitzer. In '81, his duo collaboration with pianist Katrina Krimsky produced the excellent **Stella Malu**.

Albums:

Amalgam, Another Time (—/Vinyl)
Amalgam, Mad (—/Syntohn—Holland)
Amalgam, Over The Rainbow (—/Arc)
Amalgam, Wipe Out (—/Impetus)
Katrina Krimsky-Trevor Watts, Stella Malu (ECM/ECM)
Trevor Watts' Moiré Music (—/Arc)

Trevor Watts and Amalgam, Over The Rainbow (courtesy Arc).

Above: Wayne Shorter—already influential through his work with Miles Davis in the 1960s; then, in '71, he formed Weather Report with Joe Zawinul...

Weather Report

The fusion of two formidably creative and volatile talents — Joe Zawinul and Wayne Shorter — created Weather Report, one of the finest jazz-rock groups, triggering off an unprecedented chain reaction, their collective influence resulting in the universal proliferation of bands exploring similar directions.

Shorter's work has always been impressive, from his period with Art Blakey's Jazz Messengers when he wrote **Lester Left Town (The Big Beat), Children Of The Night (Mosaic), This Is For Albert (Thermo)** and the title track, **Free For All**. At this time his tenor was a personal amalgam of Sonny Rollins and John Coltrane, a coarse-toned and unbelievably savage rip-saw, playing weirdly asymmetrical lines. In the '60s, he joined Miles Davis and his style changed. He wrote meticulously precise structures, often modal, that swiveled and snaked to allow room for the drummer. Pieces like **Nefertiti (Nefertiti)** or **Orbits, Dolores (Miles Smiles)** avoid the old statement-solo-reprise format in favor of densely plaited unison statements that prowl like a wolfpack.

Zawinul came to New York in 1959 from Vienna and joined the popular Cannonball Adderley band, contributing numbers like **Mercy Mercy Mercy** to Adderley's book.

Zawinul and Shorter met in the Maynard Ferguson Orchestra and then, more significantly, in the Miles Davis group for the seminal album **In A Silent Way**, the title track being a Zawinul composition. The combination of Zawinul's harmonically strong yet economic themes and Shorter's sinuous soprano saxophone was responsible for much of the success of Miles' new direction and with the departure of Zawinul after **Bitches Brew**, the group lost much of its flexibility.

In 1971, Shorter, Zawinul and Czech bassist Miroslav Vitous established Weather Report to extend some of the implications of Miles Davis' fusion with rock. The role of the soloist was subordinated to an ensemble attack, a great premium was placed upon instrumental texture and group sound, and great care was taken over the themes which had to be strong enough to support fragmented interpretation.

Adding drummer Alphonse Mouzon and percussionist Airto Moreira, their début album **Weather Report** remains one of their best. The sumptuous chiming effect on **Milky Way**, and the sheer beauty of Zawinul's **Orange Lady**, showed that this was a Rolls-Royce of fusion music.

The next album, despite the substitution of Eric Gravatt and Dom Um Romao for Mouzon and Moreira, was even better, especially on the choppily driving **Directions (I Sing The Body Electric)** while Zawinul's **Dr Honoris Causa** gets a shorter, sharper workout than on his own album, **Zawinul**.

The third album proved to be their biggest seller **(Sweetnighter)** though artistically less successful and more riff-bound. Friction was already blowing up in the rhythm section — a common hazard in jazz-rock outfits — and Gravatt's absence from three tracks was patched over with multiple percussion. Titled in honor of an anti-bed-wetting prescription, **Sweetnighter** is their least flexible work.

Gravatt was briefly replaced by Gregg Errico, and then Ishmael Wilburn — a fast, light drummer well suited to group needs. A great return to form resulted **(Mysterious Traveller)** and excellent themes like **American Tango** and **Blackthorn Rose** received imaginative treatment, the electronic effects from Zawinul's battery of keyboards — Moog synthesizer, electric piano, piano — always to the point. Two of the tunes, **Jungle Book** and **Nubian Sundance**, grew out of Zawinul's improvisations at home which he normally tapes as source material.

Bassist Vitous left in '73 and problems in the drum department kept Weather Report from public performance for a year. By 1975, with Alphonso Johnson on bass, Ngudu drums and Alyrio Lima percussion, the group recorded **Tail Spinnin'** which, in many ways, marked a return to solo routines. Shorter's tenor excursion on **Lusitanos,** and the tenor-keyboard duets of **Five Short Stories**, imply a reliance on the strength of the founders rather than on group interaction. The next album **(Black Market)** breaks no new ground but has many of Weather Report's virtues—for example, the way that Zawinul establishes a change of tempo with one attacking chord after the introduction to **Gibraltar**.

New virtuoso bassist Jaco Pastorius contributed enormously to the greatly improved group sound of 1977's **Heavy Weather** and Alejandro Neciosup Acuna and Badrena made an extremely flexible rhythm section. Shorter dispensed with the showy lyricon to make a lyrical return to acoustic saxophones, while Zawinul's pen-and-ink and delicate gold leaf approach to synthesizer on the ballad **A Remark You Made** exemplified his sensitive economy. **Heavy Weather** produced probably the most famous Weather Report number, **Birdland**. Three years later, Manhattan Transfer's vocal version was a worldwide hit (becoming Zawinul's favorite version of his own tune).

With **Mr Gone** in '78, the percussion disappeared; in its place, the tight drum mastery of the skilled Pete Erskine. Weather Report remained a four-piece for nearly four years and the **8.30** double album ('79) featured live and studio material.

Rumors abounded about Weather Report's collective future in '82 when Pastorius formed his Word of Mouth band and Erskine left to work solo and with just about everybody. Their replacements for the '83 **Procession** were chosen for a combination of youth and experience: bassist Victor Bailey (ex-Larry Coryell, Tom Browne and Hugh Masekela), drummer Omar Hakim (ex-David Sanborn, George Benson and Roy Ayres) and, of particular interest, percussionist José Rossy (a former classical musician from Puerto Rico).

Weather Report activities into the mid-'80s were registering further winds of change. Separate projects in '85 from Zawinul **(Dialects)** and Shorter **(Atlantis)** were tentatively received while the world waited with baited breath. However, true to form, Weather Report's **This Is This** album appeared in the summer of '86 — with Zawinul and Shorter together — plus bassist Victor Bailey, drummer Pete Erskine (one track with drummer Omar Hakim) and noted Miles Davis percussionist Mino Cinelu. The interesting addition of an 'honored guest' in the form of guitarist Carlos Santana, and vocalists, were regarded as a potential indicator of an intriguing new direction. As the album was launched, Zawinul was touring the international festivals with his special '86 'Weather Update' line-up: drummer Pete Erskine, percussionist Bobby Thomas Jr and bassist Victor Bailey plus the surprise but delightful addition of guitarist Steve Khan. Shorter's own quartet, meanwhile, was touring simultaneously but separately.

Albums:

Wayne Shorter:

- Night Dreamer (Blue Note/Blue Note)
- Ju Ju (Blue Note/Blue Note)
- Speak No Evil (Blue Note/Blue Note)
- All Seeing Eye (Blue Note/Blue Note)
- Adam's Apple (Blue Note/Blue Note)
- Schizophrenia (Blue Note/Blue Note)
- Super Nova (Blue Note/Blue Note)
- Odyssey Of Iska (Blue Note/Blue Note)

Weather Report, I Sing The Body Electric (courtesy CBS)—the second superb album from a group which has led the field of jazz-rock. Widely influential.

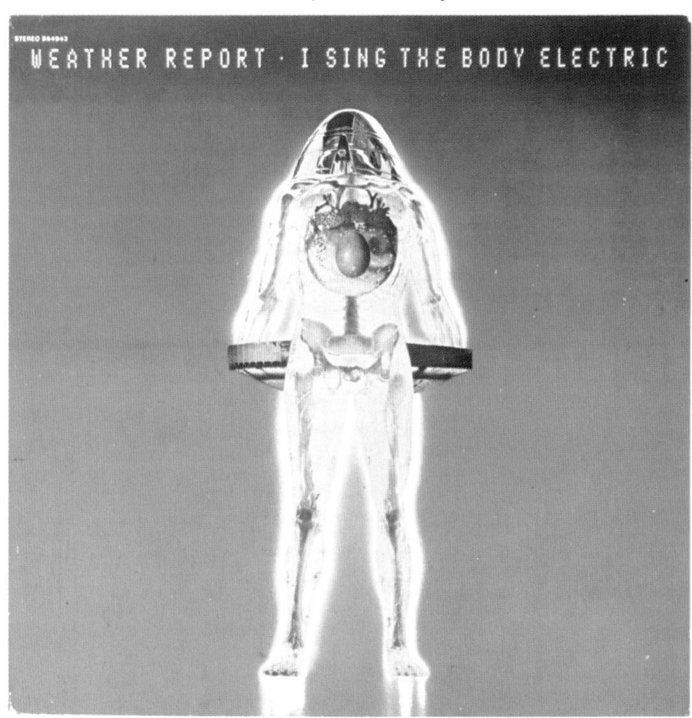

Native Dancer (Columbia/CBS)
Joe Zawinul:
Zawinul (Atlantic/Atlantic)
Concerto (Atlantic/Atlantic)
Weather Report:
Weather Report (Columbia/CBS)
I Sing The Body Electric (Columbia/CBS)
Sweetnighter (Columbia/CBS)
Mysterious Traveller (Columbia/CBS)
Tail Spinnin' (Columbia/CBS)
Black Market (Columbia/CBS)
Heavy Weather (Columbia/CBS)
Mr Gone (Columbia/CBS)
8:30 (Columbia/CBS)
Night Passage (Columbia/CBS)
Weather Report (Columbia/CBS)
Procession (Columbia/CBS)
Domino Theory (Columbia/CBS)
Sportin' Life (Columbia/CBS)
Joe Zawinul, Dialects (Columbia/CBS)
Wayne Shorter, Atlantis (Columbia/CBS)
This Is This (Columbia/CBS)

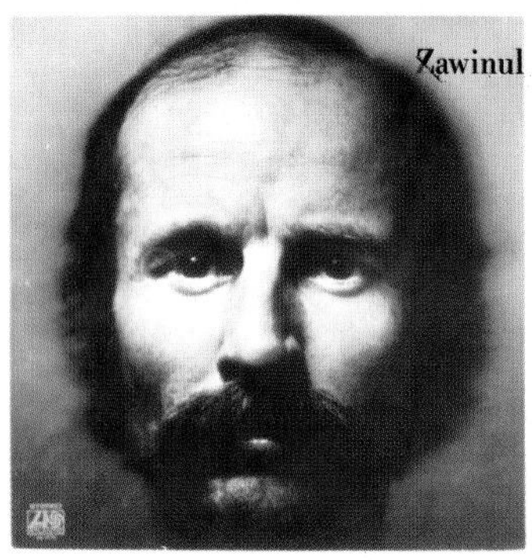

Zawinul (courtesy Atlantic)—Weather Report's keyboard magician, solo.

Eberhard Weber

The distinctive and individual style of German bassist-composer Eberhard Weber has earned him the title 'the Poet of Sound and Space' and an international reputation. Using a custom-built solid five-string bass fitted with an array of electric pick-ups, which he plays using upright bass techniques, Weber has created new acoustic freedoms for the instrument.

Born in Stuttgart, Germany, in 1940, Weber played cello from age 7, switching to bass at 17. Before he became a professional musician, he worked as a photographer and film director. In '74 his album **The Colours Of Chloë** immediately established him as one of Europe's most identifiable bassists. The following year he formed Colours (which has included multi-reeds-played Charlie Mariano, keyboardist Rainer Bruninghaus, drummers Jon Christensen and John Marshall).

Weber has continued to lead his own groups into the '80s and has contributed to ECM recordings by Gary Burton, Wolfgang Dauner, Pat Metheny, Michael Naura and Ralph Towner. He has also worked with Hampton Hawes, Lucky Thompson, Jean-Luc Ponty, Joe Pass, Keith Jarrett and Mal Waldron. Since the mid-'70s, Weber has been an integral part of the German-based 'Band of Band-leaders', the United Jazz+Rock Ensemble.

Albums:
Ralph Towner, Solstice (ECM/ECM)
Gary Burton, Ring (ECM/ECM)
United Jazz+Rock Ensemble, 10 Years (—/Mood Records—Germany)
The Colours Of Chloë (ECM/ECM)
Yellow Fields (ECM/ECM)
The Following Morning (ECM/ECM)
Silent Feet (ECM/ECM)
Fluid Rustle (ECM/ECM)
Little Movements (ECM/ECM)
Chorus (ECM/ECM)
Works (ECM/ECM)

Below: German bassist Eberhard Weber (second left), 'the Poet of Sound and Space'—an asset in any ensemble. Here, with the Jan Garbarek group.

Ben Webster

Benjamin Francis 'Ben' Webster (born Kansas City, 1909) was a mostly self-taught saxophonist. The Websterian sound was individualistic and instantly identifiable: on the uptempo, more overtly rhythmic numbers, the tone was coarse, threatening and fierce, the swing huge; on ballads, the tonal quality became breathy, tender and sumptuous — rather like the muted roar of a contented lion.

Influenced by Coleman Hawkins, then by Johnny Hodges, Webster was an influential and rewarding soloist from the '30s.

Played piano in an Amarillo, Texas, silent-movie house; Webster was an accomplished stride pianist. Chronologically, Webster worked with bands of W. H. Young (father of Lester Young); Gene Coy (playing alto as well as tenor); Jap Allen, 1930; Blanche Calloway, 1931; Bennie Moten, 1931-33; Andy Kirk, 1933; Fletcher Henderson; Benny Carter, 1934; Willie Bryant, 1935; Cab Calloway, 1936-37; Fletcher Henderson, again, 1937; Stuff Smith, Roy Eldridge, 1938; and Teddy Wilson, 1939-40.

Above: Ben Webster—his sumptuous and majestic tenor saxophone remains one of the most unforgettable sounds in jazz; he was also an accomplished pianist.

Webster's reputation became part of jazz legend when, in January 1940, he joined Duke Ellington Orchestra as featured tenor saxophonist. With Ellington, Webster produced some of his greatest recorded solos, including those on **Cotton Tail** (a classic showcase for his fierce up-tempo playing), **All Too Soon, Conga Brava, Bojangles** (all **The Works Of Duke, Vol 10); Sepia Panorama (The Works Of Duke, Vol 11); Just A-Settin' & A-Rockin' (The Works Of Duke, Vol 16*); The Girl In My Dreams (The Works Of Duke, Vol 17); Chelsea Bridge (The Works Of Duke, Vol 17*) Blue Serge (The Works Of Duke, Vol 16*)**.

Webster's contribution to the blues section of **Black, Brown & Beige** at its Carnegie Hall première in January, '43, was major. He also worked with Billie Holiday **(The Golden Years, Vol 1** and **The Voice Of Jazz, Vols 6-9)**; Jack Teagarden **(Jack Teagarden/Pee Wee Russell)**; Dizzy Gillespie **(The Gilespie Jam Sessions)**; Red Norvo **(The Greatest Of The Small Bands, Vol 1)**; Benny Carter **(Jazz Giant)** and Gerry Mulligan **(...Meets The Sax Giants, Vols 1-3)**. His gentle-raucous double-edged approach to tenor was ready-made for Norman Granz' Jazz At The Philharmonic concerts **(JATP In Tokyo)**. Also recorded productively with Don Byas **(Ben Webster Meets Don Byas)**; Johnny Hodges **(Blue Summit/Side By Side — Back To Back)**; Oscar Peterson **(Soulville)**; Coleman Hawkins **(Blue Saxophones)**; and Harry Edison **(Walkin' With Sweets** and **Blues For Basie)**.

Probably the most satisfying of Webster's studio dates was that which Granz supervised in 1955. The results **(The Tatum Group Masterpieces)** were glorious, with Tatum at peak form and Webster, ignoring pianist's 'solo-accompaniments', producing one solo after another of great warmth and beauty.

Webster, one of the true giants on saxophone, lived in Denmark for the last nine years of his life. His majestic horn was silenced, finally, in Amsterdam in 1973.

Albums:
Bennie Moten, Moten's Swing, Vol 5 (1929-1932) (RCA Victor—France)
Willie Bryant/(Jimmy Lunceford) & Their Orchestras (Bluebird/RCA Victor—France)
The Fletcher Henderson Story (Columbia)/ The Fletcher Henderson Story, Vol 4 (CBS)
Duke Ellington, The Works Of Duke, Vols 9-18 (RCA Victor—France)
Duke Ellington, Black, Brown & Beige (Ariston—Italy)
Billie Holiday, The Golden Years, Vol 1 (Columbia/CBS)
Billie Holiday, The Voice Of Jazz, Vols 6-9 (Verve/Verve)
Various, Jack Teagarden/Pee Wee Russell (BYG—France)
Ben Webster — A Tribute To A Great Jazzman (Jazz Archives/—)
Various, The Charlie Parker Sides (Verve)/ The Parker Jam Session (Verve)
Various, JATP In Tokyo (Pablo/Pablo)
Red Norvo, The Greatest Of The Small Bands, Vol 1 (RCA Victor—France)
Benny Carter, Jazz Giant (Contemporary/Vogue—Contemporary)
Coleman Hawkins/Ben Webster, Blue Saxophones (Verve/Verve)
Barney Kessel, Let's Cook! (Contemporary/Vogue—Contemporary)
Ben Webster/Oscar Peterson, Soulville (Verve/Verve)
Jimmy Witherspoon, At The Renaissance (HiFi/Ember)
Jimmy Witherspoon & Ben Webster (Atlantic/Atlantic)
Giants Of The Tenor Saxophone/The Genius Of Ben Webster & Coleman Hawkins (Columbia/CBS)
Duke Ellington/Johnny Hodges, Blues Summit (Verve)/
Side By Side—Back To Back (Metro)
John Lewis-Kenny Clarke-Ben Webster-Milt Jackson (Ozone/—)
Bill Harris & Friends (Fantasy/Vocalion)
Teddy Wilson & His Big Band 1939-40 (Tax—Sweden)
Art Tatum, The Tatum Group Masterpieces (Pablo/Pablo)
Ben Webster & Associates (Verve)/ Ben Webster & Friends (Verve)
Ballads By Ben Webster (Verve/Verve)
Harry Edison, Walkin' With Sweets (—/Verve)
Harry Edison, Blues For Basie (—/Verve)
Ben Webster, Atmosphere For Lovers & Thieves (Black Lion/Black Lion)
Ben Webster, Days Of Wine & Roses (Black Lion/Black Lion)
Ben Webster, Duke's In Bed! (Black Lion/Black Lion)
Ben Webster, Saturday Night At The Montmartre (Black Lion/Black Lion)
*There are two separate issues of Volume 16 (has been withdrawn but nevertheless was officially released by RCA Victor — France). Same applies to at least two other volumes in this series, including Volume 17.

Ben Webster, Duke's In Bed! (courtesy Black Lion)—a true giant.

Above: Mike and Kate Westbrook—dramatic performances from two of the UK's most original artists.

Kate Westbrook

A multi-faceted musican, Kate Westbrook has emerged as one of the most distinguished, original and individualistic performers in Britain. An accomplished tenor horn and piccolo-player, and a gifted lyric writer, she is also a captivating multi-lingual vocalist with a spell-binding sense of theater.

Born in Britain, Kate Westbrook was raised in the United States and Canada before returning to England to study at Dartington Hall School, Bath Academy of Art and Reading University. The first of numerous major exhibitions of her paintings was held in Santa Barbara Museum of Art, California, in '63. (Her career in art is documented by the Arts Council of Great Britain film, *Kate Barnard and her Work*.) After travelling in Mexico, she became a teacher at Leeds College of Art in England.

In '74, she joined the Mike Westbrook Brass Band jazz-cabaret group, singing and playing tenor horn and piccolo, giving up teaching to concentrate on painting and music. Since '78, she has written lyrics for many of the Brass Band's songs and, in collaboration with Mike Westbrook, has worked on scenarios for the group's productions, notably **Mama Chicago, Bien Sur** and **Hotel Amigo**. Kate Westbrook's imaginative adaptations of European texts, including those of Lorca and Rimbaud poems, were featured in **The Cortege**. Since '82, she has been an important part of the trio A Little Westbrook Music with Mike Westbrook and saxophonist Chris Biscoe.

In '85, she was commissioned by the Bloomsbury Festival to present a music-theater piece, *Revenge Suite*, performed by the five-piece Kate Westbrook Ensemble. The suite — 'musical episodes in a picaresque heroine's life' — included original songs by Kate and Mike Westbrook, music from Rossini's *Otello*, the Brecht-Weill *Seerauber-Jenny*, texts by Lorca and Saarikoski and her interpretations of Billy Strayhorn's *Lush Life*, Cole Porter's *Love For Sale* and Rodgers & Hart's *Ten Cents A Dance*. Her performing group included Trevor Allan (accordion), Chris Biscoe, Lindsay Cooper (reeds), Georgie Born (cello) and Mike Westbrook (piano, tuba).

Kate Westbrook's later work in the '80s also includes co-writing, with Mike Westbrook, two extraordinary and highly acclaimed music-theater pieces — *The Ass* and **Pier Rides**.

A Little Westbrook Music (courtesy Westbrook Records).

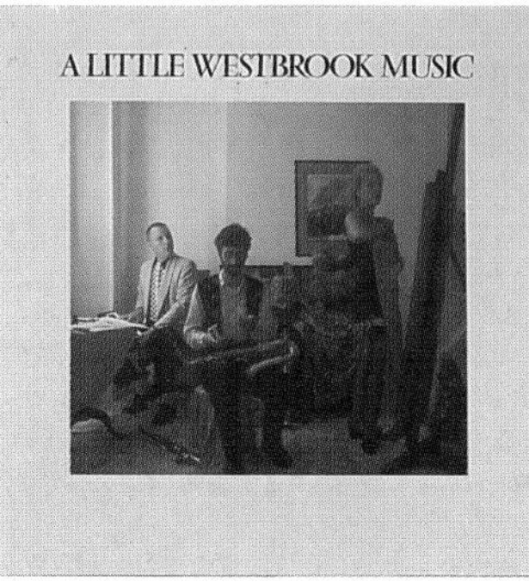

Albums:
For The Record (Transatlantic/Transatlantic)
Goose Sauce (—/Original)
Mama Chicago (—/RCA—UK; Teldec—Germany)
The Westbrook Blake (Europa/Original)
The Paris Album (—/Polydor—France)
The Cortege (—/Original)
A Little Westbrook Music (—/Westbrook Records)
On Duke's Birthday (—/hatArt—Switzerland)
Pier Rides (—/Westbrook Music)
Love For Sale (—hatArt)

Mike Westbrook

The multi-dimensional composer and bandleader Mike Westbrook has been one of the most important energy-centers in contemporary British music since the early 1960s. His wide-ranging musical inspirations have produced enduring works for a series of diverse and original ensembles.

Born in High Wycombe, England, Westbrook was raised in Torquay, Devon. In '58, while at art school in Plymouth, he formed his first band which included saxophonist John Surman. He has led and composed for his own bands since, moving to London in '62. From the mid-'60s, Westbrook — who also plays piano and tuba — has regularly assembled large groups (10 to 25 musicians) to play his extended compositions like **Celebration** and **Marching Song** ('67), **Release** ('68),

Metropolis ('69) and **Citadel/Room 315** ('74). **Citadel/Room 315**, commissioned by Swedish Radio, remains one of Westbrook's finest works from the '70s, making brilliant use of soloists like baritone saxophonist John Surman on **Outgoing**, tenorist Alan Wakeman on the driving **Pastorale**, as well as blending inspirations from Duke Ellington and Gil Evans.

In '79, he formed a 16-piece orchestra for his large-scale **The Cortege** (the first part of a trilogy on the theme of Life-Death-Life based on the New Orleans jazz funeral). Westbrook has also composed extensively for voice including his settings for the poetry of William Blake **(The Westbrook Blake),** Rimbaud, Lorca and Hesse **(The Cortege)**, as well as the spirited jazz-cabaret **Mama Chicago** ('78) with lyrics by his wife Kate Westbrook and Michael Kustow.

From '70 to '72, Westbrook co-directed (with John Fox) the multi-media company Cosmic Circus and led the rock group Solid Gold Cadillac from '71 to '74. In '73, with trumpeter and voice-performer extraordinaire Phil Minton, Westbrook formed his regular and popular Brass Band (later to include Kate Westbrook—voice, tenor horn and piccolo, multi-saxophonist Chris Biscoe and drummer Tony Marsh). (The Brass Band is featured in the Arts Council of Great Britain documentary film *Work In Progress*.)

In the '80s, Westbrook has performed in a many-faceted trio alongside Kate Westbrook and Chris Biscoe — with their unique combination of music and drama — recording **A Little Westbrook Music** and the double **Love For Sale**. A major Westbrook orchestral work, **After Smith's Hotel — The Young Person's Guide To The Jazz Orchestra**, was commissioned by the Aldeburgh Foundation and premièred in October '83. Westbrook's spectacular **On Duke's Birthday** (marking the 10th anniversary of Ellington's death) was performed by an 11-piece orchestra at the Amiens and Angoulême festivals in '84.

More recent projects (all written in collaboration with Kate Westbrook) include *Westbrook-Rossini* (his jazz and rock variations on Rossini opera), *The Ass* (based on D. H. Lawrence's poem) and **Pier Rides** (an unusual interpretation of the mythology of the nine Muses using dance, theater, music and song). The highly acclaimed *Pier Rides* toured the UK widely with Emlyn Claid's Extemporary Dance Company in '86.

Much of Westbrook's later work has become as important for its visual and dramatic impact as for its dynamic and inventive music. He has evolved a style of theater and music which, in its originality and scope, is unsurpassed.

Albums:
Celebration (—/Deram)
Release (—/Deram)
Marching Song Vols 1 & 2 (—/Deram)
Love Songs (—/Deram)
Metropolis (RCA/RCA)
Tyger (RCA/RCA)
Solid Gold Cadillac (RCA/RCA)
Mike Westbrook Live (—/Cadillac)
Brain Damage (RCA/RCA)
Citadel/Room 315 (RCA/RCA)
Love/Dream And Variations (Transatlantic/Transatlantic)
Goose Sauce (—/Original)
Mike Westbrook Piano (—/Original)
Mama Chicago (—/RCA—UK; Teldec—Germany)
The Westbrook Blake (Europa/Original)
The Paris Album (—/Polydor—France)
The Cortege (—/Original)
A Little Westbrook Music (—/Westbrook Records)
On Duke's Birthday (—/hatArt—Switzerland)
Pier Rides (—/Westbrook Music)
Love For Sale (—/hatArt)

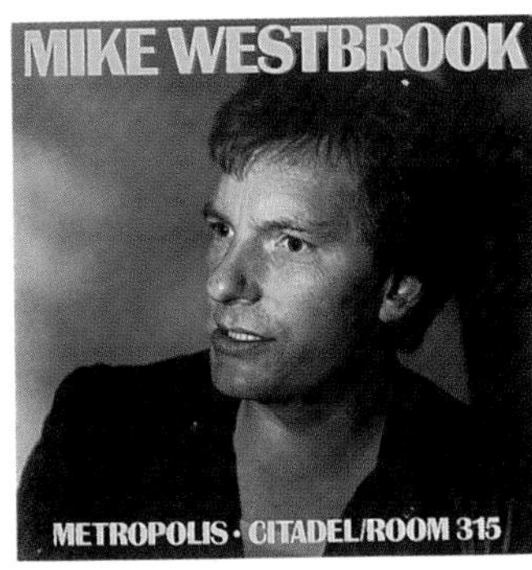

Mike Westbrook, Metropolis/Citadel 315 (courtesy RCA)—combined classics.

Randy Weston

Randy Weston ran a restaurant in Brooklyn frequented by the giants of bebop and was encouraged by customers like Bird and Max Roach to take up the piano. Like his friends Herbie Nichols and Valdo Williams, Weston idolized Thelonious Monk, and that influence—along with Duke Ellington and Fats Waller — can be found in his style.

After R&B experience with Bull Moose Jackson and Eddie Cleanhead Vinson, he launched out on a jazz career, winning the *Downbeat* New Star category in 1955. A Blue Note album **(Little Niles)** reveals the strength and charm of his keyboar and compositions. **Pam's Waltz** and **Little Niles** are classics of impressionistic writing.

In 1961, Weston — always deeply conscious of his African heritage — took a band to Africa, the first of several visits leading to his settling in Morocco in 1968. An album made in 1964, **African Cookbook**, shows the all-pervading African influence. **Congolese Children** is adapted from a traditional Bashai folk song, though the outstanding piece is **Portrait Of Vivian** — a vehicle for the overwhelming tenor of Booker Ervin.

Other albums have featured works dedicated to Africa and Ellington **(Blues** and **Carnival)**, and the solo piano album **Blues To Africa** shows the spectrum of his talents from stride to bebop.

A highly articulate man, and a trail-blazer in terms of the Afro-American search for cultural heritage, Randy Weston has been performing in Europe since 1974. His music is as distinctive as his 6 foot 7 inch frame.

Albums:
Little Niles (Blue Note/Blue Note)
African Cookbook (Atlantic/Atlantic)
Blues (Trip/—)
Carnival (Freedom/Freedom)
Blues To Africa (Freedom/Freedom)
Nuits Americaine (—/Enja—Germany)
Blue (1750 Arch Records/1750 Arch Records)

Kenny Wheeler

Based in Britain, Canadian-born Kenny Wheeler has become one of Europe's most formidable and in-demand trumpeters, with an international reputation.

Born in St Catherine, Canada, in 1930, Wheeler was encouraged to become a musician by his trombonist father. His earliest influences were Buck Clayton and Roy Eldridge, followed by Miles Davis and Fats Navarro. Working in Britain with musicians like Joe Harriott and Ronnie Scott led to his joining the Johnny Dankworth band in '59.

In '66, Wheeler became associated with John Stevens' ground-breaking group improvisations in the Spontaneous Music Ensemble and worked with drummer Tony Oxley. Through saxophonist Evan Parker and guitarist Derek Bailey, Wheeler became part of Alexander Von Schlippenbach's German-based Globe Unity Orchestra and, in '71, joined the Anthony Braxton group.

Since the mid-'70s, Wheeler has recorded steadily for the German ECM label. His first ECM album, **Gnu High** ('75), featured pianist Keith Jarrett, followed by **Deer Wan** (with saxophonist Jan Garbarek and guitarist John Abercrombie), **Around 6** (with Evan Parker, trombonist Eje Thelin, vibist Tom Van Der Geld, bassist J. F. Jenny-Clark and drummer Edward Vesala) and **Double, Double You** ('84, with saxophonist Mike Brecker and pianist John Taylor). Most recently, Wheeler has also worked with vocalist Norma Winstone and pianist John Taylor (in the trio Azimuth), bassist Dave Holland, and is part of the German-based 'Band of Band-leaders', the United Jazz+Rock Ensemble.

Above: The self-effacing Canadian-born Kenny Wheeler has become one of Europe's most respected and sought-after trumpet-players. A musician to cherish.

Albums:
Globe Unity Orchestra, Improvisation (Japo/Japo)
Globe Unity Orchestra, Compositions (Japo/Japo)
Globe Unity Orchestra, Intergalactic Blow (Japo/Japo)
Anthony Braxton, The Complete Braxton (Freedom/Freedom)
Azimuth, Azimuth (ECM/ECM)
Azimuth, The Touchstone (ECM/ECM)
Azimuth, Départ (ECM/ECM)
Azimuth, Azimuth '85 (ECM/ECM)
Dave Holland, Jumpin' In (ECM/ECM)
Dave Holland, Seeds Of Time (ECM/ECM)
United Jazz+Rock Ensemble, 10 Years (—/Mood Records—Germany)
Gnu High (ECM/ECM)
Deer Wan (ECM/ECM)
Around 6 (ECM/ECM)
Double, Double You (ECM/ECM)

Kenny Wheeler, Double, Double You (courtesy ECM)—all his own work.

Annie Whitehead

Trombonist Annie Whitehead has emerged as one of the brightest and most versatile young musicians in Britain in the 1980s, working with her own groups and a diversity of British jazz luminaries.

Annie Whitehead learned trombone at age 14, in Oldham, Lancashire, playing with her school brass band. At 16, she joined the Ivy Benson band, traveling the exhausting European big-band circuit for two years. In the late '70s, after a long sabbatical in Jersey, the Channel Islands, she arrived in London and found herself in great demand as a session musician. Her excellent writing and arranging skills also brought her regular live work with Latin-based bands like Valdez, Dave Bitelli's Onward Internationals and Working Week, and the Afro-pop band Orchestre Jazira.

She has worked with a wide range of jazz groups — the Lydia D'Ustebyn Orchestra (the women's big band), the Guest Stars, drummer John Stevens' Folkus and Freebop, pianist Chris McGregor's Brotherhood of Breath, bassist Paul Rogers' 7RPM, and with vocalist Maggie Nichols and saxophonist Evan Parker.

Annie Whitehead's first album as leader, **Mix-Up** — an eclectic and lively blend of jazz funk, ska and salsa — was released in '85.

Albums:
John Stevens' Folkus, The Life Of Riley (—/Affinity)
Mix-Up (Paladin/Paladin)

Trombonist Annie Whitehead, Mix-Up (courtesy Paladin)—her début.

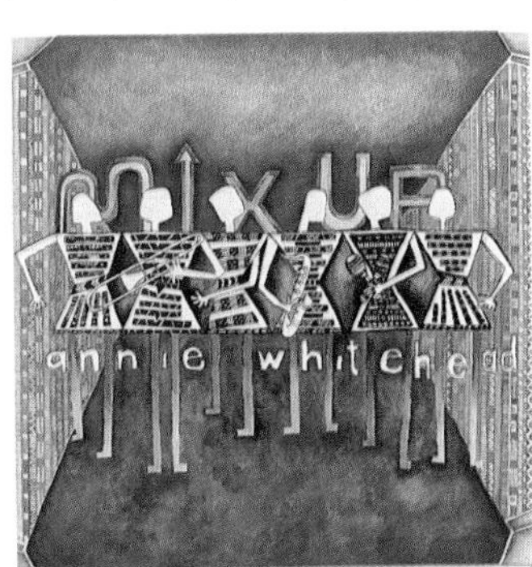

Above: The eclectic British trombonist Annie Whitehead—making a lively blend of jazz, funk, Latin, ska and salsa. A promising future.

Clarence Williams

New Orleans pianist-composer Clarence Williams (1893-1965) tended to be eclipsed by the musical company he kept. He accompanied Bessie Smith on her recording début **Downhearted Blues** and **Gulf Coast Blues (The World's Greatest Blues Singer)** and worked with her on and off throughout her career, writing or co-writing many of her songs including **Baby Won't You Please Come Home**.

Based in New York, he managed Okeh's race label, arranging recording sessions and recruiting talent, adapting the New Orleans style to the new environment and market. His ensemble-writing for various combinations was always professional and often highly resourceful, while his piano-playing remained retiring and functional. Williams turns up on numerous sessions featuring Sidney Bechet, Louis Armstrong, Coleman Hawkins, Buster Bailey, King Oliver, Eddie Lang and Tommy Ladnier, lending his distinctive touch to the arrangements.

Albums:

Bessie Smith, The World's Greatest Blues Singer (Columbia/CBS)
Clarence Williams! Jazz Kings 1927-9 (/—VJM)
Louis Armstrong, Sidney Bechet With The Clarence Williams Blue Five (—/CBS—France)
Adam & Eve Had The Blues (—/CBS—France)
Jugs & Washboards (—/Ace Of Hearts)
West End Blues (—/CBS—France)
Clarence Williams & His Washboard Band, Vols 1 & 2 (—/Classic Jazz Masters)

Cootie Williams

Charlie Melvin 'Cootie' Williams was one of the Duke Ellington Orchestra's most potent and important soloists.

Williams (born Mobile, Alabama, 1910), first joined Ellington in 1929, after gaining playing experience with Fletcher Henderson, Chick Webb and James P. Johnson (on record, at least), as well as with the exquisitely named Eagle Eye Shields. Remained an Ellingtonian until 1940 when he accepted lucrative offer to join Benny Goodman as featured soloist. Williams' departure from Ellington shocked the jazz schene at the time, an event documented by bandleader-composer Raymond Scott, who composed **When Cootie Left The Duke**.

During his stay with Goodman, Williams (together with the youthful Charlie Christian), gave immeasurable inspiration to the clarinettist's sextets and septets of 1940-41 period.

Between the Goodman sojourn and the reunion with Ellington, Williams fronted own big band. This band, often R&B-oriented, was only partially successful, in terms of commercial acceptance. Both big band and small combo of 1944 were recorded and results **(Cootie Williams Sextet & Orchestra)** show it was a more than capable band.

From the earlier days, Williams' fierce blowing stood out on many dates including several hosted during late-1930s by Lionel Hampton **(The Complete Lionel Hampton/Lionel Hampton's Best Records, Vols 1, 5)** and those celebrating annual jazz popularity polls (in which Williams has featured strongly) including **Benny Carter 1945+Metronome All-Stars** and **The Metronome All Stars/ The Esquire All Stars**.

Of numerous solos by Williams in his pre-Goodman period with Ellington, many feature his superb use of plunger mute. Williams replaced Bubber Miley in this role, and made himself as irreplaceable as his predecessor.

His post-1962 work sometimes lacked flexibility of a quarter-century before but was, perhaps, more powerful. Both on record and in person he contributed torrid solos, including **Let's Get Together (Recollections Of The Big Band Era); Tutti For Cootie** and a reworking of **Concerto For Cootie (The Great Paris Concert); Intimacy of The Blues (...And His Mother Called Him Bill); Night Flock** and another **Tutti For Cootie (Greatest Jazz Concert In The World); Satin Doll (Duke Ellington's 70th Birthday Concert); Portrait Of Louis Armstrong, Portrait Of Mahalia Jackson (New Orleans Suite)**; and **I Got It Bad, C-Jam Blues, In A Mellotone (Togo Brava Suite/ The English Concert)**.

In later years, Williams was dogged by ill health and his playing tended to be intermittent. Significantly, perhaps, Cootie Williams' trenchant trumpet playing was heard on the first album to be made **(Continuum)** following Duke Ellington's death, when son Mercer Ellington had taken over.

Although Williams toured briefly with Mercer Ellington, he was totally inactive for the last five years of his life. Cootie Williams died in New York on September 14, 1985, after a long illness during which he had undergone treatment for a kidney ailment. He was 77. His passing was to leave trombonist Lawrence Brown as the only surviving member of Ellington's legendary late '30s orchestra.

Albums:

Duke Ellington, The Works Of Duke, Vols 3-5, 8, 10, 11 (RCA Victor—France)
Duke Ellington, The Ellington Era, 1927-1940, Vols 1, 2 (Columbia/CBS)
Duke Ellington, The Complete Duke Ellington, Vols 2-7 (CBS—France)
Duke Ellington, Cotton Club Days—1938, Vols 1, 2 (Jazz Archives/—)
Duke Ellington, Recollections Of The Big Band Era (Atlantic/—)
Duke Ellington, The Great Paris Concert (Atlantic/—)
Duke Ellington,...And His Mother Called Him Bill (RCA Victor/RCA Victor)
Duke Ellington's 70th Birthday Concert (Solid State/United Artists)
Duke Ellington, New Orleans Suite (Atlantic/Atlantic)
Various (Including Duke Ellington), The Greatest Jazz Concert In The World (Pablo/Pablo)
Duke Ellington, Togo Brava Suite (United Artists)/The English Concert (United Artists)
Charlie Christian With The Benny Goodman Sextet & Orchestra (Columbia/CBS)
Charlie Christian/Benny Goodman, Solo Flight —The Genius Of Charlie Christian (Columbia)/Solo Flight (CBS)
Benny Goodman Plays Solid Instrumental Hits (Columbia/CBS)
The Complete Lionel Hampton (Bluebird)/ Lionel Hampton's Best Records, Vols 1, 5 (RCA Victor—France)
Johnny Hodges, Hodge Podge (Epic/CBS-Realm)
Various, The Metronome All Stars/Esquire All Stars (RCA Victor—France)
Various, Benny Carter 1945+The Metronome All-Stars (Queen Disc—Italy)
Various (Including Cootie Williams), The New York Scene In The '40s: From Be-Bop To Cool (CBS—France)
Cootie Williams Sextet & Orchestra (Phoenix)
Cootie Williams/(Hot Lips Page), Big Sound Trumpets (RCA Victor—France)
Cootie Williams/Rex Stewart, The Big Challenge (Jazztone/Concert Hall)
Various (Including Cootie Williams), Big Band Bounce (Capitol/Capitol-Holland)
Cootie Williams, Cootie & The Boys From Harlem (Tax—Sweden)
Cootie Williams, Cootie & His Rug Cutters (Tax—Sweden)

Mary Lou Williams

Pianist Mary Lou Williams' contribution to jazz cannot be underestimated or understated. She was instrumental in the development of Kansas City swing and one of the few jazz musicians who successfully weathered the changes in the music—from spirituals and ragtime to jazz in all its later forms—and still retained an international following. Mary Lou Williams' keyboard acumen, as Duke Ellington remarked, 'possessed a timeless musical quality'.

Mary Lou Williams (born Mary Elfrieda Winn, Atlanta, Georgia, 1910) was a gifted jazz composer and arranger as well as producing more extended works, including religious masses. Her arranging skill is demonstrated in the repertoire of many famous bands including Duke Ellington, Benny Goodman, Louis Armstrong, Tommy Dorsey, Earl Hines, Glen Gray and Andy Kirk. She first played for, and recorded with, a band led by Kirk as early as 1929 but Mary Lou Williams was leading her own band two years before that date.

Her piano-playing and writing were subsequently to run the whole history of jazz from stride to boogie-woogie to bop to post-bop impressionism **(History Of Jazz: Ragtime To Avant Garde)**.

Together with mother and sister, Mary Lou Williams moved from Atlanta to Pittsburgh when she was four. Studied piano at four and was playing live engagements a few years later. Toured with TOBA circuit as pianist-accompanist, working under name of Mary Lou Burleigh (surname was stepfather's).

Toured with several other bands, including one led by John Williams. It was this band with which Mary Lou Williams made her bandleading début when Williams left (1928). Contributed arrangements in 1929 to a band led by Andy Kirk, occasionally sitting in on piano at recording dates and gigs. Joined full-time, as pianist and chief arranger, in 1931; she was to remain with Kirk's band (soon to be known as his 12 Clouds of Joy) from 1931-42. Amongst her first charts for Kirk, **Messa Stomp, Corky Stomp** and **Blue Clarinet Stomp** (all **Clouds Of Joy)** register far more convincingly than the band which plays them.

By 1936, both as pianist and writer, she had improved. There is a freshness and originality about items like **Walkin' & Swingin', Lotta Sax Appeal, Bearcat Shuffle** and **Steppin' Pretty** (all **Andy Kirk & His 12 Clouds Of Joy—March 1936)**, that makes them sound good even today. Also during '36, Williams recorded (together with Booker Collins and Ben Thigpen, her rhythm section colleagues with Kirk) a series of piano tracks of which **Overhand, Swingin' For Joy** and the inappropriately titled **Corny Rhythm** (all **Jazz Pioneers 1933-36/Andy Kirk & His 12 Clouds Of Joy—March 1936)** exemplify her instrumental talents.

Married trumpeter Harold 'Shorty' Baker and the two co-led own small combo before Baker joined Duke Ellington Orchestra and in 1945 Williams contributed an electrifying **Trumpet No End (The Golden Duke)** to Ellington book. (In 1937 she had enhanced repertoire of Benny Goodman band by producing **Camel Hop, Roll 'Em** (both **Benny Goodman, Vol 7)** writing superior arrangements

Above: A tremendously exciting player, Cootie Williams' deft use of plunger mute attracted much admiration.

for both.) Also in the '40s, led a superb women's combo including Mary Osborne (guitar), Marjorie Hyam (vibes), June Rotenburg and Vivian Garry (bass) and Bridget O'Flynn (drums) **(The Greatest Of The Small Bands, Vol 2)**.

Became deeply involved in bebop evolution during 1945, having become close friends with Dizzy Gillespie, Thelonious Monk and Bud Powell. Her **Zodiac Suite** was premièred at New York's Town Hall, played by New York Philharmonic; 12 years later, Gillespie persuaded her to sit in on piano during performance (featuring his big band) of the work, played at Newport Jazz Festival **(Dizzy Gillespie At Newport)**. Between 1944-48, became more or less resident at both Café Society clubs, New York.

During early 1950s, active in New York clubs before leaving US to spend time (1952-54) in Britain and France. Recorded in Paris with Don Byas **(Don Carlos Meets Mary Lou)** and in London took part in two separate piano-quartet dates **(Mary Lou Williams Plays In London** and **I Love A Piano)**.

Back in US she decided to leave music business altogether, becoming deeping immersed in religious instruction and charity work for needy musicians. Her musical comeback, in August 1957, led to regular work mostly with own combos at clubs, concerts and festivals. A 1971 solo piano date **(From The Heart)** provides a perfect showcase for her timeless artistry, improvising brilliantly on a varied selection of her own compositions: old **(Scratchin' In The Gravel, Little Joe From Chicago, Morning Glory)** and new **(Blues For John, Offertory, A Fungus Amungus)**. In a different vein, she was involved—writing, arranging, playing — with two splendid masses **(Black Christ Of The Andes** and **Music For Peace)**.

Since '77, Williams taught jazz history and improvisation full-time at Duke University, Durham, South Carolina. Mary Lou Williams died of cancer on May 29, 1981, aged 71, in Durham. She bequeathed her entire estate to the Mary Lou Williams Foundation (set up just a year before) to enable gifted young children to study with professional jazz musicians.

Albums:

Andy Kirk, Clouds Of Joy (Ace of Hearts/Ace of Hearts)
Various (Including Mary Lou Williams), Jazz Pioneers, 1933-36 (Prestige)/Andy Kirk & His 12 Clouds Of Joy—March 1936 (Parlophone)
Andy Kirk, Twelve Clouds Of Joy (Ace of Hearts/Ace of Hearts)
Benny Goodman, Vol 7: 'The Kingdom Of Swing' (1935-1939) (RCA Victor—France)
Duke Ellington, The Golden Duke (Prestige/Prestige)
Various (Including Mary Lou Williams), The Greatest Of The Small Bands, Vol 2 (RCA Victor—France)
Dizzy Gillespie At Newport (Verve/Columbia-Clef)
Don Byas/Mary Lou Williams, Don Carlos Meets Mary Lou (Storyville/Vogue—EP)
Various (Including Mary Lou Williams), I Love A Piano (—/Esquire)
Mary Lou Williams, Black Christ Of The Andes (MPS)
Various (Including Mary Lou Williams), Café Society (Onyx/—)
Dizzy Gillespie/Bobby Hackett, Giants (Perception)
Buddy Tate, Buddy & His Buddies (Chiaroscuro/—)
Mary Lou Williams, From The Heart (Chiaroscuro/Storyville)
History Of Jazz: Ragtime To Avant Garde (Folkways/—)
Mary Lou's Mass (Mary/—)
My Mama Pinned A Rose On Me (Pablo/Pablo)
Praise The Lord In Many Voices (Avan Garde/—)
Solo Recital/Montreux Jazz Festival 1978 (Pablo/Pablo)
Zodiac Suite (Folkways/—)
Zoning (Mary/—)

Tony Williams

At just 17, Tony Williams astonished the jazz world with his revolutionary and totally fresh rhythmic concept on drums. His work with Miles Davis (1963-69) and Eric Dolphy **(Out To Lunch**, '64), plus his own early albums for Blue Note **(Life Time** and **Spring)**, combined to confirm his status as the most advanced drummer of the age.

Born in Chicago on December 12, 1945, Anthony 'Tony' Williams—the son of tenor

The Mary Lou Williams Quartet (courtesy Esquire): collectors's item! An old EP from 1953 with Britain's Ray Dempsey (guitar), Rupert Nurse (bass) and Tony Kinsey (drums).

saxophonist Tillmon Williams—was raised in Boston. At age 17, after a brief but devastating début with Jacie McLean **(One Step Beyond)**, Williams came to international attention and acclaim through the Miles Davis Quintet, his new free-ranging rhythmic explorations sweeping away much of what had gone before.

Leaving Miles in the late '60s, Williams formed the trio Lifetime with guitarist John McLaughlin and organist Larry Young plus, later, bassist Jack Bruce. One of the pioneers in early fusion, Lifetime was to be influential in spite of its short existence.

In '76, Williams was reunited with his old Miles Davis Quintet colleagues—pianist Herbie Hancock, bassist Ron Carter and saxophonist Wayne Shorter—touring widely with the all-acoustic VSOP recreating the music of a classic, pre-electric era.

Considering Williams' early reputation as a musical pathfinder, not surprisingly he has been one of the reactivated Blue Note label's new signings producing **Foreign Intrigue** in '86.

Albums:
Jackie McLean, One Step Beyond (Blue Note/Blue Note)
Granchan Moncurr III, Evolution (Blue Note/Blue Note)
Eric Dolphy, Out To Lunch (Blue Note/Blue Note)
Sam Rivers, Fuchsia Swing Song (Blue Note/Blue Note)
Life Time (Blue Note/Blue Note)
Spring (Blue Note/Blue Note)
Miles Davis, My Funny Valentine (Columbia/CBS)
Miles Davis, Miles Smiles (Columbia/CBS)
Miles Davis, ESP (Columbia/CBS)
Miles Davis, Sorcerer (Columbia/CBS)
Miles Davis, Nefertiti (Columbia/CBS)
Miles Davis, Filles De Kilimanjaro (Columbia/CBS)
Tony Williams' Lifetime, Emergency (Polydor/Polydor)
Tony Williams' Lifetime, Turn It Over (Polydor/Polydor)
Ego (Columbia/CBS)
Million Dollar Legs (Columbia/CBS)
VSOP, VSOP (Columbia/CBS)
McCoy Tyner, Supertrios (Milestone/Milestone)
The Joy Of Flying (Columbia/CBS)
Foreign Intrigue (Blue Note/Blue Note)

Above: The inspirational Teddy Wilson. His death in July 1986 left a gaping hole in the music.

Teddy Wilson

Theodore 'Teddy' Wilson (born Austin, Texas, 1912) was one of the music's finest keyboard soloists. Wilson's style was a personal refinement of the more virtuoso and extrovert interpretations of Art Tatum and Earl Hines (with a passing reference to the basic deliberations of Fats Waller and James P. Johnson). He worked and recorded with most of the great innovators in jazz from beginning of the 1930s up to the bop era.

His experiences in fronting own big band lasted only a year (1939-40). As good as it was—and its personnel included Ben Webster, Doc Cheatham, J.C. Heard and Harold 'Shorty' Baker, with arrangements by Wilson, Edgar Sampson, Buster Harding and Webster—its music was too refined and lacked real dynamics and basic excitement **(Teddy Wilson & His Big Band 1939/40)**.

Wilson was celebrated for providing exquisite accompaniments for an impressive number of jazz or jazz-based vocalists: Billie Holiday, Mildred Bailey, Ella Fitzgerald, Sarah Vaughan, Lena Horne, Midge Williams and Putney Dandridge. The accompaniments Wilson provided for Holiday — especially between 1935-38 — were superb, reaching heights of sublimity with Lester Young. Wilson undoubtedly helped make the majority of Billie Holiday recordings (at this important time during her career) masterpieces **(Billie Holiday, The Golden Years, Vols 1, 2, The Lester Young Story, Vol 1** and **The Billie Holiday Story, Vol 1)**.

Wilson was also an important pianist with Benny Goodman's trio and quartet, from 1936-39. (He was to rejoin Goodman in '45, for record dates and to appear on Broadway production of *Seven Lively Arts*.)

After demise of his own big band, Wilson led a succession of superior small combos, including a 1944 sextet which included Hot Lips Page and Benny Morton **(The Radio Years/Teddy Wilson & His Orchestra 1944)** and another the following year which included Charlie Shavers and Red Norvo **(Stompin' At The Savoy)**. Started work for CBS radio in 1946; he was studio musician at WNEW four years, from 1949. Had recorded with Charlie Parker and Dizzy Gillespie in 1945 **(Red Norvo's Fabulous Jam Session)** but had made no attempt to adjust his style to meet the demands of the 'new music'.

Played well-received concerts in Scandinavia (1952), and visited Britain (1953). Took part in 1955 biopic, *The Benny Goodman Story*. In Hollywood was reunited for recorded tribute to Goodman with Lionel Hampton and Gene Krupa **(Krupa-Wilson-Hampton/Kings Of Swing, Vol 1)** which produced some of his finest playing of past 25 years.

Continued to record, including two exceptional sessions—one quartet, one septet—headlined by Lester Young **(Pres & Teddy & Oscar/Pres & Tedd)** in January 1956. Latter-day recording **Runnin' Wild!,** taped live at 1973 Montreux Jazz Festival, with trio of British musicians; plus two excellent solo albums; **Striding After Fats** and **With Billie In Mind**.

Teddy Wilson's last engagement was a reunion concert with Benny Goodman in New York in October '85. This most universally admired pianist died at his home in New Britain, Connecticut, on 31st July, 1986. He was 73.

Albums:
Willie Bryant & His Orchestra (RCA Victor—France)
Benny Carter—1933 (Prestige)/Various (Including Benny Carter), Ridin' In Rhythm (World Records)
The Teddy Wilson Piano Solos (CBS—France)
The Complete Benny Goodman, Vols 1-3 (RCA/Bluebird)/Benny Goodman, Vols 1-3 (RCA Victor—France)
Benny Goodman Trio & Quartet, Vols I, II (CBS—France)
Various (Including Benny Goodman/Lionel Hampton/Gene Krupa/Teddy Wilson), Kings Of Swing, Vol 1 (Verve/Verve)
Benny Goodman, 1938 Carnegie Hall Jazz Concert (Columbia/CBS)
Billie Holiday, The Golden Years, Vols 1, 2 (Columbia/CBS)
The Billie Holiday Story, Vol 1 (Columbia/CBS)
The Lester Young Story, Vols 1-3 (Columbia/CBS)
Mildred Bailey: Her Greatest Performances 1929-1946, Vols 1-3 (Columbia/CBS)
Various (Including Ella Fitzgerald/Billie Holiday/Lena Horne), Ella, Billie, Lena, Sarah; 4 Grandes Dames Du Jäzz (CBS—France)
Teddy Wilson & His Big Band 1939/40 (Tax—Sweden)
The Teddy Wilson (CBS/Sony—Japan)
Teddy Wilson & His All Stars (Columbia/CBS)
The Radio Years/Teddy Wilson & His Orchestra 1944 (—/London)
Teddy Wilson, Stompin' At The Savoy (—/Ember)
Sarah Vaughan, Tenderly (—/Bulldog)

Red Norvo's Fabulous Jam Session (Charlie Parker)
Krupa-Wilson-Hampton (—/Verve)
Lester Young/Teddy Wilson, Pres & Teddy & Oscar (Verve)/Pres & Teddy (Verve)
Benny Goodman In Moscow, Vols 1, 2 (RCA Victor/RCA Victor)
Teddy Wilson, Runnin' Wild! (Black Lion/Black Lion)
Teddy Wilson, Striding After Fats (Black Lion/Black Lion)
Teddy Wilson, With Billie In Mind (Chiaroscuro)/Body & Soul (Vogue)
Mr Wilson And Mr Gershwin (Columbia/CBS)

Jimmy Witherspoon

James 'Jimmy' Witherspoon (born Gurdon, Arkansas, 1923) is one of the most compeling blues singers. 'Spoon' received no formal music training and started in music at seven, as member of local Baptist choir. His musical education came from church music as well as from blues instrumentalists and singers who visited Arkansas.

At 18, was drafted into US Merchant Marines, serving (1941-43) in Pacific area. On leave in Calcutta, met pianist Teddy Weatherford, who had lived in Far East since 1926. Sang with Weatherford's band. Following release from Marines, decided to make career out of blues singing.

Joined Jay McShann Orchestra in place of Walter Brown. For next four years, Witherspoon gained valuable experience as McShann's principal blues vocalist. Record début, with band, in 1947, for Down Beat-Swing Time label. Apart from first-class interpretations of blues classics like **How Long, How Long Blues** and **Ain't Nobody's Business**, his expressive voice was well served by two of his own compositions: **Skidrow Blues** and **Money's Getting Cheaper** (all **Ain't Nobody's Business!**). Same year, Witherspoon-McShann combination put together equally fine versions of **Frog-I-More, In The Evening**, and **Backwater Blues (Ain't Nobody's Business!)**. In 1948, came Spoon originals, **Spoon Calls Hootie** and **Destruction Blues**.

Pursuing a solo career, progress was slow but steady. A hit record in 1952—a re-recording of **Ain't Nobody's Business**—helped make his one of the big names in R&B; other successes came later (eg **Big Fine Girl, The Wind Is Blowing** and **No Rollin' Blues**). His overall acceptance by a more jazz-type market came at end of 1950s, when Witherspoon produced two of his greatest recordings. The first **(Singin' The Blues/There's Good Rockin' Tonight)** was for World Pacific, with Spoon's vibrant singing complemented by Harry Edison, Teddy Edwards, Gerald Wilson, and Henry McDode.

A live recording from late-1950s **(Witherspoon At The Renaissance)** found Spoon, in magnificent voice, supported by a rhythm section (Jimmie Rowles, Mel Lewis, Leroy Vinnegar) and with exceptional solos and obbligatos from Ben Webster and Gerry Mulligan. Webster was to be a catalyst during recording of two LPs made for Reprise in 1961, 1962, with **Jimmy Witherspoon & Ben Webster**.

In the early '80s, Witherspoon underwent treatment for cancer of the throat but made a remarkable recovery, returning to tour and record with all his of old spirit. A Norman Granz-instigated 'blues summit' in '85, with veteran blues-shouter Big Joe Turner and saxophonist Red Holloway, showed Witherspoon as indomitable as ever.

Albums:
Jimmy Witherspoon, Ain't Nobody's Business (—/Black Lion)
Jimmy Witherspoon, A Spoonful Of Blues (RCA Victor—France)
Jimmy Witherspoon/(Count Basie), Blue Moods In The Shade Of Kansas City (RCA Victor—France)
Jimmy Witherspoon, The Spoon Concerts (Fantasy)/1959 Monterey Jazz Festival (Ember)
Witherspoon At The Renaissance (HiFi/Ember)
Buck Clayton & Jimmy Witherspoon Live In Paris (Vogue/Vogue)
Evenin' Blues (Prestige/Stateside)
Baby, Baby, Baby (Prestige/—)
Blues Around The Clock (Prestige/Stateside)
Some Of My Best Friends Are The Blues (Prestige/—)
Blue Spoon (Prestige/—)
Singin' The Blues (World Pacific)/ There's Good Rockin' Tonight (Fontana)
Jimmy Witherspoon & Ben Webster (Atlantic/Atlantic)
Jimmy Witherspoon/Wilbur De Paris, Callin' The Blues (Atlantic/London)
Spoonful (Blue Note/—)
Handbags & Gladrags (Probe/Probe)
Love Is A Five Letter Word (Capitol/Capitol)

Below: Jimmy Witherspoon—his magnificent voice, his personal charisma and an enduring stage presence make him a memorable blues musician.

Phil Woods

Born 1931 in Massachusetts, Phil Woods inherited his first alto from a deceased uncle. His spent four years at Juilliard Music College and gained experience with Charlie Barnet, Neal Hefti and Jimmy Raney, before cutting his début album with trumpeter Jon Eardley in 1955.

A Charlie Parker disciple, Woods is a direct, charging player who conveys few of the emotional depths of a contemporary like Jackie McLean but can dominate the session with his fiercely strident tone and sense of structure.

The re-release of hard bop sessions from the '50s shows Woods as one of the most inventive swingers around, from the excellent George Wallington Quintet **(The New York Scene** and **Jazz For The Carriage Trade)**; the Donald Byrd-Phil Woods-Al Haig session,

Below: Hard-blowing altoist Phil Woods. Resident in Europe for many years, his return to the States was a celebrated home-coming in the 1970s.

House Of Byrd; to the chases with fellow altoist Gene Quill, **Phil Woods**. He was completely at home with mainstream musicians like Benny Carter and Coleman Hawkins **(Further Definitions)** and undaunted by the challenging Thelonious Monk scores **(In Person)** in an orchestral setting, where his jumping attack dominates **Friday The 13th**.

Woods leads a large group through his own extended composition, **Rights Of Swing**, which features beautiful trumpet from Benny Bailey, some darkly somber voicings for baritone and French horn, and Woods' own linking alto.

In 1968, Phil Woods left America for Paris where he formed a new quartet, The Rhythm Machine, which included composer-pianist Gordon Beck, bassist Ron Mathewson and drummer Daniel Humair. A recording from 1972 **(Live From Montreux)** shows all the old ebullience and the incorporation of some of the New Thing's expressive tonal devices. **The Executive Suite** is a *tou de force* of alto playing—unaccompanied sections, great command from sceaming top to plangent bottom of the horn. Later work with Michel Legrand **(The Concert Legrand)**, tends to be submerged in the string sections.

In '72, Phil Woods returned to the States, settling in Pennsylvania's Pocono Mountains and recording Grammy-winning albums like **Images** (with Michel Legrand) and **Live From The Showboat**, as well as consistently topping the polls in the alto section. In the '80s, Woods continued to exert a compeling influence on young alto saxophonists, recording the excellent **Birds Of A Feather** in '81 with a superb quartet including pianist Hal Galper, bassist Steve Gilmore and drummer Bill Goodwin. The live album **Phil Woods Quartet At The Vanguard** ('83) finds this quartet in top form with an exceptional performance from Woods.

Albums:

George Wallington Quintet: The New York Scene (Prestige/—)
Jazz For The Carriage Trade (Prestige/—)
Donald Byrd, House Of Byrd (Prestige/Prestige)
Phil Woods (Prestige/Prestige)
Thelonious Monk, In Person (Milestone/Milestone)
Benny Carter, Further Definitions (Impulse/Impulse)
Rights Of Swing (CBS-Barnaby/CBS-Barnaby)
Live From Montreux (Verve/Verve)
The Concert Legrand (RCA/RCA)
Musique Du Bois (Muse/—)
Three For All (—/Enja—Germany)
European Rhythm Machine, At The Frankfurt Jazz Festival (Embryo/Embryo)
Birds Of A Feather (Antilles/Antilles)
The Phil Woods Quartet At The Vanguard (Antilles/Antilles)
Integrity—The New Phil Woods Quintet Live (Red/Red)

The Phil Woods Quartet, Birds Of A Feather (courtesy Antilles).

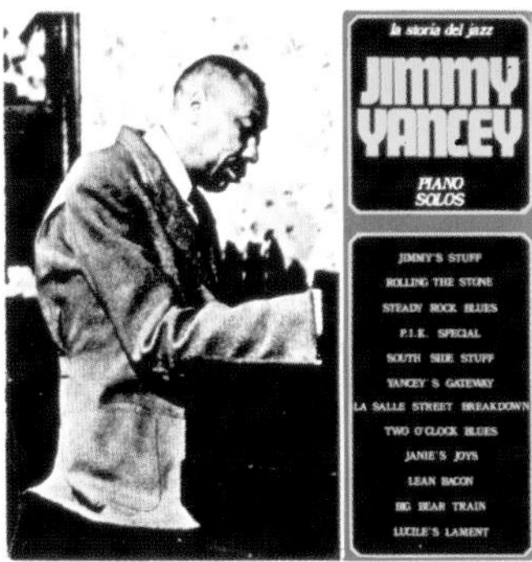

The artistry of Jimmy Yancey, Piano Solos (courtesy Joker-Italy).

Jimmy Yancey

James Edward 'Jimmy' Yancey (born Chicago, Illinois, 1894) was a pianist with limited technical skills and musical vocabulary. Yet he was a master of understatement and a great blues-player within an area bounded by boogie-woogie and basic blues. His playing—often poignant and invariably full of expression—was so personal as to give a sense of intruding into Yancey's private world.

Yancey came from a musical family—father was musician and singer, brother a pianist—and before World War I, starting when he was 6, had been a dancer-singer. He visited Europe as a dancer prior to 1914. Back in Chicago (1915), he taught himself to play piano. Worked at rent parties and clubs in Chicago until 1925 when he retired to become groundsman at headquarters of Chicago White Sox baseball club. Rediscovered after late-1930s success of **Yancey Special**, written by fellow pianist Meade Lux Lewis.

Yancey's comeback was achieved first by records. In 1939 he recorded a series of piano solos for Solo Arts, of which **Yancey's Getaway, Lucille's Lament, 2 O'Clock Blues** and **Janye's Joys** are superior illustrations of Yancey's sensitivity, combining two-handed strength with delicacy of touch **(Lost Recording Date/Piano Solos)**. Recorded later same year **(Boogie Woogie Man)** with outstanding piano-playing on **Yancey Stomp, Five O'Clock Blues** and **State Street Special,** plus moving vocal performances by Yancey on **Death Letter Blues** and **Crying In My Sleep**. Recorded equally moving performances for Session in 1943 **(The Immortal: 1898-1951)**, including **35th & Dearborn, I Love To Hear My Baby Call My Name** (another Jimmy Yancey vocal), plus three examples of his wife Mama Yancey's singing but topped by Jimmy's pain-filled **How Long, How Long Blues**.

In spite of failing health in '51, Yancey was able to make just one more recording before he died in Chicago that year. Accompanied by fellow Chicagoan Israel Crosby, Yancey's final record date was memorable for his best playing **(Lowdown Dirty Blues)**.

Albums:

Jimmy Yancey, Lost Recording Date (Riverside)/Piano Solos (Joker—Italy)
Various (Including Jimmy Yancey); Boogie Woogie Man (RCA Victor—France)
Various (Including Jimmy Yancey), Boogie Woogie Man Originaux (RCA Victor—France)
Jimmy Yancey, 'The Immortal' (1898-1951) (Oldie Blues—Holland)
Jimmy Yancey/(Cripple Clarence Lofton), The Yancey/Lofton Sessions, Vols 1,2 (Storyville)
Jimmy Yancey, Lowdown Dirty Blues (Atlantic)

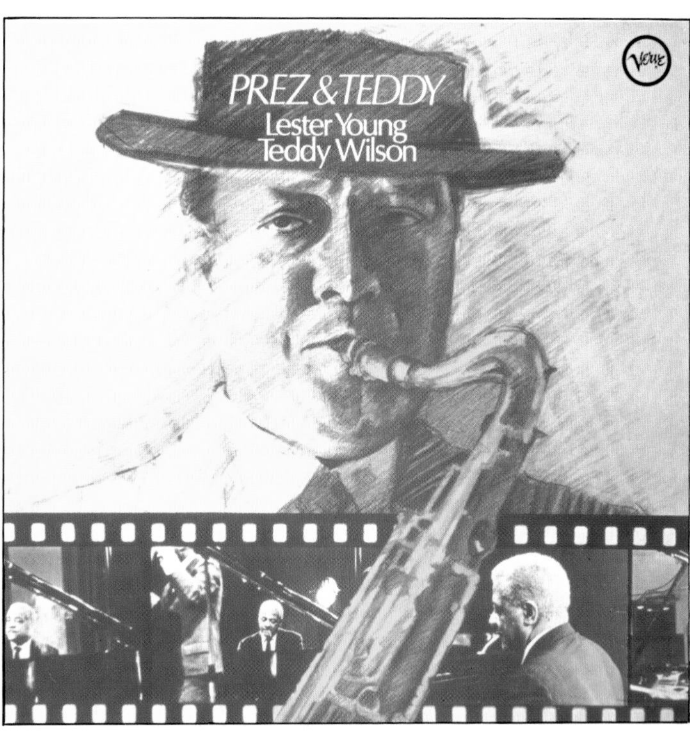

The influential Lester Young with Teddy Wilson, Prez & Teddy (courtesy Verve)—both musicians contributed immeasurably to Billie Holiday's career.

Lester Young

When Lester Willis Young (born Woodville, Mississippi, 1909) came to prominence in mid-1930s, his talent seemed fully developed. That was in 1936, recording for first time with a small band calling itself Smith-Jones, Inc (actually, a contingent from Count Basie Orchestra of which Young was soon its most important soloist). Those early Young solos, on **Shoe Shine Boy, Evenin', Boogie Woogie** and **Lady Be Good**, have provided constant inspiration to generations of saxophonists.

But Young's strongest influence came over ten years after those 1936 recordings. His playing was a prime mover in helping shape styles and approach taken by numerous (mostly white) tenor players, notably Stan Getz, Brew Moore, Al Cohn, Allen Eager and Zoot Sims.

Young—whose brother, Lee Young, was a drummer during 1930s-1950s—came from a musical family. His father gave Lester, Lee and sister Irma a basic music education. Lester Young tried drums (at 10), giving them up after three years because he grew tired of packing and unpacking the kit at each gig. Admired Frankie Trumbauer's playing and tried to assimilate his flowing lines on C-melody sax on first, alto, then tenor.

At 18, Young joined Art Bronson's Bostonians; on baritone sax, then switching to tenor. After returning to Young family band for a while, rejoined Bronson, in 1930. Subsequently, worked with various bands around Minneapolis, Minnesota, playing alto, baritone but mostly tenor. Became member of Original Blue Devils in 1932, leaving following year to link up with Bennie Moten. Other engagements followed, including short spell with a then fading King Oliver. After first-time work with a Count Basie band, he was offered the chance to replace Coleman Hawkins with the prestigious Fletcher Henderson Orchestra. Joined Henderson at beginning of '34—only to leave three-and-a-half months later because some of Henderson's musicians found Young's more airy, almost bland tone no substitute for the rich, majestic one of Hawkins.

Young then became member of Andy Kirk Orchestra, thence to Boyd Atkins and others. Finally, in 1936, joined Basie again, in Kansas City, establishing an enviable reputation as valid and vital alternative to the tenor saxophone styles of, say, Hawkins, Ben Webster and Bud Freeman.

During four-and-a-half years with Basie, Young became its most celebrated soloist and one of the great instrumental voices in jazz. Young produced a series of remarkable solos that helped re-write the art of saxophone-playing and did much to point in the directions jazz would take during the next decade. His solos with full Basie orchestra are numerous but those of inestimable importance are **Honeysuckle Rose, Roseland Shuffle, Every Tub (The Best Of Count Basie, 1937-38); Panassie Stomp, Jive At Five, Swinging The Blues, You Can Depend On Me** (a Basie Sextet track), **Jumpin' At The Woodside (You Can Depend On Basie)**; and **Taxi War Dance, Clap Hands, Here Comes Charlie, Ham 'N' Eggs, Pound Cake, Hollywood Jump, Blow Top, Tickle-Toe, Moten Swing, Let Me See, I Never Knew, Broadway** (all **Lester Young With Count Basie & His Orchestra)**.

During the late-1930s the unforgettable Lester Young-Billie Holiday partnership was forged. Holiday had much in common with Young, not the least of which was impeccable, subtle time. Holiday's matchless singing was perfectly complemented by the tenorist's totally sympathetic, equally poignant contributions. And Young's solos themselves often sounded like an extension of the vocal.

During 1939, he was brilliant at recordings featuring Count Basie & His Kansas City Seven **(Lester Young With Count Basie & His Orchestra)**, gloriously so on his own **Lester Leaps In**. Apart from tenor-sax, Young occasionally soloed on a metal clarinet, producing a haunting, wistful, almost eerie sound. Used this instrument on earlier Basie sides like **Blue & Sentimental, Texas Shuffle (Jumpin' At The Woodside)**, also on a 1938 edition of **Kansas City Six (Lester Young & The Kansas City Five)**; and equally beguiling on **I Want A Little Girl, Pagin' The Devil** and **Countless Blues**.

Left Basie in 1940; worked with own bands,

first in New York (at Kelly's Stables), then, with brother Lee on drums, in California (at Billy Berg's). Recorded in Los Angeles with pianist Nat Cole **(Nat Cole Meets The Master Saxes)** including a tender **I Can't Get Started**. Back in New York summer of '42, Young worked with tenorist Al Sears' big band following year, also with Dizzy Gillespie on 52nd Street; then, for nearly a year, back with Basie.

In October, '44, Young was inducted into US army. Apparently, he suffered degradation, mental and physical hardship during his approximate one year as serviceman; certainly, the experience was traumatic, affecting him personally; it also changed him musically. A particularly sensitive man, Young's demeanor had changed dramatically following a court-martial, period of detention and subsequent discharge. He became withdrawn and prone to eccentricities in dress, speech and behavior (including a drink problem).

His first recordings following his return **(The Aladdin Sessions)** show the change he had undergone personally. His playing had become laconic, indolent—even morose in places. There was a wry, sometimes caustic humor and an overall feeling of resignation that later was to approach despair.Much of the lightness in his playing prior to army service would rarely return, likewise with the quicksilver dexterity of **Lester Leaps In** or **Jumpin' At The Woodside** of a few years before. There was a difference in approach between **D.B. Blues** (a reference to his incarceration in army detention block), **After You've Gone** and **Jumpin' At Mesners** and pre-army recordings such as **Blue Lester, Jump Lester Jump, Basie English (Pres/The Complete Savoy Recordings); I Never Knew, Lester Leaps Again, Just You, Just Me (Lester Young Leaps Again!)**; or his uniformly superb playing during a celebrated jazz movie *Jammin' The Blues* **(Jamming With Lester)**.

However, his playing had become even more emotionally enriched, as was personified in Jazz At The Philharmonic in 1946 on **I Can't Get Started (Jazz At The Philharmonic, 1946, Vol 2)**. He had lost none of the running excitement at faster tempos as can be judged from **After You've Gone (Jazz At The Philharmonic 1944-46)**. True, subsequent recordings tended to be inconsistent but there was sufficient top-class tenor-playing during his 'declining' years to negate accusations that he was a pale shadow of his former great self.

Of later years, his finest recordings took place in 1956, on two consecutive dates. On both, he was reunited with Teddy Wilson with whom he had worked during memorable Billie Holiday sessions. The second of the '56 dates was in quartet setting with Wilson pacing Young's tenor in masterfully sympathetic fashion. For the first, Wilson, Young and the same rhythm section (Jo Jones, Gene Ramey) were joined by Vic Dickenson, Roy Eldridge and Basie's long-serving guitarist Freddie Green. On the slower numbers (eg **This Year's Kisses, I Didn't Know What Time It Was)** Young's phrasing was masterful, the emotional content deeply moving.

Poor health dogged Young during the last years of his life. After a not altogether successful engagement at Blue Note Club, Paris, he returned to New York; one day later (on March 15, 1959) he was dead. Lester Young (known affectionately as 'Prez' or 'Pres') was a significant link between pre-war jazz and bebop of the 1940s. He was an important influence on bop musicians—particularly Charlie Parker—as well as younger musicians who were as much influenced by Young (sometimes more so) as Parker. Young's innovations paralleled those of guitarist Charlie Christian making their recordings together interesting and instructive **(Charlie Christian/Lester Young: Together, 1940)**.

The Lester Young Story Volume 1 (courtesy CBS)—the tenor genius.

Albums:
Lester Young With Count Basie & His Orchestra (Epic/Epic—France)
Count Basie, The Best Of Count Basie 1937-1938 (MCA Coral—Germany)
Count Basie, You Can Depend On Basie (—/Coral)
Various, 1938 Carnegie Hall Jazz Concert (Columbia/CBS)
Count Basie, Jumpin' At The Woodside (Brunswick/Ace of Clubs)
Lester Young & The Kansas City Five (sic) (Mainstream/Stateside)
Various, Nat Cole Meets The Master Saxes (Phoenix/Spotlite)
Various (Including Lester Young), Jammin' With Lester (Jazz Archives)
Lester Young, Lester Leaps Again! (EmArcy/Fontana)
Charlie Christian/Lester Young: Together, 1940 (Jazz Archives/—)
Lester Young, Pres/The Complete Savoy Recordings (Savoy/—)
Various, Jazz At The Philharmonic 1944-46 (—/Verve)
Various, Jazz At The Philharmonic 1946, Vol 2 (—/Verve)
Lester Young/(Coleman Hawkins), Classic Tenors (Contact/Stateside)
Lester Young/(Coleman Hawkins/Ben Webster), The Big Three (Bob Thiele Music/RCA Victor)
The Lester Young Story, Vols 1-3 (Columbia/CBS)
Lester Young, The Genius Of...(Verve)
Coleman Hawkins/Lester Young (Zim/Spotlite)
Lester Young, The Aladdin Sessions (Blue Note/—)
Lester Young, Prez In Europe (Onyx/Onyx)
Lester Young, Pres & Teddy & Oscar (Verve/—)
Lester Young, Prez & Teddy (—/Verve)
Jimmy Rushing/Count Basie, Blues I Love To Sing (Ace of Hearts)

Frank Zappa

The extraordinary and unclassifiable guitarist-composer Frank Zappa wasn't initially inspired to become a musician through jazz, or blues, or rock (although his music was to contain all these elements) but through the works of modern classical composer Edgar Varese. Indeed, in the early 1950s, Zappa attended the Courses in Contemporary Music at Darmstadt in Germany which attracted many new-music composers (both as students and lecturers) like Stockhausen, Ligeti and Berio.

Frank Zappa was born Francis Vincent Zappa Jr (to Sicilian-Greek parents) in Baltimore, Maryland, on December 21, 1940. At 18, he bought a guitar and tried to emulate the styles of Johnny 'Guitar' Watson, Clarence 'Gatemouth' Brown and Matt Murphy. In '65, Zappa joined the Soul Giants which he renamed the following year The Mothers (the 'of Invention' was added after record-company pressure). Tim Wilson, an early Zappa producer, had worked with avant-garde pianist Cecil Taylor as well as Bob Dylan and the Velvet Underground.

On the '67-'68 **Uncle Meat** album, Zappa brilliantly used the available studio technology to create a 'brass sound', explaining that the 'things that sound like trumpets are actually clarinets played through an electric device...'

Below: The individualistic and uncategorizable Frank Zappa. Since the late 1960s, an extraordinarily influential musician, composer and 'organizer'.

The subsequently influential **Hot Rats** ('69) featured the jazz-oriented violins of Sugar Cane Harris and Jean-Luc Ponty. Zappa was to work closely with Ponty the following year on the exceptional **King Kong**—an album which would include a 'classical' section **(Music For Electric Violin And Low Budget Orchestra). King Kong** also included the distinguished input of keyboardist George Duke (a long-time associate), bassist Buell Neidlinger (ex-Cecil Taylor, Gil Evans and the Boston Symphony), saxophonist Ernie Watts and the Crusaders' (saxophonist) Wilton Felder on bass.

In '72, Zappa's **The Grand Wazoo** gave a further insight into his eclectic musicality, listing a string of influences including Miles Davis, John McLaughlin and Gil Evans (alongside Manitas De Plata, Prokofiev, Stravinsky and Kurt Weill...). **Waka/Jawaka** (also that year) produced its 'big-band effects' through a multi-track playback process, while a favorite from '76 is **Zappa In New York** featuring jazz-funk luminaries the Brecker Brothers, Mike and Randy.

The uncategorizable Frank Zappa—a musician who acknowledges no musical barriers, no frontiers to his creativity—is a fitting end to this *jazz* encyclopedia. The wide-ranging spirit in which Zappa has created an all-embracing music-without-labels is an object lesson in the way music should be received in any age of enlightenment.

Frank Zappa, Hot Rats (courtesy Reprise)—with Captain Beefheart.

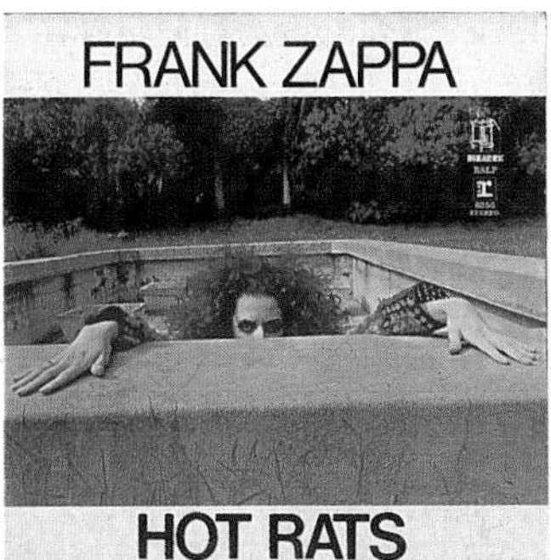

King Kong (courtesy Liberty): Jean-Luc Ponty plays the music of Frank Zappa.

Albums:
Uncle Meat (Bizarre/Transatlantic)
Hot Rats (Bizarre/Reprise)
Jean-Luc Ponty, King Kong (Liberty/Liberty)
The Grand Wazoo (Bizarre/Reprise)
Waka/Jawaka (Bizarre/Reprise)
Zappa In New York (DiscReet/DiscReet)
Chamber Works (HMV/HMV)

Joe Zawinul

see Weather Report

Appendix

Lack of space prevents us from including a full entry on the following performers. Nevertheless they cannot be ignored, for all have made their own original contributions to the development of the music.

A

BERNARD S. ADDISON—b. Annapolis, Maryland, 1905. Fine '20s guitarist. Rec. with Louis Armstrong, Bubber Miley, Fletcher Henderson, Jelly Roll Morton, Benny Carter, Mezz Mezzrow, Coleman Hawkins, Pete Brown etc. Toured with vocal groups Mills Bros ('36-'38) and Ink Spots (late '50s).

DOROTHY ASHBY—b. Detroit, 1932. Accomplished classically trained musician, one of few gifted jazz harpists. Worked with Louis Armstrong, Woody Herman *et al*. Author of book on jazz and modern harmony for harp and cello. Died, 1986.

GEORGIE (GEORGE) AULD—b. Toronto, Canada, 1919. All-round, accomplished tenorist. Rec. with Bunny Berigan, Artie Shaw, Charlie Christian, Benny Goodman, Dizzy Gillespie, Count Basie *et al*. In '77, took supporting acting role in film *New York, New York*; also ghosted tenor-playing for main star Robert De Niro.

B

BUSTER BAILEY—b. Memphis, 1902. One of most accomplished clarinettists in jazz history, also fine saxophonist. Rec. with Louis Armstrong, Fletcher Henderson, Alberta Hunter, Ma Rainey, Bessie Smith, King Oliver, John Kirby, Bubber Miley etc. Died, 1967.

SHORTY BAKER—b. St Louis, 1914. First-rate big-band trumpeter who came to prominence late '30s, notably with Ellington band. Also rec. with Billy Strayhorn, Johnny Hodges, Doc Cheatham etc. Died, 1966.

PAUL BARBARIN—b. New Orleans, 1901. One of most gifted Crescent City drummers of '20s. Rec. with King Oliver, Luis Russell, Louis Armstrong, Henry 'Red' Allen, Sharkey Bonano etc. Died, on New Orleans parade, 1969.

DANNY BARKER—b. New Orleans, 1909. Notable '30s guitarist-banjoist, joined Cab Calloway's band '39. Also rec. with King Oliver, Chu Berry, Lionel Hampton, Louis Armstrong, Sidney Bechet-Mezz Mezzrow, Billie Holiday etc. Autobiography published 1986.

EVERETT BARKSDALE—b. Detroit, 1910. Veteran guitarist, worked with Erskine Tate early '30s. Associated with Art Tatum ('45-'55. Died, 1986.

GEORGE BARNES—b. Chicago Heights, 1921. influential '40s guitarist of Van Eps-Kress-McDonough school, noted for sympathetic collaboration with Ruby Braff ('73-'75). Died, 1977.

CLYDE BERNHARDT—b. Goldhill, North Carolina, 1905. Trombonist-blues singer, worked with King Oliver, Vernon Andrade, Edgar Hayes, Jay McShann and Claude Hopkins. Died, 1986.

Paul Barbarin and his New Orleans Band (courtesy Vogue).

EMMETT BERRY—b. Macon, Georgia, 1916. Trumpeter who came to prominence late '30s with Fletcher Henderson. Also rec. with Basie, Teddy Wilson, Jo Jones, Sammy Price, Buck Clayton, Buddy Tate etc.

LENNY BREAU—b. Auburn, Maine 1941. Fine country-based guitarist who developed an individual voice between Chet Atkins' finger-style and Bill Evans' pianistic approach. Notable for 'bebop' collaborations with pedal-steel guitarist Buddy Emmons. Died, 1984.

LAWRENCE BROWN — b. Lawrence, Kansas, 1905. Distinguished tombonist and Ellington side musician for 30 years. Also rec. with Johnny Hodges, Joe Turner, Earl Hines, Lionel Hampton etc.

PETE BROWN—b. Baltimore, 1906. Definitive, hard-swinging, jump-blues altoist, an influence on Charlie Barnet, Louis Jordan and Bruce Turner. Rec. with own bands, Willie 'The Lion' Smith, Jimmy Noone, Frankie Newton, Joe Turner *et al*. Died, 1963.

GEORGE BRUNIS—b. New Orleans, 1900. One of first white musicians to latch on to art of tailgate trombone-playing *à la* Kid Ory. Rec. with his own New Rhythm Kings, Bix Beiderbecke, Eddie Condon, Muggsy Spanier, Wild Bill Davison *et al*. Died, 1984.

C

LEROY CARR—b. Nashville, 1905. Pianist-singer-composer who with guitarist Scrapper Blackwell provided an all-time great blues partnership. Most famous composition, **How Long, How Long**. Died, 1935.

WAYMAN CARR—b. Portsmouth, Virginia, 1905. Fine '30s reeds-player and composer, credited as first to make extensive use of flute as jazz solo instrument. Rec. with Chick Webb, King Oliver-Dave Nelso, Spike Hughes etc. Died, 1967.

BIG SID CATLETT—b. Evansville, Indiana, 1910. One of '30s finest and most influential drummers with a larger-than-life personality. Rec. with Benny Carter, Spike Hughes, Fletcher Henderson, Sidney Bechet, Henry 'Red' Allen, Louis Armstrong, Benny Goodman, Coleman Hawkins, Dizzy Gillespie etc. Died, 1951.

KENNY 'KLOOK' CLARKE—b. Pittsburg, 1914. One of prime movers—with Parker and Gillespie—in the birth of bebop. Pre-bebop associations Roy Eldridge, Edgar Hayes, Claude Hopkins, Louis Armstrong, Ella Fitzgerald, Henry 'Red' Allen etc. Died, 1985.

ROD (GEORGE RODERICK) CLESS—b. Lennox, Iowa, 1907. One of school of white clarinettists who emerged mid/late-'20s. Rec. with Muggsy Spanier, Eddie Condon, Art Hodes, Max Kaminsky, Yank Lawson etc. Died, 1944.

LARRY CLINTON—b. Brooklyn, 1909. Popular swing-era band-leader, best known for **The Dipsey Doodle**, originally a trumpeter. He became an arranger for Tommy and Jimmy Dorsey, Louis Armstrong and Bunny Berigan. Died, 1985.

BILL (WILLIAM JOHNSON) COLEMAN—b. Paris, Kentucky, 1904. Sensitive, melodic, Armstrong-influenced trumpeter who came to prominence late '20s with Lloyd and Cecil Scott, Luis Russell and Lucky Millinder. Rec. with the Scotts, Russell, Django Reinhardt, Lester Young *et al*.

Above: Trumpet veteran Bill Coleman learnt a lot from Louis Armstrong.

LEE COLLINS—b. New Orleans, 1901. Archetypal '20s-'30s New Orleans trumpeter. Rec. with Jelly Roll Morton, Mezz Mezzrow etc. Died, 1960.

JIMMY (JAMES STRICKLAND) CRAWFORD—b. Memphis, 1910. Driving drummer, primarily associated with Jimmy Lunceford Orchestra ('33-'40).

Blues Before Sunrise (courtesy Columbia) by Leroy Carr, a blues legend as singer, pianist and especially composer.

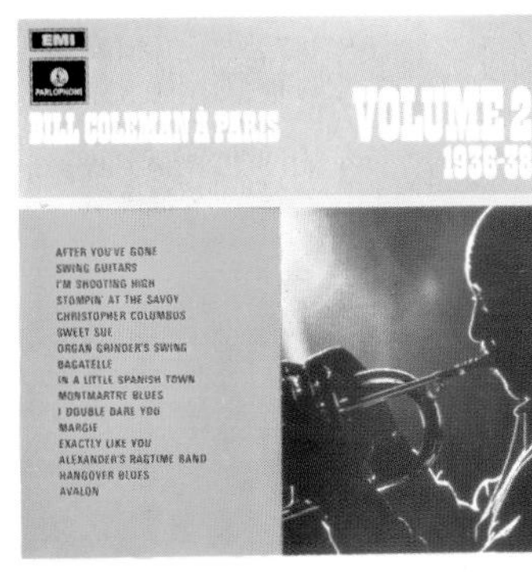

Bill Coleman à Paris, Volume 2 (1936-38) (Parlohone/EMI).

PEE WEE CRAYTON—b. Rockdale, Texas, 1914. Blues singer-guitarist of '40s, noted for his stage guitar-battles with T-Bone Walker. Worked with Johnny Otis to good effect in '70s. Died, 1986.

D

JOE DARENSBOURG—b. Baton Rouge, 1906. Warm-toned clarinettist, associate of Kid Ory and Louis Armstrong. Died, 1985.

Soprano Summit, Chalumeau Blue (courtesy Pye) featuring Kenny Davern.

KENNY (JOHN KENNETH) DAVERN—b. Huntingdon, Long Island, 1935. Impressive, all-round clarinettist-saxophonist, celebrated for his Soprano Summit partnership with Bob Wilber. Led own band Salty Dogs, '58.

WILD BILL (WILLIAM) DAVISON—b. Defiance, Ohio, 1906. Cornetist (also played mandolin, banjo and guitar), integral part of white Dixieland scene in '30s. Rec. with Sidney Bechet, Tony Parenti, Eddie Condon etc.

SIDNEY DE PARIS—b. Crawfordsville, Indiana, 1905. Gifted tumpeter of '30s and '40s. Rec. with brother Wilbur De Paris, Lloyd Cecil Scott, McKinney's Cotton Pickers, Don Redman, Sidney Bechet, Jelly Roll Morton etc. Died, 1967.

VIC (VICTOR) DICKENSON—b. Xenia, Ohio, 1906. Gifted trombonist and soloist who came to prominence with Benny Carter and Basie bands late '30s-early '40s. Also rec. with Bechet, Ruby Braff, Buck Clayton, Bobby Hackett, World's Greatest Jazz Band *et al*. Died, 1984.

NATTY (ANATIE) DOMINIQUE—b. New Orleans, 1896. Warm-toned trumpeter of '20s, closely associated with Jonny Dodds. Also rec. with Sippie Wallace, Jelly Roll Morton *et al*.

HANK (HENRY) DUNCAN—b. Bowling Green, Kentucky, 1896. Under-appreciated but enduring stride pianist. Led his first band '18-'19, working with King Oliver and Bechet in '30s and '40s. Also rec. with Fats Waller, Wild Bill Davison and Tony Parenti. Died 1968.

EDDIE DURHAM—b. St Marcos, Texas, 1906. Widely gifted guitarist (among first to use electric instrument), trombonist, arranger and composer. Worked with innumerable big bands, including all-women International Sweethearts of Rhythm ('41-'43). Compositions inc. **I Don't Want To Set The World On Fire, Topsy** etc. Rec. with Bennie Moten, Jimmie Lunceford, Basie, Glenn Miller *et al*.

GEORGE DUVIVIER—b. New York, 1920. Renowned bassist and respected composer-arranger. Came to prominence with Coleman Hawkins, Lucky Millinder, Jimmy Lunceford and Sy Oliver. Died, 1986.

E

BOOKER TELLEFERRO ERVIN—b. Texas, 1930. Big-toned tenorist who came to prominence as featured soloist with Charlie Mingus ('58-'60). Died, 1970.

HERSCHEL EVANS—b. Denton, Texas, 1909. Fine '30s tenorist who came to prominence with Basie band a few years before his early death in '39. Also rec. with Lionel Hampton, Harry James, Mildred Bailey etc.

F

IRVING HENRY FAZOLA—b. New Orleans, 1912. Liquid-toned,. '30s clarinettist who skilfully adapted to swing era. Rec. with Bob Crosby, Claude Thornhill, Muggsy Spanier, Harry James etc. Died, 1949.

G

LLOYD GLENN—b. San Antonio, Texas, 1909. Blues pianist who worked with Kid Ory and rec. with Lowell Fulson, B. B. King and Joe Turner. Died, 1985.

TYREE GLENN—b. Corsicana, Texas, 1912. Big-band trombonist with impressive plunger technique, vibes-player and occasional vocalist who came to prominence mid-late '30s. Rec. with Ellington, Cab Calloway, Benny Carter, Ethel Waters, Don Redman, Al Sears *et al*. Died, 1974.

PAUL GONSALVES—b. Boston, 1920. former guitarist who became one of jazz's leading saxophonists, immortal for his 27-chorus solo on **Diminuendo & Crescendo In Blue** with Ellington at Newport '56. Died, 1974.

The Chase And The Steeplechase (MCA), Wardell Gray and Dexter Gordon.

WARDELL GRAY—b. Oklahoma City, 1921. Versatile tenorist whose solo on **Twisted** was immortalized by Annie Ross' vocalised version Died, 1955.

SONNY (WILLIAM) GREER - b. Long Branch, New Jersey, 1903. Classic Ellington drummer from '23-'51. Claimed to be first drummer to fix leader's name and monogram on bass drum. Died, 1982.

TINY (LLOYD) GRIMES—b. Newport News, Virginia, 1917. Solid, blues-based guitarist (originally drummer, pianist and dancer), playing amplified instrument as early as '39. Rec. with Art Tatum, Ike Quebec, Charlie Parker, Roy Eldridge, Coleman Hawkins, Earl Hines etc.

JOHNNY (JOHN A.) GUARNIERI—b. New York, 1917. Gifted pianist and prolific composer who came to attention with Artie Shaw in '41, notably for his use of harpsichord.

Vic Dickenson Plays Bessie Smith 'Trombone Cholly' (courtesy Sonet). Great jazz trombonist salutes a great blues singer...

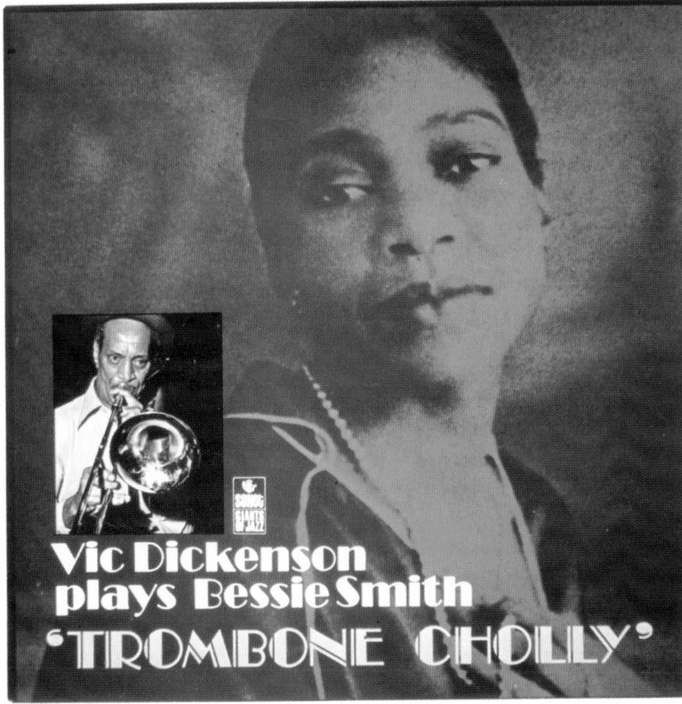

Below: Paul Gonsalves, tenor saxophonist of distinction, who learnt his craft over 24 years with the Ellington Orchestra.

H

BOBBY (ROBERT LEO) HACKETT—b. Providence, Rhode Island, 1915. Distinguished, highly respected trumpeter (also guitarist) who came to prominence in '30s. Rec. with Benny Goodman, Teddy Wilson, Louis Armstrong, Eddie Condon, Dizzy Gillespie etc. Died, 1976.

EDMOND HALL—b. New Orleans, 1901. Clarinettist (formerly guitarist) who, stylistically, encompassed New Orleans, Dixieland and mainstream. Rec. with Claude Hopkins, Joe Sullivan, Henry 'Red' Allen, Art Hodes, Celestial Express, Sidney De Paris, Eddie Condon *et al.* Died, 1967.

JIMMY (JAMES) HAMILTON—b. Dillon, South Carolina, 1917. Smooth, elegant clarinettist and R&B-influenced tenorist featured with Ellington Orchestra for a quarter of a century. Also rec. with Johnny Hodges and Earl Hines.

TOBY (OTTO) HARWICKE—b. Washington, DC, 1904. Gifted, multi-reeds-player and founder-member of Ellington band.

BILL (WILLARD PALMER) HARRIS—b. Philadelphia, 1916. One of great individual voices on tombone (formerly saxophonist and trumpeter), notably with various Herman's Herds. Also rec. with Charlie Ventura, Serge Chaloff, Terry Gibbs, Gene Krupa etc. Died, 1974.

JIMMY (JAMES HENRY) HARRISON—b. Louisville, Kentucky, 1900. One of first tombone stylists, notably with Fletcher Henderson's band. Also rec. with Charlie Johnson, Chocolate Dandies, Chick Webb etc. Died, 1931.

HORACE HENDERSON—b. Cuthbert, Georgia, 1904. Pianist, composer, arranger, band-leader, accompanist. Rec. with older brother Fletcher Henderson, Coleman Hawkins, Chocolate Dandies, Benny Goodman, Don Redman, Charlie Barnet etc.

ERNIE (ERNEST ALBERT) HENRY—b. Brooklyn, 1926. Distinctive, Parker-influenced altoist who came to prominence late '40s with Tadd Dameron Septet and may have influenced Eric Dolphy. Rec. with Howard McGhee-Fats Navarro, Thelonious Monk, Kenny Dorham etc. Died, 1957.

EDDIE (EDWARD) HEYWOOD JR—b. Atlanta, Georgia, 1915. Neat, economic pianist, band-leader, and gifted accompanist who emerged early '30s. Rec. with Shelly Manne, Billie Holiday etc. Had big 'pop' hits with **Begin The Beguine** and **Canadian Sunset.**

J.C. HIGGINBOTHAM—b. Georgia, 1906. Gutsy, extrovert trombonist who came to prominence as soloist with Luis Russell orchestra ('28). Also rec. with King Oliver, Chocolate Dandies, Louis Armstrong, Henry 'Red' Allen, Fletcher Henderson *et al.*

CHARLIE HOLMES—b. Boston, 1910. Veteran altoist known principally for his association with Luis Russell Orchestra in '30s. Died, 1985.

CLAUDE D. HOPKINS—b. Washington, DC, 1903. All-round musician, pianist, band-leader, composer-arranger prominent in '30s and '40s. Rec. with own bands, Ma Rainey, Coleman Hawkins-Pee Wee Russell.

NOAH HOWARD—b. New Orleans, 1943. Altoist, one of the second generation of New Thing players, making his mark with Archie Shepp **(Black Gipsy)**. Also rec. with Frank Wright.

Right: Alto saxophonist Noah Howard taking the air outside a well-known venue, along with (l-r) Juma Sultan, Frank Lowe, Rashied Ali, Bob Bruno and Earl Freeman.

Clarinet, Jimmy Hamilton (Jazz Kings). An invaluable Ellingtonian.

J

BUTTER (QUENTIN LEONARD) JACKSON—b. Springfield, Ohio, 1909. Trombonist and notable Ellington section-player from '48, specializing in plunger-mute solos in 'Tricky Sam' Nanton tradition. Also rec. with McKinney's Cotton Pickers, Don Redman, Cab Calloway, Johnny Hodges, Billy Strayhorn, Thad Jones-Mel Lewis, Charles Mingus. Died, 1976.

CALVIN JACKSON—b. Philadelphia, c. 1919. Jazz and classical painist, composer, conductor, hailed as 'the Art Tatum of 1942'. One of first black musicians to compose for MGM musicals. One of the best-known works, **Profile Of An American**, dedicated to President Kennedy. Died, 1985.

BLIND LEMON JEFFERSON—b. Texas, 1897. Influential and seminal country-blues singer-guitarist. Worked regularly with Leadbelly. Died, age 33, in a snowstorm, 1930.

HILTON JEFFERSON—b. Danberry, Connecticut, 1903. Former banjoist, later altoist, who became distinguished big-band sax-section leader and soloist, Rec. with King Oliver, Fletcher Henderson, Benny Carter, Henry 'Red' Allen, Cab Calloway, Coleman Hawkins, Jimmy Witherspoon. Died, 1968.

BUDD (ALBERT J.) JOHNSON—b. Dallas, 1910. Supremely versatile multi-reeds-player and fine composer-arranger. Rec. with Louis Armstrong, Earl Hines, Coleman Hawkins, Billy Eckstine, Woody Herman, Al Sears, Gil Evans, Ben Webster, Dizzy Gillespie *et al.*

Above: Trombonist 'Butter' Jackson, plunger-mute specialist and Ellington Orchestra stalwart for over a decade of fine music.

BUNK (WILLIAM GEARY) JOHNSON—b. New Orleans, 1879. Early cornetist-trombonist and Buddy Bolden associate whose work was a legend till recorded in '42, age 63. Rec. with Lu Watters, Sidney Bechet and own groups. Died, 1949.

JO JONES—b. Chicago, 1911. Known as 'Kansas City Jo Jones' after working there with Basie. Also worked with Illinois Jacquet, Lester Young, Benny Carter, Joe Bushkin, Milt Buckner *et al.* Died, 1985.

JONAH (ROBERT ELLIOTT) JONES—b. Louisville, Kentucky, 1909. First-rate trumpeter, soloist and big-band section-player. Rec. with Stuff Smith, Benny Carter, Cab Calloway, Billie Holiday, Sidney Bechet etc.

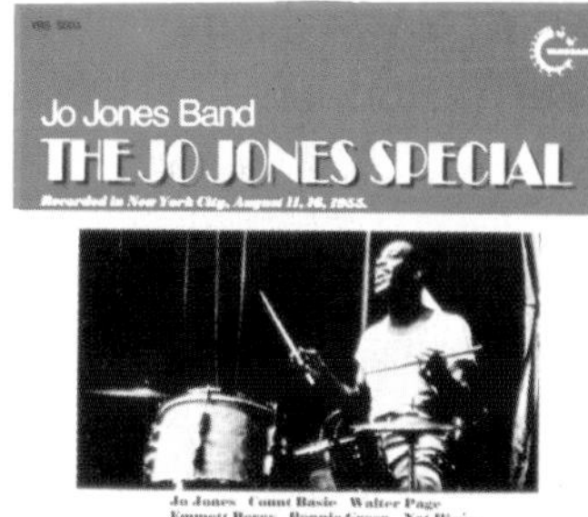

The Jo Jones Special (Vanguard).

PHILLY JOE JONES—b. Philadelphia, 1923. Exceptional drummer, part of classic mid-'50s Miles Davis Quintet and a favorite attraction at Birdland late '50s. Worked with Bill Evans, Gil Evans, Tadd Dameron, Ellington *et al.* Died, 1985.

K

MAX KAMINSKY—b. Brockton, Massachusetts, 1908. Distinguished trumpeter and band-leader from early '20s. Revealing biography, **My Life In Jazz** ('63). Rec. with the Chocolate Dandies, Tommy Dorsey, Artie Shaw, Art Hodes, Eddie Condon, Sidney Bechet, Bud Freeman (Summa Cum Laude Orchestra).

JOHN KIRBY—b. Baltimore, 1908. Probably most accomplished bassist until arrival of Jimmy Blanton late '30s. Rec. with Fletcher Henderson, Chick Webb, Billie Holiday, Teddy Wilson, Lionel Hampton, Henry 'Red' Allen, Frankie Newton *et al.* Died, 1952.

ANDY (ANDREW DEWEY) KIRK—b. Newport, 1898. Saxophonist and tuba-player noted for his excellent 12 Clouds of Joy band important to career of pianist-arranger Mary Lou Williams.

BILLY (WILLIAM OSBORNE) KYLE—b. Philadelphia, 1914. Neat, precise, Teddy Wilson-reminiscent pianist who played vital role in John Kirby Sextet ('38-'42). Also rec. with Buck Clayton, Lionel Hampton, Jack Teagarden-Pee Wee Russell, Louis Armstrong. Died, touring with Armstrong, 1966.

L

CLIFFORD LEEMAN—b. Portland, Maine, 1913. One of swing era's best drummers, started as xylophonist. Worked with Artie Shaw, Tommy Dorsey, Charlie Barnet, Woody Herman, John Kirby, Raymond Rushing *et al.* Died, 1986.

YANK LAWSON (JOHN R. LAUSEN)—b. Trenton, Missouri, 1911. Strong-blowing, hard-hitting trumpeter, notably with Ben Pollack early '30s. Rec with Bob Crosby, Tommy Dorsey, Bob Haggart (World's Greatest Jazz Band) etc.

Mc

HOWARD McGHEE—b. Tulsa, Oklahoma, 1918. One of leading bebop trumpeters. Rec. with Coleman Hawkins, Charlie Parker, Fats Navarro, Illinois Jacquet etc.

M

SHELLY MANNE—b. New York, 1920. Versatile drummer—from small groups to big bands—and frequent poll-winner. Worked with Joe Marsala, Les Brown, Stan Kenton, Bill Harris, Woody Herman, Shory Rogers, Barney Kessell, Jimmy Giuffre, Stan Getz, Lee Konitz *et al.* Made notable appearance in '55 film *The Man With The Golden Arm* (also Frank Sinatra's drum instuctor for the role). Died, 1985.

Below: Reluctant soloist Billy Kyle, a band pianist of unimpeachable reliability and crisp economy, the foundation stone of the John Kirby Sextet for four years. A total professional.

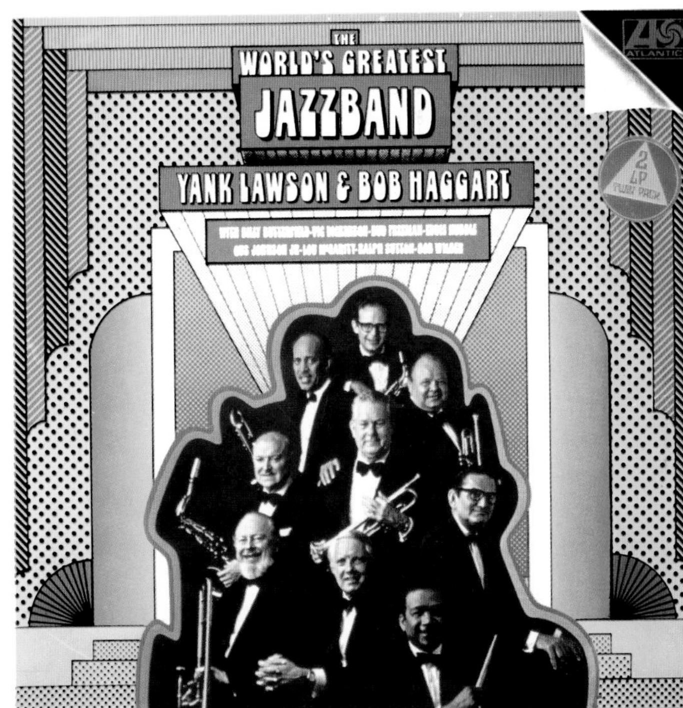

World's Greatest Jazz Band (courtesy Atlantic). Modestly-titled aggregation featuring the forceful trumpet of Yank Lawson.

WINGY (JOEPH) MANONE—b. New Orleans, 1904. Dynamic '20s trumpeter, first musician to record a 'riff tune', **Tar Paper Stomp** ('29), later to become famous as **In The Mood**.

DODO MARMAROSA—b. Pittsburg, 1925. Under-rated bebop pianist, succeeded Joe Albany as Charlie Parker group pianist. Also rec. with Howard McGhee, Gene Ammons etc.

JOE (JOSEPH FRANCIS) MARSALA—b. Chicago, 1907. Clarinettist-altoist long associated with Wingy Manone. Also rec. with Adrian Rollini, Jack Teagarden, Eddie Condon, Chu Berry etc.

EDDIE MILLER—b. New Orleans, 1911. Tenorist and clarinettist with unmistakable Cresent City Sound, founder-member of Bob Crosby band ('35-'42). Also rec. with Ben Pollack, Jack Teagarden, Bunny Berigan, Wingy Manone, Harry James and own big band.

ERNEST 'KID PUNCH' MILLER—b. Raceland, Louisiana, 1897. One of early jazz's most gifted and articulate trumpeters-cornetists. Worked with Kid Ory, Jack Carey, Fate Marable, Jelly Roll Morton, Tiny Parham, Freddie Keppard, George Lewis and led own groups. Died, 1971.

Jazz Rarities 1929-1930, by virtuoso trumpeter 'Kid Punch' Miller (Herwin).

GEORGE MITCHELL—b. Louisville, Kentucky, 1899. Gifted trumpeter-cornetist who came to prominence in '20s and '30s, consolidating reputation with Jonny Dodds-Kid Ory (New Orleans Wanderers and Bootblacks). Rec. with Jelly Roll Morton, Earl Hines, Cookie's Ginger Snaps, Luis Russell, Jimmie Noone, Richard M. Jones etc. Died, 1972.

MIFF (IRVING MILFRED) MOLE—b. Roosevelt, Long Island, New York, 1898. Major tombone influence during '20s. Closely associated with Red Nichols. Also rec. with Ladd's Black Aces, Eddie Condon etc. Died, 1961.

MONK MONTGOMERY—b. Indianapolis, 1921 (brother of Wes and Buddy). Electric-bass pioneer with Lionel Hampton's orchestra in early '50s. In '75, founder of and principal activist in the World Jazz Association. Died, 1982.

N

FRANKIE (WILLIAM FRANK) NEWTON—b. Emory, Virginia, 1906. Gifted trumpeter soloist who came to attention with Lloyd Scott's band, '26. Notable for sterling solos on Bessie Smith's last record session. Also rec. with Teddy Hill, Willie 'The Lion' Smith, Sidney Bechet, Mary Lou Williams, Big Joe Turner etc. Died, 1954.

P

TONY (ANTHONY) PARENTI—b. New Orleans, 1900. Piping clarinettist often heard in ragtime context. Rec. with own groups, Eddie Condon, Wild Bill Davison-George Brunis, Jimmy Rushing and many others. Died, 1972.

WILLIAM 'PIANO RED' PERRYMAN—b. Hampton, Georgia, 1911 brother of Speckled Red. Pianist-singer, dubbed 'Dr Feelgood' after his hit song. Some aficionados credit him with first 'rock and roll' record (**Rockin' With Red**, '50). Died, 1986.

BEN POLLACK—b. Chicago, 1903. Good drummer who came to prominence during Chicago's hey-day. Fronted succession of bands noted for strong soloists. Rec. with New Orleans Rhythm Kings, Jack Teagarden, Harry James. Committed suicide, 1971.

SAMMY (SAMMY BLYTHE) PRICE—b. Honey Grove, Texas, 1908. Accomplished blues-based pianist who helped pioneer jazz on radio in '20s and accompanied numerous Decca blues artists. Rec. with Cousin Joe, Trixie Smith Cow Cow Davenport, Sidney Bechet-Mezz Mezzrow, Jimmy Rushing, Henry 'Red' Allen *et al.*

RUSSELL PROCOPE—b. New York, 1908. New Orleans-influenced altoist-clarinettist who established leading reputation with Ellington band. Also rec. with Fletcher Henderson, Coleman Hawkins, Jelly Roll Morton, Clarence Williams, Earl Hines, John Kirby etc.

R

RON REDMAN—b. Piedmont, West Virginia, 1900. Arranger and gifted multi-instrumentalist, influential pioneer of '30s big-band jazz. Rec. with Fletcher Henderson, McKinney's Cotton Pickers, Chocolate Dandies, Louis Armstrong, Bessie Smith etc. Died, 1941.

BIG JIM ROBINSON—b. Deeringe, Louisiana, 1892. Probably finest and most important trombonist, along with Kid Ory, in New Orleans jazz. Rec. with Sam Morgan, Bunk Johnson, George Lewis, Wooden Joe Nicholas, Sweet Emma Barrett and own groups. Died, 1976.

LUIS RUSSELL—b. Carreening Cay, nr Bocos Del Toro, Panama, 1902. Fine pianist who led superb orchestra, '30s and '40s. Rec. with King Oliver, Louis Armstrong, Henry 'Red' Allen etc. Died, 1963.

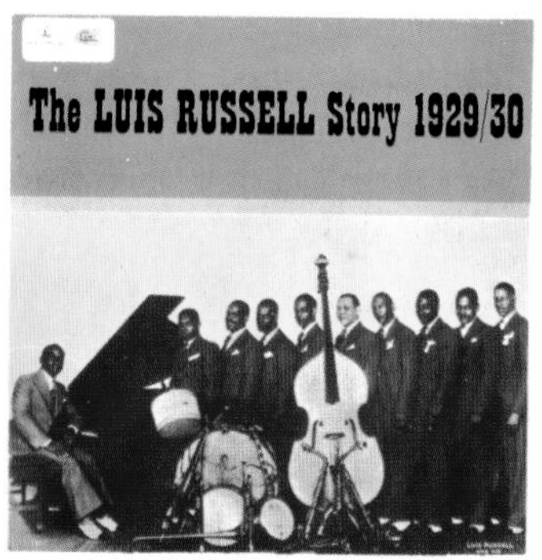

Luis Russell and his Louisiana Swing Orchestra in their heyday (Parlophone).

S

EDGAR MELVIN SAMPSON—b. New York, 1907. Excellent altoist and reasonable violinist, best remembered as a composer-arranger **(Don't Be That Way, Stompin' At The Savoy, Blue Lou, If Dreams Come True)** for bands like Chick Webb's, Benny Goodman's, Teddy Wilson's, Artie Shaw's. Also rec. with Charlie Johnson, Bunny Berigan, Lionel Hampton. Died, 1973.

EDDIE (EDWARD ERNEST) SAUTER—b. Brooklyn, 1914. noted as one of jazz's most gifted and imaginative writers-arrangers, associated with Red Norvo, Mildred Bailey, Benny Goodman, Ray Mckinney, Artie Shaw, Woody Herman, Stan Getz, Peggy Lee etc.

AL (ALBERT OMEGA) SEARS—b. Macomb, Illinois, 1910. R&B-influenced tenorist who became an attraction with Ellington band as Ben Webster's successor. Later associated with Johnny Hodges, writing R&B hit **Castle Rock**.

Above: Big-toned Al Sears' R&B-influenced tenor sax became a feature of the Ellington orchestra during the 1940s.

Right: Charlie Shavers in action; an emotional, technically brilliant player.

CHARLIE (CHARLES JAMES) SHAVERS—b. New York, 1917. One of jazz's most dazzlingly gifted trumpeters and composers (notable for **Undecided**), first recorded during tenure with John Kirby, '38. Also rec. with Billie Holiday, Jimmie Noone, Coleman Hawkins, Tommy Dorsey, Sidney Bechet, Charlie Parker *et al.* Died, 1971.

ROBERT SHAW—b. Stafford, Texas, 1908. Legendary barrelhouse-style singer-pianist, made record début '63 after being tracked down by Mack McCormick. Died, 1985.

PAT SMYTHE—b. 1923. Exceptional British pianist who co-founded legendary quintet with saxophonist Joe Harricott in '60s, pioneering **Indo-Jazz Fusions** with John Major. After his death in '83, the Pat Smythe Memorial Trust and Award was established (the first such British commemorative award in Jazz). First recipient, pianist Steve Melling in '86.

OMER VICTOR SIMEON—b. New Orleans, 1902. One of great dynasty of New Orleans clarinettists, he remained a major solo voice on that instrumen for three decades. Rec. with King Oliver, Jabbo Smith, Jelly Roll Morton (Red Hot Peppers), Earl Hines, Tiny Parham, Jimmie Lunceford, Kid Ory, Wilbur De Paris *et al.* Died, 1959.

SONNY SIMMONS—b. Louisiana, 1933. Altoist and early associate of Ornette Coleman, noted for his contributions to Eric Dolphy's **Memorial Album, Iron Man**, and his fierce outing on his own '69 **Manhattan Egos**.

JOE SMITH—b. Ripley, Ohio, 1902. Alleged to have been Bessie Smith's favorite trumpeter. Also rec. with Ma Rainey, Ethel Waters, McKinney's Cotton Pickers, Fletcher Henderson etc. Died, 1937.

WILLIE (WILLIAM McLEISH) SMITH—b. Charleston, South Carolina, 1908. Along with Johnny Hodges and Benny Carter, one of most important pre-Parker altoists. Rec. with Jimmie Lunceford, Ellington, (replacing Hodges), Harry James, Nat Cole, Charlie Barnet etc. Died, 1967.

EDDIE SOUTH—b. Louisiana, 1904. Technically skilful violinist who came to prominence late '30s. Rec. with Django Reinhardt, Stephane Grappelli etc, 1962.

Jess Stacy playing in a quartet setting (courtesy Ace of Hearts).

JESS ALEXANDRIA STACY—b. Cape Girardeau, Missouri, 1904. Individual yet under-rated, he was a perfect big-band pianist working/recording with Benny Goodman, Lionel Hampton, Harry James, Eddie Condon, Bob Crosby, Ralph Sutton etc.

JEREMY STEIG—excellent technician on flute, specializing in 'Roland Kirk-style' overblowing. Led pioneering jazz-rock band Jeremy and the Satyrs during late '60s.

JOE SULLIVAN (DENNIS PATRICK TERENCE JOSEPH O'SULLIVAN)—b. Chicago, 1906. One of the first white pianists in '20s and '30s completely to understand—and play—hard-driving, two-fisted style made famous by Fats Waller, Willie 'The Lion' Smith and Earl Hines. Rec. with Bob Crosby (featured on **Big Noise From Winetka**) *et al.* Died, 1971.

GABOR SZABO—b. Budapest, Hungary, 1936. Superb guitarist, he learned jazz from Voice of America broadcasts to Europe. Came to attention in US in mid '50s working with Chico Hamilton, Gary McFarland and Charles Lloyd. Died, 1982.

T

CHARLIE (CHARLES) TEAGARDEN—b. Vernon, Texas, 1913. Reliable, melodic and lyrical trumpeter whose career too often unfairly came under the shadow of brother Jack.

FRANK TESCHEMACHER—b. Kansas City, 1906. Influential clarinettist (tenor and alto saxophonist, banjoist and violinist), member of 'Austin High School Gang' in '20s.

CLAUDE THORNHILL—b. Terre Haute, Indiana, 1909. Pianist-arranger whose influential late '40s bands, with Gil Evans' futuristic orchestrations, provided a starting point for Miles Davis' 'Birth of the Cool' band in '48 Died, 1965.

FRANKIE TRUMBAUER—b. Carbondale, Illinois, 1900. First-rate multi-instrumentalist, best remembered as a distinctive C-melody saxophonist and major influence on Lester Young.

The Memorable Claude Thornhill (courtesy Columbia).

The Very Best Of Dinah Washington (courtesy Philips).

W

GEORGE WALLINGTON (GEORGIO FIGLIA)—b. Palermo, Sicily, 1924. Technically adroit pianist and songwriter, early bebop revolutionary, composer of classics like **Godchild** and **Lemon Drop**.

DINAH WASHINGTON (RUTH JONES)—b. Tuscaloosa, Albama, 1924. Gospel-inspired vocalist who made big impact fronting Lionel Hampton's band in '43, particularly with **Salty Papa Blues**. Influence extended to Aretha Franklin and Esther Phillips. Died, from accidental sleeping-pill overdose, 1963.

ETHEL WATERS—b. Chester, Pennsylvania, 1900. Popular 'Race records' vocalist of '20s and '30s, nicknamed 'Sweet Mama Stringbean'. Worked with Tommy Dorsey, Fletcher Henderson, Duke Ellington, Benny Goodman *et al.* Died, 1977.

CHICK (WILLIAM) WEBB—b. Baltimore, c. 1902. One of '30s greatest drummers and a powerful force as big-band leader (introducing Ella Fitzergerald). Major influence on Gene Krupa and Buddy Rich. Died, 1939.

DICKY (WILLIAM) WELLS—b. Centerville, Tennessee, 1909. Important, if undersung, trombonist and Basie band soloist; much of his best work was with tenorist Lester Young. Also rec. with Charlie Johnson-Lloyd Scott-Cecil Scott, Fletcher Henderson, Buck Clayton, Buddy Tate etc. Died, 1985.

DICK (RICHARD McQUEEN) WELLSTOOD—b. Greenwich Connecticut, 1927. Superior, Waller-inspired stride pianist. Rec. with own groups, Bob Wilber, Sidney Bechet, Eddie Condon, Billy Butterfield *et al.*

ARTHUR PARKER WHETSOL—b. Punta Gorda, Florida, 1905. Individualistic but under-rated trumpet soloist with Ellington ('28-'36). Died, 1940.

PAUL WHITEMAN—b. Denver, Colorado, 1890. Band-leader of '30s and '40s, billed as the 'King of Jazz' (a title since often challenged as his 'symphonic jazz' bears little comparison with bands led by Fletcher Henderson, Duke Ellington and Don Redman). However, line-up included such immortals as Bix Beiderbecke, Charlie and Jack Teagarden, Frankie Trumbauer, Mildred Bailey, Buddy Berigan, Joe Venuti, Tommy-and Jimmy Dorsey and Eddie Lang. Died, 1967.

BOB (ROBERT SAGE) WILBER—b. New York, 1928. Distinctive saxist-clarinettist whose Wild Cats band was important to the post-New Orleans revival. Rec. with Sidney Bechet, Maxine Sullivan, Buck Clayton, World's Greatest Jazz Band, Kenny Davern (Soprano Summit), Bud Freeman etc.

LEE WILEY—b. Port Gibson, Oklahoma, 1915. Popular '30s vocalist-composer with a distinctive wide vibrato. From '39, closely associated with Eddie Condon's band. Her **Any Time, Any Day Anywhere** became hit for R&B's Joe Morris and Laurie Tate in '60s.

ERNIE WILLIAMS — b. Winston-Salem, North Carolina. Vocalist and drummer, contributor to early Kansas City jazz. Worked with Harlem Leonard's Rockets and Chocolate Dandies. Appeared in '80 film *The Last of the Blue Devils* (was, in fact, band's last surviving member). Died, 1986.

Above: Dinah Washington. A true individualist, she sang jazz, blues, gospel, R&B, even pop. Her death at age 39 in 1963 was a great loss.

SAM WOODING—b. Philadelphia, 1896. Widely travelled pioneer pianist, arranger and band-leader, noted for his historic visit to the Soviet Union in '26. Worked with Tommy Ladnier, Sidney Bechet, Doc Cheatham *et al.* Died, 1986.

FRANK WRIGHT—b. Grenada, Mississippi, 1935. Second generation, free-playing tenorist strongly inspired by Albert Ayler's experiments, and an important contributor to the Paris-based coterie of self-exiled avant-gardists.

Y

MARTHA YOUNG—b. Los Angeles, c. 1930. Daughter of saxophonist Irma Young and niece of Lester Young. Although she studied all reed instruments, she was noted professional pianist from mid '40s. Died, 1985.

Jazzin' Babies' Blues, Ethel Waters (courtesy Biograph). Classic recordings by a singer whose talent encompassed a broad range of styles.

Index

An *italic* figure refers to the page number of a performer's entry in the book.

A

B

C

D

E

F

N

R

S

U

Z

Picture Credits

The publishers wish the thank the following photographers, picture agencies and companies who have supplied photographs for this book. The photographs have been credited by page number, and position on the page where appropriate: B (Bottom), T (Top), BL (Bottom Left) etc.

Arista Records: 37 (BR)
Beggars Banquet Records: 132 (T)
Blue Note Records: 41 (T), 71 (BR) (Benno Friedman), 142 (BR) (Harrison Funk), 160 (T) (Caroline Greyshock), 180 (TL) (Carol Friedman)
Kwame Brathwaite: 108 (T)
CBS Records: 195 (B)
Columbia Records: 34 (TR) (Bruce Lawrence), 61 (B) (Anthony Barboza), 66 (C) (Bill Fewsmith), 66 (T), 73 (BR) (David Gahr), 98 (R) (Bill King), 123 (BL) (Deborah Feingold)
Concord Records: 149 (B), 151 (B), 154 (BL)
ECM Records: 19 (B), 78 (R), 95 (B), 122 (T), 187 (TR), 187 (B)
Elektra Records: 155 (T) (Ron Slenzak)
Phil Gorton: Endpapers, 2-3, 4-5, 6-7, 8-9, 10-11, 12-13, 196-197
Ironic Records: 146 (B)
Island Records: 150 (T) (Nick White)
Jazz Centre UK: 148 (B)
Jak Kilby: 135 (B), 185 (BR)
Mike Laye: 92 (T), 178 (TL)
Manhattan Records: 62 (TR)
MCA Records 51 (BL), 169
Milestone Records: 21 (Michele Clement)
National Film Archive: 33 (T), 109 (BR), 134 (TR), 141 (T)
Matt Rose: 59 (T)
Rough Trade Records: 181 (T) (Anton Corbijn)
Jonathan Sa'adah: 56 (BR)
Sonet Records: 176 (TL), 177 (B)
Allan Titmuss: 82 (B), 106 (TL), 125 (T), 131 (T)
Warner Bros: 49 (BR), 99 (B), 121 (T), 161 (TR)
WEA Records: 65 (TR), 121 (B), 184 (T)
Nick White: 17 (BR), 53 (B), 83 (T), 117 (BR), 124 (T), 188 (T)
Val Wilmer: 15 (B), 19 (T), 24, 26, (T), 30, 31 (L), 31 (R), 35 (T), 36 (T), 37 (T), 39 (T), 40 (T), 41 (BL), 42, 44, 45, 47 (T), 48 (B), 49 (BL), 51 (B), 54 (L), 55 (T), 59 (R), 60 (B), 61 (T), 63 (T), 64 (T), 67 (T), 68, 69 (B), 73 (T), 74 (L), 77 (R), 78 (L), 79, 80, 81 (T), 82 (T), 83 (B), 84, 86, 87 (T), 88 (B), 90 (T), 90 (B), 91 (T), 91 (B), 93 (B), 94, 96 (L), 97 (T), 98 TL), 100 (L), 101 (TL), 102 (T), 103, 104 (L), 105 (T), 107 (BL), 110, 112 (B), 113 (TR), 116 (TR), 116 (BL), 117 (T), 118 (B), 120 (B) 125 (B), 127 (T), 129 (T), 129 (B), 130 (BL), 130 (BR), 131 (B), 132 (B), 136 (TL), 137 (BL), 138 (B), 140 (L), 142 (B), 143 (T), 149 (TR), 151 (T), 153 (BL), 155 (B), 156 (T), 159 (T), 159 (Br), 161 (BL), 162 (L), 163 (T), 164 (T), 165 (B), 166 (B), 167 (TL), 168 (BL), 169 (BR), 170 (T), 171 (BL), 173 (R), 175 (T), 177 (T), 183, 185 (T), 186 (T), 187 (R), 191 (T), 192, 193 (L), 193 (R), 198, 199, 200, 201, 202, 203.

PRINTED IN BELGIUM BY proost INTERNATIONAL BOOK PRODUCTION